THE GREEK COMMONWEALTH

THE GREEK
COMMONWEALTH

Politics and Economics in Fifth-Century Athens

ALFRED ZIMMERN

FIFTH EDITION, REVISED

OXFORD UNIVERSITY PRESS

LONDON   OXFORD   NEW YORK

OXFORD UNIVERSITY PRESS

Oxford London New York
Glasgow Toronto Melbourne Wellington
Cape Town Salisbury Ibadan Nairobi Lusaka Addis Ababa
Bombay Calcutta Madras Karachi Lahore Dacca
Kuala Lumpur Hong Kong Tokyo

938·
Z

701828

First published, 1911
Fifth edition published, 1931
First issued as an Oxford University Press paperback, 1961

This reprint, 1969

Printed in the United States of America

TO THE TWO

ST. MARY WINTON COLLEGES

PREFACE TO FIFTH EDITION

A few slight changes have been made in this edition, but I have not attempted on this occasion to deal with the recent literature. I would like to express my acknowledgements to Professor Victor Ehrenberg for his notice of the book in *Gnomon* (vol. i, no. 3, 1925).

A. Z.

Oxford,
August 1931.

PREFACE TO FOURTH EDITION

Since the publication of the third edition I have done my best to keep abreast of the recent literature over the wide range covered in the book. But it has not been altogether easy to decide how best to make use of the gleanings thus gathered up. The natural course would be that followed in previous editions, of embodying the new material in the text and foot-notes. But as the years go on I am carried farther and farther away, not indeed from the subject of the book, which remains a κτῆμα ἐς ἀεί, but from the state of mind in which I wrote it. When I sat in my room at the British School at Athens with my well-thumbed texts around me I had been soaked in the details of the subject for ten years and more ; and when I came to a decision on a disputed point, it was the resultant of a host of considerations many of which are necessarily no longer present in my mind. Experience in following up criticisms either of my general treatment or of special points has convinced me that I shall do the book, and my own earlier judgement, an injustice if I tamper with them too freely. On the other hand, it would obviously be foolish to ignore the recent literature and to allow the book to become stereotyped and out of date. I have therefore decided to leave the text unaltered except in a very few cases (such as the date of the Parthenon sculptures) where questions of ascertained fact are involved and to deal with the recent literature and considerations suggested by it in a separate Appendix. This seems to me the best way of doing justice at once to the writer of the book, of whom, to adopt the phrase of an Irish writer, I am the nearest living representative, to my own conscience as a scholar, and to the requirements of an ever-growing subject.

I have also added an index of Greek words and phrases.

LONDON,
April 1924.

PREFACE TO THIRD EDITION

IN revising the book for a third edition I have been chiefly indebted to my friend Mr. Shirley C. Atchley, of H.M. Legation at Athens, who has not only applied his unrivalled knowledge of the Greek countryside to the revision of the text, but has also corrected the map of Attica in the light of knowledge gained in his many wanderings. I am also indebted to the distinguished Spanish scholar, writer, and patriot, Don Miguel de Unamuno of the University of Salamanca, for a number of helpful suggestions. The other changes and additions relate chiefly to the recent literature on the subject and to later applications of ideas or tendencies referred to in the text.

Oakhill Drive.
Surbiton.
March 20, 1921.

PREFACE TO SECOND EDITION

I AM indebted to a number of friendly critics for enabling me to correct certain errors and obscurities in the first edition. My thanks are due especially to the Warden of Wadham College, Oxford, to Canon Cruikshank, Mr. H. J. Cunningham, Mr. G. Dickins, to reviewers in *The Times* and the *Journal of Hellenic Studies*, to Professor Francotte of the University of Liège and, above all and in spite of all, to Professor von Wilamowitz-Moellendorff of the University of Berlin. I have also made use of the opportunity to add references to the literature of the subject since 1911, and an occasional comment on recent events, as on pp. 98 and 245–7. But the great addition to the book is the map of Attica by my friend Mr. Arnold J. Toynbee.

The book as a whole remains unchanged. I cannot pretend to be satisfied with the discussion of slavery as it is left by Part III, Chapters XIV and XV, on the juxtaposition of which some critics have fastened. But I have come no nearer a final solution than when I wrote them. Perhaps some one else may make a better use of the evidence to which I have called attention.[1]

While the book has been passing through the press war has broken out, bringing Great Britain face to face, for the first time since she has become a Democracy, with the full ultimate meaning of the civic responsibilities, both of thought and action, with which, in the narrower field of the City-State, the fifth-century Athenians were so familiar. Greek ideas and Greek inspiration can help us to-day, not only in facing the duties of the moment, but in the work of deepening and extending the range and the meaning of Democracy and Citizenship, Liberty and Law, which would seem to be the chief political task before mankind in the new epoch of history on which we have suddenly entered.

Board of Education,
   Whitehall, S.W.
      Dec. 2, 1914.

[1] 1924. Mr. Heitland has now gone more fully over the ground, at least as regards agricultural work, and has arrived at the same conclusion. See his remarks (*Agricola*, pp. 446–7) on the reasons why slavery in the mines and on the Roman *latifundia* differed in character from slavery in domestic, industrial, and professional occupations.

PREFACE TO FIRST EDITION

THIS book is the result of an attempt to make clear to myself what fifth-century Athens was really like. Most educated people have their own vision of ancient Greece. I have tried to convey mine in the form of a study of the nature, influence, and inter-action of two great forces in Athenian life.

A few words may explain what has dictated this choice of treatment.

It is now generally admitted that neither an individual nor a nation can be properly understood without a knowledge of their surroundings and means of support—in other words, of their geographical and economic conditions. This doctrine, obvious though it seems to-day, was somewhat slow in winning acceptance in connexion with the study of ancient Greece. The traditions of classical learning and the lack of relevant evidence combined to keep Greek scholars out of touch with newer methods of social inquiry. But during the last two generations, thanks mainly to the archaeologists, this defect has been steadily repaired; and we now possess, and are entitled to draw con-clusions from, a large and increasing mass of information about the economic side of Greek life. It is this accumulation of new evidence which, more than any other single factor, distinguishes the Greece of modern scholarship from the Greece of Grote and our grandfathers.

Classical scholarship, therefore, on the Continent at any rate, can no longer be reproached with neglecting the application of modern methods. The special dangers to which it is exposed to-day, and which determined my choice of treatment, lie rather in the opposite direction. There is, firstly, the tendency to over-specialization and one-sidedness, the inclination to forget the wood for the trees. This is a temptation which besets every science at a stage when knowledge is accumulating very rapidly : but it is particularly insidious in such a study as that of ancient Greece, where for the student everything depends upon remaining steadily conscious, in and through the smallest detail, of the wonder and greatness of the whole. It is so easy, for instance, in studying the Erechtheum building inscriptions to become absorbed in their interesting information about work and wages, and to forget that they relate to the Erechtheum. Yet when that is forgotten all is forgotten.

Books and articles written in this spirit are easily detected and can be allowed for accordingly. But there is a second tendency to error, against which it is more difficult to guard. It arises from the application of modern methods and ideas to ancient times without a sufficient estimate of the difference between ancient Greek and modern conditions. To take an obvious instance. It has long been clear to historians that economic circumstances had a good deal to do with the Peloponnesian War ; yet we have no right to pass from this to an explanation of the whole struggle in modern economic terms. What is misleading in such explanations is not the details but the background. They seem to be based upon a wrong or at least an inadequate conception of the normal economic life of ancient Greece. The only safe road to the solution of this and kindred problems is to go back to first beginnings, to the careful analysis of ordinary ancient terms and processes. This must be my excuse for the disproportionate length of the third section of the book.

Some further explanation is perhaps necessary as to the attitude I have adopted towards the fourth-century philosophers. Plato and Aristotle used often to be regarded, in the comparative lack of other evidence, as first-rate authorities upon the life of the City State. It is perhaps not even yet sufficiently recognized that they are not. They only knew the City State in the days of its decline, and their view of it is coloured by their own personal ideas and doctrines. It is as unsafe to rely upon them for the facts and spirit of the fifth and preceding centuries as it would be to rely upon Carlyle and Ruskin for the facts and spirit of English life before the Great Reform Bill and the Industrial Revolution. The right method is exactly the reverse, to apply the history of the generation that preceded them to the interpretation of their own doctrines. No interpretation of either the political or the ethical theories of the later philosophers can be satisfactory which does not take into account the impression left upon their minds by the social development which I have attempted to describe. I had originally planned to close the book with a section dealing with this subject—one of great importance in the history of European political speculation—but eventually abandoned it as beyond the proper limits of my scheme. I have, however, allowed myself occasionally to touch upon the subject in the footnotes, as a glance at the Index will show.

I have tried to arrange the book so as to make it useful to students with the least possible distraction to the general reader. It seemed inconvenient to group the footnotes together at the end of the book or the chapters, but I hope that their arrangement in paragraphs will make it easy for the general reader to skip them. My ancient references are, so far as possible, to well-known authors. Modern writers I have generally quoted either to support some statement that seemed to need confirmation, or because I thought the reference might be helpful to the reader. I have never referred to a writer simply because I disagreed with him, and have not troubled to multiply modern witnesses when I had good ancient testimony on my side. In a work involving so many decisions on points of detail I cannot hope to have avoided errors of judgement, but I have done my best to play no tricks with the evidence. Indeed, as those who care to look up the references will realize, there are comparatively few special points on which I can claim to have contributed anything novel.

I have to thank a great number of friends for kind help and encouragement, notably Professor Gilbert Murray, Professor Myres, Mr. Reginald Coupland, Mr. R. H. Dundas, Mr. Arnold J. Toynbee, Mr. Richard Jennings, Mr. W. C. Barton, the Rev. J. M. Murphy, S.J., of the National University of Ireland, and, last but not least, my old teacher and present colleague, Mr. Graham Wallas. My acknowledgements are also due to the authorities of the British School at Athens, who by making me an Associate of the School enabled me to write the greater part of the book under the pleasantest and most favourable conditions.

Oakhill Drive,
Surbiton, 1911.

CONTENTS

PAGE

INTRODUCTORY NOTE 13

PART I: GEOGRAPHY

CHAPTER
- I. The Mediterranean Area 17
- II. The Sea 24
- III. The Climate 36
- IV. The Soil 43

PART II: POLITICS

THE DEVELOPMENT OF CITIZENSHIP

- I. Fellowship, or the Rule of Public Opinion . . 59
- II. Custom, or the Rule of the Family . . . 69
- III. Efficiency, or the Rule of the Magistrate . . 83
- IV. Gentleness, or the Rule of Religion . . . 107
- V. Law, or the Rule of Fair Play 125
- VI. Self-Government, or the Rule of the People . . 139
- VII. Liberty, or the Rule of Empire 180

THE IDEAL OF CITIZENSHIP

- VIII. Happiness, or the Rule of Love 198

PART III: ECONOMICS

- I. Poverty 213
- II. Use and Wont 220

THE GROWING CITY

- III. Work on the Land 228
- IV. Hunting or Robbery 236
- V. Warfare 244
- VI. Colonization 252

CITY ECONOMICS

- VII. Craftsmen and Workmen 257
- VIII. Retail Trade 279
- IX. Public and Private Property 286

CHAPTER		PAGE
X.	Money	301
XI.	Foreign Trade	314
XII.	Population	325

IMPERIAL ECONOMICS

XIII.	Sea-Power	350
XIV.	Free Intercourse	366
XV.	The Fellow Workers	380
XVI.	The Silver-Mines	397
XVII.	Finance	403

CONCLUSION

The Peloponnesian War	420
APPENDIX	445
CHRONOLOGICAL TABLE	452
NOTE ON ABBREVIATIONS	458
INDEX OF MODERN WRITERS CITED	459
INDEX OF GREEK WORDS AND PHRASES	463
GENERAL INDEX	465

MAPS

Greece and adjoining lands	14
Map of Attica	*face p.* 40
Attica, Megara, and parts of Corinth and Boeotia, with Yorkshire to same scale	156

INTRODUCTORY NOTE

IT is not the purpose of this book to tell any part of the story of Greek history. That lies within the province of the narrative historian. Our object here is a more modest one—to group together certain facts and to trace the course of certain ideas which may help to make that story and the men who acted in it more intelligible to modern readers.

Greek civilization differs from our own both in its material environment and in its feelings and ideas. Our method will be to deal first with the main features of that environment ; next with the political institutions which the Greeks established within it ; next with their means of livelihood, that is with their ' economics ' or housekeeping ; and lastly with the conflict which arose, as it has arisen in many modern civilized communities, between the driving necessities of economic development and the accepted institutions and ideals of national life—a conflict which brought inward unhappiness and outward disaster upon the foremost Greek community at the very height of her greatness and left its mark upon the mind and writings of the men who laid the foundations of European political thought.

We shall thus be approaching Greek civilization from a direction contrary to that often taken by modern writers, approaching it from the side on which its differences from our own are most apparent and from which its unique characteristics are most easily seized.

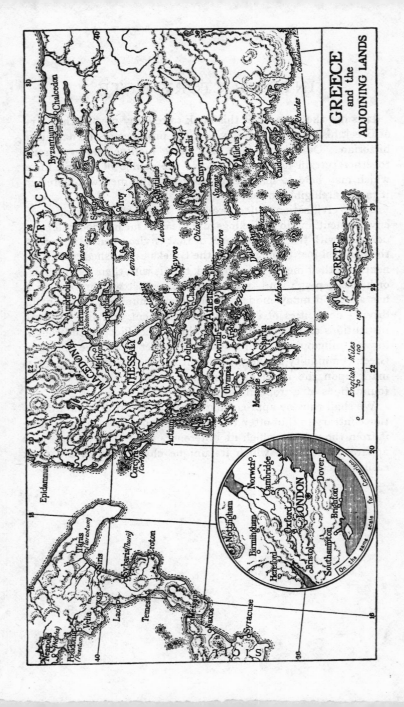

GREECE
and the
ADJOINING LANDS

THE GREEK COMMONWEALTH

Die Griechen sind, wie das Genie, *einfach*: deshalb sind sie die unsterblichen Lehrer.—NIETZSCHE.

The Greeks are like Genius, simple: that is why they are the immortal teachers.

PART I. GEOGRAPHY

Two Voices are there; one is of the sea,
One of the mountains, each a mighty voice:
In both from age to age thou didst rejoice,
They were thy chosen music, Liberty.

CHAPTER I

THE MEDITERRANEAN AREA [1]

Ἡ Ἑλλὰς τὰς ὥρας πολλόν τι κάλλιστα κεχρημένας ἔλαχε.

HERODOTUS, iii. 106.

Greece enjoys by far the best tempered climate.

Τὸ τῶν Ἑλλήνων γένος μεσεύει κατὰ τοὺς τόπους.

ARISTOTLE, *Politics* 1327.

The Hellenic race occupies an intermediate situation geographically.

GREECE is a Mediterranean country, placed, as Aristotle says, in an intermediate position, half-way between the Tropics and the cold lands of the North. It shares with the other Mediterranean lands, as compared with Europe beyond the Alps and Africa beyond the Atlas, a distinctive climate, distinctive scenery, and, as a necessary consequence, a distinctive mode of life.

It is the scenery which first attracts the passing traveller of to-day; and so it has been with the invading hosts of all ages. From the days before history, when the first barbarians thrust their way southwards, the men of the North have always been susceptible to the peculiar beauty of the Mediterranean lands. To us in the North, if we are book-learned and home-keeping, Greece and Italy spell Athens and Rome. They are associated in our minds with a host of inherited ideas, with Art and Freedom and Law and Empire. They are familiar to us as the cradle of some of the strongest forces in our national life, as the first and most congenial home of our distinctively Western civilization. But to the prehistoric Achaeans and Dorians, and to the Galatians and Goths and Longbeards and Vandals and Avars who followed them, this abstract appeal would have had no meaning. Yet they too, in their cold Northern homes, heard

---

[1] In this and the following sections I have made much use of Philippson's *Das Mittelmeergebiet*, a popularly written book by a standard authority on Mediterranean Geography. So far as I know, there is no similar book in English, although one is greatly needed. It is to be hoped that Professor Myres's inaugural lecture on *Greek Lands and the Greek People* marks the beginning of a new era for English classical teaching in this respect.

the call of the South, and thousands of them obeyed it. For months or years they pushed sunwards with their families and possessions and household gods, trusting in tribesmen's tales of a wonderful land behind the hills. When they emerged at length out of the last rough Balkan defile and pitched camp one evening on level Greek ground between the mountains and the sea, it was the sheer beauty of this new world which made them feel that they had found a home. Upon their Northern eyes, unused to a region of sharp outlines and strong colours, the Southern landscape worked like magic. They felt they had come to fairyland, and that they must stay there for ever.

The poets of their race, from the bards of the early invaders, out of whom our Homer grew, to Goethe and Byron, Ibsen and Browning, bear constant witness to this spell. Yet it is hard, except just at twilight when the magic is working, to feel quite at home in fairyland. Romance and Imagination sway us powerfully at moments ; but Habit and Affection are stronger forces in our nature and are not to be won over by superficial enticements. The gulf between North and South is too great to be bridged in a single visit or a single lifetime. It takes more than one generation to live a new country into the blood. Our Northern poets who have sung of the South have sung as strangers and sojourners : they have been Romantics not Realists, enthusiastic bystanders rather than quiet inhabitants going about their business and speaking naturally of their life and feelings. The spirit of the South remains for them something strange and picturesque and external, which attracts their wonder and curiosity without winning its way into their understanding or laying its hold upon their devotion. And sometimes they are honest enough to confess it. ' Oh to be in England,' cried Browning, letting pass before his mind's eye all the dear familiar sights that he was missing—

> Oh to be in England
> Now that April 's there,
> And whoever wakes in England
> Sees, some morning, unaware,
> That the lowest boughs and the brushwood sheaf
> Round the elm-tree bole are in tiny leaf,
> While the chaffinch sings on the orchard bough
> In England—now !

That tells us something of what men have to renounce when they go southward. At the outset of our journey it is well to have it brought to mind.

Where even the poets feel homesick, plain men will fare worse. Often and often must the conquering invader have repented of having obeyed the call, and cursed himself for a fool as he opened his eyes in the morning, after a hot and troubled night, upon the metallic sky above him and the baked ground beneath. It was not for a mere whim that many a Frankish baron of mediaeval Greece abandoned his hard-won domains and went ' home ' to die by the Rhine or the Loire. What could be more attractive to the possessive spirit of a Northern noble than to have Athens for his very own and to look forward to leaving it to his heir ? Otho de la Roche, first feudal lord of Attica and Boeotia, had the Acropolis for his castle and the Parthenon for his minster. Yet he gave up all in his old age and went back with his sons to the rolling plains of Burgundy.[1]

If the Northerner who has come and seen and yielded to the spell cannot easily adapt his mind to Southern conditions, it is still harder for those who can only enter into contact with it indirectly through books and pictures. They can only understand Mediterranean life and the literature to which it gave birth, whether in Greece or Palestine, by a deliberate effort of the imagination. No doubt the effort is worth making, but its difficulty (especially for young and untrained minds) is very great ; and in England, at any rate, our educational traditions do little to overcome it. For the uncorrected imagination of the Northerner the olive-groves of Colonus are an English park and the plane-trees of the Ilissus a Thames promenade, while ' Sunium's marbled steep ', like the chalk cliffs of the South coast, runs down to long stretches of tidal beach.

These mistakes are all the harder to correct because the Greek poets who have come down to us seldom pause to describe the scenery of their country, and are never detailed or Wordsworthian in their treatment of it. Landscape poetry, like land-

[1] Miller, *Latins in the Levant*, pp. 91–2, cf. 68, 74. Count Berthold of Katzenellenbogen, the Crusader who gave the signal for setting fire to Constantinople, is another instance of the same home-sickness. Both their modest castles still stand. Otho's is La Roche-sur-Ognon on the Haute-Saône : Katzenellenbogen looks down on a little village in Nassau.

scape painting, belongs to the reflective period in a nation's life, when it has learnt to see itself in its own surroundings. Greek writers, at least up to the end of the fifth century, had not yet fully entered upon this stage of self-consciousness. Like all simple folk, they take a knowledge of their scenery and surroundings for granted in all who listen to them. The Mediterranean landscape, like the institutions of the City State, forms a permanent background to Greek life and thought. Its influence is omnipresent, but it is seldom expressed. It is left to show itself, more spontaneously and truthfully, in the chance idiom or detail that slips out as the setting of a story, in what is implied or hinted rather than consciously stated, in the many little significant touches which to the careful observer, of nations as of men, are always the surest and happiest revelation of character.

Thus the traveller in Southern lands, if he is prepared to forget all he ever knew and begin learning it afresh, will constantly be discovering the real meaning of words and phrases and metaphors which he had been accustomed from his school-days to regard as ' classical tags ' or romantic properties, or had perhaps never noticed at all. A man must have overcome his first strangeness and grown used to going up the Acropolis for his evening walk before he can know why Pericles said that his Athens ' cheered the heart and delighted the eye day by day '. He must have stood on an island peak after sunset before he can truly understand the words of Alcman's evening hymn :—

> The hills have fallen asleep.
> O'er cleft and crag
> Onè quiet spreads,
> O'er rocks that face the deep
> And stony torrent beds.[1]

or appreciate the masterful subtlety with which Goethe adapted it to his Northern purpose in *Über allen Gipfeln ist Ruh*. He must have sailed through the straits of Salamis and landed to look across at the hills of Attica to feel what Euripides' hearers felt when the chorus sang :—

---

[1] Alcman, *Frag.* 65, beginning

εὕδουσιν δ' ὀρέων κορυφαί τε καὶ φάραγγες,
πρώονές τε καὶ χαράδραι,

where every word should call up a picture.

In Salamis, filled with the foaming
  Of billows and murmur of bees,
Old Telamon stayed from his roaming,
  Long ago, on a throne of the seas ;
Looking out on the hills olive-laden,
  Enchanted, where first from the earth
The grey-gleaming fruit of the Maiden
  Athena had birth.[1]

But what seems simple and obvious to the man on the spot
often entirely escapes the notice of the Northern reader ; or, if
his attention is directed to it, seems unnatural and mysterious.
The traveller, if he is teachable, gradually learns what to look
for : he is living in the atmosphere, and a sense of the world in
which the old books were written settles on him like thin dust
and is with him all day long. When he returns to his study or
class-room and takes up Sophocles or Aristophanes his mind is
alive with pictures. He can hear the chorus of village elders
holding forth by the fountain ; he can almost smell the garlic.
His stay-at-home fellow student cannot follow him there without
guidance, if he can ever really follow him at all. Travellers'
tales, alas, are very different from travel, and geography is a
poor substitute for personal experience. Books and lectures and
lantern slides cannot take the place of life. Still, unless we are
to despair of classical education, the attempt at guidance is
worth making. Let us try, therefore, before describing Greek
institutions in detail, to make clear some of the simpler features
of the world in which the Greeks lived.[2]

We are taught from early youth to divide the world into continents, and are apt to think of the Mediterranean, which washes
three of the five, as marking a boundary line between Europe,
Asia, and Africa. We think of Europe as ' civilized ', Asia as
Oriental or stagnant, and Africa as barbarous ; or, making the

[1] Eur. *Troad.* 799 ff., tr. Murray.
[2] This is not the place in which to marshal the arguments for and against
using the languages and literatures of Greece and Rome as a means of training
the young. But it is worth pointing out that the analogous attempt to use the
English language and literature as a means of education in India is severely
criticized by some of the very people who defend the ' classical ' tradition in
English education.—1921. See on this point the masterly report of the
Sadler Commission on the University of Calcutta, which is likely to remain
for long the *locus classicus*, not only on the problem of education in Bengal
but on kindred problems in other countries.

frontier one of religion rather than of 'progress', we regard Europe as Christian and Nearer Asia and Africa as Mohammedan. In either case we 'think in continents', making the land our centre of vision.

This view is natural enough in London, but appears strange in Constantinople, where business men cross twice daily, in suburban steamers, from one continent to the other. It has always been misleading from the point of view of physical geography, for the countries round the Mediterranean form, both structurally and climatically, a distinct region of the world's surface. But it is historically and politically misleading also. Since the French occupation of Algiers, North Africa is no longer Barbary; and with a Parliament in Angora and a railway to the Prophet's Tomb at Medina, Nearer Asia can no longer be called 'stagnant'. We are returning, in fact, to normal conditions. For to the Greeks the Mediterranean area was always a unity, and the Mediterranean itself not a frontier, but a highway; they saw the world as 'a rim of convergent coastlands encircling the Midland Sea, which is Our Sea'. 'Our Sea' or 'This Sea' was indeed their only name for it. With the countries immediately round it they were tolerably familiar; but the *hinterland* beyond, which differed in climate, structure, and manners, always remained to them mysterious. Herodotus penetrated behind the true Mediterranean region to Scythia and Babylon and inland Egypt and Libya; so we can see from his book what non-Mediterranean lands looked like when observed through Greek spectacles.[1]

This Mediterranean area differs structurally from the countries round it. It is *younger* than they. A geological map shows the greater part to consist of chains of sharp, recently folded mountains, formed mainly of limestone; and only in isolated patches,

---

[1] 'Convergent coastlands': Myres in *Anthropology and the Classics*, p. 121. The reference is to Hdt. iv. 36–45. Herodotus could not understand (ch. 45) why 'the earth, being single, should be divided into three parts with names called after women'. The names Europe, Asia, and Libya are unknown to Homer and appear first in Pindar and Aeschylus (e. g. *P. V.* 412). Compare Myres's paper on *The Geographical Aspect of Greek Colonization*, published in *Proceedings of the Classical Association*, vol. viii (1911), where he dwells on 'the persistent Greekness', even now, of the Mediterranean seaboard, and shows how 'in all the chief functions of human life and in all the principal relations between its several parts' the ancient world, which was even in Roman times a predominantly Greek world, 'faced inwards upon the shores of a Midland Sea.'

as in the ' blunt bowheaded Downs ' round Constantinople, does the traveller find the tame contours to which he is accustomed in England. This adds to the grandeur of the scenery ; but also to the difficulty of communications by land, which is a constant feature of Mediterranean life. Sometimes, for instance, as in Dalmatia, the Chile of Europe, a strip of land is entirely cut off from the regions behind the mountains, and leads a separate life through the greater part of history.

The sea in its present dimensions is even younger than the rocks. Proofs of various sorts, amongst others the occurrence of fossils of dwarf elephants in Malta, Sicily, and Sardinia, have convinced geologists that at some (geologically) very recent period there was a great subsidence of land over large parts of the area, accompanied, of course, by a corresponding encroach-ment of sea. To this are attributed the deep depressions which interrupt the mountain chains at many points and cause the irregular coastline and the countless larger and smaller islands and sunken rocks of the Aegean. The cliffs that rise out of what Sophocles called the ' sea-ravines ' of the Cyclades are simply the continuation, across a submerged depression, of the mountain chains of the mainland. Hence, too, the curious straits which we find in Greek lands, which bear little resemblance to our narrow seas at Dover or Stranraer. The Bosporus, the Helles-pont, and the Euripus are close and intricate pathways full of twists and corners ; they have, in fact, been eroded, and are simply submerged river-valleys. The famous Golden Horn was once a tributary stream.[1]

Moreover, this process of subsidence is not yet completed, as Calabria and Sicily know only too well. Mediterranean man has always been familiar with earthquakes and volcanoes. Herodotus remarks it as noteworthy that in Scythia ' if an earthquake takes place, either in summer or winter, it is regarded as a wonder '. This found its reflection in religion and literature : and *terra firma* to the Greeks was never quite what it is to us.

But we must turn first to the sea, which deserves precedence over *terra firma* in Mediterranean geography.[2]

---

[1] Sea-ravines *Trachiniae* 100.
[2] Hdt. iv. 28. Strabo, 57–9, gives a list of catastrophes by earthquake and volcano. For the general feeling cf. Eur. *Bacchae* 391, and numerous other similar passages.

CHAPTER II

THE SEA

Φέρε γὰρ
σήμαιν' ὅ τι χρή σοι συμπράσσειν·
οὐ γάρ ποτ' ἐρεῖς ὡς Ὠκεανοῦ
φίλος ἐστὶ βεβαιότερός σοι.
AESCHYLUS, *Prometheus Vinctus* 294.

Πῶς δὴ ἄνδρες γεωργοὶ καὶ οὐ θαλάσσιοι ... ἄξιον ἄν τι δρῶεν ;—Pericles in
Thuc. i. 142. 7.

How can mere farmers, with no knowledge of the sea, achieve anything
worthy of note ?

EVERY Englishman is familiar with ' the sea ' ; but the sea of
the Greeks is not the sea that we know.   Landlocked on all sides,
as its name implies, except for the narrow exits at Gibraltar and
the Dardanelles, the Mediterranean seems in summer as gentle as
an inland lake.   Yet to call it a lake is to belie its possibilities.
It is in fact double-natured, sometimes a lake far better adapted
to oars than to sails, sometimes an ocean, not adapted, as a timid
Greek navigator might say, for either : or to put it in his own
language, a lake when the gods are kind, and an ocean when they
are spiteful.   This double-natured sea has its own peculiarities,
some of which have interesting bearings upon the life of those
who dwell round it.

To begin with, it is not self-sufficing.   It is a warm inland sea
subject to constant shrinkage by evaporation, and its supplies of
fresh water are not enough to make up the deficiency.   Only three
large rivers—the Nile, the Po, and the Rhone—flow into it, and
there is comparatively little rain.

If the Mediterranean were entirely landlocked, this constant
evaporation would gradually dry up parts of it altogether and
reduce it to a chain of salt lakes, as some geologists say it once
has been.   As it is, it is considerably more salt than the outer
ocean and becomes increasingly salt in its more eastern portions.
Hence the collection of salt in salt-pans or ' salt-fixings ', as the
Greeks called them, is a simple process, and a trade in salt from
the coast to the saltless people of the hinterland went on all

through antiquity ; salt was commonly exchanged for slaves, so commonly that a certain kind of cheap slave was known as a ' saltling '. Only two of the Roman roads were not called after their constructors : the Via Latina and the Via *Salaria,* the old highway by which salt was conveyed up the Tiber valley from Ostia to the interior.[1]

The deficiency of water is, of course, made up at both ends— from the outer ocean and from the big fresh-water supplies brought by the Russian rivers and the Danube into the Black Sea. But the straits of Gibraltar narrow to a little over seven miles and are comparatively shallow ; and in antiquity they were a little narrower and shallower still. They do not let in nearly enough water to equalize the levels of the Mediterranean and the Atlantic. The Dardanelles and the Bosporus are still narrower. Hence there is a strong current at both exits of the Mediterranean, and this, together with the rush of wind through the straits, made both the Atlantic and the Black Sea passages difficult for seamen before the days of steam.

The Greeks as a whole, before the Hellenistic age, knew little of the Atlantic. For a long time their knowledge ceased absolutely at Gibraltar or, as the Greeks named it, the Pillars of Heracles. The name itself suggests the first impression made upon a mariner from the East : for the long ridge of the Rock, throwing out a tongue, or, as the Greeks called it elsewhere, a Dog's Tail, into the strait, looks anything but a pillar to seamen approaching from the West. Then stray traders were blown by the Levanter through the funnel of the straits, past Trafalgar, into the bay of Cadiz, and discovered the ' virgin market ' of Tarshish on the Guadalquivir. But beyond Cape St. Vincent they knew nothing at all ; even Heracles got no further than Geryon's island in Cadiz Bay ; ' man cannot sail into the darkness West of Cadiz ; turn back the ship to the land of Europe,' says Pindar, as one of his many ways of breaking off a long tale.

---

[1] Teiresias in *Od.* xi. 123 speaks of inland people who eat their food without salt. He is probably talking (as a prophet should) not without good information : for hunting and pastoral people, who live on meat and milk, do not need salt. It is only the eating of cereals that makes salt indispensable. Hence even in Greece traditions survived of a time when no salt was eaten, and meat offered to the gods was always unsalted. For ἀλώνητον (saltling) see Suidas. Another word derived from salt is *salarium* (salary), originally the money given to soldiers for salt with their rations. [See Appendix.]

Herodotus had heard stories of tin being brought from the Tin Islands, but he could find out nothing definite. Moreover, it is significant that he tells us of two different pioneering companies who found their way to Tartessus—the Phocaeans and the Samian Colaeus. This is probably not because, as with the North Pole, there was a competition for the honour of discovery, but because the route was so hazardous that communications had not been properly kept up.[1]

It was, however, not only the difficulty of the Gibraltar passage but the competition of Carthage which kept Greeks out of the Atlantic. The Carthaginians traded all along the nearer coasts of the Atlantic, both in Spain and Africa. They had rounded the Cape of Good Hope and sailed far into the Northern sea for the tin of Cornwall and the Scillies. A Carthaginian account of the West African route is extant in Greek—the so-called Itinerary of Hanno. Rudyard Kipling seems to have made use of it for his story ' The Joyous Venture' in *Puck of Pook's Hill* : it speaks of reaching an island inhabited by shaggy women who bit and scratched and whom the interpreters called ' Gorillas '.[2]

It was of course to the interest of the Carthaginians, as of all pioneer sea powers, to keep their voyages secret and to exaggerate their danger. It was a long time before their next rivals, the Romans, found their way to the British tin mines. The geographer Strabo has an interesting passage about this British trade and how its monopoly was safeguarded :—

The Tin Islands, he says, are ten in number. . . . One of them is desert, but the others are inhabited by men in black cloaks, clad in tunics reaching to the feet, girt about the breast and

[1] The name Atlantic appears first in Herodotus (i. 203) in the form ἡ ἔξω στηλέων ἡ 'Ατλαντὶς καλεομένη (θάλασσα). Pind. *Nem.* iv. 69 (turning back from Cadiz). But he speaks elsewhere in the same way of the Pillar : *Ol.* iii. 44 ; *Nem.* iii. 21 (cf. Eur. *Hipp.* 744) ; Hdt. iii. 115 (Tin Islands). For Geryon's island *vide* Hdt. iv. 8 ; Hesiod *Theog.* 287 and 979 ; and for the two explorers Hdt. i. 163 ; iv. 152 (ἀκήρατον ἐμπόριον). There is a Dog's Tail (κυνόσουρα), for instance, at Marathon and another at Salamis.

[2] Ἅννωνος περίπλους in *Geographi Graeci Minores* (ed. Didot). Its date is probably between 466 and 450 B.C. For Gorillas see i. 13 with an interesting note. Gorilla Island is off the coast of Sierra Leone. The honour of having first discovered England probably belongs to Greek sailors from Marseilles, but their city, which lived a life quite apart from the Eastern Greeks, was not strong enough to keep others out of the discovery.

walking with sticks, like Furies in a tragedy. They subsist by their cattle, leading for the most part a wandering life. Of the metals they have tin and lead, which with skins they barter with the merchants for earthenware, salt, and brazen vessels. Formerly the Phoenicians alone carried on this traffic from Gades, concealing the passage from every one ; and when the Romans followed a certain skipper in order to discover the market for themselves, the skipper purposely ran his vessel on to a shoal, luring the Romans to the same fate. He himself escaped on a piece of wreckage and received from the State the value of the cargo he had lost. Nevertheless the Romans persevered until they discovered the passage.

Parallels to this story could be found in the annals of early Dutch and English seamanship, when the passage into perilous and monopolized seas was being made in the opposite direction.[1]

The Dardanelles and the Bosporus were even more difficult to navigate than the straits of Gibraltar. Down both there flows a strong current accompanied generally by a high wind.[2] In the Dardanelles or Hellespont, which is considerably broader and a little deeper than the Bosporus, the current attains an average speed of nearly two miles an hour and a maximum of six ; when Byron swam across at the narrowest point he covered four miles to make one. In the Bosporus the average is as high as three, and it beats round the corners with such violence that at some points there is a regular towpath.

Polybius has left us a description of the Black Sea passage which can be checked from the sailing directions in the *Pilot* published by the British Admiralty.[3]

In the Hellespont the main difficulty was to pass the first corner by Cape Sigeum, which Pisistratus occupied for Athens at the very beginning of her sea power ; for here the current rushes out along the Asiatic shore with great velocity, and there are no back-eddies to counteract it. To this fact some writers attribute the importance of Troy in early times. When boats

---

[1] Strabo, 175–6. It was these Carthaginian mystifications which were probably responsible for the legend of Atlantis—a name which still lives on men's lips, for it is borne, appropriately enough, by a prominent Greek news paper published in New York. [See Appendix.]

[2] As Kinglake remarks in *Eothen* (chap. iii, *ad init.*) in language too picturesque to be quoted here.

[3] Polyb. iv. 43–4 (written, he says, to refute the traders' tales of his day). *Med. Pilot*, vol. iv, pp. 111–18 (ed. 1908), *Sailing Directions for Dardanelles*, &c., pp. 26 ff. (Dardanelles), pp. 94 ff. (Bosporus)

were small, it is argued, they did not attempt to round the Cape, but disembarked in the small bay opposite the island of Tenedos and carried their goods over by land to the bay just round the corner. The hill of Troy is so placed as to command this land route, and its chieftains kept up the road and levied toll on all who used it. Once inside the strait, modern sailing ships 'work up in the eddy, taking care to tack short of the main current, which may be distinctly seen ', and, after the narrows, hugging the European shore to avoid the prevalent north wind, right up to Byzantium. Ancient ships did the same, except for the tacking : for they suffered from the additional inconvenience of not being able to sail into the wind.[1]

The Bosporus presents considerably greater difficulties than the Dardanelles ; its winding channel extends for some fifteen miles, varying from a mile and a quarter to half a mile in breadth, and the current sets in a zigzag, sweeping round no less than seven times from corner to corner. The last of these zigzags sets from Scutari or Chrysopolis on the Asiatic shore, the spot where Io landed in the myth and Alcibiades established his custom-house in 410, across to Seraglio Point at the entrance of the Golden Horn, under the old acropolis of Byzantium, where a wreck protrudes out of the current to-day. Here it is divided into two, a small part entering the Golden Horn, but most of it sweeping back again towards mid-channel. But this time it does not set right across to Chalcedon opposite, for the land

[1] *Med. Pilot*, ed. 1908, vol. iv, p. 118, ed. 1831, pp. 275 and 280 ; Polyb. iv. 44-6. Of course the current is responsible, as in a river, for many dangerous shoals. This explanation of the importance of Troy was first given by Bérard, *Les Phéniciens et l'Odyssée*, vol. i, pp. 79-82. Compare Murray, *Rise of the Greek Epic*, p. 38 (2nd ed., p. 59). For Sigeum see Hdt. v. 94-5. The Dardanelles wind was responsible for the Turkish capture of Constantinople in 1453. A relieving squadron was kept at Tenedos for a whole month. See the *Destruction of the Greek Empire*, by Sir Edwin Pears (an old Constantinople resident), p. 352. Both this and the author's other work on the Venetian capture in 1204 are full of interesting sidelights on the influence exercised by the geography of this unique neighbourhood on its history.—1914. I have left the passage in the text practically unaltered, since the mention of Troy is after all only incidental. But Leaf, in his *Troy, A Study in Homeric Geography* (1912), pp. 257 ff., argues convincingly that Besika Bay in the Tenedos channel was an impossible place for the beginning of an Isthmus route, and that Troy was rather a castle, blocking the sea-passage of the Dardanelles by its command of the land and of the supplies for passing ships, than a toll station in an isthmus land-passage. Hence, in his view, it became the seat of a great annual fair (p. 314), attended by traders from all quarters. —1921. See also Leaf, *Homer and History*, p. 72.

recedes, but into the Sea of Marmora or Propontis. Chalcedon
remains well outside its sweep. In fact, as Polybius says, ' you
always get to Byzantium whether you wish to or not, but however much you wish it is very hard to get to Chalcedon.' This is
true, as he says, both of the upward and downward voyages ; for
the natural course through the Propontis is to hug the northern
rather than the southern shore. On approaching Constantinople,
' should the wind be unfavourable, the current too strong, or
both united, you may anchor,' say the sailing directions, by the
southern wall of the city. So it was not for nothing that Apollo
called the Megarians blind when they founded their colony at
Chalcedon in preference to Byzantium. Prospecting for an
agricultural colony only, they preferred the quiet coves and fruitful shores of the Gulf of Ismid, where the villa dwellings of Constantinople are spreading to-day, to one of the best trading and
strategic sites in the world.[1]

Here, for the present, we must leave the Eastern Passage and
return westwards. Two other results follow from the nature of
the straits of Gibraltar. They are too shallow for the cold deep-
sea water, which circulates from polar regions through the oceans
of the world, to make its way in, and the bottom temperature of
the Mediterranean is thus almost the same as that just below
the surface. How warm that is every traveller knows who has
disregarded local warnings and braved it when ' it is far too cold
to bathe '. Here the naturalist would add a section on the
curious effects of this on the deep-sea life of the Mediterranean,
which we will omit.

Secondly, the Mediterranean has nothing that the Northerner
would call a tide. It has a small ebb and flow of its own, which
can be measured everywhere and is just noticeable in some places,
but our big ocean tides scarcely penetrate beyond the entrance.
The absence of tides is convenient in many ways. It simplifies

---

[1] Apollo, for once, is convicted of plagiarism. His advice to the Byzan-
tines to found their city ' opposite the blind men ' is preserved in Strabo
(320) and made a good ' foundation legend ' such as every Greek colony
needed. But unfortunately Herodotus (iv. 144) tells us that the remark was
made by the Persian general Megabazus, who visited the city many years
after its foundation, adding that it was remembered in the district. The
' isthmus ' of Stamboul is the Bosporus counterpart to Troy ; but as the site
has been continuously occupied there is no evidence that it was a ' fortified
centre of exchange ' in early times. Scutari : Xen. *Hell.* i. 1. 22. Southern
anchorage : *Med. Pilot,* ed. 1831, p. 278.

the use of harbours and landing-places, the construction of docks, and the laying out of seaport towns. It is no more difficult to put to sea or put ashore in a boat in the Mediterranean than on an English river. Small Greek boats, and even triremes and merchant-vessels, were just run ashore and hauled up a few feet out of the water, ready for embarkation. Hence the many ' Battles at the Ships ' we read of in Greek history and legend, in which, like Aeschylus's brother at Marathon, men could get their hands chopped off while hanging on to the stern of a warship which was being pushed into the water. Hence, too, a Greek port looks very different from an English one. There are no high quays or sea-wall with a long expanse of shingle and seaweed below. Everything is much neater and more closely packed. The villa dwellers on the Bosporus can have their bow-windows over the sea, and Aeginetan fishermen tumble out their sponges straight on to the high road. Nausicaa, who liked things tidy, thus describes the arrangement of her father's model port in Phaeacia. ' There is a fine harbour on each side of the city ; the entrance between them is narrow, and the curved ships are drawn up along the road : for each man has a special slip assigned to him.' And there too, she goes on, is the market-place, with the stores of the ship chandlers and the workshops for the oars near by. The same arrangement is found to-day in many an island port, where there is just room to squeeze the town between the harbour and the hills ; and the effect of neatness given by the orderly arrangement of the ships along the low quay is heightened by the sharpness of the coast-line (as any one will soon discover who tries to pick his way, English-fashion, ' by the beach ') and by the edging that seems drawn so boldly and clearly along it where red-brown rocks and brimming water meet.[1]

On the other hand, a tide brings with it advantages of its own which the Greeks would have known how to appreciate. It supplies a perpetual motive power upon which the seaman can reckon with complete assurance in order to save himself trouble : and he can counteract it in a moment by the use of that oldest of all brakes, the anchor. Putting out to sea from a windless harbour was always a trouble to the Greeks. They would have

[1] *Od.* vi. 263–9 (Phaeacia) ; Hdt. vi. 114 (Battle at the Ships) ; vii. 198 (tide in the Malian Gulf) ; the tide is also particularly noticeable at the Lido in Venice.

gazed with envy on the shipping that glides lazily with the ti⟨
up and down our northern estuaries.

However, if the Mediterranean has not tides, it makes up, to
some extent, for the deficiency by its currents. These the
navigator has continually to reckon with, particularly in narrow
waters. 'Currents have more than one way of running through
a strait,' as Strabo remarks, and their different peculiarities were
a constant source of preoccupation. The two best known are
those at the Straits of Messina and in the Euripus.

Scylla and Charybdis present no difficulty to modern steam-
ships ; and the little whirlpool off the harbour of Messina which
has been identified as Charybdis can never by itself have been
very alarming. But the currents set up by the meeting of the
two seas, together with the wind, made the passage an awkward
one for ancient ships, and Thucydides, who had observed it, and
always makes sense of a legend when he can, wisely extends the
name Charybdis to the entire strait. In any case, Charybdis,
wherever the exact scene of her operations, made the fortune of
one of the richest towns of antiquity. For skippers who feared
the straits, and perhaps too the strong arm of the Chalcidian
colonists at Rhegium and Messina who commanded them, preferred to deliver their Western-bound goods in a port on the
Eastern coast and have them conveyed across the toe of Italy by
land. The shortest and most convenient way of doing this was
up the valley of the Crathis from Sybaris ; and the wealth of
Sybaris, which became proverbial, was due mainly to her command and use of this ' isthmus ' road, which led across in two
days' journey to her colony of Laos on the Western coast. Here
the goods were re-embarked for the ports of Etruria on the
further West. That is why, when Sybaris had been destroyed by
her neighbour Croton, ' the Milesians of every age shaved their
heads and displayed marks of deep mourning : for these two cities
had been more closely befriended than any others we know of.'
Miletus was the chief Greek trading city at that time. Manchester
would be as sorry, though she might show it differently, if the
Cape were in foreign hands and we then lost control of the Suez
Canal.[1]

---

[1] Hdt. vi. 21. Cf. *Mélanges d'archéologie et d'histoire,* xxvii. 250 ff.,
describing the ' portage ' : there was a turning to Temesa, and a rival road
from Siris to Pyxos and thence to Velia and Posidonia. Charybdis : Thuc.
iv. 24. 5, cf. vi. 2. 4.

The currents of the Euripus at the narrows of Chalcis are the most famous in the Mediterranean. The passage was [1] not so broad as a cricket-pitch, and the current, which in a gale can run at over eight miles an hour, changes four times in the twenty-four hours. Yet the Euripus was probably the ordinary road for northward bound ships from Piraeus, for the Eastern coast of Euboea, in the summary language of the old pilot, ' is rocky, irregular, precipitous, and destitute of harbours ; therefore must always be avoided.' Towards the end of the Peloponnesian War the rebellious Chalcidians blocked the strait by building a bridge and half-filling the passage with earth—a severe blow, of course, to the sea power of Athens. The bridge has stood in various forms from that day to this. Its permanence shows that the traffic between Euboea and the mainland, which the Athenians used to conduct in small boats between Eretria and Oropus, has in all ages been as important as the sea road through.[2]

But currents, especially when he had known them from boyhood, were by no means the greatest difficulty with which the Greek navigator had to contend. His real enemy was ignorance. We are apt to reproach him for his timidity, and think ill of him for lying up during the winter months ; but we forget the narrow limits of his knowledge and experience. We should remember that he set sail without either map or compass : that if once he got blown out of his familiar course he could never tell where he was, what current he might find sweeping him along, or what submerged prehistoric peak he might not encounter. So far as we know, none of the sunken reefs in the Aegean, of which the modern *Pilot* is full, bore sea-marks, and the Greeks must have

[1] ' Was ' because it has recently been widened to 129 feet, by the blasting away of a rock with a mediaeval castle on it in the centre of the channel. The new bridge opens to let vessels through.

[2] *Med. Pilot*, ed. 1831, p. 218 (East coast of Euboea). For the sea road cf. Thuc. vii. 29. 2 ; Aesch. *Ag.* 190 : why Agamemnon, King of Argos, should have selected the port of Aulis opposite Chalcis to start from we shall never know : on its drawbacks as a naval base see Leaf, *Homer and History*, p. 103. ' A fleet is worthless unless it is kept together, and how is such a fleet (of 1,200 ships) to be kept together when each ship has to wait for slack water four times a day to make the passage.' Leaf suggests that Aulis appears in the epic as the choice of a Boeotian poet desiring ' to make his own country the scene of the muster ' ; and Hdt. vii. 173, viii. 66. For the boat traffic, Thuc. vii. 28, viii. 95. 2. Thucydides did not live to write, and Xenophon omits, the account of the first bridge, which is only in Diodorus, xiii. 47. Athens must have held both sides of the strait before the revolt of Chalcis. There is a map of the Euripus channel and the surrounding country in Leaf, p. 102.

been astonished when they saw the Persians bringing out a pillar to set up on the famous Myrmex or Ant off Sciathus. Map-making was still regarded as a branch of geometry, and it was not inclined to descend from its diagrams of continents and big rivers, in which the Nile flowed parallel to the Danube and the circular fast-flowing Ocean (imagined as a river with a swift current) neatly rounded off the whole, to the laborious task of locating every detail in a coasting voyage. To some extent this was done by Itineraries (περίπλοι) like that of Hanno : but probably these were not widely used by unlettered Greek seamen, who preferred to rely on experience and oral guidance and tradition. Hence the sea to them was by no means what it seems to the landsman surveying it from the cliff—an unmeasured expanse of navigable water. Their sea roads were as rigidly marked out to them, by the limits of their knowledge, as land roads. They seldom ventured out of sight of land, even when it involved a long way round : the high road to the West, for instance, went up to Corcyra and across to the heel of Italy. So, too, they seldom ventured into strange seas, and when they were blown there against their will they were quick to engage a guide. Naviga-tion naturally tended to be a local affair, and an Aegean seaman knew as little of the routes of the Adriatic as a Swiss guide generally knows of the climbs in the Tyrol.[1]

It was only a spirit of real adventure which, in the language of the Funeral Speech, ' forced a way into every sea ' ; and it was only the larger sea powers, or Sea Lords, as the Greeks called them, who took pains to attract much-travelled mariners to their harbours and so brought distant seas within the sphere of their trade and influence. Smaller maritime communities lived in a narrower circle, and if this, as was natural, gave them few openings for legitimate trade, they fell back on piracy and

[1] Myrmex : Hdt. vii. 183. The rock (which bears no mark to-day) was pointed out to them by a man of Scyros. Probably the people of Scyros and the other Sporades made fine play with the Myrmex. A few years later the Scyrians were turned out of their island by Athens, at the request of the Amphictions, for incorrigible piracy (Thuc. i. 98 ; Plut. *Cimon* 8, who gives details). For sunken rocks as a metaphor cf. Aesch. *Ag.* 1007, *Eum.* 565. Maps : see the scene in the *Clouds* (206 ff.) and Hdt. ii. 33. It is the natural tendency of unscientific man to imagine the world much tidier and less complicated than it is. Compare the early study of astronomy (Ptolemy's map of the heavens), chemistry (the four elements), political science (the three forms of government), industrial organization (universal competition as against universal socialism).

wrecking. So that the history of the Mediterranean from Minos down to the bombardment of Algiers has been a story of the struggle between the ' bad men ' of the rocky islands and coastlands and the vigilant policing of the dominant power.[1]

But the sea is not only a means of transit but a source of production. In some seas the latter element predominates : the North Sea herrings, the salmon of Norway, and the cod of Newfoundland are indispensable to the prosperity of those countries. The Mediterranean, however, has no such staple fisheries ; Yarmouth herrings are eaten to-day by the poor of the Piraeus. The chief Mediterranean fish are the tunny, the anchovy, and the sardine—all familiar to readers of Aristophanes. The Greeks caught them close inshore : they used to watch from the rocks for shoals of tunny and then put out and drag for them or harpoon them with tridents. Readers of the *Persae* will remember Aeschylus's description of how the Persians at Salamis as they struggled ashore were knocked on the head with oars ' like tunnies or some draught of fishes '. But in Greek life the fisherman plays a subordinate part ; in Attica he hardly counts. We have a picture of Attic fishermen in the *Rudens* of Plautus, and from their soliloquy one may gather that to an Athenian audience a fisherman was anything but a millionaire.[2]

One other Mediterranean product is, however, worth a brief mention—the ' purple ' dye which is obtained from a secretion of

[1] Pilots (τοῦ πλοῦ ἡγεμόνες, i. e. guides) : Thuc. vii. 50. 2 (North Africa). Bérard, vol. ii, pp. 543 ff., thinks the geographical accuracy of the *Odyssey*, which he has certainly shown to be remarkable as regards knowledge of winds and weather as well as of places, was due to information derived from an early Phoenician or Greek itinerary. But he gives no evidence. The earliest known work of the sort was that of Hecataeus, the sixth-century predecessor of Herodotus. Thalassocracy or sea lordship : the word is constantly occurring in the Greek historians, e. g. Hdt. v. 83. See Thuc. i. 8. 3 on Minos and the island κακοῦργοι, and Murray's *Greek Epic*, Appendix C.

[2] The short account of the Norwegian fisheries in Demolins, *Comment la route crée le type social*, vol. ii, p. 468, is so suggestive as to be worth a reference. Tunnies : *Persae* 424, Ar. *Eq.* 313. The so-called ' Party of the Shore ' which we hear of in Attica in Pisistratus's time were not fishermen, but the inhabitants of the Paralia or Southern portion of Attica. Places in the Greek world in which we hear of a ' fishing interest ', as at Grimsby or Yarmouth, are Tarentum, Cyzicus, and Byzantium (where the current drove the shoals close inshore) : cf. Ar. *Pol.* 1291 b 23 ; See Appendix. There is a great variety of fishes in the Bosporus, as can be seen in Abdul Hamid's collection of them at Yildiz. Poseidon's trident (which he has bequeathed to the Britannia on our coppers) was originally simply a long fork, such as is still used, for spearing fish. Afterwards he used it (as can still be seen at the Erechtheum) for striking holes in the ground, and even for goading his horses. English residents in Greece find the trident useful as a toasting fork. See Daremberg s.v.

two molluscs, the *purpura* and the *murex*. The ancients had, of
course, no mineral dyes, and this therefore was the only really
firm dye which they possessed, and is often contrasted, in the
poets and elsewhere, with the treacherous dyes obtained from
herbs. Hence the word ' purple ' was loosely applied to all the
colours which the creatures produced, from deep red to violet,
and was regarded throughout antiquity as a great luxury and
mark of distinction. As such it was of course forbidden to the
Spartans under the régime of Lycurgus, although the Spartiate
uniform included a dark red military cloak and Laconia offered
some of the finest fishing grounds. Herodotus tells us that when
an Ionian ambassador came to Sparta he put on a purple robe
to secure an audience. The dye was said to have been discovered
by the Phoenicians, whose god Melkart (so the story went)
noticed one day that his dog had got his nose red by poking
about among the shells. The Greeks learnt it from them early,
but it was totally lost in the Dark Ages and only rediscovered
in 1858 by a French investigator, who traced some violet stains
on Minorca fishermen's clothes.[1]

The question of the nature of Phoenician settlements in early
Greece is curiously bound up with the habits of these little
marine animals; for they hide in the height of summer and
give no good colour in the spring, so that fishing is only possible in the autumn and winter. As the ancients did not go
to sea in the winter, it must have been left either to natives or to
strangers with regular establishments on the coast. Moreover, the
colouring matter could only be extracted while the creatures
were still alive. Hence the complicated business of preparing
the dye had to be undertaken on the spot; and purple works
can still be recognized by masses of crushed shells throughout the
tideless coasts of the Aegean. It is highly probable, therefore,
that the Greeks were right in believing that, before their own
maritime days, their coasts were studded, like those of Sicily,
with little Phoenician settlements on convenient islands and
defensible promontories.[2]

[1] Hdt. i. 152. Spartan uniform : Ar. *Pax* 303 ; maps and description of
the Laconian fishing grounds : Bérard, vol. i, pp. 415 ff. Cf. also Daremberg
and Saglio, s.v. *Purpura*. The Phoenicians were not actually the discoverers
of the purple dye. Crushed murex-shell has been found in a Minoan deposit
in Crete. See the *Annual of the British School at Athens*, ix. 276.

[2] Thuc. vi. 2. 6: cf. Hdt. ii. 44 and Eur. *I. T.* 263 (purple-fishers' encampment).
Hdt. iv. 151 mentions a purple fisher who had been driven astray in a storm.

CHAPTER III

THE CLIMATE

Αὗται γάρ τοι μόναι εἰσὶ θεαί· τἄλλα δὲ πάντ' ἐστὶ φλύαρος.

ARISTOPHANES, *Clouds* 365.

The Clouds are our only goddesses : the others are all vain talk.

IT has been said that the British Islands have no climate, only
weather ', and certainly our climate is so stable in essentials and
so uncertain from day to day that we take it for granted and
ignore its general influence. The climate of the Mediterranean
has for the greater part of the year exactly the opposite char-
acterics ; it is fixed from day to day but varies very greatly
between season and season. Hence its importance as a social
factor is much more apparent and calculable.

The three main points to consider in dealing with climate are
wind, rainfall, and temperature. We naturally tend to think
of temperature first : for us summer means (or ought to mean)
hot weather and winter cold weather. But in the South men
think less of heat and cold than of dryness and moisture, and
less whether a wind is gentle or rough, or warm or chilling, than
whether or not it is likely to bring rain.

The Mediterranean area is, climatically speaking, a border-
land ; it is half-way between the tropics and the steady ' temperate ' climate of North and Central Europe. Its boundaries
are best given in the rainfall maps, which mark off the area
of ' little rain in summer ' : they show that this line mostly
follows, even in its deviations, the limits of Greek colonization,
including, for instance, an island of Mediterranean climate in the
North-West corner of the Black Sea.[1]

Throughout this area it may be said that there is not one
climate but at least two, the effects of two different wind-states
or conditions of atmospheric pressure. The climate changes, not
from day to day, but with startling suddenness in spring and

[1] This explains why the Greeks avoided the Adriatic. See Philippson,
Map VI. His limit of average summer rains is four inches. [See Appendix.]

autumn. As Herodotus remarks, these changes are very trying and are the cause of most illnesses. The Ethiopians, safe in rainless Libya, are the healthiest of mankind, and live to 120, because they have no rainy season. Thucydides was not pedantic but merely sensible and scientific in dividing up his history into summers and winters instead of reckoning by Olympiads or priestesses or archonships. Summer and winter are real and well-marked divisions. Every autumn, when the clouds collected on the mountains and the first rains began, the Greeks put away the comfortable sunny open-air life, gave up fighting and sailing and lying out on the warm stones discussing politics and philosophy; the shepherds came down from the mountain pastures and the traders stayed in town for their lawsuits; the neighbours dropped in to the blacksmith's for a chat round his forge; cloaks and warm shoes were brought out and every one prepared, if necessary, to shiver till the spring. To go to sea in the winter months was madness, and to go to war, as Philip did, was, to say the least, unsportsmanlike.[1]

Still, to the Greeks as to hibernating animals, winter was merely an interlude, and no attempt was made to organize a winter mode of life. Their institutions were arranged for summer conditions. There was as little home-life in winter in their cold draughty houses as in the hot summer evenings. Work went on as usual in the country, for there were olives to be picked, a slow and toilsome process very cold for the fingers. The Parliament and the law-courts were still held in the open air, and Aristophanes' plays were generally performed in January before any foreign visitors dared cross the sea. Dwellers in Mediterranean lands are tough and hardy, and the Greeks could stand cold, if need be, as well as most men. It is only casual observers, visiting favoured spots like Corfu or the Riviera, or judging the activity of the Southerner by the sleeping forms in the streets on a hot afternoon, who have spread the legend that the ' Latin races ' are soft. Xenophon's Ten Thousand survived the snows of Armenia, and many of the highlands of Greece (such for instance as the plain of Tegea, where the corn is not reaped till August) hardly

---

[1] ' It must be the weather ': Hdt. ii. 77, iii. 23. So Thuc. vii. 87. 1 : but cf. vii. 47. 2. Close season : Hesiod, *Erga* 674 ; Dem. ix. 50. Clouds : cf. *Clouds* 275 ff. The smithy as ' public house ' : Hesiod, *Erga* 493 ; *Od.* xviii. 328 ; Hdt. i. 68.

enjoy the true warmth of the summer climate at all.   At Athens
itself snow falls, on the average, only about once a year, but the
surrounding hills are covered with snow about five times during
the winter season.[1]

The marks of the summer in Greek lands are a steady NNE.
wind and a clear sky.   It is a combination which is strange to
us ; for our rough winds are mostly rain-bearers from the
Atlantic. To see the Aegean tossing at midsummer in a ' shining ' gale seems uncanny to an Englishman unless he happens
to have watched the Föhn blowing on a Swiss lake.   But the
' Etesian ' or periodic winds (the Greek ' trade winds '), which
generally prevail throughout the summer, at the least from June
to September, are the Greek sailor's main stand-by.   When
they failed, as in the year of the great plague, Greece became
like a tropical country.   They blow so strongly over some
of the islands as to interfere with the growth of trees on their
northern slopes, and Herodotus is at pains to refute the suggestion that the cause of the Nile flood in the autumn is that the
Etesians will not let the water out all the summer.   So the Corcyraeans were urging quite a credible excuse when they said
that the Etesians blowing round the rough headland of Malea
had unfortunately prevented them from being present at the
engagement of Salamis.   It was this same NNE. wind off Malea
which was the beginning of all Odysseus's troubles.   As the
Greeks did not go to sea in the winter, they selected their
harbours with a view to the North wind only ; hence many
of them face south and are as exposed in the winter as the open
sea.   Readers of the Acts will remember how Paul's ship managed, with difficulty, to reach a harbour ironically called ' the
Fair Havens ', only to find, as the apostle told them, that they
were caught in a trap and that it ' was not commodious to
winter in '.[2]

---

[1] Ar. *Ach.* 505 (the Comedian's *tête-à-tête* before the tourist season).

[2] No Etesians in 430 B.C. : Diod. xii. 58. 4, who of course attributes the
plague to this.   Thucydides omits this and merely points out that the year
had been an unusually healthy one (ii. 49).   Nile-flood : Hdt. ii. 21 ; Corcyraeans at Malea : vii. 168 ; cf. *Od.* ix. 80–1, but Odysseus's North wind
was an autumn or winter one.   See Polyb. v. 5. 3–6 for the influence of the
Etesians on campaign plans, and Hdt. vi. 140 for how to get carried by
the Etesians from Attica to Lemnos.   The Fair Havens : Acts xxvii. 8–12.
The whole chapter is full of interesting detail and well illustrates the dangers
of sailing in the close season.

For in the winter the winds blow from every point of the
compass and cannot be relied upon from one day to the next,
'a great trouble to mortals', as Hesiod says. The Greeks had
names for them all; every variety in the bag of Aeolus was
known and discussed, and the local coast-winds and mountain
hurricanes or 'snatchers' (ἅρπυιαι) besides. These Harpies
were indeed the most dangerous and deceptive of all, for they
could tear down at any season, and make havoc, as at Arginusae,
on an August afternoon, of the well-earned fruits of a fight.
Coast-winds, on the other hand, are known and calculable. As
the sea is warmer than the land by night and cooler by day,
there is a displacement of air after sunrise and sunset. In the
evening the breeze is off the land : in the morning off the sea.
That is why the wise Phaeacians sent Odysseus off in the evening
after supper, although the Greeks as a rule did not like being on
board at night, and why Telemachus and the suitors, who could
rely on their sailors, both set sail after sunset. So Phormio,
the best seaman Athens ever had, waited in the Gulf of Corinth
for the local morning breeze to throw the Peloponnesians into
confusion and then let his old sea-dogs show that experience and
training count for more in warfare than all the native manliness
in the world.[1]

Winds and rainfall go together. The rainless season in Greece
lasts from the middle of May to the middle of September. In
one year out of three, on the average, there is practically no rain
then at all. In the other two the quantity which falls is very
slight. Greece, like Palestine, relies for its moisture on the unsettled weather of winter and the big rainfalls in the autumn
and spring, the 'former' and 'latter' rains of the Bible. It is
on these seasonal rains, this marriage of Earth and Sky, as
legend called it, that everything depends. Herodotus, who
travelled both North and South of the Mediterranean rain zone,
expresses his surprise at the local conditions in each case. In
Egypt he found a country in whose annals it was written, ' In this
king's time rain fell at Thebes.' When the Egyptians asked him
how Greece would fare if Zeus sent no rain, he shrugged his

---

[1] Hesiod on winter winds : *Theog.* 872. Night voyages in the *Odyssey* :
ii. 388, iv. 786, xiii. 70. For the sailors' view of it see *Od.* xii. 279. Phormio :
Thuc. ii. 84. 2. Contrast Thuc. ii. 87. 6 with 39. 1 ; Thucydides is, of course,
quite aware of the contradiction, and so was Pericles.

shoulders and replied with an obvious *tu quoque* about the Nile.
As for Scythia, ' its winter is different from the winter in all
other places : for there is no rain at the proper time, at least
none worth speaking of, but during the summer it never leaves
off raining.' ' All other places' is too confidently phrased. Herodotus was forgetting for a moment how much country he had left
unvisited and falling back into the parochial ways of which he
was trying to cure his audience.[1]

If rain falls in this torrential manner, its effect must naturally
be marked in the behaviour of springs and rivers. Indeed it is
due to this that Greece possesses practically no rivers, in our
sense of the word at all. As the Admiralty *Pilot* remarks, with
ill-concealed irony, ' The rivers that empty into the Aegean Sea
are more deserving of notice from their classical associations
than from their commercial importance.' In winter Greece has
torrents : in summer dry stony beds, with perhaps a trickle in
the middle ; but rivers such as we know which flow, in the Greek
phrase, ' equal themselves with themselves,' all the year round
are unknown. Some of the larger streams are deep enough to
bathe in during the summer, but the majority could be mistaken
by the unwary traveller for an unusually rough road, or sometimes, when there are oleanders in blossom there, for a very
neglected garden. One of the lawsuits in Demosthenes turns
upon the question whether a certain piece of ground was a water-
course, a public highway, or a private garden. Where the rock is
hard, the river banks are steep and form what Thucydides calls
a ' not-to-be-got-out-of ' torrent-bed, as the Athenians found in
their retreat from Syracuse ; while sometimes the river disperses
its bull-headed strength into a wide and stony basin.[2]

Three characteristics, in any case, all Greek rivers share in
common. Firstly, they are not navigable. Home-keeping Greeks
did not know what a navigable river was. Herodotus is delighted
with the navigation of the Euphrates and the Nile, which he
describes in great detail. Yet the Thames-side dweller would
hardly describe these as navigable rivers, since neither of them

[1] Cf. Hdt. ii. 13, iii. 10, iv. 28. Connected with this is the answer to the
conundrum, ' Why have the Nile and the Danube got different habits ? '
(iv. 50).
[2] Torrent-beds : Dem. lv, esp. § 13 ; Thuc. vii. 84. 4. ; cf. iii. 98 : ἀνέκβατος
is the word : most travellers in Greece know what it means.

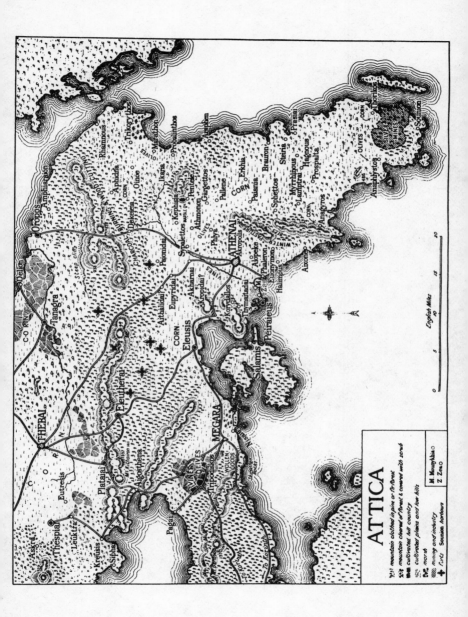

ATTICA

Legend:
- mountain clothed in pine or fir-forest
- mountain cleared of forest & covered with scrub
- cultivated hill country
- cultivated plains and low hills
- marsh
- mining and industry
- ford

M. Mouphkbia ◌
Z. Zeno ◌
Soumn harbour

English Miles
0   5   10   15   20

Place names:
Askra, Thespia, Leuktra, Kreusis, Eutresis, THEBAI, Plataiai, Oropos, Delion, Tanagra, Amphiareion, Rhamnous, Aphidna, Dekeleia, Oinoe, Trikoryntos, Marathon, Probalinthos, Eleutherai, Athmonia, Phyle, Panakton, Spendeios, Kephisia, Acharnai, Akropotamoi, Athalidai, Eupyridai, Kolynaios, Thriaiatai, Eleusis, MEGARA, Nisaia, Pagai, Aigosthena, Plataiai, Philaidai, VINES, WOOLLEN GOODS, Mt. Geraneia, Pentele, Brauron, Gargettos, Pallene, Pausania, Sphettos, Steiria, Myrrhinous, Lamptrai, Hagnous, Prospalta, AGRA, ATHENAI, Akropolis, Alopeke, Phaleron, Peiraieus, Salamis, Hymettos, Euonymon, Halimous, Aixone, Anaphlystos, LAURION MINE, OLIVES, CORN, Prasai, Thorikos, Sounion

allowed small boats to go up stream, and the Euphrates boatmen had to take donkeys on board to carry the boat back by land. Roads and rivers were indeed connected in the Greek mind; for where there was a river there was probably a land-road too. Goods came down from the North along the big rivers, such as the Strymon, which flowed into the North Aegean. But, with the possible exception of timber, they came *by* the rivers, not *on* them. It was only the rivers of Russia and Central Europe which were really useful as beasts of burden, and it is no wonder that Herodotus extols them. There are three special wonders, he tells his audience, in Scythia: the rivers, the vast plain, and a footprint of Heracles.[1]

Secondly, Greek rivers are not easy to cross. In summer there is no great difficulty in going over stony torrent-beds; but they are very difficult to bridge, and become quite impassable in winter. Thus they were as inconvenient for land as for water transport. A few hours' rain might block an important high-road, as the Thebans found when they marched on Plataea in two detachments on a wet night. The first crossed the Asopus easily: the second was stopped and could hardly get through. When a Greek river is in flood there is nothing to do but to wait, like Horace's rustic, till it has passed; it is the roaring bull which river-dwellers often put on their coins. The idea of taming a strong-flowing river and performing engineering feats with it, which Herodotus found prevalent in countries where streams flowed more steadily, appealed greatly to his Greek imagination, and he makes the most of the story-telling possi-bilities of Mesopotamia.[2]

---

[1] Euphrates: Hdt. i. 194, on which see Myres, *Class. Ass.* 1911, p. 56. John Eldred saw the same donkey business in 1583 (Hakluyt's *Voyages*, Maclehose's ed., vol. vi, pp. 5–6). Nile: Hdt. ii. 96. Scythian rivers: iv. 48–9, 82. As regards the navigability of Greek rivers, Mr. S. C. Atchley writes: 'The Louros in Epirus is navigable for a few miles and was used for transport during the operations in the war of 1912 against the Turks. A few other streams, e. g. the Acheron, are navigable for small boats for a few miles.'

[2] Asopus: Thuc. ii. 5. 2. See the coins of Gela and Thurii, and Soph. *Trach.* 11, where Achelous is described as 'sometimes a manifest bull, some-times a shining, winding snake, sometimes bull-headed with a man's body'. Very different from 'Father Thames'. River-engineering: Hdt. i. 75, 189, iii. 9, 117. The Greeks could play with springs, as we know from the tunnel at Samos (iii. 60) and the Pisistratid drains at Enneacrounos; but they did not play with rivers except when they were so tame that it was doubtful which way they flowed. For the troublesome river at Tegea see Thuc. v. 65. 4;

There is another reason why the Greeks did not play with rivers. They are generally too muddy to drink. Hence when the Greeks laid pipes underground, they were directed, not to lakes or rivers, but to the mountain springs ; these alone were pure enough to be the resort of maiden spirits. There were no river-nymphs in Greece.

The fact that Mediterranean rivers flow brown and muddy is more important than it seems. For it means that they deposit all the silt at their mouths and that, in a tideless sea, this is never washed away. To quote the *Pilot* again: 'all [Greek rivers] are obstructed at their entrance by shoals, and few will admit boats.' Hence all through the Mediterranean the ports are never at river-mouths, though, as the river-valley is a road, they are often *by* them. Venice is not at the mouth of the Po, or Marseilles of the Rhone, or Salonica of the Axius, or Alexandria of the Nile, or Smyrna of the Hermus. The alluvial strips or plains thus formed are of particular importance in Greece, but their discussion belongs to a different section.[1]

Xen. *Hell.* v. 2. 4 ; this mighty ($ε\mathring{υ}μεγέθης$) stream, when turned into the streets of Mantinea, was so deep as to wet the foundations of the houses. There are remarkably few remains of old bridges in Greece, and several of these are near Mycenae and pre-Hellenic.

[1] Smyrna has recently only narrowly escaped the silting up of its gulf, and Venice is said to be threatened by the steady filling up of the North Adriatic. See Thuc. ii. 102 for the conundrum, ' When is a land not a land ? '.—1921. Pella, the ancient port of Macedonia, is now many miles from the sea. Salonica port is destined to be closed, in default of counter-measures, by the silt from the Axius and other rivers. The same is true of the port of Haifa in Palestine, the silting up of which it is one of the first tasks of the new government of that country to counteract. These silt-deposits seem to date from the destruction of the forests. Thermopylae is now 3½–4 miles broad, whereas in 480 it was hardly so many yards. Yet the rainfall then was as great as now. It seems, therefore, that the process of denudation followed on the deforestation which began on a large scale after the Slav barbarian invasions of the fifth century A. D.

CHAPTER IV

THE SOIL [1]

Τρηχεῖ', ἀλλ' ἀγαθὴ κουροτρόφος· οὔ τοι ἐγώ γε
ἧς γαίης δύναμαι γλυκερώτερον ἄλλο ἰδέσθαι.
HOMER, *Odyssey* ix. 27.
Rough, but a mother of men, and the sweetest of lands to me.

By soil we do not mean the surface of the earth in general,
but only such of it as is neither too hard nor too dry to nourish
vegetable life. The rocks of the high Alps have no soil; and
it was only a diplomatist referring to an unequal exchange of
territory who spoke of the ' rather light soil ' of an African
desert.

This seems a platitude in England, but it is not so in Greece.
People sometimes speak of the ' fertile South '. They do not
realize that there is far more rock and dry grit and far less
life-giving earth in the Mediterranean lands than in North-
Western Europe. Only a very small proportion of the total
area of Greece is cultivable, and much of that it would be an
exaggeration to call fertile.

In order to understand how the Greeks lived, it is necessary
to take a general survey of their country and see to what uses
it can be put. We might take as the basis of our classifica-
tion, the description, or bird's-eye view, given by the chorus of
Birds in Aristophanes. But they seem to be singing of Attica
only, since they say nothing of the forests. Or we might take
the picture of it on the shield of Achilles in the *Iliad*. But this
is economic rather than geographical, and describes rather what
people do than the country they live in. But its plan of
arranging Greek life in separate departments is not so artificial
as it seems. The features of the Greek country-side can be far
more clearly defined and distinguished than those of our own,
and do really correspond, in a measure, with the demands of
a symmetrical design.[2]

[1] See the map of Attica facing p. 41.
[2] *Iliad* xviii. 490–589; *Birds* 230 ff.; cf. *Clouds* 275. This threefold

Leaving Homer and Aristophanes, we find modern geographers marking off the Greek country into four divisions : the unproductive, the forest, the pasture, and the cultivable. Roughly speaking, these divisions start from the highlands and pass gradually down into the plains. This will become clearer as we deal with them in order.

The unproductive area is mainly rock and the weathering of rock, and now includes about a third, and of course the most conspicuous part, of the entire country. For Greece is not fat and well-fed like England, but a naked land with all her bones showing. She is a land of sharp forms and pure outlines— a land for sculptors and architects, for men who could feel the dignity and repose in the plain folds of her mountains, and see perfect building-sites in her still unlevelled rocks. It is not merely because Greece is mountainous that she is bare ; few of her peaks are above the Alpine level of vegetation, and in the South vegetation might be expected to grow higher still. It is because there is not enough permanent moisture at any elevation to counteract the constant weathering that denudes the surface, as the traveller can realize by comparing the bare sides of a Greek railway cutting with the green walls to which he is accustomed on an ordinary English journey. In the tropics men spend their time weeding ; in England they plant and tend ; in Greece they often have first to make the soil. And even when it is made its maintenance is often precarious. Devastation or neglect may take the life out of it and reduce it once more to useless grit. Hence the effects of a really serious devastation, as in the Decelean years of the Peloponnesian war, are far more lasting than with us. Attica never recovered from it, though she recovered at once from the desultory burnings of the first ten years. Where Nature has her own way in the North she makes a tangled wilderness ; over a large part of Greece she has made a lifeless desert. It is true that men have helped her. They have cut and burnt down and are still burning down the forests which retain the moisture in their roots, and have thus helped the storms to sweep the mountains dry ; and they have neglected the river-mouths and allowed good soil to remain

division is as true of Palestine as of Greece. Compare the Parable of the Sower, with its ' rock ', ' thorns ' (i. e. pasture), and ' good soil '.

swamp. But even in ancient times, when men were thriftier, a large part of the Greek area was naked and lifeless. Corn never grew on the low rocky hill which became the Acropolis of Athens.[1]

We pass from rock to forest. Here perhaps is the greatest outward difference between ancient and modern Greece. A hundred generations of careless peasants have dealt with the country since the days of Plato and Pericles, and it seems probable that they have been watching the trees diminishing all the time. Good observers estimate that the area of the country under forest has actually been reduced by more than one-half in the last thirty years. The peasants kill the trees by burning them, and the process is assisted by the gashing of pine trunks to extract resin. The dry trees are then removed for firewood, and the goats deal with the young shoots. In this way a hill-side can be cleared in a few years. At the present time there are few forests left in Eastern Greece, though parts of North-Western Greece and of Euboea are still well wooded, and thus preserve, far better than the more familiar provinces, the outward aspect of Ancient Greece.[2]

But we must not imagine that Greece was then a forest country in the German sense of the word. Goats have always been goats, and their appetite for dry wood was as vigorous then as now. One of the lost plays of Aristophanes' predecessor Eupolis had a chorus of Goats, and a few lines of their bleat about their favourite bushes have been preserved, showing that they were already well started on their age-long nibble up the mountains.[3]

[1] Devastation of Attica : cf. Thuc. vii. 27. 4 with *Hellenica Oxyrhynchia* xii. 5.—1921. Mr. Atchley tells me that such virgin clumps can be seen to-day in Epirus.

[2] It is very baffling not to be able to find out more definitely what fifth-century Greece looked like, but it is a point on which isolated bits of evidence count for little. I append two. Sophocles speaks of Sunium as a ' wooded promontory ' (*Ajax* 1217) : there are no trees on it to-day. According to Wilamowitz (*Orestie*, p. 228) the ἄλσος or clump of trees round the shrine of a god (corresponding to the cypresses in Southern churchyards to-day) was originally not planted but left ' virgin ' (cf. Eur. *Hipp.* 74), while a clearing for settlements was made round them. Later on, in historical times, when trees had become the exception, they were specially planted.

[3] *ap.* Macrobius, vii. 5. 9 ; cf. the expression ' forest cattle ', e. g. Eur. *I. T.* 261. Tricoupis made a brave attempt to restrain the Greek goat and his master, but with no success. No real effort has been made to enforce the paper provisions of more recent laws. The Greek peasant seems to regard trees as his mortal enemies. Even in Plato's time Attica looked bare and treeless, and there were traditions about the great trees which had been cut

Besides the goats there were the charcoal burners to help to thin the trees. The ancients burnt no coal and all their fuel was wood, either dry or charred. So that in the neighbourhood of every settlement the fringe of trees would be cut down, while the goats would be there to prevent them from growing up again. Athens drew her fuel from the woods around Acharnae, some seven miles out.

But though Athens had fuel enough at home, she had not the timber she needed for her ships. That came mainly from the true forest belt outside the Greek peninsula. For the soil of Greece is not capable of supporting such forest as we know in the North. The trees are both smaller in themselves and grow less close together. The majority of them are evergreens, such as the pine, the fir, and the prickly oak, and of our familiar Northern trees with spreading leaves none but the plane, oak, and chest-nut are at all common. A Greek forest is rarely so thick that the sun cannot get in; the trees grow, in fact, in ' open order '. Moreover, much of what the Greeks call wood we should rather call copse. The most characteristic wild Greek trees are really bushes : the bay, the lentisk, the oleander, the myrtle, the maple, the juniper, the strawberry-tree. Euripides needed to go to Macedonia to find forests high enough to make a dignified procession when ' Orpheus with his lute ' made the trees follow him. Indeed the Greeks had no proper word for tree. ὕλη, which they used of wild wood, refers to bushes and trees in-discriminately; while δένδρον, which we translate ' tree ', means properly fruit-tree. Unlike the Turks and the English, they have no particular love for big trees, and would have regarded a typical English park landscape, bristling with useless giants, as ' shaggy ' and uncivilized.[1]

Below or among the forests on the mountain slopes, or, where the trees have disappeared, immediately under the bare rock,

down. See a very interesting passage, *Critias* 111. But probably the mischief was not very widespread till the advent of the Gauls in the third century B. C. with their large herds of nomadic cattle.

[1] Cf. Eur. *Bacchae* 560, also 677 ff. (the messenger's speech) ; there is nothing of the German forest sentiment (*Waldzauber*) in the description of the Maenads on the mountains. The two things are as wide apart as is the Parthenon from a Gothic cathedral. δένδρον and ὕλη : Thuc. iv. 69. 2, i. 108. 2 ; Hdt. i. 193 (where the vine is a δένδρον) ; *Od.* xi. 588 (the ' high spreading trees ' that tantalized Tantalus).

come the pasture-lands.   Pasture with us calls up a picture
of a lush green meadow on the levels, hedged in from a field of
vegetables or arable near by.   Some of our pasture-land is on
moors or downs ; but most of it is amongst the cultivable land,
with which it is continually rotating, and nearly all of it is grass.
Not so in Greece.   There pasture is on soil which is not good
enough to be sown or planted ; it tends to be a separate ring on
the shield, a separate region of its own away from the settlements on the plain.   That is why undesirable infants, like
Oedipus or Cyrus, were so easily passed on by shepherds to
another country.   For frontiers ' marched together ' on the
pasture-lands, and the shepherds of Thebes and Corinth spent
their summer months in company on the upper slopes of
Cithaeron, descending to their respective countries in the autumn.
That too is why wars so often began, well beyond the arm of
justice, with the stealing of flocks.[1]

Greece pastured a few cows, but mainly goats and sheep, and,
where there were oak trees (as in Arcadia), pigs.   The goats
clamber highest and find dry wood to nibble where the slope
seems almost bare ; and the sheep, too, find sustenance which
ours would certainly disdain.   For what the Greek mountains
offer is mostly not grass but scrub or ' dry-stuff ' ($\phi\rho\acute{\upsilon}\gamma\alpha\nu\alpha$),
all of it stiff and hard and most of it prickly, growing wherever
it can find a hold in the stony soil.   Even in Elysium the
' meadows ' are not all green, but red with spring anemones or
ghostly pale with asphodel.[2]

For though Greek pasture keeps the animals thin, it provides

---

[1] Shepherds : Soph. *O. T.* 1136 ; Hdt. i. 110. Cf. p. 230 below.
[2] The asphodel is one of the commonest scrub flowers.   There are two kinds,
one a fine tall white flower, the other flesh-coloured and shorter.   To the
ordinary Greek farmer the name conveyed nothing of the romance which
our poets have woven round it.   The asphodel meadow became a conventional
Epic phrase for the Elysian Fields, but Pindar, in the beautiful fragment of
one of his dirges, says of the dead : ' the fields outside their city are scarlet
with roses ' ($\phi\omega\nu\kappa\rho\acute{o}\delta\omega\iota\varsigma$ $\dot{\epsilon}\nu\grave{\iota}$ $\lambda\epsilon\iota\mu\acute{\omega}\nu\epsilon\sigma\sigma\iota$ $\pi\rho\omicron\acute{\alpha}\sigma\tau\iota\omicron\nu$ $\alpha\grave{\upsilon}\tau\acute{\omega}\nu$) : cf. Ar. *Frogs* 373.
On the ' scrub ' see Myres, *Greek Lands and the Greek People*, p. 24, who is,
however, in error in saying that, owing to the absence of berry-bearing plants,
' the Greek world is, in general, a jamless world.'   ' On the contrary,' writes
Mr. Atchley, ' it is *par excellence* a berry-bearing country.   Blackberries are
abundant, whilst myrtle, lentisk, arbutus, juniper, bryony, all produce
quantities of berries.   Wild pears are abundant all over Greece, wild plums
are not uncommon, while raspberries and strawberries abound in Pindus.'
It was the lack of sugar, not of berries, which made ancient Greece jamless.

labour for multitudes of bees. The 'dry-stuff' flowers unex-
pectedly and in abundance, like our English gorse, and Greece has
always been a land of goats' milk and honey. Honey indeed
was a necessity, not a luxury, to the ancients ; for they had no
sugar or other sweetening matter, and introduced honey, as
students of Homeric gastronomy will remember, into the strangest
mixtures.

In winter, of course, snow lies on the high pastures and the
shepherds come down into the lower lands, on to the borders and
sometimes even over the edge of the arable. That edge, the last
line on the concentric shield, is very clearly marked in the rainy
season. 'Any one who will go in spring-time,' says Professor
Myres, 'and look round from the Acropolis upon Attica, will
recognize that abrupt change from the emerald green to the
purple and brown which tells where plain and cornland end and
the goats of the mountain slopes begin.' For the Greek levels
are not trimly set about with hedges to prevent the flocks from
eating what they should not ; and goats used to mountain
climbing will surmount most petty obstacles. Hence the dogs
are trained to be very quick and savage. For both the dogs and
their masters have a good deal more to do.[1]

We have at last descended to the level of the cultivable land,
which, with the exception of the forests, forms the smallest of all
the four belts of country. But it is the most important of all, for
without it Greece would hardly be habitable, and certainly would
never have become the home of civilization.

The conformation of these plains is important : for on it
depends much of the political history of Greece. We think of
a mountainous country as a land of ridges and valleys, running
more or less parallel and broadening out as the streams grow
larger. Such, for instance, is Switzerland, whose struggle for
political independence starts from the easy co-operation of the
men in the valleys round the Lake of Lucerne. But in Greece
the land falls, not into valleys, but into plains or levels (πεδία).
Seen from above, the mountain-ranges do not run in straight

---

[1] See *Anthropology and the Classics*, p. 165. Our hedges of course date
only from the time when the mediaeval system was abandoned and arable
and pasture intermingled. The goats that are milked from door to door, as
so often in Southern towns, must often pasture amid the arable. Cf. *Od.* x. 82,
xvii. 170.

lines but, very roughly speaking, rectangularly, enclosing the land into little square boxes. These plains are generally entirely flat, as flat as the English Fens, or, if they rise at all, they rise not at the base of the mountains, but towards their own centre, like upturned saucers. They are watered by streams from the slopes, but these do not flow down lordly valleys in easy stages to the sea, but make their way out as ' foiled circuitous wanderers '. Sometimes, like the Eurotas below Sparta or the Peneus at Tempe, they escape into a deep ravine and disappear like the Mole at Box Hill : sometimes, as in the case of the Stymphalus, the Peneus, and the rivers that run into Lake Copais, they form a lake ; sometimes, like the famous river in the Tegean plain, which caused so many disputes, they settle the matter by drying up and disappearing altogether.

Hence the cultivable land in Greece is divided into compartments well sealed against easy entrance. Some, and the most important of these, are formed partly on alluvial soil, with one side open to the sea. Such are the plains of Argos, Athens, and Eleusis. Others, like the plains of Sparta, Thessaly, and the central plain of Arcadia, are shut in by mountains on all sides. Both formations equally promoted isolation in early times ; for, before the sea was policed, there were no regular maritime communications, and all cities were built, like Athens and Argos, well away from the shore. Greek institutions and Greek patriotism grew up during long centuries of isolation in these boxes of cultivable land with their rigid mountain frontiers.[1]

It was on the products of these little plains that the Greeks lived, ever since they had settled down and ceased to be a purely pastoral and nomadic people. Three stood out above the rest as necessary to human existence—corn, wine, and oil, which have been called ' the Mediterranean triad '.

Corn comes first in point both of time and necessity. For before men felt firm enough in their homes to plant olive-trees, or even vines, they sowed corn for the next harvest, ready to pass on when they had reaped and prepared it. σῖτος, that is wheat or barley, was the staple Greek food. Meat they seldom ate, except at festival times, when the sacrificial animals were dis-

---

[1] See Grundy's map of Greece (Murray's Handy Classical Maps) which marks the plains at all elevations green.

tributed; and everything else that was not σῖτος was regarded as dessert (ὄψον). Persians, who were not used to Greek meals, complained that there was nothing worth eating after the flour course and that they left the table hungry; and later visitors have re-echoed their complaint. The Greeks ate flour food in great quantities and in many varieties. As a rule only the wheat was made into bread: the barley was kneaded but not baked, and eaten as a sort of porridge with water; these are the 'noble cakes' Plato provides in the spare dietary of his Guardians in the ideal city. The Greeks have never been either gluttons or drunkards. Then as now most of them only took two meals— lunch (ἄριστον) towards midday, after half a day's work, and supper (δεῖπνον) in the evening. But these meals, like rare holidays, are all the more needed when they come, and the arrangements of the day, even in war time, tended to revolve round them. There were few Greek commanders (outside the Epic) who could make their men fight during the usual luncheon interval. When they arranged to do so they generally won a decisive victory.[1]

Every Greek city grew, or tried to grow, its own corn. When the demand exceeded the supply and the city was no longer self-sufficient very serious political difficulties arose, as we shall see. The corn is sown in October, and reaped in May and June. It is grown wherever the state of the ground permits, and it is not unusual to see oxen ploughing on little terraces of rock which look far too small and inaccessible to be worth the trouble. Thucydides, who objected to dating by the awkward Athenian months (for most Greek states had different names for their months), fixes his events during each season, as is natural for country readers, by the state of the crops.

[1] Corn-growing: Thuc. i. 2. 2. Cf. Hdt. iv. 42 on 'How could the Phoenicians carry enough fresh provisions to go round the Cape of Good Hope?' See Isocr. vii. 29 on the steady increase in the number of festivals at which sacrifices were required. Also [Xen.] Ath. Pol. (henceforward referred to as 'Old Oligarch') iii. 8 and Thuc. ii. 38. Persian meals: Hdt. i. 133; Ar. Ach. 77–8. Cakes: Rep. 372 B: the details are all taken from daily life. Fighting in the luncheon interval: Xen. Hell. ii. 1. 27 (Aegospotami). Other instances: Thuc. vii. 39. 2, viii. 95. 3; Hdt. i. 63, vi. 78. Compare the account of the battle of Trebia (a winter battle) in Polyb. iii. 71–2. Clytemnestra (Aesch. Ag. 331) enlarges on how the Greeks must be enjoying their first good meal in Troy; cf. Thuc. viii. 101. 2. One can work or walk for many hours in Greece on an empty stomach, but when hunger suddenly comes it is quite paralysing. Cf. Murray, Greek Epic, p. 27 (2nd ed. p. 47).

After corn, wine. It is curious that the chief commercial importance of the vine in modern Greece should not be alcoholic at all. The largest article of export is currants (or, as the Germans more correctly call them, Corinths), a small variety of grape which was not known in Greece till the fourteenth century. In its older forms, however, the vine has been in Greece from the earliest times, and wine has always been the national drink. Herodotus was surprised when he found himself in a new zone of drinks, and saw Egyptians drinking beer ' because they had no vines ', and Babylonians drinking palm-wine. The Greeks were not a drunken nation, though wine played a large part in their social and religious life. They always drank it mixed, generally in the proportion of three of water to two of wine, and they thought it uncivilized to take it neat. But they could not do without it.[1]

The third member of the triad is the olive, the only one of the three which is characteristically Mediterranean. While the vine grows as far North as Cologne and Vienna, and can even grow in England, the olive follows very closely the frontier of the ' practically rainless summer '. Hence its uses are unfamiliar to us, and it is worth while to explain them. For in Greek life the ' little oil-flask ' was as indispensable, and as easily mislaid, as the umbrella is with us.

Olive-oil to the Greeks played three separate rôles—those of butter, soap, and gas. It was used for cooking, for washing, and for lighting. No one in Greece (outside fashionable hotels at Athens) eats butter; bread and olives or bread and goats' cheese are their ' bread and butter ', and Herodotus thinks it necessary, for the information of his readers, to give a minute description of

---

[1] Drink-zones : Hdt. ii. 77 (but cf. ii. 60), i. 193. κρασί, the modern Greek word for wine, means ' mixture '. The Temperance Question of course assumes very different aspects in different drink-zones—e. g. in Greece and Scandinavia. For a thoughtful Greek view see the discussion by Plato in the *Laws* (Book i), who sums up (650) that wine ' is a fair test of character, and cheaper, safer, and speedier than any other ', and that it is also a ' cheap and innocent ' way of *training* character, ' if care be taken in the use of it.' The Greeks used the word ' drunk ' far more loosely than we do, at any rate in our police courts. For instance, the ' inopportune man ' in Theophrastus ' when he is minded to dance, will seize upon another person *who is not yet drunk* '. So clearly a ' drunken man ' was considered by no means incapable of executing the complicated manœuvres of a Greek dance. (Theophr. ix, Jebb's 2nd ed., which will be used in subsequent references, p. 77.)

a Scythian butter-making or literally ' cow-cheese-making '.[1]
Hence oil is used in almost every dish, and every Greek cook
would be lost without it. Again, the Greeks used no soap,
but rubbed themselves with oil and, if that was insufficient, put
scents on above it. Lastly, if they outstayed the sun (which
they did far less than we), they had no other light but oil or
resinous torches. Hence the multitudes of oil-lamps in every
classical museum. For each of these purposes thrifty house-
keepers used a different quality of oil. The olives were squeezed
in presses : the first squeeze produced eating oil, the second
anointing oil, the third burning oil, and, finally, the remainder,
skins and all, was used as fuel.[2]

The olive used to be regarded as a comparatively late comer
into the Greek world, for legend spoke of how Athena introduced

[1] Hdt. iv. 2.   Butter is probably simply βού-τυρος.   The Babylonians'
substitute for butter is Aladdin's Sesame, i. 193.

[2] Scents : it must be remembered that home-spun clothes, unlike ours, last
a very long time.   Fullers and laundrymen used a rough kind of soap for
getting out bad stains (hence the metaphor in *Republic* 430), but oil was
used, like camphor with us, for keeping clothes fresh (*Il.* xviii. 595). Sometimes the fine ashes from the hearth were mixed with oil, which made a soap
(Ar. *Lys.* 470 Schol. : cf. Ar. *Ach.* 17–18). But the Greeks were not, judged
by our unusually high English standard, a clean race. To wear linen clothes
was regarded as a luxury, partly because they required constant washing.
Hence, after a short excursion into linen underclothing, even the Athenians
reverted to woollens, which are not the cleanest wear in a hot country.
(Cf. Thuc. i. 6. 3 with Hdt. ii. 37 and *Od.* vi. 64–5. Bérard, vol. i, p. 556,
exaggerates this point in an interesting passage on Nausicaa's clothes-washing.)
One of the marks of Theophrastus's ' Man of Petty Ambition ' (Jebb, p. 63)
is his excessive cleanliness. ' He will have his hair cut very frequently and
will keep his teeth white ; he will change his clothes, too, while still good, and
will anoint himself with unguent.' On Greek washing arrangements see
Sudhoff, *Aus dem antiken Badewesen*, with a most attractive collection of
vase illustrations, showing e. g. the flimsiness of the ' washhand stands ' in
private houses and the simplicity of the arrangements in the public baths.
There were public baths for women, too, whither they resorted perhaps
about weekly (p. 63). We can see towel, scraper, oil-flask, sponge, but no
trace of soap. On a piece of an Athenian Vase in the Louvre (*Louvre Album*,
vol. ii, Plate 78, F 203) there is a women's swimming-bath, perhaps the well-
house of the Enneacrounos during certain hours. Cf. also Lysias, i. 9, and
Furtwängler and Reichhold, Fig. 107, and *Text*, vol. ii, pp. 237–41, with some
interesting psychology. The fourth-century vase there represented shows
two women at a washing basin which is like a large holy-water stoup. There
is another like it on a kylix in the British Museum, dating from about 480.—
The first ' corner ' recorded in Greek history was made by Thales the philosopher, in olive presses. According to the story, his knowledge of the stars
enabled him to predict a good crop, and he bought up all the presses, ' just
to show that a philosopher can make money if he likes.' Ar. *Pol.* 1259 a. 16.
See Daremberg and Saglio, s. v. *Olea*, Fig. 5388.

it into Attica at a time when it existed in no other part of Greece. But the archaeologists have corrected this idea, which may have been due to the slow growth of olive cultivation. There are clear signs of an olive press in the Palace of Minos at Cnossos, another has been found under the pumice of the prehistoric eruption at Thera, and olive kernels are being discovered in deep levels in Crete. So the olive may now be regarded as indigenous, and the Olympian ' crown of wild olive ' as a truly Hellenic prize. The tree grows in all parts of Greece, wherever it can find soil, up to a level of 1,800 feet, often in most inaccessible spots in the mountains. But it flourished best in Attica, and in Athenian poetry. The olive is generally not a big tree ; it is not allowed to grow larger than a pollarded willow, and its trunk is even more gnarled ; its charm lies in the wonderful shimmer of its leaves, which flash from grey to silvery white in a sunny wind. From Greece it went the round of the Mediterranean, past Cyrene and Magna Graecia. It began to be extensively cultivated in Italy about the second century before Christ. It spread widely in North Africa, and we know that at the time of the Arab conquest there was a ' forest of olives ' right along from Tripoli to Tangier.[1]

Greek and Roman writers have left us directions, which can be verified in Greece or Italy on a country walk, as to the planting of olives. An ' olive grove ' is not a forest but an open orchard. The trees are planted tidily in rows, and on good soil it is wise to leave forty feet between each tree in the row and sixty feet between row and row. Thus there is plenty of room to sow corn between the trees, and the peasant has not to choose between two forms of cultivation, but simply which of the two he is to make his staple.

As Virgil remarks, the olive wants very little looking after, beyond digging round the roots. Hence, once planted in a country, they are a very favourite form of cultivation ; for Southern man (and every man) enjoys sitting complacently beneath his fruit-trees. It is only in the late autumn that work

---

[1] Olives : Hdt. v. 82. Athena's first olive was planted on the Acropolis and its first cutting in the Academy. Cf. Wilamowitz, *Aristoteles und Athen* (henceforward referred to as *A. A.*), vol. i, p. 240. See the fine simile in *Il.* xvii. 53, and, of course, the Sophocles chorus (*O. C.* 694). Also Hehn, p. 111.

begins, in a convenient interval when other crops give no trouble ; for the olives ripen later than the figs and the grapes. 'Such olives as you can reach with the hand or from ladders are better pulled than shaken from the tree,' says a professional Roman agriculturist. 'Those branches that cannot be reached by the hand should be beaten with a rod rather than with a pole, for a heavy blow demands a doctor.' There were no rejoicings at the olive harvest as there were for the vintage. It was as laborious as English hopping or strawberry picking, and hired labourers went out from the city to do it in the familiar Kentish way.[1]

But there is another important factor. It is a long time after they are planted before olives come to maturity. They do not bear a full crop for sixteen or eighteen years, and it is forty to sixty years before they are at their best. As with forests, therefore, it is difficult to introduce them except under a strong central government and with a country population which can afford to wait. This explains the slow progress made in their cultivation in early times and the difficulties that Solon and Pisistratus experienced when the Athenian Government favoured their spread. Probably they would never have spread widely in Attica at all had not Pisistratus made advances to the proprietors out of his own private purse.[2]

Hence, too, the seriousness of the devastation of an olive-country. An olive-yard well destroyed is not, like a cornfield, the destruction of a year's income, but the destruction of capital as well. Sophocles, writing in 406, after seven years of the constant occupation of Attica by the enemy, might bravely call the olive ' self-renewing and unsubdued ', carrying the minds of his hearers back to how the sacred olive on the Acropolis sprouted after the Persians left. But the farmers who heard him knew the hollowness of the words, and when at the end of the war they left their ruined farms with their charred olive-stumps and went soldiering side by side with their late enemies for a living, they must have felt a lump in their throats as they sang his chorus round their camp fires.[3]

[1] Varro, *Rerum Rusticarum* i. 55. Olive pickers : Ar. *Wasps* 712. They are represented on a vase in the British Museum, reproduced in Daremberg and Saglio, s. v. *Olea*, Fig. 5385. Cultivation : *Georgic* ii. 420.

[2] *Ath. Pol.* xvi. 2.

[3] Soph. *O. C.* 699 alluding to the story in Hdt. viii. 55. For camp-fire talk between Athenians and Spartans see Xen. *Anab.* iv. 6. 7–19. That the

Modern geographers mention another department of cultivation in present-day Greece—that of so-called sub-tropical products, which require constantly irrigated soil. The chief of these are cotton and tobacco, both of which are grown in the country to-day, the latter in considerable quantities.

This sub-tropical cultivation played no part in ancient Greece. Cotton they only knew as a strange and rare kind of ' tree-wool ', and tobacco, rooted as it appears to be to-day, like coffee, in the life of the Near East, they did not know at all. It is only worth while mentioning them in order to point out that the systems of intensive cultivation and gang-labour with which they have else-where been associated are equally foreign to ancient Greece. If the Greeks had had sugar instead of honey, they might have been turned from a race of yeomen into a race of planters. It is only fair to add that, if they had eaten rice instead of wheat and barley-flour, they would have saved their women-folk a great deal of hard labour at the mill. But we have already crossed the narrow line between geography and economics—between products of the earth and the use man makes of them, and it is time to bring this section to a close.[1]

Peloponnesians in Attica addressed their devastation mainly to olive-trees seems clear (*inter alia*) from the wording of Thuc. iii. 26. 3 : ' they ravaged what had sprouted in the parts previously ravaged ' (τά τε πρότερον τετμημένα εἴ τι ἐβεβλαστήκει) : there would be no point in adding ' what had sprouted ' in the case of corn, which there had been plenty of time to sow since they were there last. It was the new olive-yards which made the Italians reluctant to go to war when Caesar crossed the Rubicon ; the first oil had been exported from Italy three years previously : Pliny, *N. H.* xv. 1. 3. The Law of Moses forbade the Jews to cut down ' trees for meat ' in warfare : Deut. xx. 19–20, but cf. 2 Kings iii. 19.

[1] Cotton (εἴριον ἀπὸ ξύλου = German *Baumwolle*) : Hdt. iii. 47 and 106. Flax was grown to a small extent in ancient Greece. In Thuc. iv. 26 the Helots carried ground linseed, such as we give to cattle, to the prisoners in Sphacteria. Hemp was not grown. It was strange to Herodotus, who found the Thracians using it for clothing and the Scythians for vapour baths (iv. 74–5). Of familiar garden products the Greek had neither cherries, oranges, lemons, tomatoes, nor, till after Alexander, peaches and apricots. The first silkworms for fine silk were brought West in 536 A. D., though silk goods were known to the Romans. An inferior silk was, however, manufac-tured in Cos from the cocoon of a native species of *bombyx* in much earlier times. The chief Greek fruits were figs (easily first), apples, pears, and pomegranates ; cf. *Od.* xi. 588 (Tantalos) and xxiv. 246 (Laertes' garden). One point about animals : cocks and hens, which the Athenians called the ' Persian bird ' (and the Romans the ' bird from Gaul '), came to Greece from Asia in the sixth century B. C. So there was a time in Greece when neither Asclepius nor the weary traveller was offered cock or ' chicken '. On all these points see Hehn, *Kulturpflanzen und Haustiere* (7th ed., Berlin, 1902), E. T. (of earlier edition), London, 1888.

PART II. POLITICS

Τοῖς μὲν σώμασιν ἀλλοτριωτάτοις ὑπὲρ τῆς πόλεως χρῶνται,
τῇ δὲ γνώμῃ οἰκειοτάτῃ ἐς τὸ πράττειν τι ὑπὲρ αὐτῆς.

They spend their bodies, as mere external tools, in the City's service, and
count their minds as most truly their own when employed on her behalf.

SUCH, then, are the material foundations on which Greek institutions were built up. Such is the permanent background against which the drama of Greek history was played out. It is time to introduce the characters. What manner of men were they, and what did they make of the rough country in which they came to live?

The greatest legacy which the Greeks have left to the after-world is their City State patriotism. The City State was the centre and inspiration of all their most characteristic achievements, culminating in the great outpouring of literature and art and practical energy, of great men and great deeds, in fifth-century Athens. The world has seen nothing comparable to it either before or since. When the Sovereign City passed away in the fourth century before Christ, the emotions and affections which it had kindled and fed passed away too, and it needs an effort of imagination in the modern man to recapture not them but their shadow. Yet without some dim understanding of how the Athenian felt towards Athens the best of ancient Greece remains sealed to us. Let us try to disentangle patiently and carefully—for it is a delicate task—the several strands of the tie which linked the Greek citizen to his city, using geography and history and all the other helpers we can find to play the commentator to that highest expression of the art of life in the City State, the Funeral Speech of Pericles.

CHAPTER I

THE DEVELOPMENT OF CITIZENSHIP

FELLOWSHIP, OR THE RULE OF PUBLIC OPINION
(τὸ κοινόν)

Idem sentire de republica was with them a principal ground of friendship and attachment ; nor do I know any other capable of forming firmer, dearer, more pleasing, more honourable, and more virtuous habitudes.—Burke.

How would geographical conditions influence the dweller in Greek lands ?

Life in Greek lands is at once very hard and very easy : or rather, dwellers in Greek lands are at once very hardy and very easy-going. The roughness and barrenness of the country, the changes between the seasons and the severity of the winters, promote the survival of the fittest, and have made the Greeks of all ages simple, tough, and abstemious. But the long cloudless summers and the ease with which life is sustained on very little have greatly simplified the problem of existence. The Greek need not, and does not, labour from morning to night to keep body and soul together. He has never needed and never liked sustained and monotonous activity of the kind which Northern workers and Northern economists tend to regard as the inevitable lot of all mankind. The Greek has never known what it is to be, in the common sense of the word, either in his habits or his ideals, an economic man. The Greek word for unemployment is ' scholê ', which means ' leisure ' : while for business he has no better word than the negative ' ascholia ', which means ' absence of leisure '. The hours and weeks of unemployment he regards as the best and most natural part of his life. Men who live among vines and olives fall naturally into this free and irresponsible frame of mind. Nature ripens the fruit, and man has only to wait and pick it. The Greeks always lived with a fine margin of leisure ; and leisure is the mother of art and contemplation, as necessity is the mother of the technical devices we call 'inventions'. The Greek peasant understood and enjoyed the depth and subtlety of Euripides, but he had never thought of so simple a contrivance as a windmill.[1]

Our steady monotonous economic activity mostly goes on indoors, generally in cramped and sedentary postures. We do not do this from choice, but because the nature of the climate and of our work compels it. Most of us would spend all our time out of doors if we could. So would the Greeks, and there was nothing to prevent them. ' I never spend my time indoors,' says the typical Athenian in Xenophon. ' My wife is quite able to manage the household by herself,' and he went out cheerfully to spend his day in the fields, or the market-place, or the wrestling-ground, or the law-courts, or the assembly, or wherever else duty or pleasure called him. All the chief institutions of Greek life took place in the open. The Greek was seldom at home. He only used his house for sleeping and eating. You will not find him in his private garden : for a Greek city, crushed within the circuit of its walls, has no room for gardens, and what was the use of them with orchards just outside the walls ? He will be at work or along with the other men in some public place.[2]

But supposing it rained ? Every self-respecting city provided for that by the erection of colonnades or covered walks, similar to those put up in some of our watering-places to-day. Strabo tells a story of how the inhabitants of Cyme in Asia Minor pledged their colonnades as security for the repayment of a State debt. When they could not repay, they were prohibited from walking

[1] Of course climatic conditions must be such as not to interfere with the right use of leisure. As Myres points out (*Greek Lands*, p. 28), ' Aegean contemplation differs from Indian in this, that it is seldom too hot for one to think with a view to action.'
[2] Xen. *Oec.* vii. 3. The Babylonians even had their hospitals in the open, and Herodotus (i. 197) thought it a very sensible arrangement, promoting the diffusion of useful medical knowledge. It was not general in Greece, probably because the Greeks did not like looking at sick people. But the Orestes of Euripides who lies ill in bed in the yard outside his own front door is probably copied from the life. For beds in the market-place see also Mark vi. 56. Gardens reveal a desire for privacy which was foreign to the City State. It is characteristic that the first people to make a regular use of private gardens, and to look upon them as indispensable, should have been the philosophers. The Academy and the Lyceum were not so much a training for City State life as a substitute for it. Socrates taught in the market-place and in public wrestling-grounds : Plato and Aristotle ' moved out into the country '. [See Appendix.]

in them. But when it rained the creditors felt so much ashamed
of the city's plight that they sent out the town-crier to remove
the interdict. The men of Cyme could not possibly do as we
should and receive their friends in their own houses. In the first
place there would be women there and they could not talk at
their ease ; and, secondly, if a Greek house is uncomfortable in
sunny weather it is still more uncomfortable in wet, for it was,
of course, not heated. Consequently the market-place and the
covered walks were to the Greek what his club is to the Northern
townsman : only he used them much more frequently. The
Greek was, in fact, not a 'family man', but, as Aristotle called
him, a political animal, or rather, for we are still quite outside
the sphere of politics, a 'man in the street'. But his wife, to
make up, was all the more home-keeping. For she had food and
clothes to prepare : nor was it safe to admit her to the free and
easy society of the market-place. So the Greeks regarded the
man's club as a law of nature. 'The god has ordained and the
law approves that each should follow his capacity,' says Xenophon. 'It is not so good for a woman to be out-of-doors as in,
and it is more dishonourable for a man to stay in than to attend
to his affairs outside.' So when Herodotus found men weavers
in Egypt and women doing their own shopping and even selling
goods in the market-place, he felt himself to be in a topsy-turvy
society. 'A house, a wife, and an ox to plough with are the first
needs of life,' sang Hesiod as a man to men : and Aristotle,
centuries later, picked out the sanctified phrase, perhaps because
he liked the order in which the commodities were arranged, and
made it one of the foundation-stones of his political theory.[1]

Club-life promotes good fellowship. The Greeks, like most
peoples in similar climates, were sociable and gregarious and
enjoyed mixing in large companies. Some Northerners think
it wrong to speak before they have been introduced. A Greek
thought it rude to let a stranger pass without a welcome, and
foolish not to gratify a natural curiosity by asking him his business. The single line question and answer dialogues (στιχομυθία)
in the Tragedy when a new character enters assume a fresh meaning to the traveller who has run the gauntlet of a Greek village.

[1] Xen. Oec. vii. 30; Hdt. ii. 35 ; Hesiod, Erga 405 ; Ar. Pol. 1052 b 11 ;
Strabo, 622.

Few Northern Sunday-school boys are so mercilessly catechized as the casual stranger in Greek lands. It is part of the club system, and goes back to the unsettled days when even pirates and brigands were not ashamed to tell the catechists their calling. Solitude to a Greek means what homesickness would mean to us. Having always lived in a kind of natural College they cannot adapt themselves to conditions which cut them off from their fellows. Hence when they emigrate, whether, as of old, to Sicily and Italy, or, as now, to the United States, they go, ' not as single spies, but in battalions,' or rather, as Plato said, in swarms, all friends together. And when they reach the other side they are more concerned to find social than economic conditions which suit them. If one of the two must be sacrificed it will not be the community life. If the immigrant can only practise agriculture in a dreary American farm miles away from the next homestead, he will prefer to remain pent up in the city, ' where he soon forgets his cunning in regard to silk-worms and olive-trees, but continues his old social habits to the extent of filling an entire tenement-house with the people from one village.' A skyscraper is a poor substitute for a sunny market-place : but beggars cannot be choosers.[1]

All this has an important influence on Greek political life. Fellowship means Equality, not the fictitious Equality which has served as a watchword for Western Republics, but the inbred feeling which has always found a home, in common needs and common intercourse, at the springs and the well-heads, the cross-roads and market-places, the temples, shrines, and mosques, of the Near East. There was more true equality in Turkey under Abdul Hamid than in the United States under Roosevelt. One illustration must suffice to emphasize what is after all one of the commonplaces of travel. A British officer is describing his reception by a Turkish Agha in a small town near the upper Tigris :—

An example of that delightful spirit of true equality which is inherent in Orientals was shown in the company present at my reception—the Agha himself, the captain in command of the

---

[1] See the whole chapter on ' Immigrants in City Government' in Jane Addams's *Newer Ideals of Peace*, pp. 62 ff. Cf. Thuc. i. 5. 1 (pirates), vii. 75. 6 (gregariousness) ; Plato, *Laws* 708 B (colonization).

troops, a blind beggar, a Christian shopkeeper, a telegraph clerk, a couple of servants, Jacob (the writer's own servant), myself, and, lastly, a butcher who came to settle the price of a sheep with my servant, which he discussed across the Agha over a cup of coffee.[1]

The scene is a typical one, not least the bargain at the end. A society which needs no ' introductions ' and knows no shyness has no reticences either. It says what it thinks, as men do in clubs, whether about money or marriage or anything else.

Equality like this is a good basis for political institutions. It is good for all the men of a community to meet and talk, for they will naturally talk about things of general interest. Now the chief thing of general interest in a small simple-minded community with a settled climate is not the weather, or money, or marriages, but the State. The State is in fact, as the Greeks called it, τὸ κοινόν, ' the common interest,' or, as the Romans said, ' Res publica,' ' everybody's business.' If a man talks about your wife and daughters, especially in a clannish society like that of Greece, you can tell him to mind his own business. But in politics every problem and every personality is fair game. It is one of the privileges of club-life to have all its questions threshed out in public—to fling everything ' into the midst ' (εἰς μέσον), as the Greeks said. Their great objection to an absolute ruler was not that he governed badly—for they admitted that a man who decided things by himself might be very efficient—but that ' he kept himself to himself '. To be governed by an absolute ruler took all the life out of society. It reduced Ionians to talking metaphysics, or, if their tastes did not run in that direction, to relieving the dullness of life by paying excessive attention to their clothes. And indeed when, after Alexander, the discussion of politics ceased to be real, the men who had something to think about ceased coming to the market-place and conversation degenerated into frivolities and superstition. The Athens of St. Paul is the Athens of Pericles with one great interest taken out of its life.[2]

[1] *Dar-ul-Islam*, by Mark Sykes, p. 188.
[2] Cf. Hdt. iii. 80, 82 (the monarch σιγῶτό τε ἂν βουλεύματα : Demosthenes says the same of Philip). A king who was easy to talk to was considered to be behaving ' in an unkingly way '. See Hdt. ii. 173, where Amasis makes himself as accessible as an American President. Also Thuc. i. 130 (Pausanias's

Community life, lived under these conditions, created the force
which we call public opinion.   We know it as focused or manufactured by the newspapers or in its outbursts at elections and
public meetings.   After 700 years of Parliamentary government it is a force with which politicians have to reckon in
England : in a lesser degree it exists in all constitutional countries.   But we little know the range and intensity of its influence
in a community like those of Greece.   The political animal
discussed everything that was put before him.   ' To say everything ' (παρρησία) was one of his most cherished rights, and he
exercised it in a large and liberal spirit, which our public men
and even our Press cannot hope to rival.   The ingenious way in
which Demosthenes interlards his speeches with smoking-room
topics seems to us both shocking and irrelevant, and we cannot
understand why contemporary critics all seem anxious to tell us
that Euripides' mother was an apple-woman.   Yet why, after all,
should the free-speaking citizen refrain from ' personal remarks ' ?
For the game of politics in Greece, then as now, consisted mainly
of personal rivalries, and everything that a man did or said or
bought or wore might be of political consequence.   Athens
prided herself, as opposed to other City States, on the free
scope which she allowed to individual idiosyncrasies.   Yet even
in Athens Demosthenes thinks it necessary to excuse a client for
' walking fast, talking loud, and carrying a walking-stick '.   And
how strangely the words of Pericles, commending the freedom of
Athenian social life, read to Englishmen brought up to believe,
as a matter of course, that ' every man may do as he likes with
his own ' !   ' We have no black looks or angry words for our
neighbour if he enjoys himself in his own way, and we abstain
from the little acts of churlishness which, though they leave
no mark, yet cause annoyance to whoso notes them.'   One can
imagine that Pericles would have had to face more than ' little
acts of churlishness which leave no mark ' if he had tried to
drive a motor-car through an Attic township.   Really it was
not worth while trying to get rich when public opinion con-

Oriental manners).   It is one of the marks of Theophrastus's ' arrogant man '
that he is ' not likely to admit a visitor when he is anointing himself or
washing ' (Jebb, p. 50).   The Ionians were always ahead of the fashion in
clothes, as the vases and monuments show : cf. Hdt. iii. 139 (Syloson's ' fancy
waistcoat ' and what it led to).

trolled the use one made of one's money. In such a society men, even, as Pericles says, old men, count honour better than riches. For to have what the Greeks called a good ' estimation ' (ἀξίωσις) probably contributed, more than anything else which lay within a man's own power, to the happiness of his life. No wonder Greeks were tempted to think that virtue consisted not in being good but in ' seeming good '.[1]

Perhaps the best way of emphasizing the place of public opinion in Greek life is by following up the meanings of the words connected with the market-place, where it reigned supreme. The original meaning of Agora is not market-place but assembly : for the Greeks were gregarious long before they lived in towns. Then it means a *place* of assembly, where meetings and trials were held, and then, as life became more complicated, a place for buying and selling. But an Agora or public meeting can take place anywhere. When Odysseus had to settle a question of policy on shipboard it was put before the ' assembly ' of the seamen : and one of the crew, Eurylochus, is a perfectly recognizable leader of the Opposition, who succeeds, on one unfortunate occasion, in placing the skipper in a minority of one. Readers of *Eothen* will remember the chapter on *Greek Mariners*, with the description of the gloomy Hydriot mate who acted as ' counter-captain, or leader of the Opposition, denouncing the first symptoms of tyranny, and protecting even the cabin-boy from oppression '. But Ἀγορά not only stands for the debate, but suggests the closure, for it came to be used as a mark of time. Ἀγορᾶς πληθυνούσης, ' full Agora,' means the forenoon before lunch. When they had talked themselves hungry they needed no town clocks to send them home. The verbal form, ἀγοράζειν, is an almost equally interesting word. It means ' to frequent the market-place', 'to lounge', 'to buy ', and, above all, in an almost untranslatable phrase, ' to disport oneself ' or ' be in good Agora form '. When Democedes the Greek doctor escaped from the Persian court to his home in Croton, the emissaries from Darius found him, in the centre of an admiring crowd, ἀγοράζοντα. Some strange stories must have taken root in Croton about life at the Persian court from those mornings' work. Such a society needed neither books nor newspapers. It picked up its new

[1] Thuc. ii. 37. 2 ; 44. 4 ; Dem. xxxvii. 52 ; Pl. *Rep.* 365.

ideas, whether serious or frivolous, from Aeschylus or from
Democedes, at first hand by word of mouth.[1]

So far we have been speaking of influences common to most
Mediterranean lands. Wherever life is easy and open there is
a certain natural equality. The sun shines alike upon the high-
born and the low. Distinctions of first, second, and third class
are either unknown or, where they have been introduced, are
only maintained by constant effort. Moreover, this equality will
tend to create a constant and vigorous public opinion and an
interest in public affairs.

This is not the same as to say that all the Mediterranean
regions enjoy a natural Home Rule, still less that they are
bound to develop some form of popular government. These
may not be secured, and indeed are seldom secured together,
except towards the close of a long and complex development.
Towards this, as we shall see in the sequel, many other factors
must co-operate beyond the few simple forces which we have so
far introduced. The history of nations is not to be written
offhand by easy generalizations from their environment. Palestine has fared very differently at the hands of her rulers from
Greece, and the delta of the Nile from the coastlands of Asia
Minor. Still it is true to assert of all these regions that, even if
they have not preserved their independence or attained to popular
government, they yet provide conditions which will prove helpful
at any time to their successful exercise.

All these conditions exist in Greece : but here their influence
is strengthened, in contrast to other Mediterranean lands, by
physical characteristics to which we have already referred.
Nature gave to Greece, as to her neighbours, the tendency to
equality together with abundant opportunities for the growth of
public opinion, and then intensified these forces by strictly
limiting the areas in which they could operate. Each little plain,
rigidly sealed within its mountain-barriers and with its population concentrated upon its small portion of good soil, seems
formed to be a complete world of its own. Make your way up
the pastureland, over the pass and down on to the fields and
orchards on the other side, and you will find new traditions and

---

[1] *Od.* x. 188 (ἀγορὴν θέμενος μετὰ πᾶσιν ἔειπον), xii. 297 ; Hdt. iii. 137
(Democedes) ; cf. another good story in iv. 78

customs, new laws and new gods, and most probably a new dialect. You will be in a new nation. For what else is nationality but a combination of all these? You will find a fierce and obstinate national spirit that knows of no allegiance to a sovereign beyond its horizon and regards Home Rule as the very breath of its being. The Greeks were not painfully taught to value local independence. They grew up unable to conceive of any other state of government. It was a legacy slowly deposited through the long period of isolation which intervened between the first settlement of the Hellenic invaders and their emergence centuries later as a civilized race. They never themselves realized, even their greatest writers did not realize, how unique and remarkable their political institutions were. For Herodotus and Thucydides, as for Plato and Aristotle, men who are not living under City State conditions are the exceptions, not the rule. It is the basis upon which all their feeling and thinking on political matters is built up; and, through their genius and infection, it has coloured and confused the political thinking of the Western world ever since.

It is this isolation and intensification of local feeling which distinguishes the Greeks from other dwellers in Mediterranean lands. Every Syrian or Arab township on the Mecca pilgrimage route is a club; but its members know that it is not the only or even the best club in the world. The Greek citizen grew up, like the members of some exclusive and favoured institutions, in a different atmosphere. English schoolboys and Italian villagers sometimes believe that there is no other school or no other saint but theirs. Greek patriotism fused the emotions of school and family, of inheritance and early training, of religion and politics— all the best of boyhood with all the best of manhood—into one passionate whole. His city was the only city, and her ways the only ways. He loved every rock and spring in the folds of her mountains, every shrine and haunt within the circuit of her walls. He had watched every day from his childhood the shadow creeping slowly across the market-place and the old men shifting their seats when the sun grew too hot. He could tell the voice of the town-crier from the other end of the city, and had made a special study, for private performance, of the favourite butt of the comedian in his last year's play. He knew every foothold and

handhold on the back way up to the citadel, and all the tricks
for getting into the city after the gates were locked.   And of
course he was very religious.   He never forgot the festival of
a god or a hero, and could tell you the rites, especially the sacrifices, appropriate to each.   He was never tired of listening to
his father and his uncles telling stories of raids and battles
against the men from beyond the range, or to some skilful
professional who could work them up into ballads.   And when
his city brought forth not merely fighters and bards, but architects and sculptors, and all the resources of art reinforced the
influence of early association and natural beauty, small wonder
that the Greek citizen, as Pericles said, needed but to look at his
city to fall in love with her.   The Athenian had loved the
Acropolis rock while it was still rough and unlevelled, when the
sun, peeping over Hymettus, found only ruddy crags and rude
Pelasgian blocks to illumine.   He loved it tenfold more now,
when its marble temples caught the first gleam of the morning
or stood out, in the dignity of perfect line, against a flaming
sunset over the mountains of the West.[1]

[1] *Od.* vi. 267 (market-place) ; Ar. *Pol.* 1326 b 7 (town-crier) ; Hdt. i. 84,
viii. 53 (back way up Acropolis) ; Thuc. ii. 4. 3 and Aen. Tact. 18–19 (tricks
with bars and bolts).
   With the educational conditions described above contrast those provided
by cities of the modern type, as described by writers familiar with the growth
and needs of the youthful imagination. See, for instance, the chapters on the
South London boy in *Across the Bridges*, by Alexander Paterson (London,
1911), and especially *The Spirit of Youth and the City Streets*, by Jane Addams
(New York, 1910), who shows, with poignant illustrations out of her own
experience, how the industries, the amusements, and, in general, all the
habits of life in a modern city tend to crush out or pervert just those moral
qualities by which the Greeks set such store. ' It is neither a short nor an
easy undertaking,' says Miss Addams (p. 30), following Plato, ' to substitute
the love of beauty for mere desire, to place the mind above the senses,' nor
have our rulers yet realized the need for making any corporate effort to do so.
See further, on this point, the note on p. 368 below.

CHAPTER II

THE DEVELOPMENT OF CITIZENSHIP

CUSTOM, OR THE RULE OF THE FAMILY

(τὸ πάτριον)

Οὐ γάρ τι νῦν γε κἀχθές, ἀλλ' ἀεί ποτε
ζῇ ταῦτα, κοὐδεὶς οἶδεν ἐξ ὅτου 'φάνη.

SOPHOCLES, *Antigone* 456.

'Tell me, when was Custom born,
Yester eve or yester year ? '
'Days and years she knoweth not,
She was always here.'

So much for the influence of environment upon Greek institutions. It is time to turn to the temperament and character of the Greeks themselves. Environment will not explain more than a small part of a nation's history : for the rest we must explore the secrets of national psychology. It is a more difficult and delicate, but a more interesting, inquiry ; for most men, being men, find the human more interesting than the natural sciences.

What use did the Greeks make of the conditions in which they were placed? No two races use the same environment alike. The scenery of Greece altered little between Homer and the Latin conquest of Constantinople. There were the same mountains and plains, the same summer and the same Aegean, to set the same tendencies to work. The Parthenon was standing uninjured on the Acropolis. Yet the Frankish invaders had no ideas of organization except the territorial feudalism in which they had been nurtured, and succeeded, in their sturdy Western way, in applying the principles of Domesday and grouping Greece, like England or France, into fiefs and duchies. If they had not done so, many people would say that, in the face of the physical difficulties, it was an impossible thing to do. It would not be hard to point out some who, knowing the earlier history of Greece and having skipped the later, say so still.[1]

[1] See the maps in Miller, *The Latins in the Levant.* This and Sir Rennell Rodd's *The Princes of Achaia and the Chronicles of Morea* are the two most recent general books in English about mediaeval Greece. But both are

When the Greeks entered Greece in numerous separate detachments during the second millennium before Christ, they were
what we should call savages. By the time when Pericles delivered
his Funeral Speech their foremost communities were, in most
essential respects, more civilized than ourselves. Can we form
any idea of how this change came about ? The best way of doing
so is to watch closely the development, not of their art and literature, or of their inventions and sciences, but of their political
institutions and the ideas associated with them. For by 431 the
City State, and the statesmen and ' men of action ' who lived the
political life, had so drawn the ' men of words ' and the artists,
Sophocles and Aristophanes, Pheidias and Mnesicles, into their
service, that Pericles can speak of their works, which we regard
as models for all time, as though they were the mere ornaments
and superfluities of political greatness. Aeschylus to us is a poet
and nothing more. To his contemporaries he was first and
foremost a patriot. When he died in Sicily, this is what men
chose to write on his tomb—unless, as one tradition says, he
wrote it himself when he knew death was near :—

> This tomb hides Aeschylus, Athenian born,
> Euphorion's son, amid far Gela's corn—
> How good a fighter, Marathon could tell,
> The long-haired Persian knows it but too well

The poet is swallowed up in the citizen. Some present-day
Hellenists regard all war as wicked and politics as a ' dirty
business '. But until they understand how the generation of
Aeschylus regarded them they have not begun to understand the
Greek spirit.

Greek history begins with the migrations of peoples in Central
and South-Eastern Europe which resulted in the entry of the
Hellenes into Greece. The incomers were ' savages '. But they

rather bewildering from their mass of detail, and the reader who knows Greek
will enjoy going on to read *The Chronicle of Morea* in the original. It has
been admirably edited by Schmitt (pub. Methuen, 1904, with a useful glossary),
and is full of interest to those who are interested in the clash of East and
West. See also Bury's Romanes Lecture, *Romances of Chivalry on Greek Soil*
(Oxford, 1911). There is a suggestive account of the Norman organization
of South Italy in Demolins, *Comment la route crée le type social*, vol. ii,
pp. 313 ff.

were far from being the free and innocent children of Nature to
whom the eighteenth-century philosophers and the men of the
French Revolution looked so wistfully back. On the contrary,
the rights of individual freedom, as of individual property-
holding, were things utterly unknown. A complex system of
social and religious custom, which they never dreamed of ques-
tioning, hedged them in on every side. How elaborate this
patriarchal system was, and how minutely and intimately it
affected their lives at every point, we are only just beginning
to realize through the sympathetic researches of the anthropologists. It seems impossible to give any general account of it,
laying stress on those elements which survived and were merged
into the life of the Athenian City State, without appearing
to over-simplify. Yet those elements are of such importance
to a proper understanding of our subject that the attempt must
be made.

The life of the early Greeks was enclosed, for political purposes, within what may be described as concentric circles of
loyalty. Outside they had the nation (or what in Jewish history
is called the Tribe) ; within that the tribe in the narrower sense ;
within that the ' brotherhood ' or ' companionship ' of tent and
messmates ; and within that the still narrower circle of the immediate family. When the fighting-men of the nation went out to
battle they went out, as Nestor reminds Agamemnon, not as an
undisciplined horde, but ' divided into tribes and brotherhoods,
so that brotherhood may bring help to brotherhood and tribe to
tribe '.[1]

It was with these inner circles, and, above all, with the family,
that the individual was in closest touch in daily life ; and it was
here that the Greek received his first training in citizenship. All
his life long, from his initiation in early boyhood, he was wrapped

---

[1] *Il.* ii. 362. The word ' tribe ' is generally used in English, by travellers
and others, in the Jewish sense, which corresponds with the Greek ἔθνος or
' nation '. We shall use it in the Greek and Roman sense, as there is no other
English word to render φυλή (in its strict use) and *tribus*. Each of the ' twelve
Tribes ' of Israel was a Greek ' nation '.   Under normal savage conditions
these ' nations ' seem to be more or less under the control of the personage
known to anthropologists as the Divine King or the Medicine King, whose
memory survived in Greece in many curious forms, e. g. in the story about
Ouranos, Cronos, and Zeus in Hesiod's *Theogony*. But this and other features
of savage life lie outside our scope.

round with the patriarchal system, moving stiffly and timidly in
a world full of hidden fears and forces, clinging to beliefs and
observances and taboos which to us have long since become
meaningless. When the anthropologists go out hunting and
bring us home strange spoils from savage lands, these are apt to
seem, to our disillusioned modern minds, merely something to
stare at—foolish and a little uncanny. Yet there is more in
us of them than we know. For many of the roots of our Conservatism go back to that early life. When an English family is
assembled at evening round the fireside it is not often conscious
of the romance which, for the lover of the past, will always en-
circle such a gathering. It does not cast its mind back to the
nameless savages who first established the religion of the hearth
and tamed the natural man into acquiescence in the institution
of monogamy. The Greek saw clearer, for he had not so far to
look. Natural Radicals as they were, as all men who are fond
of exercising their intellect on political questions are tempted to
be, they knew and felt the difference between the deep-seated
moralities which their ancestors had handed down to them and
the institutions which they or their lawgivers had recently
devised. The former they observed not out of calculation but
out of ' reverence ' : they were not ' fallible contrivances of
reason ' but ' unwritten ordinances whose transgression brings
admitted shame ' : and not all the codes of Delphi and the Seven
Sages were as dear to them. For they went down to levels which
reason had not yet plumbed and embodied the elemental unsel-
fishness—the sense of one human being's natural relation to
another—which was the germ of Greek citizenship as of all good
citizenship since. Fraternity sits ill on the banner of the anar-
chist ; there is no true fraternity which does not grow, as it grew
in Greece, out of the plain primaeval emotions of friendship or
family.[1]

We can recover to some extent the simple and homely life
these old ' savages ' led with their gods and their cattle. Hesiod
seems to preserve many memories and even phrases and nick-

[1] Ἑστία or Vesta, the Hearth-Goddess, goes back as early as anything we
know of the Greeks ; cf. *Od*. xix. 304 and the use of ' hearth ' for ' family '
(e. g. Hdt. i. 176, v. 72). Unwritten Laws : Thuc. ii. 37. 3 ; Soph. *Ant*. 454 ;
O. T. 863, with Jebb's note. Cf. the use of the word πάτριον in the historians
and orators (πάτριόν ἐστιν ἡμῖν, &c.).

names that go back to it. We know how, as in the beautiful painter's tradition of the Nativity, the animals formed part of this early family circle. But our best evidence is derived from the ideas and practices of the later Greeks. There are regions of life into which the modern state has hardly dared to intrude, or, if it has ventured in at all, has crept in on tiptoe. There are solemn moments when the modern man feels himself stripped bare of his citizenship, when even the statesman used to living, like a Greek, in the world's eye, retires into privacy and feels himself just a man alone with his God or his kin, in a world of strangers. At such moments, at birth, at marriage, and particularly at death, the old patriarchal system resumed its sway. The Greek was not baptized or married or buried by the Church. There was no such thing as a Church as distinct from the religion of the family or of the State or of Hellas. There were no death-bed consolations or hopes of a glorified immortality. Nor did the State, which embraced so much of the sphere since annexed by the modern Churches, cast its hallowing aegis over such moments. The Greek city kept no register of births : it took no account of the young till they were old enough to be trained as soldiers. Marriage was always in Greece, as in Mohammedan lands, a purely domestic ceremony. And the dead the State only cared for when they had earned a public funeral, and even then, as we see from Thucydides' account, it was careful to allow full scope for the ancestral family ritual. The women, debarred from walking through the streets in the procession, go by themselves to the graveside to perform their domestic lamentations. So whenever the Tragedy, as being Tragedy it must, brings us face to face with the elemental facts of life, we find ourselves suddenly in an atmosphere of prehistoric pieties and observances. To us these long-drawn ritual scenes and weird half-savage plots, of which Sophocles especially was so fond, sometimes seem, as they seemed to some of the matter-of-fact Stoic philosophers, tedious and even slightly absurd. It is our want of imagination. Orestes and Electra exchanging alternate invocations at the barrow of Agamemnon, Teucer wrangling with kings to secure burial for his brother Ajax, and that last almost unbearable scene between the child-murderess Medea and her childless husband—these do not yield their full meaning until we understand something of the old patriarchal world into which they transported their audience.[1]

Matricide and incest, the stories of Orestes and Oedipus, are still terrible to us. But let us consider another calamity whose peculiar sting has passed away : it will bring us to the heart of that old world and show how the City State entered in and took possession of its holiest conceptions. We have forgotten, and find it hard to reimagine, what 'childlessness', as the Greeks called it, that is, the absence of legitimate male offspring, meant in the religion of the hearth. There was nothing probably in the whole range of life which the Greek dreaded more. No one to tend him in old age, to close his eyes in death and give him ritual burial, to give the daughters in marriage within the customary and honourable circle, to cherish the memory of the dead and keep alive the institutions that were so dear to him—in a word, to ' save the hearth '. Greek law and custom are full of curious vetos and fictions to avoid this most dreaded disaster. Such was the sentiment which originated divorce, which allowed a childless widow to ' raise up seed ', in a second marriage, for her first husband, which gave rise to the facility and frequency of adoption. Celibacy, always forbidden in Greece by custom and often by specific enactment, was regarded not only as a misfortune but as an impiety, and how many expectant parents must have grieved over the birth of a girl ! All this Pericles, the friend of Sophocles, knew and felt far better than we when it fell to his lot to speak words of comfort to an audience of Athenians bereaved of their sons. ' Keep a brave heart,' he said, ' in the hope of other children : for the new-comers will help you to forget the vacancy in your own home circle and will help the city to fill the gaps in her ranks.' We have no reason to think these parents winced as they listened. They had been trained from the dateless ages to put individual affections and sorrows aside. In the

[1] Murray, *Greek Epic*, ch. iii, and references to Hesiod (nicknames). Aesch. *Choeph.* 315 ff. ; Soph. *Ajax* 866 (where a modern play would end) to 1419. There were ' nonconformists ' in Greece, who made Judgement and Immortality an important part of their official creed. But, speaking generally, their influence on Greek life is small, though their influence on later thought, through Plato (who, as Nietzsche puts it, ' went to school with the Egyptians ' or, as some think, the Indians), is considerable. In Greece to-day weddings still take place in private houses. Boys are still so much more desired than girls that it is sometimes necessary to conceal from the mother that her child is female, for fear the disappointment should lead to fatal results. [See Appendix.]

patriarchal days the son was made for the hearth, not the hearth for the son. Now that the hearth has become a city, and its humble flicker a consuming fire, shall any citizen dare think of Athens as a respecter of persons ? Athenians were made for the city, not the city for Athenians. Some, who have listened to the Sophists, have whispered to the contrary, but their tongues are tied on a day of burial.[1]

Such was the world in which the early Greek lived before he moved into his historic abode. Let us now consider briefly this movement and its results.

In times of disorder and migration the routine and observances of daily life were interrupted and the ties of tribal and national organization more closely knit. The invaders moved South, as the legends tell us, not in small bodies but in nations, planting, not a tribe here and a tribe there, but generally, so far as we can trace it, detachments of all their tribes wherever the nation settled. This is the explanation of what seems at first sight a puzzle, the common divisions on the map of ancient Greece. The maps in ordinary use do not cut Greece up into City States or recognize the political divisions between one sovereign plain or valley and another, but show much larger units. The Peloponnese, for instance, is divided into Argolis, Laconia, Messenia, Elis, Achaea, and Arcadia, and islands like Crete, Euboea, and Lesbos are shown as single states. This is, of course, profoundly misleading. Arcadian history is nothing if not a record of the quarrels between the states in her several small plains. Crete, in historical times, had forty-three independent City States, Euboea ten, and Lesbos six. But these large divisions (which very roughly correspond to the present provinces of the Kingdom of Greece) are a legacy from the early days of the first settlement of the immigrants. Partly, no doubt, they are due also to the previous organization of the country into ' kingdoms ' under ' Mycenaean ' rulers. At any rate they still survived in some

---

[1] Thuc. ii. 44. 3. Childlessness : Hdt. v. 48 (ἀπέθανε ἄπαις θυγατέρα μούνην λιπών), vi. 86 fin. ; Aesch. *Choeph.* 264, *Ag.* 896 ff. Divorce : Hdt. v. 39, vi. 61. The family organization which the Greeks found among the ' Mycenaeans ' when they reached Greece was not patriarchal but matriarchal, and its influence can be traced in worship and legend ; see Murray, pp. 73-8 (2nd ed., pp. 96-101) ; but recent preoccupation with Mycenaean data has tempted scholars to exaggerate the importance of these pre-Greek elements in Greek life.

vigour at the time when the Homeric catalogue of the ships was written ; and though the whole history of ' mediaeval ' Greece down to the sixth century, and in backward cases even later, was a process of crystallization into City States, the old names and a breath of the old tradition lived on. It was in the religious sphere, of course, that it was remembered best. Men worshipped together as Boeotians at the All-Boeotian feast at Coronea centuries after they had been fighting one another as Thebans and Plataeans and Orchomenians ; and the goddess they worshipped there, though they knew her as ' Athena ', had come with them from the North.[1]

When the Greek tribes entered Greece they had been accustomed to a nomadic or semi-nomadic life. They were not wholly pastoral, like Abraham or the Scythians of the Russian steppe ; for they seem to have used their cattle for ploughing as well as for milk. But agriculture is compatible with a very unsettled mode of life. Like Herodotus's Phoenicians on their way round the Cape of Good Hope, the early Greeks reckoned to stop just long enough in one place to sow and reap a single harvest. They were too unsettled and insecure to think it worth while to plant fruit-trees or build good houses or make any other permanent provision for the future. Thucydides, in the first pages of his history, has imagined for himself, without any of our scientific aids, this early semi-nomadic economic stage, and modern investigation has done little more than amplify his brief account.[2]

Spiritual progress in Greece really begins, as Gilbert Murray has pointed out, with the chaos of the migrations. The morality of the *Iliad* goes back to a time when men were fighting far away

[1] Cf. Thuc. i. 12. 3 (migrating ' nations ' : e. g. ' Boeotians ', ' Thessalians ') ; Strabo 411 (the Παμβοιώτια) ; cf. Roscher, s.v. Itonia. On the centrifugal tendency see Meyer, *Forschungen*, vol. ii, pp. 512 ff. Two ' cities ' on a small island : *Od.* xv. 412. Maps have been made of Greece as it appears from the catalogue of the ships : see Freeman's *Historical Geography of Europe*, vol. ii ; Monro's *Iliad*, i–xii, and Chadwick, *The Heroic Age* (Cambridge, 1912). Thucydides, who worked on it as a comparatively trustworthy historical document, had a perfectly clear picture in his mind of what Greece was like in this age : he had thought out for himself, for instance, such a knotty problem as the relation between Diomed, who led the men of Argos, and Agamemnon, ' King of Argos and many islands.' He was not able, as we are, to regard the Epic account of the Trojan war as presenting a series of literary rather than historical problems, and thus to feel justified in taking it clean out of his picture of early Greece.

[2] Thuc. i. 2 ; Hdt. iv. 42.

from gods and family, beyond the sway of the old sanctions of
tribe and custom. Man finds himself for the first time a free
agent in the world, with no one to control him but other fighters
as reckless and uncontrolled as himself. ' The only powers over
him are the powers within his own breast,' the conceptions of
duty and honour which he somehow recognizes. But this phase
of development, immortalized in the literature, lasted but for
a few short generations in the history of Greece. Early man is
never destined to know freedom for long. New attachments
awaited the invaders in the country of their adoption. Once
they had settled in Greek lands, links were slowly forged with
the ' Mycenaeans ' whom they discovered in possession upon
their arrival. Victors and vanquished were gradually merged
into one race, and the distinctions between them, as in England
after the Saxon conquest, soon almost altogether disappeared.
There are conquered populations, Helots and others, in historical
Greece ; but their condition was not due to the early migrations
so much as to social and political causes that had since intervened. The ' mediaeval ' institutions of Greece, and above all of
Attica, are the result of a harmonious fusion between the patriarchal system and gods of the Northern immigrants and the
vaguer and more unfixed traditions of the populations on whose
lands and among whose gods they settled.[1]

How did the invaders settle on their new lands ? We have no
historical record for this early time, only legend and tradition
and ' traditional books '—poems revised, like the Jewish scrip-
tures, from generation to generation. But one thing is quite
clear both from the books and from survivals. The early Greeks
did not live together in towns but scattered about in villages.
The urban habit which we think so characteristic of the Greeks
was of later growth. The State existed, in rudimentary form,
before the city. The invaders were used to moving about in
bodies with flocks and herds, but they were not used to being
packed close inside a wall. When they found themselves in the
little plains of Greece, they went off in parties to build groups of

---

[1] Cf. Murray, chap. ii (who, I think, makes too much of the *effects* of the
chaos upon the later history) ; Wilamowitz, *Orestie*, Introduction to Choephoroe, especially pp. 121–4 ; E. Meyer, *Geschichte des Altertums*, ii, § 176
(the English parallel).

huts wherever there was water and good soil. In these early
centuries one must picture the cultivable areas of Greece not,
as they became later, as wide spaces of open country with a
walled town in the centre, or as dotted about with isolated
farmsteads like the Scottish lowlands, but as showing a definite
number of well-marked villages each with its land attached.
To a fifth-century Greek ' to live in old-fashioned style ' meant
to live in open villages (κατὰ κώμας ἀτειχίστους). The people
of Elis lived in this way till after the Persian War, and many of
the backward peoples of North-Western Greece were still so
living in the time of Thucydides. Indeed, ' to reduce a town
to villages,' that is, to destroy it and its fortifications and disperse
the inhabitants over the country-side, was the severest penalty
that a conqueror could inflict. The Spartans were particularly
fond of this punishment; for Lacedaemon itself remained (for
peculiar reasons) a group of unwalled villages. Xenophon gives
a good account of one of their punitive operations. When their
king, Agesipolis, had captured Mantinea by turning in the river
to wet the foundations of the wall and houses,

' he destroyed the wall and broke up Mantinea into four parts as it
was in the old days. At first the Mantineans were very angry,
because they had to destroy their existing houses and build new
ones. But when the landed proprietors found themselves living
nearer their properties, which were out by the villages, and being
governed by an aristocracy, and rid of the troublesome demagogues, they were well pleased with the change.'

This is not quite an impartial account, for Xenophon holds
a brief for the Spartans, but it shows how natural and convenient
the old system was for a nation of farmers. The later town-
dwellers had often to walk many miles every day to reach and
return from their fields, leaving before dawn and coming back
after dark, as late as the gates were left open. The same may be
observed in South Italy and Spain to-day; and there are few
bicycles, or smooth roads to ride them on, to help the peasants
over the difficulty.[1]

[1] Xen. *Hell.* v. 2. 7, cf. Thuc. i. 90. 1 ; v. 4. 3 (returning after dark). κῶμαι:
Thuc. i. 10. 2, iii. 94. 4 ; Strabo, 337 ; cf. Meyer, ii, § 193. In spite of these
and other passages Thucydides does not properly emphasize the process of
centralization in the City (Synoecism) as one of the main factors in the mediaeval development of ancient Greece. This was another difficulty caused by

Why then did the Greeks, as time went on, deliberately put themselves to the inconvenience of living in towns ? We must delay till the next chapter the answer to this obvious question. But it is worth while saying here that (in spite of Aristotle) not all of them did. The most new-fashioned of them all, the Athenians, never did so completely, at least down to the Peloponnesian War. Thucydides pauses to tell us so in order to emphasize how hard they felt it to come into Athens at the beginning of hostilities.

' The Athenians,' he says, ' had from early times lived scattered over the country-side in groups of independent dwellings ; after the centralization of government at Athens the old habit still prevailed, and right down to the present war the majority of Athenians were used to living in the country with their wives and families. Consequently they were not at all inclined to move now, especially as they had only just got their buildings into repair after the Persian invasion.'

It was forty-eight years since the Persian invasion, years in which civilization moved faster than ever before or since. But in this matter the historian treats time in the lavish leisurely spirit of the true country-dweller.[1]

One more point we must notice about these old-fashioned villages. As the Mantinean story shows, they were not defensible. They date from a time when there was no regular warfare between state and state, but only raiding and robbery. Hence

the Trojan war, which forced him to believe that city life existed far earlier than he would otherwise have put it. Hence in his early chapters he speaks throughout of ' cities ' ; in one place, conscious of his difficulty, he calls them πόλεις ἀτείχιστοι κατὰ κώμας οἰκουμέναι, as if Homeric Greece had been full of Spartas ; cf. i. 5. 1, and especially i. 9. 2, on Pelops as a demagogue. This is probably why he is betrayed into speaking of the Synoecism of Athens as a union of ' cities ' instead of villages (ii. 15. 2).

[1] Thuc. ii. 16 (and 15). The passage gains in point when one recollects how the artistic temperament abhors systematic repairs. Where a ' piece of string ' will not do, it prefers to design the whole thing afresh. Ask any one who has employed a Greek or Italian joiner. Although they lived all over the country-side (ἐν τοῖς ἀγροῖς) the inhabitants of Attica never called themselves ' Atticans ' (on the analogy of ' Boeotians ' or ' Arcadians '), but always, except in the very outlying parts, Athenians. This is almost certainly an unbroken survival from the Mycenaean period (cf. Thuc. i. 2. 5, and Meyer, *Forschungen*, vol. ii, p. 516). Hence Thucydides, in describing how Theseus centralized Attica, leaves unanswered the prime question—Whence did Theseus get his authority ? For he was not *made* king (like Deioces, p. 97 below), but appears armed with immemorial authority (see Francotte, *La Polis grecque*, Paderborn, 1907, p. 7).

there was no organized military system to repel an organized invasion. Every man carried his own weapons, and used them in his own way, like men over parts of the Balkans to-day or the pioneers in the mining camps of Australia or the Far West. 'The whole of Hellas,' says Thucydides, 'used once to carry arms, their habitations being unprotected and their communications with each other unsafe : indeed, to wear arms was as much a part of every-day life with them as with the barbarians.' And he goes on to say that the Athenians (although they remained country-dwellers) were the first Greeks to go unarmed—no doubt partly because their country was so little exposed to invasion.[1]

If a raid occurred which was too formidable to be repelled in this haphazard way, the early Greeks would leave their villages and retire to an inaccessible stronghold, sometimes high up in the mountains, till the enemy withdrew. These fortresses were very different in character from those needed in the ages before and after them. They were not citadels so much as refuges. Thus the inhabitants of the plain of Argolis abandoned the mound of Tiryns, in spite of its cyclopean walls, and fled up to the Larisa of Argos, 950 feet high. The people of the isthmus used Acrocorinth, an unequalled tower of refuge, with a pure spring at the very top, but uncomfortably high for a permanent home. The people in the plain of the Ilissus and Cephissus had to content themselves with the Acropolis. It was not so good a refuge as Acrocorinth, but their turn came later. These early strongholds bore a famous name : they were called Poleis (πόλεις), the word round which later the associations of City State patriotism gathered. 'For this reason,' says Thucydides, 'the Acropolis is to this day known to Athenians as the City.' Athens, like London, had a City within a city. So Aristotle was talking good history (though he may not have known it) when he said the City had come into being in order to preserve life.[2]

But we must not anticipate the process of centralization. So much only was necessary as a preface to the development we are

[1] See Thuc. i. 6. 1, i. 2. 6.
[2] Thuc. ii. 15. 6 ; Meyer, *Gesch.* ii, § 193 ; Francotte, *La Polis grecque,* p. 106. The word Polites (the later ' citizen ') originally meant ' citadel-man ', i. e. look-out man. It is no accident that Priam's son Polites was so employed (*Il.* ii. 792).

about to trace—the steady crystallization of Greek feeling round the City State. The process was twofold—both centrifugal and centripetal. Of the former, the gradual break-up of the old nations into smaller units, we have already spoken. What we have now to watch is the gradual snapping of the lesser loyalties which form the intermediate links between the State and the individual, till the citizen stands, free and independent, face to face with the city.

' The city,' says Aristotle in the first paragraph of his *Politics*, ' is the highest of all forms of association and embraces all the rest.' It is easily said on paper, and as glibly repeated by those who do not make clear to themselves what it means or how seldom in history its meaning has been realized. It is not an easy thing but well-nigh impossible to train civilized men, not merely in the hour of danger but in the work and leisure of every day, to set country before wife and family, or lifelong companions, or fellow-craftsmen and fellow-worshippers, ' to bring the dispositions that are lovely in private life into the service and conduct of the commonwealth,' to ' spend their bodies, as mere external tools, in the city's service, and count their minds as most truly their own when employed on her behalf '.

This amazing result, to which Japan in these latter days seems alone to offer a parallel, was not achieved without a long rivalry between the city and all subordinate claims on men's devotion. The conflict, which was being waged all through the Greek middle ages, is obscured in the later writers, because to them it was a dead issue. Yet both the victors and the vanquished in that forgotten struggle contributed to the making of Pericles' perfect Athenian.[1]

---

[1] Burke, *Present Discontents, sub fin.* ; Thuc. i. 70. 6.   Japan, as revealed by the intimate records of the Russo-Japanese War, is the only *national* parallel, but there are many professional parallels. The best is, perhaps, the modern naval officer, especially on a submarine, whose daily and hourly training in courage and self-control is lit up for us in a flash at moments of crisis or disaster. For Japan cf. Uyehara, *The Political Development of Japan*, 1867–1909, p. 15 : ' To a western people of migratory nature, Ego or I is the first of all things. They say, " I came out here, tilled the soil, and made my home." The case is quite different with the Japanese. The *Kokku-kwa* or " country and home " stand to him before all things : they are to him a higher and greater reality than his " Self ". He says, " It is the country and home that protected the life of my ancestors, and will do the same for me and my posterity." Hence loyalty to the Emperor, who is identical in the mind of the Japanese masses with the country ' (as Athena was with

Athens), 'constitutes the basis of Japanese morality.' Hence, too, Japan, like Athens, is quite capable of putting a Socrates to death.—A full account of the patriarchal system is given in Fustel de Coulanges' *La Cité antique.* This well-known book was written in 1864, but the first half of it is still the best general account, not of the City State in itself but of the lesser loyalties out of which it grew. It may be worth while briefly suggesting some of the defects which time has revealed. (1) It is, like many French books, too tidy and logical, it simplifies the old world and its beliefs too much. (2) It tries to deal with Greece and Rome at the same time—an impossible design which survives from the days when people believed in a parent Aryan civilization ; hence its generalizations sometimes fall between two stools and fit neither. 'Greece and Rome,' as a witty American woman has recently said, ' have in fact suffered the fate that, according to Madame Cardinal, has overtaken Voltaire and Rousseau : *Il paraît que de leur vivant ils ne pourraient pas se sentir, qu'ils ont passé leur existence à se dire des sottises. Ce n'est que depuis leur mort que les deux font la paire* ' (*The Lady*, by Emily James Putnam, p. 39). (3) It greatly exaggerates the influence of the Conservative as opposed to the Radical elements in Greek life. So far as Athens is concerned its story admittedly ends with Cleisthenes (see p. 337, ed. 1906). It is, for instance, a gross exaggeration, or misuse of words, to say, as on p. 269, that ancient man never possessed liberty or even ' the idea of it '. (4) It ignores one of the most interesting sides of patriarchal life, its system of criminal law. Here it has recently been supplemented by the work of Glotz (*La Solidarité de la famille dans le droit criminel en Grèce*), who has made detailed use of the evidence of mythology. His book is a model of the way in which science can extract truth out of fiction. See also the same author's shorter work : *Études sociales et juridiques sur l'antiquité grecque.* [See Appendix.]

CHAPTER III

THE DEVELOPMENT OF CITIZENSHIP

EFFICIENCY, OR THE RULE OF THE MAGISTRATE

(τὸ εὖ ζῆν)

Ἰὼ θεοὶ νεώτεροι, παλαιοὺς νόμους
καθιππάσασθε κἀκ χερῶν εἵλεσθέ μου.

AESCHYLUS, *Eumenides* 778.

Our fathers worshipped in this mountain ; and ye say that in Jerusalem is the place where men ought to worship.

WE have watched the Greek becoming transformed from a nomad tribesman into a villager. We have now to watch his further progress from a villager to a citizen.

Perhaps the chief external difference between what is known as the Middle Age of Greece and the mediaeval period in England is that in ancient Greece mediaeval man, whatever his occupation, was predominantly a town-dweller. There were towns in England from the Roman period onwards ; but they never became the homes of the main agricultural population. All through our Middle Ages the mass of the cultivators lived scattered over the open country-side : the boroughs, which received charters and were thus distinguished from the villages and rural townships, under the influence of the Gilds became increasingly associated with commerce and industry. This is even more markedly the case with the great French and Flemish communes, such as Ghent and Ypres, and with the cities of North and Central Italy. In the history of mediaeval Greece we find no such distinction. From the earliest times we can watch the working of the forces that drove the village-dwellers, whatever their occupation, into the towns. Already in the Epic, city life seems to be regarded as the natural mode of existence for the mass of mankind. Not only the Phaeacians and the Ithacans, but even the savage Laestrygonians and the misty Cimmerians of the *Odyssey* are confirmed city-dwellers. The centripetal tendency thus early set up remained uninterrupted throughout the whole history of the City State.[1]

[1] *Od.* x. 103–8, xi. 14 ; cf. ix. 114, where the Cyclops stands as the type of the extinct race of independent patriarchal fathers.

The Greek City, as we find it in the sixth or fifth century, towards the close of a long development, is thus very different from a Borough or Commune at the end of our own Middle Ages. It is in essence not a marketing or manufacturing centre, but an overgrown agricultural village. It is mainly inhabited, not by shop-keepers and craftsmen, but by cultivators of the soil who have, in the Greek phrase, 'set up house together.' Its sacred calendar shows a round of country festivals. Its drama is set in a framework of country custom. Tragedy grew (or the Greeks thought it grew[1]) out of a chorus of men in goatskins singing in honour of the wine god, and comedy out of the mumming of the vintage and the harvest home. The full-grown city never forgot its country origin, nor did its citizens lose contact with the fields outside its walls. Everywhere in theory, and almost everywhere in practice, the City State remained, through all its days, predominantly agricultural.[2]

It is time to answer the question already raised in the last chapter : Why did the Greeks come in from the villages to ' set up house together ' ?

They went to find Efficiency. They discovered, in the phrase of Aristotle, that though, with a stronghold in reserve, they could live out in the country, they could only ' live well' in the city. The formation of these agricultural cities is an important factor

---

[1] The traditional account, canonized by Aristotle, of the origins of Greek tragedy has lately been called in question by Ridgeway, Gilbert Murray and others, who connect it with Tomb ritual or initiation ceremonies.

[2] There is a complete discussion of the process of setting up house together (' Synoecism ') in Greece in Francotte's *Polis grecque*, pp. 95 ff., especially p. 110. He points out that there were very great varieties of the process in individual cases, and that it did not always denote an actual geographical migration, as the later Greek writers thought. Attica is a case to the contrary, and there are others. The main point is the transference of the seat of government from the villages to the city. But the domiciles were generally transferred too, and the Mantinea story shows how movable they were. The Greek agricultural town is, of course, not a unique phenomenon. One of its most interesting counterparts is to be found in Palestine. ' The synoecismus of Attica by " Theseus " is evidently in some sort parallel to the Deuteronomic legislation of Josiah. . . . One of our objects in tracing the history of Israel will be to show that it is a record of a City State in the making.' This point of view is attractively presented in *Politics and Religion in Ancient Israel*, by Canon J. C. Todd (London, 1904), and, more authoritatively, by Wellhausen in his standard *Israelitische und jüdische Geschichte* (6th ed., 1907), especially ch. vi, on the old Jewish village life, and pp. 134 ff. The Temple summed up the City State patriotism of Judah as the Parthenon summed up that of Attica.

in the development which Thucydides so well describes—the gradual growth of the material resources and powers of the Greek States, culminating in the Persian and Peloponnesian wars. It is not enough for him or for Pericles that a State should be good or beautiful; it must also be strong. The Persian war is not a victory of the weak over the strong, but of the strong over the incapable. The Greeks, unlike the Jews, have nothing quixotic in their nature. They never lead a forlorn hope, unless they can persuade themselves that it is not forlorn. It is the *power* of the city which the Athenians, going about their city and ' falling in love with her ', behold embodied in her institutions and in the monuments of the Acropolis. The Doric columns of the Parthenon still give that sense of power to-day.[1]

The most obvious reason for the change is a military one. Instead of retiring to their ' city ' whenever the need arose, they found it safer and more economical to go and live by it permanently. So they came together and grouped their dwellings round the foot of their Acropolis, or, where that was too inaccessible, set to and fortified another in a more convenient situation. But they did not yet go to the trouble of defending their houses or their fields. The wall was built round the citadel, not round the new-formed city itself, which lay huddled just beneath it. It was only later on, when the city had increased in size and citizens had become more conscious of their unity and the central government of its strength, that they called all hands to the work, including even women and children if the need was urgent, and swept a lordly circuit round all their habitations, and sometimes even round some open fields besides. When the Persians landed at Marathon, Athens was still practically an open city. She had no real fortifications except her Acropolis until Themistocles had a proper city wall built after the Persian retreat. Sparta remained true to the old ways and never built a wall at all. What use would it have been to her? Her real enemies, the Helots, had to come in every day to bring food to

---

[1] See the argument of Phormio's speech in Thuc. ii. 89. The most recent authorities (e. g. Grundy, *Persian War*, pp. 293 ff., and Macan) do not allow us to regard even Thermopylae as a forlorn hope. The unfamiliarity of the idea clearly puzzled Herodotus (see vii. 220–1). Watch the uses of the words connoting power and bigness in Thucydides, e. g. vi. 31, i. 17 : he liked ἔργα ἀξιόλογα, things on a scale worth talking about.

their masters' mess. A city divided against itself cannot be
saved by a wall.[1]

This tendency to acquiesce in the old methods of defence, even
when the new city had far outgrown its citadel, suggests that
defence was after all only a secondary factor in its foundation.
The real motive force that drove men into it was not the need for
efficiency in time of war so much as the need for efficiency in
time of peace. They came together not so much for safety as for
Justice. This is the oldest and perhaps the strongest of the city's
claims to men's devotion. It is emphasized again and again in
City State writers of every age. Pericles gives it the first place
in his eulogy of Athenian institutions. Plato, in the beautiful
myth which he puts into the mouth of Protagoras, describes
how, to the first city dwellers who were ignorant of ' the art of
city life ', Zeus sent down Hermes, ' bearing in his hands
Reverence and Justice to be the ordering principles of cities and
the bonds of friendship and conciliation '.[2]

Like many other myths, this mistakes the cause for the consequence ; men felt the need of ' the art of city life ' before they
lived in cities. But Plato's account of the early city, whether in
the mouth of Protagoras or of Socrates, is in its essentials historically true. Turn back to the *Iliad*. The old epic writer who
wrought out his sociology on the shield of Achilles shows us this
early city, as he would like his hero to picture it as he goes into
battle on its behalf. A marriage procession with music and

---

[1] Athenian wall : Thuc. i. 89–93 ; women and children : 90. 3 (wrongly
bracketed in Oxford text, cf. v. 82. 6). The question as to whether Athens
had a defensible city wall before 478 has been much discussed. I follow
Wilamowitz (*Aus Kydathen*, pp. 97 ff.), Dörpfeld, Körnemann (*Klio*, vol. v,
p. 78), and, more recently, Cavaignac (*Histoire de l'antiquité*, ii. 40). Dörpfeld
thinks the Acropolis too was refortified after 480, and that the Periclean
Propylaea stand on the site of the last of the old ' Seven Gates '. The old
Acropolis fortifications extended on the south and west a little beyond the
hill itself (Thuc. ii. 15. 3) That a wall was not part of the original equipment of a city is clear from Thuc. i. 8. 3 (' some of the richer cities began to
build walls ') and Hdt. i. 15, 141, and 163 (a grateful Spanish chieftain gives
the Phocaeans money to build a wall, as an Indian rajah has had a well
sunk at Stoke Row in the Chilterns as a thank-offering to his engineer).
Homer's Phaeacians have only a provisional wall of earth and wood (*Od.*
vii. 44 ; v. Bérard, vol. i, p. 543). Cf. Ar. *Pol.* 1330 b 32 with criticism of the
more old-fashioned view in Plato, *Laws* 778 D.
[2] Thuc. ii. 37. 1. Compare Polybius's account of country life in Elis,
rendered possible by the fact that the statesmen there had arranged for
Justice to be administered ' on the spot '. (iv. 73. 8.)

dancing and lighted torches and all the old patriarchal ceremonial is passing through the streets. The women working in the inner chamber start up at the noise and stand staring from the window or the threshold—they are not allowed to go further—as the rout goes by. It emerges into the open market-place. But here its progress is stayed, for there is another crowd assembled. Standing on tiptoe, the revellers can see a group of old men with staves in their hands, sitting round in a half-circle on the well-worn stone seats. Before them stand two heated and angry disputants : at their feet lie two lumps of glowing gold. What is it all about ? The story soon goes round. There has been a murder, and the dead man's representative refuses to accept the money compensation which the murderer's family after due conclave decided to offer. So they have submitted their case to the ' right judgement ' of the elders of the city. Then those talents of gold are the compensation that was offered ? The crowd is not quite sure. It seems rather little for a good man's life—no more than the fourth prize in the chariot race at the big funeral last year. Here's a friend with a likelier theory. They are both so certain of winning that they have laid a wager on the result, and the loser will have to pay up the money as a fee to the best spokesman among the elders.[1]

Who are these old men and how do they come to have this authority ? Our friend in the street will give no help here. He will only inform us that, as every one knows, they have the blood of gods and heroes in their veins, and therefore know the rights and wrongs of things far better than common folk. For a more lucid explanation we must go back a little and watch how, in the course of a few generations on Greek soil, an aristocracy of

[1] *Il.* xviii. 490 ff. with Monro's note on l. 507, also xxiii. 269 ; compare *Ruth* iv. 1. For Plato on the early city see *Protagoras* 322 C and *Laws* 680 ff. (where the Trojan war, as usual, confuses the development). The *Republic* does not even pretend to be historical, but its argument and the sub-title commonly attached to it (πολιτεία ἢ περὶ δικαίου) embody the same idea. For the proximity of the Seat of Justice and the Bazaar in early Athens see Wilamowitz, *Aus Kydathen*, pp. 195 ff. The fee is interesting : it is not given to all the justices on the bench, but only to the ' straightest speaker '. It is the lineal ancestor of the much-abused fees which were paid to the large popular juries in fifth-century Athens. In early times these were called πρυτανεῖα (Guildhall Fees), and were paid by κωλακρέται. (' Carvers ') : so it is clear wherein they consisted. The public servant was counted worthy of his bread and butter. So he was in the fifth century (cf. Meyer, ii, §§ 209, 225). [See p. 175 and Appendix below.]

capable city magistrates grew up among the old equal patriarchal families.

When the invaders entered Greece, they were used to being patriarchally but not aristocratically governed. They obeyed the commands of the heads of the family or the brotherhood : they followed their leader in time of war and accepted the decisions of his council of wise men ; but they did not regard one family or brotherhood or section of the community as any better than another. This democratic tradition was adhered to in their settlement on the soil. The cultivable land was divided into equal ' lots ' (κλῆροι), and every adult received a share which he held in trust for his family and his descendants ; for private property originated not in rights but in duties. The family which enjoyed the temporary usufruct of this property included women, children, and sometimes a few slaves captured in raids, more often women than men. These ' houselings ' (οἰκέται) had their recognized place and duties in the home, into which, on arrival, they were solemnly initiated by the pouring of libations. They were the lowest people in the household, but their position was infinitely preferable to that of the ' unhonoured vagrants ' who had no place or lot in the world at all. They and all who may be dependent upon them are, in the world of the Homeric poems, the most to be pitied of all mankind. Eumaeus, the slave swineherd, can afford to be kind and patronizing to a wanderer like the disguised Odysseus, and one of the suitors shows his charity by offering him a job as a wage-earner, for board and lodging and his clothes, at planting trees and making stone walls—work for which obviously he could not spare the superior services of a slave. The ' lotless ' man may be trying to earn a bare living on a bit of land that he has reclaimed for himself ; or he may be a beggar or exile ; or simply a rebel and a brigand with his hand against every man. In any case he is ' outside all brotherhoods and all binding customs and all hearths ', and the patriarchal organization rides rough-shod over him. Society has no place as yet for men who ' make their own way in the world '. But with these exceptions all heads of families were thought of as equal, and were symmetrically grouped on the land and in the state as a community of equals. Equal lands and equal rights were deep-rooted and persistent traditions of Greek life. All through the history of the City State, whenever a colony was founded, the old equal arrangement was maintained, whatever the inequalities that had supervened in the mother state. And at home, too, the dream of a new sharing-out of the land never died out of men's minds. In the *Clouds* of Aristophanes some one asks a pupil of the mock Socrates what is the use of geometry. 'Why, for measuring land into equal portions,' he replies. 'Do you mean colonists' land?' 'No, I mean all the land.' 'A capital idea, thoroughly practical and public-spirited.' [1]

But equal lands never remain equal for long—least of all in a society in which the tradition of equality is strongly developed. For the Greeks, unlike ourselves, did not recognize the prior rights of the eldest son : they divided their property at death equally between all their male issue. The results of this upon a society in which land is the chief form of wealth are manifest. In a few generations there will be a marked division in the community, and it will not be long before the more skilful or fortunate members have begun to take rank as a hereditary aristocracy.[2]

These are the Zeus-born ' kings ' whom we know so well from the epic. They were Zeus-born in a very special and peculiar sense. In historical Greece every one was in the habit of claiming divine descent from the god or hero to whom his community was believed to go back. Athenians, for instance, claimed to be descended from Zeus through Ion the son of Apollo. But aristo-

---

[1] Of course the Patriarchal idea of equality was modified by practical exigencies. The immigrant nations had Kings and Witenagemots (βασιλεῖς and γέροντες), and some families were richer and more honoured than others. But their aristocracy was only skin deep and kept for emergencies. Βασιλεύς means a ' war-leader '. See Meyer, vol. ii, § 53. Refs. : Aesch. *Ag.* 1035 (Cassandra's initiation into the household) ; *Od.* xiv. 56 (Eumaeus's pretty speech to Odysseus), xviii. 357 (Eurymachus's offer of relief work), xi. 490 (to work for a lotless man) ; *Il.* ix. 63 (ἀφρήτωρ ἀθέμιστος ἀνέστιος) ; Hesiod, *Erga* 602 (don't engage hired labourers with young children) ; *Il.* ix. 648, xvi. 59 (ἀτίμητος μετανάστης) ; Ar. *Clouds* 202 (geometry) ; Thuc. iii. 50. 2 (κλῆροι). See in Dittenberger's *Sylloge*, No. 933, a fourth-century colonization inscription, where the colonists are still grouped under the old Dorian tribes. [See Appendix.]

[2] Cf. Hesiod, *Erga* 376. The Aryan theory, and the Greek tendency to have only one son, led Fustel de Coulanges astray on the question of primo-geniture ; cf. p. 90 (ed. 1906) with Meyer, vol. ii, § 197. I have followed Meyer in ignoring the possible influence of migrations and conquests in the rise of aristocracy. I am aware that this is very probably to oversimplify the problem ; but in the present state of the evidence no other treatment seemed possible within the limits of the book. See also note on p. 111.

crats disdained the pedigrees of common folk and traced themselves back to the All-Father by lines of their own—some of
them going back a suspiciously short way. We know from
Pindar, who wrote in the Saint Martin's summer of this aristocratic régime, how much these pedigrees meant to them ; and old
Herodotus has made many a democratic reader chuckle by telling
how the Egyptian priest used simple arithmetic to shame the
parvenu aristocrat Hecataeus when he boasted of being ' the sixteenth from a god '. These convenient fictions, which may in
many cases have been deliberate inventions, seem childish to us,
who are inclined to be amused at our College of Heralds. But
the Greeks went to work at their political institutions with
a radical thoroughness in all ages. ' Their legislators work like
architects with rule and compass ' : they like order and sym-
metry, councils of 5,000 and tribes made up of ' hundred-ships ',
everything as neat and logical as the plan of an American city.
So a noble family without an ancestor must needs procure one,
just as when Cleisthenes turned the four Attic tribes into ten he
got Apollo to tell him after what heroes he was to name them.[1]

In Homer and Pindar, who embody the great literature of this
period, we see little of mediaeval Greece but these ' kings ' and
their dependants. They have monopolized all the glamour, as
they monopolized the authority, of their age. The government,
as Thucydides says, ' was in the hands of hereditary kings with
fixed prerogatives.' If kingship meant then what it does now,
it would be hard, and indeed impossible, to explain how this
came about. A community of patriarchal families is a bad basis
for a hereditary monarchy. But we must be careful not to widen
the gap between these ' kings ' and their ' subjects '. They were
only kings in a very limited and peculiar sense. Their kingship
was one which admitted, for instance, of degrees : you could

---

[1] Hdt. ii. 143 ; Plato, *Euthyd.* 302 B (where Socrates is cornered over his
Ζεὺς πατρῷος) ; Eur. *Med.* 825 : Ἐρεχθεῖδαι and θεῶν παῖδες (O Sons of
Erechtheus the olden Whom the high gods planted of yore . . .) ; it was
a later and more democratic Athenian boast to be ' earth-born ' (αὐτόχθων) ;
Francotte, *Polis*, pp. 125, 147 ; Meyer, vol. ii, § 203. Meyer points out that
these ' Zeus-born kings ' with their superior pedigrees seem to be peculiar to
Greece. Jewish and Arabian pedigrees all go back to the All-Father through
the father of the whole race, e. g. through Abraham or ' Israel ', who correspond to the Greek Hellen. No Benjamite or even Levite would venture to
claim special descent by a line of his own, like a Heraclid or a Neleid.

speak of one king as being 'more kingly' than another. There were kings who were poorer than many of the commoners in their city, and whose sons, some day to be kings themselves, were not ashamed of working in the fields or going out, like David, with the sheep. When Athena went to meet Odysseus on his landing in Ithaca, she came in the likeness of a young shepherd, 'very delicate of countenance such as are the sons of kings.' You could tell a king's son then from a plain man when he sat piping to his flocks, not so much by his clothes as by his face. So sang the epic poet, mindful as always of his audience. But no one would have told the old hero Laertes, working away in his garden in gloves and gaiters, from the plain peasants amongst whom he lived.[1]

Such touches as this and a hundred others, concealed for the careless reader beneath the easy magnificence of epic diction or the Biblical English of the modern translator, help to bring the heroes of Homer into relation with the common life of their time. We were apt to forget, until the paradoxical common sense of Samuel Butler reminded us, that it is strange for kings like Menelaus to ask their guests to bring their own food with them, or for princesses to look after their brothers' washing. The truth is that, in mainland Greece at any rate, there was no such wide separation as the epic tale leads our Northern imagination to suppose between the nobles and the people. Except in the sphere of law and government, the old patriarchal equality lived on, in spite of all the new influences of wealth and rank. In Lacedaemon, where Helen and Menelaus held high state, there are hardly any traces of aristocracy surviving in our records at all. The institutions of Lycurgus well-nigh blotted it out of Spartiate life. Attica has its Whig families, its Philaids and Alcmaeonids, with all their pride of descent. Yet the mediaeval period laid the foundations for the fabric of fifth-century democracy, which could never have been erected over a chasm of classes. It is the familiar English analogy—closest perhaps to just those Englishmen who have most loved Homer—which is apt to mislead us. Our class distinctions, not between noble

---

[1] *Od.* xxiv. 226, xiii. 222, ii. 77 (cf. 386, where Telemachus borrows a ship from a commoner), ii. 127. Cf. Hdt. viii. 137 (a queen who did her own cooking). For βασιλεύτερος *v. Il.* ix. 160, 392, x. 239 ; *Od.* xv. 533.

and commoner but between ' lady ' and ' gentleman ' and ' man '
and ' woman ', or, in old English speech, between ' gentle ' and
' simple ', are deeply rooted and of immemorial antiquity. We
are only slowly emerging, with painful self-consciousness, into
the free atmosphere of a real democracy. We have behind us
and still lurking in obscure corners of our minds, not the simple
and easy equality of the patriarchal village, but respectful
memories of the hierarchy of the feudal manor. The Greek
aristocrat had not our traditions of social exclusiveness, as he
had not our economic resources, our first-class carriages and
a hundred other luxurious conveniences, for preserving and
emphasizing them : for his chariots, never at home on Greek
soil, were feeble substitutes, and even his boasted mediaeval
cavalry could not maintain its predominance for long. To understand aright either Pindar the aristocrat or Pericles the democrat,
one the servant of nobles, the other a noble himself, we must
sweep away our feudal cobwebs. The fifth-century Athenian
had indeed abolished aristocracy not only in substance but even
in form. Pericles could trace his pedigree to Nestor and beyond,
and only two generations back Pindar had written odes for his
family. But in 431, when he is chosen ' for his public estimation ' to give an address over the city's dead, he is for Thucydides no longer Pericles the Alcmaeonid, but ' Pericles the son
of Xanthippus '. The Marquis of Salisbury has become plain
Robert Cecil. By that time Athens had done away, except in
the case of a few priesthoods, with hereditary titles.[1]

<hr/>

[1] On Athenian nomenclature see below, p. 157. The Spartan senate was
confined to aged Spartiates from certain families ; but this only trace of the
old régime never appears as of any consequence. For cavalry cf. Thuc. vii.
27. 5 with Ar. *Pol.* 1297 b 18. To keep horses in Greece was what to keep a
motor-car is with us (Thuc. vi. 15. 3). Samuel Butler's *The Authoress of the
Odyssey* and his translations of the *Iliad* and *Odyssey* are too little known books.
His plain English brings out numberless points which are apt to escape our
notice in their Greek dress. The passages referred to above are *Od.* iv. 621,
vi. 64.—There is a second source of misconception about Greek aristocracy
besides that referred to above. We confuse the aristocracy of the Greek
Middle Age and of Pindar with the ' oligarchy ' so familiar in fifth-century constitutional strife, thus exaggerating the depth and persistence of the aristocratic elements in the City State. Mediaeval aristocracy and fifth-century
' oligarchy ' belong to quite different stages of City State development. The
Oligarchs (who sometimes no doubt labelled themselves ' Aristocrats ') were
a political party in a constitutionally governed state. Their programme was
to limit the franchise, restricting it, however, not simply to nobles but to
land- and property-owners as opposed to the poorer trading and industrial

Such then are the nobles whom we saw sitting, in all the dignity of age and office, on that Homeric Judgement-seat. But what of the litigants who plead before them ? What sort of men are they, and what has brought them to accept the decisions of that tribunal ? In order to answer these questions we must leave the newly settled town and go back once more to the old village.

The legendary account of early Attica classifies the population of that region in three divisions—nobles, yeomen, and craftsmen. The mere names should serve to remind us that there is another world besides that with which the poets of the *Iliad* and the *Odyssey* have made us familiar. Fortunately it has left us its epic spokesman too. Besides Homer there is Hesiod. Kings and nobles play a very small part in the *Works and Days*. We are no longer living at the centre of government, passing our days giving judgements in the market-place, earning an appetite for supper and hoping that Alcinous, or some other ' king ' amongst us, may offer us a banquet in the king's hall or vary our monotony by arranging sports in honour of a distinguished stranger. We have passed into a quieter world, where the very word monotony is unknown and the kings and nobles of the metropolis are seen, not as they themselves or their poets, but as the plain yeomen saw them. It is a toilsome life, very near to the earth, in the poor and backward village of Ascra under Helicon, ' a miserable place, bad in winter, unpleasant in summer, never good to live in.' The Muses to whom Hesiod appeals for inspiration seem to have no political message to give us. They speak neither of the old patriarchal loyalties of tribe and brother-hood, nor of the new divinely descended clans of the noblemen. They have never heard of the City State. Their citizenship is rudimentary. Yet it is very real, and the statesman will have to deal with it in due time. In their little world the bond between

population. Their motto was a word of which Homer's heroes had never heard, for it presupposed the existence of a written constitution : their policy claimed to be ἰσόνομος, to give ' equality before the law '. We shall meet them again in chap. v, where, having contributed their part in the development of the Periclean City State, they drop out of the running. A third source of misconception is no doubt provided by the aristocratic theories of fourth-century philosophers.—' Gentle ' and ' simple ' was the true old division in English life, as opposed to ' nobles ' and ' people ' in feudal societies on the Continent. See, e. g., Trevelyan, *England under the Stuarts*, p. 4.

man and man is not tribal but territorial, based not on blood
but on situation.   They have neither the time nor the pride to
remember that they are brothers.   They only know, like the
humble peasants in Tolstoy's *Village Tales*, that they live and
work and suffer side by side.   It was the modest Muses of Hesiod
who first spoke to Greeks of their duty to their neighbour.[1]

Among simple men, far removed from the seat of government,
and too poor and too busy to stir outside their native valley,
neighbourliness takes the place of citizenship.   It is only the
hurry and confusion and moroseness of modern life which boxes
men up in rows of suburban houses, too proud or too shy to
borrow a neighbour's frying-pan, or even in common humanity
to put their blinds down for his funeral.   The cottagers of Ascra
had not much to give, but they gave what they could, and for
very shrewd reasons.

Ask your friend to a meal, but leave your enemy hungry ;
Never forget above all to invite your next-door neighbour :
For you know that if things go wrong and there's need for
     help in the village,
Neighbours come post haste while kinsfolk stop to put cloaks on.

To have a little coolness with your cousin does not matter,
but anything is better than a bad neighbour : for the wiseacres of
Ascra know by experience that

Anything may happen to the ox when you're on bad terms
     with the neighbour.[2]

And in their meditative moments, lying out on the hill-side at
midday, or gathered round the smithy fire on winter evenings, as
they think over what they saw in the city when they went in
years ago to settle a dispute, they are glad that they are still
villagers.   City life is too dishonest and artificial and pretentious.
We have our little quarrels at Ascra which loom large for the
moment.   A new potter set up last year at the further end of the

---

[1] ' Up in the village ' : Hesiod, *Erga* 639.   ' Down in the city ' : *Od.* xii. 439,
viii. 40.   Alcinous asks all the other sceptre-bearing kings to his palace.   Glotz,
Études, p. 250, points out that the palace here is what the Prytaneum was at
Athens.   Distinguished strangers and benefactors, such as Socrates claims to
be in his *Apology*, were entertained there.   The intermediate link is supplied
by the stated public dinners we hear of at Naucratis (Hermias frag. 2 in
Frag. Hist. Graec., vol. ii, p. 80).   At Cnidos the guildhall where the magistrates
messed was called the δαμιόργιον, or Public Servants' Hall.

[2] *Erga* 342, 348.

village, and his rival's temper has been unendurable ever since. There is trouble, too, among the carpenters. The younger son of the old man who has the land near the hero's barrow has just set up a second joiner's shop. Hephaestus, he says, should really be the god for him, because he has always been too lame for field-work; but he owes the blacksmith so many pleasant hours that he does not like to interfere with his trade. Besides, the present carpenter is getting old, and never was any good at his craft. Those images he made last holiday were a disgrace to the artistic traditions of the village. We should never have got inside Troy if *he* had had the making of the wooden horse.[1]

All this is very harassing sometimes, especially after a long day's work. But it is better than life in the city, where men are too grasping to settle, with their own help and the gods', a plain dispute about the ownership of a strip of borderland or the mark on a sheep's back. They must needs go to law and spend most of what they stand to gain on fees to a lot of kings.

Babes ! who never have learnt that a half is more than a
    whole loaf ;
Never enjoyed the delights of a mallow and asphodel banquet,

which is better and homelier far than the high feeding and min-strelsy up at the palace.[2]

Yet these comfortable country methods had perforce to give way. Disputes cannot always be settled by recourse to the gods and ancient custom. Why should the beaten party accept so haphazard a decision ? He is a Greek who thinks for himself, and it is in his nature to accept nothing without a reason. He demands an impartial human arbitrator who can exercise his judgement with intelligence as well as clothe it with authority. In olden days, when the heads of families and brotherhoods reigned supreme, their words were a binding custom ($\theta\acute{\epsilon}\mu\iota\sigma\tau\epsilon\varsigma$) and no member dreamed of disputing them. But when custom conflicts with custom, or when there is a dispute between equals on a question of fact, some newer and higher authority is needed. There is a call for law. And who so fit to interpret law—it is still interpretation, for the age of law-*makers* is not yet—as the

---

[1] *Erga* 493 (note the distinction between sun-heat and fire-heat), 25. At this time statues were made of wood ($\xi\acute{o}\alpha\nu\alpha$) : cf. Hdt. v. 82.
[2] *Erga* 33–41.

kings in whose veins runs fresh and strong the blood of the All-Father. To-day we are slowly rising to the conception of international law, the only basis and guarantee of international organization. Let us watch how the poet of the *Theogony*, in his smaller world, taught men to take the longer step, not from the nation to the world but from the family to the state. The words that are falling from those old men's lips embody not ancient right (θέμις), but something totally new in Greek life—justice (δίκη).

'Whomsoever,' says the old poet, 'the Muses, the daughters of Zeus, see fit to honour, beholding him sprung from the loins of Zeus-born kings, upon his tongue they pour sweet dew, and forth from his mouth flow honey-sweet words : upon him all the people gaze as he gives binding decisions, clear and just. This man, with his knowledge and with sureness of speech, can abate in a moment even the mightiest contention. For to this end were kings granted wisdom, that they might bring redress in the market-place to men of the people who suffer wrong, quietly and easily, persuading them with gentle words. As he walks to and fro in the city they seek his favour as they would a god's, softly and reverently, and his head is high in the assembly. Such is the holy gift of the Muses to mankind. For from the Muses, daughters of Zeus, and from far-darting Apollo, come singers and harpers upon the earth, and from Zeus, too, come kings; and he is blessed whom the Muses love, and sweet is the voice that flows from his mouth.' [1]

This is the poet's account of how a strong government first arose among Greeks. It explains in the poet's way why the mediaeval Greeks gathered in cities and gladly hearkened to their new magistrates, founding that tradition of ' obedience to whosoever is set in authority ', which remained an integral part of the City State tradition long after the halo which encircled these early kings had gone the way of most other superstitions. But we have another account in plain prose by the prince of story-tellers, in one of those political allegories of which, like Abimelech and

[1] Hesiod, *Theog.* 81-97. Judges are said to be inspired by the Muses because they remember precedents : ' full of wise saws and modern instances.' In the same way the Registrars (keepers of archives, contracts, &c.) were often called ' Remembrancers ' (μνήμονες) ; before writing came into use their memory was the real State Archive.

Menenius Agrippa and other early political thinkers, Herodotus
was so fond. It is entitled ' How the Medes got their Kings ',
but there is nothing Median in it but the names. The rest is
pure Greek, as the audience slowly began to realize when the
story drew on to its inevitable climax ; but the scientific modern
reader must be careful as usual to distinguish (as a good story-
teller finds it so hard to do) between designed and undesigned
consequences.

  ' Now there lived in Media a certain wise man named Deioces,
son of Phraortes. This Deioces conceived a passion to become
king, and this is how he achieved his wish. The Medes of that
time lived scattered about in villages. Deioces, who had already
won honour in his own district, showed himself continually
zealous in the promotion of justice. This he did, since at that
time there prevailed great lawlessness throughout the whole of
Media, knowing that justice and injustice must ever be enemies.
The Medes of his own village, marking his ways, chose him to be
their judge ; and he, being desirous of the chief power, was clear
and upright in his judgements. By this means he won no small
praise from the citizens, so that the men from the other villages,
who had hitherto been oppressed by wicked decisions, came
gladly themselves to Deioces for judgement, until at last none
would go before any other judge. As the concourse became ever
greater and greater, since men heard that his decisions were
rightfully given, Deioces, perceiving that everything was passing
into his hands, gave it out that he would no longer sit where he
had been used to sit, saying that he would deliver no more judgements, for it was not worth his while to neglect his own affairs
and to sit judging for his neighbours from morning to night.
When after this, therefore, robbery and lawlessness prevailed
far more widely than ever before among the villages, the Medes
assembled together to discuss the affairs of their nation. And
then, as I suppose, the friends of Deioces took the lead in
the argument. " It is not possible for us to go on dwelling in the
land as it is now. Come, let us set up a king over us, so that the
land may be well governed, and we may turn to our own labours,
and no longer suffer havoc at the hands of lawless men." By
some such words they persuaded them to accept a kingly government. Thereupon, when they put forward names as to whom

they should set up as king, the name of Deioces was put forward and commended by every man present, so that at last they agreed that he should be their king. And he bade them build him a dwelling suitable to his kingship, and give him guards for the security of his person. When he had received the chief power he compelled the Medes to establish a single city and, having provided all things needful for it, to think less of the other townships.' [1]

Here we can trace every stage in the growth of the influence of state law. First Deioces is only a casual arbitrator, chosen on grounds of respect and reputation, to settle a chance quarrel between two fellow villagers. In the same way the King of England has occasionally adjudicated between two lesser states, and disinterested public men are sometimes called in to settle labour disputes. Then the arbitrator comes to be generally recognized as a person of guaranteed impartiality, and his judgement-seat becomes the favourite place of resort for disputants in difficult cases. Next Deioces turns his judgement-seat into a court in permanent session, superseding all others of the same kind. Lastly, it is transformed from a court of arbitration, to which disputants may, if they wish, submit their case, to a court of law whose judgements they are forced to accept. At this stage Deioces becomes a tyrant : for whether the quarrel ruffled pride or wounded honour, or was only a plain dispute on a question of fact, men had no choice but to bring it to him. City law has abolished fisticuffs, as some day, when mankind has become conscious of a common citizenship in the world and a common need for a World-Law, the World-State will abolish war.[2]

Here we might leave the City State, efficiently launched, with its first strong governors at the helm, to face the dangers that have beset the government of the few in all ages. But there is one more point to be explained before we can talk at our ease with the men in that Homeric market-place which first roused our curiosity. It concerns the most remarkable and difficult of the achievements of these early magistrates—the intrusion of

---

[1] Hdt. i. 96.   [2] The pioneers of town life and state justice, like Deioces or Theseus (or the Roman Numa and Servius Tullius), must not of course be confused with the later ' tyrants ', who did all they could to discourage town life and send people ' back to the land '. They come much later in the development. For all-day sessions see *Od*. xii. 439–40.

their jurisdiction into the sphere of what we know as the criminal law. Aeschylus wrote his *Trilogy* to show us what a great advance of the human spirit the first city criminal court embodied; but we are so used to State justice that we prefer the murder to the trial—the *Agamemnon* to the *Eumenides*—and think his lesson an anti-climax. It is not so very difficult after all—once they have lighted on the idea—for men to agree to bring a simple quarrel about *meum* and *tuum* before Alcinous or Deioces. But when blood has been shed or primitive taboos infringed things bear a different aspect. There are passions to be slaked and ghosts to be appeased and rites to be performed, before the deed is expiated. An age-long custom, which even Apollo dare not disregard, preaches to all the house of the member sinned against the bounden duty of vendetta—an eye for an eye and a life for a life.

If the offence is committed within the circle of the family the family can deal with it out of its own resources. The ' jurisdiction of the father ' went on in Greece, as at Rome, side by side with state law, all through the City-State period, as it still goes on in China. ' Thou shalt not commit adultery ' was in Greece not merely, as with us, a command to the conscience, a moral rule with the breach of which the courts are only indirectly concerned, but a law. But that law was neither made nor enforced by the state. The city was slow to interfere with the inner doings of the household, and even its ' Thou shalt not murder ' was never applied, even in enlightened Athens, to new-born infants.[1]

But if the murderer is not one of us, how are we to deal with him? He is outside our family and brotherhood. There has never been, or there subsists no longer, any bond of law or custom between our people and his. By the act of murder he has set up a state of war. We are not merely his enemies but the enemies of all his kin, who are collectively responsible for the evil he does. It is war to the bitter end between Orsini and Colonna, between Montagu and Capulet; and it is bound to go on till due expiation has been made (and the debt is for ever accumulating) or till one or other has been rooted out. The sins of the older generation live on. Their sons are born, like

---

[1] For the list of rights which made up the *patria potestas* see Fustel de Coulanges (ed. 1906), p. 98. It died, of course, far harder in Rome than in Athens, or indeed in Greece generally. For China see note at end of chapter.

Orestes, into a heritage of blood-feud. 'The fathers have eaten sour grapes and the children's teeth are set on edge.'

The Jewish spirit fought a long and bitter struggle with the idea of collective responsibility ; and Aeschylus, who, in his day, was a reformer too, wrote his *Trilogy* in order to root it finally and triumphantly out of the minds of his Athenians. But it was not so easy to turn the Furies into the kindly Goddesses and conduct them in procession to their new home beneath the Areopagus. The criminal court on Ares' Hill was not set up in a day. This great and characteristic invention of Athena—first of women lawyers—was the fruit (like most 'inventions') of a long and painful development of which we have but intermittent glimpses. The Greek spirit took centuries to shake off the barbarities of the vendetta.

The *Iliad* of course is a tale of vendetta, an incident, as Herodotus puts it, in a long course of reprisals between rival tribes. But it is a tale of Greece, not of Corsica, and gives us many a glimpse, as Gilbert Murray has shown us, of how its story outlived itself. We can feel the breezes of humanity blowing in to purify the atmosphere of the blood-feud. We are at a stage of development at which clans no longer fight till, in the old Roman phrase, they have 'extirpated their enemies root and branch ', but are content to be reconciled after a fair and chivalrous ordeal. And we can watch in these ceremonies of peace-making, where each side reverently and tolerantly accepts the pious usages of its adversaries, the beginning, both in the letter and the spirit, of international law. For in all societies in all ages the law of the larger unit tends to be held in less esteem than that of the smaller, and progress consists in making the spirit of the smaller, with its appropriate ideas and customs, transmute and inspire the larger. The oaths and the libations, the sacrifices and the banquets of the *Iliad*, are family ceremonies transferred, as in the peace-making between Achilles and Agamemnon, to a wider sphere. The two are not born friends, they are made friends. What makes them friends ? Partly the mere communion or sacrament of the common meal. They have dined together and like rival modern politicians, they can never feel so bitter or misunderstand or misrepresent one another so harshly again. It is the handshake between buyer and vendor in the Eastern bazaar, when after a long and lying wrangle they have come to an agreement—or what the modern Greeks call a ' symphony '—upon their price. But, more than that, it is the feeling that they have each become ' members of one another ', parts together of a larger whole. For the word we translate ' friend ' or ' dear one ', the word the Greeks use in these ceremonies of ' making friends ', has a subtler and more intimate meaning. It means not ' my friend ' or ' my dear ', but ' my own '. When a Homeric hero talks of his ' dear knees ' and his ' dear spirit ' he is not talking affectedly, as we might say ' my poor head '. He means his own knees and spirit, which are, as we say, ' near and dear to him '—perhaps, if he is fighting in desperate case, almost the only things he has left. ' A Homeric man,' says a recent writer, ' calls his wife or his house " dear " because they belong to him. His heart has nothing to do with it.' That is why when Homer wants to say ' dear ' in our sense he is obliged to be precise and say ' dear to my heart '. A stranger, therefore, becomes ' dear ' only when, by some ritual ceremony, he has become part of a man's own society, or is bound to him by some definite agreement. So Hector and Achilles, when they make an arrangement before their duel as to the disposal of the victim's body, are ' friends ' for the moment. With such an intrusion as this of the forms of peace into the usage of warfare the days of the vendetta were already numbered.[1]

---

[1] *Iliad* vii. 302 and Glotz, *Études*, pp. 21–2. Cf. *Il.* ix. 115, where Agamemnon not only offers Achilles ' unlimited reparation ' of a material kind, but is prepared to compensate him for ' moral and intellectual damages ' by ' making a clean breast of it ' (as our language expressively puts it) in the most generous manner. ἀασάμην (*Il.* ix. 116, 119) really needs a strong expletive to render its full meaning in plain English prose. For Herodotus on the *Iliad* see i, chaps. 1–4. His fifth-century mind cannot see why men bothered to keep up the reprisals for the carrying off of Io, Medea, and Helen, for ' it is clear they would never have been carried off if they had not been ready to go '. It is interesting to watch the use made of the conception of ' dearness ' (φιλότης) in the debates of the Peloponnesian War. The natural relation between Athens and her allies is one of fellow membership, as the Funeral Speech says (ii. 40. 4). It is therefore quite logical and (accepting Athens as Head of the Family) quite just that the rebellious Mytileneans should be punished with all the severity that a ' tyrant ' or master of a household had at his command. This is how Cleon argues, from the high moral point of view of many masters before and since (iii. 40). His opponent Diodotus eschews moral arguments and the judicial traditions of the household altogether and simply discusses the *expediency* of the proposed action. His speech is very impious, but also very enlightened. The one thing it is not is (what it looks at first sight) cynical.

Let us watch it disappearing. The first resistance it met with was not active but passive. One day, when a murderer fled home for refuge, a Greek dared to say aloud ' Am I my brother's keeper ? ' The family listened and thought it over—and refused to go to war. Let him suffer for his own act. As he sinned alone, let him go forth alone to meet his own enemies. So they closed the doors on him and on mercy and sent him to his doom. There is only one hope for him now—a new and impartial tribunal.

But something more was required to hearten patriarchal man to this act of progress and impiety. It was supplied by the appearance of a new religious theory, that of the physical horror and infection of blood-guiltiness. It is a novel idea. We do not find it in the Homeric poems ; Telemachus on his way home from Sparta ships a murderer as a passenger without a qualm of mis-giving. Like many other novel doctrines, especially in the sphere of religion, it was at once socially convenient and held with intense moral earnestness. We read the story of Oedipus and think of the polluted beggar-king, whose innocent intentions Sophocles is at such pains to bring out, as a primitive figure, victim, as some of the later Greeks held, of an unreasonable superstition. It is primitive perhaps to us, but it was not primi-tive to Greece. The real primitive Greeks, the men of the earlier *Iliad*, lived too much in the atmosphere of feud and danger to feel repugnance at bloodshed. The everyday happenings of one age became the fairy-tales of the next but one. Herodotus and his fifth-century audience were as fond as the men of the *Iliad* of hearing tales of murder ; but in the stories that he told them, as in the *Arabian Nights*, the murderers are not expected to feel remorse, because they never really existed. Men had completely forgotten that in the earliest version of one of their favourite legends Oedipus killed his father, married his mother, and even after he had made these two dire discoveries was allowed to con-tinue living among his fellow men and to go on ruling over Thebes.[1]

---

[1] *Od*. xi. 271 ff. (earliest version of Oedipus story) ; *Od*. xv. 222 ff., especially 257 (before the idea of blood-guiltiness has arisen) ; Hdt. iii. 50–3 (a tale of its obstinate survival). For the conception of blood-guiltiness (first found, according to Glotz, *Études*, p. 39, in the second half of the eighth century) see Wilamowitz's introductions to his translations of the *Eumenides* and the *Oedipus Tyrannus*. In the latter he points out how the ' church-going

Between that early tale of Oedipus and the gay and unblushing short stories of Herodotus lies the age of blood-guiltiness, when the impiety of bloodshed lay heavy on men's minds and inspired them with something like a real physical revulsion against the murderer and the homicide. They have stained their hands in human life-blood and not all the perfumes of Arabia can wash them clean. They must be cut off forthwith from the common life of men, till the god has found them a way out and has cleansed them solemnly from their guilt. We know that stage of feeling about offences against society, for it still lingers on in our midst from our own Middle Ages. It would not be hard to point to offences for which society still preserves the mediaeval bell, book, and candle, which are scandalous in general without being blame-worthy in the particular case. To thinking modern minds the interdict is a barbarous and uncivilized institution. But it is more advanced and more humane than that which it replaced. For, in the slow process by which society affixes individual responsibility, there is a stage at which ' it is expedient that one

Sophocles ', unlike the intellectuals round him, held strongly to the traditional ideas of blood-guiltiness, yet emphasizes throughout in every detail the inno-cence of Oedipus's motives. Herein precisely lies the tragedy. Sophocles' difficulty is the problem of *suffering*, as Aeschylus's is the problem of *sin*. Familiarity with bloodshed is apt to produce a strange callousness even among men brought up amid civilized conditions, as any one may observe in the literature of modern warfare and exploration. There was no sense of blood-guiltiness among the Europeans employed by the Putumayo rubber companies, many of whom must have ' reverted ' to the level of the savages they oppressed. This, together with the mental habits of our civilized stay-at-homes, is raising up serious difficulties in the colonial policy of modern democratic states. A city-dwelling public finds it easier to see the tropics through a haze of story-book romance than to use its own imagination on the facts. Thus a taste for exciting fiction actually makes it harder for a civilized democracy to govern an uncivilized empire justly—and the better the fiction the greater the difficulty. This was as true in Rome of Caesar's *Commentaries*, which, though not fiction, were probably deliberately written for the ' man in the Italian verandah ', as it is of *Soldiers Three* and *King Solomon's Mines*. The best of these blood-curdling stories in Herodotus is ' Rhampsinitus and the Thieves ', a tale of fratricide and mutilation and midnight meetings, where the hero ends by marrying the king's daughter. It is interesting as showing that even Herodotus's enlightened listeners still felt uneasy about unburied corpses ; it is all in the day's work to kill your brother, but you simply must get him buried. Are there any similar ' No thoroughfare ' posts in the modern reader's mind ? Probably not, if the subject is treated with sufficient absence of seriousness. ' Rhampsinitus and the Thieves ' is also interesting as revealing the germ of the modern detective story. But Herodo-tus's audience had not yet reached the pitch of sophistication and respectability attained by our modern city-dwellers ; its natural sympathies are with the thief, who therefore defeats all efforts at detection.

man should die for the people, and that the whole nation perish not '.[1]

But if this ritualistic conception of crime is at a certain stage expedient, it is, as we shall see in a moment, still very far from being moral. It is not surprising that, then as now, it should lend itself easily to unscrupulous piety and to the sophistries of priest and soothsayer. If the *Agamemnon* shows us the stained and innocent figure of the prophetess Cassandra, who shrank from the blood-stained halls of the son of Atreus as from a charnel-house, it tells us also of the prophet Calchas, who murdered or rather ' sacrificed ' Iphigenia. Thucydides preserves a typical instance of this ritualism. Alcmaeon the son of Amphiaraus had killed his mother. Apollo supplies him with a prescription to cure his infection. He is to search all Greece for a land which was not being shone on by the sun when the murder was committed. He has wit enough to solve the riddle, and settles down and lives happy ever after as king of Oeneadae on the new alluvial flats at the mouth of the Achelous. Herodotus is even more light-hearted. He tells us of a Phrygian who arrived at the Court of Croesus with polluted hands, having suffered a family misfortune. ' O King,' he says, ' I am the son of a friend of yours and I have had to leave home because I killed my brother.' ' You are come to friends,' replies Croesus, ' among whom you shall want nothing. Take your misfortune as lightly as possible, and you will find yourself best off.' [2]

But not every one was so fortunate as Alcmaeon in washing off his infection and finding a refuge from his murderers. If the murdered man is rejected by his kinsfolk there is as yet no expiation. The vendetta continues. Only it is war against an individual instead of war against a clan.

It is at this point, apparently, that the City State and its magistrates first intervened decisively in criminal affairs. We know little of the details. But one interesting document has

[1] See this point of view clearly put, in connexion with the familiar Agamemnon murders, by Clytemnestra's respectable old father in Eur. *Or.* 500. Orestes' right course would have been to drive his mother out. To kill her only made matters worse. Interdict : Soph. *O. T.* 236 ; *Ant.* 203 : it issues of course from the State, not from the Church.

[2] Thuc. ii. 102 ; Hdt. 1. 35. The *Odyssey* (xv. 247) knows nothing of Alcmaeon's wanderings. Aesch. *Ag.* 1309, 1311, 122–59. See also Leaf, *Homer and History*, p. 165, with map of the Achelous flats.

come to light which reveals these early magistrates trying to grapple with their new responsibilities. It embodies the first City State regulations we know of—the parent of those of which Pericles speaks at Athens—' in relief of those who are being oppressed '. It is an inscription incised on a thin plate of bronze which was discovered at Olympia in 1880. It runs as follows : ' Peace and safety to the fatherland, the family, and the goods of the accursed ! If any one has issued a sacred proclamation against a man of Elis who is in enjoyment of civic rights, should the supreme magistrate and the kings fail to apply the means of right, let each of them who have incurred the forfeit pay ten minae to the sacred treasure of Olympian Zeus.' Then follow some difficult details, and the inscription closes with the words, ' the tablet is sacred to the gods at Olympia.' [1]

The whole document is only ten lines long ; but every crabbed Doric word in it is precious. Here is the state of Elis throwing its aegis over any Alcmaeon or Orestes among its citizens and decreeing penalties against its magistrates should they fail to secure him a fair trial. Amongst these magistrates is one called a δημιουργός or public worker. It is the same name as the early Greeks applied to their craftsmen—the smith who kept the village in horseshoes and the potter who kept them in water-jugs. This inscription explains why we find a magistrate in such company. He too is a man who performs public as opposed to private services, for he takes the side of the State as against the tribe and the clan. The name lasted on as a memory of a great step forward in Greek political life.[2]

---

[1] ' Laws in relief of those who *are being* oppressed ' (the present tense has puzzled some commentators) are grouped with ' unwritten laws ' in Thuc. ii. 37. 5. For the Olympia inscription and full commentary see Glotz, *Solidarité*, pp. 248 ff.

[2] δημιουργοί as magistrates : Thuc. v. 47. 9, i. 56. 2 ; *I. G. A.* 113, 471, 544, and esp. 506, where we find a woman δημιουργός (at Aspendos, second cent. B. C.). Full list in Pauly, s.v. δημιουργός is derived from δήμιος, ' public ', not δῆμος, ' people '. The distinction between public and private duty is a familiar one to the Greeks of this age : e. g. *Od.* iii. 82 (Telemachus is travelling on private not public business : so iv. 314). Homer's ' public workers ' include soothsayers, doctors, joiners, poets, singers, and heralds, but on consideration he rejects beggars (*Od.* xvii. 383, xix. 134). But the most interesting mention of δημιουργοί is in an inscription found at Mycenae (given in Wilamowitz, *A. A.* vol. ii, p. 48) which provides that, where there is no magistracy, certain ἱερομνήμονες (i. e. religious officials) are to act as judges. This suggests an obvious question. Why did not the religious authorities step in, as in Israel,

'For this Olympian inscription,' says the French scholar to whom we owe its elucidation, 'is of inestimable value, not merely for the study of Greek law, not merely for the study of comparative law, but still more for its place in the history of the fundamental ideas on which modern societies repose. When the great historian of Israel (Renan) reaches in his narrative the reforms carried out by the Hebrew code of 622, after having emphasized the capital importance of the rule abolishing vicarious punishment, he turns to Greece to ask her what she has at that moment to set against the dawn of justice which has risen over Jerusalem. Well, Greece need not be ashamed of facing the comparison. She can not only point to the code of Draco, which is, for all its stringency to the individual, a milestone on the road of progress. She can point besides to this authentic document from her past in which, perhaps in the same year as the men of the East, the men of the West declare that they will no longer see the son punished for the father, and proclaim the great principle of individual responsibility. "The tablet is sacred to the gods at Olympia." Yes, this tablet is sacred. For the decree of the government of Elis forms, together with the book of Deuteronomy, a double link in the chain of gold which ends in the Declaration of the Rights of Man.' [1]

But it is high time we passed on from rights to duties.

to act as the interpreters and then the makers or revealers of law ? Why did not Olympia or Delphi become like Jerusalem or mediaeval Rome ? Instead the whole development of Greek political institutions (with which, of course, official religion was intimately bound up) was in a secular direction. Greek political thought from Solon to Aristotle was equally secular. They preferred laymen to priests, and thinking about this world to getting ready for the next.

[1] Glotz, *Solidarité*, p. 259. The transition from family to state justice is going on in China at the present moment, and it is interesting to hear what it looks like at close quarters. A well-informed writer in the *Nation* (Dec. 25, 1909), discussing the proposed new State Courts of Justice to be set up there, remarks : 'The question faces us : How far will the Government be able to enforce its penal code upon the villages, and sweep into the new Courts of Justice forms of lawlessness that have been dealt with in the villages by the elders themselves for scores of generations ? The village elders are really magistrates chosen by the heads of the groups of families in which they live, without the intervention of either a Lord Chancellor or Lord Lieutenants of the counties, and they sometimes inflict death sentences. ... My impression is that village justice which arises from the all but absolute power of the parent for life or death over children and descendants is better than that of the official courts. If I were a Chinaman I should prefer trial by a bench of great-uncles and a grandfather to trial in some of the Yamens into which I have had glimpses.'

CHAPTER IV

THE DEVELOPMENT OF CITIZENSHIP

GENTLENESS, OR THE RULE OF RELIGION

(σωφροσύνη)

στέργοι δέ με σωφροσύνα,
δώρημα κάλλιστον θεῶν.—EURIPIDES, *Medea* 636.
Give unto us made lowly wise
The spirit of self-sacrifice.—WORDSWORTH.

WE have seen how the Greeks gradually learnt to be citizens and to submit themselves to the rule of authorized magistrates. We have now to examine the problems and hardships in which their submission involved them, and to watch their long struggle to free themselves from the yoke that they had thus accepted. For it was here that the growing City State gained an experience of difficulties, and acquired qualities of statesmanship, which left a permanent mark upon her spirit and history in the fifth century.

The record of civilized States seems to show that no sub-division of the community, either a dynasty or a rank or a class or an army or a priesthood, is sufficiently well informed or wise or tolerant or unselfish to be entrusted for long, without control or responsibility, with the powers and temptations of government. The Greeks learnt this lesson from their Zeus-born aristocracy. They were not, as is often said, democrats by nature : they became so by necessity. By nature, environment, and tradition they believed in equality and fraternity. It was a slow and pain-ful development which drove them to self-government.

So long as the tribunal of Deioces was only a place of arbitra-tion, he had every reason to judge justly, for if his decisions were unfair he would lose his custom. It is when his authority became binding that the temptation began, and the instrument of efficiency became the handy tool of oppression.

We cannot trace the process in detail. But we know its con-sequences. They are writ large in the history of seventh-century Greece. It is with them and the painful crisis they ushered in that our narrative records of Greek history begin. The curtain rises on what the old Boeotian poet calls the Iron Age—a generation of chaos and bewilderment, when, not for the first or the last time in the life of the Greek nation, its institutions were no longer in harmony with the natural bent of its life and thoughts. We of the twentieth century know well what such a disharmony means, for we have it in our midst—misgiving and bitterness on the one side, suffering and rebellion on the other. But our society is large and complex; we are used to its contradictions and have learnt to shake down together in its confusion. In Greece it was different. The Greeks had yet to learn that society is not a work of art and that the perfect city is a poet's dream. Artists and thinkers by nature, lovers of order and reason, they asked for harmony in the world without as in the world within. 'Order' and 'world' are the same word (κόσμος) in their language. 'The love of man rises as upon stepping-stones,' says the high priest of this political doctrine in one of his noblest passages, 'from beautiful bodies to beautiful institutions and from beautiful institutions to beautiful ideas, until from beautiful ideas it attains to the idea of absolute beauty and at last knows what the essence of beauty is; this, my dear Socrates, is the life above all others which man should live.' It is such a life as only an ancient Greek could dream of living. But even he cannot do so in a period of transition.

In seventh-century Greece the whole scene is disordered. Men stand, as a poet complains, at the cross-roads. Ancient right points one way and newborn necessity another. Some good men are for one road, and some for the other. But the greater part stand puzzled and unhappy, looking in vain for a living guide. Meanwhile the brigands that lie in wait for every society in difficulties have stolen down from the hills and are looting the cherished store of the caravan. The fate of the whole venture is in peril. Only one thing can save it and bring a happy ending— the intervention of a god.[1]

---

[1] Theognis 911 (cross-roads—I have, however, altered the sign-posts); Plat. *Symp.* 211 (Plato's 'best life' is above the level of 'beautiful institutions'; that comes of his being a high priest and not a statesman). Thucydides has nothing to say about this crisis in his introduction. It is not part of his subject. Nor does the author of *The Expansion of England* waste words on the misery of the Industrial Revolution.

While we are waiting for the god, let us look round carefully at the company. The régime of the Zeus-born, prolonged through generations, has broken up the growing City State into two parties. It is important to be clear as to who is in each. The division is not one between nobles and non-nobles, or ' patricians ' and ' plebeians ', for, if it were, the nobles would soon go under. They are not rich or numerous enough to maintain themselves, and their cavalry is not a match for the bronze-clad ranks of the city's infantry. Nor is it the familiar division between rich and poor—the rich trying to maintain stability and the poor clamouring for revolution. For here it is the rich who are the radicals, whilst men who call themselves poor lift up their voices against change. The true division is not between wealth and poverty but between old and new forms of wealth, or—for it is almost the same thing—between town and country.

The breach between town and country had been widening, in the more progressive communities, all through the Middle Ages. Every generation increased the gulf between the families who followed Deioces into the city and those who stayed behind. Hesiod writes for one world, the poet of the *Odyssey* for the other. The men of Ithaca call themselves city folk (ἀστοί or δῆμος), while Hesiod's neighbours were outsiders or, as the late Romans called their village folk, Pagans ; the Greek name was Dwellers-round (περίοικοι). Despised by all the progressive and governing elements, they mope and languish in their old-world villages, and gradually sink into a position of inferiority and dependence. When our narrative records begin, most of them are not exactly slaves, but, to use the convenient South African phrase, in a ' condition of service or residence of a servile character '.[1]

We cannot trace the various stages of their decline. But it seems to have been most marked and rapid in the communities which laid most stress on military organization—particularly in the Dorian states of the Peloponnese. To the fifth-century Greeks the Dorians stood for a great military tradition. Whether

[1] Cf. the Homeric expression δῆμός τε πόλις τε (e. g. *Od.* xi. 14). See Solon ii (ed. Hiller), lines 6, 7, 23 (ἀστοί and δήμου ἡγεμόνες, nobles and demagogues, on one side against πενιχροί, paupers, on the other).

they really came of a sturdier stock than the other Hellenes it is still impossible to say; but if so we must admit that some of their outlying members, particularly in the West, showed marks of degeneracy. Certainly in the big Dorian settlements in the Peloponnese their natural bent, if such it was, was confirmed by circumstances. They were the last comers among the immigrants, and the memory of their community as a body of warriors cleaving their way through Greece was always lively in their minds. The old gathering of equal and disciplined fighting men, the Agora, which is the only form under which the people appear in the *Iliad*, lasted on all through the mediaeval period, and was transformed at its break-up into a democratic assembly. In Sparta especially the military tradition was always vigorous; her aristocracy won but a precarious foothold in the government, and her foot-soldiers were the first in Greece to recover their pre-rogatives when the transition came. We do not know when the five villages which made up the unwalled city of Lacedaemon were first gathered together under Taygetus. But they soon felt their superiority over the scattered settlements round them, and the fear of famine in their narrow valley drilled them early into a career of conquest. Like the Romans, they pushed back their borders year by year, dividing the land as they took it in lots among their families. Amyclae, a few miles down the valley, was their Veii; next came Helos by the sea, and next the rich Messenian plain over the other side of Taygetus. Finally, in the early part of the sixth century, they absorbed the eastern sea-board of Laconia. Henceforward their only way was northward. But here their advance was stayed for good on the mountain borders of Arcadia, and by the middle of the sixth century they realized that they had ' bitten off as much as they could chew ' and had abandoned the quest for new lands with which to keep their fighters in food and muscle.[1]

But the men of the city of Lacedaemon were not the only citizen fighters who reduced villagers to dependence, although undoubtedly they were the most active of all in the work, and the system that they established the most durable and barbarous.

---

[1] The Dorians, as opposed to the ' Ionians ', are a ' greatly wandering race ': Hdt. i. 56, who still has details to give. ἐκ παλαιτάτου ηὐνομήθη, Thuc. i. 18. [See Appendix.]

There were ' outsiders ', under various names and no doubt with various histories, in most of the growing Greek states at the end of the mediaeval period. Argos, the premier Dorian community, lorded it not only over the villages of her plain, but over the hill-town of Mycenae, the old capital of the region, and over Cleonae and Hysiae across the mountain barriers. The Epidaurians nick-named their Dwellers-round Dustfoots, the Sicyonians theirs Club-carriers or Smock-weavers, and the Corinthians theirs Wearers of dogskin caps. Crete and Thessaly, Delphi and Heraclea in Trachis had their own village dependants each with an appropriate designation. And in Attica we know from the first page of Aristotle's *Constitution of Athens* that, when our detailed history begins, ' the poor were enslaved to the rich, they, their children and their wives, being called " clients and sixth-parters ", for this was the hire for which they laboured on the fields of the rich ; and the land was in the hands of the few.' [1]

What exactly was this ' condition of service or residence of a servile character ' to which these country folk were reduced ? It differed in different places, mainly according to the nature of the land. But in every case it was intimately connected with the loss or lack of political rights. The principal reason why they were slaves was because they were not full citizens. They had not yet discovered democracy as a safeguard of economic freedom.

---

[1] See Wallon, *Histoire de l'esclavage dans l'antiquité* (2nd ed., Paris, 1879, a thorough book but antiquated in treatment), vol. i, pp. 130–4, for references to these κονίποδες, κορυνηφόροι, κατωνακοφόροι, κυνόφιλοι, &c., and their parallels in the Greek colonial communities. We know little more of them than their nicknames, which amused the later lexicographers. For ' Orneates ' as a general name for Argive Perioeci see Hdt. viii. 73, probably adopted because it was the first important place the Argives subdued. Helots may owe their name to Helos in the same way. Meyer, *Gesch.* vol. ii, § 355 (cf. § 176), especially emphasizes the fact that the status of the Helots and Perioeci had nothing to do with the original immigration, but was due to later conquest from Lacedaemon. There is no *evidence* for any difference of race or dialect between them and the Spartans. The same is true of the other ' serf ' populations. In some cases they may have been, in large measure, pre-Hellenic by blood ; but it is impossible to test Bury's statement (*History of Greece*, large ed., vol. i, p. 157) that the revolutions which raised the tyrants to power in Sicyon, Corinth, and Megara ' seem to have been partly movements of the pre-Dorian popu-lation against the dominant Dorian families '. The Cretan serfs were some-times called κληρῶται, i. e. men on lots. They may be compared with the conquered Mytileneans who cultivated their old lands, in this case for a money payment, on behalf of the Athenian lot-holders or κληροῦχοι : Thuc. iii. 50. 2. [See Appendix.]

Hesiod's villagers and many others like them lost their opportunities by neglect, but did not yet know themselves as inferiors.
Side by side with them we can observe at least three varieties of
official and recognized dependence. The first and simplest is that
of the people who were technically known, by a purely Peloponnesian usage, as Perioeci or Dwellers-round. These were villagers
or even inhabitants of small townships, whose land was not worth
coveting. When the citizens of Lacedaemon, or, to call them by
their own name, the Spartiates, conquered and absorbed Laconia,
much of the land that they overran was too poor to be divided
out. So they left it to the villagers. These stayed in the same
position as before, only with the added sense that henceforward
they were definitely in a position of inferiority and remained
excluded from all share in the government of the City State.
Not that they would ever have made much use of the privilege of trudging into Lacedaemon and voting in the assembly.
They were too busy fighting starvation on their miserable
acres.

The second variety is the ' serfdom ' which we find in Laconia,
Crete, Thessaly, and other places. To a fifth-century Greek like
Thucydides the status of the Helot or the Thessalian Pauper
(πενέστης) was hardly distinguishable from that of a bought foreign
slave. But both the political origin and the economic operation
of the system were very different. The serfs of Laconia (which
includes the fertile plain of Messenia) and of Thessaly, like the
Laconian Perioeci, are conquered villagers ; but the lands on
which they live are no longer their own. They have been divided
out in lots among their citizen conquerors. But the citizens have
neither the leisure nor the inclination to cultivate them in person.
They are soldiers first and politicians second ; and in these two
activities they have gradually forgotten to be farmers. A democratic community is always faced with the big difficulty which,
as we saw, faced Deioces too, how the individual citizen can
combine public and private work. The Spartans settled it, in
a manner approved, strange to say, by the moralists of the fourth
century, by leaving their private work undone, and using their
public authority to get others to do it for them.

When Pericles boasts that the Athenians find time both for
public and private work, he is contrasting them in his mind with

the lordly Spartans who spend their mornings drilling and their afternoons, after the unappetizing meal which the Helots have brought in to them from their farms, hunting or boxing or making themselves beautiful. The Helots were forced to keep their masters in provisions. The arrangement was so drawn up that if there was not enough for their master there was not enough for them ; for they were bound to supply him, as a very jerky old poet tells us, with ' half of the yield of the corn grown on the soil that they tend '. If a Spartan could not supply his quota from his farm to the common mess, he was disfranchised till he did so : he had broken the rules of the club. Presumably he retired to his farm, whipped his Helots into activity, and cumbered them with his burdensome presence till they had restored it to prosperity. But he would never forget those misspent months, or how near he had been to total expulsion. With this memory in his mind he would take good care that there were not too many sons amongst whom the property must be divided. Seen in this light, it is not difficult to understand—what was such a puzzle to Xenophon—that Sparta, the most powerful and famous of the Greek states of his day, had also one of the smallest citizen bodies : or, as he puts it, disdaining even to mention the dependent classes, ' was one of the least populous.' [1]

In all other respects the Helot, like his fellow serfs, lived pretty much as he liked—or rather as he could. His master had no power (as in the case of a slave near at hand) to prevent him

---

[1] Xen. *Pol. Lac.* i. 1 : on serfs as ordinary slaves cf. Hdt. vi. 83 (δοῦλοι) ; Thuc. viii. 40. 2 (οἰκέται). To supply his master with ἥμισυ παντὸς ὅσον καρπὸν ἄρουρα φέρει is the Helot's task (Tyrt. *Frag.* 6). Though the Spartans lived so simply, they seem, like the Montenegrins to-day, to have paid a good deal of attention to their personal appearance ; cf. Hdt. vii. 208 ; Ar. *Pol.* 1269 b 25 (γυναικοκρατούμενοι). One of the chief impressions a passing tourist receives at Cettigne is that the fine-looking and finely uniformed Montenegrins whom he sees strutting about the streets or drinking and smoking in their back-kitchens have nothing in the world to do. Probably an Athenian stranger would receive the same impression at Sparta. Perhaps this is what prompted Plato to his playful suggestion (*Protagoras* 342) that they spent their leisure hours talking philosophy—a passage which Pater adopts as the motto of his beautiful chapter on Lacedaemon in *Plato and Platonism*. Not all the languid charm of Pater's style can persuade us that the young Spartans were ' monastic ' in spirit ; if he had told one so to his face out of school hours, he would probably have paid dear for it. On the Thessalians see Athenaeus, xii. p. 527. They had no Lycurgus to restrain their habits. Hence the Pharsalians, for instance, are ' both the laziest and the most extravagant of mankind '. [See Appendix.]

from marrying and having children, and, however poor he was, the youngsters could pick up a living somehow on his own or the neighbouring farms. Thus, while the Spartans, when there were no new lands to be won, aimed at keeping their population stationary and in reality suffered a steady decline, the number of the Helots increased rapidly, till the disproportion between rulers and ruled became the central anxiety of Spartan states-manship. But the serf's obligation to feed his master limited his freedom by keeping him tied to the soil. Moreover, the Helot at any rate had long since lost his legal rights. He might be ' weeded out ' any day by the Spartan secret police, with the acquiescence and approval of the city magistrate. Thucydides tells us without a tremor that two thousand Helots ' disappeared ' in this way during the crisis of the Peloponnesian War. It was the only means left of partly redressing the unequal balance which left one Spartan citizen face to face with some seventy-five dependants.[1]

But there is a third variety of dependence which concerns us most particularly. It was the most painful and degrading of all : for it came swiftly and without warning, and affected principally the most progressive of the Greek communities, and amongst them Athens. It is bound up with one of the greatest advances in material civilization—the introduction of a metal currency.

The early Greeks paid for their transactions in kind, or in bars of metal of unfixed weight. The first currency stamped as bear-

---

[1] Thuc. iv. 80. Meyer, *Gesch.* vol. iii, §§ 263–4, estimates the total popula-tion of Laconia (including Messenia) in the fifth century, before the losses sustained at the time of the earthquake in 464, at roughly :

Spartans	12,000 (i. e. 3,000–4,000 adult males)
Perioeci	80,000
Helots	190,000
Total :—	282,000–300,000.

For the disproportion between the citizens and non-citizens cf. Xen. *Hell.* iii. 3. 5. The Cretan ' serfs ' (οἰκεῖς) had certain customary rights which in the age of law-making were formally recognized. For details see commentary on the laws of Gortyn in *Inscriptions juridiques grecques*, vol. i, p. 423, espe-cially the interesting tariff of fines for offences against freemen, freedmen, serfs, and slaves (p. 419). But Lycurgus did nothing similar for the Helots. Consequently the Cretan outsiders remain faithful, but the Helots are always rebelling (Ar. *Pol.* 1272 b 18). For the tariff compare our own earliest laws, those of Æthelbert, which are similarly graded for different classes of the population. They consist of a tariff of ninety short sentences : e. g. ' If a man strike another with the fist on the nose—three shillings ' ; ' If the eye be struck out let amends be made with fifty shillings,' &c.

ing a fixed weight to serve as a convenient medium of exchange was issued by the Lydian kings in the seventh century. Like the plough and the printing-press it was one of those simple inventions which, once discovered, humanity cannot imagine itself without. It spread rapidly to Greece. In the course of one or two generations all the leading Greek states, both in Greece proper and in the West, are coining their own money, and every creditor is asking to be paid his debts in gold and silver.

It seems a simple change. But its effect upon the villager is as disastrous as the invention of the steam-engine. It created an economic revolution in the Mediterranean communities comparable to that from which Europe is only just recovering (if she is recovering) to-day. We can watch it in Greece, in Palestine, and in Italy, and see the temper of the sufferers reflected in Hesiod and Theognis, Amos and Hosea, and in the legends of early Rome.

For consider what the change means in the life of a peasant who is living from hand to mouth on his yearly harvests. He used to take his stuff to market and exchange it for the goods he needed—wool for the wife to spin, children's shoes for the winter, or tiles to mend the roof ; or he would pay the smith and the joiner in kind for repairing his plough or his cart. But now most of them will not accept his corn and wine till he has turned it into money. How much is it worth ? He has not the least idea : for it depends on factors outside his range and which he has no means of controlling. He takes what the middleman gives him ; and the middleman makes a living on his commission. At the end of the first year he is alarmed to find he has not as much margin in hand as usual. When the inevitable lean year comes he has no margin at all. In fact he cannot see his way through the winter without help. His only resource is to borrow.

So he applies to the Big House (for the day of the professional Shylock is not yet). The Well-born or Eupatrid (as the Athenians called him) is most accommodating. His heroic ancestors used to take their gold with them to the grave, in masks and such like. He is delighted to have found a better use for it. Certainly he will keep him through the winter. But of course he must be repaid punctually next harvest. And he wants a little extra as well to make up for what he might have been doing with his money in the meantime—say twenty per cent. for the six months. It is only fair, seeing that money, like seed, multiplies and bears fruit. The old ' garlic-smelling Acharnian ' scratches his head. ' Money-breeding' (τόκος) seems an unnatural idea, somehow. But it will find its way into current speech soon enough : and he has no head just now to anticipate Aristotle and Ruskin in discussing the morality of interest. So he agrees. One more detail before the transaction is concluded. Is he sure he can repay ? The Eupatrid has his oath, but he wants some more substantial security. Can he produce a friendly neighbour to go bail for him ? He fears not. They have all grown cautious these days—ever since on market-day there was a stranger from Laconia, telling all and sundry about the miserable state of the peasants there. The wisest man in Sparta, he said, summed up the position in five words—they never waste words in Sparta— ' Go bail and see ruin.' They did not believe him at the time ; but since he died they have found out how wise he was, and now they worship him as a hero. So neighbours are no good. He is thrown back on his own resources. What has he got to offer ? Only his land and his labour. He had never really thought of his land as his own : properly speaking it belongs to the family, to his ancestors and descendants as much as to himself. Still, the neighbours keep telling him this is an old-fashioned idea, and that nowadays land can be bought and sold and sliced and pieced together just like any of the ordinary wares in the market-place. What will the children do if he has no land to leave them when he dies ? And what about all the religious associations ? Well, necessity knows no religion, and his children must pray for happier times. So he consents, reluctantly, to make a bargain about his land. If he does not repay next spring, let the Eupa-trid take it over : he will cultivate it as his tenant, and pay him a sixth of the produce as rent. Done. He goes away with his money, and the Eupatrid sets up an eyesore of a pillar, with letters on it, in full view of the house. He cannot read the letters but he supposes they are to keep him in mind of his bargain.[1]

---

[1] ἐγγύα παρὰ δ' ἄτα is Chilon's laconic advice. The British School has recently discovered a relief bearing the letters ⟨X⟩ΙΛΩΝ which formed part of his shrine at Sparta. On borrowing cf. also Hes. *Erga* 394. On the reluctance to treat land as an ordinary commodity cf. Genesis xxiii. 11, where the children of Heth do not like to *sell* the Cave of Machpelah to Abraham : also the story

Alas, he needs no such reminder ! Lean years have a way of running in cycles. Next spring the harvest is as bad as its predecessor. By the end of the year his land is no longer his own, and he has joined the ranks of the ' clients ' or ' sixth-parters '. For some time all goes well. Then there comes a bad year, when expenses are heavy and he cannot pay his sixth ; or perhaps the Eupatrid discovers him cheating over the division of the produce. What remedy has the landlord ? He could no doubt evict him. But, besides being impious, this is to neither party's advantage. For the landlord could not easily replace his tenant, nor the peasant his home. Anything is better than being homeless. What has the peasant left to offer ? Like the modern proletarian, nothing but his labour. So he makes another and still more humiliating bargain. Unless his rent is repaid (of course with interest) by next spring, the whole produce of his labour shall henceforward belong to the Eupatrid. In other words, he will become his slave. And who will keep his family if the breadwinner is removed ? The Eupatrid will keep them, provided they work for his household and continue to give satisfaction.[1]

Such, roughly speaking, is the history of many of the debt-slaves whose bitter cry goes up in seventh-century Greece and in the prophecies of Israel—perhaps the bitterest of all forms of slavery, because its victims are suffering in the midst of increasing abundance. They are like the labourers who are driven out of work by the invention of new machinery, whose starvation passes unnoticed amid the swelling statistics of industry. Very often

of Naboth, 1 Kings xxi. Meyer, in his *Wirtschaftliche Entwickelung des Altertums* (reprinted in *Kleine Schriften*), first emphasized the parallel between Theognis and Amos. Cunningham's *Western Civilization in its Economic Aspects* (especially pp. 73–5) is also worth a mention because of its suggestive references to our own mediaeval period. See also Wilamowitz, *A. A.* vol. ii, pp. 57–8, especially on the pillars. To correct any apparent over-simplification in the above account see note on p. 303 below.

[1] The status of the Attic sixth-parters (ἐκτημόροι) has been much disputed. I follow E. M. Walker (whose view is adopted by the editors in the note on p. 14 of Routledge's condensed edition of Grote's *History of Greece*). But I differ from him and agree with De Sanctis, Ἀτθίς, 2nd ed., 1912, p. 196, n. 2, in regarding this peculiar tenancy as itself provisional and a badge of ' slavery' and ' dependence ' (see *Ath. Pol.* ii), the first step down the abyss. The traditional system in Attica, as elsewhere, was the peasant proprietorship which Solon re-established. Cf. a similar descent in two steps in an interesting parallel story in Genesis xlvii. 13 ff.

as the years go on they are sold out of the country ; their masters prefer to realize rather than to have these sullen fellow-country-men hanging about their farms. As defaulting debtors they have no remedy ; the master who owns their labour owns their bodies, and they are in all respects like the captured or kidnapped foreigners who are now beginning to be brought into the city as slaves from abroad.[1]

Moreover, the landlord himself is in difficulties. The economic crisis has not passed him by untouched. He too needs money to keep up his style of living, and he too pays his tribute to the man with the table in the market-place. He is beginning to discover, as all landed aristocracies discover at a certain phase of development, that though the land may yield him a living it will not yield him a fortune. However extensive the lands he con-trols, however numerous his unhappy labourers, he cannot rival his younger brother who has taken to seafaring. The bigger his property the harder it is to supervise ; and, as he remarked one day after a disheartening round (and the remark was treasured up in the family till his great-great-grandson put it in a book), the best of all animal foods is ' Master's Eye '. His brother, on the other hand, once he got his ship, made a fortune in a few years by the simple process of dangling before foolish people things that their own country does not happen to produce. In the olden days we were satisfied with our own country and despised foreign products. Now the idea is abroad that all the things most worth possessing come from the ends of the earth. It was clever of my brother to exploit this innocent foible, and for the first few voyages he did so at the risk of his life and live-lihood. But now that he has amassed some money it is time he turned farmer. He has as much as he needs. Why risk his life and ruin his character and waste the few short years of life for more ? [2]

---

[1] Solon, xxxii. 7.

[2] Hesiod, *Erga* 618, 686 ; Theognis, 1202 (dangers of trading) ; Hdt. iii. 106 (' the most valuable things come from the ends of the earth ' : not having an ' economic mind ' he has not stopped to ask why). Effect of the crisis on farming : Hdt. v. 29 (when the Parians were called in to settle the political and economic crisis which had distracted Miletus for two generations they examined all the estates and found very few well-farmed : it is clear from the account that there were still a fair number of proprietors). Xen. *Oec.* xii. 20 (' Master's Eye '—the friend of Cyrus gives the remark a Persian colouring,

The question has often been asked since, in many a dollar-ridden society. But these early Greek traders were facing it for the first time ; and to us who think we know the answer there is a charming ingenuousness about their questionings. The queer thing about money, says Theognis over and over again, is that you can never have too much of it. Herein it is different from any of the things you can buy with it. Food, clothing, houses, above all wine—there is a limit to them all. But to money there is no limit. There is only one thing like it, and that is wisdom.

> Two powers there are against whom evermore
>   Man's spirit fights in vain,
> Riches and knowledge. Seemeth crammed thy store ?
>   Greed whispers : ' Pour again.'
> Wisest of men, look inward : lo, thou art
>   Thrall to Queen Wisdom's will.
> Bid her begone ! Thou knowest in thy heart
>   Thou lov'st her still.[1]

No one but a Greek could have coupled Wisdom and Riches in such a fashion at such a time. You will not find this note in old Cato, shrewd and worldly wise though he was, still less in Amos and Hosea. Yet the traveller might hear it to-day in a Peloponnesian village on the lips of a returned and discontented emigrant. It bears all the stamp of the Greek spirit : its calm way of sitting down to think things over, its ' hard matter-of-factness ', and its ' feeling for the best things '. It is an artist's phrase, this last, but it serves better than any other. For

but it is true enough all the same). The idea that landed property was more respectable than any other kind died hard, with the ancients as with us. Cf. Xen. *Oec.* passim (e. g. iv. 4) ; Ar. *Pol.* 1278 a 25 (at Thebes you only become respectable when you have been ten years out of ' business ') ; and the well-known passage of Cicero, *De Off.* i. 42, recommending wholesale merchants to buy land and a ' position '—advice frequently taken even by those unfamiliar with the *novus homo* who fathered it. Of course Plato and Aristotle gave this, like so many other conservative ideas, a fillip.

[1] Theogn. 1157. I append the lines in their native dress :—

> Πλοῦτος καὶ σοφίη θνητοῖς ἀμαχώτατον ἀεί,
>   οὔτε γὰρ ἂν πλούτου θυμὸν ὑπερκορέσαις·
> ὡς δ' αὔτως σοφίην ὁ σοφώτατος οὐκ ἀποφεύγει,
>   ἀλλ' ἔραται, θυμὸν δ' οὐ δύναται τελέσαι.

I have purposely wavered between ' Wisdom ' and ' Knowledge ', for these older Greeks, living before the day of universities and encyclopaedias, did not know the distinction. It was not till a century later that Heracleitus told a surprised world that ' A man may learn and learn yet stay a fool ' (πουλυμαθίη νόον οὐ διδάσκει).

Theognis was not a preacher or a philosopher, but only a quiet artist in bewilderment.[1]

But the intrusion of the commercial spirit did more than make men think. It made them suffer, and it sent them to the high gods for redress. For the new lords of the city, the parvenu aristocracy, who lorded it with their money-bags and their ' silver-bought slaves ' over the old country folk and their traditions, unlike the godlike judges of old, knew neither mercy nor justice. Gold and silver were in their houses, but, as old Hesiod said, it was iron that was in their hearts. His beautiful lament is familiar to many English readers. So let us turn rather to its weaker counterpart in the elegiac verses of poets who, unlike the old Boeotian, have come to live in the city, nearer to the seat of injustice.

> Good Hope alone of kindly powers remains amongst us now,
> All other gods have fled away to high Olympus' brow,
> She of the saving temper and Faith whose touch can bind,
> And Grace that makes life lovely, friend : but we are left behind.
> No more do men deal justly or keep the plighted word,
> The immortal gods are far away : their anger is not stirred.
> The good are dead and buried, and no man now feels awe
> For the wisdom of our fathers and our ordered city law.

So sings one who has watched the rise of the ' rights of property ' and of the generation of business men. Here is another cry from one who has been drawn into the current of the new wealth, as he looks back, as many a European has looked back from New York, on the ruined country-side from which he is driven forth.

> The years I dropped my pitcher in the clear dark village spring
>   How sweet and good the water's taste did seem.
> But now the rains have flooded it, the mountain streams have
>   muddied it,
>   I'll drink another spring, a larger stream.

---

[1] Drunkenness is the most simple and obvious temptation for a nation or class with money newly in its pocket. The Greeks were not drunkards, but there is a great deal about wine in Theognis and Archilochus. These early citizen-soldiers called it their ' breast-plate '. ' You'll feel ever so much lighter when you've got your breast-plate on,' said some wag at a party (v. Theognis, 882–4 and 413, note that even this wine is not unmixed). Compare Arch. fr. 2 and 4 (wine in camp and on shipboard) and Hosea and Amos, *passim* (e. g. Hos. iii. 1). The Romans at this stage of development were the grossest of all. Their magistrates are said to have had jars put at the street-corners to take a drink from as they went by. See Ferrero, *Greatness and Decline of Rome* (E.T.), vol. i, p. 23.

It is a typical metaphor. We speak of living under a strange sky ; but the Greek, whose city or village grew up round a spring, by Peirene or Castalia or Dirce or Callirrhoe, speaks of ' drinking strange waters '.[1]

' The good are dead and buried.' There is no more goodness or piety (for the two still mean the same) among men. Nothing is left, as Hesiod tells us, but Aidôs, that vague sense of respect for gods and men, and shame of wrong-doing before earth and sky, which is the last expiring flicker of good in bad men's hearts. There is no legacy here for fifth-century Athens ; for this shame is too vague and impalpable to be counted as part of the body politic. Its positive meaning—the particular uttermost wickedness which it checks men from committing—varies from age to age. The shame of the *Iliad* and of the migrations was simpler and wilder than the shame of Theognis, as his would seem meaningless and old-fashioned to the age of the Peloponnesian War. The men of the migrations feel shame as they fling away the last shreds of patriarchal custom, the contemporaries of Theognis when they break loose from city law. But to Thucydides shame is the last sanction and safeguard of a whole system of personal and political morality. It is the foundation on which Pericles bases his whole Funeral Speech. But the foundations are not visible while the building still stands. It is only when it has been overthrown in a crisis greater than that through which Theognis passed that Thucydides, in the bitterest section

---

[1] Theognis, 1135 and 959 (the two poems *may* be by the same hand, but I do not think so). Cf. Hdt. ii. 18 ; Eur. *Med.* 69. I append the second poem from Hiller's text :—

> Ἔστε μὲν αὐτὸς ἔπινον ἀπὸ κρήνης μελανύδρου,
> ἡδύ τί μοι δόκεεν καὶ καλὸν ἔμμεν ὕδωρ·
> νῦν δ' ἤδη τεθόλωται, ὕδωρ δ' ἀναμίσγεται ἰλυῖ,
> ἄλλης δὴ κρήνης πίομαι ἢ ποταμοῦ.

The spring is ' dark ' because, as one can still see at Peirene, it is covered in to keep it from the sun and make it a shady resting-place. A modern romantic would have been tempted to add that there was gold dust in the mud brought down. But the ' classical ' poet refrains. He only gives one hint of his inner meaning—in his last word : for men do not drink from rivers in Greece. If they did, they would drink mud in winter and go thirsty in summer. On ' silver-bought ' slaves, first introduced at this period, see the *locus classicus* in Athen. 265 b. For Hesiod's beautiful lines see *Erga* 174 and Murray's *Greek Epic*, p. 79 (2nd ed., p. 102). I follow Glotz in referring them to this period.

of his book, makes a speaker think of shame—to make mock of it.[1]

But the crisis of the seventh century has still a positive message for the fifth. That is why it was necessary to describe it. For the gods had not all fled to Olympus. One still cared for the men in turmoil in the cities, and showed them a way of safety. It was just when things were darkest that the Delphic Oracle began to speak.

We know Apollo only in the days of his decline, when he had sacrificed his authority by siding with the Persian invader. That was after he had founded what we may almost call a church. In the seventh century Delphi was not the seat of a church but of a gospel ; and it was a gospel to which Greece was drawn to listen. For its good tidings were very simple—so simple indeed and so sensible that only a Greek oracle would have dared proclaim them—the duty of self-control. They are summed up in two sayings of two words each : *Know yourself* and *Be moderate*. The self-knowledge which Apollo preached to his visitants, and wrote up in large letters over the entrance to his sanctuary, is not the careful self-analysis which Socrates, misinterpreting the god, as his manner was, made the basis of his philosophical teaching. It was a plainer lesson—merely that which the Egyptians taught their guests when they brought in a skeleton to their banquets : ' Know that you are a feeble and short-lived creature. Naked you came into this world, and naked you will leave it. What is the use of much riches, much honour, much pleasure, much anything ? Be moderate.' But how can I be moderate while men rage furiously around me ? asks the worshipper. ' By Gentleness,' replied the god, using a word which does not bear translation, ' by controlling your temper, by thinking good of men and not evil, by cultivating thoughts and habits of mind which " save " instead of those that excite and corrode.' For this is the meaning of that gentleness or self-control (σωφροσύνη) which henceforth ranked as one of the cardinal marks of the Greek spirit.[2]

---

[1] See v. 111. 3 τὴν πλεῖστα διαφθείρουσαν ἀνθρώπους αἰσχύνην : the phrase is intended to remind the reader of i. 122. 4, a very different atmosphere. Nemesis is as shifting in its positive content as Αἰδώς. For the origin of the meaning familiar in Aeschylus and Herodotus (' Though the mills of God grind slowly yet they grind exceeding small ') see Theognis, 659.

[2] Cf. Murray, *Greek Epic*, pp. 27–8 (2nd ed., p. 48) ; Hdt. ii. 78 (Egyptian banquets) ; Plato, *Charm.* 164.

Yet, in the form in which we know it, it was no older than the seventh century. It was Apollo's invention. The gospel of Delphi is indeed a new religion, like the gospel of Amos and Isaiah. Like theirs, and that of St. Francis, it was attached to an old name—for great religious teachers, like great statesmen, never build on new ground—but the Apollo of Homer, the god of the silver quiver and the arrows of pestilence, is as remote from the Apollo of the oracle as is the Yahweh of Jael from the Yahweh of Isaiah. It was a religion which sprang up, so far as we can tell, simply out of the needs of the age. Its story, for it had a story, was simple enough. Apollo was the son of Zeus and the appointed mediator, by means of his oracle at Delphi, ' the navel of the earth,' between the All-Father and helpless mankind. But nothing in the story, and no material circumstances in the environment of Delphi, explain the rapid rise of the Oracle till it became for several generations the greatest spiritual force in the Greek world. And not only a spiritual force, but (as the two were not yet dissociated in men's minds) a temporal power as well. It was Apollo to whom, as to a Pope, kings and people came for advice, who encouraged and directed that great impulse of colonial expansion which, however different in pretext and appearance, is yet in some measure akin to the Crusades ; above all it was Apollo who, as tradition affirmed, not merely by his preaching but by detailed suggestion and regulation, helped some of the most ' diseased ' of Greek states to recover health and strength. There were clever shufflers at Delphi in the fifth century. They were the unworthy offspring of men who, in spite of their motto, did not compromise but originated. The very names of these early prophets have passed away. They were content to cast their work upon Apollo, as the bards were content to cast theirs upon Homer. Yet prophets there must have been, as truly inspired as those of Israel. In spite of the priests who succeeded them their work lived on : ' the fire of their spirit illumined and warmed the whole religious life of the Hellenes.' None of the great names of the greatest age of Greece but shows marks of their influence, though Pindar and Sophocles, Aeschylus and Herodotus, Thucydides and Euripides, Plato and Aristotle (to group them roughly in couples) each let the leaven work in the way that best suited their own genius. It is a far cry

from ' Be Moderate ' to Aristotle's ' Virtue is a Mean ' and
Plato's canonization of Apollo as the god of his New Republic.
But the same ' saving temper ' is at work in them all.   So too
we can feel it in the Funeral Speech, despite all its superlatives ;
and when, at Pericles' exit from the story, Thucydides is trying
to sum up his work in a sentence, this is what came into his
mind, like a breath from the older Delphi : ' So long as he held
supreme authority in the city in time of peace, he led her with
moderation and fenced her with security.   So under him she
attained her greatest power.' [1]

But it is time to pass on to Apollo's more immediate achievement in the building up of the fifth-century city—his work
as a lawgiver.   For the prophets who ' speak out ' at Delphi,
like the prophets of Israel, precede and make straight the way
for written law.[2]

[1] Thuc. ii. 65. 5 : μετρίως here means either ' moderately ' or ' fittingly ',
' appropriately ' : both expressions recall the Delphic way of looking at things.
For Plato's use of Apollo (which many a Christian reader must have thought
strange) see *Rep.* 427.   Not even the ' city in the heavens ' can do without
Apollo's saving influence.   For Sophocles (who is far nearer the seventh-
century spirit) cf. *O. T.* 863 ff.   νοσεῖν (to be ill) is the ordinary Greek word to
denote internal trouble in a city.   To people who have no medical science
the causes of bodily illness are no less obscure, often more obscure, than
those of social unrest.

[2] ' Prophet ' (προφήτης) of course means ' one who speaks out ', not ' one
who predicts '.   For the prophets of Delphi see Wilamowitz, *Orestie*, Introduction to *Choephoroe*, especially pp. 133-4.   For an appreciation of their
influence see the chapter on ' The Unity of Greece ' in Curtius's *History
of Greece*, E. T., vol. ii, ch. i (not up to date in its details).   The best monument
to the colonizing influence of Delphi is Pindar's Fourth Pythian Ode.   See
also Hdt. v. 43.

CHAPTER V

THE DEVELOPMENT OF CITIZENSHIP

LAW, OR THE RULE OF FAIR PLAY

(ἰσονομία)

Ἐλεύθεροι γὰρ ἐόντες οὐ πάντα ἐλεύθεροί εἰσι· ἔπεστι γάρ σφι δεσπότης νόμος.

HERODOTUS, vii. 104.

Though free they are not absolutely free; for they have a master over them, the law.

I will no longer hate the government but obey its commands willingly, since I feel sure they are laid down for the good of all of us. The policeman I will no longer regard as an enemy but as a friend.—*Yiddish-English Conversation Manual*, compiled in connexion with the Russo-Jewish Committee, p. 196.

THAT the Greek states recovered from the confusion caused by the economic crisis of the seventh century was due in the main, as we have seen, to the influence of the Delphic oracle. Apollo's gentle doctrine of self-control and moderation became an integral part of Greek political life. But we must be careful not to exaggerate the rapidity of its working. Bitter passions once aroused by injustice and suffering are not easily assuaged, and it would be too much to expect them to lie down in Greece at the magic of a single phrase. Moreover the surest remedies, in the body politic as elsewhere, are not always those which act most quickly. Apollo was no revivalist, and he could afford to wait.

Thus in the majority of the Greek states the recovery from chaos was slow and halting, and there were many quarters where the bitterness was at first too great for Apollo's message to penetrate. Between the confusion of the seventh century and the lawgivers who followed upon it there is a period of transition, during which Greece was adapting herself to the new economic conditions and accustoming her mind to the new teachings of Delphi. This period is marked by the emergence of personal rule under what are known as the ' tyrants '.

In the development which we are tracing—the growth of the influences which culminated in the political life of fifth-century

Athens—the tyrants are an interlude. As Herodotus and Thucydides both tell us, each in his own characteristic way, they did ' nothing noteworthy '. They made no special contribution to the spiritual development of Greece : for they brought no reinforcement either to the corporate sense of the community or to the liberty of the individual. And in the material sphere too, in spite of all their grand designs, they were felt to be an incubus. ' The Athenians,' says Herodotus, who knew the spirit of his adopted countrymen, ' when governed by tyrants were superior in war to none of their neighbours ; but when freed from tyrants became by far the first. This, then, shows that as long as they were oppressed they purposely acted as cowards, because they were labouring for a master ; but when they were free every man was zealous to labour for himself.' [1]

Yet, because of the part that they play in the development of our story, we cannot ignore them altogether. For it was they who set before the Greeks in the clearest light their need for written law, and who thus pressed them to apply, and to embody in permanent form, the somewhat vague and general teachings of Delphi.

The rise of the tyrants is easily explained. The gathering discontent in the various Greek states was bound to lead, sooner or later, to popular uprisings. But the oppressed and suffering people had no natural leaders, and the crisis was a golden opportunity for men of vigour and ability to espouse the popular cause and lead their party to victory. Once masters of the multitude, and with the reins of power within their grip, it was not difficult for them to maintain and regularize their position, and even to hand on their authority to their lineal successors. Personal governments of this sort were established in the seventh and sixth centuries in numerous states of Greece and Asia Minor, for instance at Ephesus, Miletus, Mytilene, and Samos, at Corinth, Sicyon, Megara, and Epidaurus. Athens, too, had her tyrants, although, as we shall see, at a slightly different phase of her development.

Most of these ' tyrannies ' were, as Aristotle remarks, ' exceedingly shortlived ' : the longest, that of Orthagoras and his

---

[1] Hdt. v. 78 ; Thuc. i. 17. The wholly different account given by Isocrates (*Paneg.* 75–84) must be taken *cum grano.*

successors at Sicyon, lasted barely a century. Its survival was due, we are told, to their exceptional moderation! For the ordinary tyrant, especially in the second generation, found it impossible to resist the temptations of power, and often yielded to them in their grossest and most violent forms. It was hardly to be expected, thought the Greeks, that a man entirely free from all corporate and customary restraints should act otherwise. ' Indeed,' asks a speaker in Herodotus, who is surely expressing the historian's own point of view, ' how can an autocracy be a well-constituted government where one man is allowed to do whatever he pleases without having to answer for his actions ? Even the best of men, were he granted such power, would alter the train of his thoughts. Insolence will be engendered in him by the advantages of his position : and envy he has already, implanted in him, as in all men, from his birth. With these two in his soul he is filled with every wickedness ; for insolence will cause him to break out into many acts of wantonness, and envy into many more. One would expect a man who holds the sovereign power to be free from envy, since he already possesses every advantage ; but he is a standing proof to the contrary in his behaviour towards the public, for he envies the best of those who survive under his rule and delights in the worst of the citizens. He very readily listens to calumny and is the most inconsistent of all men. If you show him respect in moderation he is offended because he is not sufficiently honoured ; and if any one pays him particular honours he regards the flattery as offensive.' There are no definite accusations here, and the account is consistent with an able and successful administration. A ruler may be haughty and sensitive and capricious in his personal likings and yet remain active and clear-sighted. The whole tone of the complaint is rather social than political. It shows us, what many will recognize in other spheres, club-life at its worst, and throws a lurid light on that spirit of petty meanness which always lies ready below the surface in all little communities. No better soil could be found for it than was provided by the conditions of Greek life. Greece only conquered these temptations and kept the air of her cities sweet by keeping men's minds full, and their hands busy, with large impersonal issues.[1]

[1] Hdt. iii. 80 ; Ar. *Pol.* 1315 b 13, 38.

But the speaker in Herodotus has not yet concluded his indictment. ' I proceed to mention,' he continues, ' what is most important of all. The tyrant changes the rights and customs of our ancestors, violates women, and puts men to death without trial.' The tyrants, in other words, cared neither for the immemorial rights of Greek life nor for the city-made rules and precedents which had gradually grown up around them. They trampled down both without thought or discrimination. They offended against all the sanctities and cut men's holiest feelings to the quick.

Yet the laws against which they sinned were not laws to which appeal could be made against them. All men knew them ; but they were nowhere to be found. Their old interpreters were dead : and the words of the oracle were not clear enough to be cited in the market-place. The times cried aloud for something more permanent and definite, for some impersonal authority, wise with the wisdom of years and invested with a perpetual validity, to which the citizen could make a sure and triumphant appeal in times of distress. ' The law,' says Aristotle, ' has a compulsory power, and is at the same time a rational ordinance proceeding from a kind of prudence or reason. And whereas we take offence at individuals who oppose our inclinations, even though their opposition is right, we do not feel aggrieved when the law bids us do what is right.' What was needed in the Greek states at this time, both as a stimulus and a safeguard, was a table of written commandments.[1]

Thus we have reached at length what seemed to the fifth-century Greeks, looking backwards, the misty age of law-making. The art of writing spread through the Greek world in the seventh century. Fortunately for Greece and for the world, the need and the opportunity brought forth the men. What Solon achieved for Athens, the mysterious Lycurgus achieved for Sparta, and a host of other lawgivers, few of whose names we know, achieved for many other City States both in the East and in the West. The fundamental laws which they established through the greater part of the Greek world formed the basis, well-laid and unshakable, of the famous and familiar fifth-century system of government.[2]

[1] Ar. *Eth.* 1180 a 21.
[2] Lycurgus is still as mysterious a figure as he was to Thucydides, who

It is hard for us to realize what part ' the Laws ' played in the life of a fifth-century Athenian. We have our constitution, written or unwritten, and the ever-changing body of our Statute Law. But they are remote from our daily life. We do not ourselves enforce them or even know them. We entrust their care to others—to representatives and experts and their agents. Between us and the enforcement of law stand the policeman and the magistrate : between us and the making of law stand Parliament and the Government. But in Athens there was no such thing as ' the Government ' as distinct from the people.

' Who is the lord and shepherd of their flock? ' asks the Queen-Mother of Persia in Aeschylus about the strange Western people against whom her son Xerxes is fighting : and straight comes the answer, worded, not for the Persian court, but for the quick audience of Athenians in the theatre under the Acropolis : ' They are not slaves : they bow to no man's rule.' We can almost hear the cheering ! Fifty years later, the Theseus of Euripides, the ideal hero-king of Athens, uses almost the same words to rebuke the envoy of an autocrat :—

> Nay, peace, Sir Stranger ! Ill hast thou begun,
> Seeking a master here. No will of one
> Holdeth this land ; it is a city and free.
> The whole folk year by year, in parity
> Of service is our king.

There is no ' Government ' in Athens, for the people is ' the Government '. [1]

But though the people has no living master, it is not without control. The fifth-century Athenian did not yet know, either in his individual or his corporate life, what it was to live without control. With all the liberty that he enjoyed, obedience was still the law of his being. Only the master whom he acknowledged and with whom he was in close and daily relation, was no human being like himself, but the Laws of the Constitution, copied out on stone pillars so as to be constantly before his

takes especial pains to avoid mentioning his name. But it is now quite certain that his work was done, not at the very beginning of Spartan history, but at the close of a long period of disturbance, as Thucydides suggests (i. 18. 1).

[1] Aesch. *Pers.* 241-2 ; Eur. *Suppl.* 403 ff. (transl. Murray).

eyes. He obeyed their commands willingly, for they embodied
the work of human reason without the defects of human caprice.
Their voice was ever the same and their commands were just.
For laws written out on stone and handed down from the past
can be no respecters of persons :—

> With written laws, the humblest in the state
> Is sure of equal Justice with the great,

says the Theseus of Euripides. So Athenians found it easy
to live justly and peaceably together under the ruling principle
of Solon's laws. 'Why,' says Herodotus, 'the very name of
it is beautiful—Isonomiê,' 'Fair Play.' We can understand
now why it was no pedantic scruple but the habit and devotion
of a lifetime which made Socrates so indignantly reject his
friends' suggestion that he should escape from prison. No one
was freer in mind than he : yet, like the Spartans at Thermopylae, he ' was not absolutely free ' : for he ' had a master over
him, the law '.[1]

Only the wisest and most successful of the makers of these
written laws is known to us as a personality, the Athenian Solon.
The others are merely shadowy 'wise men'. But we have
evidence enough to be able to descry the general lines of their
work and to recognize their peculiar spirit. The pithy sayings
which the after-time preserved as having fallen from the lips of
the 'Seven Sages' bear the marks of the healing influence of
Apollo. They did not, like the Jews, call in a god to father their
work ; but they pursued it in a frame of mind pleasing to the
god they worshipped. Sayings like ' It is hard to be good ', or
' Call no man happy till his life be ended ', and many others
which we know as current coin, from the mint of the Sages, in

---

[1] Eur. *Suppl.* 433 ff. ; Hdt. iii. 80, vii. 104 ; cf. v. 78, i. 29 ; Plato, *Crito* 50.
Cf. Wilamowitz, *Aus Kydathen*, pp. 47 ff. ; *A. A.* i. 45. Plato and Aristotle
took up again the hopeless quest for the ' philosopher-king ', and the modern
Anarchists have reinvented ' unwritten laws '. Theseus knew better.—' Fair
Play ' was the foundation on which Athenian self-government was built up :
hence it was a natural battle-cry for the party which was opposed to the
extension of popular government, the ' oligarchs ' or ' aristocrats ' referred to
on p. 90. If Fair Play is secured, what need of Self-government or Empire ?
Cf. Thuc. viii. 97 (the ὀλιγαρχία ἰσόνομος in 411), iii. 62. 3 (Boeotia, as to which
we have recently secured the only extant account of the detailed working of
an ὀλιγαρχία ἰσόνομος : see p. 167 below), and viii. 48. 6, where Phrynichus
points out how unlikely it is that such an oligarchy will really ensure ' fair
play ' to all sections of the population.

fifth-century Athens, testify to the influence of the gentle and
mellow and pleasantly ironical wisaom which spoke from the
sanctuary at Delphi. Its strangely simple and philosophical
teaching had penetrated deep into the heart of the Greeks : for
they had a nature ready to receive it.[1]

One feature we can trace in the work of all these lawgivers—
an attempt to restore the unity of the state by restricting the
use of wealth. It was the sudden discovery of gold and silver,
or rather of what can be bought with gold and silver, which
had tempted the aristocracy into injustice. The Sages were
wise enough to see that the best way to cure the disease was,
so far as possible, to remove the temptation. Hence we find
them enjoining, not only moderation of spirit, but sobriety of
demeanour and simplicity in outward appearance, and going
so far as they dared, and as the independent spirit of their
fellow-countrymen allowed, in legislation against luxury. While
Lycurgus could put all his Spartans in uniform and prescribe
their daily menu and how they were to eat it, Solon went no
further than to limit an Athenian girl's trousseau to three dresses,
and to forbid hired mourners at funerals or the interment of
more than three suits of clothes with the dead. But the aim in
both cases was the same—to redress the inequalities of wealth
in the state, not merely by making just laws, but by causing the
rich to *look* as much like the poor as possible. Men were to feel
themselves plain citizens, not nobles or dependants. It was the
outward and visible sign of the democracy that was to come.
Solon was wise enough to have discovered, two and a half centuries before Aristotle, that it is more important to form good
habits than to frame good laws.[2]

[1] e. g. Hdt. i. 30 (Solon and Croesus). Of course this story does not record
what Solon really said to Croesus, whom he probably never met, but ' what
he ought to have said '. In Book I alone there are several other ' moral
stories ' which seem to belong to this cycle, e. g. ' Arion and the Pirates, or
Art's unexpected resources ' (ch. 23–24), ' The Tomb of Nitocris, or How to
hoax posterity ' (ch. 187), ' Candaules and Gyges, or Things one had better
keep to oneself ' (σκοπέειν τινὰ τὰ ἑωυτοῦ, ch. 8) ; note the particular delight
taken in discomfiting money-grubbers (as in the Rhampsinitus story). Compare Plato, *Protag.* 343.

[2] Plut. *Solon* 21. The best account of Solon, because it connects his work
with his personality, is Wilamowitz's in *A. A.*, vol. ii, pp. 59 ff. Details in
Gilliard, *Quelques réformes de Solon*, Lausanne, 1907, who reprints the poems
in a convenient form. With Solon's sumptuary legislation compare Mahmud

We have reached a point in our story when we can afford
to concentrate our attention on Athens. So far we have been
trying to understand those elements in the Funeral Speech
which are typically Greek. From Solon onwards our commentary is concerned with what is pre-eminently Athenian.
For henceforward Athens's leading rivals gradually drop out
of the running. All over Greece there were lawgivers, but
Solon laid the best foundations. Moreover, it is just at this
point in the development that Sparta made the great refusal,
which caused her to fall gradually into the familiar fifth-century
rôle, that of the champion of reaction. She had not the
courage to extend her new code of justice to all who lived
within her borders. She established fair play, but only for
Spartiates or full citizens ; so that her lawgiver, instead of ' cast-
ing his strong shield ', like Solon, ' over both contending parties ',
strengthened the one still further at the expense of the other,
and made a permanent division between citizens and subjects
or rulers and ruled. This explains, of course, the peculiar and
ferocious asceticism of the Spartan code. It is not the sober
simplicity intended to reconcile rich and poor in a common
mode of life, but the rigid barrack-room uniformity of a nation
of soldiers encamped for ever as a minority amid irreconcilable
enemies. There is no room here for the gentle moderation of
Apollo ; Sôphrosynê is interpreted, not as the ' saving temper '
of Solon, but as a discipline so strict and inhuman that no
race of human beings can be loyal to it in their hearts. The
Spartans are only obedient for lack of opportunity to transgress.
' When an Athenian is good,' says a Spartan in the *Laws*, ' he
is very very good ; ... for Athenians are the only people who are
good by nature, truly and genuinely good, without compulsion,
by some happy dispensation of Providence.' ' As for your laws,'
says an Athenian speaker in Thucydides to the assembled
Spartans, ' no city outside Sparta has any use for them, and when
any of you are outside Sparta yourselves you do not observe
them ; but neither do you observe those of the ordinary Greeks.'
Naturally not : for life in the barrack-room or the cloister (to

the Reformer's introduction of the fez for all Ottoman subjects. Any one
who has watched the crowd on the Galata Bridge or attended service in a
Turkish mosque will have been struck by its levelling influence.

misuse an idyllic word) affords a poor preparation to grown men for the rough and tumble of the world.[1]

Let us examine then the nature of the laws which Solon ' commanded the Athenians to obey ', remembering that Sparta's were very different, but that between Lycurgus and Solon there was a host of intermediate Hellenic lawgivers whose work approximated, in greater or less degree, to the Athenian standard.[2]

What does fair play mean ? The Aristotelian *Constitution of Athens*, whose writer, whoever he was, had Solon's poems to guide him, singled out three of Solon's achievements as specially far-reaching. ' First, and most important of all, he forbade men to borrow money on the security of their own persons. Secondly, he allowed any one who wished to exact legal vengeance for those who were suffering wrong. Thirdly, and this is what they say gave the mass of the people their greatest leverage, there was the appeal to the people's court ; for once the mass of the people are masters of the verdict they become masters of the constitution.' Let us take these three points in order.[3]

When Solon was called in to put Athens to rights he did not find himself with a clean slate, or at liberty to compose a fancy constitution of his own. His first duty was to save Athens from the poverty and disorder into which she had sunk through the distress of the agricultural population. The poor were calling out, as they always did in Greece whenever trouble arose, for a redivision of the land into equal slices. The richer landowners were tired of trying to work their farms with debt-slaves and were also ready for a change. Solon saw it was a case for surgery. He cancelled at one stroke the entire debts of the agricultural population by proclaiming what went down to history, in

[1] Thuc. i. 77. 6 ; Plato, *Laws* 642 C. [See Appendix.]
[2] The best known of these constitutions is that of Gortyn in Crete, discovered in 1884. Parts of it go back to the seventh century, but it was finally put together in the first part of the fifth. For other lawgivers, e. g. Zaleucos, Charondas, Pheidon, cf. Meyer, *Gesch.*, vol. ii, § 360 and references. The constitutional movement probably originated, like Greek poetry and philosophy, in Ionia ; but all that is left of its Ionian origin is a broken stone pillar from Chios. It shows traces, not only of an early written constitution, but also of a popular law court. See Wilamowitz, *Nord-Ionische Steine*, pp. 64–71, *Staat und Gesellschaft*, p. 78 (2nd ed., p. 81).
[3] *Ath. Pol.* ix. 1.

Pilgrim's Progress language, as a 'Shaking Off of Burdens'. He then took steps to redeem the Athenians who had been sold into slavery abroad, using public and any private funds he could secure for the purpose, and made it illegal for a man to barter away his personal liberty for money. The farmers were re-established as freeholders on their ancestral holdings (though the old tradition of inalienability was of course swept away), a number of practical enactments were passed for the improvement of agriculture, and Attica was launched again on her course, not without more troubles ahead, as a land of peasant proprietors. The men whom Solon set on their feet were the ancestors of the farmers we meet in Aristophanes, who objected so strongly to having to leave their vines and olive-trees to the mercy of the Peloponnesians. They made their country famous, in spite of the poverty of its soil, as the best cultivated in Greece.[1]

Solon's two other chief achievements were connected not with political but with judicial administration. For, as we have seen, Solon was not the founder of the fifth-century democracy because he gave the people power in public policy, but because he secured them justice or fair play. If we think of Athens in connexion with democracy rather than with justice, it is because, through the usage of centuries, we regard justice between man and man in a court of law as a matter of course. But in Athens at Solon's advent it was not so. There were two great changes to be made before every individual Athenian could be assured of fair play.

---

[1] Solon, frag. xxxii ; Plut. *Solon* 23 (on wells, olive-planting, beehives, &c.) ; *Hellenica Oxyrhynchia* xii. 4 (cultivation of Attica). It was an act of piety to ransom a fellow-citizen from slavery. Names like Λύσανδρος (Lysander) and many others beginning in Λυσι- attest the practice. Glotz, *Solidarité*, pp. 329 ff., following Grote, has, I think, disproved the view (based on a careless reading of Ar. *Pol.* 1266 b 17) that Solon limited the amount of land a man might hold, as is virtually done in some cantons of Switzerland. It was contrary to his ideas to impose fresh restrictions on trade in land or anything else. That he should impose restrictions on borrowing was inevitable, but it led to fresh trouble none the less, as we shall see, just as the abolition of imprisonment for debt, for which Dickens pleaded, has led to the bankruptcy scandals of to-day. As a matter of fact, debt-slavery was not entirely extirpated from Athenian life. It, or something very like it, crops up again later. For instance, in Menander's *Hero* we hear of a freedman shepherd who borrowed money in a bad year, could not repay, and died leaving his freeborn children to work off the debt. These live in the creditor's household together with his recognized slaves, and are described as being ' in a sort of way slaves ' (*Hero* 20 ff., Teubner). Of course there was borrowing both before and after the troubles of the Solonian era : but it was very much more widespread just after the introduction of money.

The city must step in finally, as we have seen it beginning to step in at Elis, to free its members from the tyranny of lesser loyalties ; and her voice must be clothed with the impartial authority, not of a class or a caste, but of the people.

These were the two chief ideas which Solon, following the lines roughly traced by his predecessor Draco, embodied in the Athenian commonwealth. Except in the case of certain peculiarly intimate offences such' as parricide, he allowed ' any one who wished ' to set on foot a prosecution for a criminal offence. To understand what this means one must think away the whole of the modern state's apparatus of policemen and ministers of justice, and imagine oneself back in a world where men were slowly being schooled to accept a wider authority than that of the household and the clan. Solon was once asked which was the best policed city. ' The city,' he replied, ' where all citizens, whether they have suffered injury or not, equally pursue and punish injustice.' His aim was to make every Athenian feel and act up to his responsibility for the administration of justice, feel it as a duty he owed, not as an individual to a friend in need, but as a citizen of a free state. For it is only in a state where men are jealous for the maintenance of justice that the freedom of the individual can permanently be secured. We can trace the success of Solon's endeavour in the rapid and continuous development of the Athenian system of criminal law down to the days when we know it best—the period of the fourth-century orators.[1]

This is not the place to discuss this system in detail. But it is worth noting that those parts of it which go back most certainly to Solon and were the first to be worked out in greatest detail are those that afford protection to the weak and helpless. ' It is probable, indeed, that Solon began by allowing any citizen to open a criminal prosecution in cases where the persons wronged were legally incapable or positively unable to secure justice for themselves, and could not secure from their families the indispensable measure of support. Plutarch says that it was to succour the helpless that Solon allowed any citizen to act on

---

[1] *Ath. Pol.* ix ; Plut. *Solon* 18. Criminal prosecutions undertaken by the state in this way through the instrumentality of ' any one who wished ' were known as written suits (γραφαί), because they were the first to be put in written form, as opposed to δίκαι, civil suits, the sort of quarrels which we saw Deioces deciding. [See Appendix.]

behalf of a victim of oppression. The actions for neglect (κακώσεως γραφαί) are logically the first in date. These public actions, by which the state took under its wing poor or aged parents, orphaned minors and heiresses, were always surrounded by an old-world atmosphere. The prosecutor appealed to the Archon, who had been the chief magistrate in the city's earliest days. His suit was specially privileged, and the procedure specially simple and expeditious. The case was opened within five days and was the only kind of suit which involved no danger to the accuser. There was no deposit to be made ; no risk of a fine for a frivolous prosecution ; not even a time limit for the pleadings. The punishment in case of conviction was loss of political rights. So far from being a violent usurpation, a revolutionary measure directed against the rights of the family, the power to step in and avenge wrongs done to others served at first to protect the family and to fill a gap in its rights.' No doubt this is what Solon tried to make it seem to conservative spirits at the time ; but he was probably wise enough to realize from the first the full consequences that were involved in bringing in the city as the defender of the helpless. For he was doing what many social reformers, wise or unwise in their methods, are trying to do to-day : he was associating the State with ideas not only of power but of kindness. No part of his work took firmer root. He succeeded in perpetuating a tradition of mercy and generosity which to the Athenian of the fifth century seemed one of Athens's oldest and most natural boasts. Not only Sophocles in the *Oedipus Coloneus* and Euripides in the *Supplices* but even the inflexible Thucydides accept and glory in it. If it had not been for Solon, the most bitterly ironical passage of the Funeral Speech could never have been penned : ' in doing good we are the exact opposite of the rest of mankind. We secure our friends not by accepting favours but by doing them.' [1]

But it is no use bringing wrongdoers before the judgement-seat if the Zeus-born noble still sat there to deliver ' crooked judgements '. Solon's third and greatest achievement was to ' make the people master of the verdict '. We led up to this early in our history by the institution of the jury system. But the

---

[1] Glotz, *Solidarité*, pp. 371-2 expanded in Daremberg, s.v. κακώσεως γραφή ; Thuc. i. 2. 6, ii. 40. 4 ; Isaeus iii. 46 ; Murray, *Euripides*, Introduction, p. xxvi.

Greeks did not care, if they could avoid it, to work through so
small a body of representatives. If the people was to give its
verdict, the people in a body, or at least a large section of the
people, must sit in judgement. Of course, they had neither the
time nor the knowledge to do so every day or in every case.
The ordinary administration must still be left to the magistrates,
who had now however a written code and not an unwritten
tradition to interpret. But in exceptional cases, where the law
was not clear or the decision hotly disputed, Solon granted an
appeal to a large popular court of several thousand citizens—
a sort of Grand Assize of the nation sitting under open heaven
by the market-place. The exact powers and composition of this
body, the Heliaea as it was called, are not known; we only
become familiar with popular justice when the Heliaea had been
split up into the numerous courts, consisting of several hundreds,
instead of thousands, of judges, which we find in the time of
Pericles. We do not know who decided what cases should be
submitted to it. But Solon enacted one provision which made it
quite certain that, in case of friction, the people had the whip-
hand of their magistrates. He ordained that every magistrate
when he went out of office should give an account before the
assembly of the people of his conduct during its tenure. With
this inquisition before him from a jealous constituency of natural
hecklers it was not likely that a magistrate would deliberately
incur popular displeasure. The danger indeed was all the other
way. Although the popular assembly had not yet realized its
power, Solon had embarked Athens, for good or ill, on the
troubled waters of democracy.[1]

These were the most momentous of Solon's Laws. But there
were many more of smaller importance—all designed with the
same double object, to free the individual from lesser ties and
bind him closely to the city. The most significant perhaps is
the enactment of testamentary freedom. Athenians were henceforward allowed to leave their money as they liked, inside the
clan or out, ' if there are no legitimate male heirs.' The exception was of course in practice more important than the rule. But

---

[1] References for Heliaea in Busolt, *Griechische Geschichte*, vol. ii (2nd ed.),
pp. 283 ff. Wilamowitz's attractive derivation for ἡλιαία, ' sunny meeting-
place ', has unfortunately not found favour.

it was not so in principle. Testamentary freedom, even in this qualified form, was a new thing in the Greek world, and we can watch its irresistible spread from Solonian Athens to the remotest parts of Greece.[1]

Only one more feature of Solon's work is worth emphasizing, for it points ahead. Plutarch tells us that Solon gave facilities for acquiring Athenian citizenship to foreigners who were willing to settle permanently in the country with their families in order to exercise some skilled manual trade. Encouragement of immigration is not uncommon among growing communities in the modern world. We are familiar with states which advertise 'situations vacant' in the Press, like employers asking for new hands. But the states of the Greek world had not been trained by generations of competition to regard the foreigner as a unit of labour. They were in their nature select and exclusive corporations, rigidly subdivided into lesser and still selecter circles ; and there was no place in them for outsiders. Solon's policy, therefore, marks the beginning of a far-reaching change of attitude. Henceforward newcomers are no longer to be despised, as in the old days, as 'cityless vagrants without hearth-fire or lands', but welcomed as useful comrades and helpers in the work of the community. In other words, Athens was now willing to accept new blood on its merits, quite apart from questions of religion and nationality. We shall watch the fruits of this policy in the twofold development of the next few generations, in the increase of trade and industry, which these landless immigrants naturally exercised, side by side with agriculture, and in the gradual relaxing of the ties that still bound the native-born Athenian to his clan and his local district. In both these directions Solon's careful yet courageous statesmanship paved the way for 'that amazing revolutionary Cleisthenes'.

---

[1] Glotz, *Solidarité*, pp. 342–5. Compare the converse, pp. 359 ff., on the duties of sons under Solon's régime. Plato's testamentary regulations (*Laws* 922 ff.) are a good measure of his old-fashionedness.

CHAPTER VI

THE DEVELOPMENT OF CITIZENSHIP

SELF-GOVERNMENT, OR THE RULE OF THE PEOPLE
(δημοκρατία)

'Αρχὴ ἄνδρα δείξει.—Greek Proverb.
Office will bring out the man.

'Αμήχανον δὲ παντὸς ἀνδρὸς ἐκμαθεῖν
ψυχήν τε καὶ φρόνημα καὶ γνώμην, πρὶν ἂν
ἀρχαῖς τε καὶ νόμοισιν ἐντριβὴς φανῇ.

SOPHOCLES, *Antigone* 175-7.

There is no way to know of any man
The spirit and the wisdom and the will,
Till he stands proved, ruler and lawgiver.

tr. WHITELAW.

IT is a constant source of astonishment to hot-headed Radicals that communities with an extended franchise should tolerate government by a superior class. It seems only natural, when power has been placed in the hands of the masses, that they should at once make use of it, particularly when it can be used so greatly in their own interest. Why any one earning under thirty shillings a week should vote Conservative and submit to the pretensions of a hereditary aristocracy passes their understanding. Logically, this point of view seems reasonable enough, and Periclean Athens seems to give it the confirmation of experience ; but in truth it is contradicted both by the warnings of history and by the hard facts of political human nature. History suggests—what many an 'advanced' candidate has discovered to his cost—that it takes generations of teaching, not by argument but by suffering, before a people, however politically gifted, can be induced to take the trouble to govern itself. The Athenians took to politics as easily, and were as politically gifted, as any community in history. Yet their acceptance of self-government was tentative and hesitating. It came late, and almost as an after-thought, in the development of their polity. If they could have lived happy and undisturbed under any other form of government, they would as willingly have turned their energies into other channels as the ' silent middle-class voter ' to-day, or their own easy-going compatriots on the coast of Asia Minor. Careful political observers, who are not blinded by catchwords or by the glamour of fifth-century Athens, have known this in all ages. Rhodes, like Venice, grew to be the greatest port in her sea without embracing democracy. Her merchant princes, as Strabo puts it, ' paid attention to the people ' without being democrats, which means that they supplied them with food and circuses. ' The example of the people of Taras,' says Aristotle, ' is especially deserving of imitation ; they keep the poor in a good temper by sharing the use of their property with them. Moreover, they divide all their offices into two classes, one half of them being elected by vote, the other by lot ; the former to ensure good administration, the latter to allow the people some share in it.' The Tarentines are not the only people who have used dummy officials for their own purposes. The device is as old as Pisistratus and as new as yesterday's caucus. Those who use it have on their side a factor that political thinkers too often forget—the dead weight of human indolence. It is wholesome for the idealist to lay aside for a moment his Grote and his Mazzini and to turn over the pages of an election number of *Punch*. He will then be in a better position to follow the ups and downs of Athenian development from fair play to self-government.[1]

When Solon had made his laws he went abroad for ten years, so as to give his constitution a fair run. When he returned he found that everything was once more in confusion. As usual, the trouble was economic. The other parts of his system had stood the strain well enough ; we hear no complaints of injustice or impiety. The new judicial powers were not only exercised but extended, and Conservatives had acquiesced in the loosening of family ties. But the village population was unhappy and restless. The peasants had been put back on their holdings, and plied with good advice as to how to manage their vines and olive-trees ; but they had no capital to go on with and of course they could not borrow. The craftsmen and small traders, whose

[1] Ar. *Pol.* 1320 b 9 ; Strabo, 652 fin.

interests were bound up with theirs, were equally clamorous. Their complaints were directed, not against Solon and his laws, but against the city magistrates who administered them. The chief Magistrates or Governors (ἄρχοντες) were no longer necessarily members of the nobility. The 'old men' of the Homeric market-place had gradually developed into a fixed number of state officials, holding office for a year. Solon had gone further by throwing open the nine Governorships or Archonships to the wealthier citizens irrespective of birth, and allowing their fellow-citizens, voting in tribes, to elect them. But still the poor complained that the aristocracy were over-represented in the seats of authority. A compromise was arrived at for a few years by which there were to be ten Governors, five of whom must be nobles, three peasants, and two craftsmen. But the trouble was too deep-seated to be righted by any such ingenious balancing. Discontent grew more and more fierce, till finally the state was openly divided into three hostile parties, each prepared to fight for its own economic and territorial interests. There was the rich population living in Athens, the Men of the Plain, with their city interests. There were the Men of the Shore, that is, the population living in the country villages and small ports of South-Eastern Attica, from the settlements behind Hymettus down to Sunium. Thirdly, there were the Men of the Mountains, the poorer peasants and shepherds and woodcutters and charcoal-burners from the rough region of Northern Attica. It seemed for a moment as if Theseus had attempted too much in trying to make a united nation out of a territory larger than that of any other Greek City State. But fortunately for Athens 'a man arose in Israel'. The Mountaineers had at their head a leader, Pisistratus, who was not only a friend of the poor but also a noted soldier and a man of large private means and influential connexions. He succeeded, after some vicissitudes, in making his party supreme in the State, as he had already made himself supreme in his party. Like Deioces, he took a body-guard; then he seized the Acropolis, and became absolute master of the country.[1]

Once in power he exercised his authority 'constitutionally rather than tyrannically'. That is to say, he respected constitu-

---

[1] *Ath. Pol.* vii, xiii, xiv.

tional forms. In the sphere of justice he made no important changes. In the sphere of policy he allowed the old machinery to go on working under his own guidance and persuasion. The assembly still sat, the magistrates were still elected annually ; but it was the tyrant, with his wise schemes of foreign policy and his connexions beyond the seas, who told the puppets how to dance. If by the end of the sixth century Athens was a figure in international politics, if she commanded the Hellespont, drew wealth from gold mines in Thrace, and had become a resort of architects, poets, and sculptors, she owed it to the initiative of her tyrant and his sons.[1]

But Pisistratus's most durable achievement was his settlement of the economic difficulties. He solved them once and for all by advancing capital out of his private fortune to the poorer landowners, largely of course his own political supporters. Once they had margin enough to keep them through lean years, or while their trees were growing to maturity, their troubles were at an end. There is no more land question in Attica till the Spartans came and ruined the cultivation one hundred and fifty years later. 'The Attic peasant sat quite contented under his vine and fig-tree, and looked with reverence upon his goddess's gift, the olive, whose planting the State was now promoting, as it had done of old, so that this most important of home products brought in more every year. This result he owed most of all to the peace ; there was no foreign enemy about to put the axe to his trees. But there was peace too within the borders, and justice was near at hand and easy to obtain. True, there was a five per cent. tax on his produce, and that was a warning that there was a master in the land. But the peasant could go to the elections every year, and every month to the assembly ; the forms of self-government were preserved both in Parish Council and in the Council at the capital, and so he did not mind voting for the government candidate.' One does not need to have tramped about Attica during 1909 and discussed the veiled dictatorship of the Military League at well-heads or in sailing boats, or over bread and olives in village coffee-houses, to know how the country-folk acquiesced in the rule of Pisistratus. One can imagine it for oneself from conversations about democracy

[1] *Ath. Pol.* xiv. 3, xv. 2, xviii. 1 ; Hdt. i. 59, 64.

nearer home. Even the glories of self-government did not wholly obscure its memory, and the peasants long looked back to the rule of Pisistratus as to a golden age.[1]

But Pisistratus died, and his sons could not manage the people so skilfully as their father. A personal quarrel led to the murder of Hipparchus, and embittered the mind of his elder brother Hippias. Harmodius and Aristogeiton, who were concerned in it, were not, what later legend made them, martyrs in the cause of freedom ; they belonged to the tyrants' own circle and were not even democrats. But their action did result, through an unforeseen chain of events, in the expulsion of the tyrants. Hippias grew tired, as a Greek well might, of ruling over an uncongenial people. When Sparta, on the advice of the oracle, sent a force against him, he could easily have held out on the Acropolis ; but he preferred to surprise both parties by surrendering his power and withdrawing to Sigeum.[2]

Athens was now ' free '. But who was to rule her—the nobles or the people, the Plain or the Mountain ? Cleisthenes the Alcmaeonid, the leader of the popular party, who had been mainly responsible for the oracle's action against Hippias, made a bid for power. But Isagoras, head of the Plain, who had connexions with Sparta, was too strong for him. Isagoras, however, was no Pisistratus. He did not understand the temper of the growing nation that he essayed to govern. He made a fatal mistake, which sufficed at length to convert Athens for good to the democratic creed. He called in a Spartan army to strengthen his hands, and proceeded to secure his régime by dissolving the popular council and banishing seven hundred families. This roused the people to fury. They were used to being ruled by nobles, but to have a regiment of dirty Spartans encamped on the Acropolis, among the shrines and statues of Pisistratus, was more than they could stand. Cleisthenes and the councillors called the people to arms and blockaded the rock. For two days and nights they sat watching every exit : on the third the foreigners surrendered. Athens never forgot the sight they pre-

---

[1] Wilamowitz, *A. A.*, vol. ii, p. 70 ; *Ath. Pol.* xvi. 4 (who says ten per cent. tax, but see Thuc. vi. 54. 5). Pisistratus made himself popular by granting exemptions from his tax when the peasants were too poor to pay it. [See Appendix.]   [2] Hdt. v. 64–5.

sented as they came down the slope.   A century later the chorus
of old men in one of the plays of Aristophanes rejoices to recall—

> How for all his loud fire-eating
> The old Spartan got his beating,
> And in sorry plight retreating
>   Left his spear and shield with me.
> Then with only his poor shirt on,
> And who knows what years of dirt on,
> All betowzled and besmeared
> With a bristling bush of beard,
>   Slunk away and left us free.[1]

Cleisthenes was now master of the situation.   He had already
been leader of the popular party.   He had now all the obstinate
spirit of national independence behind him too.   Athens felt herself for the moment a united nation.   Cleisthenes was determined
to make her continue to do so.   Like Solon, he refused to assume
the supreme position.   He preferred to continue Solon's work by
completing in the sphere of executive government what Solon
had achieved in the sphere of justice.   Athens was already half
a democracy in spirit ; he made her wholly one both in fact
and in name.   The political constitution under which Athens
flourished in the fifth century is in the main, and except for
certain inevitable developments, the work of Cleisthenes.   This
therefore is the moment to pause and take stock of it as a whole.

Cleisthenes' work falls into two parts, for he reorganized both
the local and the central government of Athens.   We will consider each of these separately, keeping in our minds in each case
the two main questions suggested by the Funeral Speech : how
much power was actually placed in the hands of the individual
common citizen, and how great was the sacrifice of time and
thought which his public duties involved.   For it was Pericles'
boast that his fellow-citizens found time to do justice both to
public and private responsibilities, that they were at once (what is
nowadays considered impossible) the most active political workers
and the most many-sided individuals of their time.

We will take Athenian local government first.   It is the
sphere of Cleisthenes' most daring achievement and presents
many features of interest.   But it is only of late years that its

---

[1] Ar. *Lys.* 275 ; *Ath. Pol.* xx, who, as Wilamowitz says, gives the order of
events better than Hdt. v. 72.

working has become comparatively clear, more through the discovery of the *Constitution of Athens* and the acuteness of scholars
than from the accumulation of inscriptions : for these small local
authorities had not much money to spend on stone-cutting. The
system which we are about to describe was in full working order
all through the Periclean period ; but men took it for granted
and the great writers say little of it. Thucydides is inclined to
pass it over altogether. No one would gather from the Funeral
Speech that it existed at all, if it were not incidentally mentioned in the introductory chapter that the ashes of each dead
soldier were laid in the coffin of his ' tribe '.

The problems of local government were, if not peculiar to
Attica, at least far more perplexing there than elsewhere. This
was due both to the unusual size of the territory, and to the fact
that, even after political unification, the people went on living in
villages. The difficulties which Cleisthenes had to face were two
in number. Firstly, how to combine an efficient local administration with a strong central government. Secondly, how to
reconcile in the country the conflicting claims of family and
territorial interest.

Let us take the second first, as it is the more old-fashioned
difficulty of the two.

We have seen that, of the lesser loyalties which hampered the
growth of the City State in the Middle Ages, two stand out
prominently. The Zeus-born noble is not wholly a patriot,
because of his duty to his clan. The poor villager is not wholly
a patriot—is in fact hardly a patriot at all—because of his duty
to his neighbour. Oddly enough, it is the ignorant villager, as
has happened elsewhere, who held the more progressive of the
two ideas. The blood-tie of the clan went back to nomadic
days ; the territorial tie of the village street was young beside it.
But both were strong and deeply rooted principles and fought
hard for supremacy in the local government of Attica.

Let us compare their working. Supposing Theseus, or any
other chief magistrate at the head of the central government,
wanted money to build ships to fetch Ariadne from Crete, he
could do one of two things. He could command the head of a
clan or a tribe to collect ship-money from his fellow clansmen,
who might be living in various parts of Attica ; or he could send

round the villages and fix the responsibility upon some headman of his own or the villagers' selection.

Obviously, from Theseus's point of view, the latter course was the more convenient. He knew exactly with whom he was dealing in each case and could make sure that every village paid. Consequently, as the central government increased its influence, the territorial principle took firmer root, and men became accustomed to think of themselves more and more not as clansmen but as parishioners. These early parishes managed their affairs through councils, which dealt with matters of parish interest, such as the making of roads and wells, or with business (no doubt generally financial) submitted to them from the central government. The chairman of the parish council or village headman was an important person, for he managed the village finances and saw to the raising of the money. He was known as a Naucraros or ship-maker, because it was generally for ships that money was wanted. Fleets cost more, and therefore tax the energy of the central authority more, than armies, because ships are more expensive to provide than spears and shields. Hence a parish in Attica became known, from its most important national duty, as a Naucrary or ship-district. Every parish furnished one ship and one sailor for each unit of the fleet : so that, as the ships of those days were fifty-oared galleys, there needed to be about fifty parishes.[1]

But fifty was a large number, and some of the ship districts were a long way off ; there was an obvious danger lest the country parishes should lose touch with the central government. This was averted in early Attica in two ways. Firstly, by grafting the naucraries on to the older division by tribes and clans, to which we shall recur in a moment. Secondly, by giving the

[1] *Ath. Pol.* viii. 3 ; Glotz, *Études*, pp. 243 ff. (who takes Ναύκραροι from *Od.* viii. 391 to mean ships' captains) ; Wilamowitz, *A. A.*, vol. i, p. 96 ; Cavaignac, *Études sur l'histoire financière d'Athènes au V*ᵉ *siècle* (1908), p. 7 ; and refs. in Daremberg and Saglio, s. v. Naukraria. The exact number of Naucraries was forty-eight. Perhaps the central government supplied the two extra men ; cf. Eur. *Suppl.* 657–8 and Murray's note in the Oxford text, where Theseus, like the Macedonian kings, has a corps of Companions apart from his territorial army. A possible parallel to the Attic ' ship-makers ' are the 'Αειναῦται (' very-sailors ' : unless the word is connected, as some think, with ναίω) at Miletus and Chalcis : refs. in Wilhelm, *Beiträge zur griechischen Inschriftenkunde*, p. 123 (a book which the leisurely student who knows how to use an index will find full of interest).

village headmen themselves a position in the central government. Unlike so many other 'Dwellers-Round', they were summoned to Athens, to a national 'council'; and they sat in the chiefs' place (πρυτανεῖον) under the presidency of one of the city magistrates or 'governors'. As forty-eight was too large a number for the convenient dispatch of the business that came before them, they did much of it through a small committee of four out of their own number, who were known as 'chiefs of the ship-makers'. The exact relation between their duties and those of the city 'governors' was forgotten later, and became a subject of dispute among fifth-century writers. Herodotus speaks of the chiefs of the ship-makers as 'managing Athens' in the seventh century; but Thucydides, who liked centralization, corrects him and gives the governors the foremost place.[1]

Let us now turn to the older and less practical divisions based on blood-relationship.

When the immigrants entered Attica and associated with the native population, they brought with them their own grouping. As we have seen, they were divided into families, 'brotherhoods,' and 'tribes', and members of each of these felt themselves united to their fellows, like Highland clansmen, by the tie of blood. This organization persisted all through the aristocratic period, and we find it still vigorous and (like so many Greek institutions) symmetrical at the time of Cleisthenes. Ask one of Cleisthenes' contemporaries how Attica is divided, and he will reply, out of the *Statesman's Year-book* of his time: 'Attica is divided into four tribes, twelve brotherhoods, 360 families' (as they are no longer round one hearth we had better henceforward call them clans) 'and 10,800 citizens' (that is, there are supposed to be thirty adult males to each clan). Press him further and he will add that Attica also consists of forty-eight parishes and twelve thirds, so called because three together make up a single tribe.

[1] Hdt. v. 71; Thuc. i. 126. Herodotus has reasons of his own for dissociating the chief governor of the time from the incident in question. Bringing of the 'chiefs' to Athens from their local 'town halls': Thuc. ii. 15 (ἐν βουλευτήριον ἀποδείξας καὶ πρυτανεῖον: from which one might too hastily conclude that 'Theseus' abolished local government in Attica altogether). There are probably parallels to this council of village headmen in other City States; cf. refs. in Meyer, *Gesch.* vol. ii, § 233 note, who agrees that the πρυτάνεις were a standing General Purposes Committee, as their rotating successors were in the fifth century.

One question immediately presents itself. What has become of the division between nobles and people or town and country of which we heard so much ? Did the poor peasants in the villages, survivors in most cases of the older population, secure for themselves, and retain through the whole mediaeval period, the rights and privileges of ' tribesmen ' side by side with the Zeus-born aristocracy which grew up among the wealthier immigrants ? This raises one of the most disputed problems of early Attic history, but, briefly, the answer appears to be that they gained and kept the rights but not the privileges. For, towards the close of the mediaeval period, when our scanty evidence begins, we find the brotherhoods consisting, no longer of ' brothers ', as their name implies, but of what Wilamowitz calls first and second class members. The first-class members, out of whom alone the chiefs and priests of the tribe are selected, are known as γεννῆται (clansmen) or ὁμογάλακτες (foster-sons) : the others as ὀργεῶνες (worshippers). This seems to show that, though the nobles, as their power grew, could not keep or turn the people out of the tribes and brotherhoods, they succeeded in putting them in an inferior position there and in keeping or turning them out of the families or clans. Probably, as the names of particular brother-hoods and their symmetrical arrangement seem to show, they reconstructed the whole organization to suit their own preten-sions. The poor Athenian, like his wealthier fellow-tribesman, was an Athenian once and for all : nothing could alter that, for he was the child of Zeus and Apollo. But he did not belong to one of the ' good families ' who traced their descent through a noble ancestor, and so his humble lineage gradually ceased to count at all. While his noble neighbour's family was elevated into a clan, and the noble himself into a clansman, the poor villager lost his parentage or only remembered it in private when he felt superstitious about his dead ancestors. At brotherhood meetings he was taught to feel himself only a sort of courtesy member. But he held his ground : and it was good that he did, for his status formed a useful precedent for Cleisthenes' statesmanship.[1]

[1] See Francotte, *Polis*, pp. 10 ff. ; Meyer, vol. ii, § 204 (who points out the radicalism of these early aristocrats all over the Greek world in constructing symmetrical tribes and subdivisions of tribes) ; Wilamowitz, *A. A.*, vol. ii, pp. 272 ff. Early Attic history was as obscure to fifth-century Athenians as

What was the point of this elaborate organization into tribes and brotherhoods with the tail of clans attached to it ? What happened at a brotherhood meeting ?

The first thing that happened, as in the House of Commons to-day, was prayers, or rather, in official language, orgies (ὄργια). But it was also the most important thing. ' Like all associations of every sort in Greece ' (for it was equally true of gatherings of craftsmen and traders) ' its first object was the celebration of public worship.' Only, of course, every association had its own special god or hero. The patron saints of a brotherhood meeting were Zeus of the brotherhood and Athena of the brotherhood (Ζεὺς φράτριος καὶ 'Αθηνᾶ φρατρία), and their annual saint's day was called ' the Feast of All-Fathers ', which Athenians celebrated together with their supposed Ionian cousins over the water Some brotherhoods, of course, had special saints of their own as well.[1]

What else did they do ? There does not seem much else to be done, beyond eating the sacrificial food. Many English associations have reached a hearty old age on dining alone, even without the elaborate grace before meat of a Greek brotherhood. Still there was some ' public business ' after dinner. Many brotherhoods had land and property to administer. We have an inscription of the Proceedings of the Brotherhood of the Demotionidae (whose patron saint was the hero Demotion) which, under the skilful handling of Wilamowitz, has been made to throw a flood of light upon brotherhood meetings. The chief thing that the brothers did at this period (the inscription dates from the fourth century, long after Cleisthenes) was to amend their own rules, particularly with regard to the admission and expulsion of members. It is clear, from a comparison of their organization with what we know of other brotherhoods, that in

it is to us, only they were more easily put off with names which explain nothing.   See Hdt. viii. 44.   ὁμογάλακτες : Ar. *Pol.* 1252 b 18, who seems to misunderstand the development.   With his head full of the ' logical priority ' of the Polis he is not interested in the stages of its growth.

[1] Hdt. i. 147 ; Francotte, pp. 24, 25.   'Απατόρια = 'Ομοπατ(ό)ρια (Schol. Ar. *Ach.* 146) : but it is noteworthy that by the fifth century the meaning of the festival had so far been forgotten that the official derivation was from 'Απάτη (deceit), and a legend had been made up to account for it.   The feast was held in the autumn, and when there had been fighting in the summer the state funeral was held in connexion with it.   Funeral speeches were thus delivered on ' All Souls' Day '.

Attica, at any rate, a brotherhood, like any other association formally recognized by the state, was left very free to make and alter its own statutes. The worshippers of Demotion did not have to put up with the Roman prejudice against secret societies, which made a prayer meeting of early Christians a breach of the combination laws. Athens had more civilized and far more effective ways of combating lesser loyalties.[1]

How were these tribes and brotherhoods spread over the country? Although membership went by blood and not by geographical situation, still fellow tribesmen and brothers would mostly be found in the same districts. The difference between the tribal and territorial division would come to this : that a parish map of Attica would be divided up into forty-eight constituencies with fixed lines, whereas a tribal map, which would alter of course, however slightly, from year to year, would show a number of points marked in twelve different colours for the different brotherhoods, where the greater number of brothers and clansmen were to be found.[2]

[1] Wilamowitz, *A. A.*, vol. ii, pp. 259-79, on the Demotionidae. Cf. the eloquent passage in Renan's *Origines du Christianisme*, vol. ii, pp. 355-7, which is worth quoting at some length because of its bearing on very similar psychological problems to-day. ' One of the chief objects of Caesar and of Augustus was to prevent the formation of new associations and to destroy those which had been already formed. . . . They were forbidden to meet more than once a month or to concern themselves with any other business than the burial of deceased members : under no pretext whatsoever might they enlarge their activities. The Empire was attempting, in desperation, an impossible task. It was trying, out of homage to an exaggerated idea of the State, to isolate the individual, to snap every moral tie between man and man, to defeat a legitimate desire of the poor, the desire to press together in a little corner of their own to keep one another warm. In ancient Greece the city was very tyrannical ; but in exchange for her vexatious demands she gave so much pleasure, so much light, so much glory, that no one thought of complaining. Men died joyfully on her behalf ; men submitted without revolt to her most unjust caprices. But the Roman Empire was too large to be a country. It offered to all men great material advantages ; it gave them nothing to love. The intolerable sadness inseparable from such a life seemed worse than death. Thus, despite all the efforts of the statesmen, the confraternities developed an immense activity. . . . Our texts reveal them to us as consisting of slaves, of ex-soldiers, of poorer citizens. Complete equality reigned there between freemen, freedmen, and slaves. There were many women members. At the risk of a thousand petty annoyances, and sometimes of the severest penalties, men wished to be members of such an association, where they could live on terms of delightful brotherhood, find mutual help and encouragement, and contract ties which lasted till death and beyond it. . . . That is why Christianity at Rome seemed for a long time to be a sort of burial club, and why the earliest Christian sanctuaries were the tombs of the martyrs.'

[2] Francotte, p. 29.

This was the position when, at some date before the time of
Solon, these two symmetrical systems were fused. It was not
very difficult to fuse them, for the four tribes were so large that
they had practically come to be considered as territorial divisions.
Except on the border-land, men did not easily, in those early
agricultural days, move their dwellings into another tribal area.
Once regard the four tribes as territorial and they are easily
reconciled with the forty-eight parishes. All that is needed is
an intermediate link, corresponding, on the territorial side, with
the three brotherhoods in each tribe. This was supplied by
dividing each tribe up into three districts or thirds. These
cannot have been the same as the brotherhoods, since a third
consisted of land and a brotherhood of persons ; but they were
so nearly the same in practice that later writers could say
they were.[1]

The tribes and the parishes worked together in harness for at
least a century (probably a good deal longer) before the time of
Cleisthenes. While the parish sent up its ship-makers to the
city, the other magistrates, the governors, were, at any rate from
Solon onwards, elected by the people voting by tribes—though
their selection was, of course, limited to candidates of a certain
status. One of Solon's innovations, inevitable with the progress
of trade and industry, was to reckon status by wealth instead of
by birth—a change which did much to help Cleisthenes in his
struggle against family feeling.

Such was the organization during the sixth century, in the
troubled times preceding the supremacy of Cleisthenes. The
root of those troubles, as we have seen, was economic ; but they
had taken the form of a division of one part of Attica against
another, in other words, of a conflict between tribe and tribe and
clan and clan. The movements in the preceding years had been
headed by clan leaders—Pisistratus of Brauron, Megacles the
Alcmaeonid, Miltiades the Philaid, Isagoras, whe worshipped the
' Carian Zeus ', apparently a saint of Boeotian origin. Cleisthenes

---

[1] The puzzling point about the difference between reckoning by land and
by persons, which Aristotle's compiler overlooked (*Ath. Pol.* frag. 6), cropped
up lately in the debates on the new land taxes. Should the increment tax be
charged on a piece of land which had fallen in value and then risen again,
having changed hands in the interval, i. e. should the State think in terms of
land or of persons ? See *Parliamentary Debates*, July 5, 1909.

himself was an Alcmaeonid, but he was first of all an Athenian. He decided to break down the local Baals who distracted his countrymen, and make them, before all things, Athenians like himself.

Cleisthenes was a revolutionary, though he knew also how to construct. The time was ripe for drastic measures. He struck first at the root of the evil, the four ancient tribes. They and all their associations disappeared for ever from Athenian politics. A few generations later Athenians still knew their names, but had not the least idea what they meant. Nor have scholars yet been able to discover. Their destroyer replaced them so skilfully that nobody even wrote their epitaph.[1]

He also destroyed the parishes, and the name ship-district disappears from Athenian terminology. For he wished to put naval and military affairs entirely into the hands of the central government. One would not know from Thucydides that it had ever been otherwise.[2]

This was all that he destroyed. The brotherhoods he did not touch : nor of course did he interfere with the deep-seated moralities of the family. With the disappearance of the tribes, which had connected them with the central government, the brotherhoods were left suspended in mid-air. As they had never had any important work to do, there was no need to attack them. To ignore them was far more blighting to their influence on men's lives. Every Athenian still belonged to a brotherhood, as every Englishman may be supposed to belong to the Church of England. He did not become a citizen till he was eighteen, but he was inscribed as a member of his brotherhood at the Feast of All-Fathers at the first opportunity after he was born. He was presented to the ' brothers ' again at the age of puberty, two years before he came of age—just as young Englishmen are often ' confirmed ' some time before they cease to be minors ; and he came before them again to offer a ' wedding sacrifice ', so that the

---

[1] The mysterious names are Hopletes, Geleontes, Argadeis, and Aigikoreis. All sorts of theories used to be held about them, e. g. that they were like the Egyptian caste-divisions. Of the last two Wilamowitz remarks (*Aus Kydathen*, pp. 122–3) : ' they sound as if they meant something, and probably once did, though who shall guarantee that it would prove more edifying than Hogfellows and Boarites (Hdt. v. 68) or Schnuck Puckelig Schimmelsumpf and Schnuck Puckelig Erbsenscheucher ? '

[2] We actually know the name of only one ship-district—Κωλιάς.

brothers might take due note of the domestic ceremony of his marriage. All these small observances were part of the fifth-century Athenian's life. It is a mark of a man of Athenian blood, as Herodotus still says, to keep the All-Fathers' Days. But what was their connexion with the City State ? Purely technical. By becoming a brother an Athenian was put into touch with his national ancestors, Zeus and Apollo. The fifth-century Athenian had no great regard for this connexion. His deeper reverence was for Athena or, at lonely moments, when his citizenship dropped from him, for the gods or saints of his own hearth. But the constitution ordained that, if ever he was elected to office, he must assure his electors in the viva voce examination before he entered upon his duties that he honoured his two national ancestors. It was a mere formality : still Cleisthenes let it stay. It was the only link that still tied the growing city to the ancient religion of the brotherhood.[1]

In all other respects the state was now cut off from ' the Church ' : or perhaps it would be truer to say that, by being cut off from the state, the religion of the brotherhood might have become what we call a Church, if the Athenian had attempted, as we have been attempting since the era of organized Christianity, to distinguish between the spheres of political and religious organization, and to pay allegiance to both. But this was beyond his inclinations : and even if it had not been, there was no other corporate power in Athens, outside the narrow circle of the hearth, which could appeal to him. Certainly the religion of the brotherhood had neither the influence nor the inspiration to stand by the side of Athena. Hence, even if it was not technically disestablished by Cleisthenes, it very soon became so in practice. Fifth-century Athenians still keep the Apaturia, though they had forgotten what its name signified. But, as time went on, men began to ask themselves whether the trouble of joining and attending a brotherhood was really worth their while. What was the use of it ? The rules for admission had gradually become so relaxed—here again it was Cleisthenes who applied the thin end of the wedge—that anybody could join and there were no distinctions between members : for Athens had now become very democratic, and one might even perhaps run across

[1] Hdt. i. 147.

ex-slaves amongst one's brothers. And when all was 'said and done', the speeches and ceremonial got safely through, what did it lead to? So far as the city was concerned it was a blind alley, which men only continued to walk down for a time, because it used once to lead out on to the state high road.[1]

So far we have seen Cleisthenes as a destroyer. What did he set up instead of the tribes and ship-districts?

The first thing he did was to create new tribes; for no Athenian could imagine Athens without tribes, any more than we can imagine a borough without a mayor and corporation. They were indeed 'tribes' only in name: for they were on a territorial basis. They were really counties or constituencies. But to give them a religious status they were each called after the name of some well-known hero, the names being selected by the Delphic oracle, out of a list of a hundred submitted to it.[2]

The old tribes, too, had been practically territorial; but Cleisthenes did more than just draw the lines a little differently. He adopted the daring device of splitting up every tribe into three divisions, situated in the three different parts of the country. This enabled him to make use of the old thirds, in name if not in fact. Every tribe was made up of three separate thirds or territorial units, one of which was situated in or near the city, a second in the interior of the country, and a third on the coast. It is as though every constituency in England consisted of three parts—one in London or the home counties, another in the agricultural midlands, and a third in the industrial north. This was his heroic and entirely successful remedy (would it have been successful anywhere but in Radical Greece?) for the territorial conflicts of the previous years. We can determine roughly of what the three zones consisted. The city zone in-

---

[1] Francotte, *Polis*, p. 80; *v.* Ar. *Pax* 416 ff. Cf. Ferguson, *Classical Philology*, 1910, pp. 257 ff., and *Hellenistic Athens*, 1911, p. 220, who has pointed out how 'when politics ceased, with the Macedonian suzerainty, to monopolize the energies of the Athenians, the aboriginal family associations', brotherhoods, &c., returned to a prominent place in their lives.

[2] There is a still odder instance of this device in the Athenian constitution. Each of the forty-two years of the military age, from eighteen to sixty, had its own 'eponymous' hero, and troops would be ordered out, as it were, 'from Moses to Solomon.' (*Ath. Pol.* liii. 4 and 7.) The Greeks were curiously fond of such picturesque devices. We can barely make them a success in our street names: and nobody thought the break up of the London County Council fleet of steamers an act of impiety to the great Englishmen whose names they bore.

cluded the southern end of the plain of Athens from Lycabettus
down to the sea, and across from Mount Corydallus to Hymettus.
The coast zone included the whole of the plain of Eleusis up to
Cithaeron, and then ran right round the coast in a narrow strip
(interrupted at Piraeus) to Oropus in the north. The ' interior '
included all the remainder—the inside of South-Eastern Attica
down to Laureion, a large piece of the plain of Athens, and most
of the mountainous country of Parnes and Pentelicus. So they
might seem to correspond with the old ' plain ', ' shore ', and
' mountain '; but detailed examination has shown the corre-
spondence to be a very rough one. Cleisthenes did his best to
avoid anything which could reawaken old controversies.[1]

We will leave aside for the moment the part which these new
tribes and thirds were called upon to play, together with their
subdivisions, in the central government, as we are dealing first
with the local administration.

Tribes and even thirds were obviously too large to take over
the duties of parish councils. Something smaller was required in
the place of the old ship-districts. Cleisthenes supplied it in the
form of the demes or ' peoples ', which formed the commune or
unit of local administration all through the great period of
Athenian history. He divided the country up afresh into over a
hundred demes—we do not know exactly how many—which were
roughly grouped into ten divisions so as to form part of the ten
tribes. These demes, as administrative areas, were an entirely
new creation, but, like the tribes, they had to be given a religious
sanction. Each deme was supplied with its own ' hero founder ',
who thus gave it a sort of shadowy past existence. Sometimes
he was the heroic ancestor of a local clan, adapted for the purpose,
sometimes an entirely new creation : in the latter case the per-
sonification occasionally failed to ' catch on ', and we find demes
paying honour to a nameless hero chief. The best evidence for
all this consists in the names of the demes themselves. Some,
like Piraeus, Eleusis, Rhamnus, are simply place-names :
Rhamnus means ' thorn ', and, unlike Glastonbury, never
acclimatized a saint to it. In other cases, where the hero was

[1] Wilamowitz, *A. A.*, vol. ii, pp. 148–68, who points out that the thirds
never ' caught on ' in the popular mind or developed ' heroes ' or sentimental
associations of their own : they were merely a practical convenience. *Ath.
Pol.* xxi ; Hdt. v. 69 (the two *loci classici* for Cleisthenes' work).

ready to hand, the deme was called by his name and sentiment
crystallized around it.[1]

These new demes formed the groundwork of the Athenian
state in the fifth century. Every Athenian was a demesman,
and officially known by the name of his deme. Cleisthenes

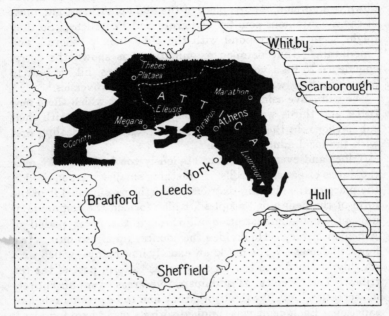

**Attica, the Megarid, and parts of Corinth and Boeotia, with Yorkshire
on the same scale.**

wished to secure that when a man thought and spoke, in our
slang phrase, of his ' people '—the close inner circle of his life—
he should think and speak of his deme. ' He made those who

---

[1] Wilamowitz, vol. ii, pp. 149–51. He reads the much disputed passage
of Herodotus (v. 69) δέκα[χα] δὲ καὶ τοὺς δήμους κατένειμεν ἐς τὰς φυλάς. If
Herodotus really said that there were exactly a hundred demes, he was
mistaken. *Ath. Pol.* xxi. 5 says that the demes were given heroic names
when there were no place-names available—just the converse of what probably
happened. The word ' deme ' or ' people ' was of course not a novelty in
Attica any more than the word ' Union ' was in England before the Reform
of the Poor Law in 1834 : it is the demes as administrative areas which were
the new creation.

lived in each of the demes demesmen one of another, in order to prevent their calling one another by their fathers and so convicting the newly admitted citizens. Hence Athenians give their deme when introducing themselves one to another.' What Cleisthenes attempted to do was, in fact, to alter the Athenian form of surname. Before his time the Athenians, like so many people, as for instance in Wales and Scotland, distinguished one another by their fathers : Herodotus distinguishes, for example, between ' Miltiades the son of Cypselus ' and ' Miltiades the son of Cimon '. Cleisthenes tried to turn John Jones and Edward Edwards into John Montgomery and Edward Radnor, and so to break down all feeling of common clan ancestry. He was only partially successful. Herodotus generally, and Thucydides (who admitted nothing between Athens and the individual) always, ignored the new practice, and we distinguish Thucydides himself from his less famous namesake by the latter's father Melesias. But, as time went on, men became more used to the custom, and when, a hundred years after Cleisthenes, there were two prominent statesmen called Thrasybulus, they were distinguished by their ' people ' at Steiria and Collytus. And everybody, of course, knows the deme of Demosthenes—Paeania behind Hymettus. The best evidence, perhaps, is the comedy. In Aristophanes the characters always introduce themselves to one another by their demes : and Strepsiades in the *Clouds*, when he is being beaten by his son, calls for help to his ' neighbours and relatives and demesmen '.[1]

So the deme maintained and ever increased its hold ; but only because Cleisthenes submitted to what seems to us a surprising compromise. He made membership of a deme hereditary. Once of Collytus a family was always of Collytus, even if it went to live at Steiria. A demesman living away from his ' people ' would just count as a ' resident alien ' : he would have no part in the public affairs of the deme, but merely be set down, like an enfranchised slave, or an Italian *civis sine suffragio*, as ' dwelling ' there. It was a striking concession : and Cleisthenes can only have made it in the expectation that the deme arrangements would be periodically revised. But fifth-century Athens had

---

[1] Wilamowitz, *A. A.*, vol. ii, pp. 169 ff. ; *Ath. Pol.* xxi. 4 ; Ar. *Clouds* 1322, 134 ; *Ach.* 406, 1028 ; *Peace* 190 ; *Lys.* 852 ; *Thesm.* 898.

other things to think of, and for this among other reasons the deme organization, like our own local authorities, worked with varying success in different parts of the country.[1]

What did these demes do ?

In local matters their powers were very much the same as those of the old ship-districts : the mayor or demarch (the name and type—mostly stout and well-to-do—still survive in the modern kingdom) took over the duties of the old ship-maker. He presided over the assembly of demesmen which managed the local affairs of the neighbourhood, and saw to the raising of the rates, and, if necessary, of the taxes. So far as the scanty inscriptions which their frugality has left us reveal, parish affairs in fifth-century Attica fall into five classes : the annual election and examination of officials and priests, the management of parish lands or ' glebe ', ' sacred ' affairs (keeping up shrines, festivals, &c.), granting honours to benefactors (these of course were always inscribed on stone), and justice. This last was a new category which had come back to the demes from Deioces' judgement-seat in the city. But the judicial powers of the general jury, or Heliaea, of the demes were very slight : they could only act in purely local cases, and only then when they were specially referred to them. These local courts evidently did not do their work well, for about fifty years later, following a precedent set by Pisistratus, we find the central authorities sending expert judges on circuit round the demes to supplement them.[2]

[1] *Ath. Pol.* lxii : ' when the demes got corrupt.' Hereditary demes are only surprising to us because we have grown accustomed to taking local ties so lightly. Yet the general substitution of a local for a birth qualification for the ' freedom ' of an English borough only dates from 1835. Membership of the seventeen parishes of Siena is still hereditary, although they are so small that families are constantly moving house from one to another. When the parish flags are flown from the houses on the day of the big horse-race in the square, these transmigrants make themselves very noticeable by hanging out their hereditary colours amid a streetful of rivals.

[2] Pauly, s.v. Δῆμοι, who gives a full list of all the known demes. Well-to-do Demarchs : Sundwall, *Epigraphische Beiträge zur sozialpolitischen Geschichte Athens*, p. 57. (This Finnish writer has gone exhaustively into the *personnel* of the whole Athenian administration and entirely dispelled the legend, which originated from Aristotle, that Athens was almost wholly in the hands of demagogues either in the fifth or the fourth century. A large and constant proportion of the official names belong to well-to-do families, who showed not the least inclination to be ' driven out of public life '. This throws an interesting light on the old controversy as to the influence of Plato and

But more important than their local duties was the position occupied by the demes in the central organization, for this is what gave them their permanent place in the Athenian citizen's life.

Firstly, the deme kept the registers of citizenship. The State took cognizance of the individual only through his deme. From birth to eighteen an Athenian was nothing to Athena. He might be a ' brother ', but he was not yet a citizen or even a semi-citizen. When he became eighteen he was inscribed on the roll of his deme, like his father before him, and henceforth he enjoyed the privileges of citizenship, such as a seat in the Central Assembly, or Ecclesia, and was called upon for its duties, such as military service.

Secondly, when direct taxation was necessary—as was only the case in times of emergency—it was raised by the demes, who, like our local surveyors of taxes, were in closer contact than the central power with the wealthier members of the locality. Here the deme was merely carrying on the duties of the old ship-districts.[1]

But the most important work the deme had to do was to keep the central state supplied with men to do its public work. We often hear it laid down as an axiom that Greek democracy differs from modern because it did not use the representative principle. This is of course a complete mistake : and it could never have won acceptance but for the foolish idea (to which so many nineteenth-century thinkers gave currency) that the only public work that a democracy requires of its citizens is an occasional vote either in or for Parliament. The Greeks were not so shortsighted. They knew that government does not

Isocrates respectively upon their contemporaries. It is clear that few Athenians followed Plato in despairing of the Republic and retiring into private life to wait for more Utopian times.) Circuit judges : *Ath. Pol.* xvi. 5, xxvi. 3, liii. 1. There were originally thirty, but when the thirty tyrants had made thirty an unlucky number they were increased to forty. Even in their most practical arrangements the Greeks were apt to be childishly superstitious. For the demarch or village Bumble see the unkind remark in *Clouds* 37. See also B.S.A. xxiv (1920–1), p. 157.

[1] As we know from the orators, fourth-century Athenians sometimes concealed their wealth in order to evade taxation. We, with our traditions of ' doing what we like with our own ' are much more averse to the ' inquisition ' of local tax-collecting officials. It is noteworthy that the super-tax on large incomes—a tax for which the Greeks would certainly have used their local collectors—should have been carefully entrusted to a class of central officials.

consist of rights, irrespective of their exercise, but of something
a great deal more practical. A governor, whether amateur (as
in Greece) or professional (as so often with us), is a man with
a job to perform, a man who is not so much engaged in exercising
rights (though of course he is only doing what he has a right to
do) as in carrying on public business. So, as Theseus has told
us, it was not the Ecclesia, whether it met weekly or monthly,
which made Athens a democracy : nor is it Adult Suffrage or
the Referendum which will make England one. Democracy is
meaningless unless it involves the serious and steady co-operation
of large numbers of citizens in the actual work of government.
No state has ever been composed of citizens all of whom have the
leisure or the desire or the knowledge to attend to public affairs.
The Greek City State differs from our modern democracies in
enlisting not all but merely a far larger proportion of its representatives in active public work. Whereas with us, however
democratic our constitution, the few do the work for the many,
in Greece the many did it themselves. As the Funeral Speech
says : ' We call our constitution a democracy because its working
is in the hands not of the few but of the many,' or, to quote the
paradox at the close of Herodotus's eulogy of democracy, ' in
the many all things are found.' Fifth-century Athens knew very
well that it was a paradox : that it was impossible in this imperfect world to secure a fair share of power, not merely for organized
minorities, like the young ' aristocrats ' in Syracuse, but for the
minority in a man's self (when it is a minority), ' the little bit
of him that cares for his country.' But the Greeks were practical
people, unconcerned as yet with the metaphysics of politics, and
Cleisthenes' organization was designed, like some of our own
recent social legislation, to sweep into the political net just so
much of the political talent and energy of his Athenians as he
could conveniently secure.[1])

---

[1] Thuc. ii. 37. 1 ; Hdt. iii. 80 *fin.* ; cf. Thuc. vi. 39. 1. For a modern
measure designed with the same object as Cleisthenes' compare (to take but
a single, and non-contentious, example) the Probation of Offenders Act.
Probation officers are generally unpaid. Does the principle become different
when they have their expenses paid, or even when they are given a small fee ?
The difference between amateur and professional is, after all, as our cricketers
know, only a matter of degree. Note the proverbial Greek remark about
judging a man's character : ἀρχὴ ἄνδρα δείξει, i. e. ' Wait till he is a magistrate '. It is like our public school ' Wait till he is a prefect ' ; nearly every

Let us cast our eye over the central government of fifth-century Athens and see how it worked. The system we are about to describe was established, in its essentials, by Cleisthenes, though Pericles and others made necessary and logical additions. We shall therefore omit, as not germane to our purpose, which is to understand the Athenian of the Funeral Speech, those parts of his work, such as his treatment of the Areopagus, which proved to be of merely temporary importance, and concentrate our attention on its essentials. All through we shall find it based on two simple ideas. Firstly, the people is, under its own laws, sovereign, and the people's will, whether expressed in the assembly or the law courts, is, under the law, supreme and responsible to none. Secondly, as the people has many other things to do besides to rule, its work must be done by representatives, as many as can be conveniently secured, subject, at stated intervals, to its own approval and correction. Complete self-government was the ideal ; but Athenians realized, to adapt the famous saying of Lincoln, that you can make some of the people rule all the time, and all the people rule some of the time, but that you will never get all the people to rule all the time.

Government consists of three parts, the legislative, the administrative, and the judicial. This is not strictly correct for Athens : for, since Solon, she had her ' laws ' complete and was not supposed to need to make new ones. She only did so, as the

one became one and had a chance of ' showing the stuff he was made of '. It recurs in Soph. *Ant.* 175–7, also quoted at the head of this chapter, where, as Jebb says, the poet is thinking of the Athens of his day.

1914. I leave this note and the paragraph in the text as it was written in the days before I was myself a professional Servant of the State. But I feel bound to quote the following, from a pamphlet by a friendly anonymous critic, in qualification of what is said about the representative principle above : ' Representation is used to cover two wholly different things, the confusion of which constantly operates to obscure the discussion of political questions. Men are said to be " represented " in court by counsel, and governments are said to be " represented " by ambassadors. In these cases representatives are mainly vehicles of intercommunication. As a rule, they can settle nothing except by particular and special reference to their principals. Edward I made the English Parliament a reality when he stipulated that the representatives who met there . . . *should carry in their own persons the full authority of the constituents who sent them.* . . . Edward I thus converted Parliament into a practical organ of government, which could, and gradually did, take over the governing powers of the king himself, and became responsible to an electorate which was extended from time to time till it included a large proportion of the male inhabitants of England.' Representation of this sort was, of course, unknown to the Athenians, as the failure of the Delian Parliament illustrates. See p. 188 below.

Americans alter their constitution, with extreme circumspection. Her Parliament met, as our English word implies, not to pass laws but to discuss policy. But these discussions were not mere academic debates. They ended in a vote which was embodied in a decree : and these decrees were really the counterpart, in the simpler and stabler conditions of Greek life, to our Acts.[1]

Let us take the judicial side first, for we have already seen it at work under Solon. Cleisthenes upheld and perhaps even extended the rule of the people in the big popular juries, or, as we should call them, Benches, which were based, as we saw, on the idea of calling the people in to act as judge ; what we have to note here is how he selected the judges. Like ours, they lived scattered about the country. The natural authority to collect them was the deme. Cleisthenes arranged that the demes between them should present 6,000 judges (600 from each tribe) to the central authorities, who should then draw lots as to whose services were required. As the population of the different demes varied considerably, a system of proportional representation was established between them. But how did the demes get their candidates ? They *elected* them, no doubt taking all those—if they had room for them—who were known to be willing to serve. When the work of the courts increased and they sat more frequently, it was not always easy to find men who could spare the time. Pericles overcame this difficulty by paying every judge a decent day's wage for his services. They were elected to serve for a year. So every morning of the year, except on the numerous feast-days (more numerous, foreign litigants used to complain, than anywhere else in Greece), these 6,000 would trudge into Athens, if they lived in the country, and present themselves at their old judge Theseus' temple—unless Parliament happened to be sitting that day and they were required there instead. Here they would be told if the courts had work for them : if they had, lots would be drawn, and, unless they were very unlucky, they would go off to court in batches of hundreds, sure of their meals for the day, to hear cases from every part of the Athenian Empire. So far as we know, they did their work very well ; amid much grumbling on other matters no complaint on the score of corruption or unfairness in individual cases has come down to us. No court consisted of less than 201

[1] Thuc. iii. 38 ; cf. Glotz, *Cité*, pp. 193–5.

jurymen and, as one of these grumblers remarked, so far as corruption is concerned, there is safety in numbers.[1]

Let us pass to administration. Athens had no permanent civil service, at least in the higher branches, and, except for military officers and for the council, no man might hold the same position twice. She had professional policemen and clerks and town-criers; but all her important public work was done by a rapid succession of amateurs. The theory was, as Pericles tells us, that quick wits are worth more than experience of routine: and the best statesmen were those who, as Thucydides says of Themistocles, were best at 'improvising policy' in emergencies. These 'dilettante' public servants held office for a year and, in the fifth century at any rate, never as single officials but as members of a board, so as to assist or control one another. Some of them were chosen by lot, like the judges, out of a list of selected candidates—the nine governors, for instance, were drawn for (after 487 B.C.) out of 500 candidates selected by the demes; others, whose work required more expert knowledge, were definitely elected by show of hands in the Assembly. Officials whose functions involved 'matters of life and death to the people', as a grumbler puts it, that is, military and financial officials, were always elected. No officials were appointed, as so many with us, on the nomination of other officials or of 'the government'; for in Athens, as we have heard Theseus declare, there was no 'government' in this sense of the word—

> The whole folk year by year, in parity
> Of service is our King.[2]

But some permanent central authority there must be. A foreign envoy coming to Athens must find one 'holding the seals of authority'. Even in the dead season, when Whitehall is deserted, there is some permanent secretary on duty in the Foreign Office. Who kept the machine of government working at Athens? Surely it cannot have been left to the slave clerks.

---

[1] Pauly, s. v. Δῆμοι; Wilamowitz, A. A., vol. ii, p. 96 note, Sundwall, p. 69; Old Oligarch, iii. 7; Ath. Pol. lxiii; Ar. Wasps 304 (' if the courts are not sitting, what shall we do for a breakfast?' say the chorus: they do not contemplate being done out of it by the lot: the risk was clearly too trifling). According to Diodorus (xiii, 64. 6) the first instance of the corruption of an Athenian jury was in 409. It is possible that the number 6,000, the fifth-century figure, was higher than that fixed by Cleisthenes: see Wasps 661 ff.

[2] Thuc. i. 138. 3; Ath. Pol. xxii. 5; Old Oligarch, i. 3; Eur. Suppl. 406.

The real permanent force which kept the machine working was what was known as the Council, a body established by Solon and reformed by Cleisthenes in the place of the old council of the ship-makers with its General Purposes Committee of chiefs. The Council consisted of 500 members (fifty from each tribe) who were chosen by lot, in the same way as the judges, out of candidates elected, on a proportional system, by the demes. These annual parish elections of candidates for the council were the most exciting political event of the Athenian year, for the political complexion of the council was, generally speaking, the decisive factor in state policy. Any citizen was allowed to stand, provided he had not already served twice as a councillor : and in this way a large proportion of the citizen body found its way by rotation on to the council.[1]

This ' council ' had a twofold function. It had a number of independent executive duties of its own, which it performed, like any other board of officials, subject to the approval of the people. But it also served as a standing representation, or General Purposes Committee, of the assembly : and as in this its most characteristic function it was, in theory, a mere section or mirror of the people, the individual councillor, like the individual voter in the assembly, was not called upon, as every other official, to give an account of his stewardship. · The council discussed and put into shape all the business which was to come before its sovereign, and sent up the agenda in the shape of προβουλεύματα or council minutes. No decree could be passed unless it had been through committee, i.e. unless, in Athenian official language,

[1] *Ath. Pol.* lxii. 3 (no second re-election). Acharnae, the biggest of the demes (cf. Thuc. ii. 19. 2), is known to have supplied twenty-two out of the fifty councillors of its tribe (Oeneis) : some small demes took turns to send one (as we find in the case of Boeotarchs in the newly found Boeotian constitution). Reckoning the citizen body at 40,000, one citizen out of every eighty would be a councillor at any given time. Reckoning thirty years to a generation, two out of every five would reach office. But allowance must be made for re-elections. We have no means of judging to what extent the candidates generally exceeded the places and how far the use of the lot was a reality. On the deme elections of council candidates see Wilamowitz, *A. A.*, vol. ii, p. 111 note. On the question of the lot see Headlam, *Election by Lot at Athens*, Cambridge, 1891, is still worth consulting for its practical insight into the detailed working of Athenian government. He emphasizes the importance of the lot in securing rotation for office. See esp. pp. 49–51. See also his clear account of the working of the judicial system, pp. 145–53. See also Glotz, *Cité*, p. 248. [See Appendix.]

'it seemed good to the council and the people.' The council sat daily to transact current business on behalf of the sovereign people between assembly and assembly, and any one who wished to have dealings with the sovereign—from a foreign ambassador to a citizen with a motion to move at the next meeting of the assembly—had to appear before the councillors. For these purposes the council was divided into ten sub-committees, one for each tribe, each of whom was on duty for a tenth part of the year. The members of these sub-committees were called by the old name of πρυτάνεις or chiefs, and their period of office was known as a prytany. One-third of the sub-committee had always to be in attendance, and from amongst it was chosen by lot every day an official called the president (ἐπιστάτης), who acted as chairman in the council or the assembly. During his single day of office (for he was not eligible for re-election) he had in his keeping the keys of the citadel, the public archives, and the state seal, and was thus for twenty-four hours the acting head of the country. The attendance of the whole sub-committee of fifty was necessary at every council meeting, that of other councillors was voluntary with the exception of one representative chosen by lot from each of these nine tribes. This was a provision to ensure that, even under the system of tribal organization by 'thirds', there should be no undue dominance of tribal interests.

But the council had also a large number of executive functions, some of which it had taken over from the old council of magistrates which sat on the Areopagus. For instance, it managed the finance—after 453 imperial as well as national finance—made all the arrangements for the election or sortition of officials, and kept a watch, in the case of all civil officials, over the performance of their duties. We do not know how often it met in full session in the council chamber, as opposed to the daily sittings of its sub-committee; but its work was sufficiently exacting to keep the councillors in the city for their whole year and to make it necessary for Pericles to make them an allowance for their work, in addition to the public dinners in the new council chamber, or Round House as it was now called, to which the 'chiefs' were entitled according to old custom.[1]

---

[1] *Ath. Pol.* xliii. 2 ff.; Daremberg, s.v. βουλή, with refs.; Wilamowitz, *A. A.*, vol. ii, pp. 95, 106. Round House: Plato, *Apology* 32, with the account of

We have seen how the sovereign people judged and administered by delegating power to representatives. Let us watch
Demos now in full session, as he assembles in the Ecclesia on
Pnyx Hill to 'decide or debate, carefully and in person, all
matters of policy ', ' holding,' as Pericles says, ' not that words
and deeds go ill together, but that acts are foredoomed to failure
when undertaken undiscussed.' These acts are not merely feats
on the field of battle, but also the decrees enacted—transformed,
as Thucydides would say, from ' words ' into ' deeds '—by the
sovereign in council.

The nineteenth century had a great veneration for ' the voice
of the people ', as if men could all shout together without
deafening one another. When it discovered that, under modern
conditions, nations cannot meet in council, it sanctified the
election of representatives to do the governing for them ; and
thus transferred its veneration from peoples to Parliaments. The
twentieth century is discovering, to its surprise, that the capacity
of Parliaments has been over-estimated : that, however well they
may shout, they find it difficult to govern. Our modern democrats might have saved themselves this disillusionment if they
had cared to listen to the psychologists. Public business is much
the same as private ; and men are not able to transact business in
hordes. Large companies are much the same as small, only
more uncomfortable. No one likes to sit for hours listening to
other men talking ; nor does the situation become very much
more tolerable when hundreds of others are listening too. Hence
the atmosphere of boredom and languor so conspicuous (as seen
from the galleries) in most modern Parliaments as in all large
committees, a vision of men striving desperately after the
unattainable—to waste none of their own time and yet to follow
conscientiously the main thread of the discussion. And hence
the ever-increasing tendency to concentrate the real power and

---

Socrates' behaviour as a ' chief ', the only office of state he ever held. The
old Athenian year consisted of twelve lunar months (354 days), with an extra
month three years out of every eight. So that Cleisthenes' adoption of the
decimal system by dividing the year (calculated as 360 days) into ten pry-
tanies involved ' dethroning the moon as a measure of time ': *Staat und
Gesellschaft*, p. 98, 2nd ed., p. 102. The *control*, as opposed to the management, of finance lay, of course, with the Assembly and its advisers. Speakers
were regarded as responsible, not only for their proposals, but for the expenditure entailed by them. See Headlam, *Lot*, pp. 112 ff.

the real work in more business-like quarters—in the hands of cabinets and committees and ' civil servants '.[1]

The same difficulties were felt in the Ecclesia ; and for that reason, as we have seen, current business was not transacted there. In some states Parliament did not meet regularly at all, but was only summoned from time to time for special emergency gatherings. In Athens it met in regular session ten times a year (once a prytany), and though the number of extraordinary sittings gradually increased throughout the fifth century to three or four during the prytany, even this did not mean a meeting

---

[1] We are still without a book on ' the psychology of committee work ' ; but the right number to discuss a complex matter of business is about seven, ' because that number of men can sit round a small table, talk with each other informally, without waste of words or any display of pretence, provide an adequate diversity of points of view and modes of dealing with the subject in hand, and be prompt and efficient in the discharge of business.'   Eliot, *University Administration*, pp. 64–5. (Compare the latest experiment in our system of government, the secret conference of party leaders.—1924. Also the Council of the League of Nations, which, by the admission of first four, then six so-called representatives of smaller states has, or will eventually, become just a little too large.) So the smaller boards at Athens, consisting generally of ten persons, were really more satisfactory than the Council. When, as in the case of the Ecclesia, complex business is only reported and hardly discussed, the exact size is of less consequence—those who are interested attend, the rest stay away. The Greeks were quite aware of the defects of ' a nation in debate '. How can a mob govern ? was a staple oligarchic argument. ' Why,' says the speaker in Herodotus's debate (iii. 81), ' it tumbles headlong into business like a winter torrent, upsetting everything as it goes along. It is stupid and violent and there is no use to be made of it.' Hence oligarchies dispensed with popular assemblies and carried on government through councils alone. See the interesting constitution, proposed for Athens in 411, in *Ath. Pol.* xxx. There is no assembly : instead the citizen-body is divided into four councils, each of which governs for one year out of four : thus (according to modern ideas) three-quarters of the citizen-body are, at any given moment, ' disfranchised.' But this legislator was not thinking of ' rights ' but of work, so he added a proviso that if the council so desired each of its members might bring in another citizen, some Pericles or Themistocles whose services they were anxious to keep, to assist in its deliberations. One year in four seems a large tax on time : but the council was only to meet one day in five. There was no pay attached, and any one who came late was fined a drachma. Similarly, in the Boeotian Confederation at the end of the fifth century both central and local affairs were managed entirely by Committees. For local purposes the restricted citizen-body was divided into four large committees working in rotation—a necessary arrangement, since oligarchies made no provision for their public servants—and important matters were decided in a full session of all four. The central federal council was similarly divided : it consisted of 660 members, i.e. of four committees of 165 each, fifteen from each of the eleven cantons or federal districts. Within each district the fifteen members were apportioned, by a system of proportional representation, between the different townships. See Thuc. v. 38 ; *Hellenica Oxyrhynchia* xi. 2 ff., elucidated by Glotz, *Bulletin de Correspondance Hellénique*, xxxii. 271 ff. ; cf. Wilamowitz, *Staat und Gesellschaft*, p. 129, 2nd ed., pp. 132–4.

more than once every ten days. Yet the Ecclesia met under
more favourable circumstances than our modern Parliaments.
It is the stuffiness of our council chambers, quite as much as the
business done there, which sends our legislators home tired out
after a few hours' work. The Athenian assembly came together
in the open air, and yet not, for all that, under conditions of
physical discomfort : for the orators of Athens did not compel
their victims, like our park and street-corner gatherings, to listen
standing up. The Athenians came to their popular assembly
unlike the Romans, in order to think, not to gape ; and no man
(except a Socrates) can think hard standing upright for hours.
On an assembly morning citizens would come together soon after
sunrise, having left their beds in the country, or in Salamis
across the water, long before it was light enough to see their
way into their cloak and shoes. Once safely on Pnyx Hill they
would dispose themselves as they liked among their friends and
acquaintances ; for Demos in Council knew of no tribes or thirds
or any subdivisions of his sovereignty. There they would sit
grumbling and yawning and scratching their heads, going over
their olive-trees or composing letters to absent friends, wishing
they had stopped for a mixed drink on their way up, above all
lamenting the square meal they will not get till to-morrow (for
it will be too late when they get home to have a supper worth
eating), till the lazy townsfolk stroll up from Athens and the
Piraeus, and, last of all, the unpunctual councillors come bustling
through the crowd. Then, at last, when our countryman has
not a curse left in his quiver, prayers are announced, and the
proceedings begin.[1]

All this does not lead us to expect to find a full meeting,

---

[1] Aristotle, *Pol.* 1275 b 8 (emergency Parliaments) ; Ar. *Eccl.* 331 ff., 289 ff.
(early rising on an assembly day) ; *Ach.* 20 (arriving early on the Pnyx) ;
Lys. 59 (crossing from Salamis) ; *Eccl.* 85 (prayers) ; Theophrastus, Jebb,
p. 86 (countrymen's drinks). All Greek Parliaments sat *sitting*, even the
Spartans (Thuc. i. 87. 2 ἀναστήτω). ' The House of Commons is a place where
a man can neither work nor rest,' said a well-known statesman lately.—1921.
Cf. the following passage from *Der Weltkrieg* (vol. ii, p. 227) by Karl Helfferich,
the best organizing head in Germany during the war, in the course of which he
held the posts of Finance Minister, Minister of the Interior, and Deputy
Chancellor : ' I may sometimes have been short and brusque in the Reichstag,
but this was generally the expression of my inward irritation, which I kept
under with difficulty, at the time and ability wasted in sterile debates, while
tasks of far greater importance and urgency were kept waiting and suffered
damage.'

except on an occasion of very exceptional importance. Nor was it necessary that there should be, provided the sense of the whole people was fairly represented. For that, after all, is what Parliaments mainly exist for ; and as all business concerns people as well as things, Parliaments will always continue to be necessary, however ' expert ' a task the work of governing may become. The duty of a member of the national assembly is not so much to know about things (though such knowledge is never wasted) as to know about people, and to keep the men who are managing things in touch with what he knows. The danger in Athens was, of course (as we can see from the care taken in the composition of the council), lest the urban population living close at hand should drown the voice of the men from the more distant country districts. We cannot tell what proportion of the citizens attended on an average ; but the only record we have of an actual division shows 3,461 for and 155 against, total 3,616, a very small proportion of the electorate. There was no quorum required for ordinary business. When a decree was proposed affecting a single individual ($\nu\acute{o}\mu os\ \grave{\epsilon}\pi'\ \grave{a}\nu\delta\rho\acute{\iota}$) 6,000 must be present, and in the special case of ostracism a six thousand majority was perhaps needed for the decree of banishment to be issued. But it is certain that the average attendance fell far below this figure. During the later years of the Peloponnesian War it was impossible to bring 5,000 citizens together, however important the business. After its close it was so difficult to secure a respectable quorum that payment was introduced for attendance, and the fee was several times increased (perhaps with the decline in the value of money) in the course of the fourth century, till it reached a drachma and a half (about an ordinary day's wage) for the ten regular, and a drachma for all exceptional, sittings. No one was eligible for attendance till he was twenty years old.[1]

[1] Thuc. viii. 72. 1. On ostracism see Carcopino's exhaustive essay in *Mélanges d'histoire ancienne* (Paris, 1909) and H. J. Cunningham's criticisms in the *Classical Review*, February 1911. It is still an open question whether the 6,000 votes were required as a quorum or as a majority : see *Mélanges*, pp. 150 ff., also pp. 145–6, for reproductions of the four extant ostraka or potsherds on which the offending statesman's name was scratched. They all differ both in shape and dimensions, and were not supplied to the voter by the state, but provided by him and filled in at leisure beforehand. So, though the actual voting was secret, an illiterate voter could get help from his neighbours. This is clear from Plutarch's story of the countryman who wanted to have his vote written out against Aristeides because he was

The *Constitution of Athens* has given us a glimpse into the conduct of Parliamentary business. The agenda were drawn up by the council, and circulated when notice of the meeting was sent out. Nothing could be brought forward which did not appear in them. But the meeting had the right of selecting in what order matters could be debated, and thus preventing the council from burking discussion by putting down awkward subjects at the bottom of a long list. Public business was arranged under three heads : ' sacred ', ' profane ', and ' foreign affairs '. Business began after sunrise and could go on till dusk ; but no doubt the impatience increased as the afternoon wore on. Steps were therefore taken (our evidence for this dates from after the introduction of pay) to secure that a reasonable amount of business must be got through. We hear of a provision (not adopted at every meeting) requiring at least nine points on the agenda, three under each head, to be dealt with in the day.[1]

What was the spirit of this assembly ? Much the same, as Nietzsche has pointed out, as that of the audience in the theatre. In both cases men turned up (as at Ober-Ammergau) with a healthy ' early morning feeling ', ready to listen attentively and to judge fairly, with their perceptions heightened and clarified by the solemnity of the occasion and the natural grandeur of the scene. Many, if not most, of those present had already been councillors, and understood the nature and details of the necessary business. So, on ordinary occasions, when nothing special was on, business was run through sensibly and satisfactorily, ' as the laws ordained,' although perhaps (Greeks being Greeks) with some little unnecessary palaver. But on exceptional occasions, when matters involving principle or rousing excitement were to be discussed, affairs assumed a different aspect. The business men retired into the background, the teachers and talkers came to the front, and all Athens flocked in to listen, as at a big debate in a modern Parliament. For questions of

tired of hearing him called the Just (Plut. *Arist.* 7). Athenians' acquiescence in the institution of ostracism shows how, as a matter of course, they put the city first and the individual nowhere. A man was ostracized for no offence whatsoever, but simply because a large proportion of his fellow-citizens thought he would be better out of the way. Nowadays such powers cannot be exercised even by schoolmasters. Cf. Thuc. viii. 73. 3.

[1] *Ath. Pol.* xliii. 4, Wilamowitz, *A. A.*, vol. ii, pp. 252 ff. ; cf. Pauly, s. v. *Ekklesia.* Division list : Pauly, p. 2170.

principle and morality affect the responsibility of every citizen, and call upon him to act, not as an expert, but as a plain man. There must have been stirring debates on Parliament Hill at the time of the Persian wars and later ; but no historian has recorded them, and only small fragments of their eloquence have come down to us. We must judge their character from Thucydides, who has condensed for us the drift and arguments of several of the discussions on the Peloponnesian War. But the best of his reports relate to the time when Athens had outgrown her idealism and show us the dangers rather than the dignity of these great popular occasions. We see an excited populace, forgetting the common sense which was the bedrock of its constitution, allowing its subtle and inquisitive intellect full play, and turning an assembly intended to transact serious business into a dazzling display of argument and casuistry. Such occasions brought to the fore a new type of public man, who had served no apprenticeship of responsibility in the business offices of state, at best the thinker and the moralist, but too often only the accomplished Parliamentarian whom we know so well from our own newspapers. The Ecclesia, and, as we know from Aristophanes, the theatre of Dionysus too, had its well-known *habitués*, who made themselves conspicuous, and gathered a host of friends and enemies, by the acuteness of their criticisms and their smart and ready way of putting them. So that ministers, engrossed in their affairs and perhaps a little forgetful of their constituents, would come down to the assembly to find that they had lost, in the last week or two, the support of their fellow-citizens, and that men were beginning to group themselves in parties under the personal leadership of some 'watchdog of the people' and master of biting speech. Then would begin the long wrangle, which we know so well, between the men of words and the men of business, ending in the sulky challenge : ' Go and take on the job yourself.' And sometimes the Parliamentarian, like other critics and journalists since, picked up the glove and put the careful minister to shame.[1]

[1] Nietzsche, *Works*, vol. xvii, p. 303. After the sophists came in, men began to bring with them a debating-society atmosphere (as Cleon complained) instead of the old simple matter-of-fact state of mind. Cleon, as depicted by Thucydides, was, in his coarse way, the worst sophist of them all. The best Athenian Parliamentary debates in Thucydides are iii. 37–48

Nicias on this famous occasion was, like Pericles throughout his career, not a civil servant, that is a civilian minister, but a soldier. Soldiering is a no less essential part of ' public work ' than inspecting markets or doing state accounts. It is necessary, therefore, to examine how the Athenians succeeded in adapting the prevailing methods of their administration to this most exacting of duties. For we are not accustomed to think of generalship, still less of admiralty, as a business for amateurs.

Athens, of course, had a conscript army. At Marathon, as we know, the Athenians went out to battle in tribes, led by the generals or colonels of their tribe, who were elected by the tribesmen. Elected officers sound strange, but who else was there to choose them ? It was a concession to efficiency that the subalterns, instead of being also chosen by the rank and file, were appointed by their superiors. When they had an Empire to administer this tribal arrangement was no longer practicable, for their generals were no longer at home, needed only for summer campaigning or for posting sentries round the walls, but were required on foreign service, sometimes continuous for the twelve months, with fleets or garrisons in different parts of the Greek world. ' No enemy has ever met us in full strength,' boasts Pericles, for half of us are on land, and the other half at sea, and ' our soldiers are sent on service to many scattered possessions '. So the leadership of the tribal regiments passed necessarily out of their hands, and was left to inferior officers whom they appointed. For the generals, alone among higher Athenian officials, the tribal war was broken down. They were allowed to be elected out of the whole body of the people. For work of such importance, involving questions of life and death for the whole people, the primary consideration was to secure the best man : as the Old Oligarch remarked with a sneer, ' the people knows that it gains more by being shut out from these

(ch. 38 on sophists) and vi. 9–23. Cf. also Plut. *Per.* 11 for the discussion on the use of the tribute-money after the peace with Persia : also the Ecclesia, or rather Heliaea, in Eur. *Or.* 866 ff., and the part played by the countryman (917 ff.) ; Thuc. iv. 28. 1 (critics *v.* ministers). Cleon was a typical ' champion of popular rights '. Like some modern editors, he would ' take on anybody ' : and even in the lower regions he was expected to help landladies to get their bills paid (Ar. *Frogs* 569). In a small society like that of a Greek city it was not so necessary for Parliament to lay stress on its function of expressing and keeping alive the conscience of the people.

positions and letting the most capable men hold them.' The special qualifications of each elected general were known and valued. Though they still numbered ten and were in theory all equal, they were sent abroad or kept at home according to the work there was to be done and the people's estimate of their abilities. The painstaking, trusty man was sent on distant service, where he might have to fight or negotiate, at short notice, on behalf of the city. The abler of the ten were kept at home, to help in directing foreign policy and to be ready to carry it out. All the ten were in a measure (alone among Athenian officials) emancipated from the authority of the council; they were often compelled to take action at a distance without consulting it; and by being subject to re-election they could escape the ordeal of examination. They were the only servants of the people who were ever given full power and allowed for a time to be ' autocrats '. But all the worse was the ordeal if they returned home defeated!

Hence it was the military officials, the men who led the people in emergencies, who were really the most powerful men in the State, in peace as well as war time. It was as General, not as Prime Minister or ' President of the Council ', that Pericles dominated the assembly and directed Athenian foreign policy for more than a generation. Sometimes he went abroad at the head of an expedition. But nearly all the long months of his thirty years of office he spent at Athens, in touch with the Parliament whose moods he knew so well. Nothing could show more clearly, what we guessed at already when we read the epitaph of Aeschylus, how large a place war held in the life and thoughts of a Greek citizen.[1]

We have seen the democracy at work. Only one thing remains now before this long review is ended—to see how many there were to do the work.

[1] Thuc. ii. 59. 3; Old Oligarch, i. 3; Zen. *Mem.* iii. 4. 1; Meyer iii. § 201 with refs.; Wilamowitz, *A. A.* ii, pp. 107 ff.; General's responsibility: Aesch. *Persae* 213; cf. Nicias's dispatch: Thuc. vii. 11, 48. 3, viii. 1. 1. A general could prevent the Ecclesia from meeting (as Pericles did in 431, Thuc. ii. 22. 1) by calling out the army (i. e. in this case, sending the citizens on sentry-go). Subalterns: Lys. xxi. 10, steersman, i. e. navy subaltern: army subalterns, as Wilamowitz has noticed (*Aus Kydathen*, p. 79), are kept very much in the background. In an army managed on Funeral Speech principles this is not surprising. No state has ever been freer from a ' military caste '.

Democracy involves the co-operation of large numbers of citizens in the active work of government. It means payment to the state not only in taxes but in time and thought. Rich Athenians gave free gifts of money for ships or choruses or public monuments ; poor Athenians (and they were mostly poor) gave their widow's mite—themselves. How great was the call which their city made upon them ? [1]

Great enough, by all accounts, to be a serious element in their lives. For the contrast between public and private activity is a familiar one in all democratic writing. Work with us means always, unless stated to the contrary, our own professional work : work in Athens might mean either your own or the State's unless you made your meaning clear.

Ancient statistics are flimsy things ; but it is worth while trying to present some definite figures to show how this great machine of democracy was managed. For the *Constitution of Athens* has lately given us some fair evidence for our use.[2]

One of the latest writers on the population of fifth-century Athens, Cavaignac, gives the following estimate for 431, the year of the outbreak of the Peloponnesian War :—

Heavy-armed troops (comprising the first three classes of Solon's census)	25–30,000
Light-armed troops and rowers (fourth class) .	20,000
Total	45–50,000

In this estimate he includes the colonists or out-residents on conquered territory in different parts of the Athenian Empire, who were drawn from the poorer class, and numbered from 6,000 to 10,000. Subtracting them, we find the resident citizen population of adult males reduced to a maximum of 44,000, or a minimum of 35,000.[3]

---

[1] Λειτουργία is probably derived from λεώς (people). So a λειτουργός was the same as a δημιουργός : only he paid in money.

[2] *Ath. Pol.* xxiv, discussed in Wilamowitz, *A. A.*, vol. ii, pp. 201–11.

[3] Cavaignac, *Études sur l'histoire financière d'Athènes au Ve siècle*, pp. 161 ff. Wilamowitz, whom I follow in the details, is inclined to put it higher, and Meyer's figure (*Forschungen*, vol. ii, p. 179) is 55,500 without the cleruchs. But three other recent writers, Delbrück, Fawcus (*J. H. S.*, 1909), and Gernet (*Mélanges d'histoire ancienne*, 1909, p. 283), agree with Beloch, *Griechische Geschichte*, 1st ed., vol. i, p. 404, note 1, in putting it lower, between 30,000 and 40,000. Multiply by four to turn fighting-men into men, women, and children. The above discussions are based on Thucydides' figures for fighting-men (ii. 13). There is very little other *evidence* ; but 20,000 and 30,000 (δισμύριοι and

Out of this population of adult males Wilamowitz reckons that 7,500, or more than one man out of six, were, at any given moment, engaged on regular daily State duty, 1,500 as civil administrators, and 6,000 as soldiers, sailors, and city police. This does not include the 6,000 judges who might be called upon any day during the year for which they were selected. If these are added in the proportion mounts up to one out of four or even one out of three.

These figures are so startling that it may be well to give them in detail.

The *Constitution of Athens* says that ' more than 20,000 men ' were ' eating public bread ' ; that is, they were either receiving state pay as judges and councillors, or being ' maintained at the public expense ' as public servants or benefactors.[1]

These 20,000 are then said to be made up as follows :—

First : Judges	6,000
Bowmen	1,600
Horsemen [including 200 horse-archers, Thuc. ii. 13. 7]	1,200
Council	500
Dockyard guard	500
Acropolis guard	50
Home Civil Service	700
Imperial Civil Service	? 300 [2]
Total, about	10,850

τρισμύριοι) are expressions commonly, almost proverbially, used of the citizen-body : e. g. Hdt. v. 97 ; Ar. *Eccl.* 1132 ; *Dem.* xxv. 51 ; Plato, *Symp.* 175 E.
[1] See Wilamowitz, *A. A.*, vol. i, p. 196, note 20. Socrates, it will be remembered, suggested that he had a claim to such maintenance : Plato, *Apol.* 36–7. Regular pay for state work, such as Pericles instituted for jurymen and councillors, is not ' corruption ' but a great advance (comparable to King Darius's fixed tribute instead of exactions or ' benevolences ') on the old Eastern system of tipping and pilfering, or the new Western system of secret commissions. ' The labourer is worthy of his hire ' : and Athenians were sensible enough not to be ashamed of receiving it. The effect of its introduction was not so much to tempt poor men into public life as to compensate the moderately well-to-do for their time and trouble (Sundwall, p. 18). But the ' old Eastern system ' survived at Athens, as with us, only more widely, for the work of subordinates. One can see the ' inspectors of markets ' carrying off their pay, so to speak, in paper bags. As Wilamowitz says : ' καρποῦσθαι τὴν ἀρχήν (to make your office bear fruit) is a pretty expression : one only begins to feel uncomfortable when there is a till concerned.' The two systems are mentioned together in the Old Oligarch, i. 3 : ' the people is eager for the offices which bring pay or help to the folk at home ' (i. e. paper bags). Of course he and other wealthy people objected to State payments : but that was because he objected to popular government altogether. As he says in his opening sentences, it all stands and falls together. The oligarchical idea was ' voluntary taxation and unpaid personal service ' (τοῖς σώμασιν καὶ τοῖς χρήμασιν λητουργεῖν, *Ath. Pol.* xxix. 5).
[2] Number corrupt in MS. Wilamowitz estimates it at ' a few hundreds '.

These are all apparently regarded as *civil officials*, since the armed men amongst them are either police or reservists not on active service.[1]

Next comes, in a corrupt passage, *the peace establishment of armed forces on active service* :—

Army (heavy-armed troops)	2,500
Navy (guardships and tributeships), about . .	3,500
Total	6,000

Lastly, benefactors, subordinate officials (e. g. prison warders) and others (not being slaves) maintained at ' the public expense ', including, as we see from the concluding paragraph of the Funeral Speech, the ' orphans ' of men who had died on the State's behalf, say 3,150.

Total under the three heads	20,000

The separate totals are :—

All persons maintained	20,000
Adults maintained for public work, about . .	17,000

[1] The standing troop of citizen-bowmen must not be confused with the corps of Scythian state slaves who acted as police at Athens from 470 (Andoc. iii. 5) onwards, and lived in tents on the Areopagus. They acted as police or ushers for the Ecclesia, where they must have looked very much out of place in their native trousers (Ar. *Ach.* 54, *Lys.* 184, *Thesm.* 923 ff. ; Wilamowitz, vol. ii, pp. 202, 334, *Staat und Ges.* 103, 2nd ed., p. 109). The Acropolis guards were, however, citizen-bowmen. A fifth-century inscription about the repairing of the Acropolis wall (Dittenberger, 16) speaks of ' three bowmen-sentries from the tribe on duty in Council ' ($\pi\rho\upsilon\tau\alpha\nu\epsilon\upsilon o\upsilon\sigma\eta\varsigma$). There were probably more than three (see Dittenberger's note) ; but the tribute-money may not have yet been brought there. The 1,200 horsemen included (what corresponded to our mounted infantry) horse-archers (Thuc. ii. 13. 8). In the case of these standing horsemen (as opposed to the ' knights ') the State paid for the upkeep of the horses. One of the duties of the council was to inspect the public horses (*Ath. Pol.* xlix). There were thus two sorts of cavalry, one with public and one with private horses, one democratic, the other inclined to be aristocratic. The distinction is marked in the Parthenon frieze where, out of seven rows of horsemen, six are in uniform, each row (i. e. squadron) different. Those in mufti are the rich young ' knights ' we know from Aristophanes. (See Keil, *Anonymus Argentinensis*, p. 141.) Despite the frieze and the beautiful riders on the vases, Athenian horsemanship does not seem to have been particularly good. Xenophon gives it away badly in his tract on the *Duties of a Cavalry Commander*, e. g. ch. i, § 17, ' the art of leaping on to horseback is one which we would persuade the younger members of the corps to learn for themselves,' &c., &c. (cf. Wilamowitz, *Aus Kydathen*, p. 24, note 45, who admits that things were probably not so bad in the fifth century, and Dakyns' Introduction to his translation of Xenophon's treatise). Alexander was the first great Greek cavalry commander. We must remember that the Greeks rode practically bareback and without stirrups. It is difficult to imagine an effective cavalry charge of lancers without stirrups. [See Appendix.]

These last may be regrouped as follows :—

Civil Service [1] (with council and juries and a few subordinate free officials), about   .   .   .   7,650
Military Service (army and fleet, cavalry-reserve and
police)   9,350

But these figures by themselves do not give a fair representation of the working of the Athenian community. For though
one out of every six citizens may have been engaged as public
civil servants, there were in addition to the slaves, whom we
must leave aside for the present, a large number of other adults
contributing to the resources of the community who were relieved
from this tax on time. These were the Resident Aliens or
Outlanders (μέτοικοι) who, although not citizens themselves,
formed in every other respect, economically and, it may almost
be said, sentimentally, an integral part of the Athenian state.
For they, and not any ' friends ' or ' allies ' outside were, as
Nicias reminded them in the hour of trial, ' the only free partners
with the Athenians in their Empire ' : and it was but fitting that
they should form part, not as a privilege but as a right, of the
audience that listened to the Funeral Speech.[2]

For though the Outlanders were exempt from some of the
civil duties of citizenship, they took their place, when called
upon, in the conscript army, and fought for Athens in the field
as readily as any of her citizens. Some of them (not included in
the above reckoning) must have served as rowers on the standing
establishment. The adult male Outlanders are reckoned at
about 24,000, of whom 8,000 were rich enough to fight as
heavy-armed troops and the remainder served as rowers or
light-armed men. But none of the richer would form part of
the peace military establishment.[3]

[1] For details as to the multifarious duties of these civil officials see Wilamowitz, *A. A.*, vol. ii, pp. 202–4.

[2] Thuc. ii. 36. 4, vii. 63. 3–4. For their part in the Panathenaic procession, sometimes represented as humiliating, see Headlam, *J. H. S.*, 1906,
pp. 268 ff., on Aesch. *Eum.* 1028–31 (who notes the use of εὔφρων instead of
φίλος : cf. p. 101 above). The Outlander men, dressed in military red, carried
sacrificial vessels, filled with cakes, their wives carried pitchers, and their
daughters parasols.

[3] The question of the Outlander population is complicated by two apparently conflicting passages in Thucydides (ii. 13. 7 and ii. 31. 1). My total
follows Clerc, *Les Métèques athéniens*, p. 373. His estimate for the army
approximates to that of Francotte, *L'Industrie dans la Grèce antique*, vol. i,
pp. 173 ff., who, however, omits the metic rowers (cf. Thuc. i. 143. 1 and vii.

It is worth while returning for comment in conclusion to the remarkable words which Nicias addressed to the Outlanders in his army before Syracuse, for they throw light on the nature and spirit of the Athenian community. ' You Outlanders,' he says, ' are all but Athenians : and by your knowledge of our speech and your assimilation of our ways you have won the admiration of Greece.' By living under the shadow of the Acropolis, or even at Piraeus, they have partaken of the spirit of Athens. Pericles himself strikes the same note. ' We practise no periodical deportations, like the Spartans, nor do we,' he goes on, ' interfere with our visitors.' And again : ' Athens has become the school of Greece.'

All this sounds quite natural to an admiring posterity, but it was Athens and, above all, Cleisthenes who made it so. For it marks the complete breakdown, never in Athens to be restored, of the old exclusive patriarchal idea of the State as a corporation. It marks the recognition of a principle far more valuable than free trade, and, in an early and suspicious society, far more difficult to safeguard, that of free intercourse between men of different peoples. Athens was glad to see her aliens, encouraged their coming, not merely for the wealth they brought, and made them part of her community. Cleisthenes, indeed, when he established his new tribes, seized a golden opportunity and enrolled many aliens as citizens.

From the nature of the case this was difficult to repeat. But Themistocles, who inherited his ideas, and knew how to apply them in a wider sphere, did all he could to encourage aliens by freeing them from burdens ; and this policy was continued all through the fifth and fourth centuries. For Athens needed her aliens, whether they were free men or slaves (and many of these aliens had begun life as slaves), to enable her to sustain the great burden of her responsibilities, to supply her with the resources in men and things, in labour and capital, without which her ideals must be but empty dreams. Many a community

63. 3) in his total : and his estimate for the fleet to Meyer, *Forschungen*, vol. ii, pp. 149 ff., who puts their army numbers much lower. See further p. 416 below. Multiply by four, as always, to turn fighting-men into total population. The slaves will be discussed later. Their total number of all ages was between 75,000 (Francotte's minimum) and 150,000 (Meyer's maximum). This gives a total population for Attica, free and slave, of maximum 425,000, minimum 310,000.

since has been 'kept going' by its immigrants; but never was hospitality so wisely extended, for never was the work which the state demanded from its citizens so arduous and so important. When one citizen in four is called away on public service, men may well set a value on every additional brain and hand. Even the slave, as we shall see, shared in this politic welcome.[1]

---

[1] Ar. *Pol.* 1275 b 36 Κλεισθένης . . . πολλοὺς ἐφυλέτευσε ξένους καὶ δούλους μετοίκους : the two classes are ordinary aliens and freed slaves, who became 'metics' on manumission ; that is why we hear of no 'freedmen' at Athens. Cf. Diod. xi. 43. 3. Cleisthenes' reorganization of the tribes was not repeated, so there was no further opportunity for the wholesale enfranchisement of Outlanders. But they enjoyed the full rights of local government in the deme in which they lived, and in this way many of them may have crept on to the citizen register in the early part of the fifth century. This, however, became impossible after a law passed in 451, limiting citizen rights henceforward to those 'born of Athenians on both sides'. When this was made retrospective on the occasion of a distribution of a present of grain from the King of Egypt, 5,000 names were struck off : Plutarch, *Pericles* 37, elucidated by O. Müller (cited p. 339 below), pp. 815–20. It is wrong to regard this isolated measure as marking a reversal of the Athenian attitude to aliens. See pp. 380 ff., below. One little fact to show what a wonderful revolution the Athenian attitude to Outlanders implies. *Ath. Pol.* lviii. 2 says : 'The duties the chief governor performs (i. e. as judge, arbitrator, &c.) for citizens are performed for metics by the Polemarch', that is, the commander-in-chief of the city's early days. He did not administer justice to aliens in those days : he chased them. See Phillipson, *The International Law and Custom of Ancient Greece and Rome* (2 vols., London, 1911, with bibliography), pp. 171 and 199, with the Phaselis inscription there cited, also given in Hicks and Hill, *Greek Historical Inscriptions*, 2nd ed., no. 36. Amongst the Outlanders we must not forget Herodotus of Halicarnassus, who was at Athens from about 466 till 443.

CHAPTER VII

THE DEVELOPMENT OF CITIZENSHIP

LIBERTY, OR THE RULE OF EMPIRE
(ἐλευθερία)

Μόνοι οὐ τοῦ ξυμφέροντος μᾶλλον λογισμῷ ἢ τῆς ἐλευθερίας τῷ πιστῷ ἀδεῶς τινὰ ὠφελοῦμεν.—PERICLES.

Slavery they can have anywhere. It is a weed that grows in every soil. . . . Freedom they can have from none but you. This is the commodity of price of which you have the monopoly.—BURKE, *On Conciliation with America.*

WE have watched Athens become a democracy. But before our commentary is complete one last and greatest step remains to be taken. We must see her as an Empire. For the Athens of the Funeral Speech was not an ordinary City State like Plataea or Corcyra, but the metropolis or mistress of some 250 dependent communities.

The first important thing that happened after the expulsion of the tyrants and the constitutional settlement of Cleisthenes was, as Thucydides says, the battle of Marathon. 'Ten years after that,' he continues, that is, just a generation after Cleisthenes, 'the Barbarian came over with his big Armada to enslave Greece. In this hour of national danger the Lacedaemonians, as being the strongest state, took command of the Greek confederate forces, and the Athenians, who had decided, on the approach of the Persians, to break up their homes and leave their city, went on shipboard and became sailors. The Confederates repulsed the barbarian; but not long afterwards they and the Greeks who had thrown off the Persian yoke grouped themselves into two parties, one round the Athenians and one round the Lacedaemonians. For these two states had been shown to be the most powerful : the strength of the one was on land and that of the other in her ships.' [1]

[1] Thuc. i. 18.

This brief paragraph, carefully examined, is a full and sufficient introduction to the history of the Athenian Empire. It
tells the tale of a great material change, and a still greater
spiritual transformation, in the affairs of Greece.

When the Athenians sent twenty ships to help their Ionian
kinsmen in their rebellion and so provoked Darius to send over
a punitive expedition, the Greek states still seemed to themselves and to the world around them very small and insignificant compared with the Empires of the East. Not only the
cringing priests at Delphi, but the common Greek citizen looked
up with reverential awe to great Moguls like Croesus and Cam-
byses. Greece could never hope to be so large or so strong
or so rich or so artistic or so generally refined and civilized
as these masters of millions of money and dependants. We
can see all this reflected in the pages of Herodotus, writing for
a public which had found out, once and for all, that the glories
of Xerxes and the wisdom of Egypt were ' only wind and boast-
ing ', but liked hearing about them all the more for that. But
it needed real pluck for a Solon, a mere country cousin come
to town, not to be dazzled by the treasures which a Croesus
was able to display to him. The sixth century stared at the
treasures ; but it was not they but their grandsons who discovered what they were worth—that, as Pericles was fond of
putting it, ' money does not own men, but men money.' [1]

[1] Thuc. i. 143. 5, undoubtedly one of Pericles' own phrases, repeated with
tragic irony by Nicias in his last speech before Syracuse (vii. 77. 7) : Sophocles had heard him say it too (cf. O. T. 56–7) ; Hdt. i. 50, where one can hear
the luscious voice of the Delphian priest pointing out the evidences of the
Great King's piety. Herodotus was ready to give Egypt credit for the
origins of anything, human or divine (e. g. ii. 50) : even ape ancestors would
not have ruffled his belief in his own countrymen. The point was, what did
the chosen race do with what it had, whether it had got it from home or
abroad, from Prometheus or Cadmus ? See this point developed in Myres,
Anthropology and the Classics, e. g. p. 151. ' The treatment of Hellenic
civilization by Herodotus stands in marked contrast with his treatment of
the civilizations of Egypt and Outland. . . . Only in Greece is there mastery
of man over nature, and that not because nature is less strong, but because
Greek man is strong enough to dominate it.' Herodotus believed in ' the
transmission of culture ', and hence preached ' the conception of progress in
civilization '. In this department Darwin is not a pioneer : he has only taught
our scholars to use their eyes. ' The Greeks had no word for Progress.'
No, because the words they used (e. g. μετεβαλον, μετεμαθον) were not so
misleading. Cf. Hdt. i. 57, vii. 170. The fifth-century Greeks had none of
the post-Exilic Jews' fear of assimilating foreign elements. This conflict is
still being fought out in Jewry ; cf. a remarkable volume of essays by Achad

This change was due to the Persian wars, above all to the
repulse of the Armada at Salamis. The Greeks did not beat
the Persians by a fluke or a miracle. Thucydides and the men
of the fifth century are emphatic on that point. It was not
a fluke, because it happened many times over, in four or five
big battles, both by land and by sea, in Greece, in Asia, and
in Sicily. It was not a miracle, because the gods had drawn
a bye and were taking no part. Apollo tried hard, by explain-
ing and patching his oracles after the event, to clear himself
and his fellow Olympians of their disgraceful neutrality; but
he failed. It was the death-blow to his national influence, and
for the present at any rate, to the influence of supernatural
religion in Greek national affairs. It was men and not gods
who won Marathon and Salamis, and it was men and not gods
who made and sustained the Empire of Athens. So at least
said Pericles, as emphatically as he could, considering that he
was speaking, so to say, in Church. True, he associated with
foreign philosophers and was tainted with heresy, but he would
not have been chosen to speak at the most solemn of all the
ceremonies of the Athenian year if men had minded his being
a heretic. Sophocles at least was above suspicion on the score
of piety, and his great chorus in the *Antigone* breathes the same
defiant human note. There were backwaters in Greece where
men did not yet know that the power of the old gods was
broken; but for all the progressive and leading communities
the lesson of Salamis was final. The victory of Greece was not
a ' crowning mercy' but a natural and reasonable development.[1]

Haam (' One of the People ', nom de plume of Dr. Asher Ginzberg), esp. one
on ' Imitation and Assimilation ' (translated from the original Hebrew by
Leon Simon, Philadelphia, 1912, pp. 107 ff.). The writer preaches substantially the same doctrine as Herodotus. Cf. the tone of the Persian scene
in the *Acharnians* (64 ff.), though all Athens knew what a sham Persian
magnificence was. Conversely, Persian and Egyptian ideas about the Greeks
underwent a transformation too. They used to be known to them simply
as rough adventurers, little better than Pisidians and other hill-tribesmen.
Now they had become respectable and respected.

[1] Thuc. ii. 43. 1 ἄνδρες αὐτὰ ἐκτήσαντο: cf. i. 76. 3. So i. 73. 1 οὐκ ἀπεικό-
τως ἔχομεν ἃ κεκτήμεθα, Aesch. *Persae* 235 ff. See the same point of view, in
a very different mood, v. 105. Enlightened people never took the oracle
quite seriously in the fifth century, as we can see from Herodotus, though
the Greeks were more prone than we to sudden attacks of superstition. But
they went on consulting it, because, as with modern oracles, it was convenient to have it on their side. So they made it as easy for Apollo as they
could. Instead of asking, ' Shall I go to war ?' they put it, ' Don't you think

It is impossible to describe what a transformation this implies. No phrases or analogies can adequately depict the difference between the small native communities on the outskirts of the Persian Empire, as the Greeks seemed to Darius and to themselves at the end of the sixth century, and the pioneers of the civilization not of Europe or of the West, but of the whole of mankind. It is the difference, or rather far greater than the difference, between what modern Japan meant to an uneducated Russian before the Russo-Japanese War and what Greece means to ourselves. For sixth-century Greece was not like one of the small powers of our own day, like Denmark or Switzerland, with a fixed character and tradition of her own. She was still in the making, still greedily absorbing foreign elements, still ready, as we can see from Ionia, to be swallowed up body and soul by any stronger force which came her way. She had not yet found herself. As the philosophers put it, she had not yet come to self-consciousness; or, to speak with the preachers, she had not yet been ' born again '. The Persian wars woke her up. Henceforward she is the Greece we know. And just because the force that stung her into new life was not intellectual or religious or artistic but political, her ideals for the conduct of that new life were political too. Nothing else really mattered. There might be Pyramids in Egypt and hanging gardens in Babylon; the Medes might promenade with parasols and the Egyptians wear clean linen every day. These were only the externals and ornaments of life. What mattered was that Greece was free and powerful and could bestride the world like a Colossus, that her citizens found their way into every sea and every land, leaving there, not temples or Pyramids

I ought to go to war ? ' The answer no doubt depended on the offertory. See Thuc. i. 25. 1, iii. 92. 5 (a reply which, though Thucydides is too indifferent to point it out, proved hopelessly wrong). Of course, till the idea of Providential interposition is dispelled, it is impossible not merely to write history but to think coolly about politics. Hence Thucydides' continual insistence on psychology and on the necessity of statesmen understanding human nature; cf. i. 140. 1 with ii. 59. 3, and especially iii. 45 where, as Cornford has shown in his *Thucydides Mythistoricus*, mythology is transformed into psychology. For Science, like the Devil, can quote Scripture for her own purposes. Wilamowitz, *A. A.*, vol. ii, p. 64 note, points out that Zeus was not worshipped as 'Ελευθέριος (God of Freedom) at Athens till after 480. But the extra title does not seem to have increased the popularity of his worship.

or books of verse or story, but memorials of their actions as men of a proud and ruling race.

It was at Athens that the change was felt most vividly, for Athens had suffered most to bring it about. While Sparta had lingered in her peninsula fastness Athens had borne the brunt of the barbarian attack. At Marathon she had discovered, to her own intense surprise, that the spear and the shield could conquer the bow, even against superior numbers; and ten years later, when the odds were overwhelming, she had dared to face the ordeals both of fire and of water. Her citizens had left their homes and their sacred places, and had stood on the cliffs of Salamis watching the flames lick the shrine of Pisistratus on the Acropolis and make a bonfire of the scaffolding round their new temple of Athena. When they came back victorious to their ruined city it was to a new life and with new ideals. They found the unfinished blocks of last year's projects lying about on the Acropolis; but they did not go on with them; they built them into the wall, with their old fears and weaknesses, where they could make mock of them daily as they passed by. They were the milestones of their old life; and nothing so 'cheers the heart and delights the eye' as to look down and back over a stretch of difficult road. When they had finished their fortifications, Acropolis and City Wall and Piraeus, and had made sure of town and port, they set their hand to beautify their levelled citadel in the spirit of their new career. For by that time they had an Empire which deserved a fine capital and could inspire artists to create one.[1]

For the confederate forces of 480 could not remain a unity. In the heat of the conflict, when the barriers of city patriotism were broken down and Greeks found themselves fighting, to their astonishment, not against but with their neighbours, they had dreamed for a moment of making Greece a single state. 'Surely,' they argued round their camp-fires, 'she has all the makings of a nation. What is there between you and me? We have the same blood in our veins, from Zeus and Father

---

[1] Thuc. i. 69. 5, 73, 74 (contrast between Athenian and Spartan behaviour in the Persian War and consequent difference in what it *meant*, psychologically, to the two parties). Marathon (however great the disparity in numbers) was no more a 'crowning mercy' than Plassy. The blocks of the unfinished 'pre-Persian' temple are still in the Acropolis wall and visible to passers-by.

Hellen. We speak the same language, else we could not be chatting, albeit with difficulty, round this fire. We worship the same gods, as we remember when we go to Delphi or Olympia ; and we have much the same habits and understand one another's ways. When we have finished with these barbarians let us form a common state.' [1]

But these dreams soon faded ; for what centuries have put asunder two summers' fighting cannot bind fast. There was quarrelling even during the fighting, though men made light of it at the time ; but when the campaigns were over and the time for reorganization arrived, all the old differences revealed themselves and the ' Panhellenic confederacy ' disappeared into the limbo of forgotten things.

Yet things in Greece could never again be what they had been before the trial came. The Greeks had learnt that, though love of country may make men brave, it is only organization that can make them strong. Moreover, for the liberated cities of Asia Minor, still technically part of the Persian Empire, and liable to be dunned any day by a satrap for tribute, some concerted system of defence was urgently necessary. Sparta had neither the men nor the money to meet this need. So she retired from a position where, after all, her famous land forces would have been of very little good to her, and left the field open for the newly made sailors of Athens. Within half a decade, almost before slow Spartan wits had time to grasp what was going on, ' the alliance of the Athenians ' had been provisionally organized, and the first great civilized attempt to form a state of many cities was an accomplished fact.[2]

Like other great things the Athenian Empire was the child of necessity, and its creators did not know what they were doing. It had its origin in an alliance drawn up between the Athenians and the Ionians in the familiar traditional terms. ' In the third year after the sea-fight at Salamis, when Timosthenes was chief Governor, Aristeides ' (commander of the Athenian forces) ' swore

[1] Hdt. viii. 144 ; Plut. *Aristeides*, 21 (details of proposed permanent confederacy : their authenticity is denied, but why ?).

[2] Persia, who learnt nothing and forgot nothing, quietly demanded her old tribute from the Greek cities in 412 (Thuc. viii. 5. 5), sixty-eight years after Salamis. Spartan minds, as Alcibiades knew, moved very slowly. One had to make their flesh creep before they would take in a new idea (cf. the improvised sensationalism of the schemes in Thuc. vi. 90).

an oath to the Ionians to have the same friends and enemies
as they, to seal which they cast lumps of lead into the sea.'
How innocent it all sounds ! But let us see what it implies and
think out the logic of the situation.[1]

What was the object of the alliance ? Not merely to be ready
to repel the Persians if they renewed the attack. This was too
tame a mood for the men who had just sent them flying at
Salamis and Mycale. Its watchword was not Defence but
Freedom. They wished to push the war into the enemy's
country, to revenge and indemnify themselves by plundering
for the losses they had sustained and (to use a phrase familiar to
the Athenian leader-writers of to-day) to complete the liberation
of their enslaved brothers. They were ready and eager to be
led to the attack.[2]

But campaigning costs money : for soldiers cannot live on
plunder alone, certainly not when they are engaged in ' liberat-
ing '. And if half the allies are islanders and warfare is to be
waged by sea, ships will be needed too. How were these two
immediate needs to be met ?

Few of the members of the new alliance had any ships to offer.
Many of them had lost their navies twice over in the last twenty
years, first in the ill-starred ' Ionian Revolt ', and then again,
after they had been forced to beat up contingents against their
own kinsmen, at Salamis and Mycale. It was not easy for them
to build new ones, for, unlike the Phoenicians, they had not the
forests of Lebanon just behind them. Moreover, such ships as
they had were not of much use, for the Athenians had been
introducing improvements in the armament and construction of
triremes with which they had not kept pace. So, with the exception of the big islands, Samos, Lesbos, and Chios, which had
a naval tradition to maintain, the allies gave up the idea of
supplying ships and were driven back on to a substitute for their
share in the enterprise.[3]

Nor were they very anxious to give their personal service on

---

[1] *Ath. Pol.* xxiii. 5. Cavaignac, p. 37.
[2] Thuc. i. 96 πρόσχημα γὰρ ἦν ἀμύνασθαι ὧν ἔπαθον δῃοῦντας τὴν βασιλέως
χώραν. Cyprus was to that generation of Greeks what Crete is to this.
[3] Details in Cavaignac, pp. 38–41. Cf. Thuc. i. 14. 3. The new type of
trireme had 170 rowers : the older triremes (themselves a great improvement
on fifty-oared ships) had probably fewer.

the other allies' ships, nor, if the truth must be told, to serve by
their side in the field. They had never beaten the Persians in
fair fight, like the Greeks across the water. Artemisium and
Mycale to them called up very different memories : and at Lade,
which might have been their Salamis, there was no Themistocles
to overcome their jealousies and want of discipline. So the
Athenians were not over-urgent in pressing them to take the
field. They preferred comrades more accustomed to the hardship and discipline of naval service.[1]

There was one natural way of settling these difficulties. The
smaller allies were to pay the piper, while Athens and the large
islands could call the tune. This was the plan which was
adopted, on the suggestion of Aristeides, to settle the immediate
needs of the first campaign. As the island of Delos had been
fixed as the rendezvous of the allied forces the Delian temple of
Apollo formed a convenient bank, and the first contributions were
paid in there. The scheme pleased both parties, and it was determined to regularize it. Aristeides ' the upright ' was entrusted
with the task of fixing a scale of contributions. ' It was a long
business, necessitating much travelling ' and (unless the Greeks
have utterly changed their nature) even more tact than upright-
ness : also ' in the absence of precedents, many difficult inquiries,
for only the cities which had formed part of the Persian Empire
for some considerable time had a census of wealth which he could
use '. But by 470 the work was done. The total sum needed
annually for the operations of the Alliance had been fixed at
460 talents. Aristeides divided this out on a proportional scale
amongst the two hundred or so allies, and the scale was faithfully
adhered to, as the charter of membership, until Cleon turned
financier in 425.[2]

---

[1] Hdt. vi. 12.

[2] *Ath. Pol.* xxiii. 5 τοὺς πρώτους φόρους, the provisional contributions of
478, not to be confused with ὁ πρῶτος φόρος ταχθείς of Thuc. i. 96. 2 ;
Cavaignac, pp. 42–3 ; Hdt. vi. 42 (Ionian census) ; Thuc. v. 18. 5. Later
there were reassessments, to meet altered circumstances, every Panathenaic
festival (i. e. every four years), made by the Athenian Council and confirmed
by the jury court (Old Oligarch, iii. 5). In disputed cases, especially where
large sums were at stake, a specially large court of 1,501 judges was convened.
See Wilhelm, *Urkunden des attischen Reiches*, who, by fitting in a broken bit,
has shown that the *I. G.* i. 266 quoted in Hill's *Sources for Greek History*,
ch. i, § 76, giving the quota-list for 427–6, reads πόλεϛ ἂϛ ἐ βολὲ καὶ οἱ πεντα-
κόσιοι καὶ χίλιοι ἔταχσαν. [See Appendix.]

Thus the allies had, without knowing it, slipped into financial centralization and established the first Greek Imperial Exchequer. Moreover, it was centralization of a peculiarly insidious kind, for the predominant partners, and especially Athens, who did most of the work and bore the chief responsibility, did not contribute a penny to the costs.

Who controlled the spending of the money? Officially, of course, the allies themselves. For this purpose they elected representatives to a Parliament at Delos, which, like the Ecclesia or any other city assembly, was to discuss and decide upon all matters of policy. But in practice little importance attached to its deliberations, for its executive officers, the Athenian generals, were themselves responsible to their own Sovereign People; so, if the two sovereigns decided differently, a deadlock would ensue. The Imperial Parliament, therefore, could do little more than ratify, if it wished to be zealous, anticipate, the decisions of the Athenians. Moreover, the money itself was put into the hands of Athenian officials. Clearly it could not be husbanded by all the allies together. One treasurer would be suspect, but a commission of ten was more than enough. They bore an imperial title, 'Stewards of the Greeks,' but they were Athenians by nationality and elected by the Athenian people.[1]

There was another sphere where centralization, if it advanced more slowly, produced even more permanent effects, that of legal and commercial intercourse.

Technically speaking, an alliance for military purposes had nothing to do with commerce or the administration of justice. Commercial and legal relations could only be established by separate conventions between two states for those purposes. The City-State tradition was that every community should live in haughty isolation from its neighbours; and even in Ionia it was not till a year or two before Marathon that a Persian governor summoned representatives from the cities and induced the Ionians to establish conventions amongst themselves and to administer justice to one another instead of settling everything by reprisals. An eye for an eye, or rather an ox for an ox, or

---

[1] συνέδριον, Diod. xi. 70. 4 and Plut. *Arist.* 25 (the Samians propose the transference of the treasury to Athens in 454–3). 'Sophocles of Colonus' was Steward in 443.

a wreck for a wreck, was the morality handed down from those of old for use in international affairs.[1]

But, side by side with the new military alliance, Athens set to work to establish a network of commercial treaties between herself and each individual member of the league. This she was able to do, not merely because of her newly won prestige, but because of the acknowledged excellence of the Solonian laws and institutions under which she lived. These formed a natural starting-point for a process of unification ; and as there were scores and hundreds of different forms of law and custom and procedure in use among her allies, such a process could not but be felt as a convenience. So the time was ripe, as in Germany in the 'sixties, for common action in numerous departments of life.

These commercial treaties varied greatly in their details, according to the resources or prejudices of the other party and according to the date at which they were made. But certain general features were common to them all. By piecing together the scattered evidence we can watch the gradual encroachment of the predominant partner till, as Isocrates put it, ' she governed all the cities by the same laws.' [2]

Let us look first at the sphere of civil jurisdiction. The motto of the alliance was Freedom. Athens was engaged, not only in clearing the seaboard of Persians, but in clearing the sea itself of pirates and evildoers. This was a duty which had devolved, from time immemorial, upon the chief sea-power of the Aegean— unless, like Polycrates, it was itself piratical. So Athens stood, not only for freedom from the barbarian, but for freedom of intercourse and freedom of trade ; and it was to the interest of the allies to encourage her in promoting them. To police the Aegean with her triremes was only the first step. It was an obvious corollary to add to traders' convenience by simplifying

---

[1] Hdt. vi. 42 (the Homeric ἄγειν καὶ φέρειν).

[2] Is. *Pan.* 104. A commercial or extradition treaty was called a ξυμβολή, and a case heard in connexion with one a δίκη ἀπὸ ξυμβόλων, from the ξύμβολα, ' symbols,' or tallies, which were formally broken and exchanged between representatives of the two states, as, at a still earlier stage of international intercourse, between individual ' guest-friends ' : cf. Eur. *Med.* 613 and Daremberg, s. v. *Ephesis*, notes 64 and 65. Athens had of course such treaties in the fifth century with states not in her alliance, cf. Antiphon, v. 78. They generally provided that the defendant should be tried (as foreigners were until lately in the Turkish Empire) by his own countrymen. [See Appendix.]

the procedure in business disputes. Athens was able, therefore, to insert in her treaties a provision that all disputes arising out of business contracts entered into at Athens must be tried by Athenian law before Athenian judges, thus removing the defendant from his own native court. This was accepted as early as 466 by Chios, one of the most independent of the allies. Smaller states acquiesced in still greater encroachments on their sovereign jurisdiction; and in cases of revolt or disturbance, when opportunity arose for a clean sweep, they might wake up to discover that it had almost entirely disappeared. A common plan was to provide that all disputes involving more than a certain sum of money must be heard in the metropolis.[1]

In the criminal sphere the process of unification was slower, for here the sovereign tradition was more tenacious and intimate. Even the tiniest island liked to manage its own murderers. On the other hand, Athens was all the more anxious to interfere, for she needed authority to protect her own adherents and put down mutineers. We cannot trace the development in detail. It seems to have begun with interference in cases where loss of citizen rights was involved. Athens was called in, as Rome and so many ambitious suzerains have been called in since, as the champion of a minority when party strife had become acute. Thus Athens interfered at Erythrae in 455–50 to protect the 'democrats' against a party favourable to Persia. She seized the opportunity to give the city a new constitution, enforced and defended by a garrison on the citadel. The new government had to swear not to repeal the sentence of banishment against 'those who had fled to the Persians' without the consent, not only of the people of Erythrae, but of the Athenians. They were also forbidden, in similar terms, to 'drive out any of those that remained'. In other words, Athens, not only by her garrison but also by her civil jurisdiction, enforced the maintenance of the *status quo*. Her double hold is emphasized by the mention, side by side with the commandant of the garrison, of 'Overseers', imperial civil servants appointed by the Home Government, but

---

[1] Meyer, iii, § 278 and elaborate note. For the money limit see also *I. G.* i. 29, last line. See Hicks and Hill, No. 36 (treaty with Phaselis ' on same terms as with Chios '). Business contracts were called ξυμβόλαια, and cases arising out of them ξυμβολαῖαι δίκαι (Thuc. i. 77) as distinguished from δίκαι ἀπὸ ξυμβόλων.

paid by the allies, to watch and report on the state of affairs in
the cities. This shows how easy it was for Athens, with her
overwhelming military predominance, to steal on from position
to position. By 446 we find her graciously allowing the people
of Chalcis ' to administer punishment according to their own laws,
as the Athenians do at Athens, except in cases involving exile
or death or loss of citizen rights '. And by the time of the
Sicilian expedition we read in a law court speech : ' No allied
city is allowed to condemn any one to death without the consent
of the Athenians.' [1]

One further point is worth noticing. The privileges extended
to Athenian citizens by treaty right were everywhere extended
equally to Athenian 'resident aliens', those naturalized Athenians
who were citizens in almost all but name. So that the aegis of
Athens was held over men of all bloods and languages, and one
might meet in any port of the Mediterranean, as one meets
Maltese and Cypriots and other British subjects to-day, men
whose proudest boast, and sometimes (it is to be feared) safest
excuse for wrongdoing, was their connexion with the queen
of the seas.[2]

Thus Athens had gradually formed herself, whether her pupils
liked it or no, to be ' an education to Greece '. The process was
so gradual, and the control so wisely exercised, that the allies
could not easily put their hand on any particular cause of complaint. There was plenty of grumbling, especially when the
courts were overcrowded with cases and a round of festivals
came on to double the arrears. But of practical grievances we
hear little or nothing. The Athenian courts did their work well.
The advantage of having a sensible code to deal with was too

[1] Hicks and Hill, No. 32 (Erythrae), 40 (Chalcis, where there is no mention
of civil jurisdiction : it had already been regulated). On the Overseers or
Imperial Bishops (ἐπίσκοποι) see Wilamowitz, *Aus Kydathen*, p. 75, who thinks
they were not appointed to single cities but had dioceses. They are mentioned as ἄρχοντες in Thuc. i. 115. 5 (see Classen's note) : so they worked
in committees, not singly. If we knew more about them we could form
a safer estimate of the numbers of Imperial Civilians (see p. 175 above).
Antiphon, v. 47 (murder-cases). Beginning of a typical convention about
jurisdiction : Ar. *Birds* 1035, same date as Antiphon's speech.

[2] Chalcis decree (Hicks and Hill, No. 40, line 53) ; cf. Wilamowitz, *Aus
Kydathen*, p. 36, and *Hermes*, vol. xxii, p. 249. There is, however, no instance
of Athens going to war to avenge wrongs done to Athenian subjects for
non-payment of traders' debts.

great to be despised. Moreover, surely it was worth the expense to have a fortnight in the capital and to see how the imperial money was being laid out on the Acropolis. So the law courts brought sightseers ; the Parthenon and its great Vestibule proved the best of advertisements ; and the waggoners and the lodging-house keepers found their own businesses more profitable than sitting still and listening hard for their day's pay in the courts. It is not surprising on the whole, though the fact remains to their credit, that the Athenians were able to boast, without fear of contradiction, before a hostile assembly, of the impartiality of their justice. Indeed they quickly grew accustomed to the judicial mood, and would put on the judge's wig even when it was wholly inappropriate. ' Do remember,' begs a speaker in a difficult debate on policy, ' that you are not sitting in a law court thinking out what sentence these people have deserved, but sitting in Parliament to discover what course is best for your-selves.' Euripides makes a suppliant for Athenian aid put in a similar reminder, when Theseus had given him a long lecture from the Bench. For Athens took her own duties, as she took everything, very seriously, and did her best, in an imperfect world, however complicated the problem, to mete out fair decisions. Nor had the teachers of rhetoric yet appeared to cloud the plain citizen's common sense with their intellectual monkey tricks.[1]

Athens had thus become recognized as a model State ; and Greece was in the mood to adopt or imitate her ways in small things as in great. We can see this in the rapid spread of Athenian weights and measures and the Athenian coinage, or of systems arranged so as to work in with them. Athens was standardizing Greek coinage as she was unifying Greek law. She did not, of course, compel her allies to use only Attic money, or money coined on the Attic standard. But she naturally pre-ferred that contributions should be paid in it ; and there were indirect ways by which she could encourage it. It was only decent to pay Apollo, and later Athena, in the coinage they preferred to see. And as Athenian coins could always be relied on for good weight, and as the device upon them, the famous

---

[1] Old Oligarch, i. 17 fin. (where $\zeta\epsilon\hat{v}\gamma\sigma\varsigma$ means cart-animals, i. e. the Greek equivalent for cab-horses) ; Thuc. i. 77, iii. 44. 4 ; Eur. *Suppl.* 253, 341–2, 575.

owl, was so conveniently uncouth that you could tell it at
a glance, there was really no need for a compulsion which would
have been against the principle of free exchange. Example was
better than precept. Attic silver began to be known and used
not only in the Confederacy but all over Greece and among
distant barbarians. When Gylippus, after Aegospotami, kept
back some of the Spartan State booty, and hid it under his
roof tiles, the man who denounced him merely said that there
were 'owls in the potters' quarter'. In fact, much as the
Spartans hated strangers, and Athenians above all, there were
a great many such owls' nests all over their city.[1]

Athenian influence was thus spreading, as Pericles realized,
far beyond the Aegean and the confines of the Empire. Her
traders were moving East and West, finding their way into every
land and every sea, fetching goods, and paying for them in owls
or pottery, from the iron mines of Elba or the caravans at Gaza
and Cyrene. For this also was part of the imperial mission—to
mix freely with all mankind and to give of their best to men and
nations. Friendships were knit and alliances made with Greek,
and even with barbarian, powers without a thought of the
Persians or the original object of the league. For thirty years
indeed the Persian War was carried on, in a desultory manner
and with varying success. When peace was made in 448 Cyprus

[1] Ar. *Birds* 1040 (weights and measures). Cavaignac, pp. 177 ff., has
shown that there was no compulsion to pay tribute in Attic money till 414,
when (after the loss of the Thracian mines) it was tried and failed ; cf. *I. G.*
xii. 5. 480. There was no Athenian gold till 406 (Ar. *Frogs* 720), so the
electrum (i. e. pale gold) coins of Lampsacus and Cyzicus were in constant
use. See Wilamowitz, *Aus Kydathen*, p. 30, on why the sixth-century Attic
owl, reproduced on the cover of this book, ' remained untouched by the art
of Pheidias.' Any one who has lived in a country where many different kinds
of coinage circulate (though no modern country, not even Germany before
the Zollverein, could compare with ancient Greece) will appreciate the advantages of a standard weight and an easily recognizable coin type. The
money-changers along the quays of Levantine ports were much the same
then as now. Many a newly arrived traveller has felt inclined to kick over
their tables. There are some interesting modern parallels. Maria Theresa
dollars, dated 1766, are still being coined for use in Abyssinia and Arabia.
Compare the Indian native states, where the imperial and local coins and
stamps (the railways being imperial there is generally an imperial letter-box
at the railway station) circulate side by side, and standardization is proceeding gradually without the exercise of compulsion. The same is of course
true of subordinate languages, though, fortunately, it is easier to speak two
languages than to use two coin-systems. Owls at Sparta : Plut. *Lys.* 16 ;
Plato, *Alc.* 122 E (Horace's ' vestigia nulla retrorsum '). [See Appendix.]

was still ' enslaved '. But in the course of a generation freedom
had changed its meaning; and Pericles did not feel ashamed
to make a convention with the national enemy, or even to receive
for the league and put away in its exchequer the contributions
of Carians and Lycians. Athens had now become an Empire
just like Persia or Assyria, and she did not blush to receive
tribute from her inferiors. Indeed she needed it for the fulfil-
ment of the work she had to do : and Pericles, like Darius, was
determined to see that she should secure and keep it. Already
in 454, when nearly the whole Athenian fleet had been destroyed
in Egypt and the Aegean was for a moment exposed to pirates
and Phoenicians, it was thought wiser to remove the treasury
of the allies from Delos to Athens. Ostensibly this meant no
more than a change of banker, Athena taking the place of Apollo.
But, practically, the result was to remove it once and for all
from the control of the Confederate Parliament, and to make
every one see and feel, what they had known in their hearts long
ago, that it was the money of Athens, with which she could do
what she liked. The world is still blessing her for what she did
with it.[1]

When peace was made with Persia in 448 there was indeed a
small party of ' Little Athenians ' who urged that the alliance
should be dissolved and the contributions returned. Athens had
no right to spend the money on herself ' as a proud and vain
woman decks herself out with jewels '. But their protests passed
unheeded, and their leader was sent into exile for his troublesome
conscientiousness. Plain facts were too strong. Athens could no
more step back than most Englishmen feel they can leave India.
She had woken up to find herself an Empire and was resolved
to play the part. So Pericles set about the first avowedly
imperial piece of organization, and divided the Empire into
Provinces for the more convenient collection of tribute. From

[1] Etruscan tombs are full of fifth-century Athenian vases. Samson's Gaza
(Herodotus's Cadytis) altered its coin standard to make it fit in with that of
Athens (Meyer, iii, § 85). Extra-imperial alliances : Segesta, 454 ; Rhegium
and Leontini, both 433–2 (Hicks and Hill, Nos. 51, 52) ; Naples, probably
438. Relations with Barbarians : Italian chief, Thuc. vii. 33 (an Athenian
' consul ') ; Sicilian chief, vii. 1. 4 ; Thracian prince given Athenian citizenship, ii. 29. 5. Inside the Empire proper : see ' Quota lists ' in Hill's *Sources*,
e. g. Λύκιοι καὶ συντελεῖς in that for 446. These lists do not give the contributions themselves but only Athena's ' commission '.

the year 443 onwards Athena's invoices show the names neatly grouped under five heads—contributions from Ionia, from the Hellespont, from Thrace, from Caria, and from the Islands : those from the Black Sea ports, which were not in the original assessment, are separately classified. This money was what Athens lived on, and still partly lives on. ' It may seem wickedness to have won it ; it is quite certainly folly to let it go.' [1]

But this is looking forward. For the men of these two generations of empire-building were not conscious of any wickedness. They were too busy with their work. If they stopped to think at all, as they rested on their oars, it was to reflect on the joy of achievement and how ' all things worked together for good '. For this it is which makes this short half-century perhaps the greatest and happiest period in recorded history. The world was moving onwards with extraordinary swiftness, bearing on its bosom, like a strong river in flood, all that lay within its track. And how much that was ! ' Freedom, Law, and Progress ; Truth and Beauty ; Knowledge and Virtue ; Humanity and Religion ; high things, the conflicts between which have caused most of the disruptions and despondencies of human societies, seemed all to lie in the same direction.' The men who were inspired by these greatest of human watchwords felt as yet no misgivings. They knew their work was right, that it was well and soundly laid, and that posterity would understand it.

For, though the material they worked in was the lives of men and nations, they were still Greeks and still artists ; and with the joyousness of the creator, whether in words or institutions, they banished every whisper which could reason them into unhappiness or break up, even for a moment, the harmonious pattern of their life. It was indeed very illogical of Sophocles to hymn eternal justice in his *Oedipus* and yet to take office without a scruple as

[1] Thuc. ii. 63. 2 (Pericles facing facts), ii. 65. 13 (Pericles' way of ' thinking imperially ' was to think in figures). Lovers of Thucydides will enjoy trying to detect Pericles' own phrases in the speeches : ἐρασταὶ τῆς πόλεως is certainly one (cf. Thuc. vi. 13. 1 δυσέρωτας, 24. 3, and Ar. *Ach.* 143, *Knights* 732, 1341). Another is δόξα ἀείμνηστος καταλείπεται (like Cicero's *esse videatur*), ii. 43, ii. 64. 5. We should understand the later speeches better if we caught all the ironical allusions to Pericles' plans and phrases. Plut. *Per.* 12 (arguments of the Opposition). For the classified tribute-lists see Hill's *Sources*, pp. 43 ff., and p. 156 (Black Sea fragment) ; also Cavaignac, xl–xliii, and his *Histoire de l'Antiquité*, ii. 16, who has restored one in its entirety eking out gaps from neighbouring lists, and Woodward, *B. S. A.* xv. 243 ff., on the list for 427–6.

a misappropriator of imperial funds. It was very illogical of the
Sovereign People to entice sister communities into a league of
liberty and then to punish them for their withdrawal—as illogical
as for Burke, imbued with the spirit of a later Empire, to declare
about the American Colonies that ' the more ardently they love
liberty the more perfect will be their obedience '. But such contradictions passed unnoticed by all but a few keen-sighted seers,
not merely because Athens wished and tried to champion freedom—this alone would not have sufficed to seal the eyes of her
citizens—but because, while they were serving her with ' the
fighter's daring, the wise man's understanding, and the good
man's self-discipline ', they felt free within themselves—free
and light-hearted and confident and incapable of doing
wrong.[1]

They had neither the leisure nor the desire, any more than
eighteenth-century Englishmen, to invent an imperial theory of
their own. But Thucydides, writing when most of what was
mortal in their work had already crumbled into dust, invented
one for them. It sounds absurd and vainglorious, as imperial
theories always do, to a critical posterity ; yet if the dead
could rise from the Cerameicus, or if their grave reliefs could
find voices, they would bear out, albeit with modesty, the analysis
of their historian. ' We are the leaders of civilization, the
pioneers of the human race. Our society and intercourse is the
highest blessing man can confer. To be within the circle of
our influence is not dependence but a privilege. Not all the
wealth of the East can repay the riches we bestow. So we can
work on cheerfully, using the means and money that flow in to
us, confident that, try as they will, we shall still be creditors.
For through effort and suffering and on many a stricken field we
have found out the secret of human power, which is the secret of
happiness. Men have guessed at it under many names ; but we
alone have learnt to know it and to make it at home in our city.

[1] Murray, *Euripides*, p. xxiii. Sophocles was Imperial Treasurer in 443,
just at the very time when the money began to be used for city purposes.
See p. 410 below. The members of the allied cities with whom the Athenians
would be chiefly brought into contact were the poorer classes, who served
for good pay as hired rowers on the Athenian triremes and were probably
' as enthusiastic for Athens as the Rhineland and Italian troops were for
Napoleon ' (private letter from Arnold J. Toynbee). This blinded Athens to
the feelings of the wealthier classes, who paid the bulk of the tribute.

And the name we know it by is Freedom, for it has taught us that to serve is to be free. Do you wonder why it is that " alone among mankind " (will there ever be another nation which can understand what we mean ?) " we confer our benefits, not on calculations of self-interest, but in the fearless confidence of Freedom " ?'

CHAPTER VIII

THE IDEAL OF CITIZENSHIP

HAPPINESS, OR THE RULE OF LOVE

(εὐδαιμονία)

ΚΗΡΥΞ. Πράσσειν σὺ πόλλ᾽ εἴωθας ἥ τε σὴ πόλις.
ΘΗΣΕΥΣ. τοιγὰρ πονοῦσα πολλὰ πόλλ᾽ εὐδαιμονεῖ.

> EURIPIDES, *Supplices* 576–7.

Τὸ εὔδαιμον τὸ ἐλεύθερον, τὸ δὲ ἐλεύθερον τὸ εὔψυχον κρίναντες.—PERICLES.

Was ist gut, fragt ihr? Tapfer sein ist gut.—NIETZSCHE, *Zarathustra, Vom Krieg und Kriegsvolke.*

> More brave for this that he hath much to love.
> WORDSWORTH, *The Happy Warrior.*

ONLY a few words are necessary before Thucydides speaks for himself.

Thucydides did not belong to the two generations of Empire builders. He was born just after them, and his personal memory went no further back than the peace of 445. So he shared the ideals of the age with his older contemporaries, but in a less instinctive fashion. Like them, he knew that he was living in great times. But, more thoughtful than they, he desired to record them ; for he knew, as they knew if they ever lay awake thinking, that this glory could not last and that posterity would be glad to read of it. But he little suspected *how* brief the blossom would be, or that, in his own short lifetime, he would yet see autumn and midwinter.[1]

---

[1] For Thucydides' life see Murray's *Ancient Greek Literature* and (for detailed evidence) Classen's Introduction to his edition ; also the four close-packed pages in Wilamowitz, *Platon*, vol. ii, 12–16, Berlin, 1919. The date of his book is not known. He was old enough in 431 to form a settled determination to write a history of the war (i. 1), yet young enough to learn 'style' from the Sophists. If, as I believe, he is thinking of himself when he speaks of the ardent young men in Athens in 431 (ii. 8), he cannot have been born much before 460. This agrees with ii. 65. 5 (putting the comma, as in the Oxford text, after εἰρήνῃ), where he confines his general verdict on Pericles to the later half of his career. He is very reserved about himself : e. g. he does not say who was responsible for his exile (v. 26. 5), or that he was very nearly recalled in 411 (viii. 70. 1) : he died not later than 396, probably after

Yet it was in midwinter, when the Long Walls had been dismantled and the Acropolis had housed a Spartan garrison, that he wrote his eulogy of the city in the form (what form could be more appropriate ?) of a speech over her noble dead. It is not, of course, the speech which Pericles delivered, or even, as the speaker hints, the kind of speech usually given on such occasions. There is too little in it about noble ancestors, and too much about the present day. But there is no reason to doubt that Thucydides had heard his hero speak, most probably more than once, over the city's fallen soldiers, and could recall in after years among his most sacred recollections, ' the cadence of his voice, the movement of his hand,' and the solemn hush of the vast audience, broken only by ' the sobbing of some mother of the dead.' We may feel with confidence that he has given us, with the added colour of his own experience, not merely the inner thought but much of the language of Pericles. So that here we can listen, as in all fine works of interpretation, to two great spirits at once ; and when we have learnt to use our ears we can sometimes hear them both, Pericles' voice coming through, a little faint and thin after the lapse of years, above the deep tones of the historian.[1]

The speech is written, if ever writing was, ' not in ink but in blood.' For with Thucydides, more perhaps than with any other great writer, there is not a word but *tells*. ' You must read and mark him line by line till you can read between the lines as clearly as in them. There are few thinkers with so many ideas brooding in the background.' All great art is like a ghost seeking to express more than it can utter and beckoning to regions beyond. This is as true in history, which deals with nations, as in poetry or any more personal art. That is why the Funeral Speech, written of a small provincial city in the untried youth of the world, will always find an echo

399, if, as Classen thinks probable, viii. 68. 2 contains a covert reference to the death of Socrates. Pericles knew after the Plague that Empires, like men, fade and die (ii. 64. 3 πάντα γὰρ πέφυκε καὶ ἐλαττοῦσθαι). But he does not sound this note in the earlier speeches. [See Appendix.]

[1] Wallas, *Human Nature in Politics*, p. 73. The Funeral Speech which Athenians remembered best was that delivered by Pericles in 439 at the end of the Samian War.—1921. Wilamowitz, *loc. cit.*, agrees with the view expressed above that the Funeral Speech was written late in Thucydides' life—was, in fact, the last piece he wrote.

whenever men and nations are living true to themselves, whether in the trenches of Mukden or in the cemetery of Gettysburg. Pericles and Abraham Lincoln were not very much alike. But common needs beget a common language ; and great statesmen, like great poets, speak to one another from peak to peak.

Let us stand in the valley and listen : [1]

(34) In the same winter, following the law of their fathers, the Athenians held the first public funeral of those who had fallen in the war. The ceremony is as follows. The bones of the dead are exposed on a covered platform for three days, during which any one may place his personal offerings at their side. On the third day they are laid in ten coffins of cypress wood, one for each tribe, every man's bones in the coffin of his tribe ; these are put on carriages and driven to the grave. One empty bed covered with a winding sheet is also borne for the missing whose bodies were not recovered for bur ing.[2] All who so desire, whether citizens or strangers, may join in the procession, and the women folk of the dead are at the graveside bewailing them. The interment takes place in the State burial ground, which is situated in the most beautiful suburb of the city. All Athenians who have died in war lie buried there, except those who fell at Marathon [3] ; their valour was adjudged so conspicuous that the funeral was held on the field of battle. When the coffins have been laid in the earth some speaker elected by the city for his wisdom and public estimation delivers an appropriate eulogy ; after this the gathering disperses. This is the customary ceremonial, and it was adhered to throughout the

[1] The quotation is from Nietzsche's penetrating chapter on ' What I owe to the Ancients ' (in ' Götzendämmerung ', Works, vol. viii). The extraordinary resemblance between Lincoln's speech at Gettysburg and Pericles' has often been noticed. The speech is printed in Lincoln's Speeches in the Everyman Library. I have translated from the text printed in Wilamowitz's Greek Reader, as I prefer it to the Oxford text. The most important differences are that Wilamowitz reads ἥκειν for οἰκεῖν in 37. 1, ἕτεροι ἕτερα in 40. 2, αὐτοί for οἱ αὐτοί three lines later, and ᾑρημένοι for ἡγησάμενοι in 42, four lines from end. I have mostly followed Wilamowitz's paragraphing : the bracketed numbers mark the chapters in Thucydides. I have added a few notes, some pointing to storms ahead. Thucydides could not restrain his irony even when Pericles was talking.

[2] One empty bed : compare the cenotaph at Westminster, unveiled, alas, without either a Pericles or a Lincoln.

[3] Those who fell at Marathon : The Athenians who fell at Plataea were buried on the battle-field too (Hdt. ix. 85), but this does not count as an Athenian but as an All-Greek battle.

war whenever occasion arose. It was at the funeral of this first group of fallen that Pericles the son of Xanthippus was elected to speak. When the moment came, he stepped forward from the graveside on to a high platform made for the occasion, so that his voice might carry as far as possible over the crowd, and spoke as follows :—

(35) Most of those who have stood in this place before me have commended the institution of this closing address. It is good, they have felt, that solemn words should be spoken over our fallen soldiers. I do not share this feeling. Acts deserve acts, not words, in their honour, and to me a burial at the State's charges, such as you see before you, would have appeared sufficient. Our sense of the deserts of a number of our fellow-citizens should not depend upon the felicity of one man's speech. Moreover, it is very hard for a speaker to be appropriate when many of his hearers will scarce believe that he is truthful. For those who have known and loved the dead may think his words scant justice to the memories they would hear honoured : while those who do not know will occasionally, from jealousy, suspect me of overstatement when they hear of any feat beyond their own powers. For it is only human for men not to bear praise of others beyond the point at which they still feel that they can rival their exploits. Transgress that boundary and they are jealous and distrustful. But since the wisdom of our ancestors enacted this law I too must submit and try to suit as best I can the wishes and feelings of every member of this gathering.[1]

---

[1] *Our sense . . . distrustful* (lines 13 to 24). Steup has pointed out (Classen's fourth ed., p. 221) that the thought of this passage does not dovetail in with the rest of the chapter. To ' speak appropriately ' in spite of the incredulity of the audience is one thing, to ' try to suit the wishes and feeling of every member of it ' is another. So he suggests that the passage is a later addition. *Pericles'* difficulty was to fit his ' advanced ' ideas to the conservative atmosphere of the ceremonial, which he meets, for instance, by damning the ' ancestors ' in two sentences of faint praise. (See Isocrates' *Panathenaicus* for the paint he might have laid on.) But as Thucydides read through his first draft he became conscious of *his own difficulty* in making his readers believe what the Athenian Empire had once been like. So he patched a preface of his own on to the brief opening remarks he had written for Pericles, but did not quite hide the join. Thus read, the chapter becomes full of meaning. *It is only human* : a curious little illustration of the glorious self-confidence of the fifth-century Athenian. Writers of modern ' appreciations ' do not need to be afraid of thus hurting their readers' feelings.

(36) My first words shall be for our ancestors ; for it is both just to them and seemly that on an occasion such as this our tribute of memory should be paid them. For, dwelling always in this country, generation after generation in unchanging and unbroken succession, they have handed it down to us free by their exertions. So they are worthy of our praises ; and still more so are our fathers. For they enlarged the ancestral patrimony by the Empire which we hold to-day and delivered it, not without labour, into the hands of our own generation ; while it is we ourselves, those of us who are now in middle life, who consolidated our power throughout the greater part of the Empire and secured the city's complete independence both in war and peace.[1] Of the battles which we and our fathers fought, whether in the winning of our power abroad or in bravely withstanding the warfare of barbarian or Greek at home, I do not wish to say more : they are too familiar to you all.[2] I wish rather to set forth the spirit in which we faced them, and the constitution and manners with which we rose to greatness, and to pass from them to the dead ; for I think it not unfitting that these things should be called to mind at to-day's solemnity, and expedient too that the whole gathering of citizens and strangers should listen to them.

(37) For our government is not copied from those of our neighbours [3] : we are an example to them rather than they to

[1] *Complete independence* : there is something like a quibble here on the word 'independence'. Its natural meaning is economic independence, i. e. a city is 'independent' when it grows its own corn, wine, timber for shipping, flax for sails, &c. In this sense Athens, which, like England, was dependent for its existence on foreign supplies, was the least independent city in Greece, as is pointed out in chapter 38. But by the 'consolidation' of her Empire, i. e. by exercising her sea-power, she was able to control the trade in necessaries. Note the careful distinction between (1) Ancestors, before Athens 'woke up', (2) the first or Marathon generation of Empire-builders, (3) the second generation (Pericles' own), who were rather traders. He omits to mention that (3) had lost some of the possessions handed down by (2), as the Quota lists show. They had made up for it by trade.

[2] *Familiar to you all* : very much so in the autumn of 431, with the Peloponnesian army just home from Attica. Hence the vague expression (emended by some editors) 'withstanding the warfare'. Both in 480 and in 431 Athenians withstood the warfare, but not the enemy in person.

[3] *Not copied from those of our neighbours* : a reference to the Spartans, who were not quite sure whether their constitution came from Crete or from Delphi. The next few chapters are full of covert references to Sparta, the home of Discipline, where men were afraid of Freedom and Originality, and to Corinth, the home of Licence, where men cared only for Riches. Possibly a few of the audience might remember that, about twelve years before, some

us. Our constitution is named a democracy, because it is in the hands not of the few but of the many. But our laws secure equal justice for all in their private disputes, and our public opinion welcomes and honours talent in every branch of achievement, not for any sectional reason but on grounds of excellence alone. And as we give free play to all in our public life, so we carry the same spirit into our daily relations with one another. We have no black looks or angry words for our neighbour if he enjoys himself in his own way, and we abstain from the little acts of churlishness which, though they leave no mark, yet cause annoyance to whoso notes them. Open and friendly in our private intercourse, in our public acts we keep strictly within the control of law. We acknowledge the restraint of reverence ; we are obedient to whomsoever is set in authority, and to the laws, more especially to those which offer protection to the oppressed and those unwritten ordinances whose transgression brings admitted shame. (38) Yet ours is no work-a-day city only. No other provides so many recreations for the spirit— contests and sacrifices all the year round, and beauty in our public buildings to cheer the heart and delight the eye day by day. Moreover, the city is so large and powerful that all the wealth of all the world flows in to her, so that our own Attic products seem no more homelike to us than the fruits of the labours of other nations.[1]

(39) Our military training too is different from our opponents'. The gates of our city are flung open to the world. We practise no periodical deportations, nor do we prevent our visitors from observing or discovering what an enemy might usefully apply to his own purposes. For our trust is not in the devices of material equipment, but in our own good spirits for battle.[2]

ambassadors had come from a barbarian city called Rome to learn about the Athenian laws, many of which they embodied in their own code (Meyer, iii, § 370).

[1] This paragraph contains the only mention of official religion in the whole speech. Note how it is sandwiched in amongst athletics, architecture, and commerce. For the meaning of ἰδίαις in the text see Wilamowitz's note.

[2] *Our trust is not in the devices of material equipment.* This seems to be contradicted by Pericles' words, i. 142. 9 : ' If anything is a matter of skill, it is seamanship ' ; and 7 : ' You have been practising seamanship ever since the Persian wars and are not perfect at it yet. How can a lot of farmers make any headway against us on sea ? ' Athenians got constant practice in seamanship in the warships kept afloat and in the Merchant Service (see Old Oligarch, i. 20 and Thuc. iii. 115. 4).

So too with education. They toil from early boyhood in a laborious pursuit after courage, while we, free to live and wander as we please, march out none the less to face the self-same dangers.[1] Here is the proof of my words. When the Spartans advance into our country, they do not come alone but with all their allies; but when we invade our neighbours we have little difficulty as a rule, even on foreign soil, in defeating men who are fighting for their own homes. Moreover, no enemy has ever met us in full strength, for we have our navy to attend to, and our soldiers are sent on service to many scattered possessions; but if they chance to encounter some portion of our forces and defeat a few of us, they boast that they have driven back our whole army, or, if they are defeated, that the victors were in full strength. Indeed, if we choose to face danger with an easy mind rather than after a rigorous training, and to trust rather in native manliness than in state-made courage, the advantage lies with us; for we are spared all the weariness of practising for future hardships, and when we find ourselves amongst them we are as brave as our plodding rivals. Here as elsewhere, then, the city sets an example which is deserving of admiration. (40) We are lovers of beauty without extravagance, and lovers of wisdom without unmanliness. Wealth to us is not mere material for vainglory but an opportunity for achievement; and poverty we think it no disgrace to acknowledge but a real degradation to make no effort to overcome. Our citizens attend both to public and private duties, and do not allow absorption in their own various affairs to interfere with their knowledge of the city's. We differ from other states in regarding the man who holds aloof from public life not as ' quiet ' but as useless;[2] we decide or debate, carefully and in person, all matters of policy, holding, not that words and deeds go ill together, but that acts are foredoomed to failure when undertaken undiscussed. For we are noted for being at once most adventurous in action and most reflective before-

[1] *March out none the less*: this was just what Pericles would not let them do until the enemy had retired home. So he pulls himself up and gives a rather weak explanation of what he meant.

[2] *Not as ' quiet ' but as useless*: these are the Mugwumps or small minority of Athenians who undertake no public service. ' Quiet ' ($ἀπράγμονες$) is what they like to call themselves as opposed to political ' busybodies '. But the fifth-century Athenians were proud of being busybodies (see Thuc. i. 70, and the chapter motto from Euripides).

hand. Other men are bold in ignorance, while reflection will
stop their onset. But the bravest are surely those who have the
clearest vision of what is before them, glory and danger alike, and
yet notwithstanding go out to meet it. In doing good, too, we
are the exact opposite of the rest of mankind. We secure our
friends not by accepting favours but by doing them. And so we
are naturally more firm in our attachments : [1] for we are anxious,
as creditors, to cement by kind offices our relation towards our
friends. If they do not respond with the same warmness it is
because they feel that their services will not be given spontaneously but only as the repayment of a debt.[2] We are alone
among mankind in doing men benefits, not on calculations of
self-interest, but in the fearless confidence of freedom. (41) In
a word I claim that our city as a whole is an education to Greece,
and that her members yield to none, man by man, for independence of spirit, many-sidedness of attainment, and complete
self-reliance in limbs and brain.

That this is no vainglorious phrase but actual fact the supremacy which our manners have won us itself bears testimony.
No other city of the present day goes out to her ordeal greater
than ever men dreamed ; no other is so powerful that the
invader feels no bitterness when he suffers at her hands, and
her subjects no shame at the indignity of their dependence.[3]
Great indeed are the symbols and witnesses of our supremacy,
at which posterity, as all mankind to-day, will be astonished.
We need no Homer or other man of words to praise us ; for
such give pleasure for a moment, but the truth will put to
shame their imaginings of our deeds. For our pioneers have
forced a way into every sea and every land, establishing among
all mankind, in punishment or beneficence, eternal memorials of
their settlement.[4]

[1] *More firm in our attachments* : so much so that the ' friends ' cannot
shake off the tie, but become subjects.

[2] *The repayment of a debt* : at the beginning of the Peloponnesian War
this was being repaid, in the form of tribute, at the rate of about 600 talents
a year.

[3] *Her subjects no shame at the indignity of their dependence.* This is Pericles'
theory of imperialism. The Empire is based, not on justice (as between
equals) but on sentiment ; not on rights secured to the other cities, but on the
admiring loyalty they ought to feel. If they do not happen to feel it, he has
nothing to fall back upon but naked force.

[4] *Establishing in punishment or beneficence eternal memorials of their settle-*

Such then is the city for whom, lest they should lose her, the men whom we celebrate died a soldier's death : and it is but natural that all of us, who survive them, should wish to spend ourselves in her service. (42) That, indeed, is why I have spent many words upon the city. I wished to show that we have more at stake than men who have no such inheritance, and to support my praise of the dead by making clear to you what they have done. For if I have chanted the glories of the city it was these men and their like who set hand to array her. With them, as with few among Greeks, words cannot magnify the deeds that they have done. Such an end as we have here seems indeed to show us what a good life is, from its first signs of power to its final consummation.[1] For even where life's previous record showed faults and failures it is just to weigh the last brave hour of devotion against them all.[2] There they wiped out evil with good and did the city more service as soldiers than they did her harm in private life. There no hearts grew faint because they loved riches more than honour; none shirked the issue in the poor man's dreams of wealth. All these they put aside to strike a blow for the city. Counting the quest to avenge her honour as the most glorious of all ventures, and leaving Hope, the uncertain goddess, to send them what she would, they faced the foe as they drew near him in the strength of their own manhood; and when the shock of battle came, they chose rather to suffer the uttermost than to win life by weakness.[3] So their memory has escaped the reproaches of men's lips, but they bore instead on their bodies the marks of men's hands, and in a moment of time, at the climax of their lives, were rapt away

ment : he is thinking chiefly of the settlements of Athenian citizens among barbarians in Thrace and elsewhere. Whether the barbarians remembered them kindly depended on the reception they gave to the colonists on their first arrival.

[1] *What a good life is.* This is the subject of Aristotle's *Ethics*, which is often taken as giving the standard Greek view on Virtue or the good life. But of course Thucydides is a much better authority for the fifth-century Greeks.

[2] *The last brave hour* : compare the parable of the Labourers in the Vineyard.

[3] *To suffer the uttermost rather than to win life by weakness* : he does not pretend that, like the Christian martyrs, they died joyfully : only they feel that they could not die at a better moment or in a better way. He is describing what he had himself experienced, the feelings of a heavy-armed soldier in the long-drawn moments just before the close fighting began.

from a world filled, for their dying eyes, not with terror but with glory.

(43) Such were the men who lie here and such the city that inspired them. We survivors may pray to be spared their bitter hour, but must disdain to meet the foe with a spirit less triumphant. Let us draw strength, not merely from twice-told arguments—how fair and noble a thing it is to show courage in battle—but from the busy spectacle of our great city's life as we have it before us day by day, falling in love with her as we see her, and remembering that all this greatness she owes to men with the fighter's daring, the wise man's understanding of his duty, and the good man's self-discipline in its performance—to men who, if they failed in any ordeal, disdained to deprive the city of their services, but sacrificed their lives as the best offerings on her behalf. So they gave their bodies to the commonwealth and received, each for his own memory, praise that will never die, and with it the grandest of all sepulchres, not that in which their mortal bones are laid, but a home in the minds of men, where their glory remains fresh to stir to speech or action as the occasion comes by. For the whole earth is the sepulchre of famous men ; and their story is not graven only on stone over their native earth, but lives on far away, without visible symbol, woven into the stuff of other men's lives. For you now it remains to rival what they have done and, knowing the secret of happiness to be freedom and the secret of freedom a brave heart, not idly to stand aside from the enemy's onset.[1] For it is not the poor and luckless, as having no hope of prosperity, who have most cause to reckon death as little loss, but those for whom fortune may yet keep reversal in store and who would feel the change most if trouble befell them. Moreover, weakly to decline the trial is more painful to a man of spirit than death coming sudden and unperceived in the hour of strength and enthusiasm.

(44) Therefore I do not mourn with the parents of the dead who are here with us. I will rather comfort them. For they

---

[1] *Not idly to stand aside* : this is exactly what the Athenians had just been forced to do during the Peloponnesian invasion of Attica. See Thuc. ii. 21. 2, where the same word (περιορᾶν) is used by the younger men against Pericles. The word means to look on while others are acting—the peculiar privilege of critics. It is what the later Greeks (e. g. in the Roman age) were especially good at.

know that they have been born into a world of manifold chances
and that he is to be accounted happy to whom the best lot falls—
the best sorrow, such as is yours to-day, or the best death, such
as fell to these, for whom life and happiness were cut to the
self-same measure.[1] I know it is not easy to give you comfort.
I know how often in the joy of others you will have reminders of
what was once your own, and how men feel sorrow, not for the
loss of what they have never tasted, but when something that has
grown dear to them has been snatched away. But you must keep
a brave heart in the hope of other children, those who are still of
age to bear them. For the new-comers will help you to forget
the gap in your own circle, and will help the city to fill up the
ranks of its workers and its soldiers.[2] For no man is fitted to
give fair and honest advice in council if he has not, like his
fellows, a family at stake in the hour of the city's danger.[3]
To you who are past the age of vigour I would say : count the
long years of happiness so much gain to set off against the brief
space that yet remains, and let your burden be lightened by the
glory of the dead. For the love of honour alone is not staled
by age, and it is by honour, not, as some say, by gold, that the
helpless end of life is cheered.

(45) I turn to those amongst you who are children or brothers
of the fallen, for whom I foresee a mighty contest with the
memory of the dead. Their praise is in all men's mouths, and
hardly, even for supremest heroism, you will be adjudged to have
achieved, not the same but a little less than they. For the
living have the jealousy of rivals to contend with, but the dead
are honoured with unchallenged admiration.[4]

If I must also speak a word to those who are now in widowhood on the powers and duties of women, I will cast all my
advice into one brief sentence. Great will be your glory if you

[1] *Cut to the self-same measure.* This is exactly what Solon told Croesus
in the famous parable (Hdt. i. 32).
[2] *To fill up the ranks.* See the population figures on p. 174 and pp. 415–18.
Athena missed every one of her dead.
[3] *If he has not . . . a family at stake.* No one could be a Councillor till he
was over 30, when he was almost certain to be married ; and, according to
the orator Deinarchus (§ 71), no man was allowed to speak in the national
Parliament until he had legitimate male issue.
[4] *The jealousy of rivals,* &c. : this sentiment is used by Alcibiades (vi. 16. 5),
in one of his many shameless adaptations of Periclean expressions, as an
excuse for getting into debt over horse-races.

do not lower the nature that is within you—hers greatest of all
whose praise or blame is least bruited on the lips of men.[1]

(46) I have spoken such words as I had to say according as the
law prescribes, and the graveside offerings to the dead have been
duly made.   Henceforward the city will take charge of their
children till manhood : such is the crown and benefit she holds
out to the dead and to their kin for the trials they have under-
gone for her.   For where the prize is highest, there, too, are the
best citizens to contend for it.

And now, when you have finished your lamentation, let each
of you depart.

.   .   .   .

It is time for us to depart too.   We have lingered too long in
the public place.   Let us follow the mourners as they disperse to
their separate homes, and watch them as they resume the even
tenour of their lives.   There is more of tragedy for us there than
among the graves of the soldiers.   These lived happy and died
happy, fighting the enemies of Athena.   But in the contest which
we are going to watch fighting will bring no joy and victory no
triumph.   For the battle which Athens has now to face is not
against the Lacedaemonians or any hosts of armoured men, but
against the foe in her own household, the desires and ambitions
she herself has nurtured.[2]   Shall she welcome them in their
fulness and seek to furnish them with all they need ?   Or shall
she try to put them from her, lest they corrupt her and wreck her
peace ?   Or, while she is seeking a middle course, will they lay
her glory in the dust ?

[1] *Least bruited* : i. e. women should be seen and not heard.   This was the
ordinary fifth-century view ; for citizens' wives were not citizens, or even
resident aliens.   It was only on sufferance that they formed part of this
audience.

[2] Thuc. v. 91 ἔστι δὲ οὐ πρὸς Λακεδαιμονίους ἡμῖν ὁ ἀγών : Aesch. *Ag.* 717–18

PART III. ECONOMICS

Φιλοκαλοῦμεν μετ' εὐτελείας.
We are lovers of beauty without extravagance.

CHAPTER I

POVERTY

Il y a deux sortes de peuples pauvres : ceux que la dureté du gouvernement a rendu tels ; et ces gens-là sont incapables de presque aucune vertu, parce que leur pauvreté fait une partie de leur servitude : les autres ne sont pauvres que parce qu'ils ont dédaigné, ou parce qu'ils n'ont pas connu, les commodités de la vie ; et ceux-ci peuvent faire de grandes choses, parce que cette pauvreté fait une partie de leur liberté.—MONTESQUIEU, *Esprit des Lois*, Book xx, chap. 3.

There are two sorts of poor people : those whom 'the harshness of government has impoverished, who are incapable of almost any virtue, because their poverty is part of their servitude ; and those who are only poor because they have disdained or never known the comforts of life, and can achieve great things because their poverty is part of their liberty.

Τῇ Ἑλλάδι πενίη μὲν αἰεί κοτε σύντροφός ἐστι.—HERODOTUS, vii. 102.

Hellas and Poverty have always been foster-sisters.

ONE of the most important facts about life is that human beings cannot get on without food, clothing, and shelter. Most modern men regard it as the most important fact of all, and spend most of the waking hours of a brief lifetime in trying to deal with it. The Greeks did not agree with them. It was too dull and monotonous and obvious to take precedence over the other great shining truths which life reveals to those that seek them. But they faced it, as they faced all the facts of life, and put it in its place side by side with them. They even gave their preoccupation with it a name, which has stuck to it ever since ; they called it Housekeeping or Economics.

'Political Economy or Economics,' says its leading English exponent, ' is a study of mankind in the ordinary business of life ; it examines that part of individual and social action which is most closely associated with the attainment and with the use of the material requisites of well-being.' [1] To this a fifth-century Greek would nod assent, with two reservations. Why *ordinary* business of life ? Is not business' done for the community, drilling and fighting and sitting in judgement, quite as ordinary ? So he would move to read ' private ' instead of ' ordinary ',

[1] Opening words of Marshall's *Principles of Economics*.

'private' bearing in his mind a slight suspicion of eccentricity. For he knew very well that a man who practises politics and ignores housekeeping, though he may possibly starve, at least remains sane and companionable; while men who ignored the world around them and thought only of their own four walls, were bound to degenerate into egotists. His other reservation would refer to the *or* in the opening words 'political economy *or* economics'. You may keep house for yourself, or help keep house for the city; but they are not the same thing. The one concerns individual action for individual well-being, the other concerns social action for social well-being. Of course there is a direct connexion between them and even an overlapping of the two spheres. You cannot have individual well-being, as Pericles told the Athenians in his lecture on economics, when the whole community is broken up, and you cannot have social well-being in full measure (though you may have it in part) when individuals are doing badly. But it will be better for us to follow the ordinary Greek practice and keep the two chains of activity distinct,—to think of Economics as the study first of individual and then of State housekeeping, according to its double object, the attainment and use of the material requisites of private and of public well-being.[1]

We have seen the Athenian as a citizen. It is time to look at him as an earner. For we shall not understand fifth-century Athens until we know the material requisites on which her well-being rested and have watched how they helped or hindered her in living the life of her ideals.

But two general warnings are necessary before we can allow our imagination to draw the picture in detail.

The first concerns the incredible poverty of the world in which we shall be moving.

We think of the Greeks as the pioneers of civilization, and unconsciously credit them with the material blessings and com-

[1] Thuc. ii. 60 (cf. Soph. *Ant.* 187–91), Pericles was fond of lecturing the Athenians on economics. See the lecturer's trick (σκέψασθε δέ) in i. 143. 5. They let him do it because they knew he was 'straight' (χρημάτων κρείσσων). ἰδιώτης, 'private citizen' or 'a man in his private capacity' gradually came to mean the same as Pericles' ἀχρεῖος or 'useless' 'anti-social' man. It corresponds to our 'egotist' or 'monomaniac'; but while the Greeks condemned a man for ignoring everything but his household, we generally only condemn people for ignoring every one but themselves.

forts in which we moderns have been taught, and are trying to teach Asiatics and Africans, to think that civilization consists. We forget that they were more innocent of most of these than the up-country Greeks of to-day, or than most Englishmen were before the Industrial Revolution. It is easy to think away railways and telegraphs and gasworks and tea and advertisements and bananas. But we must peel off far more than this. We must imagine houses without drains, beds without sheets or springs, rooms as cold, or as hot, as the open air, only draughtier, meals that began and ended with pudding, and cities that could boast neither gentry nor millionaires. We must learn to tell the time without watches, to cross rivers without bridges, and seas without a compass, to fasten our clothes (or rather our two pieces of cloth) with two pins instead of rows of buttons, to wear our shoes or sandals without stockings, to warm ourselves over a pot of ashes, to judge open-air plays or lawsuits on a cold winter's morning, to study poetry without books, geography without maps, and politics without newspapers. In a word we must learn how to be civilized without being comfortable. Or rather we must learn to enjoy the society of people for whom comfort meant something very different from motor-cars and arm-chairs, who, although or because they lived plainly and austerely and sat at the table of life without expecting any dessert, saw more of the use and beauty and goodness of the few things which were vouchsafed them—their minds, their bodies, and Nature outside and around them. Greek literature, like the Gospels, ' is a great protest against the modern view that the really important thing is to be comfortable. The Comfort promised by the Gospels ' (and that enjoyed by the Greeks, whether the same or somewhat different) ' and the comfort assured by modern inventions and appliances are as different as ideals can be.' [1]

[1] F. C. Burkitt in *Essays on Some Biblical Questions of the Day* (Cambridge, 1909, pp. 208–9). Let the reader run through the catalogue of a wholesale ' Stores ' and ask himself how many articles or even departments were represented in antiquity ; and then consider what an economy of thought this implies. There was no fashionable or rich man's quarter in Athens : or, at least, we know the name of none. The gracefulness of Greek dress should not blind us to its extreme simplicity, only one stage removed from the simplest dress of all, the skin of a beast. A men's and women's undergarment ($\chi\iota\tau\acute{\omega}\nu$) was simply an ' oblong piece of material ', a foot longer than the wearer and twice his width from extended elbow to elbow, fastened by a pin at each shoulder. The outer garment ($\iota\mu\acute{\alpha}\tau\iota o\nu$) was a little longer and

   This old Greek atmosphere of poverty and discomfort and
vigilant thrift in small social arrangements is revealed to us most
vividly in the *Characters* of Theophrastus, types taken from the
Athenian life of the fourth century, when, as Demosthenes complained, men lived so much more luxuriously than their grandfathers in the fifth. Here we see the Athenian going about his daily
business with all his small worries and preoccupations full upon
him. What strikes the modern reader most about the life thus
revealed is what Jebb politely described as its ' frank homeliness '.
The characters are, indeed, all of them homely, and some of them
incredibly narrow and petty. They are capable, for instance,
of quarrelling about lending one another ' salt or a lamp-wick or
cummin or verjuice or meal for sacrifice or garlands or cakes '.
When a club-dinner is held at their houses, they ' secrete some of
the firewood, lentils, vinegar, salt, and lamp-oil ' placed at their
disposal for the occasion. When one of their women-folk ' has
dropped a three-farthing piece ' they ' move the furniture and the
beds and the wardrobes and rummage in the curtains '. They
weigh out rations to their household using a measure with the
bottom dinted inwards. They borrow a neighbour's cloak and

broader and was not fastened at all. So it could be put on in a number of
ways—over the head if necessary. (' It was exceptional for Greek garments
to be shaped or fitted to the person ': C. H. Young, *American Journal of
Archaeology*, vol. iv, p. 168, after experiments with models.) ' Dressing '
was therefore a very simple process, as we can see from Homer (e. g. *Il*. ii. 42).
See Abrahams, *Greek Dress* (London, 1908), with pictures and diagrams.
Dwellers in the Near East still have a preference (dictated by the climate)
for sleeveless cloaks, which either hang loose on the back and leave the arms
free, or wrap close round the whole body in repose. The Greek wore no
head-gear, except in battle and on journeys. For the flimsiness of Greek
houses note how the Plataeans dug through the party-walls of most of their
houses in the latter half of a single night without being heard from the street
(Thuc. ii. 3. 3), and the way in which, Japanese-fashion, the tiles and woodwork were conveyed away before the Peloponnesian invasion in 431, and
stripped by the Boeotians in the Decelean War (Thuc. ii. 14, vii. 27. 5;
Hellenica Oxyrhynchia, xii. 4). Greek houses were built of sun-dried brick.
So were the early temples (as can still be seen from the remains of the
Heraeum at Olympia). That is why it became necessary to build out a
columned veranda or ' peristyle ' to protect them from the weather. It was
only public buildings which were built with the massive stone or marble blocks
so familiar to us. For the contents of a *well-to-do* fifth-century Athenian
bedroom see the inventory of Alcibiades' bedroom furniture (Hicks and Hill,
no. 72, supplemented by a second fragment published in the Austrian *Jahreshefte*, vol. vi, pp. 236 ff.). It includes everything from the leather straps to
form rough springs for the mattress to the scent-jars on the dressing-table
and the reed mat on the floor; but it is not an imposing list. There is no
hint of washing arrangements. Cf. p. 52 above. [See Appendix.]

refuse to return it, when the only one they possess has at last been sent to the cleaner's. We, too, have our ' Penurious Man ' and our ' Avaricious Man ', but they do not commonly descend to these levels. The difference between Theophrastus and our tales about Scotsmen borrowing matches to save their own, or grudging an extra penny on an important telegram, is that the characters of Theophrastus are drawn from the life, with hardly a trace of exaggeration or caricature.[1]

A simple comparison may serve to make this point still clearer. It is useless to attempt to bring the resources of Athens into relation with those of any of our advanced modern communities. The disparity would be too great. But there is one obvious mediaeval analogy. Athens was not so rich, or nearly so rich, as her sister Venice, the State which, in all history, she most closely resembles. Venice, with a population of some 40,000 adult males, built St. Mark's and the Doge's Palace and other memorials of her greatness. But she did so on the profits of her trade and industry. She took no tribute, and needed none, from the cities in her sphere of influence, which she maintained, like Athens, in an almost unbroken line down the Adriatic and round Greece to Constantinople, Asia Minor, and Syria. We shall see in the sequel how dearly Athens paid for her failure to do likewise, for her inability to rest her greatness on the solid foundations of commerce.[2]

Ancient Greek finance was indeed parochial, almost childish, in its methods. The Greek States passed with difficulty beyond the schoolboy stage at which every bit of money that comes in is regarded as a windfall, to be spent gaily as the mood will have it without thought of the morrow. The first and most obvious duty of the financial administration in a modern state is to get the Budget voted. The Budget, of course, has nothing to do with money received or spent in the past. It makes provision for the year to come, and involves an estimate of the total revenue and expenditure to be expected from all sources. Greek Parliaments never had a Budget presented to them at all. They simply

---

[1] Theophrastus, ed. Jebb, 1909, pp. 4, 121, 123, 131, 135. The three-farthing piece is supposed to be lost in a bedroom, as the details show. Compare the parable of the lost piece of silver (Luke xv. 8–10).

[2] Details in *Cambridge Modern History*, vol. i, pp. 255–7 (by Horatio Brown). Wordsworth was therefore not strictly correct when he spoke of Venice as ' holding the gorgeous East in fee '.

voted sums of money whenever occasion arose, stating in each case where the money was to come from. The State receipts might be lying in two or three or half a dozen different treasuries, looked after by different committees, these treasuries being, in the case of Delos, where the inscriptions enable us to study the financial administration in detail, simply so many jars bearing on each of them a label stating where its money came from and for what purpose it was ear-marked. In this way things jogged on from year to year, and no attempt was made—for there was no one expert and continuous authority to make it—to forecast possible expenditure ahead. The usual practice was to make both ends meet for the year and then (unless the money was sacred) to distribute the surplus among the citizens. When, in 483, valuable silver deposits were discovered at Laureion, Themistocles with difficulty persuaded the Athenians to build a fleet out of the proceeds instead of dividing them out, at ten drachmas a head, amongst themselves. The Spartans, as might be expected, were more primitive still in their ideas. When Corinth persuaded them to embark on the great war with Athens, which was likely to last many years and involve a need for ships as well as men, ' they had no resources, either private or public.' Their treasury was empty, and they had no means of filling it. So they talked vaguely of getting help from the treasures of Delphi and Olympia (which they knew they would not have the courage to use) and let the Corinthians build ships for them. But even Corinth was only wealthy in a very relative sense. And as for Athens under Pericles, the financier who always worked with a margin, she never at any time had more than 10,000 talents (£2,500,000 or about £12,000,000 purchasing power) in what seemed her inexhaustible treasury on the Acropolis. And this, it must be remembered, was not only capital money but probably more than the private wealth of all her citizens put together. When she had spent it she was exhausted. For she could not, like the meanest modern State, raise a loan to go on with. There were as yet no international financiers.[1]

[1] The most instructive text for ancient finance is Aristotle's *Economics*, Book II (on which there is now an excellent commentary by Riezler, *Über Finanzen und Monopole im alten Griechenland*, Berlin, 1907). Some of the stories told of ' clever ways of raising money ' transport one back to one's school days. School-boys have not been unknown to sell their school-books

All this will serve to remind us—what the art and literature of the Greeks and our own treacherous imaginations are constantly causing us to forget—that the pioneers who created our European civilization were stricken by poverty all their days. In all the work they did for us, and in all they wished and tried to do, they were straining the tiny human strength of their own unaided idealism against the heavy dead weight of material forces which they could neither control nor understand. When we feel tempted to reproach them with all that they left undone, let us rather remember the pluck and cheerfulness and endurance, so characteristic of the poor, with which they maintained the unequal combat. Let us not require of them overmuch, or they will return us an evil answer, like the Andrians of old. When the Athenians invested their rocky island and demanded from them heavy payment, the islanders, says Herodotus, made answer as follows :—' That the Athenians were with good reason great and prosperous and were favoured by propitious gods; since, however, the Andrians were poor in territory and had reached the lowest pitch of penury, and two unprofitable goddesses, Poverty and Impossibility, never forsook the island, but ever loved to dwell there ; therefore the Andrians being in the possession of these deities would give them nothing.' So might the Athenians answer us ; for it was the doom of Athens that Poverty and Impossibility dwelt in her midst from first to last. It is to the immortal glory of her citizens that, though they were too clear-eyed not to behold them, they bravely refused to submit, either in mind or in body, to the squalid tyranny which they have imposed upon the great mass of humankind.[1]

second-hand and buy the necessary new ones on credit. This gives the measure of many of the author's devices. They depend of course on ' the ship coming in '. Themistocles : Hdt. vii. 144 ; *Ath. Pol.* xxii. 7. The discovery of the deposit of Maronea at Laureion made all the difference to Athens. Spartan finance : Thuc. i. 141, 121, 3 (cf. Ar. *Pol.* 1271 b 11 : ' they have no money in their treasury and are bad at paying taxes ') : they had no secretaries of State either, and had recourse to the most childish methods for communicating with their officials at a distance. On Greek ear-marking as opposed to proper budgeting see Francotte, *Les Finances des cités grecques* (1909), pp. 133 ff., who seems to be unaware that the government of the United States was then still carried on without a Budget. Cf. Thuc. vi. 46. 3 on the nature of the apparent resources of Egesta. King Minos's system, in still earlier days, seems to have been similar, as is clear from the underground ' magazines ' discovered at Cnossos and Phaestos. Thucydides always thinks of public and private wealth together in reckoning up national resources : e. g. vi. 31. 5.

[1] Hdt. viii. 111, vii. 102.

CHAPTER II

USE AND WONT

Οἱ μὲν γὰρ τῶν τε νόμων σοφώτεροι βούλονται φαίνεσθαι . . . ὡς ἐν ἄλλοις μείζοσιν οὐκ ἂν δηλώσαντες τὴν γνώμην . . . καὶ μὴ ἐν ᾧ ἡ πόλις βραχέα ἡσθεῖσα μεγάλα ζημιώσεται.—THUCYDIDES, iii. 37 and 40.

Some men are always seeking to be Radicals in the wrong sphere of activity. Let them apply their reason to the attainment of high and lasting purposes, not of brief satisfactions for which the whole community will pay dear.

THE Greeks, as we have seen, were far poorer and lived far more simply than ourselves. To this initial difference in material environment and possessions there naturally corresponded a difference in thoughts and feelings and imaginative outlook. Men who live differently think differently, both about life in general and about money and housekeeping in particular. It is this latter point, the Greek attitude to economics, which we have now to examine. Let us begin our discussion, for once, not with the common man but with the philosophers.

Modern thinkers, like the Greeks, are fond of fashioning Utopias ; but the ideal society which they rejoice in setting before us is generally very different from that upon which the Greek imagination loved to dwell. It is a world swept and garnished and regulated, stocked with every variety of convenience that modern science can devise, cushioned round with insurances against all the ills that flesh is heir to, in which distance has been annihilated, disease prevented or amply provided for, destitution probed to its root-causes, regular employment guaranteed to all, and a minimum standard of comfort assured except to the undeserving. Yet nothing is more certain than that the vision of such society would make no appeal whatsoever to an ancient Greek thinker ; and that an ordinary Greek citizen, if he found himself set down in it, would feel restless and homesick and ill at ease. No lapse of time or increase of familiarity with his surroundings would enable him to find there ready to hand, as in his old uncomfortable home, that state of happiness or blessedness (εὐδαιμονία) which his thinkers set before him as the one object to be aimed at in social organization.

What reason can be assigned for this difference of outlook ? One reason at least, as we shall see, is economic : and that must be our excuse for following up a little further the line of inquiry just suggested. Our thinkers, if we cross-examine them, have no better ideal to suggest than the old Greek quest for happiness. They will admit, with Plato and Aristotle, that the object of the statesman and the political thinker is to bring into existence not a state of organization but a state of consciousness, that their ultimate concern is not with matter but with mind. But the changes and complexities of modern life have called into existence so many urgent material problems that they find it hard to keep their attention fixed upon so ultimate a goal. They are daily and hourly tempted to accept as a final ideal some working hypothesis of the passing generation of social workers, to acquiesce in creeds and theories which provide a solution for the pressing difficulties of the day, but leave many of the essential problems of social life as far from solution as ever. We live in an age of unexampled economic expansion : Natural Science and the many industries and organizations called into being by Natural Science have attracted, as is only natural, the best and most vigorous brains of our time ; and our thinkers are still so much impressed, and even bewildered, by the possibilities thus opened out to them that they have not yet recovered their steadiness of vision. They have not yet succeeded in schooling their imaginations to the fact that wealth and organization are not ends in themselves, that it is possible for a society to go back in happiness and real well-being with every step in its forward march in material prosperity and organization.

The Greek imagination lived in a freer and simpler atmosphere. The Greeks did not have to dig painfully down through problem after problem of material organization before they reached the level of ultimate social speculation. When they wished to discuss the perfect society, or rather, the perfect life for human beings in society, they did not have first to settle such business questions as whether the city or groups of private citizens should manage the gas and tramways, or what should be the proportion between direct and indirect taxation. Their Utopians would have to do without either gas or tramways; but they and their thinkers would be saved all the preoccupations that such luxuries necessarily entail. They could leave on one side as irrelevant the familiar modern problems of material organization and give their undivided attention to 'those most interesting objects to be met with in life, human beings'. So they lingered over such subjects as how to secure a right relation between the sexes, or how to find the artist his proper place in society, over the influence of professions upon character, or of environment and example upon the young, discussing them sometimes wisely and sometimes crudely, but always freshly and sincerely: and since it is human problems alone that never grow stale, Greek speculation on these topics is fruitful and suggestive to us still. If Plato had left the Communism of husbands and wives out of his *Republic* and dealt instead with the nationalization of the trade of the Aegean, who shall say that we should have gained by the exchange?

Strictly speaking, of course, there is no such thing as a problem of material organization. All problems, from gas and tramways to education and women's rights, are human problems, concerned with people rather than with things. Even dividends and output would not matter if there were no one to receive them. Yet men often act as if they had forgotten this elementary truth. Why should this be?

Here we come upon another characteristic present-day difficulty which the Greek thinkers were spared—the increase in the scale and range of the modern world and of the sphere embraced by the modern thinker. What to Plato and Aristotle were problems of city life, bounded by the walls of the country town in which they lived, are now removed for the modern thinker to the wider and more complex sphere of national and international life. In other words, these problems have not only grown in scale but, by so doing, they have changed in character. They have lost the colour and clearness of old days and have become vague and misty and impersonal.

It is this impersonality of the world in which their thought is forced to move which tempts modern political thinkers to stop one step short of reality, to think in terms of things instead of pushing the problem further back and thinking in terms of human beings. An educational administrator, for instance, is inclined, when he discusses education, to think more of desks and black-boards and apparatus and new buildings and teachers' salaries than of children and teachers ; or to think of children and teachers, not as individual living souls, but as so much accumulated human material, as ' cases ' on an agenda paper or arithmetical totals.   The Greeks were not thus in danger of losing touch with the living world around them.   Their social discussion never outran the natural range of their senses and emotions ; it was always fresh and vivid and personal, always invested with the feeling of reality which springs from a close and evident relation between the intellect and the objects of its thought.

But it is time to draw the conclusion towards which this digression has been moving.   This difference in methods of speculation between the Greek and the modern world is not due simply to the superior insight of the Greek thinkers and of the public among whom they talked and wrote. ⁄ It is due partly, if not principally, to the state of society around them, to the conditions of daily life which enabled the Greek imagination to work freely and naturally on human problems. ⧸ ' The food of the Greek imagination was the very antithesis of our own nourishment.   We are educated by our circumstances to think no revolution in appliances and economic organization incredible, our minds play freely about possibilities that would have struck the philosophers of the Academy as outrageous extravagance, and it is in regard to politico-social expedients that our imaginations fail.'   In their wildest flights of imagination about men and women, the Greek thinkers could not help keeping their feet firmly fixed upon good Greek ground.   While Sparta, and the revolution in human life and manners which she implies, seem incredible to us, even in spite of the evidence of history, it is ' a motor-car throbbing in the Agora ' which would have seemed incredible to the men who boldly speculated about the communism of wives and children.

It is wellnigh impossible for us to think ourselves back into the unearthly quietness and conservatism of this old Greek world which has for ever passed away, into a civilized society from which the stress and hurry and complexity and ceaseless change and ' progress ' of to-day are wholly absent.   Yet this is what we must do if we would put ourselves in the mood to understand the economic basis of Greek society.   We must get behind the

Industrial Revolution, which has altered the daily life of ordinary people more profoundly than any other change since recorded history began, behind wholesale production and machinery and the rush of new patents and processes, back into a sequestered and stable world where competition and unemployment are unknown terms, where hardly any one is working precariously for money wages or a salary, where life goes on without visible change or desire of change from generation to generation and century to century. The women whom Jesus watched daily grinding by the mill-stones at Nazareth were the successors of unnumbered other families and races of tired women who had done the same heavy work without a word of complaint or any hope of relief. An intelligent Lancashire mill-girl (granted she was sure of keeping her place) would not tolerate such a life for a day without setting her wits to work to think out some labour-saving contrivance. Yet even the high-spirited Athenian of the fifth century, so ready to criticize all things human and divine, pulled at the clumsy oar of his State galley without a thought of fault-finding or improvement.[1]

So we must grow accustomed to living in a different atmosphere and under different standards. We must take as our economic watchword not Progress but Stability. We must minister, if we are producers and traders, not to Fashion but to Custom. We must remember that our city has been living for

[1] I owe much of the above to H. G. Wells, *A Modern Utopia*, p. 98, who has written the most suggestive of latter-day Utopias, partly because he had allowed his imagination to run riot on machinery in earlier writings. As a matter of fact twentieth-century man is ceasing to be impressed by visions of mechanical progress. You must go to India or Turkey or Morocco to find gramophones and cinematographs properly appreciated. The conquest of the air is a week-end wonder, while human issues, like the death of a great popular figure or a moment of national danger, can still stir men, as of old, to the depths. The reason for this is not that our imaginations are *blasé* and refuse to be as impressed as they should, but that we know in our hearts that these inventions make very little real difference in our lives, and each one progressively less than its predecessor. In these matters it is ' the first step that counts ', the first flickering oil-lamp in the darkness rather than the latest electric light globe, the first slow and irregular State post rather than Universal Penny Postage or cheap telephones, the first rattling steam conveyance rather than motors and turbine-steamers and airships. James Watt and George Stephenson were greater innovators than Paulhan and Blériot, and Prometheus than Stephenson or Watt. Cf. an interesting chapter on ' Le Nivellement des Jouissances ' in d'Avenel, *Découvertes d'histoire sociale*, 1200–1910, Paris, 1910. The problem has now been definitely analysed by Graham Wallas, *The Great Society · a psychological analysis*, London, 1914.

centuries, ever since the dim days of the prehistoric migrations, in a dignified isolation of her own, that she has long since learnt to be proudly self-sufficient, to serve her own needs, to supply her own luxuries, and to do everything in her own way. She has her own tricks for shaping and colouring pots, her own peculiarities of dress and shoes, her own traditional dishes and drinks, her own 'school' of arts and crafts, just as she has her own dialect and way of writing it and her own gods and constitutions. In fact she is a little world of her own ; and if you want to do business there you must not bring her the wares of the great world and expect her to welcome them, but try to fall in with her own mood and suit her own traditional taste. Just as in Turkey to-day, where the old barriers of isolation are beginning to break down, the trader discovers no two cities alike, Damascus a world away from Aleppo and Samsun from Trebizond, so Athens and Thebes, Argos and Corinth all had tastes and productions as varied and conservative as their history and traditions. Even dull-witted Sparta had her own pots and shoes and her own special black broth.[1]

But surely the people in our Greek city were men like ourselves and subject to the same human impulses and weaknesses ? Surely the blood of the 'economic man' ran in their veins, and, like all sensible people to-day, they desired to be rich ?

That is just the point where the older Greeks differed most profoundly from ourselves, or rather from the interpretation of

[1] The so-called 'Cyrenaic' pottery is now known, from the excavations of the British School, to be Laconian ware. One of the most curious illustrations of Greek Conservatism in small things may still be observed in the doorways of the Propylaea. Door-jambs were traditionally made of wood : so, even in a building made of marble, they had still to be in the old material, and the marble was cut away to make room for the wood. Where Art was concerned the Greeks set their minds to work ; but not otherwise. With us art-forms become modified by material changes : travelling by train turns the minds of our writers to producing magazines and short stories. In Greece they became modified by changes in the spiritual sphere : it was what Aeschylus and Sophocles had to say which transformed the character of the Greek chorus. This is what makes Greek art-forms, despite their apparent stiffness and conventionality, so truly original, while ours, despite our freedom of choice, seem so artificial and unsatisfactory. Because we produce according to the laws of supply and demand, and are prepared to keep everything on tap, we have so little that is really and fundamentally our very own. For the conflict between Custom and Fashion, in its various bearings, see Tarde, Les Lois de l'Imitation, ch. vii. Many Englishmen who have experienced both will think of their Public School as a home of Custom and their University as a seat of Fashion. For details see Glotz, Travail, pp. 154 ff.

the modern man given by some of his nineteenth-century leaders. The older Greeks did not want to be rich for the sake of riches. They were too sane and well-balanced to harbour such a desire. One of the central facts about their life, expressed over and over again, in their art and conduct and institutions, was their sense of harmony and proportion. They had overcome the wild passion of the child or the savage for ' too much '. They only desired riches when they had convinced themselves that riches were necessary to social well-being. They knew, as some Eastern peoples know still, that ' a pennyworth of ease is worth a penny ', and that it is not worth while spending two pennyworths or more of worry and effort to attain it. They had sense enough to correlate the values of wealth and well-being. ' The richest of men is no more happy than he who has a sufficiency for a day, unless good fortune attend him to the grave so that he ends his life in happiness. Many men who abound in wealth are unhappy ; and many who have only a moderate competency are fortunate. He that abounds in wealth and is yet unhappy surpasses the other only in two things ; but the other surpasses the man who is wealthy and unfortunate in many things. . . . He enjoys the full use of his limbs, he is free from disease and misfortune, he is blessed with fine children and a fine body, and, if in addition to all these things he shall end his life well, he is the man you seek and may justly be called happy.' So, according to Greek tradition, spoke the sage to the millionaire, in words that were never forgotten. The older Greek tried to be faithful to the doctrine that Solon preached, and, judged by any modern standard of comparison, they were faithful indeed. What drove them into economic activity and into the development we shall have to trace was not simply our senseless greed for more, a kind of insatiable craving which would have run counter to some of their deepests instincts, but the sober conviction that they needed wealth for the purposes of their civilization. In other words, civilization, which means not yachts and motor-cars but a refined and many-sided and effort-loving society, costs money, and money cannot be had without economic activity. So there is a point in the growth of every developing society when it is driven by its own needs, however reluctant it may be, into the atmosphere of money-getting, with all its attendant temptations

towards wrong standards of living. This is what happened to
the Greeks, and, above all, to Athens, just at the culminating
point of her greatness. But we shall do well to remember, when
we feel inclined to reproach her with unscrupulous dealing, both
the lofty objects for which her riches were deliberately sought,
and the tranquil and harmonious conservatism of the world of
high thinking and plain living out of which she was just emerging.
It is not for us, with our modern comforts and our modern
business motives, to cast the first stone.[1]

[1] Hdt. i. 32 (Solon and Croesus). One testimony to the general level of
happiness among the Greeks is the uncommonness of suicide. Greeks only
killed themselves when they felt they had incurred some public disgrace, like
Ajax or Phaedra; cf. Thuc. ii. 92. 3. See on this point Westermarck, *The
Origin and Development of Moral Ideas*, vol. ii, pp. 247 ff.

CHAPTER III

THE GROWING CITY : WORK ON THE LAND

Τὸ δὲ πλεῖστον γένος τῶν ἀνθρώπων ἀπὸ τῆς γῆς ζῇ καὶ τῶν ἡμέρων καρπῶν.—
ARISTOTLE, *Politics* 1256.
Most of mankind get their living from the land and from cultivated plants.

WE turn then to our examination of the fifth-century Athenian
as an earner and a housekeeper, and of the economics or housekeeping of fifth-century Athens. What we have to ask is, firstly,
how did the fifth-century Athenian make his living as a private
individual ? secondly, how did the Athenian State support
itself ? what was the economic basis of its civilization and
achievements ?

These questions are easily asked ; but they are not so quickly
answered. Just as, in order to understand the politics of the
Funeral Speech, we had to go down to the political foundations
of Greek society, building up the City upon the Tribe and the
Empire upon the City, so, in order to understand the economy
of Athens at the opening of the Peloponnesian War, we must go
back to the economic foundations of Greek society, to the origins
and development of the City State, and to its ordinary humble
working citizens, and so build up, layer by layer, the economics
of the Athenian Empire.

Let us go back, then, once more, with Thucydides for our guide,
to the beginnings of Greek society, to the days before the Greeks
had settled down into the routine of City State life. We shall
find here some elements in their economy which remained stable
and persistent, and others which, with advancing civilization,
they were able later to discard or to develop. But all of them,
as we shall see, will prove of importance in our inquiry.

Thucydides has left us, on the first page of his book, a vivid
imaginative sketch of the economic life of the earliest Greeks in
their scattered villages just after the chaos of the great migrations. ' It is evident,' he says, ' that in ancient times the country

now called Hellas had no settled population ; on the contrary, migrations were of frequent occurrence, the several tribes readily abandoning their homes under the pressure of superior numbers. Without commerce, without safe communications either by land or sea, cultivating no more of their land than they required for bare subsistence, destitute of capital, never planting their land with fruits (for they could not tell when an invader might not come and take it all away, and when he did come they had no wall to stop him), they thought little of shifting their dwellings, and consequently neither built large cities nor attained to any other kind of greatness.'

There is very little here which is common to the society of Periclean Athens. It is Greek life reduced to its barest elements. There is no trade, no travelling, no vine and olive, no security, not even organized warfare from a settled citadel ; yet one permanent element stands out. These men made their living, so far as they made it at all, and did not merely rob it, by cultivating the soil. They lived by the land.

This is the one abiding fact about the economy of the Greeks, from their earliest days down to the fifth century ; and therefore, at the risk of anachronism, it is necessary to deal with it here, at the very outset of our inquiry. There were many possible ways in which a Greek could make a living, but there was only one which seemed entirely natural and traditional—work on the land.

The Greek writers who discuss the question of livelihood (and, in spite of what is often said, Greece did produce ' economists ') are unanimous upon this subject. All of them preach work on the land. No other occupation which fills the family store, says Xenophon, in his glowing eulogy of the farmer's life, is at once so pleasant and so healthy, and so worthy of a free man. Agriculture, says Plato, is a more natural art than politics itself, for it ' co-operates with Nature ', like medicine and physical training. And Aristotle, heedless of the life of the steppe and the forest and the fiord, actually regards agriculture of the Greek sort as the normal life of all mankind. Be that as it may, it was at any rate the right and proper occupation for the Greek father of a family. Ever since his ancestors had established themselves, centuries back, in their little enclosed plains and valleys, and gradually dropped, as Thucydides describes for us, from the old semi-

nomadic life into settled and stationary ways, he had been used
to thinking of himself as attached, first as the member of a tribe
or brotherhood and then as a father of a single household, to
a definite piece of land from which he drew his living. Greek
civilization is, in a sense, urban ; but its basis is agricultural, and
the breezes of the open country blow through the Parliament and
the market-place. The landed tradition is the strongest and most
persistent force in the inherited social economy of Greece.[1]

It is necessary to emphasize this in order to understand to
the full how fundamentally different their economy is from ours.
It is not our cloistered Hellenists and city-dwellers but our
shepherds and yokels who, in their daily occupations and habits
of housekeeping, touch most nearly the ancient Greek—not
merely the Greek of the unsettled early days and of the quiet
Middle Ages, but the alert and enterprising citizen of fifth-century
Athens. ' Let me make my meaning clear by two widely
separated quotations. Every one recalls the passage in the
Odyssey where Homer describes the founding of the city of the
Phaeacians : first they build the walls of the city, then they
divide the land into holdings. Centuries and centuries later, in
the Attic comedy, one of the characters is expounding the popular
demands. He asks for the latest news : has there been a par-
tition of lands in a colony ? Always this idea of landed property ! Thousands of things have changed since Homer. The
love of the Greeks for the land has remained the same. Go
to-day into the recesses of the Ardennes and you will still
find some of these children of the soil. You will meet the
old-fashioned peasant, systematically ignorant of everything connected with commerce and industry, an aristocrat and a conservative in his own peculiar way, protesting against every
novelty, and adding year by year to his ancestral store. An
Athenian of two thousand years ago would have understood
him : to-day he is but the last survivor of a vanishing race.' [2]

At first sight the Belgian writer may appear to be exaggerating. But when we look closer we shall see that his judgement is a true one. For we must not think of work on the land

---

[1] Xen. *Oec.* v ; Ar. *Pol.* 1256 a 38 ; Plato. *Laws* 889 ; cf. 743 and Hesiod,
Erga 683.

[2] Francotte, *L'Industrie dans la Grèce antique* (Brussels, 1901), vol. ii,
p. 53.

as it is practised, in these days of machinery and organization, by restless immigrants round Winnipeg, or even by up-to-date farmers and market-gardeners nearer home. We must think of it as what it was until a few years ago, the most stable and conservative of all economic occupations. The trader and the manufacturer rely upon their own skill and enterprise, and can transform and diversify what they handle. The shepherd and the farmer wait upon Nature's pleasure, and look, not to improvements in method, but to favouring skies and kindly gods. They learn to be patient and contemplative, and pleased with the day of small things ; they form in every society the great bulwark of Use and Wont. The Greeks, being by tradition shepherds and farmers, were brought up conservatives.

There is another reason why it is not easy for us, approaching him as economists, to understand the Greek farmer. He did not want to grow rich. He worked on the land for a livelihood and for his city, not in the hope of high prices and an ultimate fortune. His object was to provide for his household and, if need be, to help to provide also for the community ; but he had no thought of amassing wealth. The great landed fortunes so familiar to us from the eighteenth century were unknown in Greece ; or if not entirely unknown, so abnormal and odious as to fall outside the limits of a general picture. If a Greek citizen owned what seemed a disproportionately large amount of the land of the community, the public opinion of the marketplace clamoured that it should be taken away from him and ' redivided '. If a trader or a craftsman was over-wealthy nobody complained, and perhaps nobody knew. At any rate his being rich did not appear to make others poorer. But in a small City State, where land was visibly limited in amount, every additional acre to the large proprietor seemed clearly to mean an acre less for the small men. So the Greek farmer had every reason, both from tradition and policy, to eschew the dreams of avarice and develop the other sides of his nature. His pleasant household and old farm buildings and the familiar gods of the near fields and springs, together with the orderly rows of gnarled olives which his great-grandfather planted, meant more to him than all the riches his cosmopolitan younger brother might be bringing home from the Western seas. For his philosophic aim (however little he might know of it) was to be a harmonious nature, with every part of his being working together for good.[1]

How did the Greek draw his living from the land ?

Under settled City State conditions he had three sources of livelihood : pasture, tillage, and fruit. Of the shepherd we have already spoken. His life was at once the most traditional and the most harmonious ; for it was the life of his earliest ancestors, and was the most completely removed from the influence and interests of the city. Only one small economic tie kept him in touch, on his high pastures, with the City World below. He had not enough to eat unless he filled his store from the lowlands. A goat-herding population cannot subsist ' wholly on the produce of its own goats, as seems to be possible on the grassland with the herders of horses '. The shepherd and his family needed bread as well as milk and cheese : and it was this that saved them from becoming nomads, like their Scythian brothers further North. If times were unsettled they came down from the highlands and stole it ; but as the City State extended its strong arm they learnt to barter for it with milk food, for which the men below, as they grew in numbers, had an ever-increasing need. Yet even when he was thus incorporated in the economy of the City State, the shepherd continued to lead a life apart, the most old-fashioned, and also, as Aristotle says, the laziest of Greek mankind ; for shepherds ' get their subsistence without trouble from tame animals, and since their flocks have to wander from place to place in search of pasture, they are compelled to follow them, cultivating a sort of living farm '. No doubt Greek shepherds, whether they were slaves or citizens, were as open and courteous then as now, and as eager for the latest news of doings in the city. The shepherds of the *Oedipus Tyrannus*, whom we know so well as Messengers in other plays, still accost the modern traveller with that frank and dignified speech and bearing which the English reader so often regards as a mere tragedy pose. But the main body of them, who spent the summer months on the high mountain pastures, were so removed from city life that they remained outside and unaffected by the economic development

[1] See Iwan Müller, *Griechische Privataltertümer*, p. 236, on the prosperity of the Athenian agriculturist in the fifth century, owing to the increased population of Attica. Yet no large landed fortunes were made.

we have to follow. Only when war broke out and the frontier pastures became unsafe, did they come down into the plain and join the ranks of their fellows, if so entitled, as citizen soldiers.[1]

Fruit and tillage, the orchard and the ploughed field, belong together, and are looked after from one hearthfire by the proprietor. So far as we can tell, tillage everywhere predominated : for the tradition was that every state must provide its own grain. Even where, as in fifth-century Attica, the growth of population had made this plainly impossible, more corn was probably raised than oil, and the country dwellers at any rate bought little food from the town. In the time of Pericles probably at least one-third of the corn consumed in Attica was homegrown, and, in spite of other interests, the soil of Attica was the best farmed in Greece. Those who know how sterile it is now will appreciate the labour spent on it by these Athenian farmers who had so much else to do and to think about.[2]

To whom did the land belong and by what tenure was it held ?

Nearly all of it in the normal Greek State was in the hands of small proprietors, who worked the soil themselves. We are not concerned here with serfdom such as existed in Sparta and

---

[1] p. 48 above. They served at Athens as light-armed troops, not as rowers. For an extant letter, probably from a shepherd, see pp. 284–5 below. Myres, *Greek Lands*, p. 26. For the economic dependence of the highlanders on the lowlanders see Xen. *Hell*. vi. 1. 9, an interesting passage : ' Since Thessaly is very flat, all the tribes round it (i. e. on the mountains) are subject to it, when there is a strong government in power : nearly all of them are javelin men.' The connexion of thought is not clear, at first sight, to a northern reader. The speaker means that because Thessaly is very flat (i. e. unsuited for guerrilla tactics, javelin-throwing, &c.), and well-policed, *therefore* the highlanders cannot steal their food, and must needs barter for it, i. e. acknowledge the supremacy of the lowland State.

[2] *Hellenica Oxyrhynchia*, xii. 5 : Attica καθ᾽ ὑπερβολὴν ἐξήσκητο καὶ διεπεπόνητο : it is added that no expense was spared on the farm buildings. These farmers were mostly small men, ' Zeugites ' like Aristophanes' Dicaeopolis. This is clear from Thuc. ii. 16 : for further evidence see Guiraud, *La Propriété foncière en Grèce*, pp. 392–3. The New Historian's description of Attica refers to the period between 421 and 414, *after* the devastations of the Peloponnesian invasions. It would seem therefore as if Attica produced more corn than oil, for a country consisting predominantly of olive-yards could hardly have recovered so quickly. This seems to be confirmed by some fourth-century evidence in Dem. xx. 31, and by the calculations of Meyer, *Forschungen*, vol. ii, pp. 189 ff. So the passage in the papyrus, only recovered in 1906, certainly does a good deal to justify or at least explain Pericles' policy in exposing Attica to devastation. See also the note on p. 54 above. On methods of tillage see Iwan Müller, p. 237. The Greeks knew nothing of the rotation of crops, so half the corn-land was always lying fallow. [See Appendix.]

234 ECONOMICS PART III

Thessaly. That was, as we have seen, an abnormal condition,
the result of a distorted development. The overwhelming
majority of the Greek States, like Athens from Solon's day
onwards, were cultivated by freeholders. They worked the land
with their households, dividing up the estate at death among
their sons. This acted, as it does in France, as a check on the
population, at any rate until new outlets were provided for
a livelihood. Nearly every citizen in an ordinary Greek State
was a landowner, whether the piece he owned was large or small,
enough to live on or only to starve on. When in 403 it was
proposed at Athens, the leading commercial state, to limit the
citizenship to owners of land or houses, we are told that only
5,000 citizens would have been excluded by the law, and most
of these were probably returned colonists. So that even in the
confusion of the Peloponnesian War, when the economic basis of
Athenian society was being shaken to its foundations, the men
who had shouted for Cleon and sailed to Sicily for plunder felt
somehow the happier for the possession of a little plot of their
own, however worthless.[1]

Tenancy, in our sense of the word, was therefore practically
unknown in Greece. Out of the numerous inscriptions preserved
which deal, in one way or another, with land, there are only
' a very small number of contracts made between individuals '.
When a Greek is a tenant at all he is a tenant for a public body :
he is cultivating land for the State or for a god or for some
brotherhood or association ; in other words he is doing for the
landlord what the landlord is unable to do for himself. A great
number of such inscriptions have come down to us. It is worth
while quoting one, to give an idea of how the system worked. It
relates to a piece of land which belonged to the town of Poiessa
(Grassland) in the island of Ceos, and runs as follows :—

Gods !
Land belonging to the City of Poiessa.

[1] Wilamowitz, *A. A.*, vol. ii, p. 227 (comment on *Lys.* xxxiv : ὑπόθεσις).
The most typical countryman in Greek literature is the kind old peasant in
Euripides' *Electra*, who is drawn from the Peloponnesian freeholders of his
day (cf. Thuc. i. 141. 3). Like Dicaeopolis and Trygaeus he is much more
characteristic than Ischomachus, the hero of Xenophon's *Oeconomicus*.
Ischomachus is an exceptionally large landowner, one of the small number
of knights or horse-breeders who are rich enough to do the State the extra
service of providing it with a small force of cavalry. Cf. note on pp. 175–6 above.

§ 1. The occupier is to pay on the tenth of the month of Bacchion 30 drachmas ; if he does not pay he must leave.

§ 2. He is to bring his money to Poiessa.

§ 3. He is to give back the house in good repair and with the roof on.

§ 4. He is not to cut down the fruit trees.[1]

---

[1] *Inscriptions juridiques grecques*, i, p. 253 (cf. the whole section, especially p. 250) ; also Dittenberger, no. 532, cf. nos. 531–6. The only formal treatise on Greek agriculture we possess is the volume called *Geoponica*, in twenty books dealing with the different departments of agricultural life. It was drawn up about A. D. 800, and consists of extracts from numerous writers, mainly Greek, of very different date and experience. It is full of information, some of it queer and magical : the following from Book XIII, ch. xv (On Household Fleas) is as interesting as any. ' If ever you come into a place where fleas abound, cry Och, Och (ὤχ, ὤχ), and they will not touch you.' [See Appendix.]

CHAPTER IV

THE GROWING CITY: HUNTING OR ROBBERY

Οἱ μὲν γὰρ ἀπὸ θήρας ζῶσι, καὶ θήρας ἕτεροι ἑτέρας, οἷον οἱ μὲν ἀπὸ λῃστείας.
Some men live by hunting, which is of different kinds: some, for example, are pirates.—ARISTOTLE, *Politics* 1256.

WORK on the land is the traditional Greek way of earning an honest livelihood, and, since we are building up the economy of the Greek city from its lasting foundations, it necessarily stands first. But it is not the most natural way for men with ordinary human impulses, whether primitive or advanced, least of all for the Greeks, who disliked monotonous activity. They needed to be broken into it. It took unnumbered generations of social training to teach them patiently to acquiesce in earning a humble farmer's livelihood by the sweat of their brow. Some bold spirits in every generation refused to be taught at all, and preferred a life of adventure, with the risk of sudden death or slow starvation, to the dull round of trivial labours imposed on them by society. These men lived by hunting.

In the early days, just after the great migrations, when the land was still only partially settled and cleared, there was plenty of good hunting, both of beasts and men. Men went hunting singly and in hordes, greedy for good prey, and it mattered little to them whence their store was replenished—whether with boar's-meat from the forests, or with sheep or goats from across the range, or with the carefully tended produce of some thriftier neighbouring race. There were as yet no rights or laws or customs outside the morality of the tribe. Where every one is afraid of robbery every one goes armed, and feels justified in using his weapons against an outsider, for other purposes than mere defence, when opportunity offers or poverty drives. Even in the fifth century, Thucydides tells us, ' many parts of Hellas still follow the old fashion, the Ozolian Locrians, for instance, the Aetolians, the Acarnanians and that district of the mainland ; and the custom of carrying arms is still kept up among these

mainlanders from the old hunting and robbing habits.   For all
the Greeks used at one time to carry arms, as their houses were
unprotected and their communications with one another unsafe.'
No wonder that, as we have seen, it was not yet worth their while
to plant their land with fruit trees, because you never could tell
when some tribe of hunters, who preferred to ' live upon their
neighbours ', ' might not come down and take it all away '.[1]

All through the history of early Greece, before city-made law
had learnt to exercise its full powers, these hunters and robbers
are continually crossing our path.   They are the central figures
in the opening chapters of Thucydides' history, for they were the
one ever-present terror of the early unwalled cities.   It was on
their account, for instance, that cities were usually planted a safe
distance inland, to secure them from sudden assaults by the corsairs who might dart round the near promontory or slip over at
night from the rocky island across the bay.   For it was by sea
especially that these old robbers plied their trade, which became
more highly skilled and more adventurous with every forward
step in local knowledge and communications.   ' The early
Hellenes of the coastlands and islands,' says Thucydides, ' and
some barbarians, too, as communication by sea became more
common, turned into regular robber bands, with their leading
men at their head, partly from love of gain and partly to support
their helpless dependants.   They would fall upon the unwalled
cities of those days—mere collections of villages—and sack
them ;   indeed, this was the main source of their livelihood,
no disgrace being yet attached to it, but even some glory.   This
is shown by the honour with which some of the inhabitants of
the continent still regard a successful marauder, and by the
question that we find the old poets representing the people
as everywhere asking of voyagers :   " Are you pirates," as if
those who were asked would have no inclination to disclaim the

[1] Thuc. i. 5. 3, 2. 2.   The Aetolians were still ' living upon their neighbours '
in the time of Polybius, leading a ' greedy and beast-like life, regarding
nobody as one of themselves but every one as their natural foe ' :   Polyb. iv. 3.
There was very little hunting of wild animals in historic Greece, for the scrub
harbours none, and good forest land was rare.   See Xenophon's little book
On Hunting, which is mainly concerned with hunting hares (on big game,
only to be had outside Greece, see chap. xi), and Mahaffy, *Progress of Hellenism
in Alexander's Empire*, p. 9, on how Xenophon enjoyed the good hunting provided by the Persian governors in Asia Minor ;   also, p. 60, on the Macedonian
(as opposed to the Greek) type of sporting country gentleman.

suggestion or the questioners to reproach them with it. The same robbery went on also by land.' [1]

But as the growing City State became more powerful, it learnt how to extend its strong arm over the haunts of the robber folk. It explored and cleared their mountain fastnesses—those great limestone caves so common in Greece, sometimes mere indistinguishable slits in the hillside, but leading down through difficult ways into high and spacious halls. Here, where the robbers of old had lived and caroused and carved altars to their gods, quiet citizens from below, shepherds with their flocks in the summer pastures, now met to talk and pipe and sleep, or even, as we know by writing found scratched on the wall or on the potsherds strewn about the floor, to worship Pan or the Nymphs or some other peaceful power. And the sea-robbers, too, had to leave their old established hiding-places. The rocky island across the bay, with its one little cove, so convenient for small boats, and its famous spring of clear water, became just an extra piece of the city's pasture ground, very useful in winter when there was snow on the heights. No need to keep dogs there, for the island was so small that it was itself a natural tether. And the larger islands or coast towns, which had lived by robbing and wrecking, submitted in their turn. For their livelihood was gone, and ' the love of gain ', as Thucydides says—in other words, the pinch of poverty—' would reconcile the weaker to the dominion of the stronger '. Only some bold spirits resisted and moved farther afield, where as yet city law could not follow.[2]

Thus the gap slowly widened between the adventurer and the honest citizen. The mighty hunters of old days, once the pride

[1] Thuc. i. 5. There is still glory attaching to the profession when it is carried on upon the old lines. In 1910 there was still at large in the vilayet of Smyrna a noted Robin Hood who was extremely popular among the peasants, both because of his skill in defying the forces of the law and of his considerate choice of his numerous victims.—1921. In 1918–20 a certain Bekiaris (shot in May or June 1920) long successfully defied all police attempts to arrest him. He used to put up notices in the Acarnanian villages fixing the price of food and warning profiteers against overcharging the villagers. In some cases individuals were ordered to send him, by way of fine, amounts thus overcharged and he would return them to the defrauded purchasers. The villagers all protected him.

[2] Thuc. i. 8. 3. For my view on the historical interpretation of this part of Thucydides see p. 76 above. For an account of one of these caves, the Cave of Pan near Vari in Attica, see *American Journal of Archaeology*, vol. vii, pp. 263 ff., with photographs of the rude stone altar and reliefs on the rock.

of their small communities, were cut off from the society of the growing city, and became recognized outcasts.

Although our main concern is with the city and its regular inhabitants and earners, we must pause to look a little more closely at some of these adventurers. For the spirit of their calling lived on into fifth-century Athens, and we shall find, as we go on, that it has an important bearing upon our subject. These independent-minded outcasts were the earliest and truest representatives in the old Greek world of the ' economic man '. Whereas the respectable city farmer worked, as we have seen, for a livelihood, the buccaneer went out for big prizes, and when he made a lucky haul could feast and clothe himself like a king. His profession remained, until its more profitable avenues were closed, the one way of becoming really wealthy, of amassing treasure and dependants, which this early world provided for the private individual or groups of individuals. Many of its members went about with the equipment of petty kings, and it is probable that the question, ' Are you a pirate ?' really meant not ' Are you a robber or a peaceful traveller ?' but ' Are you here on a public or a private venture ?' In either case the sudden and unwelcome visitor was out to ' convey ', but the one would be warfare and the other merely robbery. Sometimes the question would be a little difficult to answer.[1]

Under what conditions did the corsair earn his livelihood ? Fortunately Homer has told us enough about him to enable us to watch him at work. Instead of the plough and the spade he has, as his instrument of production, his ship, which, whoever made it or whoever was its first owner, by now counts as the joint possession of all the partners of the venture. The Argo belonged to all the Argonauts alike.[2]

---

[1] Cf. *Od.* iii. 82, iv. 314 ; Pind. *Ol.* xiii. 69 ; Hdt. v. 63 (εἴτε ἰδίῳ στόλῳ εἴτε δημοσίῳ). How thin, even in the fifth century, was the line between warfare and private buccaneering may be seen by a careful study of Brasidas' operations in Macedonia and Thrace (e. g. Thuc. iv. 124 ff.), and by the equivocal position of the Spartan contingent sent to help the Younger Cyrus. So, too, Xenophon describes Alexander, tyrant of Pherae, as ' an unholy robber both by land and sea ' : *Hell.* vi. 4. 35. Polycrates of Samos was much the same. He designed a ship, only too well known to the Athenian naval police, which combined speed and ' belly ' for plunder in an unprecedented degree. When they captured the island the Athenians are said to have branded the Samians with the mark of its peculiar design (Hdt. iii. 39 ; Plut. *Per.* 26).

[2] I infer this from the constant insistence on a fair (though not an equal)

' This ship is small. She needs to be, for every evening she is pulled on shore, where she serves the pirates as a house, a citadel, or a rampart. Her crew is seldom less than twenty or more than fifty. As the old epic epithet tells us, she is hollow, that is to say, undecked. Her hold is open, there is no semblance of a quarter-deck or of a cabin. She is a boat pure and simple, in spite of her length. Only at each extremity there is a small raised plat-form with a barrier, but the space below these two platforms is open like all the rest and forms a continuation of the ship. On the " forecastle " stands the watch ; on the poop the captain and the pilot have their place. They are no more sheltered than the rest against wind and rain, but their relative elevation protects them from the waves and the spray. The body of the ship is occupied by the rowers, seated on little transverse benches. Down its whole length runs a sort of central track or " bridge ", along which movement is possible when it is not encumbered with merchandise. This is stowed as best it can be under the rowers' benches, in the " hollow " of the vessel, or under the front and back platforms. In the centre there is a sort of hole for the mast. When the wind is favourable the mast is fixed in the hole and attached by ropes in front and behind, perhaps, too, at the sides. Sailing is in its infancy ; the wind is not made use of unless it is behind or almost so. When the mast is no longer needed it is unfixed, taken out of its hole, and laid in the middle of the ship. For provisions the crew generally take flour and wine ; but water must also be fetched from time to time, since rowing is thirsty work and wine will not do as the only drink. When the time comes for fighting, the rowers, or at least a part of them, are transformed into fighting-men. They fight from the two castles, which are more favourable positions than the centre of the ship. In short, the Greek ship is not a comfortable abode ; but this disadvantage loses force when it is remembered that almost every night its inmates can sleep on shore. Night voyages are rare, and the leaders run the risk of raising their

division of the profits. Strictly, of course, the ship belonged to the man who fitted out the venture ; the Argo, therefore, to Jason who, as a touching old story says, went in his lonely old age to live with his old ship, now rotting on the shore. (Eur. *Medea* 1386 and Murray's note.) But probably each member of the crew had by custom a small share in the winnings.

men against them if they call upon them for this exceptional hardship.' [1]

But in spite of its discomforts it is a highly attractive life, more attractive by far than earning a respectable livelihood, under the tutelage of fellow-tribesmen and neighbours, in the stuffy plain. There is continual excitement—then, as now, a perpetual craving among all who have once tasted it—and every fresh day round every headland the possibility of untold treasure. The prize, when it came, was divided out strictly in a democratic spirit of equality ; for, in the simple code of the corsairs' morality, murder and robbery counted for nothing, but an unfair division was the gravest of social offences. When Agamemnon cheats Achilles of a favourite girl captive the whole fabric of this primitive society is loosened, and an Iliad of tragedy may ensue. Their methods of production may be peculiar, like those of some lavish modern millionaires, but custom prescribes that their methods of distribution shall be scrupulously respectable.[2]

But it is weary work as the years go on and the muscles grow stiff to tug for ever at the oar, or to live winter and summer in mountain fastnesses. So even pirates and highwaymen tended to settle down after a time and lead normal Greek lives. Sometimes, if they dare not go to their own city, they look out for a fresh home where they can live unmolesting and unmolested, with no questions asked. In this way, for instance, Messina was first occupied by pirates from Cumae in Italy. Similarly respectable in his old age was Odysseus's old grandfather Autolycus, who had a reputation, the poet tells us, for ' surpassing all mankind in stealing and the use of the oath : Hermes himself had taught him how '. And, after all, the heroes of the Trojan War,

---

[1] From *La Grèce ancienne*, by G. d'Azambuja, Paris, Bureaux de la Science sociale, 1906, p. 66, a brilliant work which exhibits all the merits and many of the weaknesses of its attempt ' to explain history by social science '. For a more detailed account of these early pirates see Bérard, *Les Phéniciens et l'Odyssée*, vol. ii, ch. 1 ; also vol. i, pp. 379 ff., on female passengers, for whom a ship so constructed offered little accommodation. Hence Clytemnestra taunts Agamemnon and Cassandra with sitting side by side on the rowers' benches : Aesch. *Ag.* 1442. Eumaeus's nursemaid, on a similar expedition, tumbled down into the hold and broke her neck : *Od.* xv. 479.

[2] *Il.* i. 122 ff. ; *Od.* ix. 42, x. 43. The Frank corsairs of the seventeenth century, as Bérard points out, led a much more disciplined life. They had regular officers on board, not elective magistrates, and mutiny was treated as such. So it was by Sir Francis Drake.

who are at such pains to come back, after ten years over one
venture, to their sorrowing wives, are little better than bandits.
For how, as Thucydides pertinently asks, did they keep themselves all those years ?   Much in the same way as the strangest
rulers Athens ever had, the Catalan Grand Company, who
settled down to govern Attica and attend service in the
Church of St. Mary on the Acropolis after some merry years
of making a living out of the Thracian Chersonese opposite
Troy.[1]

These epic adventurers were gradually scattered and thinned
out by the vigilant policing of the sea powers ; and by the fifth
century, when Athens kept watch over the Aegean, their great
days were over.   Yet they still reappeared whenever opportunity
offered, and the security of which Athenians boasted remained
relative rather than absolute.   Travelling in Greek times was
always, according to modern standards, unsafe.   Even in fifth-
century Athens itself there was the well-known footpad, nick-
named Orestes, to set upon you as you picked your way home
through the dark streets after a party.   And at sea the enemies
of the ruling power were quick to improvise as corsairs.   How
common and natural a profession it was may be seen by the
stratagem adopted by some Megarians on one occasion to
admit the Athenians into their walls.   They pretended to be
privateers, and so got leave every evening to have the gates
opened in order to carry through their boat on a cart to the
seashore, bringing it back again before daylight.   As soon as the
strong hand of Athens was removed the craft renewed their
activity, and played hide and seek with the lesser sea powers
all round the Archipelago.[2]

[1] Thuc. vi. 4. 5 (Messina), i. 11 (Trojan War commissariat) ; Od. xix. 395
(Autolycus).   For the amazing history of the Catalans see Rennell Rodd,
vol. ii, p. 66 ; also pp. 138 ff., a characteristic story of how one of these grizzled
and tender-hearted old murderers carried a royal Infant, cradle and all,
through infinite perils to his grandmother in Spain.   They would be glad to
know that Spanish is still talked in the little ports of the Chersonese, though
not their Spanish and by no descendants of theirs.—1921.   Don Miguel de
Unamuno comments on this : ' It is well known to us in Spain that fifteenth-
century Spanish is still talked in the small ports of the Chersonese.   On the
exploits of the Catalans in Greece we have the work of Ramon Montaner,
himself one of the legionaries.   It is written in Catalan and is an admirable
work.'   It has been translated into English by the Hakluyt Society, Nos. 47
and 50.
[2] Thuc. iv. 67. 3 ; cf. ii. 67. 4 and 69.   For ' Orestes ' see Birds 1491.   He

But it is time to leave them to their devices : if we follow them further we shall find ourselves encroaching upon other branches of housekeeping. For who shall draw the exact line where robbery stops and legitimate warfare and even commerce begin ? Between stealing and commandeering and ' peacefully persuading ' to sell there are the thinnest partitions : and even the modern variant, peacefully persuading to buy or ' opening a virgin market ', is sometimes strangely like them. In any case, all these activities carry our attention beyond the subject of this chapter, the early hunters and robbers, whether by land or sea. Let us now pass on to examine how the growing city learnt to enlist and use this hunting instinct to promote her own national purposes.   [See Appendix.]

was no isolated figure ; cf. Xen. *Mem*. ii. 1. 15 ταῖς ὁδοῖς ἔνθα πλεῖστοι ἀδικοῦνται.

CHAPTER V

THE GROWING CITY : WARFARE

'Αλλ', ὦ Σώκρατες, δυνατόν ἐστι καὶ ἀπὸ πολεμίων τὴν πόλιν πλουτίζειν.

Νὴ Δία σφόδρα γ', ἐάν τις αὐτῶν κρείττων ᾖ· ἥττων δὲ ὢν καὶ τὰ ὄντα προσαπο-
βάλοι ἄν.—XENOPHON, *Memorabilia*, iii. 6. 7.

But, Socrates, it is possible to procure wealth for the State from our foreign
enemies.

Yes, certainly, you may, if you are the stronger power ; but, if not, you
stand to lose even what you have already.

Ἡ πολεμικὴ φύσει κτητική πως ἔσται, ᾗ δεῖ χρῆσθαι πρός τε τὰ θηρία καὶ τῶν
ἀνθρώπων ὅσοι πεφυκότες ἄρχεσθαι μὴ θέλουσιν, ὡς φύσει δίκαιον τοῦτον ὄντα τὸν
πόλεμον.—ARISTOTLE, *Politics* 1256.

War is strictly a means of acquisition, to be employed against wild animals
and against inferior races of men, who, though intended by nature to be in
subjection to us, are unwilling to submit : for war of such a kind is just
by nature.

For many centuries, as we have seen, the growing City State
gained slowly in prosperity, bringing the distant lands under
cultivation or pasture and consolidating its authority over men's
minds and lives. Outside her were the landless adventurers,
infesting the narrow seas and barring the mountain passes ; but
within her well-marked borders the farmer and the shepherd,
and the craftsman and small trader beside them, were serving
the State and preparing themselves for self-government. We
have now reached the point in our rapid sketch of the economics
of the growing City, where, after centuries of isolation, the old
seclusion is interrupted and the states of Greece began to be
brought into relation with their neighbours.

The change was due to very simple and natural causes.
Greece is by nature, as we have seen, a poverty-stricken country.
Her bare hills and plains provide in themselves food for but
a small population. Under the rude methods of cultivation then
in use, a time was bound to come, in every City State area, when
the land could yield no more increase. It became peopled up to
its natural limits. If the slightest mischance occurred, if the

rains came late or a sudden storm spoilt the harvest, the State would be face to face with famine. This point seems to have been reached in the development of the leading City States in the eighth or seventh century before Christ. On an earlier page we watched some of the consequences to which this led in the sphere of politics or citizenship. Here we are concerned only with its economic results.[1]

When population presses upon subsistence, and there is not enough food to go round, there are only two immediate remedies —less people or more food, to send away emigrants or to bring in supplies from outside. Leaving the question of emigration aside till our next chapter, let us turn to the question of fresh supplies.

How is the food to be procured ? It cannot be bought, for there is nothing to buy it with. There are as yet no surplus products or manufactures. It must be hunted or stolen, ' led off or carried off,' as the Greek phrase ran. In other words, the city must make her peace with the hunting instinct and learn to use it in her service. She must learn how to conduct war.

War is a threadbare subject in our pulpits and newspapers. But to understand its normal place in City State society we must forget all that we have ever heard or read about either its wickedness or its romance. To the early Greeks, as to many of the Balkan highlanders to-day, it did not seem either wicked or romantic, but was simply an exciting and not unusual way of spending some weeks in early summer, a traditional part of the national economy and of the citizen's public service. For between Greek and modern Western warfare there are clear and vital distinctions ; and it is doubly necessary, both for the understanding of history and for sound policy to-day, that they should be widely recognized.

War in the modern world serves, or is supposed to serve, two separate functions. It is firstly, since we live in a world of sovereign States between which there is no binding law, the only available way of settling inter-State differences when reason and good temper have failed to adjust them, the stern arbitrament which men, conquered in body if not in spirit, must perforce accept, for the time at least, as decisive. For these purposes war has long been recognized by thinkers and

[1] See pp. 115 ff. above.

statesmen (to use an American statesman's phrase) as a
' ferocious folly '—a stupid and clumsy expedient unworthy of
our civilized life.   For civilized nations—peoples, that is, who
have acquired the self-respect which is second nature to all
true nationalities—cannot regard the arbitrament of force as
final.   Such peoples fight not for material but for moral issues,
not to avoid tribute and save their purses, but for homes and
liberties and customs and all their intimate associations.   Force
by itself can decide no moral issues.   England, for instance,
might conceivably be conquered, but she could not be held.
Men speak idly of war as ' clearing the air ' like a thunderstorm.
Napoleon, by the time he reached St. Helena, knew better : that
the sword, as he moaned, settles nothing, nothing.   You may
annex a province and secure her loyalty with fortresses, or
humble a proud people so that they long for revenge, or poison,
with the bitterness of persecution, a wellspring of young ideas ;
but you will decide no spiritual conflicts.   For though you may
think the battle is being fought out with the latest artillery on the
plains of Troy, it is up on Olympus, far from the roar of the guns
and the crash of musketry, that the gods are weighing the combatants in their scales.   In the third or fourth generation you
shall know the All-Father's verdict.

But there is another function claimed for warfare.   Modern
wars, we are told, should no longer be regarded as religious or
moral—these considerations may be waived—but as predominantly economic ; they are simply an extension to the national
sphere of the jostling competition of modern life.   Individuals
who have been bargaining against foreigners in the market-place
adjourn as soldiers to the battlefield to continue the debate.
Modern nations fight, not for provinces but for profits, for the
virgin market and the protected plantation.

This conception of war is often claimed by its advocates as
characteristically modern.   In the Middle Ages, we are told,
men fought for religion : nowadays they fight for trade.   In fact,
of course, it is war in its oldest and crudest and most thought-
less form.   It is, as some of its more outspoken advocates have
realized, simply the old state of brigandage of the Homeric chieftains and state piracy of King Polycrates, dressed up in a new
guise to suit our struggle-for-life philosophies. It is war, as

Aristotle described it, as a ' means of acquisition ' and ' a species of hunting '. Only it is carelessly transferred, without any attempt to realize the consequences, to the infinitely complex field of modern international economy. Under our sensitive system of credit-built finance, when Berlin and New York respond to every shock or shadow of shock in London or Paris, there is at least a presumption that the old doctrine of warfare should be revised. Certainly it can no longer be carried on in the same easy con-fident buccaneering manner ; for we know by experience that it touches the lives and fortunes of millions of non-combatants, the workman and the taxpayer, the shareholder and the house-wife, as surely and as closely as the fighters themselves. There are few things in public life more disastrous and demoralizing than the misplaced lightheartedness which treats serious issues as a game. The fifth-century Athenian was prone to the same fatal mistake, although with far greater ground for excuse. So it is worth while, in order to understand both the economy of ancient Greece and our own daily paper, to watch the history of the part played by warfare in the life of the older Greeks.[1]

Let us turn back once more to Thucydides. In one short but emphatic sentence he takes us through the long quiet centuries of isolation. Then, with a brief reference to colonies, he plunges into his favourite subject of the improvement of communica-tions, especially by sea. He tells us of the earliest navies, dating from the end of the eighth century and the early seventh, and of their successors down to the fifth. Then he proceeds as follows : ' The Greek navies of the period that we have traversed were what I have described. All their insignificance did not prevent

---

[1] For a good discussion of the economic conditions under which modern warfare is carried on, see *The Great Illusion* by Norman Angell (London, 1910, and many later editions). The illusion in question is the common belief that warfare between highly organized modern peoples can be economically pro-fitable to the victor. To put the author's doctrine in its simplest form : if an invading army were to loot the Bank of England, for every pound taken from its cellars the invaders would lose a thousand through the general shock to credit. He has thus caused a startling transposition of forces in an ancient controversy. The advocate of war becomes the ' sentimentalist ' whilst the ' practical man ' is ranged on the side of peace. It is important, however, to remember that opinions and impulses (especially collective impulses) do not automatically pass away by being proved to be unreasonable, or even un-profitable.—1914. I leave the above note and the passage in the text with its veiled reference to Poland and Alsace-Lorraine practically unaltered. They have been verified sooner than I expected.

them from **being** an element of the greatest power to those who cultivated them, alike in revenue and in dominion. They were the means by which the islands were reached and reduced, *especially by states that had not sufficient land of their own.* Wars by land there were none, none at least by which dominion was acquired. They were all simply border contests between neighbours, but of distant expeditions with conquest for object we hear nothing among the Hellenes. . . . What fighting there was consisted merely of local warfare between rivals.' [1]

Here we see clearly both the objects and the methods of this old Greek warfare. Its object was to secure ' revenue and dominion ', in other words, land and supplies. Its methods by sea were to reach and to occupy cultivable islands, driving out or imposing tribute on the existing population ; by land, across the range, where annexation was impossible and tribute could not be extorted, to make raids over the border and carry off what could be found.

Once the city had discovered this easy means of enrichment, she created the military and naval organization which would enable her either to pursue it herself or to defend herself against her neighbours ; and once this organization was created men were certain, as we know, to feel inclined to put it to use. Practically every Greek state had its conscript army of heavy-armed foot-soldiers, ready to be called out at need, and many of them— including Athens from a very early time—had trained seamen ready for their galleys as well. From the days of those early expeditions described by Thucydides, war, or rather State robbery, became a recognized part of City State life and economy. ' It belonged to the particular life-force of the City State,' says a recent German writer, ' to live on the products of other men's labours. This impulse did not disappear until the possibilities of satisfying it were diminished.' Glaucon, the ingenuous young man in the *Memorabilia* of Xenophon, regards it as the first and most natural source of income, ' to procure wealth for the city from her foreign enemies.' For the customs which grew up in this ancient warfare, no doubt out of the brigandage which preceded it, secured to the victor the whole property of the

---

[1] Thuc. i. 15. The translation is practically Crawley's (Temple Classics), except in the important sentence which I italicize, where he has blundered.

vanquished; and we shall have occasion to see later how Greek
financial arrangements often depended on the application of
these customs. The harder the struggle for existence became
for a City State, the more closely did its wars approximate to
freebooting expeditions. We shall not understand the imperial
position of fifth-century Athens unless we bear this temptation
very constantly in mind.[1]

We can watch many of these freebooting expeditions in the
pages of Herodotus. Two must suffice here—one by land and
one by sea. The first concerns Athens and one of her most
illustrious names. 'Through the victory of Marathon,' says
Herodotus, 'Miltiades, who was before highly esteemed among
the Athenians, still more increased his reputation. When, therefore, he asked of the Athenians seventy ships and troops and
money, without telling them what country he purposed to
invade, but saying that he would make them rich if they would
follow him, as he would take them to a country whence they
would easily obtain abundance of gold, the Athenians, elated by
these hopes, granted him the ships. Miltiades took the troops
and sailed against the island of Paros, alleging as a pretext that
the Parians had provoked hostilities by sending a galley with the
Persians to Marathon. This was his pretended reason; but, in
fact, he had a private grudge against the Parians, because Lysa-
goras, son of Tisias, a Parian, had spoken ill of him to Hydarnes
the Persian. He arrived with his forces and besieged the Parians,
who were driven within their walls; Miltiades sent a herald in to
them with a demand for a hundred talents, saying that if they did
not give him that sum he would not draw off his army until
he had destroyed them. The Parians never entertained the
thought whether they should give Miltiades any money, but
devised means by which they might defend the city; and, in
addition to other plans, raised the wall, in several of the most
exposed parts of the city, during the night, to twice its former
height. Up to this point of the story all the Greeks agree.'
Here the tale becomes confused. A Parian priestess seems to
have told Miltiades to do something which resulted in his hurting

---

[1] Riezler, *Über Finanzen und Monopole in Griechenland*, pp. 68–9. For
Glaucon see the chapter motto. The very word for enemy (ἐχθρός) means
'outsider', as opposed to ξένος, 'stranger' or guest-friend.

his leg by leaping over a wall in the dark. In any case, he
eventually ' sailed home again in a bad plight, neither bringing
money to the Athenians nor having reduced Paros, but having
besieged it for six and twenty days and ravaged the island '.[1]

The story dates from the early part of the fifth century, but
the sea-raid of which it gives so vivid a picture is of the sort that
must constantly have been going on between coastlands and
islands all through the days of the growth of the City State.
But this particular incident has a further interest, for it throws
forward an ominous shadow on the path of our special inquiry.
There was as yet no Athenian Empire when Miltiades sailed
to Paros. But the Empire, when it came, did not forget the
methods found so convenient by the City State.

The other story hails from the Peloponnese. When King
Croesus sent for help to Sparta, about the middle of the sixth
century, he received none because ' at that very time ', says
Herodotus, ' the Spartans themselves happened to have a quarrel
with the men of Argos about a tract of land called Thyrea ; for
this Thyrea, which properly belongs to the territory of Argos,
the Spartans had seized. . . . The Argives having advanced to
the territory which had thus been taken from them, both parties,
upon a conference, agreed that three hundred men on each side
should join battle, and that whichever party was victorious
should be entitled to the disputed territory.' In the event, two
Argives were left alive and one Spartan ; but the Argives,
thinking themselves victorious, ran home with the news, leaving
the Spartan to strip the corpses of the Argives in the old Homeric
fashion and carry their arms to his camp. Whereupon, of course,
the battle was renewed next day.[2]

There is one special point of interest in this famous story.
It bears the mark of a curious transition in our subject. It deals
with a border struggle of the old familiar kind, such as went on,
between citizens and outcasts and between State and State, all
through the period which we have been considering. But the
struggle is no longer carried on in the old unscrupulous buccaneering spirit. There has been a change in methods. Fighting is

[1] Hdt. vi. 132–5.
[2] Hdt. i. 82. Compare, in this connexion, the Boeotarch's speech, Thuc.
iv. 92.

now conducted according to a certain fixed code. It has an elaborate etiquette of its own. It is no longer a fierce scramble in which ' all is fair '. It is a game which is played according to rules. It has become in fact a sport as well as a ' means of acquisition '.

But war as a sport carries us beyond the limits of this chapter. For it belongs properly to a time when the old crude methods of robbery were no longer so indispensable to the life of the City State, when men could afford to be chivalrous because they had discovered other means of satisfying their immediate needs. For the present we must pass on to the growing city's second remedy, the safety-valve of emigration.[1]

[1] See Appendix.

CHAPTER VI

THE GROWING CITY : COLONIZATION

Καὶ δὴ καὶ τό γε τέλος, ἂν ἐπίχυσις ὑπερβάλλουσα ἡμῖν πολιτῶν συμβαίνῃ καὶ ἀπορῶμεν, τὸ παλαιόν που ὑπάρχει μηχάνημα, ἐκπομπὴ ἀποικιῶν.— PLATO, *Laws* 740

Last of all, if there be an excess of citizens and we are at our wits' end, there is still the old device of sending out a colony.

WE have seen that the growing Greek States were faced, in the eighth and seventh centuries, with the problem of over-population in its acutest form. Of the two obvious forms of relief—less mouths or more supplies—the latter was the easier and more natural. But it was also the less satisfactory. For, as Socrates told his young pupil, you may certainly ' grow rich upon the foreigner . . . if you are the stronger power ; but, if not, you stand to lose even what you have already '. Greece was therefore gradually driven back upon the more difficult remedy, the drastic purge of emigration. As Plato puts it, in the kindly conservatism of his old age : ' when men who have nothing, and are in want of food, show a disposition to follow their leaders in an attack on the property of the rich, these, who are the natural plague of the State, are sent away by the statesman in as friendly a spirit as possible ; and this dismissal of them is euphemistically termed a colony.' By a deliberate effort of state-craft, encouraged at every point by the healing influence of Delphi, the activities that were running riot at home were diverted into a great colonizing impulse. In the course of these two centuries the Mediterranean, from Spain to the Crimea, was girdled with a ring of cities sent out from Greece and Asia Minor.[1]

It is these circumstances of their origin, rather than the character of the Greek race, which explain the profound and characteristic differences between ancient Greek and most modern forms of colonization, between ancient Marseilles, for instance,

[1] Cf. p. 123 above. Plato, *Laws* 735–6 ; Thuc. i. 12. 4 (where the Black Sea colonies are omitted and the foundation of the Ionian cities is much post-dated).

and the modern Greek quarter in New York. A Greek colonizing expedition was not a private venture of individuals or groups of individuals, but embodied a carefully organized scheme of State-promoted emigration. A Greek colony was not founded by a few pioneers and then gradually built up by band after band of subsequent stragglers, but planted once and for all, in its proper form and numbers, by a swarm going out, like bees, with a Queen or Head-colonist of their own.[1]

Once planted, the colony became, of course, a full-fledged city, leading a new and independent life, associating much or little, according as it felt inclined, with its metropolis. To describe that life, so far as it had characteristic features of its own, does not fall within the strict limits of our subject ; the Greek colonial communities are only important to us for the part they played in connexion with fifth-century Athens. But a few words are necessary, if only to clear away misconceptions.

A Greek colony was not primarily a trading centre. The basis of its economy was agricultural, as with the cities of the homeland. It was only through the chances of later development that some of them, like some of their parent cities, attained commercial importance. The men who went out to form their citizen-body shared the old agricultural tradition : indeed, they were mostly dispossessed cultivators, who had been crying out at home for a ' redistribution of lands '. And our inscriptions show us this redistribution taking place, only on barbarian soil. ' Ten land-distributors shall be chosen, one from each tribe ; and they shall divide up the land,' say the regulations that have come down to us for an Athenian colony in Thrace. Our only other set of regulations, for a colony on the island of Curzola in Dalmatia, goes into closer details. ' Those who are the first to occupy the land and fortify the city are each to receive as a special portion a site for a house within the fortified enclosure, with the portion of land belonging to it ; and of the land outside the city each man is to receive three-quarters of an acre as his first share, besides his proportion of the land which will still remain to be divided. The men of the parties that arrive later shall each receive an acre of the land that still remains to be divided. The following occupied the land and fortified the city.'

[1] Plato, *Laws* 708, who compares over-population to a state of siege.

Here follow the names of the first settlers, arranged according to the ' tribes ' of the mother-country.[1]

These two inscriptions are all that remain to show us in detail the care and organization that was directed to the founding of a Greek colony. But we know from Herodotus the pains that were taken to select a good site, and how Apollo was called in, not only as a healing power for moral influence and support, but as a source of useful information for the details of the proposed settlement. Men went to Delphi with a string of business inquiries, and every statesman in Greece knew the chief questions to be asked.

Plato in the *Laws* and Aristotle in the *Politics* have both embodied the main conditions of the model colony—plenty of water and good land for corn and vine and olive, timber for ships, a good harbour, a town site not too near the sea, and, above all, tame natives, willing and anxious to do field-work if their masters will secure them against aggression. But the fourth-century philosophers are only copying the traditional prospectuses that have come down through many generations of Greek agricultural life. You will find the archetype in Homer, on the lips of Odysseus, when he describes to Alcinous his last bivouac before meeting the Cyclops, in an island full of woods and soft meadows, ploughland and vine-land, with unnumbered goats in its rugged glens, but which in all the long days has never known seed-time or ploughing and is just calling out for men.[2]

Here we must leave our colonists till we meet them again when we go out on a voyage with the Athenian trader. For it is time to pass on to another stage of our inquiry. Colonization begets intercourse and intercourse begets commerce. We have in fact reached the point in the economic development of the city at which, even with colonization for a safety-valve, the old self-sufficient economic life is no longer possible. Strictly speaking, indeed, we have already passed that narrow barrier. For how can Apollo issue his sailing instructions, or our colonists know

[1] Hicks and Hill, No. 41 ; Dittenberger, No. 933. Brea was founded in the fifth century, Curzola in the fourth. In general see Meyer, ii, § 284 and note, who points out how scanty our detailed evidence about Greek colonization is. There was no Greek Hakluyt to collect the early voyages.

[2] *Od.* ix. 116 ff. ; Hdt. v. 155 ff. ; Xen. *Anab.* vi. 4. 3 ff. (showing that Xenophon had a practised eye) ; Plato, *Laws* 704 ff., 740 ; Ar. *Pol.* 1327 a, 1329 a 26, 1330 a 26 ff. (tame natives)

round which headland lies their home, unless adventurous fore-
runners have already explored the field, unless some ' young
light-hearted master of the waves ' has already braved Phoenicians and natives and won his way, after an Odyssey, through
uncharted seas, to the harbour of his choice ? These pioneers,
part pirates, part dealers with the ' shy traffickers ' of the hinterland, sometimes an organized soldiery, sometimes explorers or
wandering scholars just going out ' to have a look ', are at once
the creators and the creatures of a new era of city economy. The
natives who watched them labouring shoreward from the blue
distance and brought their treasures down to the beach for
exchange at the recognized meeting-place, often dimly wondered
what drove them so far abroad from their homes and gods.
Euripides, ' most tragic of poets,' has taken the question from
their lips, and given it to a band of captive women longing for
the sight of a face from home.

> A flash of the foam, a flash of the foam,
>   A wave on the oarblade welling,
> And out they passed to the heart of the blue :
> A chariot shell that the wild winds drew.
> *Is it for passion of gold they come,*
>   *Or pride to make great their dwelling ?*

They could not tell, nor could the wanderers themselves.
Through good or evil, gain or suffering, victory or disaster, like
the Elizabethans after them, they followed the gleam.

> For sweet is Hope, yea to much mortal woe
> So sweet that none may turn from it nor go,
>   Whom once the far voice calleth,
> To wander through fierce peoples and the gleam
> Of desolate seas, in every heart a dream :
> And these she maketh empty die, and, lo,
>   To that man's hand she falleth. [1]

[1] Eur. *I. T.* 407 ff. (transl. Murray); Hdt. iv. 196 (shy traffickers). ἅμα
κατ' ἐμπορίαν καὶ κατὰ θεωρίαν (' combining business with sight-seeing ') is the
Greek voyager's account of himself : *Ath. Pol.* xi. 1 ; Is. xvii. 4 ; cf. Hdt. iii.
139 ; Thuc. vi. 24. 3. Plato, who thought travel bad for people, had yet
a weakness for the wandering scholar, having been one himself. So they are
the only people he allows to go abroad unhindered. Ordinary citizens may only
travel when they are over forty, and then only on State business ; and ' when
they come home they shall teach the young that the institutions of other states
are inferior to their own ' (*Laws* 951). It is a curious fact that, according to the

traditional dating of the 'foundation stories', the earliest Sicilian colonies, beginning with Naxos and Syracuse, were founded some time before those in Magna Graecia. Yet Magna Graecia was on the sea-road to Sicily (which was viâ Corcyra), and presented some excellent agricultural sites. It is probable, therefore, that the dates we have are in some cases not those of the foundation of the colony but of the first trading settlement (ἐμπόριον), perhaps of the first time a party of men were left during the winter. This is supported by the fact that Syracuse, and, more particularly, Naxos, are by no means the most natural sites for an agricultural colony. Naxos under Etna, as seen after rounding Spartivento, was a natural point to steer for, and Syracuse, or rather the 'off-lying' island Ortygia (such as passing traders loved : Thuc. vi. 2. 6), was welcome for its fresh-water spring, Arethusa, a few yards from the shore, at its extreme outward edge. Compare the account in Hdt. iv. 151 ff. of the way in which Cyrene was colonized from Thera through information supplied by a purple-fisher. These early trading visitors came without wives or families or gods or institutions. They were as different from the later colonizing swarm as the Hudson Bay trappers from the ordinary Canadian, or the early Vikings from the Normans. They are, in fact, not immigrants but migrants. Myres (*Proceedings of Classical Association*, 1911, p. 67) has offered another solution of this difficulty. He thinks the early colonists passed by Magna Graecia because 'Magna Graecia was preoccupied by the survivals of an earlier régime, dating back to the late Minoan Age': but this, as he admits, is only a suggestion.—1921. See now Aubrey Gwynn's Cromer Prize Essay on *The Character of Greek Colonization*, which puts together a large amount of information in convenient form. [See Appendix.]

CHAPTER VII

CITY ECONOMICS : CRAFTSMEN AND WORKMEN

Your labour only may be sold ; your soul must not.—RUSKIN, *Time and Tide*, § 81.

With the Greeks every handicraft was an art : with the Romans every art was a handicraft.—MARQUARDT.

So far, in this economic sketch, our attention has been fixed upon a process of growth. We have watched the isolated Greek states, with their purely agricultural economy, faced with the inevitable pressure of population upon subsistence and finding a heroic remedy in a wholesale process of colonization.

After this necessary bloodletting follows a quieter period, marked by a consolidation of economic forces upon a new and broader basis. We are coming into the daylight of history, to the City State which we know, not only from the regretful eulogies of Plato and Aristotle but from the poets and historians—to the economy which immediately underlay the fifth-century Empire of Athens. It seems advisable for us, therefore, to change the method of our inquiry from the dynamic to the static : to use this natural halting-point in order to make a survey of the economic features of the historical City State. We shall only be able to do so in rough and general terms, for the evidence must be collected from widely scattered fields. But without some such account it is impossible to understand the economic problems that confronted fifth-century Athens. We shall follow the arrangement suggested in a previous chapter, dealing first with individual and then with public housekeeping, first with the Athenian as an earner, and then with the political economy of the Athenian state. In this way we shall pick up and put into their proper setting a number of important factors which have necessarily been omitted in the rough sketch of the previous pages.

So far we have only encountered one kind of Greek earner, the man who made his living out of the land, the natural nursing mother of all mankind. We have now to set beside him the other types of earner which grew into importance during this period of consolidation. The first and greatest of these is the craftsman, or, as we should call him to-day, the skilled industrial worker.

We shall need to exercise our imaginations before we make his acquaintance, for there is very little in common between the working of skilled industry as we know it and its working in Greece. In the first place it occupied with the Greeks a position of relative unimportance. With us manufactures are the chief and most obvious form of national wealth, and, when the advocates of agriculture bid us place the land side by side with them, they remind us that it is our ' greatest industry '. In Greece the land was indisputably supreme. The normal citizen did not look beyond Mother Earth for a living ; and when industry pushed its way in as a possible livelihood, it was only as subordinate to her paramount position. In the state of nature, as the Greeks imagined it, every family of farmers supplied their own needs— made their own ploughs and pruning-hooks, spun and wove their own clothes, built and repaired their own houses, composed their own poetry, and mixed their own black draughts when they were taken ill. If we are to believe a certain school of economic historians, this was what the Greeks went on doing all through their history.[1]

No doubt this happy state of self-help never really existed. We know from the specimens in our museums that even the flint-knapper must have been a professional ; and as far back as our records reach, in Greece as in Palestine, we find the craftsman beside the farmer, not only Tubal-cain, the shoesmith and metal-worker, but also Jubal, who played the harp during the winter evenings. But it remains true, none the less, that these early farmers, with their wives and dependants, accomplished within the household, especially in the sphere of clothing, much that in our own day, and even in later Greek days, was sent outside to the

---

[1] Cf. Meyer, ' Die wirtschaftliche Entwickelung des Altertums ' (reprinted in *Kleine Schriften*, 1909), who deals faithfully with Rodbertus and his modern followers. Their theory is only worth mentioning because it has mingled with the general stream of contemporary ideas to reappear, for instance, in socialist and other addresses on industrial evolution. Meyer himself, by speaking of ' capitalism ' in ancient Greece without sufficiently defining what he means, has inspired another equally misguided school of popular writers, who detect everywhere in Greek life the familiar conflicts of modern industrialism. [See Appendix.]

paid specialist as a matter of course. For industry in its origin
was simply specialism. A man was lame or blind and no use for
field work ; so he devoted himself to the forge, which demanded
a strong body and brawny arms but did not tax the legs, or, if he
had the memory and the aptitude, took to reciting and improving
ancient songs. So the community became enriched with a local
Homer and Hephaestus. Soon it became an accepted thing that
it was foolish to waste valuable family time on making ploughs
and pots and baskets which the craftsmen could do far better and
more quickly, or even to risk a valuable life without calling in
expert advice about drugs and herbs. By the beginning of the
sixth century it was well recognized in Athenian society that
when a man possesses a certain skill he will naturally employ it
as a means of livelihood. Solon gives us a brief list, in one of his
poems, of some of the skilled earners of the Athens of his day.
Besides the trader and the skilled farmer, who was now busily
engaged in mastering the secrets of olive-culture, he mentions
metal-workers, weavers, poets, or rather reciters, diviners, and
doctors. The list is by no means exhaustive, for he has left out
at least two very important classes, the workers in stone and clay.
But it is full enough to serve as a useful introduction to our
inquiry. For it reminds us how, if we are to understand Greek
craftsmanship and the joyful spirit which inspired it, we need to
revise and enlarge our current conception of labour, sweeping out
of our minds many lurking prepossessions due to the narrow
specialism and, above all, to the class distinctions of modern life.
The Greeks, then as now, recognized no distinction between a
craft or ' trade ' and a ' profession '.[1]

For these modern distinctions, if once we stop to consider them,
are unreal and meaningless. The real distinction in this sphere,
as our forefathers knew, is between the man within the gild or
brotherhood who possesses certain definite knowledge, with the
trained capacity to use it, and the man who possesses none, or, to

---

[1] Solon, xii. 41 ff. (49 does not refer, as sometimes stated, to mining). For
Jubal and Tubal-cain see Genesis iv. 20 and Giotto's representations of this
early society on the base of his Campanile. Some of the early craftsmen were
prisoners, like Democedes, the doctor at the Persian court (Hdt. iii. 125,
129). Thus Epeios, the maker of the famous wooden horse (in the *Little
Iliad*), was probably a captive Epeian (a tribe which became extinct later,
when another origin was invented for him).

put it boldly, between the artist and the common labourer. In those earlier days all men who knew the joy of creation, whether with hand or brain, ranked as ' poets ' or ' artificers ' (ποιηταί, τεχνίται), and were accepted as fellow-craftsmen.

If we have unlearnt this truism and allowed our painters and our authors, our doctors and our mechanics, each to relapse dull-eyed into the separate groove of his ' trade ' or ' profession ', it is because we have lost the old happiness which kept the sense of a common purpose fresh in the craftsman's mind. Our modern industrial system, with an ingenuity so wicked that one might almost believe it to be deliberate, has contrived to take the joy out of craftsmanship, and so to choke up the very springs of art. It has replaced, wherever possible, the delicate skill of the human hand by inhuman machinery, and the independent thought of the human brain by ' soulless organization '. It has removed the maker or producer from all association with the public for whom he works, and substituted a deadening ' cash-nexus ' for the old personal relationship or sense of effort in a corporate cause. Above all, it has taken from him his liberty, and forced him to work for a master who is no artist, and to work fast and badly. It has turned Solon's weaver into a maker of shoddy, his minstrel into a journalist, and his diviner (if not his doctor) into a dispenser of quack remedies. If we are to understand aright the craftsmanship of the Greeks, we must think ourselves back into a freer air, such as blew through the homes of our own English workers until close on the Industrial Revolution. It is natural for human beings to enjoy using their own best faculties. Men never felt that enjoyment so keenly, or put so much high effort into its attainment, as in the workshops of ancient Greece. If you seek a proof, go and look through the shelves of our Greek museums. There is hardly an object that they made, however rude, but bears on it, sometimes faintly, sometimes with speaking clearness, the touch of the spirit of Art.[1]

---

[1] It is unfortunate that Greek craftsmen speak to us only through their works. They have left us none of the songs which they surely used to sing over their tools. All we have is three lines of an old mill-catch :

      Grind, mill, grind,
      For Pittacus did grind
      Who was king over great Mytilene.

                          (*Anth. Lyr.* ' *Carmina Popularia* ' 46.)

Under what conditions did these Greek craftsmen work? In answer to this question we will take two typical branches of craftsmanship, one outdoor and one indoor, our information as to which enables us to watch the work going on. Leaving aside the tanners and the lyre-makers, the jewellers and blacksmiths and glass-workers, about whom we know all too little, let us pay a brief visit to the stone-cutters and the potters. With the exercise of due caution what we learn from them may be presumed also of their fellow-craftsmen in other spheres of activity.[1]

The Greek temples and public buildings, together with all the works of art that they contained, are the most famous surviving monuments of Greek craftsmanship. Fortunately, we have now sufficient evidence from inscriptions to watch some of them in the building.

The stone-masons and sculptors who made and adorned the temples and sanctuaries, the colonnades and armouries, and other public buildings of Greece, were not State servants. They were private craftsmen, such as Socrates, whose time was in their own hands. On ordinary days, when the State did not call for their services, they worked in their own stoneyards, with four or five young apprentices, cutting those formal inscriptions and carving those quiet gravestone scenes that we know so well from our museums. But when there was a public building to claim their craftsmanship, they accepted State employment for the time being, working under an arrangement with the State Overseers or Special Commissioners of Public Works. Sometimes the master-mason became simply a foreman, and his workmen were paid direct by the State, although he still retained control over them at their work. More often he remained a small contractor, undertaking the work himself and accepting all responsibility for its performance. Some of the contracts made in this form are preserved, and show how jealously the city watched over the work it gave out to its contractors. ' He shall work continuously . . .

(Compare the song of the well-diggers in Numbers xxi. 17–18.) There is nothing like the beautiful Ceylon potters' song, quoted in Wallas, *The Great Society*, pp. 346–7, which takes the worker through every stage and process of his beloved work. Cf. Glotz, *Travail*, pp. 328–9, and illustrations.

[1] Blümner, *Technologie und Terminologie der Gewerbe und Künste bei Griechen und Römern* (Leipzig, 1875–86), collects all the evidence about the crafts (though not about the craftsmen).

working with a sufficient number of craftsmen according as the nature of the craft admits (κατὰ τὴν τέχνην), not less than five, and if he disobey any provision written down in the agreement or be discovered executing bad work (κακοτεχνῶν τι) he shall be punished by the overseers, as he shall seem to them to deserve, for not doing according to the written agreement ; and if any of the workmen employed under him be discovered executing bad work, let him be driven out from the work, and no longer take part in it ; and if he disobey this sentence he shall be punished, together with the contractor . . . and if the contractor injure any sound stone in the course of his work, he shall replace it at his own expense without interruption to the work, and shall remove the spoilt stone out of the temple enclosure within five days, or the stone shall become sacred property . . . and if the contractors have any dispute amongst themselves upon anything written in the agreement the overseers shall decide it. . . .' [1]

Here we can see plainly what kind of men these ancient contractors were, and how different from the modern organizer of hired labour who is called by the same name. The Greek contractor is himself a workman, who works by the side of his labourers, and is liable to punishment for their careless work or his own. He has neither the capital nor the labour to undertake the whole building or even a considerable part of it. He is simply a master-mason, working together on the same job with a number, perhaps scores, of other master-masons, proud to be able for a time to make the Acropolis their stoneyard, and to leave the mark of their craftsmanship, and that of the craftsmen whom they have trained, upon a great city monument. There is no competition here to keep the rival builder out of the job, and no rivalry for big winnings. Indeed, so little capital have these contractors, and so incapable are they of meeting any larger demand upon their resources, that, when a city suddenly embarked upon a work that required an exceptional supply of labour, she had to send out

[1] Dittenberger, No. 540, ll. 11, 13, 32, 42 : the building is a temple of Zeus at Lebadea : the date 175-171 B.C. But the same system and similar provisions appear in all the extant inscriptions. See Dittenberger, ii. 537 ff. (aedificationes). For the Overseers (ἐπιστάται) see Francotte, *Industrie*, vol. ii, pp. 63-4, and the whole section on public works. At Athens at the time of Pericles' building schemes they numbered three or more, and stayed in office for more than one year, probably till the building with which they were concerned was completed.

recruiting agents to bring in contractors and workmen from abroad. Neither in Athens nor elsewhere do we find any traces of unemployed skilled labourers. The danger was all the other way : that cities would lack the labour necessary to carry out their designs. Thus, when the citizens of Argos decided that, like Athens, they needed long walls down to the sea, they had to send to the Athenians for extra workers in wood and stone. The rough labour they could raise at a pinch with women, children, and household slaves ; but these skilled employments, with their inherited craft-methods, they could not so easily improvise.[1]

This should serve to prepare our minds for what will be for modern readers the most remarkable feature of the Athenian building inscriptions, because we have been taught by our economists to regard it as impossible—the appearance in them of slave-masons doing the same work and receiving the same pay as the freemasons. The fact is that in an ambitious city, anxious to build great public monuments—in a city, as we should say, with a rapidly expanding building industry—there was a constant need for fresh labour to fill the ranks of the craft. The deficiency was not easily supplied out of the free population in other walks of life, for the movement of expansion affected, in some degree, almost every branch of livelihood. It was therefore supplied from abroad. Athens in the sixth century, and still more, as we shall see, in the fifth, filled up her crafts with foreign apprentices. Some of them were free resident aliens who had been attracted to Athens, others were slaves who had received a more pressing invitation. The point that we have here to notice is that both these classes, whatever their legal status, were admitted into the craft, and are found working there on the same terms as the citizens. An analysis of the payments made by the State for the building of the Erechtheum in 409 shows that wages were paid for the work of 27 citizens, 40 free Outlanders, and 15 slaves. We can confirm these figures by confronting them with two other sets of Attic accounts dealing with the building of a sanctuary at Eleusis in the years 329–328 and 319–318. These two sets, when put together, show 36 citizens, 39 resident aliens, 12 strangers,

---

[1] Thuc. v. 82. 5. For labour recruiting-agents (κήρυκες) see Francotte, vol. ii, p 83. Compare Hiram's help to Solomon, 1 Kings v. 6 and 18.

and 2 slaves at work, besides 57 other names which are too indefinite to be put into any category.[1]

These slaves and other non-citizens (no doubt many of them freedmen) are working not only at the same trade but at identically the same tasks as the citizen workmen. In the case of the Erechtheum, for instance, one piece of work dealt with in the inscription is the fluting of the columns. Each column is being fluted by a squad of from four to six workpeople, directed by their foreman or master-mason. All of them, including the foreman master, are paid at the same rate. Citizens and non-citizens, slaves and free men, seem inextricably mixed. In one case the foreman is actually a slave ; in another, a master who acts as foreman brings two slaves of his own and another hired from some one else for the occasion. All receive the same wage, one drachma a day, or about four shillings' purchasing power. Indeed, as Francotte remarks : ' The ordinary wage for all categories of workers ' on the Erechtheum ' from the architect to the day labourer, for free men as for slaves, is a drachma a day '.[2]

This is indeed only what we should expect in a society which cared truly for art, if the theories of Aristotle and others had not confused our imaginations. All true artists are democratic in spirit, for a common interest in good work breaks down all unreal distinctions. To the Athenian craftsmen their slaves were not, as Aristotle called them, ' living instruments,' but simply ' fellow workers ', additional hands brought into the family workshop to help the masons and the potters to fulfil the city's needs. Of course the lawyer-like Aristotle is technically correct : the slave remained a Thing, not a Person, and could not assert a legal claim to the wage that he earned. But we shall see in a later chapter how his position in the household economy and his daily activities in private life reacted upon his legal status.[3]

[1] *I. G.* i. 324 analysed by Francotte, vol. ii, pp. 205–7.

[2] Francotte, vol. i, p. 316. The slave was not entitled to keep this or any other money that he might earn (e. g. by shopkeeping). His master, the slave-lord, farmed him out (as a landlord might a piece of land) for what he could make out of him, and pocketed the proceeds, which were known as the ' slave-rent ' (ἀποφορά). But in practice such slaves were able to keep a fair proportion of their earnings, out of which they hoped ultimately to buy their freedom. See pp. 390–2 below. Slaves working ' on their own ' were known as χωρὶς οἰκοῦντες (Dem. iv. 36). On purchasing power see note on p. 412 below.

[3] ' Fellow workers ' : Xen *Mem.* ii. 3. 3, an incidental passage but all the truer for that.

Those fluted columns are still in position supporting the entab-
latures for which they were made. Time has not robbed them
of their beauty, or dulled the delicacy of the work which those
aliens and slaves put into them. But it is time to leave the
Acropolis. Let us go down now to visit some friendly potter in
the Cerameicus. We need not look for a large unsightly modern
factory. We shall probably find him in his own home, like an
industrial cottager of to-day, with his children and a handful of
other young workers to help him. The home was used for so
little else that there was no objection to using it as a workshop,
and there was no reason for adding to the working expenses by
occupying another building. This workshop or ' school ' (as we
have learnt to say of Italian painters), or, as the French neatly
describe it, the ' atelier patronal ', was hardly ever on a large
scale. Twelve in all, says a French writer, was about the proper
number. The vase-painters have left us many pictures of the
homely interior of the potter's shop, with all the various processes
going on in close juxtaposition. We can see the master working as
in the stoneyard, side by side with his apprentices, superintend-
ing and encouraging their own efforts at craftsmanship. How
successfully they did so may be judged by the fact that, among
the thousands of extant specimens which fill so many museum
shelves, ' two painted vases exactly identical do not exist.' Yet
Duris and Euphronius and their many nameless fellow workers
were not in their own day counted among the immortals. They
were only honest workmen who had trained eye and hand by
a long and persevering apprenticeship, till they knew what really
good work was and enjoyed the supreme effort of doing it. The
vases they turned out were not ornaments or curios for the col-
lector—the Greeks had never heard either of collectors or of
curios—but objects for daily use. But, since they were made for
Greeks, they needed to be as beautiful as they could make them,
well-shaped, well-glazed, and well-painted, or they would not be
counted serviceable.[1]

---

[1] See Pottier's *Duris and the Painters of Greek Vases* (English translation,
1909), with illustrations, especially p. 25. Of course some branches of craftsmanship were more mechanical than others. There was not much room for
individuality in the making of shields and spears, and it is in this department
that we find the largest workshops. That of ˙Lysias and his brother is
generally said to have had a hundred and twenty workpeople ; but it is

Within these humble workshops, as among the builders up on the Acropolis, there were no social barriers. Each man did his best and was fitly honoured, and, in due course, rewarded for what he did. Many of the apprentices in the sixth-century Athens, and perhaps the majority a century later, must have been slaves or born in slavery. We know that even among the masters several, and among them some of the most famous, such as Brygos, were not Athenians or even Greeks by birth. Yet neither from the paintings nor from the inscriptions can we discern any difference of treatment. Down in the potter's workshop, as up on the Acropolis, slave and free craftsmen ate the same food, worked the same hours, and wore the same working clothes, or, when the work was hot and dirty, mutually agreed to discard them.[1]

The craftsman needed no capital beyond the simple utensils of his craft (which the vase-paintings show us, as in a Holbein picture, hanging up on the wall when not in use). For the materials that he used were seldom costly and were generally provided by the customer who gave him the order. Just as you took your own cart or plough to the joiner's or to the blacksmith's to be mended, so you took your own leather to the cobbler's, and (if an Oxford vase may be trusted) stood up on his table while he cut it to the shape of your foot, and, if you were extravagant and your wife and daughters had turned lazy, or your women-

doubtful from the passage (Lys. xii. 19) whether the 120 slaves there mentioned were all so employed. If so, it was more than three times as large as any other Greek workshop we know of. That of Demosthenes' father with 33 comes next. But both these date from a period when, as we shall see, the best Greek habits of work were in decline. Francotte (*Industrie*, vol. ii, p. 21) seems to have shown that big workshops were found not to pay so well as small ones. ' Whatsoever thou doest, do it with all thy might,' was the fifth-century spirit in the workshop, as in public affairs. Socrates preached it too (Xen. *Mem.* ii. 8. 6). See Glotz, *Travail*, p. 319.

[1] On the equal treatment of slaves and free men in workshops see Guiraud, *La Main-d'œuvre industrielle dans la Grèce ancienne*, p. 197, and Pottier, *Duris*, p. 10. The name Duris itself is not Athenian, although it is not, like so many other artists' names, barbarian. It used to be held that the naked or very scantily dressed figures of potters, blacksmiths, and others on vase-paintings were ' conventional ' : but on at least one vase there is a tunic hanging up on the wall. See Daremberg and Saglio, Fig. 2969, s. v. *Ferrum*. The fact is that, like the Avaricious Man in Theophrastus, they cannot and will not afford two. (The ancients wore no nightdresses.) Other master painters of slave origin were Scythes, Colchos, Thrax, Lydos, Sicanos, Sicelos, and Amasis, who was the first Attic vase-painter to sign his name (Pauly, s. v. *Amasis*).

slaves been given their freedom, your own wool to some outside wool-worker. The craftsman, in fact, was not a trader but simply what the Greeks called a technîtes, which means ' artist ', without any of our grand or Bohemian associations. It was not his business to buy materials, but to work them up and make them serviceable. This saved him from having to keep a large stock, and you from the complications that arise from paying a number of different profits.[1]

The craftsman, therefore, lived in close touch with the public for whom he performed services, not separated, like the modern workman, by a host of distributors and intermediaries. It was on the direct appreciation of the citizens that he depended for a livelihood. Hence he took care to set up shop in the heart of the city, where he could easily be reached and would easily attract notice, generally close to the market-place, where the public promenaded up and down. Every craft had its own quarters, in a special Row amid the maze of streets. Just as in Old London, when you turned off Cheapside, you found yourself in Bucklersbury or Wood Street, or in Ironmonger or Leather Lane, so, in an old Greek city, as you dawdled away from the Agora into the shady back alleys, you could tell by the noise or the smell, by the clanging of the hammer, the grating of the saw, or the pungent odour of the tannery, into whose domain you were intruding. You strolled past the open doors of the little workshops, crowded in friendly rivalry one next the other, and, if you were feeling contemplative or inclined for a chat, you could drop in and watch your friend the artist at his work. Socrates, himself a stone-cutter by trade, was particularly fond of spending

[1] For the Oxford cobbler vase see *Journal of Hellenic Studies*, 1908, Plate 30, and Beazley's commentary. For professional ' wool-work ' done by women see an interesting article by Tod in the *Annual of the British School at Athens*, 1901-2, p. 204, and cf. p. 339 below. The women in his inscriptions are freed-women often working by arrangement for their former masters. Lovers of Socrates will remember how he advised an unfortunate friend, who was burdened during troubled times by an influx of sisters, cousins, and nieces, to set them to work making clothes, and how, when his advice was adopted, ' they went on working during lunch and right up to supper time, and became cheerful instead of surly.' But for this vast and unusual industrial experiment money had to be borrowed to buy the apparatus and the wool. See Xen. *Mem.* ii. 7. Similarly, when Democedes the famous doctor emigrated because he could not stand his father's temper, he had a hard struggle because he had no proper surgical instruments, and was too poor to procure them (Hdt. iii. 131).

his abundant leisure in this way: while he was enticing his crafts-men friends into discussions and puzzling them with awkward questions, he was storing up in his mind that host of useful images and illustrations which we know so well from Plato's *Dialogues*. One of his shoemaker friends, called Simon, took the trouble to write down his conversations in a book called *Leather Talks*, and so became the first Boswell. It was in these humble workshops that he learnt what it is for a man really to ' know his job ', and realized how little the average politician knew of his, as the Greeks conceived it—the creation of a city which should be as perfect a work of art as a good shoe or a good plough or a good glass vase. Modern statesmen have still similar lessons to learn in the same quarter. For ' while our glass-makers proceed by vigorous and confident processes to exact results, our statesmen, like the glass-makers of ancient Athens, still trust to empirical maxims and personal skill '. So hard is it, as Socrates knew, to keep the art of government up to date.[1]

The modern tourist at Athens, when he walks down 'Shoe Lane', that last survival of the ancient Bazaar in a city of modern shops, where you can hardly pass for the masses of shoes hanging out on either side of the narrow street, while their proprietors are busy inside their little workshops making additions to the store, wonders at the unpractical arrangement by which all these com-peting cobblers live next door to one another. If they were living in an English town, they would spread themselves carefully out and be at pains to leave at least a stone's throw between competing shop and shop. The answer to the puzzle, of course, is that these old-fashioned craftsmen are not competitors at all.

[1] Graham Wallas, *Human Nature in Politics*, p. 115. This book marks, as it seems to me, the first practical attempt to do for modern politics what Socrates did for Greek, to explain to our political craftsmen the nature and use of their tools. Writers enough have told them what they are or should be working *for*; but they had forgotten to remind them what they are working *with*. No wonder modern democracy has had its disappointments. The wonder is that it survives at all. For Boswell-Simon see Diogenes Laertius, ii. 122; for Socrates in the workshop Xen. *Mem.* iii. 10 and 11; he goes suc-cessively to a well-known painter, a sculptor, and a breastplate-maker. Compare Plato, *Apology* 22. The vase-paintings often show visitors in the workshop, Agora loafers who were glad to get out of the sun. See Lysias, xxiv. 20. On the workshops round the Athenian Agora see Wilamowitz, *Aus Kydathen*, pp. 204 ff.

They are fellows and comrades, members of the same honoured craft or gild and possessors of the same art or ' mystery '. There is work enough for all : and, if any one suffers, it is rather the public for want of craftsmen than the craftsmen for want of a public. In time of war or famine the craftsmen suffered, of course, as Pericles said, together with the whole nation ; but in the stability of industrial processes they did not suffer together as a class.[1]

Because economic life was stable, craftsmen could feel them-selves to be comrades, and because they were comrades they could help to keep life stable. Every art and craft had its own Association, not a Trades Union or Employers' Association such as we know them, but a union of men who understood one another and were drawn close together by the same daily effort and the practice of the same art. The Greek θίασος, or band of associates, was a social and religious, not an economic form of grouping. Its members did not need to ' protect their own interests ', for these were sufficiently protected by custom and the constitution of society ; when they felt anxious about them they could go as citizens to the assembly. They did not need to raise prices, for they were working not for riches but for honour and a livelihood, and prices were fixed by immemorial custom. In their

---

[1] Thuc. ii. 60. 2–3. Practically the only unemployed *class* the Greek world had to deal with were the mercenary soldiers and rowers disbanded after a long war ; but this was a fourth-century problem, due to the decline of citizen armies, and was indeed one of the evil effects of the development we are tracing. Isocrates recommends the Macedonian conquest of Asia for the purpose of establishing Unemployed Farm Colonies (v. 120, cf. viii. 24). Alexander took his advice almost to the letter and planted Greeks as far East as Cabul. But the fact that there were so many thousands of unattached Greeks shows how completely the Peloponnesian War and subsequent troubles had undermined the stable fabric of City State life, the real and older Hellas which we are trying to describe. The Greek words for ' competition ' (ζῆλος in the abstract and ἀγών in the concrete) have no special commercial significance, but denote contests of skill, ' since with the Greeks rivalry in every department of life, even in art and learning, took the form of a contest,' as we know from anecdotes and inscriptions. See Soph. *O. T.* 380–2 ; Wilhelm, *Beiträge zur griechischen Inschriftenkunde*, pp. 40–2 (potters' contest) ; and the doctors' competition in Austrian *Jahreshefte*, vol. viii, pp. 133–4. Prizes were given for ' handicraft ', for the best instruments, for the best original medical writing, and the best answer to a set question. We can see from this how easy it would be for the old free contest to fade away into a mere compulsory examination test. It only needed a change of spirit. But at the time of these inscriptions (which are late) the contests were still an honour and not a burden, as is clear from the fact that Public Health Officers, who held life appointments, entered for them.

little professional conclaves they merely did honour to their god or
hero or founder, the metal-workers to Hephaestus, the doctors to
Asclepius, the epic poets and reciters to Homer, and then ' talked
shop ' about the mysteries into which they had been initiated.[1]

For the craft-secrets that they discussed were really mysteries.
The outer world, and, above all, the State, had no concern with
them. There was no State regulation of skilled industry, for
there were no industrial abuses—not, at least, in the sphere with
which we are here concerned. Nor were there State-granted
patents. Knowledge was either free for all men or religiously
confined to the craft and handed down and added to from
generation to generation. So the craftsman was honoured not
merely as a maker of beautiful things but as the member of
a school, the guardian of an ancestral tradition : almost, only the
terms are too romantic for the matter-of-fact Greek world, as
a wizard or a wonder-worker. So many streams of thought and
feeling widely separated in modern life are united in the Greek
idea of craftsmanship or technê.[2]

So, as Solon has already suggested to us, craftsmanship in
Greece covered a far wider sphere than that which we are
accustomed to associate with ' industry ' to-day. Everybody

[1] For Greek forms of association see Ziebarth, *Das griechische Vereinswesen*
(Leipzig, 1896), who has conveniently collected the inscriptions about them,
from the philosophers' schools (the nucleus of the first European University)
down to silversmiths (as we know from the *Acts*) and municipal slaves (who,
according to Aristotle, should have been far too stupid to form one). There
is now a larger work on the same subject, *Geschichte des griechischen Vereins-
wesens*, by F. Poland (Leipzig, 1909). We must beware of calling these
associations ' gilds ', in the mediaeval sense of the word : they exercised no
control over their members or would-be members ; every one at Athens was
free to exercise any craft or calling that he chose. This explains why slaves
found it so easy to develop their gifts.

[2] For State regulation see Guiraud, *Main-d'œuvre*, p. 198. He can only
find two laws, one at fastidious Sybaris, relegating noisy workshops to the
suburbs, and another at humanitarian Athens, inflicting the death penalty on
any one who employed a free-born child to turn a mill-stone. See Deinarchus,
i. 23, where it appears that a miller was actually put to death. This shows
how strongly public opinion must have felt on the subject. Slaves, of course,
were safeguarded against assault, &c., by the ordinary law, particularly so at
Athens ; cf. Glotz on ' Les esclaves et la peine du fouet en Grèce ' (*Comptes
rendus de l'Académie*, 1908, pp. 571 ff.), who believes, with good reason, that,
except under very exceptional circumstances, slaves were not allowed to
receive more than fifty strokes from the rod, corresponding to the fifty
drachma limit in the case of ordinary fines. This enactment seems to have
been peculiar to Athens, who, here as elsewhere, was more humane in her
laws than the rest of Greece.

who had some special skill or art by which he earned his living, whether by ' rendering service ' or ' producing commodities ', was accounted a craftsman, from the poet who ' built the lofty rhyme ' and the doctor who could mix herbs or perform operations down to the tanner and the cobbler. City State life was, in fact, democratic ; and we ought not to be surprised, though in fact we are, when we find doctors and sculptors and schoolmasters being paid, like masons and joiners and private soldiers, at the customary standard rate. They all earned a decent livelihood, which was all that they asked for in pay. They prefer to take the ' rise ' that the modern craftsman would demand, in honour and public estimation, or, if the city felt particularly grateful, in a golden crown and public banquet.[1]

Indeed, it was very seldom that they worked for wages at all, because, as the London clerk said of his summer holiday, it interfered so much with their daily habits. They worked as wage-earners for the city when the need arose : for they were her citizens and trained to do her bidding. But who were they, as free men, that they should work for wages from their equals ? ' Such an arrangement would have put the craftsman almost in the position of the slave. His aim in life was very different : to preserve his full personal liberty and freedom of action, to work when he felt inclined and when his duties as a citizen permitted him, to harmonize his work with all the other occupations which filled the life of a Greek, to participate in the government, to take his seat in the courts, to join in the games and festivals, to break off his work when his friends called him out to go to the market-place

---

[1] For the doctor as a ' practica artist ' ($\chi\epsilon\iota\rho\sigma\tau\epsilon\chi\nu\eta s$) see Soph. *Trach.* 1001 and Jebb's note. As in the potter's shop so in the dispensary there were both free men and slaves. See Plato, *Laws* 720, who says that slave-practitioners were much more rough-and-ready in their methods. Doctors were probably paid at the standard labourer's rate, in spite of the high bidding among different cities for the services of Democedes (Hdt. iii. 131), who was not an ordinary doctor but one of the social lions of the day. (See Pohl, *De Graecorum Medicis Publicis*, p. 68). The figures slowly rise after the end of the fifth century, partly owing to the decline in the value of money : and this provided an opportunity for the inevitable tendency to distinguish between higher and lower kinds of work. These distinctions are not always according to our notions. Curious readers may consult Dittenberger, No. 523, where, in a school at Teos, the music-master is paid nearly three times as much as the ' games-master '. For honours to a craftsman see Dittenberger, ii. 545. Greeks preferred golden crowns to titles. For sculptors and masons see *I. G.* i. 324, where there are, however, some high rates paid for piece-work.

or the wrestling school, or when his colleagues in the craft were holding a dinner—all of them things which were incompatible with a contract at a fixed wage '.[1]

So it is not altogether impossible to understand whence arose, in decadent days, the false idea that the Greeks of the great age regarded manual labour as degrading; though it is still difficult to explain how, with the Parthenon before their eyes, men can believe so still. It is, of course, grotesquely untrue, as could be seen at a glance, if there were no other evidence, from the names they gave to those who exercised it. They called them ' manual artists ' (χειροτέχναι) or ' public workers ' (δημιουργοί), a title applied also to magistrates, who, too, performed what was regarded as an indispensable public service; or ' lords of the hand ' (χειρώνακτες), a name which must surely have been struck out, in the envy of the moment, by some wistful bystander at the potter's wheel or the blacksmith's forge. In truth they honoured manual work far more than we, who are only just beginning to discover the secret and mutually helpful connexions between the workings of hand and brain. But they insisted, rather from instinct than from policy, on the duty of moderation, and objected, as artists do, against doing any more work than they needed when the joy had gone out of it. Above all, they objected to all monotonous activity, to occupations which involved sitting for long periods in cramped and unhealthy postures, especially in a hot and vitiated atmosphere. It was these occupations, those of our respectable clerks and secretaries of all grades, rather than of our rough-clad artisans, which they regarded as ' menial '. ' It is quite right,' said Xenophon, a typical Greek in his prejudices, ' that cities should rate them low; for they injure the bodies of those who spend their time on them, by compelling them to remain indoors and sedentary, and sometimes even to spend all day by the fire.' Art cannot be produced under those conditions when joy is

[1] Salvioli, *Le Capitalisme dans le monde antique*, Paris, 1906, p. 148. I have altered a word here and there, as the passage, and the work as a whole, deal with Rome. But the book is full of suggestion for Greek students also. Compare Socrates' objection to bring paid for talking to people, i. e. for teaching : he regarded such an arrangement as selling himself into slavery (Xen. *Mem.* i. 2. 6). Moreover, it would probably not pay, according to Greek ideas, from the pupil's point of view, because a paid teacher is less likely to feel that he is a friend, and ' nobody ever received any education from a man he did not care for ' (i. 2. 39).

absent ; and if it could, it would have destroyed in its coming to birth what the Greek regarded as a still greater work of art, the human body.   This was the origin of the Greek feeling against ' menial employments '.   Its real significance has been obscured by later writers, who took a current prejudice, widened its range, and transformed its meaning, till almost every method of earning a livelihood, from teaching philosophy downwards, ceased to be respectable, and no forms of activity remained worthy of a free man beyond contemplation and politics and fighting.   Small wonder that scholars nursed on these theories fell into the habit of assuming that the Greeks fed solely on honeydew and drank the milk of Paradise.[1]

Yet society cannot get on without a basis of unpleasant and monotonous labour.   There are regions of social work which can never be made artistic and only with difficulty joyful, where, with all the willingness in the world, the best that can be aimed at is often a mere humdrum conscientiousness.   There are pitchers to be filled, dinners to be cooked, clothes to be made and mended within the household.   There is rough work to be done outside, in the heat of the sun, digging and lifting, pulling and pushing and carrying, very aggravating to men accustomed to finer and more congenial forms of activity.   How was all this necessary common labour managed in our society of artists ?

Some of it, as we shall see, did not get done.   Societies which dislike irksome work must be content to live in a slovenly manner, and there are regions of Greek life into which it is wiser not to pry.   Still, even in the most neglectful City State, there remained work enough to be done by a number of those workers who earn their living, as Plato put it, by ' hiring out their bodily

[1] Xen. *Oec.* iv. 2 is the *locus classicus* for βαναυσία.   It was very wrong of Plato, for instance, to gibe at the sophists for taking money for teaching virtue, when he himself happened to be rich enough to do without it.   The later philosophers, especially when they came under the influence of well-to-do Roman patrons, pushed the prejudice against menial work to terrible lengths. They thought the connoisseur a greater man than the creator.   ' Who does not admire the Olympian Zeus of Phidias ?   And yet who would care to be Phidias ? ' says one of Gallio's friends in the excellent sketch of that society by Anatole France (*Sur la Pierre Blanche*, p. 43).   He is echoing Lucian, *Somnium*, ch. 9.   We are justly in revolt against this form of conceit, and the old academic theory of ' culture ' with which it has been associated.   The result is that we tend to forget how much truth lay concealed in the original fifth-century prejudice.

strength '.   Let us briefly put together what we can find out
about them.[1]

For the work within the household, the pitchers and the dinners
and the clothes, a few words must suffice.   In the great majority
of cases it was performed by members of the family.   While the
father and sons are out in the fields, the wife and daughters are
spinning and weaving and cooking, and picking their way, with a
pitcher balanced on their head, up and down the stony track to
the city well-house.   Xenophon has set forth for us with charming frankness, in his delightful pamphlet on housekeeping, the
attitude taken up by a Greek husband and master towards his
newly wedded young wife.   The case he gives us is not a typical
one, for the girl was the daughter of rich parents and had been
brought up with unusual care.   But it is too instructive to be
passed over.   She comes to her husband ' not yet fifteen years of
age.   All her life she has been carefully watched over, so that she
has hardly seen anything or heard anything or even said anything '.   ' When I had tamed her,' says her husband, ' and she had
overcome her shyness and would talk, I asked her, " Tell me, my
wife, have you yet thought over why I have received you into my
house and why your parents gave you to me : for I know even
you must recognize that a large choice was open to me ! " '   After
this hopeful prelude he proceeds to instruct her in her new responsibilities as a housewife and future mother, laying particular
stress upon the duty of setting a good example.   She is to lead
the way in tidiness and punctuality, in modesty and simplicity, in
obedience to her master's will and uncomplaining perseverance in
tedious and unpleasant tasks.   For upon her rests the joint responsibility with her husband of ' increasing the prosperity of the
house '.[2]

---

[1] Pl. *Rep.* 371.
[2] Xen. *Oec.* vii. 5 ff., iii, x et passim.   See Mrs. Putnam's *The Lady*, p. 300,
for an interesting comparison between Xenophon's model housewife and ' the
lady of the slaves-states ' in the days before emancipation.   ' Each was the
chief executive of a large and motley community, in duty bound to enforce
the laws. . . . Each, doubtless, if not overtaxed, derived satisfaction from the
performance of important work bearing directly on the welfare and happiness
of those she loved best ; but neither could be called a free woman.   In
the case of the Greek lady we see this plainly enough.   No sentiment had
arisen in her day to mask the issue.   If she was constrained to an exacting
profession, no one obscured the fact by calling her a queen or, with a much
stronger connotation of leisure, an angel.'

Amongst the duties assigned to the young housewife, one on which great emphasis was laid was the wise management of slaves. For in the larger cities which could afford to keep imported workers, a certain proportion of the more prosperous families would keep household slaves ; and the housewife, like the craftsman, had to learn how to train them. When they had been properly trained, and if they were kindly and tactfully treated, they would relieve the housewife and her daughters from some of their more irksome tasks. Very touching is the relation, as we see it in the tragedy and on the gravestones, between a good housewife and her servants. Some of them even came by long service to occupy respected and honourable positions in the life of the household. The trusty Paidagôgos or children's attendant, who accompanied the boys of the family out-of-doors, is a familiar figure in Greek life : and so is the faithful old nurse, whom we know both from the *Hippolytus* and the *Medea*. But this tempts us into regions which we must leave for a later chapter.[1]

Let us now turn to the men's drudgery, to the rough common labour that forms the indispensable basis of even the simplest society. Even in a Greek city, which dispensed with so many conveniences, there must be some one to make roads and walls, to fell trees and quarry stone and extract the ore from the hillside. And in a society of artists there must be some one to bring to the workshop and the stoneyard the materials in which they work. Without the help of the general labourer the craftsmen of Greece were as helpless as our own more specialized societies. Plutarch makes this very clear for us in his account of the labour employed on the Acropolis buildings. First he enumerates all

---

[1] Eur. *Alc.* 192 ff. is a touching passage illustrated on many funeral reliefs. In an average Greek city the proportion of families which kept household slaves was probably not large. For example, in fifth-century Plataea we hear of household slaves taking part in the street-fighting, but there is no further mention of them when the non-combatants are specified. (Thuc. ii. 4. 2, 70. 3, cf. 78. 4.) But the subject is one on which it is impossible to speak with assurance. In early Athens the girls went to the well themselves, because 'neither the Athenians nor the other Greeks at this time had slaves', says Herodotus (vi. 137). In his plays about town households Aristophanes makes the slaves play a prominent part ; but not in the *Acharnians* or the *Pax*. Cf. also Aristotle, *Pol.* 1323 a 5 ; Ar. *Eccl.* 593. It is estimated by Mr. Charles Booth that only eleven per cent. of the population of London belong to the servant-keeping class (*Life and Labour in London*, final volume, p. 8). Paidagôgos : Plato, *Lysis* 223 (where two of them, flushed with wine, break into their native language, i. e. they were not born in the household).

the craftsmen whose services were requisitioned : ' the different materials such as stone, brass, ivory, gold, ebony, and cypress employed carpenters, masons, brass-workers, goldsmiths, painters, turners, and other craftsmen.' Then he passes on naturally to the transport labourers. ' The conveyance of them by sea employed merchants and sailors and steersmen, and by land wheelwrights, drivers of ox-wagons and horse-carts, rope-makers, leather-cutters, road-makers, and iron-founders, and every craft had a number of these lower unskilled labourers ranged in proper subordination to it, like soldiers under a general.'[1]

It is hard for us to realize how heavy and wearisome such labour was in the days before cranes and steam-rollers and all our labour-saving contrivances. Some vivid records survive to remind us what it was like. On a fourth-century inscription from Eleusis we can read full details about the transport of the materials for an important monument. The work comprised three stages : first the preparation of the road from the quarry to the city, which had to be paved with grooved stones, with sidings at intervals; next the making of the wagons heavy enough to hold the stone blocks ; and lastly the process of transport itself. This is done by means of ox-wagons. Each pair of oxen costs four drachmas and half an obol per day ; the transport takes three days for a distance of thirty miles. To drag a single block thirty to forty pair of oxen are needed. Each block therefore costs the State from three to four hundred drachmas. When we read this and then look at the vast masses of stone used in the great State buildings at Athens, we begin to realize how much straining man-power and brute-power were expended on their construction. The men who manned those ox-wagons may have been, as Plato said (though it may be doubted), ' hardly on the level of intellectual companionship,' but they accomplished work of which no modern machine need be ashamed. The road they made from the quarries may still be seen, with its grooves, on the slope of Pentelicus, and at intervals along its upper course there still stand by the wayside vast derelict blocks of half-hewn stone which they failed to carry further.[2]

[1] Plut. Per. 12.
[2] Francotte, vol. ii, p. 86 (from I. G. i. 834 c). The men employed seem all to be free men. Cf. Ar. Frogs 167, where the trusted slave suggests that

Work such as this was costly, and could only be undertaken by cities which had command of large means. But there was a great deal of rough work which was necessary, whether the city could pay for it or no. How did an ordinary city, for instance, build its walls and towers ? In the only way possible under the circumstances, by a process of conscription. Just as, when war had been declared, there was a call to arms, and the citizen gave up his daily work and went to join his regiment, so, when there was urgent public building or digging to be done, there was a call to work, and all hands sallied forth to help, as at an English haymaking. That is how the walls of Athens were built in 479 and the walls of Argos in 417, women, children, and household servants joining in the work. A better instance still is given by Herodotus. The whole population of Cnidos, a Greek city in Asia Minor, turns out to dig a trench across the isthmus which separated them from the mainland, in order to fortify their city against an imminent Persian attack. ' And as they worked in a great body, the workers appeared to them to be subject to unreasonable and possibly heaven-sent injuries in every part of their body, and particularly in their eyes, owing to the splitting of the stone. So they sent a message to Delphi and asked what was hindering them. And the priestess (so at least the Cnidians say) replied to them in verse as follows : " Do not fortify your isthmus, or go on digging. If Zeus had wished it to be an island he would have made it so." ' So the Cnidians ceased digging and surrendered to the Persians without a struggle.[1]

This typically Greek story will illustrate better than any accumulation of further evidence the attitude which the Greeks always felt tempted to adopt towards unpleasant and monotonous forms of labour. It explains why a Greek would rather lie in the sun with nothing to eat than work underground in a mine, and why there were thus, as we shall see, certain forms of employment which were handed over, whenever possible, to slaves, freedmen,

some one else should be hired (i. e. probably a free man) to carry the heavy luggage instead of himself.   [See Appendix.]

[1] Hdt. i. 174. Cf. Thuc. i. 90. 3, v. 82. 6 (call to work) ; and cf. Dittenberger, No. 529, for a typical State call of this sort. After all, the sapper is still accounted a soldier. The story of the hasty building of the walls of Athens in 479, during Themistocles' absence at Sparta, which used to be denounced as a ' technical impossibility ', has now been vindicated by the archaeologists : see Cavaignac, pp. 18–19, and cf. Busolt in *Klio* v, pp. 255 ff.

and resident aliens.   Yet it would be a pity to leave the impression that men in Greece had not discovered, or did not relish, the satisfaction that comes of honest labour well performed.   The old garlic-smelling charcoal-burners of Acharnae enjoyed to the full, we may be sure, their rough work in the woods of Parnes.   They can speak to the reader for themselves through the lips of Aristophanes.   Let us turn instead to their obscurer comrade in labour, a woodman like them, but a Phrygian by blood and a slave by origin.   When the Peloponnesian army invaded Attica in the spring of 431 one of the first skirmishes that occurred was at a place called Phrygia, near Acharnae, a little settlement of Phrygian woodcutters.   Some of these seem to have taken part in the fight, and one of them, the head of the community (if we may take him at his own word), lost his life in the engagement.   Here is his epitaph, breathing, if ever headstone did, the spirit of a strong man ashamed neither of his origin, nor of his work, nor of his position in his adopted country—a welcome voice for the nameless thousands, who lived and worked in the same spirit but have ' left no memorial ' :

' *Mannes, son of Orymas, who was the best of the Phrygians in the broad lands of Athens, lies in this fine tomb ; and by Zeus I never saw a better woodman than myself.   He died in the war.*' [1]

[1] Best given, with commentary, in Wilhelm, *Beiträge zur griechischen Inschriftenkunde*, pp. 35–7. The stone is a healthy (and perhaps an intentional) correction of the common opinion about the Asiatics resident in Attica, canonized by Aristophanes in the *Knights* (cf. Eur. *Alc.* 675). It runs as follows :

Φρυγῶν ὃς ἄριστος ἐγένατ' ἐ-
ν εὐρυχόροισιν Ἀθήναις Μάν-
νης Ὀρύμαιος, ὃ μνῆμα τόδ' ἐστὶ καλόν· καὶ μὰ Δί' οὐκ εἶδον
ἐμαυτῶ ἀμείνω ὑλοτόμον.
ἐν τῶι πολέμωι ἀπέθανεν.

CHAPTER VIII

CITY ECONOMICS : RETAIL TRADE

Ἐστὶ χῶρος ἐν μέσῃ τῇ πόλι ἀποδεδεγμένος ἐς τὸν συλλεγόμενοι ἀλλήλους ὀμνύντες ἐξαπατῶσι.—KING CYRUS in Herodotus i. 153.

There is a special place in the middle of the city in which they meet and swear and cheat one another.

The fair and the market, those wise institutions of our forefathers, and with regard to the management of which they were so scrupulously careful, bring the producer and the consumer in contact with each other . . . the shop and the trafficker keep them apart . . . the fair and the market lay everything open.—COBBETT, *Rural Rides*, vol. ii, pp. 257–9 (ed. 1885).

So far we have been concerned with shepherds and farmers and robbers and craftsmen, with men who earn a livelihood for themselves and their household by making or taking things, or by sitting by while Nature makes things grow on their behalf. All of them, except the robber, are producers : and as the robber is so often a farmer or a fisherman in difficulties, ' eking out,' as Aristotle said, ' the deficiencies of one employment by another,' he may almost count as one too, and at any rate takes rank among the respectables. But we now come to a class of house-keepers against whom the Greeks always maintained a prejudice, chiefly because they are not producers at all, but middlemen, living in an ' unnatural ' way by distributing and exchanging the products of other people.[1]

Yet it is clear enough that society cannot get on without them. ' Supposing,' says Plato, ' that a husbandman or an artisan brings some product to market ' (on his way in, perhaps, to sit in Court or in Council), ' and he comes at a time when there is no one to exchange them with, is he to leave his calling and sit idle in the market-place ? Not at all ; he will find people there who, seeing the want, undertake the office of salesman.' But, of course, thinks the philosopher, recalling amongst other things his aesthetic objection against people who sit still all day long, ' no one will earn his living in this way if he can help it.'

[1] Ar. *Pol.* 1258 b ; cf. Dem. xxv. 46 (a typical passage).

So he proceeds, following a natural Greek train of reasoning to lay it down that ' in well-ordered states they are commonly those who are the weakest in bodily strength and therefore of little use for any other purpose. Their duty is to be in the market-place and to give money in exchange for goods to those who desire to sell, and to take money from those who desire to buy '.[1]

This sounds as harmless as it is elementary to the modern reader, in a world of shops and a nation of shopkeepers. But it is by no means harmless in the philosophers' eyes : Greek retail traders, they found by experience (and many a modern will bear them out), were no better than they ought to be, and instead of accepting this as inevitable, or merely as material for standard witticisms, as we have learnt to do with the effect of modern professions upon character, they looked about for a reason. They found it in the association of retail trading with moneymaking.[2]

For the retail traders, when one comes to think of it, were almost the only people in a Greek city who were continually handling coin, and were thus peculiarly exposed to the temptation of reckoning wealth or happiness in that fallacious medium. Their days were spent in a perpetual haggling over small change, till they came to think that everything in life could be bought, and that there was nothing too great to be expressed in terms of money. They forgot, as a witty Jewish writer has said, that ' the small change for a Napoleon is not equal to a Napoleon ', or, as the apostle put it to his business friends at Corinth, that the Word of God cannot be administered retail.[3]

However, we will see for ourselves. Let us make sure that

---

[1] Plato, *Rep.* 371.

[2] The neglect to study the effect of the different modern professions upon character, when we are always insisting, and rightly, upon the importance of a ' character-forming ' education, is one of the strangest lapses due to the sway of nineteenth-century economics. Yet we know perfectly well, as the Greeks did, that men's and women's characters are not, as parents and schoolmasters seem to assume, ' formed ' and petrified by the time they are ready to begin earning their living. It seems a pity to study (and in some cases to counteract) the physical effects of occupations and to ignore the mental, or to study the psychology of abnormal types, such as criminals or ' saints ', and to ignore the professional man.

[3] 2 Cor. ii. 1 οὐ καπηλεύοντες τὸν λόγον, translated ' corrupting ', i. e. adulterating. The Napoleon epigram is Zangwill's, addressed to the Zionists in 1905, after Herzl's death.

Parliament is not sitting, and then attach ourselves to some party of countrymen riding in on their mules to town ; or better still, get a lift on some country cart filled with wineskins or heavy produce, and so rumble in along rough roads to the city gates and then through a labyrinth of mud-brick houses and busy workshops till we emerge on to the broad market-place where our retail dealers are at work. They will be so hard at work, slaves and free men together, swearing and protesting over their bargains and, in the intervals between them, ruining what voice they have left by their stentorian yells (on the best town-criers' model), that it is useless to think of going to them for information, which moreover would cost far more than it would be worth. It will be better to use our eyes.[1]

The general plan of the market-place is a rough square. Along two sides of it there are colonnades, open towards the market-place, with brightly coloured paintings on their inner walls, depicting some battle-scene between the gods and the giants, or between the citizens and their next-door neighbours on the other side of the range. As the sun is not yet high, they are still empty, but no doubt they will fill up with loiterers later on. Already men are beginning to stream out from the narrow lanes that here and there interrupt their covered walks. Down there, as we know, for we have just come past them, are the workshops and studios of the barbers and potters and other craftsmen. On the other two sides are public buildings, on the one a temple with a big altar and a number of statues and votive offerings in front of it, on the other the Prytaneum or Government building, where the President for the day and other officials have their meals and sleep, and perhaps a prison and a public treasury as well. About half the area of the square is kept free and open for the general public, who are already beginning to come together for their morning's chatter. The other half is filled with an inextricable confusion of stalls and booths and boards and wickerwork and sunshades, and every variety of temporary erection, roughly arranged, if the word can be used

---

[1] On Ecclesia days a rope steeped in red dye was put round the market-place and gradually drawn in so as to drive every one lingering there towards the Pnyx or Parliament Hill. See Ar. *Ach.* 21–2. Slave shopkeepers were, of course, common in the larger cities. They were allowed a percentage on what they made.

of such a chaos of men and wares and such a babel of voices, in rows ' and ' circles ', according to the nature of the goods being sold on or under or round them. The greater part of these consist of foodstuffs, which cannot be sold, like boots and pots, at the place where they are produced, and so have to come to market : flour, and perhaps some baked bread as well, vegetables and cheese, honey and fruit and garlic, wine to be decanted from pig-skins, meat (for those who can afford it) freshly slaughtered and still staining the pavement with its blood, and fish on great slabs of shining marble. As we approach the fish-stalls, a perspiring busybody pushes his way through the crowd, ringing a bell with all his might. This, we are told, is one of the Clerks of the Market, and the bell is to open the fishmarket. No need to tell us this : the sudden reinforcement of noise and pushing are sufficient evidence, not to speak of the choice specimens of fishmongers' Attic which begin to be wafted to our ears. We retire in search of a more refined and rarefied atmosphere, and, hurrying past the sinister-looking money-changers with their annoying habit of clinking a coin on their table, find ourselves among a crowd of young dandies round the perfumes and frankincense. A new cargo from Arabia viâ Egypt reached port only yesterday, and here are subtle and exotic scents such as the city never knew before. But the prices asked are too high. We will wait a day or two till the first rage has passed, and trust to luck that the cargo is larger than the dealer swears. Avoiding the slave-market, being in no mood for an exhibition of naked humanity, we move on to the humble book-stalls, hidden away by themselves in the quietest corner of the market, and here we find friends who will keep us busy discussing Our Savage Ancestors, with the latest items from Scythia, or Tragedy versus Comedy, with intelligent anticipations of next playday, till it is time to go to lunch.[1]

[1] Cf. Paus. vi. 24 : We do not know to what extent the Athenian practice of keeping Parliament Hill and Market Square distinct was adopted in other cities. Plato and Aristotle are anxious to keep the two separate, not, like the Athenians, from motives of convenience, but for moral reasons. See *Politics* 1331 a 30 and *Laws* 849 for their grandfatherly regulations. In *Laws* 917 Plato actually forbids bargaining and insists on ' fixed prices ', which would have spoilt all the fun. In the fourth century and later, the public buildings (colonnades, &c.) in and round the market-place became grander and the whole scene less untidy. For details see Wachsmuth, *Stadt Athen*, ii,

A scene like this, the reader will reflect, calls for a good deal of regulation, and the Clerks of the Market fully earn their perquisites. It is worth while encroaching for a moment into the domain of State management to inquire into their duties. It will show us how hard the city tried to let every one, so far as was compatible with citizen duties, earn his own living and conduct his own private business in his own way.

The chief duty of the Clerks was to keep the market in order, and put down, if not quarrelling—that would be Utopian—at least its more dangerous and unseemly developments. They had also to inspect weights and measures, to prevent adulteration, and to collect, not themselves but through tax farmers, the rent for stalls and booths. We catch a glimpse of them, in the pages of Xenophon, weighing cottage loaves and guaranteeing the top and bottom to be, as declared, of equal weight.[1]

It was also their business to protect the citizens from famine prices in the case of absolutely necessary articles. But no attempt was made—though under similar economic conditions it is often made elsewhere—to settle prices generally. In a small almost self-sufficient community, where there is only one market and transport to another centre is expensive and difficult, grand-fatherly governments are often tempted to fix lists of fair prices. The Greek market authorities never exercised this natural power except under very special circumstances. They preferred to leave buyer and seller free to settle it out by ' persuasion ', or by the natural economic tendencies which operate so speedily among sellers of perishable wares in a hot climate. It was against their instincts to interfere with private bargaining. As Pericles said—and this example from the market gives an added

pp. 443 ff.   For a market-place in a country township see Dittenberger, No. 431, arrangements for a new market-place at Sunium. Greek men did their own marketing, unless they could afford to keep a slave. Since free women never went shopping, their husbands had to do it, even when they were on sentry-duty : Ar. *Lys.* 555–64. For the procedure in the slave-market see the vivid description in Lucian's Βίων Πρᾶσις. This reads like a special auction sale, but in reality it is simply an ordinary sale under the usual conditions of Greek publicity (*v.* Pauly, s. v. *Auctio*). This publicity enabled Greek retailers to dispense with all our apparatus of advertisement, for advertising is simply ' salesmanship plus publicity '. Our skilled advertisers try to hit us in the eye from the hoarding or the newspaper with the same kind of appeal as the old Greek salesman shouted into the passing customer's ear.

[1] Xen. *Symp.* ii. 20, where Socrates is compared to a cottage loaf.

meaning to the words—' we give free play to all in our public life, and carry the same spirit into our daily relations with one another '. And when we get the worst of a bargain (so we may read into his next sentence) we take our beating in good part and ' have no black looks or angry words for our neighbour '.[1]

There is in the Berlin Museum a small tablet of lead with a few rows of much-worn characters upon it. It is the earliest existing Greek letter. It dates probably from the end of the fifth century before Christ, but is very similar in substance to the letters we write twenty-three centuries later ; it is about making a good bargain. Here it is, restored in its entirety from the most desperate illegibility by the almost uncanny skill of Professor Wilhelm :

Carry to the Potter's Market, and deliver to Nausias or Thrasycles or my son.

Mnesiergos sends his love to all at home and hopes this may find them well as it leaves him.

[1] For Clerks of the Market cf. Ar. *Ach.* 896, where Dicaeopolis sets up a private market of his own and is his own clerk. For a typical inscription on their duties see Dittenberger, No. 503, where, at the fair connected with a festival, they have general instructions to prevent the inhabitants from being too extortionate, and to provide medical attendance for the crowd. In Greece to-day local authorities have the power to draw up a list of prices, and I have seen such a list affixed to the gate of a South Italian town. But the only evidence I can find for a tariff for *ordinary* goods (i. e. where neither moral and ' sumptuary ' considerations nor special necessities come into play) is a reference in Plautus, *Miles Gloriosus* 727, where the Roman adaptor probably goes ' just wrong '. Plautus and Terence must, of course, be used as evidence of Athenian life as cautiously as we should use English adaptations of French plays as evidence for modern Paris.

See, further, the important third-century inscription from Delos discussed in *Bulletin de Correspondance hellénique*, xxxi, 46 ff. (which, it must be remembered, is concerned with a crowded sanctuary), and the Greek and mediaeval analogies there collected. It concerns the sale of fuel, and its numerous provisions are all designed to secure the general public from fraud and extortion. For instance, merchants are not allowed to go back upon their prices when once they have fixed them. But we need not conclude from this and a similar regulation for the Athenian fish-market (and from Plato's veto referred to above) that the City State authorities insisted on ' fixed prices ' in general. But what was and still is an abuse, to be stopped by the authorities if they can, is for the merchant to tell each customer that prices are fixed when in reality they go up and down according to the apparent wits of the buyer. Just possibly it is simply this which is referred to. In any case Delos was not an ordinary City State, nor were fuel and fish (a favourite article with the Athenian poor) ordinary commodities. The inscription is also interesting for the light it throws on Greek custom-house arrangements and the meaning of the ' exemption ' granted to certain merchants. See also, in this connexion, Dittenberger, No. 936. For famine regulations see p. 365 below

Please send me a rug, either a sheepskin or a goatskin, as cheap as you can get it, and not with the hairs on, and some strong shoe-soles : I will pay some time.[1]

[1] *Jahreshefte des österr. arch. Inst.*, vol. vii, pp. 94 ff. By what happy accident the tablet has been preserved Wilhelm cannot say. It was printed first in a collection of ' Attic curse-inscriptions ', similar little thin plates of lead which were laid in graves : and perhaps it may have been mistaken for one of them and so became entombed itself. It runs as follows :

Φέρεν ἰς τὸν κέραμ-
ον τὸγ χυτρικόν·
ἀποδόναι δὲ Ναυσίαι
ἢ Θρασυκλῆι ἢ θ' υἱῶι·
Μνησίεργος
ἐπέστελε τοῖς οἴκοι
χαίρεν καὶ ὑγιαίνεν
καὶ αὐτὸς οὕτως ἔφασκε ἔχεν·
Στέγασμα εἴ τι βόλεστε
ἀποπέμψαι ἢ ὤας ἢ διφθέρας
ὡς εὐτελεστάτας καὶ μὴ σισυρωτὰς
καὶ κατύματα : τυχὸν ἀποδώσω.

A similar letter has lately turned up in Russia (probably from Olbia) and is published by Wilhelm in *Jahreshefte*, vol. xii, pp. 118 ff. : it is a little younger than its companion, dating certainly from the fourth century B.C. The opening formula is practically the same : τοῖς ἐν οἴκωι χαίρειν.

CHAPTER IX

CITY ECONOMICS

PUBLIC AND PRIVATE PROPERTY

Κοινὰ τὰ φίλων.
Friends have all things in common.—GREEK PROVERB.

Δεῖ γάρ πως μὲν εἶναι κοινά, ὅλως δ' ἴδια.—ARISTOTLE, *Politics* 1263.
There should be full legal rights for the individual, combined with customary common use by the community.

WE have watched the Greeks going about their private business within the limits of their city unaided, and, for the most part, unhindered by her rule. It is time to turn to the city herself and inquire how she watched over her private citizens. For if by the fifth century the city had become, as we have seen, the supreme element in their lives, she must have had her attitude and policy towards economic questions also. So we leave the Greek as a worker to go back to him once more as a citizen in council, and cross the frontier which separates private from political economy.

It was a tradition and a boast of Greek cities to be sovereign States wholly independent of foreign claims. Their fierce love of independence had been nourished by centuries of isolation, and was, as we have seen, one of the strongest forces in the national life. But we shall be merely following the bad example of so many nineteenth-century traders and pioneers if we interpret this sentiment in a strictly political sense. It was in origin and essence, in Greece as elsewhere, every whit as much economic as political : for politics and economics, State government and State housekeeping, are to simple people (as they should be to us) merely two aspects of the same thing. So it provided what was for centuries the bedrock of Greek economic policy. If a State was to be independent it must not only govern itself in its own way, but also feed and clothe itself in its own way. It must not only manage its own affairs but supply its own

needs.   Home Rule and Self-sufficiency (αὐτονομία and αὐτάρ-
κεια) are, in the traditional Greek view, almost convertible
terms.   How strong was the tradition may be seen by the way
it lingered on, years after Greek traders had begun pouring
in goods from East and West, in the political economy of the
philosophers.[1]

So that long before the Greek city was faced with the question (which, as we shall see, became so urgent in fifth-century
Athens) of how to add to the national resources from beyond
her own borders, she had evolved, in harmony with her political
development, a good working doctrine of how to manage and use
those which she had inherited.

What was that working doctrine ?   What was the attitude
of the normal Greek city towards what we call private property ?

Very different, we may be sure, from our own, for the economic, like the political, institutions of the Greeks had grown
up from roots very different from those of Western lands to-day.
If we wish to understand them, there is a whole thicket of
prejudices to be cleared away from our minds.   We must think
ourselves back into a world in which public ownership, and even
complete communism, seem, to serious people, more natural and
satisfactory and in harmony with the past than the ' absolute
rights ' of the individual property-owner, in which it was the
Conservatives and reactionaries who were preaching the doctrines of William Morris's *News from Nowhere* and the sentimental Socialists, while it was the Radicals who were timidly
beginning, not indeed to proclaim, but to act upon the doctrine
which still survives among our Rip Van Winkles that a free-
born citizen may ' do what he likes with his own '.   It was
a world in fact which, so far as economic theories are concerned,
was moving in exactly the opposite direction from our own, not
from anarchy to regulation, but from social control to individual
freedom.

For the Greeks set out from a different starting-point.   In
their early world of tribes and brotherhoods and families no

---

[1] See Aristotle's fancy picture of the origin of the city (*Politics* 1252 a 24
to 53 a), all leading up to ' Self-sufficiency ' which ' is the end and the best '.
Plato's *Critias* seems to have been planned on the same text.

one thought of his own 'rights' or questioned the claims of
society. Practically everything that he had belonged to his
kin. He would not claim his own life for himself, if they asked
it of him in time of need. Why should he dream of claiming
his house or his field or his cattle ? They were indeed his own,
for he needed them daily and could not live without them.
He had made them his own by making use of them, and his
chief claim upon them was that no one else could use them,
like the bow of Odysseus, so well as he, the father of the family
or head of the clan. But if it fell to him therefore to administer
the family wealth, this did not bring with it any rights over its
bestowal. He could not give them away and so beggar his
dependants, or will them away to strangers when his life interest in them ended. He held his wealth in trust for the little
society round him : and if it belonged to him, as head of the
family, rather than to them, this was simply because, in the
slow evolution of generations, it had been discovered that private
ownership, in this limited and primitive form, was better for the
community as a whole. Property held in this way did not
involve rights ; it simply bestowed duties. It was the tradition of Greek economic policy—and nowhere was the Greek
practical genius seen more happily at work—to bestow these
duties upon those best qualified to perform them and in such
a manner as to call out their best powers in doing so.[1]

Hence the double thread which we find running through the
economic as through the political development of Greece. Just
as the Greek citizen gained in individuality and personal freedom
in proportion as his ties to the city were more closely knit, so
the Greek property-owner grew in zeal and enterprise as he
became increasingly conscious of the larger society in which he
was working, and of the purposes for which the city required
his wealth. It was the policy of the city to place no new
restrictions on his freedom, and gradually, as we saw in the
legislation of Solon, to withdraw all traditional fetters that

[1] We need not discuss the vexed question as to whether the Greeks had
ever, in prehistoric days, actually lived in a state of communism. The fact
that it has seemed, both to Greek and modern writers, the 'logical' starting-
point for their economic evolution is sufficiently significant. But Spartan
institutions, on which Plato and others have relied for this theory, were not
really primitive but a case of perverted development. See p. 112 above.

interfered with the free exercise of effort. But every increase in freedom meant an enlargement of patriotism : the duties that used to be paid to the family or the clan were now paid to the city, which united all these lesser loyalties : and if he was now free to give away his riches as he liked, and even, within limits, to bequeath them, he was willing, nay eager, that the city should ever be the first to profit by his generosity. She had a claim upon his wealth, as she had upon his time. We have seen that he gave her far more than a tithe of his working hours. His wealth was as freely and as generously lavished. As the Corinthians remarked, with all the bitterness of unsuccessful trade rivals, the fifth-century Athenians were so enterprising in business that they had ' little opportunity for enjoying, being always engaged in getting ', but also so eager as citizens that ' their only idea of a holiday is to do their duty, and they are sorrier for themselves for being out of public life than over the most laborious private enterprise '.[1]

The Greek city, then, in its policy towards private property, bore this double development instinctively in mind ; and its most characteristic institutions, particularly at Athens, show how eager it was to preserve and intensify the traditions of personal freedom and generosity. For, if a man was in the habit of giving freely of his wealth to the city, he would be willing to serve her also in person, and to sacrifice, if need be, his life, as Pericles put it, on the city's subscription list.[2]

So it is not difficult to see why the Greek democracies always shrunk, unless they were driven to it by necessity, from direct taxation. It was regarded as derogatory to the dignity of a free citizen. Resident aliens and freedmen might pay a poll-tax and be thankful for the privilege ; but the citizen must be left free to help the city in his own way. Every kind of indirect tax he was indeed willing to pay, taxes in time as well as in money ; but the only direct contribution he made as a citizen to the State's resources was by preference a free gift, or what was called at Athens and elsewhere a ' liturgy ' or ' public work '. A large part of the public expenses of the Athenian State, the

[1] Thuc. i. 70. 8 ; cf. ii. 65. 7 on Thucydides' view of the temptation of pursuing ' private gains '.

[2] τοῖς σώμασιν καὶ τοῖς χρήμασιν λῃτουργεῖν, *Ath. Pol.* xxix. 5 : (τὴν ἀρετὴν τῇ πόλει) κάλλιστον ἔρανον προϊέμενοι, Thuc. ii. 43. 1

mounting of its plays, the equipment of its ships, the arrangements for its games and festivals, its chariot and horse and torch
races, its musical contests and regattas both in city and township, were defrayed by private citizens, who came forward
voluntarily, and took pride in vying with their predecessors
or with a crowd of rivals in their performance of the task. ' It
was by free gifts that the Athenians armed the fleets which were
so long supreme on the seas, by free gifts that they formed
the choirs which performed the dances and recited the songs
" taught " them by Aeschylus and Sophocles, Euripides and
Aristophanes.' There is perhaps no other institution in City
State life which brings one more vividly into touch with the
intimacies of its working. Lysicrates the ' choir-provider ' is
awarded the prize for the best choir in a boys' singing competition, and is so pleased that he erects the monument which
is still standing in the ' Street of Tripods ' to commemorate the
event : just as members nowadays present (though seldom in
rivalry) books or pictures or challenge cups to institutions in
which they feel a close personal interest. To talk of taxes
in such an atmosphere is a blunder as well as a sacrilege,
for a tax is a payment which leaves a man poorer : a ' liturgy '
leaves him richer. He still possesses what he has given, and
yet has added to the common store. For, to quote Pericles
again, ' national greatness is more for the advantage of private
citizens than any individual well-being coupled with public
need.' These are the platitudes of the Greek theory of public
finance, and only the complexity of the modern state and the
wide dispersion of private wealth prevent them from seeming
platitudes still.[1]

For here we have lighted upon an important difference
between Greek and modern feeling which has unlooked-for
bearings upon Greek economic life. Wealthy Englishmen, too,

---

[1] Thuc. ii. 60. 2. The other quotation is from Daremberg and Saglio,
s.v. *Leitourgia*, which gives details of its incidence. The institution, though
characteristically Athenian, is found all over Greece. Details in Pauly, s.v.
Choregia. See also Daremberg, s.v. *Trierarchia* on the disputed question
of the exact obligations of the ' Trierarchs ', the 400 private citizens, chosen
year by year, who were responsible for a ship each. Their duties were (1) to
recruit (but not to pay) the crew, (2) to equip and arm the ship (the materials,
&c., were provided by the State), (3) to keep the ship in repair, (4) extra
expenses in connexion with launching, prizes to rowers, &c.

tend to have a conscience about their expenditure ; but, owing
to our feudal origins, it acts in a different way. Our English
tradition is to lay stress upon right expenditure as a private and
personal matter, a duty that a man owes to his rank and position. A rich man likes to keep the control of his riches wholly
within his own hands, to give lavishly out of his superfluity, but
in his own way and to his own causes. He remains, in fact, in
other men's eyes and in his own, a baron or a ' magnate ' rather
than an ordinary private citizen a little more fortunate than his
fellows. The Greek's feeling was very different and his standard
of giving therefore very much higher. When Lysias tells us of
a citizen who has given an average of 7,000 drachmas a year (say
£1,300 purchasing power) for nine years, we must not reckon
his wealth by our own paltry standard of well-to-do generosity.
We must measure it rather by the standard of the poor, of
the widow who will spend half the leavings of the breadwinner
of the family upon his funeral and headstone, or of the devotees
of working-class causes who will stint themselves in food and
clothing to build a meeting-hall or run a newspaper.[1]

But here we are concerned not so much with the feeling that
prompted this constant stream of generosity as with its effect
upon the economy of the city which it enriched. It produced
what is to us an entirely unfamiliar relation between public and
private riches, between the resources of the city and the private
resources of the citizens. In a community so poor as an ordinary
Greek State the city not only tends to possess far larger permanent resources (quite apart from her annual revenue from
gifts and taxes) than any individual citizen, but may easily, with
her public lands and temple-treasures, be wealthier than all her
individual citizens put together. The great increase in modern
resources has fallen, not to governments or Churches or public
bodies, but to individuals, and this has led to a relative as well
as to an absolute change. It has upset, once and for all the old
Greek equilibrium between public and private resources. Private
wealth has always covered a larger area than public : the State

---

[1] It has often been observed that rich Americans give more generously to
public objects than rich Englishmen. What is more interesting, perhaps,
is that they have a different feeling about giving, just as they would have
a different feeling about selling part of their estates or retrenching on the
hounds.

or township or temple is one and the citizens or worshippers are many. A park is smaller than 10,000 back gardens and a town-hall than 10,000 parlours. But the balance was redressed in an old Greek city by the beauty and magnificence of her own courts and buildings. It is still held true in a few old-world centres, though the buildings are more often cathedrals than town-halls. Stambul spreads over countless acres, but whether he approach from the Bosporus or the Marmora the traveller's eye will rest first on the mosques which crown its heights; only when he lands and tries to reach them will he realize, with a sense of contrast strange to the Western mind, how modest and ramshackle are the wooden dwelling-houses which lie huddled around their spacious enclosures. Fifth-century Athens presented a similar and indeed more striking contrast. You would gaze with admiration, says Demosthenes, on her temples and colonnades, her armouries and her dockyards, and on those immortal buildings upon her Acropolis which, as you passed to and fro in the city, flashed over the edge of the rock on every side; but when you asked for the house of Themistocles or Cimon or Aristeides or any other of the great ones whose names were on all men's lips, you would find that men hardly knew it, and, when you reached it at last, that it was just like their next door neighbour's—a plain villa of sunbaked brick. Their real wealth, in fact, was not laid up in their own houses where moth and rust do corrupt and thieves break through the flimsy party wall and steal, but was shared with their fellow-citizens and embodied for all to enjoy in the works of their artists. For such a society, however poor, will know how to use the talents of its architects and sculptors and painters. It may be without wealthy patrons; but its public will have the zeal and its artists the inspiration. Whereas a society in which men live in finely decorated private houses but have learnt to grumble, like Demos-thenes' Athenians, about the rates, will neither plan immortal works nor, for all its improvements in technique, raise up from among its members the school of artists to perform them.[1]

---

[1] Dem. xiii. 28. Looking across from the Pnyx to the building right in face of him, he speaks of 'these Propylaea'. Pericles' idea for the Acropolis seems to have been to have a building looking out over each of the three brows. The relation between public and private wealth at Athens is dis-puted; but it is generally agreed that there was a fair equilibrium between

This suggests a natural question. If the State played so large a part, not only politically but economically, not only by the public work which it commanded but by the wealth which it possessed, in the life of its citizens, why did it not extend a fuller control over their working activities ? Why did it not secure for itself and directly administer, as in a democratic state it must surely have been tempted to do, all the private wealth within its borders ? Why, in other words, did not Athens, like her rival Venice in later days, set the world an example of municipal socialism ? [1]

One easy answer to this question has already been given. Athens never felt less like adapting a socialistic system than she did in the fifth century, for she was moving steadily away from communism and State regulation towards unfettered freedom of individual action and enterprise. But this is at bottom not a satisfactory explanation, for if the Athenian had earned his living as a municipal official he would have felt not less but more free than as a private wage-earner. In Athens, at any rate, socialism would not, as the modern assertion glibly runs, paralyse effort and enterprise, for the Athenian never worked so well or put so much hard individual thinking into his business as when he was working for the city. We must look below this surface argument for a reason.

The real reason why, in spite of the predilection of Plato and other writers for a socialist system, Athenians managed their

the two. Polybius, ii. 62. 7, says that, at a valuation taken in 378, no doubt a time of depression, the total private *capital wealth* of Attica, including land, houses, and movable property, was estimated at 5,750 talents (less than £7,000,000 purchasing power), a figure roughly confirmed by Dem. xiv. 19 (6,000 talents). This figure, about six times the annual *revenue* of the Athenian Empire, is so astonishingly low that attempts have been made to explain it away ; but the latest opinions regard it as correct, with a liberal margin for error, fraud, and dissimulation (Lécrivain in Daremberg, s.v. *Eisphora* ; Wilamowitz, *Staat und Ges.*, p. 111, 2nd ed., 116). Cavaignac, p. 125, gives reasons for estimating the private wealth of Athens in 427 at 20,000 talents. We have no means of estimating the total wealth of the fifth-century Athenian State in lands, mines, treasure, &c. The total wealth of the United Kingdom is estimated at £18–20,000,000,000 (*Quarterly Review*, 1910, p. 304), while the Exchequer revenue for the year 1908–9 was £151,500,000, and the money raised in rates in England and Wales was £59,500,000.

[1] For the Venetian State trading fleets see Horatio Brown, *Cambridge Modern History*, vol. i, p. 277. A similar proposal was made by the Athenian author of the curious and interesting fourth-century treatise on *Ways and Means*. So it was not for want of ability to think out practical applications of socialism that Athens refrained from it. Nor was it because she did not need the profits it might have brought in.

affairs on such sturdily individualistic lines was the rooted dislike
of the Greeks, and chief among the Greeks, of the Athenians, to
discipline and organization. It was not that they objected to
working in a State system : it was that they objected to working
in any system whatsoever. It was their settled inclination and
one of their proudest boasts to remain amateurs, to be supreme,
as they said of perhaps their greatest statesman, in ' improvising
right remedies for sudden emergencies ', and this inclination,
strengthened by the sudden and startling successes with which
they emerged into prominence, grew with every enlargement of
their experience, and was not repressed but only encouraged into
fresh masterstrokes of improvisation by the growing complexity
of the world in which they found themselves playing a part.
Athenian enterprise presents a picture, if ever there was one, of
the artistic temperament in action; and the artistic temperament,
as we know from its hard struggle with modern conditions, shuns,
rather by instinct than out of policy, the drudgery of office work,
the restraint of a ' settled ' position, and all the discipline and
regularity of organized service. These things are for others : and
the artists will not envy them their rewards. ' Indeed,' we can
hear them saying, after the words of their great leader, ' if
we choose to face life with an easy mind rather than after a
rigorous professional training, and to rely rather upon native
inspiration than on a State-made position, the advantage lies with
us ; for we are spared all the weariness of practising for future
appointments, and when we find ourselves in the vein we are as
happy as our plodding rivals. Let them toil from boyhood in
a laborious pursuit after efficiency, while we, free to live and
wander as we please, are ready, when the time comes, to face the
selfsame problems. For our trust is not in the devices of professional and material equipment, but in our own good spirits for
city life.' [1]

Truth to tell, their material equipment was sadly defective,
and called for the best of spirits to put up with it. Strange
indeed is the contrast between the city as mistress of men's lives
and as manager of their affairs, between Athens as the source of
energy and dispenser of wisdom and Athens as a mere municipality. It would be hard to credit some of the facts if we could

[1] After Thuc. ii. 39. For Themistocles the improviser see Thuc. i. 138. 3.

not fortify our imaginations by observing the same piquant contrast in parallel surroundings nearer home—in institutions which
shed spiritual illumination far and wide, and are reluctant to
put in the electric light, which preach ' a sound mind in a sound
body ', and employ the best architects upon buildings devoid of
the most ordinary conveniences, which expend energy and devotion in supplying unrivalled intellectual fare and will not face the
everyday problem of ensuring a cheap food supply. The Athenians lived under the Acropolis, as many generations lived under
the spires of Oxford, in ' squalid magnificence '. So hard is it for
the human spirit to do two good things at once.

For, in spite of all the talent at her disposal, asking for nothing
better than to do her bidding, her organization was more primitive than that of our most backward country town. Water
indeed she had, thanks to her tyrants : although even that almost
indispensable condition of Greek city life was not extended to the
Piraeus, which up to the time of the Great Plague relied wholly
upon cisterns. Her streets were narrow and crooked, dirty,
unlighted, and ill-paved. She had no sewers, or even cesspools,
and over the whole department of sanitation it is best to draw
a veil. Most of the police were amateurs, and the rest Scythian
barbarians, the laughing-stock of freeborn citizens. State-paid
detectives she had never heard of, and their place is taken by
private spies or 'sycophants' who, in a society full of tittle-tattle,
create more mischief than they discover. Postmen we do not
expect, though the Persians, and later the Ptolemies, had a
national post. But it is a surprise, especially if we come fresh
from the national systems of education in Plato and Aristotle, to
find that the Athens of Pericles paid no attention whatever to
her children (who did not indeed become hers till they reached
their eighteenth year), and provided no national schoolmasters
except the citizens who drilled the recruits : and these are not
permanent sergeants properly trained to do the work, but elected
from year to year, and apt, as we might expect in a system where
' to obey ' is the same as ' to be persuaded ', to win public
recognition rather for their amiability than for their efficiency.
Another surprise is to find that the city was too lazy to collect
her own money. The imperial treasury, where her ideals were
vitally concerned, was carefully looked after in every particular,

and if the contributions were late there were officials to hasten them in. But all the mere municipal moneys, the foreigners' poll-tax, the customs, the market dues, and all the various licences, were simply farmed out to ' publicans ', who made a profit on their contract. How natural this arrangement (which still survives, of course, in many parts of the East) appeared to the Athenian mind, and how great a step forward, by contrast, the imperial financial arrangements must have been, can best be illustrated by a detail accidentally preserved for us. The animals killed in the large public sacrifices, which took place many times a year, were not bought by the city, or sent in on a fixed arrangement by the tenants on the State grazing-lands, but supplied by private contractors, who catered for the ceremony at a fixed rate.[1]

Thuc. ii. 48. 2 (cisterns), Dittenberger, No. 500 (pavements). On the streets and general outward appearance of Athens see the interesting third-century description in Heracleides (*Geographi Graeci Minores*, vol. i, pp. 97 ff. ; *Fragmenta Hist. Graec.*, vol. ii, pp. 254 ff.). The Greeks did not go in for artistic town-planning till the Hellenistic age. It was one of the results of consciously thinking about the city, as the philosophers did, as a work of art. The great architectural achievements of the Periclean age were either religious or defensive, i.e. in both cases political not aesthetic. What they attempted they did perfectly, but they did not take up large sites in the thoroughgoing spirit of a modern city architect. Hippodamos's rectangular plan of the Piraeus, was not architecture at all, but simply geometry, and, as Wilamowitz remarks, ' intolerably dull ' at that. Whatever Pericles', or rather Mnesicles', plans for the Acropolis may have been, the final arrangements of buildings, largely dictated by traditional considerations, would still have looked haphazard. The big Hellenistic city, such as Alexandria or Antioch, a real metropolis in our sense of the word, and akin to our London and Paris, Vienna and New York, was totally different, in form as in spirit, architecturally, economically, and politically, from the sovereign municipalities of older Greece. Details in Schreiber, ' Zur Typologie der hellenistischen Stadtgründungen ' (*Kiepert's Festschrift*, Berlin, 1898, esp. p. 341) ; Pöhlmann, *Die Übervölkerung der antiken Grossstädte* ; and Körnemann, ' Stadtstaat und Flächenstaat des Altertums in ihren Wechselbeziehungen ' in *Neue Jahrbücher für das klassische Altertum*, 1908, pp. 233 ff., who points out suggestively (though he juggles a little with the word ' territorial ') how the desire for territorial aggrandisement (' painting the map red ') was foreign to the City State proper ; the form in which the temptation presented itself to Greek statesmen was not annexation but robbery. See also Haverfield, *Ancient Town-Planning* (Oxford, 1913), who points out that Greek town-planning began with the Processional Way (p. 28). On sanitation see Ar. *Eccl.* 311 ff. and *Plut.* 1184, which does not refer (as suggested by Daremberg and Saglio, s.v. *Latrina*) to a public latrine. Compare in that article the disproportion between the Greek and Roman sections. There is no Greek evidence, for an obvious reason. Few things impressed Greeks who visited Rome so much as the Big Sewer (Cloaca Maxima) : *v.* Strabo, p. 235 ; Dion. Hal. iii. 67. The Athenians would have been still more astonished if they had known of the elaborate and careful system of drainage

No doubt all these things, Pericles would tell us, are non-essentials on which we ought not to dwell. We should accept and enjoy the magnificence and let the squalor rest in peace; go straight for the big things, as he did, and ignore all the rest. What matters is the finished work of Athenian civilization, not the infinite petty obstacles with which it was daily contending.

But have we the finished work? Alas, Pericles himself would be the first to shake his head. The Parthenon was finished, but Athens never achieved more than three-quarters of the Propylaea or one-half of the Erectheum; and her great building design proved so hard, in its incompleteness, for posterity to accept and enjoy that it was twenty-three centuries before men found out what it really was. The fact is that Pericles and the men of the great age were dealing not only with an unprecedented movement of ideas but with an unprecedented set of material facts. Borne along on the tide of a great spiritual adventure Athens miscalculated the need for careful thought about the details of common life; and these, when their hour came, arose in judge-

---

in the prehistoric palaces of Crete. Athens seems to have had simply a big open drain or gutter which was eventually covered over (Merkel, *Ingenieurtechnik im Altertum*, p. 452). There is, of course, another side to all this. As Mr. John Burns remarked at the opening of the Town-Planning Exhibition : ' There are modern disabilities from which communities formerly escaped. Athens did not have 600 miles of railway, as London has, on ugly viaducts, creating *culs-de-sac* of mean and poor streets, with 500 ugly railway stations spoiled by vulgar advertisements ; it had no gas works, and was without the 7,000 public-houses London possesses—nearly all of them at street corners, in positions which ought only to be occupied by banks, libraries, post-offices, and police-stations. We labour under the disadvantage of having all the apparatus of light, heat, smoke, traction, and rapid communication ' (*Times*, Oct. 11, 1910). Sacrificing by contract : Is. vii. 29. On the tax-farming arrangements in detail see Böckh, *Attische Staatshaushaltung* (1886 ed.), vol. i, pp. 382 ff. After 413 the Imperial tribute was farmed out too. The classical instance of modern tax-farming is Bengal, where a hundred years ago the land revenue collection was granted by the British Government to certain tax-farmers and their heirs in perpetuity for a fixed sum. On education see Aeschines, i. 9 (Solon's regulations controlling private schools), and esp. Freeman's delightful but unfinished *Schools of Hellas* (where the difference between fifth- and fourth-century arrangements is not sufficiently emphasized : e.g. there was no ' secondary education ' at Athens during the first three-quarters of the fifth century). See also the interesting inscriptions (none out of them from the fifth century) collected in Freeman, pp. 221–3, and in Dittenberger (Nos. 518–25). One is praised (521, lines 70 ff.) for ' preserving a spirit of friendship and concord among the boys throughout the year ', for remitting the fines they had incurred, and bringing them back safe and sound from several ' marches-out ' to the frontier. It is only fair to add that the boys acknowledged his many kindnesses by publicly crowning him.

ment against her. In the first year of the Peloponnesian War the influx of population from the country districts taxed her municipal resources as they had never been taxed before. Here is Thucydides' account of how the strain was met. ' When they arrived at Athens, though a few had houses of their own to go to, or could find an asylum with friends or relatives, by far the greater part had to take up their dwelling on plots of vacant ground and in the temples and chapels of the heroes. . . . Many also encamped in the towers of the walls or wherever else they could. For, when they were all come in, the city proved too small to hold them.' The authorities, however, had no eyes for the difficulty. While the immigrants were ' dividing out for themselves the space between the Long Walls and a great part of Piraeus into lots and settling there,' they were thinking of higher matters. ' All this while,' Thucydides grimly continues, ' great attention was being paid to the war ; the allies were being mustered, and an armament of a hundred ships equipped for the Peloponnese. Such was the state of preparation at Athens.' The historian does not waste words. Only those who have endured the milder alternative of ' being received into a friend's house' in a Greek city at time of festival, and sleeping with twenty or thirty other friends on the floor of an airless room, can measure the unhappiness of those to whom such privileges were denied.[1]

Judgement was delivered eighteen months later. There was only one thing, Pericles tells the Athenians in his parting speech, which he failed to foresee; but that one thing proved for Athens her Achilles' heel. For the Plague, which ignored the magnificence and went straight for the squalor, was the first step in Athens' irresistible decline. It took one citizen out of four, and with them not only her resources, so carefully husbanded, in men and money, but her proud and confident morning courage. Athenian idealism broke for the first time under the strain, and the snapped ties were never again securely reunited. The memories were too horrible. ' The new arrivals from the country,' says the historian, sending our minds back to the earlier passage, ' were the greatest sufferers. As there were no houses to receive them, they had to be lodged in the hot season of the year in stifling cabins where the mortality raged without

[1] Thuc. ii. 17. As regards the Erechtheum design I follow Dörpfeld.

restraint. The bodies of dying men lay one upon another, and half-dead creatures reeled about the streets and gathered round all the fountains in their longing for water. The sacred places in which they had encamped were full of corpses of those who had died there just as they were; for as the disaster passed all bounds, men, not knowing what was to become of them, became utterly careless of everything, whether sacred or profane. All the burial rites before in use were entirely upset, and they buried the bodies as best they could.' Burial rites, as he expects us to remember, are the Holy of Holies in Greek life. Nothing remains sacred now.[1]

Yet even Thucydides himself, most practical head amongst all the Greek writers who have come down to us, has not the heart to reproach his Athens for neglecting the world of small things. There is his usual gentle irony playing round the confident sentences in which Pericles glorifies the Athenian amateur. But, looking back in after years, he had too great a sense of what had been accomplished to fling a gibe or a rebuke at what had been left undone. When we have seen the Athenian in his own home and known him for what he was by nature, careless, indolent, and undisciplined, a bad servant and a bad master, we can better appreciate what he accomplished abroad and for posterity; we can realize what an effort it cost Athens' chosen ' band of lovers ' to respond to her call, not only with ' the fighter's daring and the wise man's understanding of his duty ' but also with ' the good man's self-discipline in its performance '. For if ' nothing great was ever done without enthusiasm ', it is equally true that nothing lasting was ever done without hard work. The monuments that Athens has left us, whether in art or literature or in her constitution and customs and history, are records of infinite pains in the making. Only she spent them where they were most worth while. Instead of being cumbered with much serving and organizing a model municipality, she chose to put Beauty before Security, to build her temples on the Acropolis rather than lay waterpipes to the Piraeus. Yet for all that we know, as she knew when it was too late and her thinkers began

---

[1] Thuc. ii. 52, iii. 87. 3 (plague-losses : the proportion of 1 : 4 is definitely stated for the cavalry, where we should expect a smaller mortality than among the general population), ii. 64. 1 (the one unexpected event).

planning those model municipalities which are so like yet so different from their living originals—

> Not wholly in the old Greek world, nor quite
> Beyond it—

yet for all that ' these things should she have done, and not left the other undone '.

CHAPTER X

CITY ECONOMICS : MONEY

Εἰ δὲ τοῦτ' ἀγνοεῖς, ὅτι πίστις ἀφορμὴ τῶν πασῶν ἐστι μεγίστη πρὸς χρηματισμόν, πᾶν ἂν ἀγνοήσειας—DEMOSTHENES, xxxvi. 44.

The more closely one examines the basis of credit, the more clearly it becomes apparent that that basis itself consists to a considerable extent of credit.—HARTLEY WITHERS, *The Meaning of Money*, p. 264.

WE have examined the relation between public and private wealth in the City State, and the general attitude taken up by the State in dealing with economic problems. It is time now to examine into the actual nature of this wealth and into some of the problems which arose in connexion with its use.

In every society, however primitive or self-sufficient, there are at least a few individuals who have more wealth than they actually need for a bare livelihood and are able to store it up. It is a natural human inclination to lay by for a rainy day or for the use of the family when you are gone. The man who does so is a capitalist. For capital is not wealth pure and simple, but wealth considered from the point of view of future as opposed to present use. Such wealth in early Greece assumed a variety of forms. We hear of it in the living form of slaves and cattle, a highly profitable investment, for living things increase and multiply and pay dividends automatically : we hear of it in manifold treasures, such as fine linen, axes, spits, and copper cauldrons. But the most usual form was, of course, gold and silver, and especially gold. Mycenae, the capital of the army of chieftains who went marauding to Troy, was on men's lips for generations as ' the much-golden ', and the archaeologists who pried into her secrets have abundantly verified the adjective. Gold and silver, from their rarity and glitter and the way in which they lent themselves to purposes of barbaric adornment, gradually came to be recognized as wealth *par excellence*. Even when the lords of Mycenae ceased from their forays and their city became a mere ordinary country town, gold and silver

continued to be regarded, in a world of steady farmers, as a convenient measure of value. For oxen and women and even
cauldrons were not always of the same value, whereas a bar of
gold was always a bar of gold, and a good solid lump of glow to
feast your eye on besides.[1]

But lumps of gold, however attractive to look at, are of no
particular use for trading purposes with people at a distance.
The fact that men think of gold as the natural form of capital, as
the way in which a wise man would naturally store his wealth,
does not make gold any the less an ordinary commodity like
women, sheep, and cauldrons. Nor even does the fact that such
lumps may be stamped with an indication of their weight. Men
and states in Greece were collecting bullion, and storing it up as
treasure in temples and treasuries or in a corner of their field,
long before they trusted one another sufficiently to use it as a
medium of exchange. It was only in the seventh century B.C.,
when security was beginning to be established and communications had been improved, that men began seriously to feel the
need of a recognized common measure in their bargaining. They
grew tired of the tedious job of calculating the exact value of a
serving-woman in ploughing oxen, or of a suit of armour in mules,
and of eking out any deficiency with some handy piece of
bullion which had to be weighed first in the scales. So, instead
of merely weighing and stamping their gold and silver lumps and
ornaments of different sorts and sizes, States began to reduce
them to simple and portable shapes, and to issue them to their

---

[1] The best Homeric passage is perhaps the familiar χρύσεα χαλκείων,
ἑκατόμβοι᾽ ἐννεαβοίων of *Il.* vi. 236, where Glaucus gives Diomed ' gold value
for bronze, a hundred-oxen-worth for nine '. This shows men reckoning value
in oxen and in metals, and, what is more curious still, both qualitatively and
quantitatively. The difference between gold and bronze is one of quality
(you could not say off-hand what the ratio was between the two), that between
nine oxen and a hecatomb one of quantity. It is the great merit of systems
of coinage to have forced men to think quantitatively, that is, carefully and
precisely, over at least one part of the field of life. Thinking out the ' right '
price, whether in an Eastern bazaar or in London and Manchester, is a delicate
operation of thought, involving, in every case, a careful adjustment to the
particular circumstances. This is what has made economics an exact science :
it is because it deals so largely with money, i. e. with measurable and ponderable quantities, and with men thinking and acting and being influenced in
a measurable and ponderable manner, that it was the first of the human
sciences to become exact and scientific. This, of course, has in its turn led
it into pitfalls, tending to make it a branch of mathematics and to obscure
its interrelations with the other human sciences. [See Appendix.]

subjects at a recognized value for use in their daily transactions, in other words, they deliberately selected the precious metals and entrusted them with the monopoly of the work of exchange. This led, of course, at first, as we have seen, to a revolution in economic habits, whereby the weaker and more ignorant went to the wall. But it was the first and necessary step towards raising the city, securely and for good, out of the old self-sufficient stage of economic life. Coins were first ' struck and used ', first issued, that is, as a publicly recognized medium of exchange, by the kings of Lydia early in the seventh century. The first Greek state to use them, a few years afterwards, was Aegina ; her neighbour Argos had led the way some two generations before, in establishing a definite standard of weights and measures. Aegina is a poor island with little of its own to sell ; but the Aeginetans became distributing agents for all the world around them. Working as carriers by sea and as pedlars by land they were for long regarded as coin-users and retail dealers *par excellence*. The particular coin standard that they adopted was for some generations supreme, and always prominent, in the Greek world ; and their coins, with the familiar tortoise upon them, are still to be found in all parts of the Peloponnese.[1]

But the use of a regular currency soon brought with it new problems of its own ; for it involved states and their rulers in peculiar temptations. When Herodotus tells us about the first introduction of State coinage he uses a much-discussed phrase. ' The Lydians,' he says, ' were the first people we

---

[1] See above, pp. 114–15. For primitive currencies in Greece and elsewhere see Ridgeway's *Origin of Currency and Weight Standards*, Cambridge, 1892. For Pheidon's Argive weights and measures see Paus. vi. 22. 2. I adhere to the date there given, 750 B.C. On this disputed subject see Pauly, s.v. *Geld*, and compare Lehmann-Haupt in *Hermes* xxvii. 557, xxxv. 648. There is an interval of six centuries (from King Offa to Edward III) between the time when stamped metals are first known to have been used as a common measure of value in England and their first use as a trustworthy medium of exchange for foreign trade. There is a similar interval of many centuries in the Near Eastern monarchies. ' Dumps of precious metal ' have been found both at Cnossos and among late Mycenaean remains in Cyprus, showing ' that at least not later than the twelfth century B.C. a medium of currency forming the true antecedent stage to the early coinage of Ionia and Lydia had developed itself in the Minoan world '. See Evans in *J. H. S.*, 1911, p. 132, who points out that a very early Ionian electrum coin recently discovered shows ' two confronted lions with a forepaw on the capital of a column, as on the lion Gate of Mycenae '. Aegina : Thuc. v. 47. 6 ; Xen. *Hell.* v. 2. 21 ; cf. Head, *Historia Numorum*, 2nd ed., 1911, p. 395. [See Appendix.]

know of to stamp and use a current coinage of gold and silver.'
If this means that they originated a state currency by issuing
gold and silver coins, it is not strictly true ; for the first coins
that they issued were of *both* gold *and* silver, that is to say
of an alloy of the two, known as ' white gold ' or electrum. We
have these coins still on our museum shelves, and their sickly
glimmer, which is to that of a healthy English sovereign as the
moon is to the sun, is eloquent of the policy of the authors of
their being.[1]

For look more closely and you will observe that, though all
are sickly, they are not all alike, but wax and wane along the
shelf with various gradations of pallor. In fact the gold in an
electrum coinage is not a fixed proportion : it varies from 80 down
to 52 per cent. of the whole. This is what made them so convenient to City State governments : they could economize on the
gold and so, if they went carefully to work, make something out
of their citizens with every coin they issued. And that, in fact,
is the currency policy of the self-sufficient City State. The
issue of coins is a state monopoly, and it operated, like nearly
all such monopolies, as an indirect tax.[2]

Actual electrum coins are indeed not very common, for the
Greek states preferred a silver coinage. But silver blended with
lead and copper quite as well as gold with silver, and the Lydian
example was the sort of lesson that they would not forget. So
they habitually and shamelessly debased their coinage : and even
in the fourth century, when inter-state trade had grown to a
considerable volume, Demosthenes can still declare that ' the
majority of states are quite open in using silver coins diluted
with copper and lead ' ; and even when our extant coins are not
debased they are in most cases under weight. It is in fact an
honest coinage which is the exception, as we can see not only
from the frequent use of every kind of metaphor connected with
bad coins but from the expressions used to denote good ones.
The coins of Darius, we are told, were ' the purest ', that is, not
necessarily pure in general, but purer than others.[3]

---

[1] Hdt. i. 94, i. 50 ; Soph. *Ant.* 1038. [See Appendix.]

[2] Pauly, s.v. *Elektron.*

[3] Hdt. iii. 56, iv. 166 ; Dem. xxiv. 214. Compare the uses of the words
κίβδηλος and βασανίζω. I owe this section to Riezler, *Finanzen und Monopole,*
pp. 62–3. For some modern parallels and their effects see Ridgeway, pp. 223–6.
The Asiatic monarchies enjoyed bimetallism, with a fixed ratio of 13·3 : 1

Civilized modern states do not debase their coins. Sometimes their coins or paper money lose value in spite of themselves. But their object is always to keep them up to what they profess to be, to maintain them at par with their face value, at par, that is, with coins similarly stamped in the rest of the world. The reason for this policy is obvious. It would not pay modern States to debase their coinage, because their coinage is not the centre of their economic life. Their main concern is with wealth itself, not with the medium of its exchange, and in their financial policy they look first not to bullion but to credit. Any small gains they might make by penny-wise economies on bullion would be lost a thousand times over in the field of credit. They would lose caste among the nations; their money would sink in value on the international exchange; and they and every business man who owned wealth in their country would have to pay dear for their low credit in transactions with abroad. In quarters open to foreign influences prices would go up as money had gone down, and in the trading centres there would be two sets of prices—such as ruled in Greece in recent years for paper and silver—one for the local and one for the international medium of exchange.[1]

How was it, then, that the Greek states were able to pursue this policy ? The reason is to be found, once again, in their isolated situation and normal self-sufficiency. If you are issuing a medium of exchange for a strictly limited circle of users under your own control, you can issue it in any form you please, and force people to use it, whether it be in coffee-tavern tickets, or in the brass disks such as they use in cloak-rooms, or in the iron bars such as were

between silver and gold. (See Hdt. iii. 95, who, however, omits the decimal.) The chief Greek standards, i. e. those of Aegina, Euboea, Athens, and Corinth, were, however, all monometallic with a silver standard. Hence the author of the *Ways and Means* is quite right, as things then were, in saying that a glut in gold will send it down in value, but that you cannot possibly have a glut in silver (iv. 7–10). The Greek silver currencies gradually disappeared in the fourth century before the Macedonian gold standard. See Keil, *Anonymous Argentinensis*, 271 ff.

[1] See *Laws* 742, where Plato, who may have come across this system in operation on his travels, but cannot have lived under it, proposes it for his model city. Its greatest advantage is that it prevents people from going abroad without leave from the authorities. He hopes to keep grown men virtuous by the petty dodges we sometimes adopt to keep schoolboys from buying tobacco or tramps out of the public-house. Of course, he had never been to Sparta.

provided for the unfortunate Spartans. Some medium they must have, and if iron bars are all that they can get, and are issued under State authority, iron bars will circulate, however uncomfortable for daily use. Sparta is an extreme instance, and her preposterous currency was deliberately maintained in order to hamper business; her statesmen worked, as always, with disciplinary rather than economic objects in view. But the ordinary debasement that went on represents the same stage of economic life. States could debase their coins because they knew and could control all the persons who would use them, and so could take steps to prevent themselves from losing ' in the long run ' what they were making on their first issue. They gave their citizens fivepence and called it sixpence, but they could prevent their citizens and the rest of the world from playing back the same trick upon themselves.[1]

How could they prevent it ? By all sorts of clever tricks. Some of them have been preserved for us, and bring vividly before our minds both how much the Greek citizen would put up with from his city, and—what we have already emphasized—the superior position occupied in Greece by State as opposed to private concerns. For instance, the State would demand that all payments to itself should be made in full weight, following the Babylonian precedent of ' one measure for the State and another for the people '. Or it would suddenly call in its coins and pay those who brought them by their actual weight, adding insult to injury, as the tyrant Hippias did at Athens, by promptly reissuing the old coins with a view to repeating the operation. Or they could imitate a still harsher State treasurer, Dionysius of Syracuse, supposing they found themselves in debt to their foremost citizens. He simply ordered his creditors on pain of death to bring him all the silver they possessed. When

---

[1] The iron spit currency which lasted on so long at Sparta survived in name at Athens also : in the old days six of these spits or obols (ὀβελοί) made a handful or drachma (δραχμή). A bundle of iron spits about four feet long, bound together with two iron bands, has been found at the Heraeum at Argos, and confirms the old etymology of the ' handful ' of six spits. It also confirms the legend of the iron money at Sparta. The British excavators there found several of their ' lumps ' and ' bars of iron ' (B. S. A. xiii. 173). Its use may have lingered on, for when Epaminondas died, he was so poor, Plutarch tells us (Fab. Max. 27), ' that nothing was found in his possession except an iron spit '.

it arrived he stamped every drachma piece with a two-drachma surcharge, and so paid the debt in their own money. The writer of the *Economics* revels in these stories. Their moral is always the same : that where a State is omnipotent over those who use its currency, it can easily exert its power so as to gain on its transactions with them. In other words, there is nothing to prevent the city from stealing its citizens' money, as there is nothing to prevent it from stealing their lives in an unjust war. The only difference is that the ordinary currency-fraud acted so indirectly that democracies were slow to see how they were robbing themselves by their own devices. When right hand robs left it wants a trained economist to mark the score. In business it is the gifted amateurs who are tempted to cheat. It takes a professional to find out that to play fair is the ' best policy '.[1]

Yet in process of time they were bound to discover it, for they would learn it, not without bad language, from the traders who came to them from more civilized centres. It is the great advantage of Athens as a mart, says the author of the *Ways and Means*, ' that you can get good silver there. In most cities merchants are simply compelled to ship goods for the return journey, for they cannot get any money which is any use to them outside.' In other words, a bad system of coinage made foreign trade almost impossible ; the merchant would only come when he could exchange his goods for some staple export, for the money-changers on his native quay had no use for out-landish money. So we see why the states which, like Athens or Aegina or Corinth or Cyzicus, prided themselves on an honest coinage gradually extended its use over more secluded parts of the Greek world. Even when it was not used up-country, among

---

[1] [Ar.] *Oec.* 1347 a 4–11 (Hippias) ; Head, *Historia Numorum*, pp. 369–70, explains this story as a ' substitution of the light for the heavy Euboic standard ', but points out that by it Hippias ' succeeded, within his own dominions, in doubling, nominally if not actually, his own resources '. It was in a similar spirit that he confiscated as State property and sold back to the unfortunate householders the ' upper storeys of houses, steps, fences, and doors that projected or opened on to the public street ' ; 1349 b 27 (Dionysius). Small modern states sometimes play similar tricks with their postage stamps, but that is because the collectors encourage them. The Greeks had no hobbies of this sort.—1924. I leave this paragraph unaltered for the reflections of readers versed in post-war governmental finance.

shepherds and farmers who were shy of the strange design, its
obvious advantages made it the only currency down at the port.
Gradually the government would give up the cheerless task of
trying to make its unwelcome lumps of metal circulate among
a reluctant population. One reason why it had originally adopted
them was the expense and difficulty of getting good bullion.
When it found out its mistake it was too late to repair it by
issuing good money of its own. Athens or Aegina with their
prestige were already in possession of the field. So the local
mint would stop working, the money-changer would have one
less bad coin on his table and one less shaft in his quiver of evil
tricks, and the Greek world would be one step nearer to a national
as opposed to a purely municipal system of economy.[1]

But compared with her astonishing advance in other directions
Greece made but slow progress in breaking down these economic
barriers and so facilitating intercourse. The Greek City States
never became large trading communities in our sense of the term :
even fifth-century Athens, under her accomplished financier Pericles, who had a better business sense than any of the older Greeks
we know, did not succeed in overcoming the obstacles in her path.

The chief of these obstacles was of course the elementary fact
of the poverty of the Greek world. This reacted upon business
life at every point ; above all, it made impossible, what is an
indispensable condition of the modern economy, the unimpeded
and healthy circulation of money. The City State never learnt,
and never succeeded in teaching its citizens, to stop hoarding
bullion like an old-time miser and to ' give it into the bank ',
as the Jewish parable says, ' that I might have required mine
own with usury '—in other words, after it had been set in circulation for purposes of trade and enterprise. Men preferred to wrap
their talents in napkins and hide them in fields, where they might,
as we are told, be ' enjoyed ' as much as if they were being used,
and so often remained as a treasure-trove for modern museums.
Even Aristotle still gave currency to the old heresy about interest.
Yet, until money is freely put out to breed, trade and industry

---

[1] *Ways and Means* iii. 2. For the voluntary closing of local mints under
the Athenian Empire see the striking table in Cavaignac, *Études sur l'histoire
financière d'Athènes*, pp. 179 ff. The ' florins ' of Florence owed their repute
to the same cause as the owls of Athens.

must languish, and the material resources of a country will remain insignificant and precarious.[1]

Let us look a little more closely into the reasons for this obstinate prejudice about bullion, for we shall discover in the sequel that it is vitally interconnected with the special object of our inquiry.

Civilized society, we are told, is ' ultimately based on force '. It is equally true to say it is ultimately based on bullion. In both cases what is meant is that, if the worst came to the worst, we should come up against that naked fact. If the whole structure of our religious and social life, built up through centuries of moral effort, came tumbling about our ears, we should have to fight it out, with fists or the latest artillery as the case might be. So if the whole structure of our commercial life were to fall with a crash, if everybody simultaneously desired to realize, we should be thrown back upon the raw bullion which is at the base of the solid foundation of our credit and enterprise. Yet we know very well, and we do not need our banker to tell us, that, if this were to happen, there would not be enough bullion to go round. What we are really living upon is not bullion at all, but confidence and credit and security, on forms of wealth which can at a pinch of individual need, but could not if the need were universal, be transformed into bullion. The gold reserve in the Bank of England is always there, like the pistols and horsewhips which our duelling neighbours regard as so indispensable to civilization. Yet, as Demosthenes said long ago, ' if a man is really and truly ignorant that confidence is the best capital for commercial enterprise he must be ignorant of everything ' : just as, if a man is really and truly ignorant that the habitual gentleness and restraint, not the occasional violence, of the modern gentleman and citizen is the best security for civilization, he must have been asleep all his days. Now to understand business life in Greece, and indeed in the ancient world generally, we must think

---

[1] Ar. *Pol.* 1258 b ; *Ways and Means* iv. 7 ; Matt. xiii. 44, xxv. 25 ; Luke xix. 12 ff., taken, as usual, out of the heart of the life of the day. Even so up-to-date a man as Themistocles seems to have hoarded his money : Thuc. i. 137. 3. For the state hoards of antiquity see Thuc. ii. 13. 4 and the inventory of the Parthenon treasure (Hicks and Hill, No. 71) : also 2 Kings xviii. 16; showing that the temple at Jerusalem was a treasure-house just like the Parthenon. The Greeks never knew the difference between a bank and a museum.

away all this scaffolding of credit and confidence, as we must
think away our opportunities of obtaining quick and trustworthy
information about foreign firms and markets. The Greeks were
never able to live comfortably, either as states or as individuals,
under the shadow of credit. Business life to-day rides, as it were,
on pneumatic tyres ; it is inflated with confidence. The Greeks,
as they rode, felt the rims all the time. Society very seldom dared
to outrun its bullion resources. If it did it risked catastrophe; and
once or twice in ancient history, after periods of inflation, when
wealth seemed for a moment inexhaustible, such catastrophes
really occurred, bringing with them disaster far more widespread
than any bank failures of to-day.[1]

So that in Greece, so long, at any rate, as the City State
system lasted and there were no international centres like Alexandria, Antioch, and Pergamum, it was always impossible for
a community, and mostly for individuals too, to live upon loans.
Cities lived strictly upon what they had, which included of course
the private property of their inhabitants. For the citizen, as we
have seen, had no rights against his city. She was, or claimed
to be, his all in all ; and if she asked for his property at need, as
a free gift or as a forced loan, the difference was merely one of
sentiment. No true Greek would dream of investing in his
city's funds and so profiting by her need. And if she could
not borrow from within, because she could only take, neither
could she raise money from outside, either for a profitable war
or for ‘ reproductive ’ public works. There was, indeed, no one
to borrow from. The great capitalists of the day were public
bodies, the Panhellenic shrines at Delphi and Olympia and the
larger City States. But sacred gold was taboo, and no State
would lend, even at high interest, to a rival. Nor was there help
to be had from private sources. There were no interhellenic
banking firms, no Fuggers or Acciajuoli such as even our Middle
Ages could provide, and such few men as had ready money to

---

[1] Dem. xxxvi. 44 (for the Greek see chapter-motto above). The widespread
distress at Rome and throughout Italy at the time of Catiline's conspiracy
was probably due to a sudden failure of confidence after a period of over-
speculation. See Ferrero, vol. i, pp. 234 and 319 ; vol. ii, p. 231 (Engl. tr.),
and also Davis, *The Influence of Wealth in Imperial Rome* (New York, 1910),
chap. i, for a vivid, if somewhat imaginative, account of the business panic of
A.D. 33.

spare, mostly resident aliens in their states, who were not allowed
to buy land, preferred to put their money in corn-ships and
speculate in local famines rather than to be creditors of a State
from whom they might never be able to recover. For if a State
refused to pay, who was to bring her to justice ? The creditor
could no more expect his temporary city to go to war in order
to recover his debts than the Jews did in the Middle Ages.
Moreover, the investment, at best, was more risky by far than
similar engagements to-day with the shakiest Central American
communities. For there was no knowing, in a world that lived
so near the margin of destitution, whether a city might not any
year ' take sick ', as the expression went, with a bad harvest or
a war, and need every penny she possessed, interest and all, to
buy food at famine prices. Small wonder that the State loans
among our inscriptions, which date from a later time than we are
discussing, are mercilessly severe in their terms, and that whenever in the historians we hear of a State obligation duly paid it is
obviously regarded not as an act of business but of virtue.[1]

[1] *Ways and Means* iv. 9 (take sick) ; Xen. *Oec.* xx. 28, *Athenische Mitteilungen* xxxvi, p. 81 (speculating in famines). Dangers of private banking :
Hdt. vi. 86. The Delphi-Olympia War Loan suggested in Thuc. i. 121. 3 of
course never came off. These shrines never handed out money unless compelled, as Delphi by the Phocians in the fourth century. Their traditions made
it difficult for the Greeks to realize what a ' loan ' was. ' Going after a debt '
in Homeric days was a very informal proceeding, and might mean merely
' giving tit for tat '. See *Il.* xi. 687, and *Od.* xxi. 17, where Odysseus goes
'debt-collecting ', i. e. seeking amends for a cattle raid. So χρέος, the word
here used, means ' that which one needs must pay ' (Liddell and Scott), a
charmingly ambiguous term. The instances of loans between States are just
cases of helping a friend in need. Thus the Corinthians on one occasion lend the
Athenians, ' with whom they were then close friends,' twenty ships at £1 or 30s.
apiece, ' because by their laws they were forbidden to give them for nothing '
(Hdt. vi. 89). Similarly, the Spartans lent the Thirty Tyrants at Athens, who
held power by their support, a hundred talents, which the restored Democracy
afterwards repaid—a fact so remarkable that it was remembered for generations (Is. vii. 68 ; Ar. *Pol.* 1276 a 10). An instance of a State loan is recorded
by Aeschines (iii. 103). The city of Oreus had given Demosthenes a talent ' for
services rendered '. ' Having spent all their money on fighting and being
altogether poverty-stricken ' they ask it back, promising to put up a bronze
statue of him in their market-place instead. Demosthenes replied that ' he
wanted none of their bronze ', but that he would let them have it back if they
would pay him one per cent. a month on the security of their public revenues
till they could repay it. So they had to pay twelve per cent. interest on their
honorarium. For the ordinary conditions in later times, when such loans
became a common matter of business, see Dittenberger, No. 517, dealing with
the public debt at Amorgos, with notes and references. Amorgos borrows
money from a Naxian, and pledges 'the whole of its public and private property
both in and outside the island ' ; i. e. the creditor might seize any Amorgian's

Much the same difficulties apply to transactions within the city between private individuals. It was always difficult to raise money, and the arrangements made seem, from a modern point of view, childish and unsatisfactory. We have already seen what a blow was struck by Solon at the rising business community in sixth-century Athens when he made it illegal for men to borrow on the security of their own persons. It was a necessary law, and as such was copied elsewhere; still it was an interference with free contract. For men only raised capital on themselves when they had nothing else to offer; and if you might not risk slavery in order to start a business, most probably you were compelled not to start it at all. Under these circumstances, borrowing tended either to become a very expensive matter, costing anything over twelve per cent., or to be done privately amongst friends. The most usual form of security on a business transaction was land or houses. But this led to a difficulty, for resident aliens who, like the famous Pasion, were generally the people with spare cash, were for traditional reasons not allowed to own them, and this tended in its turn to act as a brake upon enterprise, or to send up the rate of interest. So the arrangements were very often of a private and friendly character, suited to the pleasant fellowship of a Greek city. A number of friends would club together to form a select private company, or what was called a common picnic (ἔρανος), receiving no interest on their capital at all, repayment by the director of the enterprise being regarded as a debt of honour. Business relations seem, in fact, to have been

ship on the high seas. For the immensely greater wealth of the Alexandrian and Pergamene period, when economic organization was no longer municipal but national, see Wilamowitz's suggestive note, unfortunately hidden away in a pamphlet on a single inscription (*Ein Gesetz von Samos*, Berlin, 1904, p. 12). The difficulty in those days was not want of capital but of a Stock Exchange to manipulate it. It lay, as it were, in large reservoirs of public and private treasure, and there were no proper means of irrigation. Finally, as he says, the Romans came and stole it in spoil or syndicates, and the improved administration under the emperors did not save Greek lands from ultimately sinking back into poverty and barbarism. ' For under the Roman emperors there was not only no Stock Exchange, but the banks of the Hellenistic age were allowed to lose their business.' There is a good description of the working of these Roman Empire-builders (who as far excelled their Greek predecessors in greed and ruthlessness as they lagged behind them in not knowing what to do with their money) in Ferrero, *Greatness and Decline of Rome*, vol. i, chap. xviii (Engl. tr., pp. 303 ff.). See also Davis, *The Influence of Wealth in Imperial Rome*. In general see Riezler, *Über Finanzen und Monopole im alten Griechenland*, pp. 56 ff.

as friendly and informal as those between the country cousin and the friend who ' knows a good thing in the city '. The money often disappeared to the bottom of the sea or into the pockets of pirates ; but as the loser had his bit of land in reserve it did not make so much difference. Yet it is strange to reflect that in an ' advanced ' society like that of Athens, where people were so fond of subtle distinctions, business life was so primitive that, as the dictionaries tell us, men had not yet learnt to distinguish between a free loan between friends and an investment of working capital.[1]

But Birmingham and Manchester are smiling at us. It is time to bring this chapter to a close.

---

[1] χρέος and δάνειον are each used in both senses. See Daremberg and Saglio, s. v. *Foenus* ; Pauly, s. v. *Eranos*, who quotes Hyperides, v. 9, on how ' debts of honour ' sometimes came home to roost (in the fourth century) after a business changed hands. The *Economics* has a story (1347 a 1) of how the city of Byzantium once sold some metic creditors the right of owning the land they had taken as a security, in return for one-third of the debt. In Egypt, according to Herodotus (ii. 136), men were at one time so hard up for a form of security that they were reduced to pawning their fathers' mummies. For an instance of the ' good thing in the city ' game see Lysias, xix. 25. Similar stories have been heard in law courts since. Our evidence for the rate of interest on private investments at Athens is all from the fourth century. Twelve per cent. is the lowest (and a not unusual) figure. The highest is exacted by the Reckless Man in Theophrastus, who lends money to market people at twenty-five per cent. *per day*, and ' will make the round of the cook-shops, the fishmongers, the fish-picklers, thrusting into his cheek the interest which he levies on their gains '. The Greeks called him Reckless (though we should not) because he had ' no restraining sense of honour ' (Theophr. xvi and Jebb's note, p. 92, on Recklessness).

CHAPTER XI

CITY ECONOMICS : FOREIGN TRADE

Αἱ ἐσχατιαί κως τῆς οἰκεομένης τὰ κάλλιστα ἔλαχον.—HERODOTUS, iii. 106.
The extreme parts of the inhabited world somehow possess the most
excellent products.

WE are at last in the position to approach the subject of
foreign trade, which played so important a part in the life of
fifth-century Athens.

The establishment of a workable, if not wholly satisfactory,
system of exchange enabled the leading City States, from the
seventh century onwards, to enter into business relations with
foreign parts. Let us watch how they did so.

The city of the seventh and sixth centuries still retains her
old tradition of self-sufficiency. She still feeds herself from her
own cornlands and clothes herself with her own wool. But she
has sent out colonists into far lands, and tales have come back to
her of the wonders that they have seen. It is her curiosity that
has been roused, rather than her desire for riches or luxury. She
would like to enliven her daily life by the novelties from over the
sea. What she hopes to gain by the establishment of commercial
relations is ' new ways of enjoying life '. ' Give me the luxuries of
life from abroad,' she said to the trader, ' and I will not ask you for
its necessities.' Trade begins with luxuries, as habits begin with
' quite exceptional cases '. But it is generally impossible for
either of them to end there. When Greece had acquired the
trading habit she never succeeded in throwing it off.[1]

But she will have some difficulty in forming the habit, for all
tradition is against her. In the world on to which she is launching her trading ventures the hand of every man and every State
is against their neighbour's. The would-be trader is mistaken,
now for a pirate, now for an explorer, now for the emissary and

[1] Old Oligarch, ii. 7. I do not remember who first inverted Benjamin
Franklin's sententious remark about not asking for luxuries.

advance guard of an invading host. It needs time and patience for him to justify and confirm and regularize his position.[1]

We have some interesting glimpses of this early period when trader, pirate, and naval officer were merged into one. Foreign relations began with war and robbery. It was a recognized right that a State which had suffered robbery or wrong in the person of any of its members, which had lost a Helen or an Io or a cargo of valuables, should ' exercise reprisals ' on its assailant or any of its assailant's ships and members, till each party was exhausted or the wrong redressed. States lived, that is, in a state of perpetual vendetta ; and the first task of internationalists was not to preach peace and goodwill to a world clamouring for adventure, but to make a few firm islands of dry land amid an ocean of buccaneering. So a treaty was not (as we are always told nowadays) an ' additional guarantee for the peace of the world ', but, at this earliest stage, simply an arrangement between States to forgo for a time (there was generally a time limit in Greek treaties, war being the natural state) the pleasure of exercising reprisals on one another, in the interest of joint operations upon a larger scale. International law, in Greece at any rate, seems to have begun with ' honour among thieves '. Here is an extract from a convention between two diminutive City States, neighbours squeezed side by side into the tiny alluvial plains between the mountains of Locris and the gulf of Crisa, whence day by day they watched with hungry eyes the rich pilgrim boats as they turned proudly in round the last corner towards Delphi. Woe to them if on a dark night they cut the corner too fine ! ' No man of Oeantheia, if he make a seizure, shall carry off a Chaleian merchant from Chaleian soil, nor a Chaleian an Oeantheian merchant from Oeantheian soil ; nor shall either Oeantheian or Chaleian seize a merchant's cargo within the territory of the other city. If any one breaks this rule it shall be lawful to seize him with impunity. The property of a foreigner may be seized on the sea without incurring the penalty, except in the actual harbour of the city.' The sting of the treaty lies, of course, in the tail. Who would not forgo the delights of robbing a fellow Locrian when there were treasure-ships in the offing ?[2]

---

[1] See above, pp. 255-6.
[2] Hicks and Hill, No. 44. The inscription is on a bronze tablet in the

So that at this early stage seafaring trade was sometimes too risky a business, and men preferred to do what exchanging they could by land. We read of ' frontier markets ' on some boundary pasture, where the shepherds would meet and exchange a few humble luxuries, the honey of Attica for the pigs and vegetables of Megara or the fresh-water fish from the plains of Boeotia, their sheep-dogs sleeping with one eye open while the bargaining proceeded. It was not easy, however, to do much trading by land. The country was too rough and the roads too bad. Even in the fifth century there was hardly a cart-road in Greece which crossed a national boundary. Merchants who travelled by land went as pedlars or tinkers, like the Breton onion-sellers who traverse England and Wales to-day with their goods slung around them, 'themselves their own carriers ', as the Greek phrase went. No doubt at Delphi and Olympia and the Isthmus, on international occasions, you would see them muster in force. But even in these centres, whither such roads as there were converged, the great majority of the dealers who have such wondrous tricks to perform or outlandish novelties to sell have made their way in by sea.[1]

British Museum. I follow Riezler's translation (*Finanzen*, p. 79) as against Meyer and Hicks. Foreigners may be seized anywhere except in the other side's harbour. Members of the ' high contracting parties ' are safe on their own soil. It is a fifth-century treaty, so we may suppose Oeantheia and Chaleion had been playing separately at this game all through Delphi's palmiest days. Oeantheia is Galaxidhi, the first stop on the steamship route from Itea to Patras : Chaleion is farther up, in a corner of the gulf. Compare Hdt. i. 1, vi. 42 ; Thuc. v. 115. 1 ; Dem. xxxv. 13 and 26, and argument of xxiv. Details in Pauly, s. v. ἀσυλία, corrected by Riezler, p. 69. The right of ' asylum ' granted by States to one another's citizens was sometimes granted to individuals by special decree. Side by side with this political idea grew a religious idea of ἀσυλία. Sanctuaries and temples became ' asylums ' for suppliants, e. g. for Opposition leaders or runaway slaves. For some modern parallels to the Greek institution of reprisals see Dareste, *Revue des études grecques*, vol. ii, pp. 305 ff. On this whole subject see Tod, *International Arbitration among the Greeks* (Oxford, 1913). Practically all the evidence is, however, later than the fifth century.

[1] Frontier ' markets ' (our market ' and ' march ' are kindred words) : Dem. xxiii. 39, quoted in Büchsenschütz, *Besitz und Erwerb*, p. 474, where see some good references also for what Delphi and Olympia must have been like. Menander sums them up in five words : ' crowd, market, thieves, acrobats, amusements.' He omits a sixth, ' beggars.' See Tenos any March 25th or August 15th (old style). The ' sacred ways ', e. g. through Phocis to Delphi, on which Laius rumbled along in state in a country cart, were the only national roads in Greece. Who was there to make any others ? They would only help an invader, as Xerxes was tempted to Delphi : see Hdt. vi. 34 ; Soph. *O. T.* 750–3, 122. Moreover, they were bound to remain

For, in the Greek area at any rate, the sea is the natural medium of travel. No one can live in Greek lands without feeling as the Greeks did, that it is the land that divides and the sea that unites. Shepherds may scramble up the mountains and spend the summer months together with friends from beyond the range ; but a wise man wishing to go afield for his living will launch his ship on the smooth blue water and head for some harbour across the channel. So the Greeks called their merchants ' Cross-channel men ', because they had watched them flickering to and fro from bay to bay and islet to islet, on the softest of all roads, where a man can turn which way he will. To travel by land was in Greek eyes always a poor second-best, just as toiling at the oar in a dead calm under a hot sun is a poor second-best for scudding along full-sail before a following breeze. Not for the Greek the slow and cumbersome ritual of the desert caravan, or the weary straining of pack-horses up the rock-strewn track to the pass. Nimble wits prefer a nimble journey ; his ship passed gently like a butterfly from one halt to the next, and he arrived at his journey's end, whether in Spain or the Crimea, having lightly grazed the edges of half a dozen foreign lands, with the agreeable consciousness that, through all the weeks of the passage, his road had never once forced him to pass through barbarian territory. For it is the great merit of sea travel, as Horace remarked long ago, that it carries you into distant parts without ruffling your social habits. You remain, unless you tranship, among your own countrymen all the time. And when you arrive, be it at the farthest Greek colony by the Guadalquivir or the Don, you can still fancy you are at home : for the men who planted it carried their country with them too.[1]

unsafe. The whole plot of the *Oedipus Tyrannus* depends on the fact that the Thebans never thought it worth while to inquire into their king's murder. ' Lost in the mountains : robbers of course ' : and they dismissed the subject. Details about sacred roads in Merkel, *Die Ingenieurtechnik im Altertum*, pp. 217 ff. See also Leaf, *Homer and History*, pp. 223–5. Pedlars : Aesch. *Choeph.* 675 (αὐτόφορτος, like Xanthias on his donkey, *Frogs* 25). The line between the pedlar carrying goods and the wandering craftsman (e. g. tinker) carrying tools is a very narrow one, as Demolins points out in his section on gipsy-economy (*Comment la route crée le type social*, vol. ii, p. 78). For land trade in Periclean Athens see *Acharnians* 870. Its volume was very small compared to the sea trade. There were apparently no customs-houses for it : *Ach.* 818 (cf. Francotte, *Finances des cités grecques*, pp. 11–12).

[1] ἔμπορος = ὁ ἐν πόρῳ from περάω. For the meanings of δεύτερος πλοῦς, the proverbial expression for ' second-best ', see Liddell and Scott ; or find out

Our merchant, then, plies his trade by sea, carrying goods to and fro between States which have given up ' exercising reprisals ' upon one another and offer a safe asylum for his ship in their harbours. He cannot venture as a trader (though he may venture in other capacities) till he is protected by treaty-rights, or has secured some citizen who will introduce him in the capacity of a guest-friend. He is therefore in a sense, although engaged on strictly private business, the representative of his country. He is protected by his nationality or, as we say, by his flag ; and though at home he may only rank as a resident alien, and for this very reason can afford to stay so long in foreign parts, yet when among Sicels and Iberians, and even at Syracuse and Cyprus, he bears himself proudly as a man of Athens. For it is 'because of the greatness of his city ' that he has a right to fetch goods for her.[1]

by practical experience. ' Caelum non animum mutant qui trans *mare* currunt ' helps to explain the nature of the colonial Greek, then and now. It is a familiar fact that Greeks and Italians hate going up country in America because they do not like losing sight of the road home. Alexander was the first statesman who succeeded in dispelling this instinct. Every one remembers how strongly it was implanted in Xenophon's Ten Thousand, and their famous cry, when they emerged from the mountains of Armenia and saw the Black Sea below them : ' Thalassa, Thalassa,' or ' Now we can go home sleeping '. For sea roads as opposed to land roads see Old Oligarch, ii. 5 : ' land-travelling is slow work, and it is impossible to take enough supplies for a long journey.' I emphasize the point because Bérard has confused it by a careless statement of his ' law of the isthmus '. He is right in holding that ancient traders often took goods by land (1) to avoid a specially dangerous or troublesome bit of sea, or (2) to save an hour's heavy rowing out of port. That is, they took roads, *when specially made for them* by an Agamemnon, or an Alcinous, either across an ' isthmus ' or from the inner port to near the point where the wind begins. But this is very different from saying that the ancients always preferred ' navigations minima' and ' routes de terre maxima ', which is not the case. See pp. 27 ff. above ; *Le Phéniciens et l'Odyssée*, vol. i, pp. 68, 178 (with refs.) ; and Leaf, *Homer and History*, p. 220. Beyond, or rather behind, the Greek fringe, caravan routes begin : witness the camels which, despite the railway, still wend their way through the streets of Smyrna. The idea of a country on shipboard, gods and all, was familiar to the maritime Greek communities. Compare Hdt. i. 165, viii. 62 (the Athenians threaten to remove to Siris) ; Thuc. viii. 76. 4–7 (which is the true Athens, the ancestral city or the movable camp ?).

[1] Thuc. ii. 38. 2. For commercial treaties see above, p. 189. Hdt. i. 163, vi. 21 (' the Phocaeans ' at Tartessus, ' the Milesians ' at Sybaris, which does not mean, as it would in a Venetian historian, that they were trading in State ships). Compare the foreign settlement at Naucratis (ii. 178), where, we may be sure, no one asked an ' Aeginetan ' or a ' Milesian ' who his father had been. Concessions were granted to individuals or groups of friends, never to large syndicates like those of Rome or our own Chartered Companies. There are many surviving traces of similar trading settlements from our own Middle Ages. For instance, the long wooden sheds for the members of the several nations who traded in Norwegian waters may still be seen at Bergen.

Let us watch his operations for a moment in detail, for they are very different from those of his modern counterpart. We are accustomed to think of the merchant as a man who sits at home in an office, directing by cable or telephone, from information similarly derived, either privately or through the press, the activities of innumerable subordinates or dependants in distant lands. At his Olympian nod from a dingy London office men gash rubber-trees in South America and load grain-ships at Odessa, sweat in the mines of South Africa, on the quays of Singapore, or, to buy shares in his company, in the jostling Stock Exchanges of the money capitals of the world. In station he is a private citizen, in power he is an emperor or at least an oligarch ; for the ever closer interweaving of the economic interests and organization of the business world all over the globe have tended to concentrate power on to the few Atlantean shoulders that have strength to meet the burden. Ambition follows opportunity as water flows downhill, and our most ambitious men to-day are not, as of old, generals and statesmen, but merchants and financiers and ' captains of industry '.

In Greece, as we know, that was not so. Merchants had but little capital, since society had but little to offer them. Nor, if they had possessed it, would they have known how to use it. They could not operate on a large scale in the absence of quick and certain information from distant markets, or with a staff of flighty, versatile, unorganizable Greeks to perform their orders. Business life in London would be difficult if a proportion of the office was always serving as juries. Yet a good deal of Greek business must have been done under these conditions and attended to in double shifts. Operations were therefore confined to a modest and restricted scale, and, down to the fifth century at any rate, partook of the amateurish and improvised character of so many other departments of Greek life.[1]

Moreover, as we have seen, ancient life lacked comforts ; and it is with comforts, rather than with luxuries or with necessaries, that the great bulk of a big modern nation's trade is concerned. Our staple imports are neither grand pianos and Old Masters, which,

---

[1] The ' bottomry ' cases in Demosthenes' private orations belong of course to a somewhat more complex stage of business life than that which we are treating here. There is no evidence for a regular system of marine insurance earlier than the fourth century. Cf. note on p. 313 above.

like King Solomon's ' ivory, apes, and peacocks ', can appeal only
to a small class, nor the food and clothing indispensable to prevent starvation and nakedness, but the long list of articles (how
long we shall only realize when we have a general tariff) such as
tea or watches or paper or the linen or cotton for our second shirt,
which have become so indispensable a part of our civilized daily
life that we have long since forgotten that they are not necessaries at all. To the Greeks such articles were neither necessaries
nor comforts : if they had them at all they ranked as rare and
expensive luxuries, and the trader who brought them had to
reckon with a public as small and precarious as that of our
painters and picture-dealers. Indeed their lot was even harder,
for to-day, if in these select branches of trade there is no business
doing, it is not because there is really no money, but because it
is being spent on other things, on charity or super-taxes or Monte
Carlo. In Greece trade would languish because society, not as a
pretext but in very truth, ' simply had not got the money.' The
familiar trade competition of modern times rages between trader
and trader and between article and article : in antiquity it raged
between two deadlier foes—the desires of man and the niggardli-
ness of nature. It was not so much his fellow merchant in his
own or any other line of business that the Greek trader feared or
hated : the merchant-skippers, like fellow craftsmen, met as
brothers in a guild and worshipped ' Zeus the Saviour ' at their
common altar. The dealer in perfumes did not rage blindly
against the dealer in frankincense, or the slave importer from the
North against his comrade who came with a cargo of negroes and
negresses from Libya. These are the fears and suspicions of our
modern system, where each man is for himself and the devil take
the hindmost. In the Greek trader's little world men's appre-
hensions were very different. If society was in a better temper
and the trading community less harassed and irritable, it was
not because the dangers that threatened their livelihood were
imaginary or far distant, or less sudden and decisive in their
working when they came. What the Greek trader dreaded as he
lay awake on his poop-castle and made his course by the stars,
what he prayed all the gods of the confraternity to avert, was
some public misfortune common to all his fellow traders—war
or famine or earthquake or some fit of asceticism or stroke of

statesmanship which might dry up at a moment's notice the whole stream of business.[1]

With these difficulties in view let us watch our merchant at his work. He will set sail from Athens or Corinth when the winter storms are safely over, on a 'round' ship of his own or one placed at his disposal by a body of friends or subscribers, manned by a small crew of some twenty citizens or resident aliens, who welcome the outing for a change and for a chance of rowing and steering practice—and perhaps of other things besides. He will be loaded with home-grown oil of various qualities in home-made jars, both plain and painted, and with a store of cheap and tempting trinkets which may come in useful for savages. His first destination is a line of ports and landing-places in Italy or Syria. But he has no fixed orders or programme, still less a time-table, and he is quite free to change his course as the wind, or a whim, or some opposition leader among the crew, or a piece of news from a passing boat, may chance to direct. When he makes a port he will sell what he can and load up with what he can find, relying on the local people to tell him how he is likely to dispose of it. So he will move about on the familiar roads of the Mediterranean, as a distributor or public carrier, making his profits not so much by his own original cargo brought from home as by the wares he buys and sells, or the commissions he executes, among local dealers by the way. He is, in fact, in our phraseology, skipper and shipper and merchant all thrown into one; and his business is not in the grain line or the oil line or any particular line of business, but in anything that happens to come handy to his ship. Being entirely his own master, or at least on his own initiative, with no firm behind him or orders to carry out, he can turn his hand to whatever he likes; and if trade is slack or the sea-police napping, there is nothing to prevent a temporary digression into other walks of life. His stock-in-trade,

---

[1] See p. 269 above. Traders' gods : *I. G.* i. 68 Ζεὺς Σωτήρ, i. 34, 35 ('Ανακες, i. e. δαίμονες, who are also Θεοὶ σωτῆρες). See a longer inscription (but later, and the merchants are Tyrians) in Michel, *Recueil*, No. 998, or (better) in Wilhelm, *Beiträge zur griechischen Inschriftenkunde*, p. 163. Traders' (and citizens') fears : Soph. *O. T.* 22 ; Plato, *Laws* 709. ' Two bad harvests or a massacre ' is the Western buyer's formula for cheap carpets in Anatolia to-day. Good for the Western bargain-hunter, but bad for the local trader who is trying to *sell* anything.—1921. All this can be read in the light of the five years' blockade of Central and Eastern Europe and its effects.

in fact, like that of his predecessor the pirate, is not his cargo but his ship, which he plies on the narrow seas as a cabman plies his horse and carriage. At the end of the season, when the days begin to draw in and the gales are due, he loads up with a final cargo, the newer and stranger the better, and so brings his vessel back to port.[1]

It is only when he reaches home that the merchant can discover whether he is likely to sell his gathered store that winter, whether, in fact, he will take rank among the affluent or the needy, the honoured or the despised. It depends on the olive crop and the harvest, on men's tempers, and on the state of politics. His best chance is that every one should be flush and cheerful and radically-minded, ready to be persuaded, regardless of consequences, into any new and startling fashion. So he will ostentatiously unload his apes and ivories and negro slaves and such other foreign wonders as he has managed to bring safe home, send word round the town by his friends, who are used to improving on the truth, and do his best to persuade an Alcibiades or some other ' man of petty

---

[1] Old Oligarch, i. 20 ; Thuc. i. 143 (mercantile marine). The ναύκληρος, ship-owner and skipper at once, was commoner, at least before the fourth century, than the φορτηγός, the dealer who carried his goods about on some one else's ship. Aristotle is careful to distinguish them, and to distinguish both from the local agent with whom they dealt at the other end, whose work is called παράστασις : Pol. 1258 b 22 ; cf. Brants in Revue de l'instruction publique en Belgique, vol. xxv, pp. 109 ff. Examples are : the trader in the Philoctetes (547), Colaeus the Samian who ' found ' Tartessus, Hdt. iv. 152, and apparently most of the Aeginetans, who were tramps par excellence, as their island produced nothing for export. Compare Laws 952 E. For a typical voyage with its vicissitudes read the argument of Dem. xxxv. Just as the trader often turned fighter, so the fighter might turn trader when he saw an opening. See Thuc. vii. 13. 2. The more primitive trade is, the greater the hold of the distributor over the producer in dealing with distant markets. Compare the way in which village producers in England were controlled by distributors in the eighteenth century under the so-called commission system. The Athenian potters, as Francotte points out (Industrie, vol. i, p. 308), must have suffered likewise, as the merchant-skipper was their only link with the Etruscan market ; but Athenian export trade was never sufficiently important for the grievance to be seriously felt. An interesting record of this trade is preserved in the merchants' marks on some of the Attic vases ; the trader went into the workshop and scratched his orders on to sample vases. These marks are many of them in Ionian characters, and show that previous to 480, during the most flourishing period of the Etruscan trade, this was in Ionian hands : we know from Herodotus (i. 163) that the way was opened by Phocaeans. It was interrupted by the Persian war of 480–79 and the Graeco-Etruscan war of 474, and later resumed by Athenians. Details in Haekl, Münchener Archäologische Studien, 1909, pp. 92 ff. and refs., to which should be added Pottier, Revue Archéologique, vol. iii (1904), pp. 45 ff.

ambition ' to set the tone in Arabian wares.   Meanwhile he will try hard, as a citizen who takes his share in the moulding of public opinion, to broaden the outlook of his fellows and break down the lingering prejudices of the elders against new-fangled habits.[1]

Thus, what the Greek importer had to fear from the city was not a tariff against foreign goods for the benefit of the home producers' pocket, but paternal legislation for the benefit of his soul. For the statesmen of the old city had not lost the instinct of self-preservation, and they knew that home-grown habits and virtues are apt to vanish with home-grown goods.   So the trader knew to his cost that they might take it into their heads to mete out to any ' honourable employment ' such treatment as we reserve for dealers in liquor or opium.   There was a party of puritans who saw in him, as he marched gaily up the quay with his tanned face and his strange merchandise, as pleased as a child displaying a new toy, only an emissary of evil and a dealer in damnation. An old Jewish fisherman (if indeed it is he) has written a curse over the trader's profession, together with a catalogue of his wares. Better for him and for his city the barley loaves and small fishes of those who toil all night and catch nothing than ' the merchandize of gold and silver and precious stones and of pearls and fine linen and purple and silk, and all sweet wood and all manner of vessels of ivory and all manner of vessels of most precious wood, and of brass and iron and marble, and cinnamon and odours, and ointments and frankincense and wine and oil and fine flour and wheat and beasts and sheep and horses and chariots and slaves and souls of men '.[2]

---

[1] See Theophrastus, vii (Jebb, p. 61), for the ' Man of Petty Ambition ' with his negro attendant, white teeth, Sicilian doves, &c.   ' Also he is very much the person to keep a monkey.'   The Greeks thought negroes very interesting-looking people and were amused at their woolly hair, but they show no trace of ' colour-prejudice '.   See the negro heads used as ornaments on the vases in the Austrian *Jahreshefte*, vol. ix, p. 321, and the Samson-among-the-Philistines scene on the vase in Furtwängler and Reichhold, vol. i, Fig. 51, where a big red Heracles is slaughtering a lot of feeble hook-nosed Egyptians, some black, others white (dressed in those famous ' newly-washed ' linen surplices), while a stalwart negro body-guard, marching beautifully in step, is arriving just too late.   The sentiment of the ' colour-bar ' appears to be of comparatively recent origin, and it has not spread to modern Greece.   See the remarks in Lord Cromer's *Ancient and Modern Imperialism*, pp. 131–43.

[2] *Rev.* xviii. 12.   The only protective measures we hear of in Greece are ' sumptuary laws ' such as Solon's, or political or religious boycotts and taboos cf. Hdt. i. 160, v. 88) and the Megarian Decree.   Sometimes it is a

commodity, sometimes the nationality of the trader, which constitutes the objection. Compare the way in which the Turks, not a trading people themselves, have lately used the weapon of the boycott against the Austrians and the Greeks. If the Brea decree (Hicks and Hill, 41) had been broken off a line higher up we should know what articles might not be imported into an Athenian settlement. Customs duties were strictly for revenue. Compare *Laws* 847, where Plato abolishes customs duties but *at the same time* restricts imports. This sounds paradoxical in our larger world ; but get into a sufficiently homely frame of mind and it is merely common sense. School hairdressers come in without paying a commission, yet they are not allowed to sell cigarettes. And this is not because the masters grow tobacco in their back gardens. Nor did the Turks keep out the Austrian fezzes because they wanted to make them themselves. Compare Guiraud, *Propriété foncière*, pp. 563–4.

CHAPTER XII

CITY ECONOMICS : POPULATION

Οὐδέν ἐστιν οὔτε πύργος οὔτε ναῦς
ἔρημος ἀνδρῶν μὴ ξυνοικούντων ἔσω.
SOPHOCLES, *O. T.* 56–7.

Οὐ γὰρ τάδε τοὺς ἄνδρας ἀλλ᾽ οἱ ἄνδρες ταῦτα κτῶνται.—Pericles in THUCYDIDES,
i. 143. 5.

Neither walled town nor ship is anything at all if it be empty and no men
dwell together therein.

For these things are made for men, not men for them.

THE statesman is concerned both with people and with things.
In Committee he has often to deal, like an engineer or a scientist,
with dead masses of material detail which only indirectly affect
human beings : while in Parliament he has to reckon with the
living forces of national life.   The political economist, gauging
and husbanding the resources of his country, has the same twofold task.   He is concerned not only with money-power but with
man-power, not only with the production and distribution of
material riches but with the human beings who produce and con-
sume them, and apart from whom they are of no value.   The
problem of population is now rightly regarded as one of the most
serious and constant preoccupations which every economist has
to face.

That problem, which we now approach, is not solely concerned,
as seems sometimes to be assumed, with questions affecting the
quantity and rate of increase of human beings within the State.
It is concerned also, if not principally, with questions affecting
their quality.   That is an old and obvious doctrine which we are
beginning to relearn from our eugenists.   The Greeks knew it
long ago : and in putting the problem of population in its due
place in our sketch of the Athenian economy, we shall therefore
find ourselves considering, not the question of numbers only, but
a group of other far more important and difficult questions bearing
upon the morale and character of Athenian social life.

But we must begin our inquiry from the side of quantity, for it was in this, its most obvious and menacing aspect, that the population question first appealed to the minds of Greek statesmen. They found themselves face to face with a great practical difficulty, the natural increase of mankind.

It was the same difficulty that stung Malthus and, through Malthus, Darwin, and which has thus become familiar, in its theoretical form, to several generations of thinking men. But to these early Greek thinkers it was no mere problem in biology or ethics, but an ever present danger to the very existence of the body politic. Nor had they our scientific knowledge or analogies to guide them. They knew nothing of the age-long struggle for life among living creatures, or of man's close physical relations with the animal kingdom; they cared nothing for the ethical issue, for the unsleeping moral effect that raises and keeps man above the level of the beasts. They only knew, in their diminutive city areas, that men tended constantly to increase, and to increase faster than their food. It was more than a difficulty: it was a terror, looming closer every year. With their primitive economy there was little margin to draw on. There was a natural limit to the numbers of a self-contained City State. Patch after patch of bare hillside was drawn into the area of cultivation, terraced and ploughed and picked over that it might yield its wretched pittance. But a time came when the pressure of population upon subsistence became too great to be withstood, and Greek statesmen were forced to seek an outlet for their people elsewhere.

The great outburst of colonization in the eighth and seventh centuries relieved the pressure. It never recurred again in so acute a form; for the economic development which followed, with the improvement of communications and the growth of foreign trade, rendered States less wholly dependent upon their agricultural resources and provided permanent activities for some of their landless members. In the period which we are now considering, the ordinary Greek State was not wholly isolated or self-sufficient. There is a certain elasticity in her provision for the natural increase of population; and, however little they may have reckoned on it, this must be borne in mind when we consider the attitude of her statesmen and thinkers with regard to this question.

Yet the old terror still remained—if not in so urgent and menacing a form as in earlier days, still far more real and constant than we can easily conceive under the international system of to-day, when we have grown used to regarding population as a fluid and mobile force. It remained as an ever present cause for anxiety, and we shall never understand the attitude of City State man towards this and kindred subjects until we have realized the strength of the unseen hold that it retained upon his thought and conduct.

It is not easy for us to do so, for the Greek writers do not help us to understand what is in their minds. Superficially read, they seem to overlook the difficulty. They prefer to speak as though population tended of itself to remain stationary, as though there were no such thing as the natural increase of mankind. The whole organization of the City State society seems based upon the idea that the numbers of its membership remain fixed. The city is made up of so and so many families and other subordinate divisions ; and the membership of all these is numerically fixed and regarded as practically unchanging. Athens, for instance, before the reorganization of Cleisthenes, was divided into four tribes, twelve brotherhoods and 360 clans, and each of the last-named was supposed to consist of thirty adult male members, making an adult citizen population of 10,800. After the changes introduced by Cleisthenes the numbers were put up, and fifth-century Athenians hesitated between 20,000 and 30,000 as the ' right figure '. But whatever the figure may be, it is regarded as constant, and as the basis upon which the city organization is built up. We can see this most clearly in the arrangements for founding new cities. The statesman's business is to discover how large a population the new territory will support, and then to stock it up to that limit. Every one will know what that limit is; sometimes it is even openly expressed in the name of the new settlement, as in the colony of Ten-Thousand-Town on the coast of Cilicia. We find the same idea in Plato and Aristotle, and it falls in very well with their general conception of the city as a work of art, and with their reluctance to allow elbow-room for the development of new forces. Plato finds the ' perfect number ' for his ideal Republic by some mathematical rigmarole : Aristotle prefers to define it as ' the largest number which suffices for the purposes of life and can be taken in at a single view '. But both agree in the necessity both for its smallness and its fixity. Few details bring before us more vividly what modern internationalism means than the contrast between these old stationary country towns and the typical modern mushroom city, our Chicagos, Johannesburgs, and Winnipegs. Such a city, the Greek would say, is no more a city than the *Olympic* or the *Aquitania* is a ship. How can you call a thing a ship when it is a furlong in length, or a city when you cannot hear the town-crier from the opposite end of the town ? [1]

Yet, if they cared to think, the Greeks knew, as well as we know, that their ordinary assumption was ungrounded. Population does not really tend of itself to remain stationary. The conditions which they had grown accustomed to speaking of as natural and necessary in civilized states were not natural at all. They were highly artificial, due to the operation of particular causes, some of which, at any rate, were within their own control.

The first and most general was a high death-rate. It is a familiar fact that medical science is now steadily increasing the ' expectation of life ' at all ages. It is impossible to estimate the difference between the Greek death-rate and our own ; but it would probably not be above the mark to say that in time of peace it was as high as that of Turkey or Russia to-day, that is to say, perhaps twice as high as that of the United Kingdom. Polybius, in a remarkable passage, rebukes the Greeks of his day for refusing to bring up more than one or two of their offspring, and so leaving no margin for war and disease, and allowing their families to become extinct. Here he clearly regards death before the marriage age as a likely chance even for children who have been

---

[1] Strabo, 673 (Μυρίανδρος), Ar. *Pol.* 1326 ; Pl. *Rep.* 546 ; *Laws* 740 (5,040 households). On the accepted Athenian figures see note on p. 174 above. A good passage showing the popular idea of fixed numbers is Menander, *Epitrepontes* 548–50, where a character speaks of the world as consisting of 1,000 cities containing 30,000 inhabitants each. For the underlying assumption that States populate up to the fixed limit of their food-supply see Hdt. i. 66 (with which compare Xen. *Pol. Lac.* i. 1, showing how Sparta's economics were as foolish as her politics) ; Hdt. i. 136 ; Xen. *Hell.* v. 2. 16, and, a most interesting passage in many ways (e. g. for light on Greek hotel life), Polyb. ii. 15. 4–7. ' The Lombard plain is so rich that you do not have to bargain for your food in the inns. *From this you may judge* (i) how populous the place must be, (ii) what fine big men they produce, (iii) how well they fight.'

deliberately picked out for survival. It is dangerous to draw conclusions from isolated passages or from general impressions, yet it is worth while remarking the frequency of references in Greek literature to what the Greeks always regarded as the most pathetic thing in their experience, the snatching away of life untimely at the height of its youth and beauty. The Greeks, as we know them, were a robust and healthy race; but we are apt to forget the ruthless selection which helped to make them so.[1]

A second cause which must not be overlooked was the prevalence of war. War acts, as has been said, as a process of reversed selection. It kills off the best stocks and promotes the survival of the less fit. Greek cities were constantly at war, and were thus constantly requiring to fill up gaps in their ranks. True, the mortality in an ordinary engagement was not great; but from time to time circumstances arose when the issue was graver than usual, when the combatants were embittered and the fight was to the death. Such, for instance, was one of the wars of which Herodotus tells us, between the Spartans and the Argives, when Cleomenes surrounded the Argives in a sacred grove and burnt them to death, leaving Argos so destitute of men ' that their slaves had the management of affairs, ruling and administering them until the sons of those who had been killed grew up '. City States were always exposed to the chance of these sudden depletions, and it was part of city patriotism to provide reserves against their occurrence. It was the Greek citizen's fixed object, in accordance, as we have seen, with the immemorial tribal tradition, that, so far as in him lay, no family should fail to give the State its quota of living souls. If temporary losses occurred, parents ' must keep a brave heart in the hope of other children, those who are still of age to bear them. For ' (listen to the ruthless economist) ' the newcomers will help you to forget the gap in your own circle, and will help the city to fill up the ranks of its workers and its soldiers '.[2]

---

[1] Polyb. xxxvi. 17. 7. Compare Myres, *Greek Lands and the Greek People*, p. 20, who points out how ' in these apparently favoured regions there is yet a physical control so efficient as to make acclimatization exceedingly difficult and slow ', and that therefore an incoming race, like the majority of the City-State Greeks, must have been exposed to severe selection by climatic and other forces. Malaria, which weakens rather than kills, is not of importance for our period.

[2] Thuc. ii. 44. 3; Hdt. vi. 82–3; Thuc. iii. 73 (a somewhat similar expe-

So far we have been dealing with causes over which the individual statesman or citizen had no control. We now pass to two others, the operation of which lay strictly within their own powers.

The first of these we need not dwell on at length, the relief of surplus of population by settlements abroad. We have already referred to colonization as the means adopted to relieve the pressure of population in the eighth and seventh centuries. All that needs to be added here is that this method of foreign settlement always remained, throughout City State history, a possible remedy in case of need. The stream of State-aided emigration never wholly dried up; there was never an age when no colonies were being sent out, from the first rush of the early navigators down to the great revival of the colonizing impulse under the inspiration of Alexander.

We pass to another set of causes, which may be set down roughly under the general head of the preventible mortality among infants. It is a difficult subject: yet, if we desire to understand Greek civilization, we must not turn away from the evidence, but seek to place it in its proper setting in relation to the rest of City State life. It has not been easy for admirers of the Greeks to admit that Greek theory and practice condoned the deliberate exercise of checks upon the growth of the population. Yet the evidence shows us that such was indeed the case. When a child was born it remained, by a custom universal, so far as we know, at least down to the fourth century, within the discretion of the father whether it should be allowed to live. On the fifth day after birth, at earliest, new-born infants were solemnly presented to the household and admitted to its membership. Up to the time of this ceremony the father had complete power of selection, and, what is more, it appears that this was quite frequently exercised, particularly in the case of female infants; for the provision of a dowry for his daughters weighed heavily on a Greek father's mind, and what was easier than to evade it by pleading inability at the outset? When it was decided that the infants were not to be ' nourished ' they would be packed in a cradle, or more often in a pot, and exposed in

dient). Cf. Hdt. vi. 27; Thuc. vii. 29 (two big disasters to school children, and the consequent loss to the State).

a public place, the poor mother, no doubt, hoping against hope, like Creusa in the *Ion*, that some merciful fellow-citizen might yet take pity on its wailing. It is strange and horrible to think that any day on your walks abroad in a Greek city you might come across a ' pot-exposed ' infant, as the Athenians called them, in a corner of the market-place or by a wrestling-ground, at the entrance of a temple or in a consecrated cave, and that you might see a slave girl timidly peeping round to look if the child might yet be saved, or running back to bear the news to the broken-hearted young mother. For though the custom was barbarous, and promoted, if not enforced, by a barbarous necessity, the Greeks who bowed before it still remained civilized men and women. ' I beg and beseech you,' writes a husband in a Greek private letter which has lately returned to us from the under-world, ' to take care of the little child; and, as soon as we receive wages, I will send them to you. When—good luck to you—you bear offspring, if it is a male, let it live ; if it is a female, expose it.' The Athenian, moreover, had a traditional abhorrence of violence, and interfered when he could on behalf of the helpless. If he consented to exercise his immemorial right over his own offspring, he did so with regret, for the sake of the city and his other children, because it was more merciful in the long run. We have no right to cast stones either at him or his fellows. They were the victims of social forces, like the thousands of civilized working mothers who are forced to neglect their babies to-day, and the thousands of Western parents who, rightly or wrongly, prefer a small family to a large one. Nature and Society between them are hard task-masters. It is not for the historian to judge, his duty is but to understand and sympathize.[1]

[1] *Oxyrhynchus Papyri*, vol. iv, pp. 243 f., reprinted with facsimile in Milligan's useful *Selections from the Greek Papyri*. The writer was at work away from home : the date is June 17, 1 B. C. Details for the City State period in Daremberg and Saglio, s.v. *Expositio* and *Infanticidium*, by Glotz, rewritten (with fewer refs.) for his *Études sociales et juridiques*. I have, if anything, understated his view of the extent to which the custom was actually practised. ' Wherever we can observe Greek manners,' he says (*Études*, pp. 188–9), ' our documents enable us to trace this murderous custom,' even in fifth-century Athens, which could make better provision than most States for an expanding population. ' Aristophanes, for instance, is a valuable guide when he speaks of it in a dispassionate tone, quite incidentally, as a natural thing.' The references here are to *Frogs* 1190, *Clouds* 531. Menander's plays, which, of course, must not be taken as evidence for the fourth century, are full of the subject (see *Four Plays of Menander*, ed. Capps, New York, 1910),

So far we have been dealing simply with the question of
numbers. We have seen that the City State needed to keep its
population fixed or nearly fixed, and have been examining the
two kinds of checks, automatic and deliberate, which were at
work to counteract the law of natural increase. But our discussion has already carried us into the second division of our
subject, that of quality as against quantity.

For the checks of which we have just been speaking did
not weed out life indiscriminately ; they were exercised, however
unscientifically, upon a certain principle of selection. The Greek
statesmen who acquiesced in their operation were not merely
aiming at fixed numbers : they desired a fine race. ' It is a very
rare and difficult thing,' says Isocrates in the course of a funeral
eulogy, ' to have both a large family and a fine family. Yet this
man achieved it.' The underlying thought in the orator's mind
is clear. The more children that a man is able to bring up the
better ; but they must all be fine children, worthy of the State of
which they are to be citizens and of the Greek race as a whole.
The Greek parent rejected, except in a few favoured instances, all
who were crippled or deformed or exceptionally delicate. Thus
easily did Greek society acquit itself of the responsibility towards

e. g. in one scene of the *Epitrepontes* there is a long dispute on the question
whether a man who has discovered an exposed child, but given it to another
man to bring up, has the right to the keepsakes (γνωρίσματα) which were
exposed with it (συνεκτιθέμενα). In spite of the many plays in which exposed
infants and their keepsakes play a part, Glotz holds that the proportion of
exposed infants thus preserved was very small. They were expensive to bring
up, and it was cheaper to buy grown slaves from abroad ; moreover, if they
did happen to be recognized by their parents, they had by law to be given
back : so they were precarious property. Tucker, *Life in Ancient Athens* (an
excellent and simply written little book on Athenian life), is too optimistic on
this point (p. 118) ; cf. Wilamowitz, *Staat und Gesellschaft*, p. 35. The only
known law against exposing infants, at Thebes, is probably of a later date
and not humanitarian but directed against the danger of depopulation. See
Aelian, *V. H.* ii. 7 and compare Polybius, xxxvi. 17. 5–8 (referred to above,
p. 327). At Sparta infants faced a double ordeal ; the State weeded out some
of those saved by the parents. Plato and Aristotle, as one might expect
from their habitual ruthlessness towards the individual, approve and recommend the practice or its equivalent, bringing in eugenics to reinforce politics
and economics (Plato, *Rep.* 459 ff. ; Ar. *Pol.* 1335 b 23). They recommend
abortion and exposure in certain cases, but say nothing about prevention.
Slave-infants of course had a more precarious chance than free, for it always
pays better to buy than to breed slaves, as Cairnes (*Slave-power*, pp. 121 ff.)
pointed out. Cf. Xen. *Oec.* ix. 5, and [Ar.] *Oec.* 1344 b 17 ; both writers
recommend that slaves should be allowed to bear children as a special reward
and encouragement after good conduct.   [See Appendix.]

those who form to-day one of the gravest problems of our social
life. The Greek city was the home of the physically fit. Weakness and infirmity found no easy entry there, and, if they came
at all, they did not influence the general tone. Over the whole
of Greek life, as over a modern residential University, there
broods a spirit of hardness, almost of callousness. Rude health
and physical energy are all around us, whether in flesh or in
marble. The tenderer emotions seem somehow out of place—
not merely the hush and compassion of the sickroom, but the
everyday considerateness and sympathy which are the natural
offspring of constant intercourse between stronger and weaker. We
grow accustomed to counting our members, as every Greek did,
in terms of fighting men, and dismissing the rest of the population, the old and the women and the children, as just useless
mouths. After all, thought the City State statistician, society, as
we know it, is very evidently based on force, and what can the
useless multitude do when, as may happen any season, the enemy
is at the gates ? ' A city,' says Thucydides, ' consists of men,
and not of walls or ships with none to man them.' Nor of women
either, we may add, filling in his unspoken thought, for what use
are women in such a crisis, except just a few to do the cooking ? [1]

Such was the world into which the Greek infant was born, and
for which the anxious parent had to estimate its fitness. Can we
wonder then that the chance of survival was greater for a boy
than it was for a girl ? If selection operated at all, on however
small a scale, it seems to follow as an inevitable consequence
that it tipped to one side the natural balance between the numbers
of the two sexes. In the turning of that balance by some continuous and steady influence, however slight it may be, lie, as we
know to-day, grave social and ethical consequences. Let us watch
them in ancient Greece, for they belong strictly to our subject.[2]

[1] Is. ix. 72 ; Thuc. vii. 77. 7, ii. 78. 3. When the ' useless multitude ' of
non-combatants was sent out of Plataea before the siege, 110 women were
left behind to do the cooking for 400 men. For the comparison between a
Greek city and a modern residential University see a fine passage in Livingstone, *The Greek Genius and its Meaning to Us* (1912), p. 137. Yet Oxford
and Cambridge, after all, are but finishing schools, in which young men are
being prepared for life, not life itself, like the Greek city. The true University
system for adults is still in the making.

[2] Take three ordinary Athenian families of which we happen to know
something. Cimon, Pericles, and Socrates all had three sons, and, apparently,
no daughters.

From such evidence as we have, it seems to be clear that in an ordinary Greek city there were always, among the citizen population, more boys than girls, and practically always, except immediately after a disastrous war, more marriageable men than women. In other words there were always more than enough husbands to go round. Girls were therefore brought up by their parents in the certain expectation of wedlock, and most of them married, or to speak more truly, were married, very early in life. Fifteen, we gather, was no exceptional age. Very few indeed of the daughters of citizens remained unmarried. Antigone and Electra, whose name itself means 'the Unmated', make us feel the tragic loneliness, in the eyes of such a true Athenian as Sophocles, of independent womanhood. True independence, indeed, they never possessed. For legal purposes a woman always remained, in Athens at any rate, under the tutelage of a man. Practically speaking, a Greek woman of the citizen class had no alternative to marriage. Let us consider the social results which follow, in the peculiar tone and temper of Greek life, from this simple fact.[1]

The women of the City State world, like the men, knew nothing of rights but only of duties, and they accepted with willing cheerfulness the duties that were laid upon them by the city. The first and greatest of these was to 'save the hearth' by bearing children for the city's service. The men went out to work and to fight, to create and defend the city's material riches ; the women stayed at home, creating and tending the rarest and truest source of wealth. Very jealously they were guarded within the peaceful shelter of the home, ringed round like precious possessions from the touch of the outer world. But when we are tempted to smile at the Greek husband's insistence upon the strictest wifely behaviour, we sometimes forget how young and careless and fiery was the masculine society in the midst of which he lived. Where man himself has not yet learnt to check each random impulse of his nature, we must not expect him to grant his women the responsibilities of freedom. Greek wives and mothers lived very quietly in their little oasis of domesticity.

[1] Cimon's sister Elpinice is an instance of a woman of the citizen class noted for her independence of mind. She did not, however, remain unmarried : she merely married exceptionally late. Fourteen is the common age at which young girls are given in marriage in provincial Greece to-day.

They have not spoken to us across the ages, for they were not skilful of speech or pen. But the poets and artists have spoken for them. Let one who has absorbed their message speak to us on their behalf.

' For a Greek maiden,' says Wilamowitz, ' her wedding-day was in truth the great festival of her life. She received a husband so early that all the feelings which to-day move a girl at her Confirmation, because they are natural and justifiable, were united with those which accompany wedlock. The time of freedom and play is over. She brings her doll and her ball to Artemis, who has watched over her years of childhood. Before her lies a time of seriousness, of work and self-denial. Forth she goes from her parents' house, a faithful servant with her for the sake of her inexperience ; but all other ties are snapped. She will wind no more wreaths for the altars before the old house ; she will carry no more offerings for her grandparents to the cemetery at new moon ; she will dance no more with her playmates, or carry the basket of the goddess in the high festival procession. She will be under the sway of other house-gods ; she will bear offerings to other graves ; and to Artemis she will cry not in play but in bitter pain. She will sit upon the hearthstone, as her good mother used to sit, turning the busy wheel, ordering the maids, working and directing, rising up in the evening, full of cheerfulness and willing service, to meet her returning husband, who is her master.' [1]

Students of Greek life have often wondered, especially in these latter days, why, when all the world around them was flowering into self-expression, woman alone in the great age of Greece remained shut out from the new life. One answer, at least, lies here. Athens had in her treasury things both new and old. Much of her greatness consisted, as we saw when we studied her citizenship, in the ennobling and strengthening of some of her most conservative social forces ; and of these the wife and the mother, the companion of the hearth and joint pillar of the household, partook in full measure. Athens valued and honoured her wives and mothers, as we can see by a hundred tokens, and she valued and honoured in them the same qualities of service as in her men : self-mastery, self-forgetfulness, courage, and gentleness.

[1] Wilamowitz, *Hippolytus* (transl.) pp. 10–11. Cf. Ar. *Lys.* 641 ff.

And, better than patronage, we too can pay them honour. When, fresh from the jarring social conflicts of to-day, we turn to the Greek wife and mother as she is portrayed for us, amid the scenes of her daily life, upon the gravestones and the vases, we moderns feel instinctively that, though those grave and gracious figures may have been lacking in knowledge and freedom and some of the essentials of human dignity, yet they were fine and noble spirits, not unworthy of their city and race.

Yet, if we are honest with ourselves and with the evidence, we feel that there is more to be said. The men of Athens did their work, and, so long as the city prospered, they were happy and satisfied. The women of Athens served too ; but their work did not leave them wholly happy ; for they felt, at first vaguely and obscurely and then with gathering clearness, that in their service was not perfect freedom. It did not satisfy all the cravings and instincts of their nature. So that, while, as we have seen, the years of Athens's greatness were for men one of the happiest periods in the whole history of the world, the women who worked beside them were restless, uneasy, and perplexed. Something was wrong ; but neither they nor the men could lay their finger on the evil. ‘ At every point where we can test it,’ writes one of our keenest-witted students of Greek life, ‘ opinion in Greece was in flux as to the rightful position of woman in civilized society.’ We do not need Aristophanes, with his up-to-date pleasantries, to underline the truth of this judgement for fifth-century Athens. It is written clear for all to see across the whole life-work of Euripides, from the *Hippolytus* and the *Heracleidae* to the rebellious defiance of the *Bacchae*. The women felt that they too were free Greek souls ; they too served the city and gave her the men she needed ; they too, at need, laid down their lives on her behalf. They were tired of hearing the old traditional story of woman's weakness and subordination. They chafed at being shut out, as inferior beings, from the better part of city life, not only from its active public work, but from its joys and refinements, its music and poetry and discussions. In the last quarter of the fifth century Athens witnessed the rise of a movement for the emancipation of woman which, because it won the heart of that arch-Conservative Plato, has left an undying mark upon the literature of the world. Yet it is Euripides rather than Plato

who is at once the truest poet and most faithful thinker for their
cause.   Listen to the war-cry of his suffering women, which falls
upon modern ears, trained by now to such discords, with a strange
thrill of reminiscence.

> Back streams the wave on the ever-running river :
>   Life, life is changed and the laws of it o'ertrod,
> Man shall be the slave, the affrighted, the low-liver !
>   Man hath forgotten God.
> And woman, yea, woman, shall be terrible in story :
>   The tales, too, meseemeth, shall be other than of yore.
> For a fear there is that cometh out of woman and a glory,
>   And the hard hating voices shall encompass her no more !
>
> The old bards shall cease and their memory that lingers
>   Of frail brides and faithless, shall be shrivelled as with
>   fire.
> For they loved us not, nor knew us, and our lips were dumb,
>   our fingers
>   Could wake not the secret of the lyre.
> Else, else, O God the singer, I had sung amid the rages
>   A long tale of man and his deeds for good and ill.
> But the old world knoweth—'tis the speech of all his ages—
>   Man's wrong and ours : he knoweth and is still.[1]

We have been carried on for the moment from the sixth-
century world to the latter days of the fifth, from the normal
City State to the society of imperial Athens.   But the digression
was necessary for our subject, for the unrest of which we have
been speaking was the natural result of causes which were already
silently at work in the society of a previous generation.
     What were those causes ?   What makes these fifth-century

---

[1] *Medea* 410 ff., transl. Murray.   Myres, *Anthropology and the Classics*,
p. 154 ; see also Bruns, *Frauenemancipation in Athen* (Kiel, 1900), reprinted
in his *Reden und Vorträge*, and Wilamowitz, *Hermes*, xxxv. 548.   All agree
in showing how much hard, inductive, fifth-century thinking lies behind Aristophanes' burlesques and Plato's essays in feminism.   On the argument that a
woman cannot die for her country see *Medea* 250, which should have given it
its *coup de grâce*.   Women were admitted to the theatre, where they sat, as
Browning says, ' Sorted, the good with good, the gay with gay,' but their
husbands and guardians did not necessarily take them.   See Schol. on Ar.
Eccl. 22 (part of which, however, Rutherford brackets : the date of the decree
there mentioned is unknown) and *Balaustion's Adventures*, which are as true
in their atmosphere as they are correct in their details.   Women also took
part, of course, in public ceremonies : witness the Parthenon frieze.   On the
general question see also Principal Donaldson's *Woman : her position and
influence in Ancient Greece and Rome and among the early Christians* (1907),
with bibliography.

women so bitter ? They were not sweated or over-driven or stung with the lash of industrialism. Who, then, are their task-masters? What are the 'hard hating voices' of which they speak? Turn back to the Funeral Speech. Pericles shall give the answer, for he has put the spirit against which they were fighting in its classic form. ' If I must also speak a word to those who are now in widowhood on the powers and duties of women, I will cast all my advice into one brief sentence. Great will be your glory if you do not lower the nature which is within you—hers most of all whose praise or blame is least bruited on the lips of men.' The words themselves are stinging enough to women of soul and spirit ; but if we would feel their full force we must bear in mind the speaker's record. The man who preached this doctrine to the assembled people of Athens was at that very time the avowed lover of Aspasia ; and Aspasia was one of the cleverest and best-known figures in Athenian society, the valued confidante, not only of statesmen, but of philosophers. How came these words, then, upon her lover's lips ? Whence this strange discrepancy between his preaching and his practice ? That is the question which we must now make an attempt to unravel.[1]

The explanation is that in Periclean Athens there were two different kinds of free women. On the one hand there were the women to whom Pericles was speaking, the wives and daughters of the citizens ; on the other the alien-born women, like Aspasia of Miletus, to whom a wholly different standard was applied. The division was being formed all through the period with which we are dealing : its origin is to be found in the immigration of unattached foreigners which was the inevitable result of the improvement of communications and the increase of trade. At first Athens welcomed them with open arms, both men and women, for she valued them as fighters and as workers. To the men, as we have seen, many privileges were granted ; and it was a natural policy to give the women too full entry into city life. Coming as many of them did from the freer life of Ionia, they made a mark in Athenian society, and some of the advanced spirits of the day exercised their freedom of choice by taking

---

[1] Thuc. ii. 45. 2. On Aspasia and her place in society as an intellectual woman, see Meyer, *Forschungen*, vol. ii, pp. 55–56 (as against Wilamowitz, *A. A.*, vol. ii, p. 99), and Xen. *Mem.* ii. 6. 36.

Ionian wives. 'Among the noble families in particular,' says
Meyer, ' such marriages were quite common. Many of the most
notable Athenian statesmen, Cleisthenes and Themistocles,
Cimon and his sons by his first marriage,' were the children
of Outlander mothers. Athens was striding forward fast to
a conception of citizenship and society in which all the old
traditional prejudices of City State life would be broken down.
She had admitted alien men to the parish and the city ; she was
now admitting alien women even into the intimate circle of the
hearth.[1]

But here the mass of the people cried halt ; for they were not
yet ready for this liberalizing intrusion upon the old sanctities of
tribal life. To take a wife outside the city seemed an act of
impiety, a dangerous breach of the old unwritten laws. In 451
this vague belief found public expression. A law was passed
that in the case of children born subsequently to that date only
those of Athenian parentage on both sides should be eligible for
citizenship ; and seven years later, on the occasion of a large gift
of corn by a foreign potentate to the Athenian people, the rule
was made retrospective and many names were struck off the
citizen lists. The effects of this measure upon those with whom
it professed to deal were not very serious. The offspring of
a mixed marriage was still a member of the parish, he still
served as an outlander in the army and the navy, and moved
freely in Athenian society. But its effects on the Outlander
woman were disastrous and irremediable. She was separated
for good from her Athenian sisters, driven out from her honoured
place by the hearth, and degraded to what was, strictly speaking,
the position of a concubine. Thus did the liberal-minded democracy of Athens, by one of those odd freaks of blindness which
afflict great peoples, check the progress of a powerful movement
towards the consolidation of city life upon a broader and better
basis. It was the same democracy which, in a similar fit of
puritanism, and in defence of the same sanctities, sent Socrates
to his death.[2]

[1] Meyer, vol. iv, § 392. Cf. Wilamowitz, *Staat und Ges.*, p. 40, 2nd ed. 41,
on how slow the Greeks were to allow *conubium* to follow *commercium*.

[2] *Ath. Pol.* xxvi. 3 ; Plut. *Per.* 37. For a full and careful treatment of this
whole subject see O. Müller, *Untersuchungen zur Geschichte des attischen
Bürger- und Eherechts*, in Fleckeisen's *Jahrbücher*, Supplementband 25, 1899 ;

Here, in this great barrier between two sections of womankind, strengthened and perpetuated by the decree of 451, we have reached one great cause of the unrest of which we have been speaking. Each of these groups needed the other for strength and encouragement and companionship, for the support that comes from the mixing of experiences and the alliance of diverse natures. Their divorce by a rigid custom, made, or at least upheld, by men, brought unhappiness upon both parties, for it took away their self-respect.

How was it possible for the democracy to maintain such a barrier? What kept the two classes apart, not only in law but in fact? Here we come back once more to the point from which we set out. One answer to this question, at any rate, is economic. As there were less native-born women than men, hardly any of them needed to earn an independent livelihood. Most of the few who did so were widows. The native-born women did not need economic independence, and the struggle for economic independence, as we know, is often the spur to further claims. It was because the Athenian wife and mother was economically secure that she remained isolated and out of touch with her alien-born sisters. In the masculine sphere citizens and strangers,

he lays great stress on the religious feeling excited by these questions, which can be traced ' like a red thread ' in all the changes of Athenian law on the subject (p. 742) : it was religious sentiment, not mere political exclusiveness (as is often said) which was responsible for the limitation of citizen rights in 451. The law led to the recognition of a ' second legally recognized union between man and woman ', called by Müller (p. 710) ' left-handed marriage '. The ' left-handed ' wife stood midway in social estimation between the γυνή or mother of citizens and the ἑταίρα ; but old Athenian law only recognized two kinds of woman with whom a man could live, wives and concubines (παλλακαί), so the left-handed wife went by the clumsy name of ' concubine for bearing free children ' (τ λλικὴ ἦν ἃν ἐπ᾽ ἐλευθέροις παισὶν ἔχῃ), pp. 729–30 ; cf. Dem. lix. 118. Aspasia, whom Pericles married after 451, was a ' left-handed wife ' of this sort (Müller, pp. 814, 823). The law was relaxed in 411 by the oligarchical party, which was favourable to mixed marriages. This explains the reference in *Frogs* 418 (date 405) to the seven-year-old citizen who had not yet ' grown a brotherhood '. Contrast with this *Birds* 1649 ff. (date 414). The law was re-enacted in 403 by the same popular leaders who condemned Socrates. On the sanctities from which alien women were to be excluded see Dem. lix. 73. After the Sicilian Expedition, when the citizen body was so much reduced that marriageable girls could not find husbands, a law was actually passed allowing double marriages. Socrates took a second wife in this way, probably much to the irritation of Xanthippe. She was a destitute widow and the daughter of a full citizen, Myrto, grand-daughter of Aristeides (Müller, p. 795 ; cf. Diog. Laert. ii. 26 and Athen. xiii. 2, p. 555). Euripides is said to have done the same. See also Donaldson, p. 213.

with their servants and apprentices, formed a friendly and homogeneous social whole. With the women this was not so ; their
lives and activities lay apart, and so they developed on different
lines. As a result they tended to become crystallized into two
separate types—the household matron under the tutelage of
a husband or some other male protector, and the independent
professional woman, who had indeed her ' guardian ' as Athenian
law demanded, but kept him for occasional use, as we keep our
solicitors.[1]

From a set of fourth-century Athenian inscriptions dedicated
by freedmen and freedwomen we know some of the occupations
which these professional women followed. No less than thirty-
three of the freedwomen are described as ' wool-workers ', a term
which includes carding, spinning, and weaving, all done in their
own houses ; a number of others are classed as market-women or
retailers, and there is even a female cobbler. But the chief and
most conspicuous profession open to an alien-born woman in
a Greek city was to be what was known as a ' companion '. It
was ' companions ', not marriageable girls, whom the young
Athenian encountered in mixed gatherings, in attendance, perhaps, on some of the most refined and distinguished men of the
day ; for it was by contributing to the success of these parties,
from which the native-born woman was rigidly excluded, that
they earned their livelihood. ' We have companions for the sake
of pleasure,' says Demosthenes, making a clear distinction in

[1] For metic women's guardians see *Frogs* 569–70, and Wilamowitz,
Hermes, vol. xxii, p. 223. Widows : Ar. *Thesm.* 446 ; also *Iliad* xii. 433.
On native-born women as earners see Dem. lvii. 31, 35, where one can see
how they are marked personages, and also Xen. *Mem.* ii. 7, especially § 10
(quoted on p. 267 above) where an Athenian citizen is reduced to destitution
because he has to provide for a number of female relations, and it has never
occurred to him to set them to any useful work, such as slave-women do
to pay for their keep. Compare the same strange idea of propriety among
the American planters. ' It filled the planter with unfeigned horror to hear
of the employment of women in the Northern states for useful purposes.
Thomas Dabney was reduced to great poverty in his old age by his determination to pay debts incurred through the bad faith of another. The touching
picture of the heroic old man and his daughters giving up such ease of life as
the war had left them shows that some illusions had survived. His chivalrous
nature (says his daughter) had always revolted from the sight of a woman
doing hard work, and he could not have survived the knowledge that his
daughters stood at the wash-tub. So he did the washing himself, beginning
in his seventieth year. So artfully is the human mind composed that he who
had complacently employed women all his life to hoe his cotton without pay
could not stand the demolition of the lady ' (Putnam, *The Lady*, p. 321).

which there is no hint of overlapping, 'and wives to bear us lawful offspring and be faithful guardians of our houses.' If we are to sit in judgement upon the profession which earned its living by giving 'pleasure', we have need to exercise both our imagination and our charity. Its members were the joy-makers and entertainers of their little world, and the qualities that it demanded were quite as much social as physical. Their repartees and witty sallies, sadly tawdry as most of them seem when written out on the cold page, were remembered and treasured up like those of the mediaeval jesters; and though Athens had no Shakespeare to help us to understand them they must often have felt as lonely and as sad at heart as the poor Fool. If they had been allowed the support of their secluded sisters who could only watch them wistfully from their windows, as they mingled with the men in the streets and in the market-place, they might have set the intercourse of the sexes, for the first time in history, on an intelligent basis, and saved the memory of Athens from a reproach of which it is not possible to clear her.[1]

[1] Dem. lix. 122. Tod, in *British School Annual*, vol. viii, pp. 197 ff. (professional women). As Mahaffy (*Social Life in Greece*, p. 284) points out, Sappho still uses the feminine word 'companion' without any specialized sense (fr. 10, Bergk): it suffered much the same degeneration as the English 'mistress'. For a typical companion's career see Hdt. ii. 135; for their character see Xen. *Mem.* iii. 11 and the letter written by one of them to Demetrius Poliorcetes, printed with a German translation by Wilamowitz in *Hermes*, vol. xlix, p. 468: it bears a third-century not a fifth-century colouring, but it is the nearest we can get. For types of their wit, Athenaeus. xiii. Of course, as in all professions, there were good and bad, respected and degraded; but we must be careful, as the Greeks were, not to tar them all with the same brush, or to confuse fifth-century Athens with Antioch and Alexandria, or even with a far less typically Greek centre, Corinth. Athens, for instance, had no female temple-slaves, and it should be added that this whole question was not then complicated by the prevalence of venereal disease. The geishas of Japan form a type analogous to the 'companions' of ancient Greece, and should help us to do them justice. It is certainly wrong to regard the fifth-century Greeks (as modern 'Pagans' tend to do) as sensualists. They were not pleasure-seekers any more than they were ascetics. They did not 'amuse themselves' any more than they did or abstained from things 'conscientiously'. These are constrained and self-conscious attitudes. The older Greeks were not self-conscious about these questions: one has only to open one's Herodotus to feel quite certain on this point. But it is hard to state the positive qualities which corresponded to these negatives. The Greeks were somehow far more *alive* than we. They possessed the gift of putting themselves, the whole of themselves, into everything that they did, or rather into everything that Nature, and social customs which tried to harmonize Nature, gave them to do. So, though they 'let themselves go' at times, and found a place in their institutions for Dionysiac routs, yet Dionysus always remained, as we see him in the vase-paintings, in spite of his baser companions, 'a model

But it is time to return once more to the main thread of our economic argument. There was another and more indirect agency which tended to check the growth of population—the comparative rarity of early marriages among men. The Greek citizen did not usually marry till he was close on thirty, or even beyond it. This practice was encouraged by public opinion and by the thinkers who directed it, and was the direct effect of the segregation of the sexes in early manhood and of the exclusion of women from the main interests of a young Greek's life. The Greek city, like an English college, was, for most purposes, a men's club ; and it was easy and natural for a Greek to pass the threshold of middle age before he became conscious of the need for any permanent attachment beyond the companionship of club-life. His youthful ideals and achievements were all shared with male companions, and it was naturally upon them that the romantic devotion of his budding nature was expended. Achilles and Patroclus, Orestes and Pylades, Harmodius and Aristogeiton, were the types which he admired and which parents and statesmen and poets encouraged and urged him to admire. One of the greatest legacies which Greece has left us is its high conception of friendship—of close fellowship for noble ends. Such attachments were cemented on the playground and on military service, and often sealed by death on the field of battle. They were as manly and fortifying as the modern friendships which, knit at our boarding-schools and Universities, continue through the vicissitudes of divergent careers, and sometimes make history. If we are startled to find that it was such friendship that their greatest philosopher selected round which to weave his discussion of love and beauty and immortality, we must reflect

of noble manners.' So did the Maenads. Read *Bacchae* 677 ff., keeping the art parallels before your mind's eye : e. g. the two lovely Maenads in Furtwängler and Reichhold's vase-reproductions, vol. i, fig. 44. What Euripides describes is not a wild debauch but an early morning ritual. See Nietzsche's profoundly suggestive remarks on this subject (*Works*, vol. xvii, pp. 297–9), and compare Murray's *Euripides*, pp. lix ff. In the city, life goes *andante*, in the measured step of the Parthenon frieze ; out in the wilds it goes *prestissimo* ; but in both cases there is an ' early morning feeling ' which is worlds away both from puritanism and its opposite. One seems to stand on a high narrow edge above two stuffy valleys—no doubt a dangerous position, but ' life itself is a dangerous thing ', and a society, like a man, must stand by its own risks. Aristotle, writing when this feeling had wellnigh vanished from Greek life, crystallizes it in his uninspiring doctrine of ' Virtue as a Mean '.

that its exaltation was due to social conditions where masculine
sentiments and interests held a natural predominance.

If we would know something of the atmosphere in which this
comradeship grew up, in which the romantic young Greek lived
and moved and had his being, let us turn for a moment, in conclusion, to the City State in time of war ; for, unless we have
seen the city so, we shall know but half of what was in her mind.
' If one studies carefully,' says one of our most thoughtful
modern writers, ' the expression of the Greek statues and the
lesson of the Greek literature, one sees clearly that the ideal
of Greek life was a very continent one : the trained male, the
athlete, the man temperate and restrained, even chaste, for the
sake of bettering his powers. It was round this conception that
the Greeks kindled their finer emotions.' What is it for which
these athletes of the statues are in training ? Not for crowns or
prizes or notoriety, but in order that they may the better serve
the city and their friends, that they may go into battle ready and
fit to lay down life for their sake.[1]

---

[1] The ' Holy Band ' of Thebes consisted entirely of close comrades : and
when the dead were collected after Chaeronea not a man among them, it is
said, was missing. Yet opinion at Thebes, we are told, was lax about the
spirit of such connexions. See Xen. *Pol. Lac.* ii. 12–14 and Plato, *Symp.* 182,
Rep. 468 : also the *Charmides* and the *Lysis*. But all these *loci classici*
about Greek friendship date from the fourth century, and are therefore too
self-conscious for our period. We must remember this in any judgement we
may be inclined to pass on the Greek attitude towards the abuse of the
physical element in such friendship—the ' black horse ' of Plato's *Phaedrus*.
The modern feeling that regards such connexions as peculiarly repugnant and
unnatural was, from the conditions of their society, entirely absent from the
Greek mind. No doubt this was partly due to the fact that the Greeks could
not contrast with them, as we can, a wholly different ideal of passion, round
which their best sentiments could concentrate. But in the fifth century, at any
rate, they did not think much about themselves : their emotions were too fresh
and quick, were too entirely without shame and embarrassment, for it to be
easy for them to separate critically the good from the bad. The subject is a
difficult one, and in such cases parallels are often the most illuminating guide.
The reader will find in Hahn's *Albanesische Studien* (Vienna, 1853), p. 166,
taken down from the lips of a young Gheg Albanian, who knew nothing of
ancient Greece, an account of a similar emotional atmosphere among the
Ghegs of Northern Albania. The details and even the phrases correspond
closely, in some cases exactly, to those of Plato and Xenophon, and the
feelings described are declared, in scornful contrast to those of the Turks
and the Southern Albanians, to be ' as pure as sunlight '. See also pp. 147–50
for two interesting Gheg love-poems. The Ghegs, like the Greeks of the
Pindaric circle, ' have no love-poetry about woman.' See also Wilamowitz,
Orestie, pp. 139 ff. ; *Staat und Ges.*, p. 91, 2nd ed. 95 ; and Edward Carpenter,
The Intermediate Sex, p. 68 (quoted above). [See Appendix.]

The city, of course, was not always at war. But she was always in training for it. For war had by now become not merely, as of old, a means of production by robbery, but a natural form of public service to which all citizens were called. But it was more even than that. It was a traditional and all-absorbing form of sport. It is hard to realize in these days, when fighting taxes the nerves and tires the limbs but has lost most of its thrills and all its animal excitement, what a fine sport it was in the days when men regarded it as the great and only game. A Greek city, as we have said, was very like a big school or college, and warfare and the training and competitions connected with warfare, were its chief forms of physical exercise. If a young man took a pride in his body and kept it hard and fit, if he flung spears in the stadium and raced round naked or in full armour, if he went off on long marches over rough country in the sun and bivouacked at night on the open hillside, or lay on a bed of rushes, watching the moon rise over the sea, after a hard day's rowing, it was all to prepare himself for the big day which might come any spring, if the city in council or the men over the range so willed it. So he and his friends lived in an atmosphere of campaigning. Their conversation ran on spears and shield-straps and camping-grounds, and where to get rations up in the hills, on rowlocks and catheads and undergirding and the boils and blisters of naval service : on how to ship horses in a trireme by cutting away the benches, or how to land on an enemy's promontory and make a fort without tools, carrying the mortar on the bent back for want of hods : or how to make a surprise attack on their chief harbour, sailing in with the night wind and making a bonfire of their bazaar to match the red of early dawn : or whether it would be fair and honourable and according to the best traditions of the old game to entrap them into a marsh or lay an ambush in a ravine or engage a corps of wild men from Thrace to eke out inferior numbers. Modern readers sometimes wonder why Thucydides and Xenophon deluge them with campaign details ; they are apt to resent or to smile at the childish particulars which these grave historians are at such pains to narrate. They should recall the conversations to which they have listened, or perhaps contributed, in smoking-rooms and quadrangles and pavilions, on yorkers and niblicks and ebenezers, on extra covers and wing three-quarters, and ask how much of it would be intelligible, however beautifully written out, to an inquiring posterity which had turned to other pastimes. War was as natural a part of Greek city life as games and recreations are of our own. No doubt there are differences of degree. You fought in bronze armour ; you needed a high degree of physical courage and self-control, and, if the luck was against you, you might be taken prisoner or even killed. But so it needs pluck to charge straight or to face a fast bowler. In both cases the object is the same, to play the man, and to do the best for your side. And if killing men is no longer sport, killing animals still remains so.[1]

There was never a period in the whole life-time of the City State when war could be regarded as exceptional. Either actual campaigning or war yesterday and war to-morrow is the natural state of the Greek city : as Herodotus, who knew their sporting temper, observes, ' states must be tied up very tight if their agreements are to be lasting.' Some quarrel arises which, in a less inflammable atmosphere, or with the troops out of training, it would be easy to compose. Perhaps there is a cattle-raid by night on the border farms. ' Cattle and sheep and horses and copper pots are raidable stuff ', as Homer remarks, and heroes and even gods set the example long ago. This will lead to private reprisals. Some cornfields are trampled, an olive-yard gashed and burnt, and perhaps a few women and some more cattle and sheep are mysteriously missing. Well before daylight the marauders, driving their ' man-legged ' and ' four-legged ' loot mercilessly before them, will be safely back over the border. The news is brought into the city, and a grave-voiced herald is sent over to complain and demand instant redress. He is met with counter complaints and counter demands, and retires

---

[1] Compare Thucydides' account of the sieges of Plataea (ii. 75–9) and Syracuse, and of the exceptionally stubborn battle in iv. 43–4, ending in 212 + 50 dead : also of the wonderful machine at Delium (iv. 100. 2) ; also iv. 4, ii. 93 ; Xen. *Hell.* v. 4. 20 ; Ar. *Knights* 594–610 and Thuc. ii. 56. 2 (horse-transport) ; Ar. *Peace* 347 (beds by sea-shore) ; *Frogs* 222, 236 (blisters). Hence we are so often told of ' record ' losses (Hdt. vii. 170 ; Thuc. iii. 113. 6), and ' record ' teams (Thuc. vi. 31. 1, iii. 17, v. 174, vii. 56. 4), and of war's ' glorious uncertainty ' (ii. 11. 4). Like all other games, it stood to be ruined by professionalism. Compare Sir George Trevelyan's delightful essay on ' An Ancient Greek War ' (printed in *Interludes in Verse and Prose*, 1905).

with unruffled dignity and sorrow rather than anger upon his
tongue. He is escorted back to the border so that he may not
see too much by the way, and before sundown on the same day
he is back in his own country.

War has been declared. The word goes round the parishes,
the farmers take shield and spear from their places in the corner
by the corn-bin and the ox-goad, and hurry to the parade-
ground, welcoming, yet dreading (how well we know the feeling)
the familiar ordeal of the battle-field, and hoping in their hearts
that it will be well over by harvest time. A few days afterwards
the two armies will be aroused at early dawn and drawn up
opposite one another in the plain not far from the city gates, and
their generals will be whiling away the last uncomfortable half-
hour before play begins with such appropriate arguments and
exhortations as rowing and football captains know. If he is an
Athenian he will tell them that brains are bound to win and that
the superior numbers of the other side only testify to their nervousness. If he is a Spartan he will remind them that Spartans
never say die and that all they have to do is to obey their trainer's
instructions. Then comes the call to attention, the slow and
steady march forward, ' shields well together '—how endless it
seems—a glitter of bronze in the near distance (thank the gods,
the sun is behind us), and then the poising of spears, the clash of
shields, and the heavy thrusting and pushing and grappling of the
mêlée.[1]

---

[1] Hdt. i. 74 ; *Il.* ix. 406 ; compare the Homeric hymn to Hermes and
a relief on the Sicyonian Treasury at Delphi ; Thuc. ii. 12 (final embassy),
ii. 89, iv. 10 (Athenian battle-speeches), ii. 87, v. 9 (Spartan ditto), v. 71
(' shields well together ' and the nervousness of the right-hand man) : for the
mêlée or ' pushing of shields ' see Thuc. iv. 96. 2, Hdt. vii. 225, ix. 62 : for
a broken army in retreat see the wonderful picture of Socrates in Plato,
Symp. 221. The fighting in the *Iliad* and Tyrtaeus is confused, combining
the champions of the older independent style of combat with the ' mail-clad
ranks ' of the ordinary City State infantry. Compare *Trachiniae* 507–21
where similarly, as Jebb says, ' the picture is not distinct,' Heracles carrying
a club, a bow, and the City State weapons, two spears. Greek history and
poetry are full of ordinary ' neighbour-wars ' : e. g. Thuc. i. 15. 2, iv. 134,
v. 32. 2 ; Hdt. i. 82 ; Eur. *Supp.* 650 ff. The battle was in the plain because
the ordinary Greek fighting man was useless on rough country. He wore
helmet, breastplate, backplate, and greaves of bronze, and carried a lance six
feet long, an oval shield three feet long, and a sword. The famous mile run
at Marathon was only a ' quick march ' ; cf. δρόμος in Thuc. iv. 78. 5. See
on this point Grundy, *Thucydides and the History of his Age*, pp. 242–4, who
writes from personal knowledge both of the weight of Greek armour and of

Such is the game as it was played when States still went to war for extra supplies or extra money, before they were tempted to make robbery their main source of revenue or to turn their farmers and craftsmen into professional fighters. All the traditional rules of the game show the same spirit at work. There is no attempt to annex or to annihilate. The enemy is at once a sovereign power and a near neighbour. He will not submit to annexation, and if you root him out there will be nothing to rob ; if it is land you want, far better go among barbarians, who will not mind submitting tamely and becoming your serfs. All that warfare involves is a fair fight with equal weapons on the plain before the city walls. When it is over, long before sundown (if it survives the luncheon interval), the victors will put up a trophy, give back the other side their dead, and go off with the spoils and with the honours of the season. If they are exceptionally enraged they may stay on for a siege. That will ruin the other side's harvest, but will also mean withdrawing a number of men from their own. They will try to take the wall by assault and will be repulsed with loss ; their mines will be uncovered, their rams will lose their noses, and the ' tortoise men ' with their ladders will retire in dismay when some one descries the round edge of a millstone peeping over the wall just where they were preparing to scale it. Fifty men behind a Greek wall—however much mud there may be in its composition—even fifty women dressed up as men, so long as they do not *throw* anything, are worth a hundred times the number outside it, and few are the sieges in City State history which ended triumphantly for the attack. It takes a city to take a city, as Nicias said ; and then, if you are away from your base, the tables may be turned on you. The besiegers' only hopes are in starvation or treachery, but most cities are well provisioned, and the firebrands of the opposition, and even the mutinous slaves, are apt to feel a return of affection for homes and masters when they see the enemy at the gates. So it is probable that the victors will count the cost and desist, like the Persian governor in the story, who was advised by the mercenary leader of the Greeks whom he was besieging to ' con-

point-to-point walking on Greek hillsides. ' The iron of the Greek helmet was extraordinarily thick, and its weight was, I should say, nearly double that of the heaviest helmet of the mediaeval period '

sider how long the operations would take, and then reckon up the working expenses. "For," said he, "I am prepared to evacuate the city at once for a smaller sum down." '[1]

The rules of the game at sea are similar, adapted to the altered circumstances. Indeed, in its naval form it is simpler, safer, and more satisfactory, for, as the Old Oligarch remarks, you can reach your destination on the alluvial plain without a tiresome march through hostile country, and you can perform an exploit that no land force dare attempt ; you can ' sometimes ravage the fields of a superior power, for you can sail along where there is no defence, or only a weak one, and then, when the troops begin to muster, retire on to shipboard and put to sea '. So it is clear that it was not considered advisable, either by land or sea, to risk an uphill fight. It sounds unsportsmanlike, but we must remember the stakes. If a man was taken prisoner in a fight which impoverished his country, it might be years before his friends could club together the money for his ransom. In one case we hear of a man who was only rescued by the chance visit of an actor from his own city ; he had been away from home so long that he had acquired a foreign accent, and his fellow-citizens nearly disowned him. But this, it must be confessed, was not after a battle with next-door neighbours.[2]

But it is time, for the present, to leave these sportsmen to themselves. We shall come upon their traces again, better organized and better led, with bigger designs and bigger booty, and regular pay besides, but never again so glad and confident as in the ringing fights of the older Greece.

---

[1] Thuc. iii. 46. 3 (nothing left to rob) : the best illustration of the Greeks' touching confidence in walls is their idea of repulsing the Persian army and fleet in 480 by defending the wall across the isthmus. The best existing ancient walls are those of Constantinople, which were only taken in 1453 after a chapter of accidents, though the odds were 150,000 to 8,000. Thuc. vi. 23. 2 (a city against a city) ; Ar. *Pol.* 1267 a 31, Hdt. i. 17 ff., Thuc. iii. 102. 4–5. The best authority on sieges is of course Aeneas Tacticus, who knew every move in the game, including the fact that ' you can tell a woman by her throwing from ever so far off ' (xl. 4–5). Any one, however ' useless ', could defend a wall, provided it was sufficiently high and thick (Thuc. i. 93. 5–6), so it was not necessary to keep heavy-armed men in the city for this purpose. Some cities drew their circuits wide so as to include cornland, as is clear from the existing remains at Messene. Compare Jonah iv. 11.

[2] Old Oligarch, ii. 4 ; Dem. lvii. 18.

CHAPTER XIII

IMPERIAL ECONOMICS : SEA-POWER

Τὴν πόλιν τοῖς πᾶσι παρεσκευάσαμεν καὶ ἐς πόλεμον καὶ ἐς εἰρήνην αὐταρκεστάτην.—
Pericles in THUCYDIDES, ii. 36. 3.

People never have had clearly explained to them the true functions of
a merchant. . . . The merchant's function is to provide for the nation.—
RUSKIN, *Unto this Last*, §§ 21, 22.

IN our account of the economy of the City State we have been
building up our structure, layer by layer, from the simplest
foundations. We have now introduced all the elements which
were essential to the life of what we have been taught by Greek
thinkers to regard as the normal or ' average ' City State. The
city is equipped with husbandmen and craftsmen, retail dealers,
and foreign traders. All that she needs for bare existence she
produces within her own borders : such extra luxuries as she
requires, in order to live as a civilized city should, she can import
from abroad. She is neither too small nor too large, neither too
poor nor too rich. If she were smaller she would be dangerously
exposed to attacks from her neighbours. If she were larger she
would lose her unity and be difficult to govern. If she were
poorer her citizens would not be leading a civilized life. If she
were richer she would be exposed to all the temptations of
excess. She has reached what appeared to the logical Greek
mind to be the limit of healthy expansion. All that seemed to
remain for her statesmen was vigilantly to maintain this fortunate
equipoise of economic forces.[1]

Such were many of the Greek cities at a certain stage in their
development. Such, for instance, was sixth-century Athens,
and such no doubt were many other States which lived so quietly
and happily that we know little of their inner history. It was
a phase which survived in men's memories to furnish a pleasant
old-world pattern for the model cities of the later philosophers.

[1] Ar. *Pol.* 1326 b.

Aristotle and Isocrates, and Plato too, when he grew gentler
in his old age, looked back to a time when men were ' industrious
and thrifty and minded their own business ', when men's wants
were such that States were ' self-sufficient and all-producing ',
and every one lived ' temperately and liberally in the enjoyment
of leisure', when the hardy virtues of asceticism were agreeably
blended with the graces and refinements of a young and growing
civilization.[1]

These fourth-century Utopias were in many essential respects,
as recent writers have shown, wholly imaginary pictures. But
even were this not so, their authors' account of them would
be misleading. For they assume that political forces can be
kept stationary, that, once the right mould has been found, there
is little more for statesmen to do but religiously to preserve and
admire it. They make the familiar mistake, so natural to the
Greek mind, of regarding the city as a work of art. They did not
stay to ask themselves why the forces which had co-operated to
produce so desirable a result should consent to abate their vehe-
mence and become trustworthy barriers against further changes.[2]

We moderns know to our cost that economic forces care
nothing for social harmony or ' natural limits ', that, once un-
chained, they are not easily arrested. Sixth-century Athens,
with her land problem solved by the statesmanship of Solon
and Pisistratus, might seem to the contemporary observer, as
she seemed to conservative thinkers two centuries later, an ideal
picture of a State comfortably settled at the happy ending of
a long and troubled course. In reality she was at the beginning
of the bitterest struggle in her history, a spiritual conflict fought
out between two of the strongest forces in human society, which
was to bring her civilization to disaster at the culminating
moment of its greatness. We are passing, in fact, from the
economics of the City State to the economics of Empire.

---

[1] Is. *Areop.*, especially §§ 24 ff., a fancy picture of early Athens ; Ar. *Pol.*
1326 b 30. Plato preferred an austerer atmosphere for his *Republic*, and
turned to Sparta for his model.

[2] For a good criticism of fourth-century Utopianism see Meyer, v, § 921,
where the ' inner contradiction ' attending all such attempts is pointed out,
viz. that ' it assumes an advanced urban civilization as its basis '. The well-
to-do ' educated townspeople ' of the fourth century, whom the philosophers
assume, and from whom their hearers were drawn, would never stand the
' simple life ', which it was sought to impose on them.

Throughout Greek lands, wherever the new economic influences penetrated, this conflict was felt, from Ionia to Aetolia, from Sicily to the Crimea.   But it was in Athens, at once so tenacious of old traditions and so sensitive to new influences, that it raged most fiercely, and left its deepest mark upon society and literature.   Here, as we have seen, men's hopes were highest, and here their failure came most quickly and the disappointment was the most sharp and stinging.   From the Funeral Speech, spoken when all was yet well with the Athenian Empire, to the *Republic* of Plato, written when even its memory seemed no longer bright, is little more than half a century.   Between the unclouded faith of Sophocles at his zenith and the dark melancholy of the later plays of Euripides there are not more than a few years.   No other Greek city rose and declined so rapidly, or has left so continuous and truthful a record of the succession of its mental states.   Let us then, henceforward, leave the lesser cities aside, and turn to Athens alone, as we turned to her in our account of the progress of the Greek as a citizen, in order to watch the onward march of the economic forces which we have mustered.[1]

The previous chapters have shown us, one by one, the elements which had become essential parts of the economy of Athens by about the middle of the sixth century.   What we have now to do is to watch and analyse the new influences which made themselves felt during the next hundred years, to understand the forces which differentiate the Athens of the Funeral Speech from the Athens of Solon and Pisistratus.

The first step in this development is not difficult to trace.   It is described for us in clear terms in Plutarch's life of Solon.   The land question was in a fair way to settlement, the seas were becoming secure, Athens had adopted convenient weights and measures, and Athenians were becoming active traders.   But they were ready not only to trade but to be traded with.   ' The city,' says Plutarch, ' was filled with persons who assembled from all parts on account of the great security in which people lived in

---

[1] See p. 132 above, and cf. Murray, *Euripides*, p. xxi.   The reader will find a general account of the conflict in Pöhlmann, *Geschichte des antiken Sozialismus und Kommunismus* (2 vols., Munich, 1893–1901, especially vol. ii), a useful work in detail, but of which Meyer rightly says (v, § 883, note) that its very title shows its author's lack of judgement.

Attica. Solon observing this, and knowing that most of the country was poor and unproductive, and that merchants who traffic by sea are not in the habit of importing goods where they can find nothing in exchange, turned the attention of the citizens to arts and crafts. For this purpose he made a law that no son should be obliged to maintain his father if he had not taught him a trade.' It was well enough for Sparta, he goes on, who admitted no strangers and whose country could feed twice as many mouths as Attica, to keep only her Helots at work, to ' set her citizens free from laborious and mechanical activities, and to employ them in arms as the only art fit for them to learn and exercise. But Solon, adapting his laws to the state of the country rather than the country to his laws, and knowing that the soil of Attica, which hardly fed its own cultivators, could not possibly suffice to feed a lazy and leisured populace, ordered that arts and crafts should be accounted honourable, and that the Council of the Areopagus should examine into every man's means of subsistence and chastise the idle.' [1]

The passage bears the colouring of a later age, but its facts are correct enough. It is not true, as Plutarch hints, that arts and crafts were not ' accounted honourable ' till Solon made them so ; but it is certain that Solon did his best to make Athens a manufacturing centre. For the prime need of the country just now was wealth—wealth to set the peasant cultivators securely upon their feet again and to assuage the bitterness of civil conflict. But the best and quickest way of obtaining wealth was from outside, through the goods and, still more, through the brains and energy of foreign traders. The goods of course must be paid for. But how ? Not in landed produce, for Athens had little or nothing to spare, but in manufactures. But here came the difficulty. Raw materials indeed she had : marble on Pentelicus, silver at Laureion, and some of the best potters' clay in Greece ; but she had few hands to work them. So she needed not only money but men, not only traders who came as summer visitors to exchange their goods, but immigrants who would come to stay and give themselves and their arms and brains to the economic service of the city. So that Plutarch is putting the cart before the horse when he says that *because* the

city was filled with immigrants Solon saw he must start manufactures so as to feed them.   In reality, as he tells us a few
pages further on, the encouragement of immigration was one of
the corner-stones of Solon's policy.   Only he wanted settlers
not traders, men who would stay to enrich Athens, instead of
mere ' gold-bugs ' who would make their pile and go home.
Plutarch again gives us the facts, though, not having our modern
analogies to guide him, he is puzzled about their meaning.   ' The
law about the naturalizing of foreigners,' he says, ' is difficult
to understand, because it forbids the bestowal of citizenship on
any but such as have been exiled from their own country for
ever, or have settled with their whole household in Athens for
the sake of exercising some manual trade.'   Plutarch had forgotten, or never realized, how hard it was for an old-world city
to introduce strangers into her corporation.   But the writer
whom he is following knew better, and inspired him to suggest
the true interpretation.   ' This was enacted,' he goes on, ' as we
are told, not in order to keep strangers at a distance, but rather
to invite them to Athens, upon the sure hope of being admitted
to the privilege of citizenship ;   and Solon imagined that he
would find faithful recruits among those who had been driven
from their country by necessity or had quitted it by free choice.' [1]

Solon and the statesmen who followed him succeeded beyond
all expectation in this line of action.   They attracted to Athens
a constant stream of immigrants, and set new-comers and old
residents at work together in developing and diffusing the national
resources.   The industrial effects to which this led we must leave
to a later chapter.   What concerns us here is that the very
success of their policy only involved these statesmen in fresh
economic difficulties.   Attica was indeed growing richer under
their auspices.   But she was also beginning to house more mouths
than she could safely feed.   Her swollen population was rapidly
outgrowing her very limited means of subsistence.   Athenians
were being taught by experience to disregard the old doctrine that
independence and self-sufficiency must necessarily go together.

No doubt it was a great step forward in practical political
economy to have discovered that a sovereign city could safely

---

[1] Plut. *Solon* 24.   For the natural resources of Attica see *Ways and Means*,
ch. i.

outgrow its own food-supply. But it brought with it for Athenian
statesmen fresh and very harassing duties. For it threw upon
them the responsibility of safeguarding a food-supply from
abroad. It forced them to cultivate foreign relations, no longer
incidentally, as of old, in order to secure openings for their traders
whenever opportunity arose, but definitely and continuously in
order to be sure of averting the ever present danger of famine.
Thus the new economic situation, created by the attraction of
immigrant labour, entirely altered the conditions of national
defence, and therewith the whole outlook of Athenian statesmanship. In other words, it gradually transformed the character of
the Athenian State.

To understand how this happened we must stop for a moment
to look more closely at the question of national defence. In the
old days a city which could defend its own fields and gather its
own harvest could rest in peace within its walls in comfortable
isolation. Provided only that its citizen soldiers were ready to
fight when called upon, it did not need to pursue any foreign
policy at all. All it needed was, tortoise like, to ' keep itself to
itself '. Its policy might be summed up in the words which those
expert neutrals, the Argives, claimed to have been addressed to
them in the year of Salamis by the temporizing oracle :

> Let the whole world hate you,
>   So the gods be kind :
> Man your wall and wait you
>   Lance at rest behind.[1]

But now those old easy hibernating days were gone past recall.
The city was driven to adopt a new and far more hazardous
system of defence. Her strength lay no longer in quietness and
confidence. She needed to look abroad for her safety, to be
active as well as vigilant, and daring as well as prudent. She
had entered upon the path, so dangerous to ambitious nations,
of Defence through Offence. Her lines of communication and
influence had gradually to be extended far across the seas, from
Euboea to the Thracian Chersonese, from the Bosporus to the
Crimea, even from Crete and Cyprus to Africa. For she now
depended, not for luxuries but for necessaries, not for her livelihood but for her life, upon the harvests of Egypt or Cyprus or

[1] Hdt. vii. 148.

the Crimea, and on the power to ensure their steady arrival in her port. Those distant and vulnerable lines, and not the homely city square within her walls with its quick pulsations of daily business, became the main arteries down which her life-blood flowed. Far away they were in strange and perilous seas, which many of her citizens knew only by hearsay, and whence, for all the racing of her galleys, news came brokenly after many weeks to the heart of her Empire. When bad tidings were brought, Athens could no longer, as of old, assemble her sentry-reserve of ' oldest and youngest ' to march out and relieve her field force at some frontier fortress. For now her sentries were posted, not on those old grey watch-towers overlooking the Megarid or astride the Boeotian passes, but in the countless harbours and vantage-points of her new domain of sea. Those six thousand soldiers and sailors, one in seven of her citizens, whom we have seen on permanent service on the peace establishment of the Athenian Empire, were not sent out to fight. Theirs was the wearier duty of lining the roadway for the city's grain-ships, or of safeguarding the money which Athens needed to pay for their cargoes. They were

> No, not combatants—only
> Details guarding the line,

and as they did not die in battle, Pericles, when he spoke over the dead, could only indirectly acknowledge their services. But they, and not the old men and boys who still stayed behind to man the frontier forts and city battlements, were the true defenders of Athens. One brief hour of carelessness in some distant roadstead and all might be ruined. It was a summer afternoon's siesta on the brown sun-baked banks of the Dardanelles which betrayed the fleet of Aegospotami and laid Athens in the dust. Once that streak of water was in the hands of her enemies, no Long Walls or watch-towers or harbour bar at the Piraeus, no revival of the temper of Marathon or vows of heroic endurance, could save the starving city. Lysander had Athens at his mercy, and he had only to calculate how many months or weeks the last feeble flicker of resistance would last.[1]

---

[1] Thuc. iii. 13. 5 (new conditions of defence), ii. 18. 2 (an old frontier fort), viii. 1 and Xen. *Hell.* ii. 2. 2–5 (bad news at Athens and Lysander's lingering before his attack). The whole colouring of the Funeral Speech is, as we

These were the realities of imperial politics in Athens. But men do not easily face realities, and when as in this case, they ran counter to so many cherished and inherited habits, both of thought and of action, they were slow to impress themselves. Pericles acted in his statesmanship upon the new conception of defence, but he never expressed it in his speeches—never, that is, in all its naked and necessary ruthlessness. We must go half a generation forward to find what have become familiar to us since as the commonplaces of a certain imperial theory. ' We make no fine profession of having a right to our Empire because we overthrew the Barbarian single-handed, or because we risked our existence for the sake of our dependants and of civilization. States, like men, cannot be blamed for providing for their proper safety. If we are now here in Sicily, it is in the interest of our own security. . . . It is Fear that forces us to cling to our Empire in Greece, and it is Fear that drives us hither, with the help of our friends, to order matters safely in Sicily.' To the outside world, to the watchful eyes of all Greece and even to all-seeing Apollo at Delphi, the Sicilian expedition of the Athenians seemed an act of wanton aggression. In Athens it ranked, or she tried to delude herself that it ranked, merely as a necessary step in the safeguarding of her defences.[1]

But we have been striding forward too fast and peeping into the future. Let us return to look more closely at the question of the Greek city's commissariat, for it forms the most natural introduction to an analysis of the imperial economy of Athens.

Perhaps it would have been more logical to have examined into it earlier, for it is a question with which every Greek State, great or small, had in some form or other to deal. To each and

have seen, conservative, and Pericles confines himself, so far as possible, to sentiments appropriate to the old theory of defence. The dead over whom he spoke were all, or nearly all, soldiers, not sailors. This leads him into some curiously unreal phrases. See Thuc. ii. 39 ; p. 203 above and the notes there. Pericles' word to characterize the old theory of defence was ἀπραγμο-σύνη (' non-intervention '). It is interesting to follow up, in Thucydides' speeches, the use made of it by Pericles and his successors. See Thuc. ii. 63. 3, 64. 4, and the Corcyraean appeal (i. 32 ff.), and compare vi. 18 (both the argument and the phraseology and iv. 61. 7). For the Athenian corn-trade in the sixth century with Cyprus and Egypt see Wilamowitz, *Reden und Vorträge*, p. 40, note 1 (3rd ed., 1913, p. 42). It is supported by Solon's journey to these countries and by recent finds in Cyprus.

[1] Thuc. vi. 83. 2-3.

all of them famine was a perpetual danger against which it was
their business vigilantly to insure. Indeed it was through this
necessity of State insurance, through its interference in the production and distribution of corn, the most vital and necessary of
all the trades within her borders, that the city first became
involved in matters of economic policy. So long as trade was
concerned with luxuries the city left the trader to himself, unless
indeed she interfered as a censor. But, by a distinction which it
was as natural for her to make as it is difficult for us to realize,
necessaries came under an entirely different law. 'If one of the
ancients were to come to life again,' says an Italian historian,
'nothing would be more incomprehensible to him than our
modern corn duties.' Russia and Canada nowadays are as eager
to sell us corn as anything else. We find it hard to imagine
(and writers who talk vaguely of 'Athenian commercial policy'
have not even tried to do so) the difference between articles of
easy transport intended for a few select citizens with money in
their pockets, and articles of bulk which are objects of common
need, but for which, in proportion as they are more needed, there
will be the less private money to pay. The modern corn-
importer, even when prices are high, flings the corn upon our
shores. In Greece the corn-importer, like so much of the labour,
had to be artificially attracted; and it is instructive to watch
some of the means that were adopted.[1]

But first it is necessary to point out that the trade policy
which we are about to describe does not concern corn alone.
Corn was the chief, but not necessarily the only, indispensable
import. There were others not so important in bulk, which were
often equally indispensable. These varied of course, in different
places, according to the policy and circumstances of the different
States. We find Delos legislating about fuel and fifth-century
Athens about cheap fish. But chief among them, at Athens
at any rate, were all the various materials for ship-building,
timber from the tall and shapely pines of Thrace and Macedonia,
flax and hemp for sails and rigging, iron and bronze and wax
and pitch. These various commodities, as the Old Oligarch says,

---

[1] Ferrero, *Greatness and Decline of Rome* (English transl.), vol. i, p. 318.—
1921. The submarine campaign and the Allied blockade will have helped to
bring these conditions home to students both in Great Britain and on the
Continent.

will most likely be found in different places, for ' where yarn is
abundant the soil will be light and devoid of timber. And in
the same way bronze and iron will not be products of the same
city. And so for the rest, never two, or at best three in one
State, but one thing here and another thing there.' All these,
in their several homes and on their several city-ward roads, are
the care of the city's ' far-flung battle-line '.[1]

Now let us turn to the business of the corn-supply. Thanks
to the inscriptions and to recent inquiries we can watch it at
every point, and we shall see the State's finger at work at every
stage.

Aristotle tells us that at Athens, when the citizens came
together for the Stated Meeting of Parliament at the beginning
of every ' Presidency ', the Agenda contained the item ' *Respect-
ing Corn* '. Ten times a year the national attention was officially
directed to this question. We shall see in a few moments how,
as a State with a large import trade, Athens proceeded to
deal with it. But first we must stop to point out that the same
item appeared duly on the Agenda and in the minds of far
smaller communities. For even if a State was ostensibly and
normally self-sufficient she might be exposed to famine any
year by a general or partial failure of her crops. National commissariat was therefore, always and everywhere in the City-

---

[1] Old Oligarch, ii. 11. For the Athenian timber-trade see Thuc. iv. 108 ;
Xen. *Hell.* v. 2. 16, vi. 1. 11 (Thrace and Macedonia ; cf. ii. 98. 1), Thuc. vii. 25.
2, vi. 90. 3 (the woods of Calabria, for use in Sicily), iv. 52. 3, i. 1. 25 (Mount
Ida in the Troad). Compare the treaty between Macedon and the Chalcidian
coast-cities, with its regulations for the right of mutually exporting timber.
Note that the coast States reserve to themselves the right (unlike the Mace-
donians who are the weaker party to the agreement) to stop the export
of *ship-building* timber at any moment by decree. The treaty is given in
Hicks and Hill, No. 95 (who do not seize this point), and Dittenberger, No. 77,
where see note 5 for further references. Athenian policy, as the Old Oligarch
points out, included also the task of preventing other States from acquiring
ship-building materials. Export of these from Athens was prohibited (perhaps
only in war-time) : *Frogs* 362 (cf. *Knights* 282 for the same word, ἀπό.ρητα,
about the export of food). One of the great difficulties of Athens' enemies in
the Peloponnesian War was ship-building. They found it hard to get the
timber—not to speak of the labour difficulty. Triremes did not require much
skill in designing and putting together, and no pride seems to have been felt
in the hulk as apart from the fittings, which were presented as a free gift by
prominent citizens. The difficulty was not the quality but the quantity of
labour required to build a fleet in a hurry. On these occasions—and indeed
generally—the wood does not seem to have been kept long enough to be
properly seasoned. Cf. Thuc. vii. 12. 3, viii. 1. 3, and viii. 15. 1 to viii. 25. 1
(six small squadrons hastily built).

State world, a matter of public interest and state control. The
export of corn was never allowed to go on unchecked ; and
careful steps were taken, as our inscriptions prove, to keep open
a cheap and steady supply either wholly from within or, if that
proved insufficient, from abroad through the help of merchants.

Two of these inscriptions are worth a mention here. A stone
found in Samos in 1903 gives some interesting details as to how
that City State managed its commissariat in the second century
before Christ. Samos drew its supplies, or an important part
of them, from a domain sacred to Hera on the mainland. These
had been taken over and farmed, in the usual way, by middlemen, who sold the grain at what were regarded as exorbitant
prices. The Samian State therefore determined to take over
the management itself, and our inscription shows her in the act
of regulating this business. She has raised the necessary capital
for working expenses, not by levying a rate but by opening
a subscription list, promising liberal interest (the exact figure has
not been recovered) to all citizens who will subscribe. The
corn will then be sold at a cheap rate to the citizens, or, to
speak more exactly, it will be doled out at this rate by the
State to all among the poorer population who apply for it.
As the editors point out, we have, in the simple and necessary
precautions of these little self-sufficient municipalities against the
ever present danger of famine-prices, the germ of the 'Bread
and Circus' policy of Imperial Rome. When Rome came into
the domain of the Kingdom of Pergamum she treated it in the
same way as Samos treated her little estate of Hera. So dangerous is it when politicians are too logical to enlarge their
imaginations with enlarged responsibilities ! Just as Cicero copied
out the political theory of Aristotle, so Caius Gracchus, with an
imperial metropolis under his charge, took his cue from the
political practice of the diminutive cities of Greece.[1]

The other inscription comes from Tauromenium or Taormina

---

[1] *Ath. Pol.* xliii. 4 (agenda) : Wilamowitz and Wiegand, *Ein Gesetz von
Samos über die Beschaffung von Brotkorn aus öffentlichen Mitteln* ; cf. *Hermes,*
vol. xxxix, pp. 604 ff. See also *Jahreshefte,* vol. x, pp. 19 ff., for an interesting
inscription of the first century B. C., in honour of a Megarian who, on the
occasion of his entry upon an office, ' dined all the citizens and strangers
and Roman residents, and all the slaves and their sons '—very different from
the elaborately organized Roman shows and distributions which took their
rise out of these pleasant little City State functions.

in Sicily—not yet then a tourist centre. Here we possess some of the actual accounts of the city over a period of several years. Amongst them are those of the 'corn-wardens', who keep the public granary and sell the corn to the citizens. This corn comes into their hands from two sources, partly from officials called ' corn-buyers ', whose business it is to stock the granary on the State's behalf by buying from merchants, and partly from other officials called ' receivers ', who draw the produce from the State lands, which are being cultivated, as at Samos, by private farmers. In time of distress, therefore, the responsibility would rest with the corn-wardens (to whom the subordinate officials were themselves responsible), who could be called to account by the people for want of foresight in making provision for them.[1]

If a small town like Taormina found it necessary to employ no less than three sets of officials to be sure of its commissariat, what of a large importing city like Athens where the problem assumed so much greater dimensions?

Let us watch the commissariat policy of Athens, as her statesmen watched it, from outwards home, from the first shipping of the corn to its sale in the Agora of Athens.

The importing city's first task, of course, is to make a commercial treaty with a corn-growing country, so that her merchants may have a right to take their ships there to fetch it. Athens' earliest connexions seem to have been with Cyprus and Egypt. When these markets were closed to her by the hostility of Persia, their ruling power, she fought hard to reopen them. She sent several expeditions to ' liberate ' Cyprus, and when Egypt seemed ready to throw off the Persian yoke she entered into relations with a native prince, who was prepared to grant her merchants ' the free run of his country '. When these schemes broke down, she forced her way through the Hellespont and the Bosporus, and established connexions with the princelets of South Russia, where, as Herodotus says, men actually ' grow corn not to eat but to sell '. This last relation, which was confirmed by a personal visit from Pericles, undertaken when the Bosporus artery had been safely joined after the temporary revolt of Byzantium, remained, for the rest of the fifth century

[1] Dittenberger, No. 515, especially note 15. The date is about 100 B. C.

and afterwards, the main source of the Athenian food-supply.
How important it was may be seen by the honours that Athens
found it politic to heap upon the native princes who controlled
it, honours at which home-keeping Athenians, who did not
appreciate the difficulties of managing restive protectorates on
the frontiers of the Empire, were inclined to chafe.[1]

Permission to trade once secured, the two next tasks are to
persuade merchants to go and fetch grain, and to safeguard the
road thither. The first of these is not so easy as it sounds ;
for grain is troublesome to transport, and, moreover, it is far less
likely than the other less bulky ' wonders ' of the barbarian
hinterland to prove a profitable investment. So that the merchants wanted managing. Athens managed them, as her manner
was, by a twofold policy of cajolement and coercion. She welcomed her merchants with open arms and was lavish of golden
crowns and honorary decrees when, by bringing in a welcome
cargo, strangers had deserved her gratitude. But in this sphere,
for once, persuasion was not enough, there must be force behind
to back it up.

Two laws preserved in Demosthenes show us what form this
compulsion took. The first reads as follows : ' It shall not be
lawful for any Athenian, or any alien residing at Athens, or any
person under their control ' (Athens, we see, made her masters
keep an eye on the use of their slaves' savings), ' to lend out

---

[1] Thuc. i. 94, i. 104. 2, i. 112. 2 (Cyprus) ; Diod. xi. 71. 4 (Egypt) ; Hdt. iv.
17 ; Plut. *Per.* 20 (Pericles in Pontus) ; no date is given, but we may confidently connect it with the events in 439 ; cf. Thuc. i. 117 ; Dem. xx. 31 ff.
(native princes).—(1921. Compare the various forms of pressure and cajolery,
black-listing and the awarding of favours and even of decorations adopted, in
somewhat similar circumstances, towards neutral states and individuals during
the War.) See Francotte, ' Le pain à bon marché et le pain gratuit dans les
cités grecques,' in *Mélanges Nicole,* Geneva, 1905, pp. 135 ff. In this article,
which should be reprinted in a form less encumbered with other matter, there
are a number of helpful references. Its conclusions have been but little
affected by the recent and more lengthy treatment of a part of the subject
in ' L'Approvisionnement d'Athènes en blé au ve et au ive siècle ', by L. Gernet
(*Mélanges d'histoire ancienne,* Paris, 1909). Gernet has brought together a
commendable number of facts and references ; but his economic foundations
are unstable. For instance, he not only upholds the old impossible figure of
300,000 slaves for Attica but quotes with approval the antiquated heresy
that economic crises in Greece were apt to be due to the influx of cheap corn
(p. 330 note), i. e. that protective corn-duties would at times have been
beneficial. This has been definitely disproved even for the far larger and
looser circumstances of Rome. See Ferrero, *Greatness and Decline of Rome,*
vol. ii, Appendix I, supplemented by Salvioli, *Capitalisme,* pp. 169 ff.

money on a ship which is not commissioned to bring corn
to Athens,—or anything else which is particularly mentioned.'
Here the last words probably do not form part of the original
law, but are substituted by the orator, for the sake of brevity, for
a long list of other specified necessaries—such as the ship-building
materials to which we have already referred. Even with this
concession, the law is stringent enough, and must have been felt
as a serious inconvenience to the trading community.

The second law is still more drastic. It prohibited any person
resident in the Athenian State from transporting grain direct to
any other harbour but the Piraeus. The effect of these two laws
is obvious. No merchant could leave the Crimea or Egypt
without grain in his hold, and this would act as a magnet to
draw him back to Athens. Even if he fell in with a lucky
famine by the way, he would not dare to touch the treasure
which he was carrying in ballast : for the one point on which all
our three texts agree is that the penalties for breaking this
particular law were severe ' to the uttermost '.[1]

The way home was, of course, safeguarded by the general sea-
power of Athens. But she took more special measures to make
sure that her commands were respected. At Sestos in the Dardanelles, the most dangerous point of her most frequented corn-
route, she stationed a special board of officials, the Wardens
of the Hellespont, to exercise control over the passing ships and
see that they headed straight for Piraeus. A decree from the
early years of the Peloponnesian War shows us Athens granting
permission to a small town on the Macedonian coast to have her
corn conveyed to her direct from Byzantium, instead of by way
of Piraeus, and giving the Wardens instructions to facilitate this
privilege. The terms of the inscription indicate how stringent
was the ordinary rule and how great and gracious the concession.[2]

---

[1] First law : Dem. xxxv. 51 ; second : xxxiv. 37, xxxv. 50 ; Lycurgus, *in Leocr* 27. The British penalty in parallel circumstances would be the refusal of bunker coal.

[2] Hicks and Hill, No. 60, who speak as though the Wardens were stationed at Byzantium. Of course their post was in the Hellespont, as their name implies, probably at Sestos (see Thuc. viii. 62. 3, 102. 1 ; Hdt. ix. 115) ; Pisistratus preferred Sigeum : Hdt. v. 94. We have no means of knowing how widely the privilege granted in the decree was extended. In Thuc. iii. 2. 2 Mytilene awaits ' archers and corn from the Black Sea ', clearly coming direct, and, so far as the corn was concerned, probably by leave of the Dardanelles officials.

So the corn-ships sailed out of the narrows, turned South with the current at the point of Sigeum, threaded their way through the islands, passed close under the cliff of Sunium, with its gleaming temple overhead, and found themselves unloading at the Piraeus. But the owners of the cargo were not yet relieved from all further regulations. The grain had to be placed in the official warehouse, where a special staff of ten inspectors was employed to ensure that two-thirds of it was conveyed direct to the Athenian market. The remaining third, under ordinary circumstances, the merchants were free to re-export.[1]

One last transaction, and we take leave of our merchant-skipper. He has still to dispose of his two-thirds to the local retailers. Here again he needs to be careful, for the State forbids him to sell more than fifty ' measures ' to any one dealer. The object of this provision was clear : to keep the grain in many hands and prevent any attempts to ' corner the market '. But, like many such laws, it was liable to produce the very results which it wished to avert. For the merchant-skipper was just as much a possible monopolist as the local retailer or miller, and if there were only one or two corn-ships in harbour and the city's store was getting low, he could set the retailers by the ears and make them run one another up for the price of their fifty measures. Hence, on one occasion at any rate, the law was temporarily set aside by a courageous official—that same sturdy old Anytus who had the misguided courage to bring Socrates to trial. Anytus empowered the retailers, on his own authority, to form a combination against the importers. These, of course, made an outcry about the illegality and engaged the best counsel of the day, Lysias, to plead their cause. His speech is still preserved, and is an admirable example of how an adroit advocate can trouble the waters so as to conceal the real point at issue. But he has now at last met

[1] *Ath. Pol.* li. 4 (fourth-century evidence : in the fifth century the duties of these special inspectors were probably still administered by the city Corn-wardens. But the point is that they were performed). Warehouse : Thuc. viii. 90. 5. Thuc. viii. 4 (cf. vii. 28. 1) speaks of Sunium being fortified in the winter of 413–412, ' to secure safety for the corn-ships on their way round.' The fortifications are on the top of the cliff, by the temple, so that it is not obvious at first sight what use they would be. To keep guardships in the neighbouring small harbour would seem more practical. But the ' safety ' spoken of is probably against the weather and attacks from the land, not against privateers : ships sailing by in the winter could put in and wait at Sunium in spite of the Peloponnesian occupation of Attica. Athens, in fact, was reduced to fortifying a sort of Pylos in her own home-country.

with an interpreter who is his match in acuteness, and Wilamowitz has succeeded (far better no doubt than Lysias' opponent at the time) in making us sorry for those ' poor devils ' the retailers.[1]

The warehouse-bargaining at length completed, the corn is carried to market. But its vicissitudes are not yet over. Whereas ordinary articles are merely under the general supervision of the Clerks of the Market, there is a special board of Corn-wardens, at first five, later as many as twenty in number, to watch over its sale. Their duty was not exactly to fix prices (though it very nearly came to that), but to secure fair play to the general public. This included, for instance, the right to prevent either the millers or the bakers from making too large a profit ; the prices of flour and loaves were to be maintained at a level strictly in proportion to the cost of the raw material. A still more delicate duty was the task of persuading the sellers of the grain to keep to the ' established price ' and forgo high profits when a scarcity placed them within their reach. ' The established price is the selling price fixed, so to speak, at the Corn Exchange, and the price at which, at a pinch, the State itself sells corn.' ' But the State never ventures on such an act of violence as to forbid individual dealers to exceed it. All it does is to employ all possible means of persuasion to induce dealers to be generous enough voluntarily to adopt this price.' In fifth-century Athens, where honour and public duty were more to most men than gold or silver, such means were still effectual. Later on they were not, as we can see, if by nothing else, by the multiplication of the officials who dealt with the corn-supply.[2]

This then is what Pericles meant, when, using the old sanctified conservative phrase, he told his hearers that the city was ' most completely self-sufficient both for war and for peace '. To the casual listener the words would suggest the creaking of the corn-wains as they bore the harvest from the fields to the granary. But Pericles, as he spoke then, saw the watchers at Sestos and the far lands of the ' Ploughing Scythians '.

[1] Lysias, xxii ; Wilamowitz, *A. A.*, vol. ii, pp. 374 ff. The date of the speech is the early months of 386, just before the signing of the King's Peace, with which the high price of corn had undoubtedly something to do.

[2] Wilamowitz, *A. A.*, vol. i, p. 220, especially note 67 ; *Ath. Pol.* li. 3 ; Dem xxxiv. 39, lvi. 8 (' established price '). Compare the inscriptions discussed by Wilhelm in *Hermes*, vol. xxiv pp. 148 ff. and Ditt. No. 152 ; also (1921) the systems of costing and maximum price established during the War.

CHAPTER XIV

IMPERIAL ECONOMICS : FREE INTERCOURSE

Ἐπεσέρχεται διὰ μέγεθος τῆς πόλεως ἐκ πάσης γῆς τὰ πάντα.—Pericles in Thuc. ii. 38.

The greatness of our City draws the produce of the world into our harbour.

L'effet naturel du commerce est de porter à la paix. Deux nations qui négocient ensemble se rendent réciproquement dépendantes : si l'une a intérêt d'acheter, l'autre a intérêt de vendre ; et toutes les unions sont fondées sur des besoins mutuels.—Montesquieu. *Esprit des Lois*, xx 2.

With her food-supply assured Athens was free to grow. The one great barrier in the path of her material progress was removed. She had transformed herself, by infinite pains, from a City to an Empire. She had only, as Pericles said, to keep what she had won, to sustain the effort her fathers had made, and however great she grew, she need never fear starvation. Her economic revolution was achieved, and, as with Western Europe at the beginning of the nineteenth century, all civilization seemed to lie before her. She had done much on small means, with tyrants to control her, and only the slender resources of Attica to draw upon. What would she not accomplish now, in the flush of liberty, with the whole world within reach to contribute to her designs ? [1]

So her prospects seemed to Pericles and his fellows, the men, and the sons of the men, who made Athens self-sufficient. They looked forward to an era of material prosperity and spiritual advance, promoted and safeguarded by the armed peace of the Athenian Empire. There must be no question about the supremacy of the Athenian navy : no sacrifice of time and money must be spared to secure its efficiency. Athenians must set the world an example of civic devotion to the famous service on which their all depended. But this was only the foundation of Pericles' imperial theory. Whatever devotion they may inspire, navies

[1] There is more than a verbal connexion, as the Funeral Speech repeated y emphasizes, between political freedom and free trade. Cf. Hdt. v. 66 : ' Athens was great before, but when she had got rid of the tyrants she became greater still ' ; Herodotus is almost apologizing, to his free trade democratic fifth-century audience, for the economic progress Athens made under the Pisistratids

and defences are only the means to a spiritual end, and Pericles never made the mistake of confusing means with ends. With the clear-sightedness of his race and time, he kept his gaze fixed upon essentials. Athens must lead the world in arms because she is to lead it also in civilization. She is to be mistress in the double sense of both ruler and teacher.[1]

What is she to teach? For the answer we must turn once more to the Funeral Speech. Not art or literature or what we moderns think of as Hellenism, but simply the practice of civic virtue, ' what a good life is, from its first signs of power to its final consummation.' But Athens, since she had become an Empire, had raised her standard of civic virtue far above the dull round of petty duties which we are apt to associate with the name. If her citizens are truly to be ' an education to Greece ', they must find room in their natures, and time in their lives, for the new world of art and of ideas which was being opened out to them by their free contact with the outside world. They must go about their work, not with the stolid conscientiousness of the Spartan, but brightly and joyfully, with ' independence of spirit, manysidedness of attainment, and ease and grace and spontaneity of behaviour '. They must welcome with open arms all that the world has to offer them—as their City, according to tradition, had always been glad to open her arms to strangers from every part. They must be lovers of all beauty and of all wisdom—the one without extravagance and the other without unmanliness. Only so would they be able, not by their words but by their deeds, to teach mankind the great secret, which no other body of citizens has ever toiled so earnestly to reveal, how men can and ought to live together in civilized society—how Liberty and Goodness, Beauty and Knowledge and Justice, can make their dwelling-place together and fill their community with happiness.[2]

---

[1] Thuc. ii. 37 41, 61. 1, cf. i. 144. 1, iv. 62. 2. Pericles regarded the Peloponnesian War as a necessary interlude to clear the air, but always seems to be looking forward to the permanent settlement which was to follow it. So did the architect whom he employed on the Propylaea and the Erechtheum.

[2] Cf. Thuc. i. 2. 6 with the similar ideas in the Funeral Speech. To welcome foreigners and to assimilate foreign ideas were kindred notions in men's minds. The Athenian community during the Periclean time must be regarded as the most successful example of social organization known to history. Its society, that is, was so arranged (' organized ' is too deliberate a word) as to

If Athens was to accomplish this great civilizing mission two material prerequisites were indispensable—absolute security and adequate wealth. We have seen that the first was guaranteed by her sea-power. How was she to secure the second ?

This question, which we must now attack, formed the standing

make the most and the best of the human material at its disposal. Without any system of national education, in our sense of the word, it 'drew out' of its members all the power and goodness that was in them. Galton noted (*Hereditary Genius*, ed. 1914, pp. 329–30, cf. the table on p. 30) what an exceptional number of 'illustrious persons' Athens produced at this time, and attempted to show that the causes favourable to their production must also have produced a corresponding and far greater number of persons who, without possessing what the world calls 'genius', were of exceptional ability : in other words, that the general spiritual level of the community was astonishingly high. ' The average ability of the Athenian race is, on the lowest possible estimate, very nearly two grades higher than our own, that is, about as much as our race is above that of the African Negro. This estimate, which may appear prodigious to some, is confirmed by the quick intelligence and high culture of the Athenian commonalty, before whom literary works were recited and works of art exhibited of a far more severe character than could possibly be appreciated by the average of our race.' This is true but the eugenic moral which Galton draws from it is not convincing : that, ' by a system of partly unconscious selection, Athens built up a magnificent breed of human animals,' which ' in the space of one century ' (530–430 B. C.) produced fourteen ' illustrious persons '. So far as Greek selection was conscious, it was exercised without any regard to mental and moral qualities (cf. p. 332 above). Breed may explain some, but by no means all of the greatness of ancient Greece. Why should all this capacity flower just at Athens and just at this time ? Clearly not because the Athenians suddenly began to be born clever, but owing to social causes. We are apt to forget that we owe the Parthenon sculptures not merely to the genius of Phidias but also to the genius of the social system which knew how to make use of him. Similarly, we owe the Albert Memorial, not to the fact that nobody was born in this country with the latent power of designing a better one, or even to the fact that nobody sent in a better design (at least one far better one was sent in and is still in existence), but to the social and industrial system which presided over its erection. It is impossible to estimate how much high capacity is thus lost to us by our own bad management ; but the marked predominance of the sturdier qualities (roughly speaking, of will-power over intellect and sensibility) in modern Western life suggests how great is the wastage. For the sins of Western ' education ' under this head see *What is and what might be* by Edmond Holmes, late Chief Inspector of Elementary Schools, whose experience has convinced him ' that under favourable conditions the *average* child can become the rare exception and attain to what is generally regarded as a remarkably high degree of mental and spiritual development ' (p. 303), a striking commentary on Galton's estimate. 1914—I leave this note unaltered. Two years' experience in the same service as Mr. Holmes has tended to confirm my belief in his dictum, which applies not only to children and adolescents but also to some extent to adults. See on this point *University Tutorial Classes*, by Albert Mansbridge (London, 1913) and an essay entitled ' Education, National and Social ' in my *Nationality and Government* (London, 1918). See also on the whole question of environment the admirable discussion in R. M. Maciver's *Community, a sociological study*, 2nd ed., 1920, pp. 373 ff.

problem of Athenian statesmanship in the fifth century. Round
it, in the many shapes which it assumed with varying circumstances, turned most of the great debates on Athenian policy.
For on the right answer to it depended, as men vaguely felt, the
whole future of Athens and of Athenian ideals.

The two wisest imperial statesmen, one the founder of the
Empire, the other its most convinced upholder, were in no doubt
as to the right reply. The best way to make Athens rich, so
they preached, was not to rest content with the resources of her
tribute-paying Empire but to develop her trade and industry. It
was not, as they knew, either the quickest or the most traditional
or the most attractive method of advance, but it was the safest,
and, above all, it embodied the new imperial ideal of freedom.

Before we ask, then, what other means of enrichment presented
themselves to the statesmen of Athens, let us turn our attention
to her commercial and industrial resources and prospects. Were
they sufficient to supply her with the material wealth that she
needed if she was to bring her schemes to fruition ?

Commerce and sea-power go naturally together. After the
battles of Salamis and Mycale, in 480 and 479, the Athenian
navy took the place, in the Aegean, of the navies of the States
of Asia Minor. The same was to be true, in the long run, of her
mercantile marine. Athens' most important trade-rivals had
been seriously affected by the Persian wars. Miletus had been
sacked and its inhabitants enslaved after the Ionian Revolt, and
Eretria had been wiped out by the Persians on their way to
Marathon. Other important trading centres, such as Phocaea,
lost some of their most active and enterprising spirits, who would
not submit to the Persian yoke.[1]

But the upward movement of Athenian commerce was slower
than that of her navy. Sea-power can be won at a blow in a
single fight, but in trade there is a momentum which lasts on
even when the original impulse has died away. Connexions and
agencies once formed, routes and methods once selected, are
adhered to for the sake of custom long after they have ceased
to be the most profitable and convenient. This is true even in
the modern world, where men are used to rapid changes and

[1] Hdt. vi. 17, 18, 101 and the beautiful epitaph on the Eretrians in captivity
in Babylonia, *Anth. Pal.* vii. 256 (Mackail, 2nd ed., p. 152).

accustomed to bow before passing fashions : four centuries have
passed since the discovery of the New World, and the metropolis
of the British Commonwealth, with its wide oceanic connexions,
still looks eastwards down the Thames towards Europe.   In
Greece, where custom controlled men so much more closely, it is
not surprising to find that the natural momentum of economic
forces exercised a powerful influence. It was only by slow degrees
that Athenian traders succeeded in securing the agencies and connexions which had originally been controlled by their rivals, and in
attracting to the Piraeus the goods which used to be transhipped
for re-export at Miletus or Samos or Phocaea. It was not till
the middle of the fourth century that Athens could be described
as the one great commercial centre and mart of the Greek world,
through which every trader was bound to pass on a long-distance
journey.   During the greatest period of her Empire, while Pericles
directed her commercial policy, ' the trade of Athens was still behind that of the Asiatic cities '—an indication, adds Wilamowitz,
of the good use these cities were able to make of the security and
justice which they enjoyed within the Athenian Empire.   In the
West, which remained outside the range of her sea-power, her
advance was even slower ; for she had a number of prosperous
rivals eager for the carrying trade, of whom the most serious,
Syracuse, was as enterprising and ambitious as herself, and had
the prestige of two successful wars against Barbarians to inspire
her efforts.[1]

With these considerations in mind, let us summarize briefly
what is known of the commercial development of fifth-century
Athens down to the Peloponnesian War, of the new relationships
which she knit, with the prestige of Salamis upon her, both in
the East and the West.

The East was nearer and more familiar to her, for here she was
working upon ground already prepared by Pisistratus. But here
she found that she had herself placed a formidable barrier in her
path. While the coast-towns of Asia Minor were still on friendly
terms with the power which held the roads up-country, the com-

---

[1] *Ways and Means*, i. 6–8 ; Wilamowitz, *Reden und Vorträge* (= *Aus
Kydathen* with different footnotes), notes to pp. 39 and 41, 3rd ed. 1913,
pp. 42 and 44, based on ' information, printed and verbal, of the discoveries
of the last few years '.   For the prosperity of fifth-century Sicily see Diod. xi.
68. 6, 72. 1 (from Timaeus).

merce of inner Asia flowed naturally down the river valleys to the Greek ports near their mouths. But since Greece and Persia had become enemies the caravan routes had been interrupted, and the inland trade of the coast-towns had not since been effectively revived. It is true that, after the first few campaigns, active hostilities languished. The Persians withdrew their armies into the interior, and the Phoenician navy did not venture to show itself in what were now regarded as Greek waters. But the land-power and the sea-power, the Persian Empire and the Athenian Confederacy, still remained nominally at war for thirty-two years from the date of Salamis, and from time to time the smouldering fires broke out into an active blaze. Themistocles, more far-sighted than his contemporaries, had the courage to set his face against the continuance of this state of war. But he was denounced by the public opinion of his day as disloyal to the national cause, and his efforts at conciliation only ended in forcing him into exile. After his death attempts were made by his successors to develop his ideas without abandoning those of his opponents—to pursue a commercial policy in Eastern waters without making peace with the national enemy. Efforts were made to keep Cyprus permanently independent of Persia and thus to make it accessible to traders. Athenian troops even seem to have made a brief incursion into Phoenicia. But the real goal of this policy was Egypt, at this time in open revolt against the Persian yoke. Athens sent out the largest force she ever collected, in order to drive the Persians out of Africa and secure an open door in Egypt. But she was playing for too high stakes. The effort failed, leaving her sea-power shaken, and even the Aegean for a moment at the mercy of a foreign fleet. The young Pericles, who had inspired it, was converted for good to Themistocles' old policy of peace and commercial intercourse. In 448 Athens and Persia became friends at last. This necessarily involved the permanent curtailment of Athenian naval ambitions in Eastern waters. Athens had indeed secured complete freedom of access, which was all that Themistocles had desired for her. Her traders and travellers could go where they liked, as we know from the itinerary of Herodotus. But she surrendered her claims to the sea-dominion of the Levant, and was forced to acquiesce for good in the competition of rival powers. Henceforward she abandoned all hope of monopolizing the Egyptian corn-supply for her own purposes, and was glad to share the Eastern carrying-trade with the experienced merchantmen of Phoenicia. Athenians must have grown used to seeing crews of Semite Barbarians at the Piraeus, taking advantage of the reciprocity which Athens was bound to offer them. We should like to know what they talked about as they stood chatting on the quays—how far they acted as intermediaries between the ideas of Greece and Palestine. But our extant fifth-century writers have all chosen to ignore them. Athens did not look upon them with favour, for her mind was set upon other things.[1]

Let us now cast a brief glance westwards. Here Athens was brought into contact, through her growing ambitions, not with

---

[1] For Themistocles' policy of developing commercial relations with Persia see Meyer, iii, § 283. It follows naturally, apart from some detailed pieces of evidence, from Thuc. i. 93. 4. Themistocles understood not only what sea-power was but what it should lead to. Themistocles had a sharp tongue and lacked the geniality of his rival Cimon, so he was never very popular within his lifetime. After his death his successors seem to have been anxious to steal his ideas and discredit his services.—Athens sent 200 + 50 ships in two detachments to Egypt as against 136 + 75 to Syracuse. While her troops were in Egypt she was also simultaneously engaged in Aegina and Megara, and, later, in Boeotia (Thuc. i. 105. 3, 107–8), although her financial resources were far inferior to what they were a generation later. We sadly miss a contemporary account of Athens during the tension of these years. Our most eloquent record of it is an inscription of the year 459–458, giving 168 names of members of the tribe Erechtheis ' who died in the war in Cyprus, in Egypt, in Phoenicia, in Halieis, in Aegina, in Megara, in the same year ', one of ten similar lists for each of the tribes (Hicks and Hill, No. 26). There is an echo of these heroic years in Thuc. vi. 17. 7, where the young Alcibiades, arguing for the Sicilian expedition, appeals to the policy of the young Pericles. By the treaty of 448 Greek waters were fixed as extending from the Cyanean islands (at the Bosporus entrance to the Black Sea) to the Chelidonian Islands off the coast of Lycia, not far from the river Eurymedon, where the Phoenician navy was broken up in 466. It was taken for granted that the Black Sea was Greek. No Persian ships ever ventured there. We know little about the commercial life of Cyprus, Egypt, and the Syrian coast in the years after 448, except what can be gathered incidentally from Herodotus, who was able to travel freely there. The relations between Athens and Persia remained good, and Athenian missions to Susa were so frequent ' as almost to assume the character of a standing Legation . . . while a knowledge of Persian and Aramaic was not unusual among Athenians' (Wilamowitz, *Reden und Vorträge*, p. 41, 3rd ed., p. 44). For the relations between Athens and Gaza, see p. 194 above ; cf. Hdt. iii. 136 for a Phoenician coasting voyage. Xen. *Oec.* viii. 11 refers in familiar terms to ' the great Phoenician vessel ', which was a model of shipshapeness. Little is known of any interchange of ideas between Athenians and Semites. There was a small resident Phoenician colony at Piraeus ; we possess some thirty inscriptions relating to it, as against one epitaph on a Carthaginian : Clerc, *Métèques ath.*, pp. 381–2 ; Francotte, *Industrie*, vol. i, p. 218 (cf. Hyper, v. 4 for an Egyptian shopkeeper at Athens). **[See Appendix.]**

Barbarian rivals, but with Greeks. The three next Greek sea-powers of the day lay straight on her Westward traders' course. The sea-road to Italy and Sicily passed through the waters, first of Corinth and her dependants, then of Corcyra, and then, on the opposite side of the Ionian Straits, through the sea-domain of Syracuse. Corinth herself commanded the gulf, and her colonies held the sea to the North-west as far as the mouth of the Ambracian Gulf. Here the trader would enter the territorial waters of Corcyra, who lived on the toll she took from the ships that put in as they passed by. Off the coast of Italy the limits of the territorial waters were not so clearly marked; but Syracuse thought herself strong enough at need to assert her sea-power as far north as the Gulf of Tarentum. If Athens was to trade westwards, she must either cripple these rivals and annex and patrol their territorial waters, or proceed by a policy of negotiation based upon considerations of mutual interest. Here, as in the East, Pericles was converted to the latter course. During the whole period of his supremacy Athens was at peace with Corcyra and Syracuse, and during the whole of the latter part of it with Corinth too.[1]

We cannot watch in detail the extension of the commercial relations which were thus established by Athens in Italian and Sicilian ports. Only a few scattered facts remain to testify to the growing activity of her merchants. We know from the merchants' marks on the Attic vases that from about 480 onwards the men who carried them to their Western market were no longer Ionians but Athenians. We know, as we might expect, that Themistocles threw his influence into this movement, that he had influential connexions in the northern Peloponnese,

---

[1] Thuc. i. 29. 3 and 30. 3 (Corinthian waters), 36. 2, 3 (Corcyraean waters), ii. 7. 2 (Athens' commercial treaties with Sicily), iii. 86. 3, iv. 64. 3, vi. 21. 2, 34. 4, with which cf. Diod. xv. 13. 1 (Syracusan waters). Athens was at war with Corinth between 459 and 451, and made incursions into her waters, even stationing warships at Pegae at the head of the Gulf. But from 445 the two were at peace, each accepting the other's supremacy in her own waters, and Corinth remained faithful to this arrangement even during the Samian Revolt in 440–439. See Thuc. i. 40. 5, 117. 1, 120. 2 (where such an arrangement is clearly alluded to). Corinth, with her good corn-land and her Peloponnesian allies at her back, had of course no reason to fear starvation, like Athens. None of the Peloponnesian States found it necessary to try to organize their oversea corn-supply. Temporary deficiencies seem to have been made up first from South Russia, and later, when Athens monopolized this source from Sicily and Egypt (Hdt. vii. 147 ; Thuc. iii. 86. 4, iv. 53).

and had knit close relations with Corcyra, and also, probably, with Hiero, the wealthy tyrant of Syracuse. We know also—for the stones themselves are preserved—that Athens began to enter into close treaty relations with Western cities, first with Segesta, in 454, and later on, in 433, with Rhegium and with Leontini. In 438, too, we find an Athenian admiral at the Greek colony of Naples, apparently helping the city against an attack from the Barbarians of the hinterland.[1]

But the most important record of the nature and extent of Athenian designs is the scheme for the colonization of Thurii. The old commercial capital of South Italy had been the famous city of Sybaris, commanding the isthmus route from the Eastern to the Western Mediterranean. Sybaris had been destroyed in 510, and her trade connexions passed into other hands. Her surviving inhabitants retired to their West-coast harbours. After a lapse of time they tried to resettle on the old site, but the jealousy of their old neighbour and enemy, Croton, made it impossible for them to do so. In 443 Athens determined to do it for them. The new colony was not to be an offshoot of Athens on the old City State lines. It was to be a Panhellenic settlement under the influence of Athens, a permanent embodiment of her new ideal of the blessings of free intercourse. Men from all the Greek States were to be merged and mingled in the new citizen body. All Greece was invited to take part in the enterprise. Colonists and visitors streamed in, not only from Athens and her Empire, but from Arcadia, Elis, and Achaea, from Boeotia, and the rest of Central Greece. Amongst them were some of the best-known figures of the day, Protagoras the sophist, Empedocles the poet and philosopher, Hippodamos the architect, and Herodotus the historian.

The city was duly founded ; Hippodamos laid out the streets in the approved rectangular fashion, and Protagoras had a hand in the model constitution. Yet not all the wise men she had gathered enabled her to live up to her ideal. The old City State

---

[1] Vases : see above, p. 322. Treaties : Hill, *Sources*, chap. iii, § 327 Hicks and Hill, Nos. 51, 52. Naples : Hill, chap. iii, §§ 381–3 ; Meyer, iv, § 435. Themistocles : Thuc. i. 135. 3, 136. 1 ; Plut. *Them.* 24 and 32 : two of his daughters were called Italia and Sybaris. Hiero died in 466, just about the time of Themistocles' flight. If we suppose that the news reached him at Corcyra, on his way to Sicily, we shall have an explanation of his roundabout route to Persia.

idiosyncrasies were too powerful to be lived down. Within a year or two the new citizen-body had divided itself into tribes, according to the previous nationality of its members, and by 440 Herodotus and other prominent upholders of the new principles retired ruefully to Athens, leaving the city in the hands of the anti-Athenian majority. The first attempt to put the educational policy of Athens into practice had ignominiously failed. The City State tradition was too firmly rooted. Greece was not fitted for Panhellenism, as Pericles understood it. Athens herself, as we shall see, was not truly fitted either.[1]

Such was the policy of Periclean Athens in the Levant and in the West. In neither of these regions was Athens, in the true Greek sense, a sea-power. She did not hold, or aim at holding, the lines of communication. She could not hope to annex to her Empire the Eastern and the Western seas. She was in fact not a ruler, but simply a missionary and a pioneer. What her traders desired, and what their statesmen tried to secure for them, was not monopolies in foreign markets for buying or selling goods, but merely access and free intercourse and power to mingle and exchange with other nations. It is this conception of free intercourse of men, of goods, and of ideas which is the distinctive contribution of the Periclean age to Athenian policy and economy. Again and again we find it emphasized in the Funeral Speech. The generation of Marathon and Salamis had given Athens the prestige of an Empire ' enlarging the ancestral patrimony ' of Attica by the membership of the Delian Confederacy. The next generation used that prestige to 'secure the complete self-sufficiency of the City both in war and peace '. ' Our pioneers,' said Pericles, ' have forced their way into every sea and every land,' and, as a consequence of the intercourse thus opened up, products from the ends of the earth find their way to Athens.

---

[1] Diod. xii. 9 ff. ; Meyer, iv, §§ 397 ff. ; and, for Herodotus, *Forschungen*, ii. 196 ff. The latest authority, however, Jacoby in Pauly-Wissowa, Supplement ii; p. 242 ff., thinks that he stayed at Thurii till his death. No Corinthians are mentioned as taking part in the colony. No doubt they had their own trade-connexions and looked askance at Athens' attempt to knit new ones. But neither Athens nor Corinth were strong enough in Western waters to dream of going to war to keep the other out. Both were only there on sufferance. At this time, according to Wilamowitz (*Reden*, p. 41 note, 3rd ed., p. 44, from Helbig), ' the Sicilian cities, and especially Syracuse, controlled the local trade with the West coast of Italy.' Pottier, however (*Revue Archéologique*, 1904, p. 46), thinks that the Etruscans shared this control with the Siceliots.

' The choice things of Sicily and Italy,' says the Old Oligarch,
' of Cyprus and Egypt and Lydia, of Pontus or Peloponnese
or wheresoever else it be, are all swept, as it were, into one
centre.' What were these ' choice things ' ? Fortunately, an Old
Comedian has given us a list of many of them, compiled in the
fourth year of the Peloponnesian War, as if to show how little
Sparta and her allies could interfere with their arrival. Here
are some of the items from regions beyond the sea-domain of
Athens : hides and vegetable relish from Cyrene, grain and
meat from Italy, pork and cheese from Syracuse, sails and
papyrus from Egypt, frankincense from Syria, cypress-wood
from Crete, ivory from inner Africa, chestnuts and almonds
from Paphlagonia, dates and fine wheat-flour from Phoenicia,
and rugs and cushions from Carthage. Athens had to do without a great deal during the Peloponnesian War, for her land was
ravaged and her land-trade was cut off. She could not get pigs
and vegetables from Megara or her favourite eels from the Boeotian lake. But with these distant delicacies Pericles was still
able to keep her supplied, until, as he tells us, they seemed ' more
home-like ' than the produce of their own poor farmsteads.[1]

All these were part of the good life which Athenians desired
to perpetuate. But, of course, they were luxuries, and from the
statesman's point of view they could be dispensed with at a pinch.
It was sufficient to secure them by the congenial Athenian
method of persuasion, by voluntary agreements and treaties.
Her real necessaries, as we have seen, Athens held by a firmer
tie, that of undisputed sea-power. Let us glance briefly, in conclusion, at this aspect of Athenian trade, for it is important for
our purpose not merely to mark clearly the extent and limits of
Athenian sea-power, but also to observe how far its maintenance
was compatible with the Periclean ideal of free intercourse.

The battles of Salamis, Mycale, and Eurymedon, followed by
the Persian Treaty of 448 and the humbling of Aegina a few
years earlier, left Athens sole and undisputed mistress of the
Aegean. In the decade before the outbreak of the Peloponnesian
War, Pericles extended this supremacy not only over the Sea of

[1] Hermippus, Frag. 63 (Kock), *ap. Athen.* i, p. 27, written in 428 ; Old
Oligarch, ii. 7 ; Ar. *Ach.* 870 ff. *et pass.*—1921. Compare the Turkish carpets
of which Germany had more than a sufficiency during the privations of the
blockade !

Marmora but over the greater part of the Black Sea. By 431 the whole expanse of water, from Crete to the Crimea, with insignificant exceptions, had been converted into an Athenian lake. It became the domain of the Athenian people, as fully and indeed even more fully theirs than the homeland of Attica, for they relied upon it more completely for their daily bread. No one might sail on it without the permission of Athens, and to trespass there against her orders was as serious an offence as to invade the soil of Attica. True, her policy, here as elsewhere, was a policy of free intercourse. She had liberated the Greek seas in order to secure freedom for the Greek cities; and the merchants of the States in her Empire, and even of those outside it, such as Corinth and Megara, could make in peace-time as full a use of it as her own. But they were only allowed there on sufferance. Athens knew, and they knew, that the moment war was declared their trade was in her hands. Athenian guardships would be posted at every point of vantage; communications would be cut off between Greece and Asia, and even between island and island; and the enemies of the suzerain power, or her rebellious subjects, could only pursue their designs by stolen journeys and furtive meetings, like pirates and conspirators.[1]

There is a passage in the Old Oligarch where that old grumbler puts before us, more vividly even than Thucydides, what this Aegean supremacy really meant. The strategic position of a sea-power, he says, is infinitely more favourable than that of a land-power. 'The subjects ruled by a land-power can come together to form one city out of several small ones and so go into battle all together, but the subjects of a sea-power, if they are islanders, cannot bring their cities together. For the sea lies between them, and their mistress is a sea-power. And even if it

---

[1] The 'insignificant exceptions' in the Aegean were the heads of the bays of Smyrna and Adramyttium . . . and a few isolated positions, such as Anaea opposite Samos (Thuc. iv. 75; Meyer, iii, § 292). The reason why Athens ignored them is probably to be found in a secret arrangement with Persia. Athenian guardships: Thuc. ii. 24. 1 (first year of the war): they were not placed permanently at the mouth of the Corinthian Gulf, to hem the Corinthians in, till the winter of 430–429, after Pericles had fallen from power (Thuc. ii. 69; cf. i. 30. 2). See in Thuc. iii. 29–33, especially 32–3, how the Peloponnesian fleet sent to help Mytilene in 427 crossed furtively to Ionia and retired almost at once 'through the open sea, determined not to put in anywhere, if it could help it, till it reached the Peloponnese'. Also Aristeus' two journeys in i. 60 and ii. 67. 1: and v. 110.

were possible for them to assemble secretly on a single island they would only do so to die of famine. Nor are the coast cities under Athenian rule in a better position. The larger of them are coerced by fear, and the smaller by the pinch of want, since there is no State in existence which is not in need of imports and exports; and these it is impossible for a State to secure unless she remains subject to the dominant sea-power. Moreover, there are many expedients open to a sea-power from which a land-power is debarred. For instance, she can invade and ravage the territory of stronger military powers than herself; for her force can sail along the coast to a spot where there are no or hardly any opposing troops, and then, when reinforcements are approaching, re-embark and sail away, leaving the land-power with considerably the worst of the bargain. Again, a sea-power can go as far away from its base as it likes, while a land-power can only move a few days' journey; for marching is slow work, and a force of foot-soldiers cannot carry rations to last very long. Moreover, a land-army must necessarily go through friendly territory or fight its way, while a naval force . . . can coast along till it reaches the territory of a friendly or a weaker power.' [1]

These arguments might be copied out of the note-book of Pericles, they correspond so closely to all that we know of his own management of Athenian policy. This is not the place to go into that policy in detail, or to show how every move in it rested upon the underlying assumption of Athens' supremacy in her Aegean and Black Sea domain. One illustration must suffice. In 423, after eight years of fighting, the Athenians and the Peloponnesians made an armistice, practically upon the basis of the *status quo*. The fourth clause in the agreement ran as follows: ' *As to the use of the sea, so far as it refers to their own coast and to that of their confederacy, the Lacedaemonians and their allies may voyage upon it in any vessel rowed by oars and of not more than five hundred talents tonnage, not a vessel of war.*' This treaty was accepted by the representatives of Sparta, Corinth, Sicyon, Megara, and Epidaurus, who thus acquiesced in the complete exclusion of their sailing ships from the whole of

---

[1] Old Oligarch, ii. 2 ; cf. Pericles' own statement in Thuc. i. 140 ff., and Archidamus in i. 81 3.

the Aegean. The contrast between the ideal of free intercourse
and the necessities of self-preservation could not well be more
clearly marked. Other ideals were soon to go on the same
road.[1]

---

[1] Thuc. iv. 118. 5 ; cf. viii. 56. 4 together with Hdt. vi. 104 (before and after
the Athenian sea-power), also Thuc. v. 47. 5. On the contrast and ultimate
incompatibility between commerce and the older kind of imperialism compare
an interesting passage in Montesquieu, *Esprit des Lois*, xx. 4. He quotes
Cicero's remark (*De Rep.* iv. 7), ' Nolo eundem populum imperatorem et
portitorem esse terrarum,' and points out that the disposition and habits of
an old-fashioned imperial race, such as the Romans under the Republic, are
wholly different from those of a nation of traders or ' facteurs '. Unfortunately,
in this as in other matters, dispositions do not disappear when they have
become harmful and antiquated. Compare note on p. 247 above. A talent
was equal to a cubic foot of water or about 57 lb., so 500 talents would equal
about 12½ ' dead-weight ' tons.

CHAPTER XV

IMPERIAL ECONOMICS: THE FELLOW WORKERS

Τὴν γὰρ πόλιν κοινὴν παρέχομεν, καὶ οὐκ ἔστιν ὅτε ξενηλασίαις ἀπείργομέν τινα.—
Pericles in THUC. ii. 39.

We throw open our city to the world and never pass decrees to exclude foreigners.

Οἰκέτας οἱ δυνάμενοι ὠνοῦνται ἵνα συνεργοὺς ἔχωσι.—XENOPHON, Memorabilia ii. 3. 3.

Those who can afford it buy slaves in order that they may have fellow workers.

Forasmuch as it is reported that the Woollen clothes dyed in Turkey be most excellent dyed, . . . you shall devise to amend the dying of England by carrying hence an apt young man in the Art . . . and if you cannot work this by ordinary means then to work it by some great base mean.—*Remembrances for a factor : what you shall do in Turkey, beside the business of your factorship.* 1582. (Hakluyt's *Voyages*, ed. Maclehose, vol. v, p. 234.)

FIFTH-CENTURY Athens had not only thrown open her doors to foreign goods, she was also attracting and importing human beings.

Population and food-supply, as we have seen, were in ancient days conditioned by one another. Once Athens had assured herself of a food-supply from abroad, she could afford to welcome immigrants. She did so gladly and without jealousy, for her statesmen were wise enough to know that all wealth is created by human brains and hands, and that every additional worker is likely to be an additional source of wealth. That indeed is one of the commonplaces of City State economists. The words of Pericles which we have placed at the head of this chapter find a constant echo in other writers. ' Themistocles,' says Diodorus, following some earlier historian, ' persuaded the people to grant the resident aliens and the craftsmen immunity from special burdens, so that many people might come to the city from all parts and that they might easily establish more crafts.' Attica, says the author of the *Ways and Means*, has many natural advantages : it has a mild climate, a favourable situation, and is specially fortunate in her marble-quarries and silver-mines : 'but

these may be added to, in the first place, by a careful handling of
our resident alien population. And for my part I can hardly conceive of a more splendid source of revenue than lies open to us in
this direction.' What does he mean by ' a careful handling ' ?
Not measures of exclusion or even of inspection, such as we are
used to at the present day, to maintain the standard of life or miti-
gate unfair competition, but steps ' to improve their goodwill ',
so that ' all people without a city of their own may aspire to the
status of an Athenian foreign resident, and thus further increase the
revenues of the city '. The Old Oligarch, writing in the early years
of the Peloponnesian War, expresses the same opinion in a still
more direct form. ' The city,' he says, ' stands in need of resident
aliens because of the multiplicity of her crafts and for the purpose
of her navy.' ' It is for this reason that we have established an
equality . . . between our resident aliens and full citizens.' The
breakdown of the old conception of the city as an exclusive
corporation could not be more bluntly stated. Under the new
economic régime Athens welcomes workers from all the world
and has adapted her institutions to their needs. Solon and Cleisthenes, Themistocles and Cimon, all contributed to the change,
until by the time of the Funeral Speech there was in Attica an
adult alien population of about 125,000, not very far short of the
numbers of the adult citizens and their women-folk.[1]

We have already met some of these immigrants, both free and
slave, working side by side with the citizens in many of the departments of the City State life. But we did not linger over them,
for in the ordinary city they were but an incidental feature. It
is only under the régime of a sea-power such as Athens that they
become a large and all-important element in the population. It
is to this point in our analysis, therefore, that it seemed natural
to reserve their fuller consideration, and especially the treatment
of that most puzzling and paradoxical phenomenon in Athenian
life, the institution of slavery.

The Old Oligarch provides a convenient starting-point for our
discussion, for, in his sweeping way, he makes a general statement which goes to the root of the whole matter. He states

[1] *Ways and Means*, ii. 1 ; Old Oligarch, i. 10–12 ; Diod. xi. 43. 3 ; also
Plut. *Sol.* 24 ; other refs. on pp. 178–9 above ; cf. also p. 399. I calculate the
adult slaves at 80,000 (well over three-quarters of the whole number), and
the adult Outlanders, men and women (rather fewer women), at 45,000.

categorically that Athens ' established a democratic equality '
between her citizen and her alien population, extending the
bearing of this statement not merely to free men but to
slaves.[1]

What does he mean ? With regard to the free Outlanders, who
numbered about a third of the settled alien population, his statement is not difficult to explain.

Not every foreigner who came to Athens acquired the status
of an Outlander or ' metic '. Many were simply birds of passage
who came for the trading season and left before the first storms.
To these Athens offered no special privileges. ' To be a metic
a man must have definitely fixed his domicile in a city, have
resided there for a stated time, and be a contributor to certain
public charges.' In other words, he must be not a passing trader
but a settler, and by preference a craftsman. For what Greek
cities desired, what Athens especially desired as her carrying-
trade increased, was craftsmen ; she needed them not merely to
meet the home needs of her increasing population, but to produce
goods for her ships to carry abroad on their summer rounds.
Athens never became, in our sense, a great industrial centre ;
most of the products manufactured in her little workshops and
' schools ' and studios were made for the home market. Still she
was now attempting to make her exports keep pace, so far as
possible, with the increase of her trade, and was sending out her
merchants and pioneers, not only with the wine and oil which
she had over in good years, but with clay jars to hold them, with
painted vases and statuettes, with shields and other forms of
metal work manufactured from imported raw material, with
silversmiths' work made from the mines at Laureion, and even
with flawless blocks of Pentelic marble for important statues in
foreign shrines. Such were the ' manufactured exports ' of fifth-
century Athens, a mere country town compared with the industrial centres of to-day, or even with cosmopolitan Hellenistic
centres like Alexandria, or with mediaeval Venice. Yet even
this she could not attain to without the importation of skilled
labour.[2]

[1] Old Oligarch, ii. 12.   The word is ἰσηγορία, the same that Herodotus uses
in his eulogy of Athenian free institutions, v. 78.

[2] Pentelic marble was used for the repairs to Phidias' pediment at Olympia
and for the metopes at the Heraeum of Argos.

These Outlanders were not full citizens, at least after the enforcement of the Law of 451. But they shared many of the privileges and responsibilities of citizens. They served in the army and in the navy, probably after a similar training ; they made the same free gifts or ' liturgies ' as the citizens, and paid the same income-tax in time of war, and in the same proportion. Their economic position too was much the same as that of the citizens. Although they were not allowed to own land (a disability which the author of the *Ways and Means* is anxious to remove), yet there were, as we know, at least a few cultivators among them. The majority became assimilated to the petty traders and craftsmen, and a small and wealthy minority ranked with the larger merchants and the rich nobility. As a class they had no special material interests of their own. They were neither, as some scholars have supposed, a rich and ambitious group of merchants nourishing sinister political designs, nor, as might have seemed more likely, a depressed and degraded class of immigrant labourers, such as some countries harbour to-day. Their social composition, in fact, made them a stable and harmonious element in Athenian life, and as such in the fifth century they are always represented ; ' neither burdensome nor in any way obnoxious to the city,' as King Adrastus says of the model metic in the *Supplices*, who finds his place there so fitly among a little gallery of Athenian portraits. Why, indeed, should they be ' obnoxious ' in such a city at such a time ? They were proud and glad to be there, even as outsiders, as we should be if we had the chance. For they had been attracted to the ' school of Greece ' not merely, we may be sure, by her policy of the ' open door ', but because they admired her ideals and were eager to co-operate in her institutions. Most of them, as we know from their gravestones, were not barbarians but Greeks, in a position to appreciate Athenian excellence, and ready, as converts always are, to be its most zealous upholders and missionaries. It is not difficult to see how ' an equality was established ' between such aliens and their citizen hosts. What needs explanation is rather why, through religion or petty jealousy, they were excluded from full citizenship.[1]

[1] Eur. *Supp.* 892. On metics see Wilamowitz in *Hermes*, 1887 (proving that they were demesmen) ; Clerc, *Les Métèques athéniens* (for points above see pp. 13, 25, 36, 382, 409–10) ; Francotte, *De la condition des étrangers dans*

But what of the slaves ? Were they, too, homogeneous in character and spirit with the free population, and ready to fall in with Athenian institutions and ideals. The Old Oligarch seems to think so, and he is the only contemporary authority who makes a direct statement on the subject. Here is the passage ; it is so full and vivid, and so agreeably ironical, that it does not bear condensation. ' Another point (about the Athenian democracy) is the extraordinary amount of licence granted to slaves and resident aliens at Athens, where a blow is illegal and a slave will not step aside to let you pass him in the street. I will explain the reason of this peculiar custom. Supposing it were legal for a slave to be beaten by a citizen, it would frequently happen that an Athenian might be mistaken for a slave or an alien and receive a beating ; since the Athenian people is not better clothed than the slave or alien, nor in personal appearance is there any superiority. Or if the fact itself that slaves in Athens are allowed to indulge in luxury, and indeed in some cases to live magnificently, be found astonishing, this too, it can be said, is done of set purpose. When you have a naval power dependent upon wealth, we must perforce be slaves to our slaves, in order that we may get in our slave-rents and let the real slave go free. Where you have wealthy slaves it ceases to be advantageous that my slave should stand in awe of you. In Lacedaemon my slave stands in awe of you. But if your slave stands in awe of me there will be a risk of his giving away his own moneys to avoid

---

les cités grecques (Louvain, 1903), on the different grades of privilege and immunity. On Outlanders as ' patrols' (περίπολοι) assisting the young citizen conscripts see Freeman, *Schools of Hellas*, pp. 215–16 and refs. ; e. g. Thuc. viii. 92. 2 together with Lys. xiii. 71 ; cf. Thuc. iv. 67. 2. Also Tod in *British School Annual*, vol. viii, pp. 197 ff., where note, on p. 205, that eight of the freedmen metics are classed as γεωργοί, ' farmers ' or ' farm-hands '. Plato and Aristotle prefer cities to be self-sufficient ; but they are both forced to admit that alien craftsmen are indispensable to ' the good life ', see *Pol.* 1326 a 20, and *Laws* 850, where Plato says that he will levy no alien tax beyond good behaviour. Theories of Athenian foreign policy based on a supposed diversity of interests between the citizens and alien populations seem to be wholly without foundation. The real distinction men felt was between the ' resident alien ' and the passing stranger (ξένος). Note how this is marked, for instance, in the *Oedipus Tyrannus*. Oedipus was (as was supposed) not Theban-born, but a metic, yet he is ' numbered a Theban among Thebans ' (l. 222 and Teiresias' taunt, l. 452). Cf. the roll of the dead in Dittenberger, No. 32, where the fallen are grouped into (i) Citizens arranged by tribes, (ii) Outlanders on the Army List (ἔγγραφοι), (iii) bowmen, i. e. probably mercenaries, (iv) strangers (ξένοι), i. e. troops from the Empire.

running a risk in his own person. It is for this reason, then, that we have established an equality between our slaves and free men.' [1]

Some of this needs further explanation ; but the main gist is clear. The slaves at Athens were so well treated, had become so integral a part of the life of the city, that they were indistinguishable in appearance from the citizens. Moreover, although we have always been taught that a slave is a thing, and a thing cannot possess another thing, the slaves at Athens were sometimes rich enough ' to indulge in luxury ', or ' to give away their own moneys ' in order to save their skins. And the reason why the slaves have to be well treated and to be allowed to become rich is not humanitarian but economic : it is because Athens needs wealth, and the slaves are wealth-producers, and will not produce wealth unless they are well treated.

Here is a very different theory of slave-labour from that which we have been accustomed to hear both from its assailants and its upholders. Slavery, as we read of it in Aristotle and in the writings of the Southern planters, is based upon a wholly different conception of slave-nature. ' The lower sort of mankind are by nature slaves,' says Aristotle, ' and it is better for them, as for all inferiors, that they should be under the rule of a master. For he who can be, and therefore is, the property of another, and he who participates in reason enough to apprehend, but not to have reason, is a slave by nature. Whereas the lower animals cannot even apprehend reason ; they obey their instincts. And indeed the use made of slaves and tame animals is not very different ; for both with their bodies minister to the needs of life.' To Aristotle and to the Southern planter the slave is halfway between free mankind and the animals, ' doomed in his own person and his posterity to live without knowledge and without the capacity to make anything his own, and to toil that another may reap the fruits.' To the fifth-century Athenian, if we may judge from the Old Oligarch, the slave is so much a man like himself that the best way to get good work out of him is to

---

[1] Old Oligarch, i. 10–12 (tr. Dakyns). The law alluded to is given in Dem. xxi. 47 and runs as follows :—' If any one commit a personal outrage upon man, woman, or child, whether free-born or slave, or commit any illegal act against any such person, let any Athenian that chooses, not being under disability, indict him before the judges.' Cf. Aeschin. *Tim.* 17.

allow him to become assimilated in spirit and appearance to the world of free men around him. ' In order that we may get in our slave-rents, we must perforce be slaves to our slaves, and *let the real slave go free.*' What is the explanation of this strange divergence of view ? [1]

The explanation is very simple. It is contained in the nature of the work which the slave is called upon to do. Where all that is required is the mere mechanical exertion of bodily power, the slave will be set to work like a machine, will be regarded by theorists as a machine, and will after no long interval be whipped and brutalized and stupefied into the miserable likeness of the dead implement he represents. Where, on the other hand, he is asked to do interesting and responsible and even artistic work, where a call is made upon his special gifts and on his natural ambition and enterprise, he is likely to develop into a valuable and active element in the working community, and to lead the theorists and apologists of his status into very different fields of argument. Broadly speaking, in fact, there are two different theories of slavery because there are two different kinds of slave-work and therefore two different kinds of slave. Athens harboured both kinds within her borders, so it is necessary to examine them somewhat closely. But first it would be well to deal briefly with the institution of slavery in general, for there is no department of Greek life on which so much confusion of thought prevails.

We have been taught to regard slavery, at all times and in all forms, as something peculiarly wrong and unnatural. If we are to understand the place of slavery in Greek life, and the Greek attitude towards it, we must cast aside this modern view. Or rather we must ascend, with the Greeks for our guide, to a higher and more philosophic level of thought. All labour-systems,

---

[1] Ar. *Pol.* 1254 b. The other quotation is from the celebrated judgement of Judge Ruffin of North Carolina, given in Cairnes' *Slave-Power*, p. 385. See also pp. 390 ff. for a paper on ' The Philosophy of Secession ', from the *Charleston Mercury* of Feb. 13, 1861, which is a most eloquent statement of the Aristotelian ideal of a slave-society ' proportioned with labour and direction, mind and matter in just relation to one another, presenting analogy to the very highest developments in animated nature. . . . The ship of state has the ballast of a disfranchised class : there is no possibility of political upheaval, therefore, and it is reasonably certain that, so steadied, it will sail erect and onward to an indefinitely distant period '. The social philosophy here embodied is not confined to slave-states.

after all, do no more than regulate relations between human
beings or groups of human beings. We have no right to pass
judgement on them till we have looked at them in this broader
light, till we have seen what human relations they involve,
what will be the spirit and morale of the human beings affected
by them. Hale the labour-systems of the world before this
tribunal, and slavery will not find itself the only or even the most
heinous offender. It is always wrong, the judge will say, for
men to oppress or exploit or overwork one another, to treat one
another as though they had only bodies and no souls. Any
system of labour which is organized on the assumption that man
is no more than one among many other machines and implements, and is to be treated accordingly, is inhuman and unnatural : it does violence, that is, to the true nature of man. But
whether this wrong takes place, to a greater extent than elsewhere, under systems of slavery, is a matter, not for inherited
belief or dogmatic assertion, but for careful and detailed
analysis.[1]

The Greeks, at any rate, did not share our modern view.
Slavery to them, so far from being unnatural, was part of the
order of nature. So far back as they knew there had always
been slaves in Greece. Master and man was to them no more
abnormal a relation than husband and wife or father and child.
In the Epic and the Tragedy, in the Bible of Greek institutions,

---

[1] The question of conditions of work is not simply a legal one. Slavery in
the broader sense of the term, i. e. treating labourers as soulless instruments,
cannot be abolished by legal enactments : it is a matter for moral forces, for
corporate feeling and opinion. In this sense, the question of slavery will
always be with us, so long as the abuse of power remains a natural human
temptation. But there remains a large sphere open to the activities of the
anti-slavery reformer, if he will consent to recognize the inadequacy of the
narrow legal definition of slavery. In the tropics, as Nevinson says in connexion with the contracted wage-labourers on the Portuguese cocoa islands
(and the remark applies equally to the free tax-payers of the Congo), ' the
whole thing will have to be faced anew, for the solutions of our grandfathers
no longer satisfy.' But so it needs to be faced anew under our more complicated industrial system at home, where exploitation can take a thousand
shapes, as any one familiar with working-class conditions knows only too well.
Sometimes it startles us by revealing itself in forms that bear a striking
resemblance to ancient conditions. ' A slave's pay is his food,' says the
author of the Aristotelian *Economics* (δούλῳ μισθὸς τροφή). There are many
modern workers, agricultural labourers, shop-assistants and others, who are
still paid largely in truck, like the slaves of ancient Greece. The chief difference
between them is that it was to the ancient employer's interest to pay them
enough to keep well on, because he bore the cost of replacement.

the slave has his place in the household, and no man dreams of blaming a master for using slaves' services without reward. To own and utilize slaves was not regarded by the Greek as a crime or as a moral offence or even as an incongruity; it was too much a part of the old world in which his society had grown up. Yet, for all the schooling of use and wont, it did not leave his sensibility quite untouched, for, unlike the modern large employer or shareholder, he had most of his living instruments close at hand, and not removed beyond the possibility of a direct appeal to the senses. So what was no sin in the master was seen, and therefore felt, to be a misfortune for the man, and the public conscience of Greece, which refused to reproach the slave-owner, yet felt pity for the slave. The literature of Greece, from Homer to Euripides and beyond him, is full of the pathos of captivity— of the cry of the strong man who, by enslavement, has lost ' half his manhood', and of the women and children whom he is help· less to protect from shame and insult. The real horror in Greek warfare, the great dread that loomed behind that glorious and exciting tournament, was the lifelong imprisonment that might await the unhappy survivors of the vanquished. Greek poets and teachers, who loved to dwell on the mutability of human things, never allowed this fear to grow dim in the minds of their public. The fifth-century Athenian, with slaves about him to help in his daily business, listened with a thrill to the story of Hecuba or Andromache or Iphigenia, and returned home from the theatre, not yet critical or resentful of the institution of slavery, but resolved to be kinder and more patient with the uncouth young barbarians who, by some strange sport of heaven, now formed part of his own household. For there still rang in his ears, as a solemn and lasting reminder, the final words of the chorus as they moved slowly off the stage :

> There be many shapes of mystery
> And many things God makes to be
> Past hope or fear.
> And the end man looked for cometh not,
> And a path is there where no man thought,
> So hath it fallen here ;

and when he felt inclined to break out against the petty thieving of the Thracian maidservant or against the incorrigible clumsiness of that young mischief-maker Xanthias, ' There,' he felt, ' but for the grace of the high gods goest thou.' [1]

But it is time to return to the economics of slave-work and to the consideration of our two classes.

Most of the slaves at Athens were imported barbarians, for it did not pay, on the whole, to breed slaves in the city itself. They had been kidnapped or taken prisoners up country, in Thrace, or Asia Minor, or Syria, or Dalmatia, and were brought to Piraeus for sale with the rest of the trader's stock. Let us follow up their careers when they have passed into the slave-merchant's hands. [2]

His first business will be to analyse the quality of his goods and to gauge their suitability for different kinds of work. He must discover which of his purchases can be induced or trained to work willingly, and which are too dangerous, or too sullen, or too weak, or too stupid to become more than brute manual workers, under strict supervision. Some of these last he may succeed in getting ransomed ; some of them will probably not survive very long ; most of the remainder will go to the silver mines, whither we cannot follow them at present. He will be left with a pack of reasonably docile pieces of property. The men of fighting age will have perished or been disposed of ; and the females, though probably a little older, on the average, than the males, will few of them be beyond the prime of life ; for there is no market for old women. This is the group of new-comers or freshmen who are now to be initiated into the working life of the city, to be trained as craftsmen or dealers or household workers or entertainers for their master's profit. [3]

---

[1]
        Πολλαὶ μορφαὶ τῶν δαιμονίων,
        πολλὰ δ' ἀέλπτως κραίνουσι θεοί·
        καὶ τὰ δοκηθέντ' οὐκ ἐτελέσθη,
        τῶν δ' ἀδοκήτων πόρον ηὗρε θεός.
        τοιόνδ' ἀπέβη τόδε πρᾶγμα.

             Bacchae 1388, transl. Murray ; cf. *Medea* 1415.
There is no trace in the fifth century of Aristotle's idea that slavery is good for the slave. That is simply a fourth-century defence, put up to stay the criticism of a sceptical age. The fifth-century Greeks did not criticize slavery, but they often felt sorry for their slaves. So it is to-day with a labour-system which is in some ways equally barbarous. An employer who reduces his staff in bad times does not criticize the industrial system, but he often feels sorry for the men he dismisses. But, like the slave-master, he feels powerless. The famous Homeric lines on slavery are *Od.* xvii. 322-3. [See Appendix.]

[2] See list of slaves, called by the land of their origin, in the household of a rich Outlander, given in Hicks and Hill, pp. 145-6.

[3] The Greek formula after the sack of a city is : ' They killed the grown

How will they be trained ?   In the true Greek way, by a process of persuasion rather than of compulsion.   They will not merely be taught to do their work but taught to take an interest in it. For the services they are required to perform are too varied and difficult, even where they are not artistic, to be learnt by a process of drill or driving.

It is here that the career of the ordinary Greek slave diverges from that of the living instrument on a tropical plantation. Picture the two scenes, and the difference is clear at a glance. ' It was a long line of men and women,' says Nevinson, ' extended at intervals of about a yard, like a company of infantry going into action.   They were clearing a coffee plantation.   Bent double over the work, they advanced slowly across the ground, hoeing it up as they went. . . . Five or six yards behind, like the officers of a company under fire, stood the overseers or gangers or drivers of the party. . . . Each carried an eight-foot stick of hard wood, pointed at the ends, and the look of those sticks quite explained the thoroughness and persistency of the work, as well as the silence, so unusual among the natives whether at work or play.' Very different this from the free and easy life in the stoneyard or the workshop or the market-place, or even from the manifold daily round of indoor domestic service.   On the tropical plantation fear is the only motive required, and physical compulsion the only stimulus applied.   But once outside the horsewhip range and man, as Plato remarks, is ' a troublesome piece of goods '. The Greek slave-master, however merciless he may wish to be, cannot rule his household simply by fear ; the work is not sufficiently mechanical, and the supervision would be too costly and irksome.   He is driven by the logic of the situation to supply his slaves with some other motive.   For the plantation slave, remember, there is, this side of the grave, nothing to be gained by working, either for himself or his family.   There is only something extra to be suffered by being idle.   It is the Greek slave-master's business, as it is of the modern employer, to make his labourers *want* to work.   He must make them feel that there is some purpose in their labours.   So he will gradually learn to

men and enslaved the children and women ' : Thuc. v. 32 and 116, iii. 36. 2 ; cf. Polyb. iii. 86. 11.   There seem to have been few *Greek* slaves at Athens itself, though no doubt they were not uncommon in Greek slave-markets. Plato himself is said to have been kidnapped and ransomed on one occasion.

lay aside (except in emergencies) the dull compelling scourge, and to make his appeal to a worthier or, at the worst, a steadier class of motives—to hope or ambition or interest or rivalry or even, if he is a good teacher, to personal affection or the true spirit of art.[1]

From this initial difference of motive-power all the other results follow. The crucial fact about a slave, in the planter's sense of the word, is that he has within his own breast no motive for working, or indeed for living at all, because he himself and all that he produces belong to another. A slave who has, somehow or other, been given some personal motive for working, and has thereby recovered some glimmering of hope and of self-respect, is an entirely different being. Both morally and economically he occupies a different position in the community. He belongs indeed to a new class of labourer, who is far more closely allied to the wage-earners and craftsmen above him in the economic scale than to the brutes and chattel-slaves beneath him. It is a long step upwards from a position as a slave-assistant in a barber's shop in the Piraeus to manumission and citizenship ; but for the economist it is the first step on the ladder, the intro-duction of a new class of motives for labour, which is all-impor-tant. A slave who will work without direct compulsion is serving his apprenticeship for freedom.

How did the Athenian slave-master persuade his slaves to work ? What steps did he take to restore them their self-respect? Our fifth-century evidence is too scanty to enable us to give a detailed answer to this question. Broadly speaking, two lines of policy were open. It was possible so to assimilate the slave into the family that he ceased to be conscious of the humiliation of his status and was proud, like a faithful servant, to work for his master till he died. That was the old Homeric method, which produced Eumaeus the swineherd and Eurycleia the family nurse ; and it lived on, with the household tradition, into the wider world of the fifth century. But, with the great influx of slave-immigrants in the period with which we are dealing, other

---

[1] Nevinson, *A Modern Slavery*, pp. 33–4 ; Plato, *Laws* 777 (δυσκολόν ἐστι τὸ θρέμμα ἄνθρωπος), a passage which shows how thoroughly Plato recognized the unity of human nature and the absurdity of dividing off mankind into two separate classes. But, in the *Laws* at any rate, he accepts the division into free and slave as fundamental and tries to make the best of it.

means became more common ; and it became generally recognized among thoughtful men that the most satisfactory way of supplying a slave with an adequate motive for working was to offer him the prospect of ultimate freedom—of being assimilated, that is, to the free alien population. This method, we know, was early adopted in Athens, for among the aliens admitted by Cleisthenes to the citizenship in 507 a certain number were ex-slaves. From that time onwards there must always have been a considerable freedmen population in Athens. It is apt to escape our notice, because the name is seldom mentioned. A freedman ranked as an Outlander, and once he had secured his rights no one raised the question of his origin. It was part of the Athenian tradition of hospitality to let bygones be bygones, and even in the excitement of the law-courts the curtain was seldom raised on a freedman's past. The great fourth-century Athenian banker Pasion, one of the richest and most public-spirited men in Athens, began life as a slave ; every one in Athens must have known it, but it might have remained hidden from us but for a phrase that slips out in a speech. ' Who are you,' cries his son, in an action against another freedman, ' that you should inquire into my father's origin ? Who would not have been indignant at such usage, men of Athens ? ' We do not know Pasion's origin, whether he was ' born in the house ' or was one of those ' Lydians and Phrygians and Syrians and other barbarians from all parts ' who, according to the author of the *Ways and Means*, formed so noticeable a part of the resident alien population. His name conceals his nationality ; but, whatever it was, he represents what was a numerous and important class in fifth- and fourth-century Athens.

That to hold out the prospect of liberty as an inducement to labour was an expedient in common use seems clear from the consensus of opinion among Greek economists upon the subject. Plato is the only writer who is content to recommend the old-fashioned fatherly method of treatment. To him it seemed sufficient that slaves should be treated kindly but firmly, as in the good old days, ' not admonished as if they were freemen, which will only make them conceited'. Even Aristotle recognized that these conservative methods provided no satisfactory solution for the servant-problem of his day. Though he must have felt that it ran counter to the whole of the rest of his slave-theory, he boldly broaches the question of freedom. ' It is expedient,' he tells us, ' that liberty should always be held out to slaves as a reward of their services.' He pledges himself indeed to further discussion of the subject, but in our text of the *Politics* this is not forthcoming. But we have a more valuable testimony—his own last will and testament. To five out of his thirteen slaves he bequeathed the gift of freedom. The more practical Xenophon had been forced to the same conclusion, though he expresses it less explicitly : ' Slaves,' he says, ' need to be filled with good hopes even more than free men, in order to keep them at their posts ' ; while the author of the Aristotelian *Economics* goes further even than Aristotle and says : ' Slaves are willing to take trouble when freedom is the prize and the time is fixed.' In other words, he advises his readers to make a definite arrangement with their slaves, pledging them their freedom after a definite term of years (or a definite contingency, such as the death of the master), rather than to keep them in a state of suspense and uncertainty. Finally, to come back within the strict limits of our period, we have the Old Oligarch's statement that it is dangerous to intimidate an Athenian slave because ' there will be a risk of his giving away his own moneys to avoid running a risk in his own person ' : that is, of his paying blackmail to an outsider to the detriment of his master's interest, or even perhaps of his demanding to buy his freedom out of his savings in order to escape ill-treatment. All this shows us not only— what we know sufficiently from other sources—that slaves at Athens were commonly allowed to possess money of their own, but suggests that the thought which was constantly in their minds as they were earning it was the ultimate purchase of their freedom. We hardly need the evidence. To slaves and prisoners at all times liberty, even liberty to starve, has loomed in the distance as the only good. Fifth-century Athens was surely no exception to this rule.[1]

[1] Dem. xlv. 81–2 (Pasion : cf. Is. xvii for his earlier life, which is vaguely described, § 22, as ' humble ') ; *Ways and Means* ii. 3 ; Plato, *Laws* 777 : in 915 he recognizes that he *must* provide for freedmen, and lays down the significant condition that they are not to be richer than their former masters. Ar. *Pol.* 1275 b 36, 1330 a 32 ; Diog. Laert. v. 1. 9 (Aristotle's will : his three successors at the Lyceum increased the proportion of manumissions. The

The material resources of Athens, then, were not built up, as
is so often said, on a foundation of slave-labour. They were

first freed five out of nine, the second four out of six, the third eleven out of
twelve). Xen. *Oec.* v. 16 ; [Ar.] *Oec.* 1344 b 15 : the whole discussion of
slavery here is full of valuable hints and suggestions. On pocket-money see
Menander, *Hero,* ll. 1–10 (Teubner), where one slave offers to look after
another's nest-egg if he has got into trouble and is to be chained and sent to the
mill (the usual threat) as a punishment. Unfortunately our detailed inscrip-
tional evidence about manumission is almost all of it later than the fifth
century. This seems to be partly accidental, as Calderini, who has collected it,
holds that the few inscriptions which have survived from the fifth century
show that manumission had by then become common in Greece. See his
La Manomissione e la condizione dei liberti in Grecia (Milan, 1908), p. 18. But
it was partly also due to the general softening of manners and the increasing
tendency to feel uncomfortable about the institution of slavery. On this
point see Ciccotti, *Il Tramonto della schiavitù nel mondo antico,* Turin, 1899,
esp. pp. 118 ff. There are some interesting details about these later manumission contracts in Francke, *de manumissionibus Delphicis* (Münster, 1904).
Two forms of contract are specially interesting. One is that which stipulates
for ' living-in ' (παραμονή), i.e. the slave is set free but remains indentured to
his master, sometimes for a fixed period varying from two to ten years,
sometimes until the whole of the purchase-money has been paid off by instal-
ments. There are all kinds of special stipulations in such cases, e. g. that
if the freedman fall ill his period of service be correspondingly lengthened
to make up for the loss of time, that in case of dispute arbitrators be called
in to settle the terms of the contract, that if a child be born to him during
the time of service he be at liberty either to strangle it (εἴ κα μὲν θέλη ἀπο νεῖξαι
ἐξουσίαν ἐχέτω) or to bring it up as a free person, &c. The other form of
contract (mostly dating from about 170 B. C.) is that by which the slave takes
over his master's debts in return for the gift of freedom. This happened
when a master had raised money on mortgage on the security of a rich slave.
Another interesting fact revealed by the Delphic inscriptions is that the
initial prices paid for slaves are considerably lower than the sums paid by
the slaves to redeem themselves. The former vary between one and three
minas, the latter between three and five. So it will be seen that the slave-
masters made their slaves pay dear for the one thing they wanted—Freedom.
Sometimes they are even required to replace themselves by training a slave-
craftsman to do their old work. Now that the evidence has been collected
by Calderini, the whole question of this intermediate status between slavery
and freedom deserves careful inquiry by an economist who is also a lawyer.
See my own very tentative articles in the *Sociological Review* (Jan. and Apr.,
1909), in the first of which I attempted a rough analysis of the wage-earning
form of slavery, and added a translation of a typical manumission contract.
A good selection of these is given in Dittenberger, Nos. 835 ff. Slave-names
are interesting as revealing the kind of sentiment that existed between master
and slave. Appended to the *Dialektinschriften* (vol. iv, pp. 311–17) is an index
of the slave-names in the Delphic inscriptions, beginning with Ἀβροσύνα
(' Delicacy ') and ending with Ὠφελίων (' Little Helper '). So named, they
would hardly know themselves for Syrians or Phrygians. They had entered
upon the novitiate of Hellenism. Cf. Dem. *de Cor.* 131, where he accuses
Aeschines of improving the names of his parents. See also Wilamowitz,
A. A., vol. ii, pp. 175–9. The only names forbidden to an Athenian slave
were Harmodius and Aristogeiton, because of their associations with liberty—
a very characteristic rule ; see Aulus Gellius, *Noctes Atticae* ix. 2. Very
interesting, too, if we had space to deal with them, are the public slaves

built up through the centuries by a society consisting mainly
of free workers ; and it was only late in her history, when the
structure of her civilization became too heavy to be sustained
by their own unaided efforts, that slaves and free immigrants
crowded in to co-operate in the task. And these she treated in
most cases, not as mere living instruments, but as 'fellow workers'
with her citizens and ' free partners in the Empire '. So we may
clear the name of Athens from one cruel reproach which has
clung to it ever since the human conscience began to concern
itself with these questions. Greek democracy, we have often
been told, was rendered possible by the leisure of a population
of slave-owners. Greek physical beauty is connected with their
distaste for manual labour ; and Greek art and literature and
philosophy owe their growth and savour to men's enviable
freedom from practical cares and preoccupations. Greek civilization, in a word, with all its wealth of thrilling achievement, is
inseparably associated with conscious cruelty and injustice ; and
we can never recapture for our own communities the spirit and
temper of that heroic time because modern man would not
tolerate its barbarous and indispensable concomitants. All this
is false, false in its interpretation of the past and in its confident
pessimism as to the future, wilfully false, above all, in its cynical
estimate of human nature. Societies, like men, cannot live in
compartments. They cannot hope to achieve greatness by making
amends in their use of leisure for the lives they have brutalized
in acquiring it. Art, literature, philosophy, and all other great
products of a nation's genius, are no mere delicate growths of
a sequestered hothouse culture; they must be sturdily rooted,
and find continual nourishment, in the broad common soil of

employed, sometimes in responsible positions, by the State or at sanctuaries.
The *Ion* of Euripides is an excellent example of the type. He sweeps the
temple courts and lives on the offerings of strangers ; but he is also steward
of the temple treasures, and enjoys a full measure of ' what is dearest to
man's heart, leisure '. He performs these manifold functions, which he is
unwilling to surrender for life as a Prince at Athens, with all the tact and
discretion of a modern verger or college porter. See ll. 54, 102, 323, 517 ff.,
esp. 544 (tact), 634 ff. On State slaves see Waszynski, *De servis Atheniensium
publicis* (Berlin, 1898), and, esp. on their legal position, his article in *Hermes*,
vol. xxxiv, pp. 553 ff., where he points out how much independence they
enjoyed : ' although each of these ὑπηρέται ' (γραμματεῖς, &c.), ' as a State
Servant, had an ἀρχή ' (Magistrate or Minister) ' over him, in private life he
was more or less his own master ', like our own Permanent Civil Servants.
[See Appendix.]

national life.   That, if we are looking for lessons, is one we might
learn from ancient Greece.[1]

[1] See Athenaeus, vi, p. 265 (from Theopompus), on the introduction of
bought slaves into Greece. The influx did not begin on a large scale till
States could afford to buy and keep them.   As Ure remarks (*J. H. S.* xxvi,
p. 135), the age of the tyrants was still an age of free labour.   See also Meyer's
two pamphlets, *Die wirtschaftliche Entwickelung des Altertums* (1895) and
Die Sklaverei im Altertum (1898), reprinted in his *Kleine Schriften* (1910),
which gave the *coup de grâce* to the old view of slavery as the foundation of
Greek life.   For an eloquent if somewhat extreme statement of this view see
Paterson's *The Nemesis of Nations*, who has tried to think out, with more
imaginative effort than the writers he follows, the implications contained in
their doctrine.

CHAPTER XVI

IMPERIAL ECONOMICS : THE SILVER MINES

The Persian Queen : Καὶ τί πρὸς τούτοισιν ἄλλο ; πλοῦτος ἐξαρκὴς δόμοις ;
Chorus : ἀργύρου πηγή τις αὐτοῖς ἐστι, θησαυρὸς χθονός.

AESCHYLUS, *Persae* 237–8.

And what else have they besides ? Is there sufficing wealth in their homes ?
They have of silver, as one might say, a spring ; a treasury in the earth.

tr. HEADLAM.

THEMISTOCLES and Pericles relied for the perpetuation of
Athenian power and influence upon the development of her resources as a trading and industrial centre. We have now briefly
examined most of these. But one still remains to be treated.

The slave-merchant landing at Piraeus with a cargo of barbarian captives sold off most of them at good prices into households and workshops. But some of his victims were by condition
or temperament not fitted for such uses. They were goods of a
lower quality, cross-grained or vicious or in some way unteach-
able. Why then did he trouble to transport them oversea ?
Because Athens had discovered a special use for this by-product
of slave-raiding. When the first auction was over, the dealer collected the base remnants for whom no master and teacher had
been found, and sold them off at cheaper rates to owners who
had no need for good character, or willingness, or intelligence, or
physical beauty, or indeed for anything more than mere vigorous
arms and legs. Within a few days or hours they would find
themselves being driven in a herd to work as living instruments
in the silver mines at Laureion.[1]

[1] We possess no account of a fifth-century slave auction. But the difference in quality between mine-slaves and ordinary slaves is clear from the
way in which the former are spoken of, e.g. in *Ways and Means* iv ; cf.
Strabo, 562 (describing some mines near Sinope : ' They were worked with
condemned criminals ' (τοῖς ἀπὸ κακουργίας ἀγοραζομένοις ἀνδραπόδοις) : the
various words for slave, ἀνδράποδον (' manfoot,' ' captive ') and σῶμα (' body ')
on the one hand and οἰκέτης (' house-slave ') and παῖς (' boy ') on the other,
suggest this distinction of quality, but they were often loosely used. Cavaignac
notes (pp. 172–3) that, amid the general rise in the prices of all commodities
in fifth-century Athens, slave-prices alone seem to show a decline. The

Athenians had always known that a possible source of wealth for their city lay in the silver and lead deposits in the extreme corner of their peninsula. But in earlier days they had done little to develop them. Free men refused to work underground, and slaves they could not afford to procure in sufficient numbers. Moreover, the location and tapping of the deposits was a troublesome and disheartening task, for they are so disposed as to baffle a community lacking in systematic knowledge or experience. Even in the fourth century the exploiter who sank a shaft still ran the risk of 'drawing a blank and losing the whole of the sum expended'. In the sixth, it appears, there were not sufficient Athenians of enterprise who had any large sum to lose. The Greek world still relied for its precious metals mainly upon the mines of Siphnos and Thasos.[1]

But in 483, towards the close of the short respite between Marathon and Salamis, the whole outlook changed. The Athenians tumbled suddenly, perhaps by accident, upon a new and very profitable vein of ore : it was found at a spot called Maronea, which is probably to be identified with what is still the most productive deposit in the district. There was a rush to the mines ; every one who had money in hand and slaves fit for use hired a concession from the State; and by the end of the year, if we may trust our authorities, the city found herself in possession of a windfall of at least fifty talents from mining royalties, apart from the profits that were being made by the exploiters themselves.[2]

---

reason is that there was now a use for a cheaper article which had scarcely been put on the market before. This affected not only mine-slaves but all slaves, for the use found for the by-product cheapened the general cost of production. Slave-raiders and dealers always have to make allowance for a very large wastage ; but this must have been considerably diminished by the demand for mine-slaves. As to prices, we hear of 200 drachmas as a normal sixth-century ransom (Hdt. v. 77), while at a household auction at Athens in 415 the average price for men is 166 drachmas and for women 170 (£33 4s. and £34) : the author of the *Ways and Means* calculates in 355 that mine-slaves could be bought at 158 drachmas each, and Demosthenes (xxxvii. 4) speaks of a transaction in which mine-slaves fetch 150 each.

[1] *Ways and Means*, iv. 29 ; Cavaignac, p. 9 (the deposits) ; Hdt. iii. 57 (Siphnos), vi. 46 (Thasos and its mainland) ; cf. i. 64, where we learn that Pisistratus relied on Attic as well as these Thracian resources. But Ure (*J. H. S.* xxvi, pp. 135 ff.) is wrong in thinking they were largely worked. Solon, xii. 49, refers to metal-work not mining, ard the Mountaineers (διάκριοι) were certainly not miners.

[2] The two texts are Hdt. vii. 144 and *Ath. Pol.* xxii. 7. The latter puts the State's windfall at 100 talents, the former at 10 drachmas a head. As

What was to be done with this enormous sum ?   According to
the traditions of Greek finance there was only one possible answer.
It must be divided among the citizens.   They had shared the
city's evil days, contributing willingly out of their scanty resources to supply her needs.   Now that she had lighted on prosperity it was *her* turn to be generous.   Greek cities were accustomed to live from hand to mouth, like their citizens.   In this case
especially, where the windfall was not merely a surprise donation
but appeared likely to recur and increase year by year, there
seemed no need to be saving.   The calculation was quickly made.
Fifty talents among 30,000 would be 10 drachmas a head ; and
so, in ordinary times and under ordinary leaders, it would have
been spent.

But Athens had not only found a treasure, she had found a
treasurer.   Themistocles, who was at that moment her leading
statesman, realized the potentialities of the situation and refused
to see the money dispersed.   He persuaded his fellow citizens to
spend it instead in bringing up the strength of their navy to two
hundred ships; and it was this fleet which three years later saved
Greece and Europe at Salamis.   Henceforward no more proposals
were made to spend the annual surplus in the old-fashioned way.
Athens had entered upon a new era, both in finance and in policy.
With the influx of slaves which followed the war, the work of
developing the mines, temporarily interrupted by the Persian
invasion, was continued with renewed activity ; and by the
beginning of the Peloponnesian War it is calculated that, out of
less than 100,000 slaves in Attica, some 20,000 were employed
there either above or below ground.   Let us watch them at work.[1]

Hdt. elsewhere (v. 79) calculates the citizen-population at 30,000, the windfall
would, on his reckoning, only amount to 50 talents, a figure which Cavaignac
accepts as the normal annual state revenue from the mines.   We have no
means of estimating the total annual production, as we do not know what
terms the city made with the concessionaries.   Cf. also Aesch. *Eum.* 947.

[1] For slave numbers cf. p. 177 above.   I follow Cavaignac (p. 172), who is
unwilling to exceed 100,000, and calculate as follows for the year 431 :—

Total number in Attica	90,000	
Mine-slaves (adult males only)	20,000	
Other slaves	70,000	
divided into—		
Adult males		35,000
Adult females		25,000
Children		10,000

But these calculations are highly conjectural.

The industry at Laureion consisted of two parts, the extraction of the ore and its carrying, crushing, and grinding above ground. The underground work was entirely in the hands of slaves, who were thus altogether cut off from the society of free men. The work was carried on either in shafts and pits or in galleries. Some 2,000 shafts and 80 to 100 miles of galleries have been discovered. The shafts are generally deep, in some cases as deep as 250 feet; the sides are smooth and almost vertical, with ledges for ladders, and the expert who has examined them calculates that, with two workmen to each shaft, they would be dug out at a rate of 16 feet per month. But most of the work was done in galleries. These galleries are winding, following the vein of the ore, and were kept very narrow, partly to save the trouble of propping, partly to obtain quick results. They are generally 2–3 feet high and 2–3 feet broad; ventilation was provided by occasional airshafts. As the galleries were quite dark the miners worked with small clay lamps, for which niches were made in the rock; these remained alight for ten hours, and almost certainly marked the length of the daily shift. It is calculated that a workman could dig out about 12 yards of rock in a month of daily shifts. They worked in chains and almost naked, and were branded with their master's stamp. In order to increase the rate of production work was continued without interruption night and day.[1]

It will be noticed at once how very closely this labour-system corresponds to the conditions with which we have already become acquainted on the tropical plantations. Unskilled underground mining is in fact a class of work which lends itself most conveniently to the perfect form of chattel-slavery. All that is required of the slave is a vigorous body, and sufficient of that lower kind of reason which, Aristotle tells us, is necessary to understand a spoken command : all that is required of the master is watchful and drastic supervision, or sufficient capital to provide efficient overseers to do this for him. The work is mechanical, unchanging, practically inexhaustible, and entirely unskilled. The

---

[1] For details see Ardaillon, *Les Mines du Laurion dans l'antiquité*, and the same author in Daremberg, s.v. *Metalla* ; also Paterson, *The Nemesis of Nations*, pp. 190 ff. For other accounts of ancient mining see Diod. iii. 13–14, v. 36–8, which attracted the attention of Marx (*Capital*, English transl., p. 219), who detected how rare such economic conditions were in antiquity.

workers are almost stationary in their places and can be chained without interfering with their efficiency. They work with only the roughest tools and appliances. The work does not involve disease (which would mean loss of capital), but is yet sufficiently exhausting to lower the vitality and so make it likely that death will follow closely upon the failure of working power. It is carried on in a number of separate pits and galleries underground, under conditions where the amount of work performed can easily be measured and tested, and where the task of supervision is extraordinarily simple and inexpensive. The overseer (generally a trusted superior slave) could probably look after the entire property of a considerable mine-owner or concessionaire. Above all, it is expended in production of silver, almost the only article for which there can be said to have been an international market and an unlimited demand.[1]

Thus Athens was gradually learning, even in the industrial sphere, to break with her old traditions. She was employing a new class of labour for a new class of product ; and she was using the one, as she was producing the other, wholesale, as we use and produce the labour and the goods of to-day. Shields and sheepskins and oil-flasks, like the craftsmen and their ' boys ' who made them, had an individuality of their own; but the owls that issued from Laureion and found their way through the Aegean were all made alike, and each bore stamped on its surface, like the brand on the slaves who mined its ore, the mark of a driving industrialism. There are still many owls on our museum shelves, but their makers have left us no message. We only know that in the crisis of the great war, when their old comrades in Athens were ready to die fighting on shipboard by their masters, the sullen crowds at Laureion felt no touch of the same spirit ; they

---

[1] Nicias paid one talent for a skilled overseer (Xen. *Mem.* ii. 5. 2). He would hardly have paid so large a sum if he had needed several : cf. Ar. *Pol.* 1255 b 35. The old are always a difficulty in a chattel-slave system. Cato, that most ruthless of economists, recommends that they shall be sold off with the other old implements for what they will fetch—' sell the old oxen the worn-out sheep and other animals, fleeces, hides, carts, implements, any old slave or diseased slave or any other waste that remains over ' (' boves vetulos, armenta delicula, oves deliculas, lanam, pelles, plostrum vetus, ferramenta vetera, servum senem, servum morbosum et siquid aliut supersit vendat '—*De Agric.* ii. 7). No Greek at any age could have written so stonily merciless a sentence as this. For a more detailed analysis of chattel-slavery see Cairnes' *Slave-power* ; also the *Sociological Review,* 1909, pp. 4–5.

only saw in the crisis an opportunity of escaping in their thousands
to what they hoped might prove an easier servitude. For the rest,
we can only imagine from modern instances what their life must
have been like. 'The doctor had come up to pay his official
visit,' writes Nevinson, in his account of that Portuguese paradise.
' " The death-rate here," he remarked, casually, during the meal,
"is twelve or fourteen per cent. among the labourers." "And what
is the chief cause," I asked. "Anaemia," he said. " That is a vague
sort of thing," I answered; "what brings on anaemia ? " " Unhappiness," he said, frankly.' That same vague disease, we may be
sure, thinned the ranks at Laureion day by day. Did their
Athenian masters when *their* turn came to die of exposure and
of broken hopes in the quarries of Syracuse think of the souls
they had sent to the same living death at home ? Surely not.
If they thought of their slaves at all it was to curse heaven for
the injustice which repaid their kindness so ill. When Nicias
their general was cruelly tortured and put to death by the victorious Syracusans, ' thus,' says Thucydides, ' died a man who of
all the Greeks in my time least deserved so miserable an end,
seeing that his conduct had always been directed with the strictest
attention to the recognized virtues of life.' Yet, this very Nicias,
the son of Niceratus, so we learn from a tell-tale writer, ' owned
a thousand men in the silver mines.' Such are the ironies of
industrialism.[1]

[1] Thuc. vii. 86. 5 (cf. Classen's note on νενομισμένην, which is not ironical) ;
Ways and Means, iv. 14, cf. 25, 43–4, on the effect of the Decelean war on
the mines ; Xen. *Mem*. ii. 5. 2 ; Thuc. vii. 27. 5 (where χειροτέχναι must refer
to mine-slaves : Thucydides, being a mine-owner himself, does not differentiate them from other workers : cf. iv. 105. 1, and vi. 91. 7, where their
desertion is foreshadowed ; the slaves inside the walls could not get away) ;
Hellenica Oxyrhynchia, xii. 4 (the runaway slaves glutted the market at
Thebes) ; slaves on shipboard : Xen. *Hell*. i. 6. 24 ; list of fallen in *I. G*. ii.
959 ; Nevinson, *A Modern Slavery*, p. 190. With the last named compare
J. K. Turner, *Barbarous Mexico* (London, 1911), who states that employers
of labour on the hemp-plantations of Yucatan estimate the death-rate among
their labourers at 66 per cent. per annum, and on the tobacco-plantations of
Valle Nacional in Oaxaca at 100 per cent. per annum (pp. 12, 63 ff.).

CHAPTER XVII

IMPERIAL ECONOMICS : FINANCE

'Ωνητὴ ἡ 'Αθηναίων δύναμις μᾶλλον ἢ οἰκεία.—The Corinthians in THUCY-
DIDES; i. 121. 3.

The power of Athens rests on money rather than on native strength.

IF Athens was to fulfil her ideals she needed adequate wealth.
We have now examined, one by one, the various methods by
which Pericles wished to enrich her. It was to commerce and
industry, and to the labour and skill which their development
would attract, that Pericles looked as the solid and lasting
foundations of Athenian prosperity ; for they alone, as he knew,
among the wealth-producing forces of his day, were in harmony
with the ideals of the City and the Empire.

But commerce and industry and immigration, especially in the
old conservative Greek world, need care and patience and, above
all, time, for their steady development ; and fifth-century Athens
was moving faster than ever community moved before or since.
More immediate and satisfying resources were needed to meet
the ambitions of the day. Athens could not live upon hopes and
prospects. It was natural for her to fall back upon the time-
honoured expedient of State robbery.

We have seen that the development of Athenian commerce
was greatly hampered in Eastern waters by the continuance for
thirty-two years after the battle of Salamis of a state of war with
Persia. It was not till 448, under the auspices of Pericles, that
peace was finally concluded, and peaceful traders and travellers,
like Herodotus, took the place of organized raiders and free-
booters. During that generation and a half many a windfall
reached Athens in the form of spoils of war. Generals sent home
gold and silver to the State treasury, and gangs of captives to
the market-place to be sold for the benefit of the city ; the
soldiers and sailors under them sent home welcome additions to
the family store. On the distribution of the booty after the
capture of Sestos and Byzantium Cimon was able to purchase

four months' provisions for his ships and send a quantity of gold besides to the Athenian treasury. The battle of Eurymedon over the Persian land and sea forces a few years later left him, we are told, with more than 20,000 men and a notable quantity of riches, 'out of which the people had enough money to build the wall on the south side of the citadel,' and to lay the foundations of the Long Walls to Piraeus. Athens was 'growing rich upon her enemies' in the old-fashioned buccaneering way.[1]

But after 448, when peace was concluded with Persia, this source of enrichment dried up. It was Pericles' ambition that Athenians should no longer rob from Persia but trade with her. No more gold and prisoners flowed in from far-off victories in Asia for the building of walls and temples. Athens must look to other means if her projects were to be carried out. She found them, not in the resources and vigour of individuals, on which Pericles, if we may believe his words, would so much have preferred to rely, but in the funds of the State. The great Acropolis buildings, into which Athenians put so much of their creative energy during the short years of their greatest happiness, were built out of the sums in the State treasury. It is necessary for us therefore to turn from the resources of individuals to those of the State, and to inquire into the nature and management of Athenian public finance.

In the general poverty of the Greek world, both States and individuals were accustomed to living from hand to mouth. States and other public bodies had large possessions, sometimes equal, or almost equal, to those of all their citizens combined ; but few of them produced money available for the current expenses of administration, and the sums on each side of the State balance-sheet, could we recover them, would seem ridiculously small. Sparta held supremacy over the Peloponnese with no regular State finances at all. Sixth-century Athens was not quite so primitive. Yet her old State treasury did its work on very limited resources. There were three regular sources of revenue : the rents from the State lands, law-court payments and fines, and the small sums that came in from the various indirect taxes and dues. Until the development of the silver mines none of these items was considerable. They were used to defray the expenses

[1] Plut. *Cim.* 9 (from Ion of Chios), 13 ; Diod. xi. 62.

of current administration, which were correspondingly simple.
They included the maintenance of public works and of the few
public slaves, ' rewards for the killing of wolves, prizes to poets
and doctors, grants to the infirm, and above all offerings and
sacrifices to national and Panhellenic deities.' This last item,
which must have formed a large proportion of the whole,
amounted in the sixth century to three talents.[1]

Thus it is easy to see how welcome to the State were the free
contributions of citizens towards ships and sacrifices and dramatic
performances and other public purposes, and how natural it
was that, when the city had a windfall, it should be distributed
amongst those who helped her. There was no thought at Athens,
down to the time of the Persian wars, of accumulating any reserve
out of the current revenue of the State.

But the old State treasury was not the only repository of
public funds at Athens. There were religious resources as well,
treasures and offerings preserved in the sanctuaries of various
deities. The chief of these was Athena, who was worshipped on
the Acropolis. Her worship, and the treasure which it had
accumulated, went back to dim and distant times. By the sixth
century the treasure was considered of sufficient public importance for the ' stewards ' who managed it to be regarded as public
officials, and Solon, in his work of constitutional reconstruction,
made fresh rules as to their mode of appointment. We cannot
estimate the value of the treasure which they guarded. We only
know that it must have grown larger year by year ; for the State
allowed the goddess to profit, though not generally in the form of
money, by some of its own sources of revenue. She received a proportion of the law-court fines and, in the case of a profitable victory,
a tithe of the windfall in spoils. As the sacred expenses were considerably less than the secular, the goddess, though far poorer than
the Panhellenic deities at Delphi and Olympia, gradually came to
hold an important position in the national economy. There were
also other treasures in various temples, as to which we can form
no estimate for the sixth century. The fifth-century financiers
lump them comprehensively together as ' the other gods '.[2]

[1] Lys. xxx. 20 ; Cavaignac, p. 5, on the δημόσιον or old State treasury.
Its treasurers were the κωλακρέται or ' carvers '. See p. 87 above.
[2] *Ath. Pol.* vii. 3 ; Hdt. v. 77 ; Cavaignac, pp. 30–1.

When the Persians occupied Athens in 480 no attempt was made to remove these sacred treasures. The pious hoped against hope that by some miracle they would be saved. The enemy laid siege to the Acropolis, found their way in by a steep side entrance, and robbed the shrines of their riches, burning all that they could not carry off. When the Athenians returned they found themselves, not only without the sacred capital which had been accumulating for centuries, but without the sanctuaries which had housed it. The goddess had indeed saved Athens, but she herself had lost everything. Her subjects came back to their ruined city with a great design in their thankful hearts—to build for their national goddess a temple worthy of Athens as the champion of Greece. They began by solemnly dedicating to her the choicest morsels from their booty—the chair of Xerxes, the scimitar of Mardonius, and other illustrious relics—and engaged on what seemed likely to be the long and difficult task of restoring the national and sacred finances.[1]

So much was necessary as an introduction to the State finance of the fifth century. Let us now examine this in detail, looking first at the City and then at the Empire.

The old State treasury had far more to pay for under Pericles than two generations earlier. There were perhaps no more rewards for wolves, but there were a large number of new and more pressing obligations—finer and more frequent festivals, larger and more numerous public works, both to make and to maintain, above all, the continual and increasing drain of payment to individual citizens for service as councillors and in the law-courts. But the sources of revenue, too, had expanded. The growth of trade was favourable to the taxes at Piraeus and in the market-place ; the licence-duties on slaves and Outlanders gained by the development of immigration ; law-court fees were swollen by the increased duties thrown on the courts ; and, above all, the city treasury was now assured of a regular revenue of some fifty talents, if not more, from the Attic silver mines, and of other large sums from new domains, including mines, in Thrace. The

[1] Hdt. viii. 51 ; Cavaignac, p. 32, who refers to other cases (at Olympia, Delphi, and Branchidae) of attempts to collect money to repair disasters to great shrines. The chair and the scimitar remained among the treasures in the Acropolis till they were abstracted by a dishonest ' Steward ' in the fourth century : Dem. xxiv. 129.

total annual revenue received by the city treasury during the supremacy of Pericles seems to have amounted to upwards of 500 talents.[1]

But Athens had now other resources to rely on. In 478 Athens was chosen to be head of an alliance or confederacy of the Greek States against Persia. The total sum annually needed for the purposes of the alliance was fixed by Aristeides the Just, to whom the task had been assigned, at 460 talents. This sum was levied on a system agreed on between the confederates, probably in most cases on a rough valuation of their lands. There were re-assessments in detail every four years ; but the main principles of the levy, as established by Aristeides, were part of the original arrangement between Athens and the cities, and could not be altered without bad faith. We have sufficient evidence to reconstruct the calculations by which Aristeides reached his total. The maximum fighting fleet of the confederates was to consist of 200 triremes. Each trireme was manned by 170 rowers, 8 officers, and 10 marines, that is, 188 in all. The year's campaigning lasted from March to October, when the season closed at Athens with the public burial of the fallen. The sum which a man required to buy food and other necessaries in the ports of the Aegean at this time was 2 obols (one-third of a drachma) per day. Aristeides' calculation then was as follows :

Each sailor cost, for season of 210 days, $\frac{1}{3} \times 210 = 70$ drachmas.
Each trireme of 188 sailors cost 13,160 drachmas.
The fleet of 200 ships cost 2,632,000 drachmas.

As the talent contains 6,000 drachmas, this works out at $438\frac{2}{3}$ talents, so that the annual levy of 460 left a sufficient margin for the replacement of ships.[2]

To whom did this money belong ? To those who controlled its expenditure. It was, and was frankly called, ' tribute,' paid to the authorities of the confederacy in the same way as most of

[1] Xen. *Anab.* vii. 1. 27 ; Cavaignac, p. 51. Francotte, *Finances des cités grecques*, p. 175, puts it as high as 600. Thuc. i. 101. 3 (new domain lands).
[2] Thuc. i. 104, i. 112. 2 ; Plut. *Cim.* 12 (200 ships), cf. Thuc. ii. 7. 2 ; Plut. *Arist*. 24 (land-valuation) ; Plut. *Them.* 10 and Ar. *Wasps* 88 (Schol.) (2 obols) ; Thuc. ii. 23. 2 (marines) ; Cavaignac, p. 44 ; Meyer, *Forschungen*, vol. ii, p. 170. If 50 talents built 200 ships in 483, 20 talents would seem an ample margin for replacement. The fittings were supplied by private generosity. The four years' interval is that between Panathenaic festivals.

the confederates had previously paid it to the King of Persia. Who were these authorities ? In theory, the representatives of the confederates themselves ; in practice, their acknowledged leader, the people of Athens. The treasurers who received the money were Athenian officials, the generals to whom it was paid were Athenian executive officers, and the body which appointed and controlled them was the Athenian people. Practically speaking, it was money contributed to the Athenians under two understood conditions : firstly, that the money should continue to be levied upon the system agreed to by the confederates and associated with the name of Aristeides ; and, secondly, that Athens should secure those who paid it from all Persian attacks. Apart from this, it belonged, says a writer who has gone into the legal question, like all tribute, to those to whom it was paid ; it became, therefore, the property of the Athenian State ; but Athens, at the outset, reserved it for the expenses of war and, to inspire the allies with more confidence, made it into a fund distinct from her ordinary revenues and deposited it at Delos.[1]

Aristeides was not only a just but a very careful financier. Indeed, as events turned out, he was over-careful. He had made up his calculation on the assumption that there would be campaigning every season, and that this campaigning would bring in no profits. Both these assumptions were soon disproved. The Persians retired up country and left it to the Greeks to take the offensive, which they were slow to do ; and when they did so, as in Thrace and at the Eurymedon, they generally made the war ' nourish itself ', and came home loaded with booty. Meanwhile the annual contributions continued to flow into the treasury, and the stewards allowed it to mount up and form an imposing Imperial Reserve. In 454–453, when, for safety or for convenience, the treasury was transferred to Athens, this reserve must have amounted to some 3,000 talents.[2]

From 453 onwards, then, Athenians were not only practically but visibly masters of the funds of the league. The money was

[1] Francotte, pp. 114 and 63 ff., on the meaning of φόρος and σύνταξις, esp. p. 117. The word φόρος (tribute) was used from the first (Thuc. i. 96. 2, v. 18. 5), and connects the finance of the confederacy with that of Persia ; cf. Hdt. iii. 89, where Darius is described as being just what Athens had become, ' a receiver of small change.'

[2] Cavaignac, pp. 68–9 (cf. p. 62 on the transference) ; Francotte, p. 161.

deposited on the Acropolis, where their other funds were kept. Athens had now, therefore, three separate treasuries, connected respectively with the City, the Goddess, and the Empire. Let us watch what came of these financial complications.

All this time Athens had been trying to collect money for the great new temple of the goddess. The State had made generous grants out of spoils and other sources of city revenue, and individual citizens had gladly borne their share. The south wall of the Acropolis, which Cimon constructed out of booty, was built to strengthen the foundations of the projected shrine. But the work made slow progress. The temple of Zeus at Olympia, which was finished in 456, was built out of a treasure which had taken a century to accumulate ; and Olympia had the contributions of all Greece to rely on. ' The temples of the wealthy cities of Magna Graecia and Sicily, which are contemporary with it, were almost all of them the result of prolonged activity several times resumed. And all these monuments are in plain stone, while the Parthenon was to be in marble.' Yet Athens was poor beside these States. It seemed that she had pitched her hopes too high.[1]

It is from about this time that we find her taking definite steps to hasten the execution of her great religious and artistic projects. ' Pericles,' says Plutarch, ' anxious to raise the spirits of the people and to encourage them to great deeds, procured a decree that all the Greeks, wheresoever they resided, whether in Europe or in Asia, whether their cities were great or small, should send representatives to Athens to confer upon the rebuilding of the Greek shrines which the barbarians had burnt, and about providing those sacrifices which had been vowed during the Persian War for the preservation of Greece ; and likewise about the sea, in order that all might sail on it without fear and maintain the peace.' This interesting decree, associating Pericles' policy of sea-power with his building projects, cannot be dated with certainty ; but it seems to belong to the decade between 460 and 450. ' It took no effect,' says Plutarch, ' nor did the cities send their representatives ; the reason of which is said to be the underhand opposition of the Lacedaemonians, for the proposal was first rejected in Peloponnesus But I was willing to

[1] Cavaignac, pp. 51-2.

give account of it as a specimen of the greatness of the orator's spirit and of his disposition to form magnificent designs.'[1]

But a second and less ambitious expedient, which Athens adopted about the same time, was more easily carried out. She made the allies contribute to her religious designs by paying in to the treasury of the Goddess the ' first-fruits ' of the tribute. The proportion thus deducted was one-sixtieth of each contribution, and it is to the records of these offerings that we owe our detailed knowledge of the imperial system. The lists were inscribed on stone slabs, many of which have come down to us.[2]

The principle thus established was quickly carried further. We cannot trace its development in detail, but we know the outlines of the story. The facts speak for themselves. In 448 peace was concluded between Athens and Persia ; but, though their contributions should no longer have been needed, the confederates were not relieved from them. In 447 the building of the great temple, the Parthenon, was begun. In 445 peace was concluded between Athens and her enemies in Greece proper. In 444 hot discussion arose in Athens as to the use of the imperial funds. The question divided the assembly, but was decisively settled early in 443 by the banishment of the statesman who opposed the financial policy of Pericles. In the year 443–442 the Confederacy, or Empire, as it had now become, was divided into five tribute districts, for the more convenient collection of funds. By 440 the reserve funds of the Goddess and of the Empire had been united in the hands of the treasurers of the Goddess. Athens had found the money for her designs.[3]

In 440–439, however, she was startled in her building projects by the sudden revolt of two of her most important allies or subjects, Samos and Byzantium. It cost her two seasons of campaigning and 1,276 talents out of her reserve (exclusive of current imperial revenue) to repress them ; and for a short time the building of the Parthenon was interrupted. But

---

[1] Plut. *Per.* 17 ; Cavaignac, p. 60, following Keil.
[2] Cavaignac, pp. 60–1. There is no evidence that a similar first-fruit offering was paid to Apollo while the treasury was at Delos.
[3] Cavaignac, pp. 76 note 2, 85 note 2, 92 note 3. [See Appendix.]

payments continued to be made for the preparation of the
gold and ivory statue which was to be the great feature of
the new temple. At the close of the war the other projects were
resumed.[1]

The following seven years, down to the outbreak of the Peloponnesian War, were the zenith of Athenian wealth and activity.
The Parthenon building was sufficiently advanced by 438 to be
inaugurated at the Panathenaic festival in the summer of that
year. The gold and ivory statue of Athena was completed by
Pheidias in time for the ceremony. The artists then turned their
attention to the approach of the Acropolis. Mnesicles drew out
the plan for the great Vestibule or Propylaea, and work began on
it in 437. Many years before a site had been fixed, on the jutting
western edge of the Acropolis, for a little temple of Athena-
Victory. The building had been delayed through lack of funds ;
but it was now taken in hand, although its plan and orientation
somewhat interfered with those of the Vestibule of Mnesicles.
A number of other temples were begun—the Erechtheum on the
north edge of the Acropolis, the temple of Hephaestus (the so-
called Theseum) down in the city, and the temples at Sunium
and Rhamnus on the coast. Besides these there were a number
of other public works, the Odeum or Singing Hall, the third or
middle Long Wall to simplify the defence of city and port, and
new docks and other works at Piraeus.[2]

Several of these buildings still remain, and attest the boldness
and patience of the perfect artists who planned and made them.
Many of the payments made in connexion with them remain
also, to attest that they were built in very truth, as Pericles tells
us, with the strictest regard to economy. It is ' visible in every
detail ', down to the careful arrangements made for selling the
wood used in the scaffolding. Every item of expenditure was
carefully discussed and rigidly controlled ; for the work was
being done, as every one knew, not out of the native or normal
resources of the city, but out of a fund which was originally
intended for military purposes, and might at any moment
be required for them again. Here is a rough calculation
of the sums that were spent upon public works between 447
and 432.

[1] Cavaignac, pp. 94-5.   [2] [See Appendix.]

Parthenon	700 talents	(£840,000)
Gold and Ivory Statue of Athena . .	1,000 ,,	(£1,200,000)
Propylaea or Vestibule (unfinished) . .	400 ,,	(£480,000)
Odeum (Singing Hall) ⎫		
Ship-houses ⎪		
Middle Wall ⎬	3,000 ,,	(£3,600,000)
Works at Piraeus ⎭		
Two Victories in gold	200 ,,	(£240,000)
Other monuments, including Nike-temple .	2,700 ,,	(£3,240,000)
Total	8,000 ,,	(£9,600,000)

This expenditure covers a period of sixteen years, from 447 to
431, but it only reached its height during the latter portion of
this period, when the Goddess had established a firm hold over
the surplus funds of the league. So far as can be judged from
the inscriptions, the average annual expenditure between 447
and 438 was between 300 and 400 talents, while between 438 and
431 it was 650 talents. This is confirmed by Thucydides' statement that at the zenith of the treasure, before the Vestibule was
begun, there were 9,700 talents of reserve in hand. It would
almost seem as if Pericles, knowing that a great war was imminent
and that he and his artists were growing old, determined to do
the work that was in them while there was yet time. By 431,
when the storm broke, most, but not all, of it was done.[2]

It is hard for us in these opulent modern days to form any
conception of the temper of Athens during these few crowded
years of creative activity. Those 8,000 talents paid to her
craftsmen and labourers represent in hard work and artistic
power, above all, in self-sacrifice, far more than can be expressed
in the feeble terms of present-day money. From our cautious
modern point of view, which puts good business before every-

[1] Francotte, p. 175, following Busolt; Cavaignac agrees generally (e. g.
as to the Parthenon, p. 99; as to the Propylaea, as against Heliodorus,
p. 102). Others, however (e. g. Dickins in a private letter), put the total as
low as 4,000 talents. I reckon the purchasing power of a drachma at 4s.
Cavaignac (p. 88) reckons it at 5s. It was, of course, sinking all through the
century.

[2] Francotte, p. 175 (annual expenditure); Thuc. ii. 13. 3 (9,700 talents);
ii. 64. 5 (running risks for glory); Cavaignac does not believe there were
ever more than 6,000 talents in hand at any one time, and gives reasons for
emending the text of Thucydides accordingly (p. 108). I have not ventured
to follow him, though it is hard to explain the existence of so large a sum just
after the Samian War and the completion of the Parthenon and its statue.
Meyer, *Forschungen*, vol. ii, p. 119, prefers not to take Thucydides' words
literally. See also Cavaignac's more recent statement in his *Histoire de l'antiquité*, ii, p. 84 note.

thing and lets in art as an afterthought, her finance was crazy. As a modern economist remarks : ' The works of Pericles served no economic purpose but that of display ; they could not be realized in money or exported to other lands, or utilized for the production of more wealth. The skill and treasure devoted to them were permanently sunk; their construction afforded a means of employing the people ; but when completed they provided no employment for industry and no incentive to trade. When large sums are laid out in productive public works like those of the Egyptians at Lake Moeris, wealth so expended not only gives employment at the time, but affords facilities for continued employment afterwards. Harbours, canals, irrigation, roads, railways, or anything else that opens up a country may have this character. Pericles, in endeavouring to find profitable employment for the people, deliberately turned their energies to unproductive public works ; the magnificent buildings which were reared under his direction absorbed the wealth of the city without developing any natural resources or trading facilities in return. The treasure was exhausted once and for all ; it was locked up in forms that are artistically superb, but economically worthless.' From the economic and political standpoints this criticism is sound, and Pericles would have admitted it. His friend Herodotus had been to Lake Moeris, and had told him, as he has told us, about reproductive Egyptian public works. Athenians were not so blind as not to know that their temples would bring in no income, except from sightseers, and that the sums out of which they were being built were only too strictly limited. They knew that they were working against time, and spending upon the work sums that wise men would have laid by for purposes of national defence and commercial and industrial development. Only on one point would they have indignantly contradicted the modern economist. He speaks as though the buildings were undertaken ' to find profitable employment for the people ', as though the Parthenon had been built as a relief work. The Parthenon was built by honest craftsmen, eager to do honour to their goddess, who were paid a frugal pittance for their devoted services. Artists do not work for money, even though they, like other men, need money to live by. But of the craftsmen and labourers employed on the temples, as of the city as a whole, the inscriptions justify us in saying that they were 'lovers of beauty together with cheapness '.[1]

We have brought this rough history of Athenian finance down to the years before the Peloponnesian War. Fortunately we now reach firm ground, for Thucydides tells us exactly how much of the treasure was left when building was stopped by the beginning of hostilities. 'Apart from the other income ' (i.e. the old city treasury), he represents Pericles as saying, 'an average revenue of six hundred talents of silver was drawn from the revenue of the allies ; and there were still six thousand talents of coined silver in the Acropolis. . . . This did not include the uncoined gold and silver in public and private offerings, the sacred vessels for the processions and games, the Median spoils, and similar resources to the amount of five hundred talents. To this Pericles added the resources of the other temples. . . . Nay, if they were absolutely driven to it, they might take even the gold ornaments of Athena herself ; for the statue held forty talents of pure gold and it was all removable. This might be used for self-preservation, and must all of it be restored. Such was their

---

[1] Hdt. ii. 149, iii. 91 (Lake Moeris) ; sightseers : Old Oligarch, i. 17 ; cf. a line preserved from the comedian Lysippus (*floruit* 434) : ' if you have not seen Athens you are a blockhead ' (εἰ μὴ τεθέασαι τὰς Ἀθήνας στέλεχος εἶ) ; Cunningham, *Western Civilization*, pp. 120–1. It is more often the Erechtheum which is spoken of as relief works, because work on it was resumed when Athens was practically in a state of siege—surely one of the most superb national achievements of the artistic temperament in the whole of history. The idea that the Athenians at the height of their greatness were grasping in money matters is very widespread. It is due partly to the strictures of Plato, who objected to the system of payment for public work, partly to the undoubted fact that the standard of money expenditure went up. This was due to the general rise in prices which was the natural result of the influx of bullion from the mines and in the shape of tribute. Athens was, as it were, living upon a standing indemnity paid in cash ; and, as has been recently pointed out, indemnities are not an unmixed blessing to the countries which receive them. (See N. Angell, *The Great Illusion*, chap. vi : in the more recent editions the chapter is rewritten in a more careful form.) Undoubtedly high prices must have done something to hamper the growth of Athenian export trade, and the rapid recuperation and subsequent expansion of Athenian trade after 404 must be connected with the fall in prices which resulted from the loss of the Empire and the closing of the mines. The subject is one which would repay closer investigation. It is difficult, for instance, to say how widely the effect of Athenian prices was felt. Cavaignac (p. 127) assumes that it was felt generally throughout the Aegean, but from Thuc. viii. 29 compared with iii. 17. 4 it would rather seem that this was not so ; cf. also v. 47. 6 (where three Aeginetan obols = five Attic in weight). No doubt the Athenians carried their own standard of prices with them, and the market-sellers of the Aegean tended to treat them accordingly.

financial position—surely a satisfactory one.' These were the resources provided for Athens by her greatest financier and described by her greatest historian as ' superfluously abundant ' —a few millions of bullion ore, and, behind them, no hope of a loan or other help from wealthy capitalists at home or abroad, but merely a National Museum to be turned into ready money. Nothing could better illustrate how pathetically frail was the basis on which Athens was attempting to build the costly fabric of a civilization.[1]

Let us now attempt to do in conclusion for Pericles what we have already done for Aristeides—to put into figures his calculations for the conduct of a possible war. In doing so we must remember that prices had been rising at Athens, and that the sum calculated by Aristeides for maintenance no longer sufficed. It will show how slender were Athens' resources not only in money but in men. It was a small handful of human beings, judged by our modern standard, which beat back the Persians, created the Empire, adorned Athens with her immortal buildings, and was ready now in 431 to take its stand, in the ranks or on shipboard, to defend and hand down its heritage. But Pericles knew how impossible it was for Athens both to fight and to do her proper work, and he did not intend that she should fight. We can best enter on the history of the war with these figures before us :

Adult male population of Attica in 431 :

Adult citizens	.	.	.	about 40,000
Outlanders .	.	.	.	„ 24,000
Slaves	.	.	.	„ 55,000
Total	.	.	.	119,000

This was the total strength of the hands and brains on which Athens depended for her maintenance as a centre of civilization. It can be seen at a glance how severely her working power would be crippled if even a small proportion of them were diverted from the arts of peace to the arts of war.

Let us now examine the same population organized for purposes

[1] Thuc. ii. 13. 3–5, 65. 13. The 600 talents probably include the indemnity paid annually by the Samians since 439 and some accessions to the Empire (e. g. in the Black Sea) since the total originally fixed by Aristeides. Compare the expedients to which the Austrian Republic was at one time reduced, in mortgaging its art treasures, &c., to secure credits for food and raw materials.

of national defence. We must subtract the 20,000 mine slaves, who would be worse than useless, and the 35,000 other slaves, who could only be called upon in the last emergency, thus reducing our total to 64,000 (citizens 40,000, Outlanders 24,000). This was the total military strength on paper of the population of Attica proper. But we should add to this the Out-residents, six to ten thousand in number, in scattered settlements in the Aegean area, who were still called upon for military duty. This gives us the following figures :

Citizens	about	48,000
Outlanders	,,	24,000
		72,000

How were these 72,000 organized for purposes of national defence ?

The nature of a man's military obligations at Athens depended on his census or property qualification. If he was rich enough to provide his own armour he served in the cavalry or as a heavy-armed soldier; if not, he served as light-armed or, more generally, as a rower. Working upon our previous estimates we reach the following figures : [1]

Heavy-armed citizens	28,000
Heavy-armed Outlanders . . .	8,000
	36,000
Light-armed citizens	20,000
Light-armed Outlanders . . .	16,000
	36,000

Side by side with these more or less conjectural estimates, let us put Pericles' own dispositions for the army, using the figures recorded by Thucydides.[2]

I. Field-Service Army		15,800
Cavalry	1,000	
Heavy-armed infantry . . .	13,000	
Light-armed mounted . . .	200	
,, on foot . . .	1,600	
Total	15,800	
II. Reserve (entirely heavy-armed)		16,000
Citizens (including oldest and youngest) .	8,000	
Outlanders	8,000	
Total	16,000	

[1] See pp. 174–5 above.   [2] Thuc. ii. 13. 6–8.

III. Garrisons in the Empire	.	.	.	.		2,500	

To which must be added :

IV. Marines on fleet	.	.	.	.		3,000	

Total (III and IV)	.	.	.	.	.	5,500

Grand total	.	.	.	.	.	37,300[1]
consisting of : Heavy-armed	.	.	.	.	.	35,500
Light-armed	.	.	.	.	.	1,800

Upon the naval establishment Thucydides is not so explicit. It appears that three hundred triremes were always kept seaworthy and that there was another hundred in reserve, for whom commanders were appointed every year in case of need. The number which actually put to sea every year in peace-time, for purposes of practice and to collect tribute and guard the sea-routes, was sixty.

The peace establishment then would be $188 \times 60 = 11,280$, of whom some 3,500 were citizens and the rest Outlanders and hired rowers.

The war establishment would be—

170 rowers × 300	.	.	.	=	51,000	
8 officers × 300	.	.	.	=	2,400	
10 heavy-armed marines × 300	.	=	3,000			

Total 188 × 300	.	.	.	=	56,400 [2]

But this was far more than the total number or citizens and Outlanders available for naval service, which only amounted to 36,000. If the whole, or even a large part, of the fleet was to be

---

[1] The garrison figures are from *Ath. Pol.* xxiv, the horse-archers (not counted separately from cavalry in Thucydides) from Meyer, *Forsch.*, vol. ii, p. 162, from whom I differ as regards the number of Outlander hoplites. There is a difficulty as to what Thucydides means by ' from the oldest and youngest ' : on my reckoning the citizen reserve would be in the proportion of 1 : 2 to the hoplites on active service, as with the Peloponnesians (Thuc. ii. 10. 2). Why the reserve for defending the walls should have consisted entirely of heavy-armed troops, as Thucydides plainly says, is hard to explain ; as Fawcus has pointed out (*J. H. S.*, vol. xxix, p. 27), light-armed troops would suffice for the work required. Possibly the explanation is to be found in the decline in the value of money, which brought a number of the poorer citizens within the limits of the ' hoplite census ', whether they could provide their own armour or not ; see Cavaignac, p. 168. Thuc. iii. 18. 4 shows that there were hoplites at Athens who had been through the oarsman's training.

[2] Thuc. ii. 13. 8 and ii. 24. 2 with Old Oligarch, iii. 4 (400 trierarchs), Plut. *Per.* 11 (60 ships in commission ; cf. Wilamowitz, *A. A.*, vol. ii, p. 206) ; Old Oligarch, i. 19 ; and Thuc. i. 142. 6–8 (naval manœuvres) ; Ar. *Ach.* 162 (citizens as superior oarsmen only) ; Thuc. i. 121. 3 and 143. 1 (hired rowers and citizen officers).

sent to sea, Athens would need to hire foreign rowers; and
everything would depend on her ability to pay them generously
for their services. Here, as her enemies knew, was the weak
spot in her defences. In the last resort, as the Corinthians said,
'the power of Athens rested upon money, not upon native
strength.'

Let us now work out with Pericles the expenditure which the
use of these forces would entail.

The pay in the army and navy had now probably risen to one
drachma a day—the same for all ranks. To keep the Field
Service Army in the field for a season's campaigning of six
months would therefore cost

$$\frac{15,800 \times 180}{6,000} = 474 \text{ talents,}$$

while to keep 300 ships at sea for a similar period would cost no
less than

$$\frac{56,000 \times 180}{6,000} = 1,680 \text{ talents.}$$

Towards such bills as these the paltry six thousand talents on
the Acropolis would not carry Athens very far in a war of
indefinite continuance. It is quite certain that Pericles never
contemplated incurring them.[1]

In conclusion, let us turn once more from the arts of war to
the arts of peace, and set out in brief tabular form the results of
our inquiries into the Athenian economy. There is no need to
sum up the work of production and distribution within the limits
of the City State proper—the work of the cultivators, the craftsmen, and the retail traders of the market-place. Those went on
in Attica in peace-time, as in every City State. Our tabular
statement can only give what went on at Athens over and above
the ordinary self-sufficient City State economy, her dealings with
abroad. It can be most conveniently expressed in the form of
a national balance sheet. The items are numbered in order of
relative importance.

---

[1] Pay : Thuc. iii. 17. 4, vi. 8. 1, 30. 3. The Potidaea campaign cost from
first to last 2,000 talents (Thuc. ii. 70. 2) : the forces employed there for the
whole 30 months were only 3,000 hoplites and less than 50 ships. Athens
was not in a position to afford many more summer-and-winter campaigns.

Cr.

(1) Tribute from allies (600 talents a year), circulated among Athenians for expenses of government, building of public works, ships, &c.

(2) Profits of carrying trade.

(3) Exports :
  (a) Silver from mines ;
  (b) Olive-oil (= butter, soap, light) ;
  (c) Painted pottery, statuettes, &c. ;
  (d) Marble ;
  (e) Manufactures from imported raw material, e. g. shields ;
  (f) Re-exported imports.
    (e) and (f) insignificant, and all except (a) hampered by rise in prices due to (1) and (3, a).

(4) Payments by visitors, coming for legal business or as sightseers.

Dr.

(1) Necessaries, including :
  (a) Two-thirds of corn-supply for 350,000 people ;
  (b) Timber for shipbuilding, and other military necessaries (e. g. iron for weapons, flax for sails).

(2) Luxuries, including :
  (a) Raw material for manufactures (except clay, marble, and wool) ;
  (b) Bought labour (i. e. slaves) for crafts, household, and mines ;
  (c) Finished products of all kinds.

When we put together all these separate facts and figures and try to imagine for ourselves their cumulative social effect, we begin to understand in some measure the meaning of Pericles' words about his fellow citizens—how 'they yield to none, man by man, for independence of spirit, many-sidedness of attainment, and complete self-reliance in limbs and brain'. For over two thousand years we have been admiring them, in their writings and monuments, for that inimitable ease and many-sidedness and cloudless serenity of spirit. Only now that we can piece together their household bills can we admire also the steady courage which put so bold a face upon the sterner realities of life. Only now can we appreciate why Athens, who has shown us, in every line she wrote and every stone she carved, how willingly she submitted to the compelling power of art, spoke with so businesslike a caution of the homage she paid in its cause—why, not out of choice but out of necessity, she 'loved beauty with cheapness'.[1]

[1] See Appendix.

CONCLUSION

THE PELOPONNESIAN WAR

'Ο πόλεμος, ὑφελὼν τὴν εὐπορίαν τοῦ καθ' ἡμέραν, βίαιος διδάσκαλος καὶ πρὸς τὰ παρόντα τὰς ὀργὰς τῶν πολλῶν ὁμοιοῖ.—THUCYDIDES, iii. 82. 2.

War, by taking away the comfortable provision of daily life, is a teacher who educates through violence ; and he makes men's characters fit their conditions.

In 434, while the workmen were still busy on the Vestibule, a cloud appeared in the West. Two years before, the small city of Epidamnus, a Corcyraean colony on the coast of Albania, had become involved in domestic troubles. A party of her citizens applied to Corcyra for assistance, but the mother-country refused to help them. So they went to Corinth instead, and the Corinthians at once consented. Thucydides informs us in detail as to the motives for this decision, setting them forth, no doubt, in what he considered to be their order of importance. They reveal a typically Greek blending of sentiment and material interest. ' Believing the colony to belong as much to themselves as to the Corcyraeans, they felt it to be a kind of duty to undertake its protection. Besides, they hated the Corcyraeans for their neglect of the mother-country. Instead of meeting with the usual honours accorded to the parent city by every other colony at public assemblies, such as precedence at sacrifices, Corinth found herself treated with contempt by a power which in point of wealth could stand comparison with the richest Greek States of the day, which possessed great military strength, and which sometimes could not repress a pride in the high naval position of an island whose nautical renown dated from the days of its old inhabitants, Homer's Phaeacians. This was one reason of the care which they lavished on their fleet, which was very powerful ; indeed they began the war with a force of 120 galleys. All these grievances made Corinth eager to send the promised aid to Epidamnus.' [1]

It was a serious decision, for between Corinth and Epidamnus lay the sea-domain of Corcyra. Corinth's acceptance of the

[1] Thuc. i. 25. [See Appendix.]

invitation was thus a direct challenge to her rebellious daughter. Corinth and Corcyra were the two chief sea-powers of Western Greece. Corcyra was the stronger of the two; her 120 ships 'held the seas' northward and westwards from the mouth of the Ambracian Gulf. But Corinth, though her fleet was smaller, had good friends and neighbours behind her, whilst Corcyra, remote from the City-State world, had hitherto always maintained herself in haughty isolation. Corinth appealed to her allies, and before long had beaten up a force of seventy-five ships and 2,000 heavy infantry. When they reached the territorial frontier, Actium, at the mouth of the Ambracian Gulf, ' where the temple of Apollo stands, the Corcyraeans,' says Thucydides, ' sent on a herald in a light boat to warn them not to sail against them. Meanwhile they proceeded to man their ships, all of which had been equipped for action, the old vessels being undergirded to make them sea-worthy. On the return of the herald without any peaceful answer from the Corinthians, their ships being now manned, they put out to sea to meet the enemy with a fleet of eighty ships (forty were engaged in the siege of Epidamnus), formed line, and went into action. They gained a decisive victory and destroyed fifteen of the Corinthian vessels. The same day saw Epidamnus compelled by its besiegers to capitulate.' [1]

The effect of this engagement was to make Corcyra as supreme on the Western seaboard of Greece as Athens was in the Aegean. ' The Corcyraeans set up a trophy on Leucimme, a headland of Corcyra, and slew all their captives except the Corinthians, whom they kept as prisoners of war. The Corinthians and their allies returned home and left the Corcyraeans masters of all the sea about those parts. Sailing to Leucas, a Corinthian colony, they ravaged their territory; they burnt Cyllene, the harbour of the Eleans, because they had furnished ships and money to Corinth. For almost the whole of the period that followed the battle they remained masters of the sea, and the allies of Corinth were harassed by Corcyraean warships. At last, towards autumn, roused by the sufferings of her allies, Corinth sent out ships and troops . . . for the protection of Leucas and the rest of the friendly cities. The Corcyraeans on their part formed a similar station

---

[1] Thuc. i. 29. On the sea-domain of Corcyra see Leaf, *Homer and History*, p. 186, with map.

on Leucimme. Neither party made any movement, but they remained confronting one another till the end of the summer, and winter was at hand before either of them returned home.'[1]

So far matters had only followed the ordinary course of a season's naval campaigning. But it was clear that things could not continue in this fashion. The issues involved were too important. Corinth could not acquiesce in the loss of her sea-power outside the Corinthian Gulf, or relinquish the smaller maritime States, who relied upon her protection, to the tender mercies of the Corcyraean buccaneers. She was prepared to stake all upon the recovery of her naval power from her undutiful daughter. So 'she spent the whole of the year after the engagement and that succeeding it in building ships and in straining every nerve to form an efficient fleet, rowers being drawn from the Peloponnese and the rest of Greece by the inducement of high pay. The Corcyraeans, alarmed at the news of their preparations, being without a single ally in Greece, . . . decided to repair to Athens,' in the autumn of 434, 'in order to enter into alliance and to endeavour to procure support from her. Hearing of their intentions, Corinth also sent an embassy to Athens, to prevent the Corcyraean navy being joined by the Athenian, and her prospect of ordering the war according to her wishes being thus impeded. An assembly was convoked and the rival advocates appeared before the people.'[2]

This is the moment which Thucydides has selected for the first of his famous set speeches or expositions of policy and opinion. It was a peculiarly difficult position with which Athens and Pericles, her chief adviser, were confronted. The arguments on either side are very narrowly balanced. To understand their full bearing we must recall other elements in the general political situation. The Greek world was divided, as it had been now for more than a generation, into two political groups, centring round Athens and Sparta. Athens, with her many hundred dependent cities round the Aegean seaboard and a few other independent allies, took rank as the chief sea-power ; Sparta, with her Peloponnesian League, which included Corinth and all Boeotia except Plataea, as the chief land-power. The two groups had been at peace, bound by a thirty years' truce, for the last eleven years ; but

[1] Thuc. i. 30.   [2] Thuc. i. 31.

feeling between them was steadily growing, and every one felt that
a final struggle could not long be delayed.   Not that there were
any special reasons of policy why they must needs come to blows.
Their interests crossed one another very little, nor could war do
much to readjust them on a satisfactory basis.   The forces which
all Greece saw to be making for a great war were sentimental
rather than material :   they concerned honour rather than trade
or riches.   In the old days Sparta, with her invincible army of
trained soldiers, had been acknowledged by all to be the chief
power in Greece.   The trained sailors of Athens had now out-
stripped her.   ' It was the growth of the power of Athens, and
the alarm which this inspired in Lacedaemon,' says Thucydides,
' which made war inevitable.' [1]

This general situation is well reflected in the arguments of the
two speakers.   The Corcyraeans boldly declare that the great
war is inevitable, and must come sooner rather than later.   Once
this is conceded, the rest of their argument is easy.   ' Remember
that there are but three considerable naval powers in Greece—
Athens, Corcyra, and Corinth, and that if you allow two of these
three to become one and Corinth to secure us for herself, you will
have to hold the sea against the united fleets of Corcyra and the
Peloponnese.   But if you receive us you will have our ships to
reinforce you in the struggle.'

Against these weighty arguments of policy Corinth had little
definite to offer.   Her envoys were indeed in a somewhat delicate
position.   For the last generation, as every one knew, the relation
between Athens and Corinth had been one of ' bitter hate ': it
was not friendship but simply expediency which had kept the
peace between them.   The bitterness dated from an occasion
some twenty years before, when Athens had interfered in a border
war between Corinth and Megara and had helped the latter to
build Long Walls and so render herself impregnable, with
Athenian help, against her Western neighbour.   So it was not without a touch of irony that the Corinthian envoys reminded their
hearers that Corinth and Athens were bound by ties of a political treaty, whereas Corcyra and Athens ' had never even been in

[1] Thuc. i. 23. 6 ; cf. i. 68. 3.   Aristophanes (*Wasps*, 707) reckons the
number of tribute-paying cities at 1,000.   This is no doubt an exaggeration ;
but considerations of grouping probably make the names on the quota lists
far from an exhaustive catalogue.

a truce '—for the simple reason that they had never been at war.
They proceeded to admit the existence of grievances which might
lead to a great war, but urged the advisability of composing them.
But their main argument rested upon a plea for spheres of sea-
power. If Athens was to be left undisturbed by Corinth in the
Aegean, she must leave Corinth free in the West. If she upset
the naval balance, she must expect reprisals.[1]

Two assemblies were held before the Sovereign People made
up its mind. Whichever way the decision fell, it involved a change
in Athenian policy. Hitherto she had abstained from interfering
in the politics of the North-West. She had been content to rely
for the safety of her trade—her only Western interest—upon the
political neutrality and commercial interests of Corcyra. But
now she could no longer do so. If she broke with Corinth, she
risked a general conflagration. But if she broke with Corcyra,
she was postponing, but not averting, this risk, with the added
fear that her Western communications would be in permanent
danger. Moreover, she was unwilling to accept the Corinthian
doctrine of spheres of sea-power, which seemed to hem her in for
all time within her Aegean domain. Outside her own Empire
she stood for a free sea and for free intercourse ; and Pericles, the
founder of Thurii, would not willingly allow Corinth to seize in
the Western waters the right Athens claimed for herself in the
Eastern. Still, he was too cautious a statesman to plunge her need-
lessly into war. The solution which was eventually adopted, no
doubt upon his suggestion, embodied an attempt at compromise.
The Athenians agreed to make an alliance with Corcyra, but of
a purely defensive character. Athens continued to observe the
Thirty Years' Truce by refusing to join Corcyra in any attack
upon Corinth, but promised to come to her assistance if her
own territory was invaded. The calculation was, as Thucydides
frankly tells us, that the two would weaken one another by mutual
conflict, and so leave the sea free for Athens as indisputably the
greatest naval power.[2]

'With these views,' the historian continues, 'Athens received
Corcyra into alliance and sent ten ships to their assistance. Their
instructions were to avoid collision with the Corinthian fleet, except
under certain circumstances. If it sailed to Corcyra and threatened

[1] Thuc. i. 32–43, 103. 4.   [2] Thuc. i. 44.

a landing on her coast, or in any of her possessions, they were to do their utmost to prevent it. These instructions were prompted by an anxiety to avoid a breach of the treaty.' But they would be very difficult to carry out, for who should decide, in a naval campaign, the exact limits between offence and defence?

So the sequel showed. The Corinthians completed their preparations, and sailed against Corcyra with 150 ships of her own and her allies. Corcyra met them with 110, the ten Athenian ships being posted in reserve. When superior numbers began to tell, the Athenians could not help joining in. ' At first, it is true, they refrained from charging any ships; but when the rout was becoming patent, and the Corinthians were pressing on, the time at last came when every one set to and all distinction was laid aside, and it came to this point that Corinthians and Athenians raised their hands against one another.' The battle ended indecisively, both sides raising a trophy of victory. The Corinthians ' put some men on a boat, and sent them without a herald's wand to the Athenians', to register a formal protest against their breach of the Thirty Years' Truce. Then they sailed home, and the operations were concluded for the time being. 'In this way,' says Thucydides, ' Corcyra maintained her political existence against Corinth, and the Athenian vessels left the island. This was the first cause of the war that Corinth had against the Athenians, namely, that they had fought against them with the Corcyraeans in time of treaty.'[1]

' Almost immediately after this,' probably in the winter of 433–432, ' fresh differences arose between the Athenians and the Peloponnesians and contributed their share to the war.' Athens having interfered in the West, ' Corinth was forming schemes of retaliation and Athens suspected her hostility.' The weak spot in the Athenian Empire was what was called the ' Thrace-ward district', comprising the cities on the north coast of the Aegean from the Gulf of Salonica to the Dardanelles. There had been some shrinkage of tribute in that district during the previous years, and there was danger of more defections, as one of the hinterland powers—the kingdom of Macedonia—was just now hostile to Athens. Athenian statesmen knew that Corinth would be hoping for trouble there, and resolved to forestall any possible attempt.

Thuc. i. 55.

Corinth's natural leverage in this quarter was through the city of Potidaea, on the isthmus of Pallene, an old colony of hers, but now, like the other coast cities, a tributary ally of Athens. Athens accordingly ordered the Potidaeans to pull down part of their walls, to give hostages, and to break off all the customary communications with their old metropolis. The Potidaeans first protested, then refused, entered into relations with the Peloponnesian Confederacy, and finally revolted from Athens. Corinth hastily raised a force to help them, which managed to slip across the Aegean while the Athenian northern squadron was engaged elsewhere, and to enter the town within forty days of its defection. The Athenians immediately sent out a force to besiege them.[1]

Corinth had now a double grievance. Athens had attacked her sailors off Corcyra and was besieging some of her soldiers at Potidaea. She found Athens prepared to maintain her Empire at all costs in the East, and to fight for the open sea, or even, perhaps, for another sea-empire, in the West. She saw no limit to Athenian designs, or to the skill and energy and devotion with which she pursued them—so different from the dull, dogged, unthinking courage and discipline of Sparta. Both anger and apprehension made her eager to precipitate the inevitable war; and she set herself to the difficult task of rousing the energy and inflaming the feelings of the slow-moving Spartan leaders.[2]

Athens was well aware of the situation. Pericles was not anxious for war, but he rightly felt that the city had gone too far to draw back. Potidaea must be reduced at all costs, Corinthians or no Corinthians, not only for the sake of Athenian prestige, but because Athens depended absolutely on the steady arrival of her tribute-money. There was only one possible way by which war might yet be averted—by a display of Athenian power which might serve as an object-lesson to the Peloponnesians as to the nature of the war on which they were being asked to engage. Pericles determined to give a demonstration of what sea-power really meant. The victims selected for the purpose were the Megarians, against whom Athens had had a grudge ever since they had ungratefully deserted her alliance and butchered their Athenian garrison at a moment of grave difficulty thirteen years

[1] Thuc. i. 56–68. [2] Thuc. i. 66–71.

before. A decree of boycott was issued closing all the harbours of the Empire and all the markets of Attica to Megarian ships and Megarian goods. Thus at a single blow Megara was practically isolated from the world, and thrown back for her subsistence upon the old self-sufficient agricultural basis. How severely she felt the pinch we know, not only by the part she played in the final deliberations at Sparta, but by Aristophanes' picture of the poor Megarian who disguises his daughters as pigs and smuggles them across the border into the Athenian market for sale. What Athens could do for Megara she could do also, so soon as war was declared, for the other maritime cities of the Peloponnesian League, and Pericles was anxious that, in their councils of war, this fact should be duly weighed.[1]

The Spartans were frightened, as well they might be. When their assembly met to discuss peace or war, the wiser heads among them frankly asked how they could expect to defeat a power which was invulnerable by land and which, by superior seamanship and superior money power, could be sure of driving them off the sea. Sparta, they said, had no resources of her own whatsoever. Athens could only be conquered by sea ; ships cost money, and good hired sailors cost even more. But the Corinthians countered these arguments by skilful appeals to Spartan pride. To acquiesce in these last acts of Athenian aggression would be to prove to all the world that they had lost their old supremacy, which had passed for good from the land-power to the sea-power. They must make a stand once and for all, make up their minds to fight, raise what money they could, and risk the consequences. This appeal was supported by the Spartan presiding magistrate and was finally approved by the Assembly, which voted that the treaty had been broken, and that war must be declared, ' not so much,' says Thucydides, ' because they were persuaded by the arguments of the allies'—they cared little enough for the particular grievances—

---

[1] Thuc. i. 67. 4, 114. 1 ; Ar. *Ach.* 530–5, 729 ff. The decree was preceded by some vexatious frontier regulations which caused the Megarians much irritation : Thuc. i. 42. 2 ; Ar. *Ach.* 519 ff. ; cf. Meyer, iv. § 539 ; *Forschungen*, vol. ii, pp. 297 ff. ; Busolt, vol. iii, p. 812. Megara relied considerably upon imported grain, which she paid for by manufactured exports, notably cheap clothing : she had little good soil, though no doubt Isocrates is, as usual, exaggerating when he says her cultivators ' have only rocks to farm ' (Is. viii. 117 ; Xen. *Mem.* ii. 7. 6). Her trade connexions with the West, viâ Pegae, were still formally open, but were probably insignificant.

' as because they feared the power of the Athenians, seeing most of Greece already subject to them.' This was in the autumn of 432. The year 431, then, was to see the opening of the decisive struggle between the two great powers for the supremacy of Greece.[1]

Embassies now passed to and fro, raking up old grievances and making impossible demands. When the last set of envoys arrived, the Sovereign People of Athens met in Parliament for the final decision between peace and war. Pericles, as chief adviser, pleaded for steadiness against the faint-hearts who were even now willing to urge a compromise, and then set forth, as General, the policy which he intended to adopt. It was based upon the principle, not of defeat, but of exhaustion. He proposed, not to attack the enemy, but to ignore them, or, if not to leave them quite uninjured, at least to spend upon hurting them as little as possible of Athens' precious resources in money and men. Athens was now, for good or for evil, a sea-power, not a land-power. She must abandon her land without a qualm to the Peloponnesian invader, and prove to him how little he could hope to bring her to terms by trampling her corn-fields and felling her olive-trees. After a few fruitless seasons of campaigning against an invisible foe, they would realize their helplessness and be prepared to accept her supremacy ; for even land campaigns cost money, and the Peloponnesian yeomen farmers would be reluctant to leave their crops just when their labour was needed. The one and only consideration for Athens must be the maintenance of her sea-power. ' Consider for a moment,' he said, with that peculiar impressiveness in his manner (Athenians called it ' Olympian ') which he always adopted when he had anything unpalatable to say. 'Suppose we were islanders : can you conceive a more impregnable position ? Well, this, in future, should as far as possible be our conception of our position. Dismissing all thought of our land and houses, we must keep guard over the sea and the city. . . . We must not cry over the loss of houses and land but of men's lives ; since it is not houses and land that make men, but men them.' With the sea and the city safe, and the treasure on the Acropolis, and the tribute coming in from the Empire, and her traders and craftsmen pursuing their peaceful and prosperous callings, and her garrisons and guard-ships keeping watch over her territorial waters and coasts, Athens

[1] Thuc. i. 80-8, 68-71.

could bid her enemies strike where they were able. She would meet the blow without flinching. Nowhere could they touch the quick.[1]

Athens obeyed Pericles to the letter. A defiant answer was returned to Sparta. Early next spring the country-folk moved into the city, bringing with them ' their children and women and the rest of their household possessions, including the woodwork of the houses themselves ; the sheep and beasts of burden were sent across to Euboea and the adjacent islands.' They found what quarters they could in the overcrowded city, and waited to see what would happen.[2]

What happened was exactly what Pericles had predicted and arranged. The Peloponnesian field army, some 30,000 strong, marched into Attica, just when the corn was ripe, ravaging the country as it went, encamped for some weeks in the plain outside Athens, engaged in a few skirmishes with flying parties of the defenders' horse, and finally, ' after remaining in Attica as long as its provisions lasted, retired home through Boeotia by a different road.'[3]

But these were stirring weeks at Athens. It was not easy for the proud Athenian people to see the enemy at their gates and yet stay crouching behind their walls. Pericles needed to exert all his powers to restrain them. He even stretched his authority as General so far as not to summon the Sovereign People to the ordinary monthly Parliament. In default of this, the constitutional safety-valve, ' knots were formed in the streets and engaged in hot discussion. . . . Oracles of the most various import were recited and found eager listeners. . . . In short, the whole city

[1] Thuc. i. 139–44. On the ' policy of exhaustion ' as a strategic principle see the interesting essay by Delbrück, *Die Strategie des Pericles erläutert durch die Strategie Friedrichs des Grossen*, who invokes the authority of Clausewitz on Pericles' behalf. There has, of course, been a whole literature of writers eager to set Pericles to rights, to some of whom Delbrück refers. As regards devastation, he points out (p. 110) that burning houses is simple enough, but to destroy corn-fields, fruit-trees, and vineyards costs time and trouble. In the Middle Ages armies used to take reapers with them for this purpose. ' To fell a single moderate-sized tree, even with the best implements, takes several hours.' This explains how it was that the Athenians ' were able to enjoy their harvests ' all through the earlier part of the war, down to the occupation of Decelea. (Thuc. vii. 27. 4.)

[2] Thuc. ii. 14–17.

[3] Thuc. ii. 18–23. It was in one of these skirmishes that the Phrygian woodcutter, whose epitaph is given above (p. 278), lost his life. Thucydides only tells us that the Peloponnesian army numbered two-thirds of their whole fighting force. I follow Meyer's estimate (iv, § 545).

was in the most excited condition; Pericles was the object of general indignation; his previous counsels were totally forgotten; he was abused for not leading out the army which he commanded, and was made responsible for the whole of the public suffering.' Pericles, of course, had foreseen this change of temper, and he had his own remedy ready. While the Spartans were still in Attica he sent out a naval force of a hundred ships round the Peloponnese, not with the object of achieving any particular success, but in order to meet pinpricks with pinpricks and to keep up the spirits of the grumbling citizens. In addition to this, he set the regular war-guards ' by land and sea at the points at which it was intended to have regular guards during the war ', thus closing the Athenian domain to all the shipping of the enemy. Henceforward, till peace was declared, all who sailed there without Athens' leave knew themselves to be privateers. Later on in the season he allowed the heavy-armed their outing too. A large force was sent into the Megarid in the early autumn to gratify its lust for vengeance by trampling the stubble-fields and vineyards of its hungry neighbours. They ravaged the greater part of the territory and then retired, resolved to repeat the incursion every year. Such, with a few minor incidents, were the events of the first season's campaigning.[1]

By the end of the season Pericles had regained his full ascendancy. In the autumn, on All Souls Day, when the army was back from Megara, he was chosen to deliver the Funeral Speech over the dead of the year. Thucydides pauses in his narrative to record it, to show us with what high hopes and undimmed ideals Athens and her leader looked forward to the second year of the Great War. Her imperial power was intact and, to all seeming, impregnable. Her allies remained her friends, bound to her by the acceptance of favours from the champion of liberty. Both in public and in private, by her free self-governing institutions and the high personal character of her citizens, Athens was an education to Greece. She was only waiting for a final peace and the definite acknowledgement of her supremacy in order to bring the whole civilized world under her lasting influence.[2]

' Such,' continues Thucydides, with almost unbearable calm, ' was the funeral that took place during this winter, with which

---

[1] Thuc. ii. 21–3, 67 fin., 31.　　　　　Thuc. ii. 34–46: cf. 61. 1.

the first year of the war came to an end.   In the first days of the
next summer, the Lacedaemonians and their allies invaded Attica
as before, and sat down and laid waste the country.   Not many
days after their arrival in Attica the Plague first began to show
itself among the Athenians. . . . All speculation as to its origin
and its causes, if causes can be found adequate to produce so
great a disturbance, I leave to other writers ; for myself I shall
simply set down its nature, and explain the symptoms by which
perhaps it may be recognized by the student, if it should ever
break out again.   This I can the better do as I was a sufferer
myself and watched its operation in others.' [1]

Its bodily symptoms find no place here.   One out of four of
the population succumbed to them, one-fourth of that precious
man-power which Athens could spare so ill.   The remaining
three-fourths survived.   But our concern is not with the body
but with the spirit, not with the citizens but with the city.   Individual Athenians grew well again. Athens herself never recovered.
For the whole of that blazing windless summer and the winter
beyond it, and another summer and another winter beyond them,
the Angel of Death stood over her, laying his hand upon whom he
would.   When he passed away at last for a brief respite, Athens
awoke to find her spirit seared.   The old hope and reverence and
self-discipline and joy had passed away as in a dream.   In their
place were anger and greed and suspicion, mean-eyed envy and
weak despair, and all the devils of disillusionment.   She awoke
clear-eyed to the realities of her position ; she saw herself, at last,
not as a missionary of Freedom but as a Tyrant.   But she had
lost her old power to think quietly and steadily and with saving
thoughts.   Henceforward not even Pericles, weakened himself by
disease, had the power to uplift the minds and hearts of her citizens.
'Fear of gods or law of man there was none to restrain them.' [2]

We must not attempt to trace the details of the long decline
of Athenian policy from the mood of the Funeral Speech, when
Athens is still a Liberator, to the mood of the great Sicilian
Expedition, when she stands self-confessed as a Robber Empire.
Thucydides has marked every step of the way with deadly pre-

Thuc. ii. 47–8.
[2] Thuc. ii. 53, 58. 3, iii. 87 ; Diod. xii. 58. 4.   There was a bad recrudescence
of plague in the winter of 427–426.

cision and quiet unsleeping irony, for he lived through it all himself. We will leave him to tell the story, to which this whole book has been an introduction. All that remains for us here is to mark the full significance of the change, and to point out, in conclusion, some of the milestones by the way.

For a whole wonderful half-century, the richest and happiest period in the recorded history of any single community, Politics and Morality, the deepest and strongest forces of national and of individual life, had moved forward hand in hand towards a common ideal, the perfect citizen in the perfect state. All the high things in human life seemed to lie along that road : ' Freedom, Law, and Progress ; Truth and Beauty ; Knowledge and Virtue ; Humanity and Religion.' Now the gods had put them asunder. Freedom, Law, Virtue, Humanity, and all the old forces of city life lay along one road : Beauty, Knowledge, Progress, and all the great new world of Civilization to which Riches and Empire held the key, along another. The gods had put them asunder. The gods have kept them asunder. Twenty-three centuries have passed ; the world has grown wiser than ever Greeks hoped, kinder than ever they dreamed, and richer far than ever they would have desired ; yet man has not been able to reunite them.

Athens now fell into a mood of childish anger and weakness. Bereft of her ideals for the future, she began to despair even of what she had. 'After the second invasion of the Peloponnesians,' says Thucydides, ' a change came over the spirit of the Athenians. Their land had been twice laid waste, and war and pestilence at once pressed heavily upon them. They began to find fault with Pericles as the author of the war and the cause of all their misfortunes, and became eager to come to terms with Lacedaemon. Indeed, they actually sent ambassadors thither, who did not however succeed in their mission. Their despair was now complete, and all vented itself upon Pericles. When he saw them exasperated at the present turn of affairs and acting exactly as he had anticipated, he called an Assembly, being (it must be remembered) still General, with the double object of restoring confidence and of leading them from these angry feelings to a calmer and more hopeful frame of mind.' [1]

[1] Thuc. ii. 59.

He only partly succeeded, and that at how great a cost ! For, though he turned their minds from an ignominious peace, it was only by setting them, once and for all, into an even more dangerous channel. He tried them first with the old imperial appeal, which he had used so often of late to hearten their resolution : ' born citizens of a great State and with a character worthy of your birth, you should be ready to face the greatest disasters and still to preserve undimmed the lustre of your name.' But the call fell upon deaf ears. The words were the same : it was the audience which had changed. ' I am the same man and do not alter : it is you who change,' said their leader sadly ; and then turned, as orators will, when the meeting is dull, to a more violent and reckless note. ' I will now reveal an advantage arising from the greatness of your dominion which I think has never yet suggested itself to you, as I myself never mentioned it among my previous arguments. It has so bold a sound that I should scarce adventure it now, were it not for the unnatural depression which I see around me. You perhaps think that your Empire extends only over your allies. I will declare to you the truth. The visible field of action has two parts, land and sea. In the whole of one of these you are completely supreme, not merely as far as you use it at present, but also to what further extent you may think fit. Your naval resources are such that your warships may go where they please, and neither the king nor any other nation on earth has power to stop them.' Thus it was that, by one of Fate's cruellest ironies, Pericles, the cautious and clear-sighted, the champion of the Free Sea and Free Intercourse, who had been warning Athens for a whole generation against the dangers of aggrandizement, was the first to preach to her the fatal doctrine of Universal Sea-power.[1]

It was his last recorded public speech. He was sick of the plague when he made it, saddened too by the loss of friends and of his last surviving legitimate son. Soon afterwards he lost his office, and, though he regained it at the next election, he never lived to resume power. It is at this point that he drops out of the history of the war. ' He outlived its commencement two years and six months,' says Thucydides, ' and the correctness of his previsions concerning it became better known by his death.'

Thuc. ii. 60–4.

Plutarch tells a story of his last hours, which reveals more clearly
than his recorded speeches the thought that was most in his
mind. ' When he was at the point of death, his surviving friends
and the principal citizens, sitting about his bed, discoursed together
concerning his excellence as a man and the great authority he
had enjoyed, and enumerated his various exploits and the number
of his victories ; for while he was General he had raised no less
than nine trophies of battle in the city's honour. These things
they talked of, supposing that he attended not to what they said,
but that his senses were gone. But he took notice of every word,
and found voice to answer them as follows : ' I am surprised that,
while you recollect and extol these acts of mine, though fortune had
her share in them and many other generals have performed the like,
you take no notice of the greatest and most honourable thing of all,
that no Athenian through my fault ever put on a mourning robe.'
Pericles died with a rebuke to the War-spirit upon his lips.[1]

With the passing of Pericles the change of spirit is complete.
Gentleness and chivalry and idealism form no part now of the
city's life. Her new-found advisers care nothing for moral issues,
and take no heed of saving thoughts. Wise or foolish, they set
their course by expediency and interest alone. The old imperial
boasts—Athens' care of the weak, her defence of the oppressed—
stir men's courage no longer. Her one faithful mainland ally,
Plataea, who alone was with her at Marathon, sends in this same
year to say that the Peloponnesians are at her gates. Shall she
risk a siege ? Her envoys return with this message, given in
the proud old style : ' The Athenians say that they have never
hitherto on any occasion abandoned us, nor will they now neglect
us, but will help us according to their ability ; and they adjure
you by the oaths which your fathers swore, to keep the alliance
unaltered.' Mindful of the oaths, the Plataeans obeyed them.
But Athens did neglect them : for it was not considered expedient to risk a battle. She was too busy extending her sea-
power in distant waters, and could not spare the money and men.
For two years Plataea held out in hope, while the Athenians
roamed the seas from Crete and Caria to the Corinthian Gulf ;
when at last she was reduced by hunger, her survivors were put to
death for their dependence on Athenian promises. Yet the little

[1] Thuc. ii. 65 ; Plut. *Per.* 36–8.

city lay but a night and a day's march from her ally, on the further
slope of the range which bounds the plain of Athens. As she
was trustful, the Athenians, watching the sun set behind her
mountain, could afford to neglect her. What would they have
done had she proved faithless ? [1]

We cannot tell, for Plataea was only an ally, not a subject :
she had no money value, for she paid no tribute. But we know
what arguments were used when a subject withdrew her allegiance.
A year after Pericles' death, Mytilene, one of the richest states
in the Empire, and one of the few which still preferred to contribute ships instead of money, suddenly revolted. Athens was
stirred to feverish activity. She sent out a large fleet, and soon
news came that all was well. The popular party in Mytilene had
reasserted itself, and the city had given its adherence. An
assembly was held to discuss what treatment should be meted
out to the rebels. Thucydides has recorded the debate, in order
that we may see the new spirit at work.[2]

It was not a contest between ideals and expediency, for no
one cared for ideals now, but between wisdom and folly. Athens'
most persuasive adviser was now a Parliamentarian called Cleon,
whom Thucydides describes as ' in all respects the most violent
man in the city ', the very embodiment of the mad war-spirit
which was driving Athens down the decline. Cleon's advice
was very simple : to give the allies a lesson in loyalty by putting
to death the whole population of Mytilene. He carried the
assembly ; but on second thoughts the debate was resumed, and
at the further sitting saner counsels prevailed. It was decided
that it would be more expedient to execute, not the entire population, but only the ringleaders. ' These,' adds Thucydides grimly,
' numbered rather more than a thousand.' The reasoning that
swayed her was financial ; for the pursuit of universal sea-power
was proving a drain on the city treasure. We must encourage

---

[1] Thuc. ii. 73, 85. 5-6, iii. 19, 20-4, 52-68. Plataea lies about thirty miles
from Athens, on the northern slope of Mount Cithaeron, overlooking the
Boeotian plain. It is within an easy day's march from the frontier fort of
Oenoe, which remained in Athenian hands all this time (Thuc. ii. 19, i ; cf.
viii. 98). No sooner had Plataea fallen than Athens began to form schemes
for the invasion of Boeotia. Ambition descried a way where loyalty could
find none. Thuc. iii. 95, iv. 77. Cithaeron is full in view from the Acropolis;
on Midsummer Day the sun sets just behind its summit.

[2] Thuc. iii. 2-18, 25-8.

cities, urged the winning speaker, to ' come to terms while they are still able to refund expenses and to pay tribute afterwards '. If we are merciless with revolted allies we shall be reduced each time to ' the expense of a siege, and when we are victorious we shall secure a ruined town from which we can no longer draw the revenue which forms our real strength against the enemy '. Athens had lost her humanity ; but so far, despite Cleon, she still retained some of her common sense.[1]

Two years later, in the seventh year of the war, the luck turned suddenly, as happened sometimes in Greek wars. Athens succeeded, by a succession of accidents, in isolating a detachment of Spartan citizens on an island off their coast, in a position where it was impossible for the land-power to relieve them. Sparta, with her diminishing citizen-body and ever in fear of a Helot revolt, could not afford to sacrifice them. The danger brought her to her knees. She sent envoys to Athens to sue humbly for peace. The terms she offered were the terms for which Pericles had advised Athens to wait. Sparta agreed to abide loyally by the *status quo*, to accept the fact of the Athenian Empire and the consequent supremacy of the sea-power over the land-power. ' The Lacedaemonians,' said their envoys, addressing the Sovereign People, ' invite you to make a treaty and to end the war, offering peace and alliance and the most friendly and intimate relations in every way.' They felt no doubt at all as to the reception of the offer. The war had already lasted far longer than was customary, and not only Sparta, but all Greece, had grown tired of the fighting mood. Moreover they knew, or could guess, how severely the Athenians were feeling the strain, in the loss of men and of treasure. ' If peace was ever desirable for both parties it is surely so at the present moment, before anything inexpiable occurs between us, before our public hostilities are transformed into a bitter and intimate personal hatred.'[2]

Before the Sovereign People give answer let us join them in their deliberations and see which way the balance inclined, towards peace or towards war.

---

[1] Thuc. iii. 36–50.

[2] Thuc. iv. 3–20, esp. 20. 1. ἀνήκεστος is a very strong word : ' inexpiable,' ' irremediable,' give only a shadow of its full religious meaning ; it is associated with the old idea of bloodguiltiness or pollution by murder ; cf. pp. 99 ff. above and Soph. *O. T.* 98.

They had been fighting now for nine seasons, dating from the affray at Corcyra, at first merely on the defensive, except for summer raids, but latterly, since Pericles died, on the offensive too, keeping ships at sea during the winter outside their own waters, and sending troops far afield, to Aetolia and even to Sicily. How had the six thousand talents of Acropolis treasure withstood these unwonted demands ?

Fortunately we are in a position to present Cleon's audience with the bill. Reconstructed from the fragmentary inscriptions of payments made to the generals, the chief heads of expenditure on campaigns, exclusive of shipbuilding and other extras, had been as follows :—

Year 433.	Corcyra	30 talents.
„ 432.	Thracian Expedition	100 „
	Siege of Potidaea (from September) . . .	500 „
„ 431.	Siege of Potidaea	1,000 „
	100 ships round Peloponnese (June to September) .	200 „
	30 ships to Locris (June to September) . • .	30 „
„ 430.	Siege of Potidaea	1,000 „
	150 ships to Peloponnese (July), then to Potidaea (up to September)	225 „
	At this point Pericles retires from power. •	
	20 ships to Naupactus (all the winter) . .	40 „
„ 429.	4,000 heavy-armed and 400 horse in Thrace up till June	120 „
	20 ships at Naupactus under Phormio, spring 429 to spring 428	120 „
	20 ships sent to Phormio via Crete (October 429– spring 428)	40 „
„ 428.	40 ships equipped for Peloponnese sent to Mytilene (pay at one dr.)	150 „
	30 ships, later reduced to 12, round Naupactus .	30 „
	100 ships to Asia Minor	100 „
„ 428.	(Winter) 5,000 heavy-armed for siege of Mytilene .	200 „
	12 ships at Naupactus	24 „
„ 427.	Siege of Mytilene (to July)	200 „
	60 ships to Corcyra (August)	30 „
	12 ships at Naupactus	75 „
	20 ships to Sicily (pay at one dr.) . . .	100 „
„ 426.	(Up to July) 12 ships at Naupactus . .	24 „
	20 ships in Sicily	80 „
	Sums advanced to generals in Sicily . . .	480 „
	2,000 heavy-armed and 60 ships under Nicias .	35 „
	30 ships and troops under Demosthenes for Aetolia	65 „

Total . . . . 4,998 talents.[1]

[1] Cavaignac, pp. 120–1, a very moderate estimate indeed, as he calculates pay at 3 obols, except where the contrary is stated. I believe the one drachma

At the beginning of the war Pericles had persuaded the People to set aside one thousand out of their six thousand talents of treasure, and to decree, on pain of death, that they should only be touched in the last resort, when Athens had suffered defeat at sea, and the enemy's fleet was advancing upon the Piraeus. Of the remaining 4,700 talents a good proportion had been spent during Pericles' leadership on the strictly necessary task of quelling the revolt of Potidaea. It was, then, with very much diminished resources, not only in men but in money, that Athens entered upon the pursuit of universal sea-power.[1]

Already three years before this time, in the spring of 428, at the news of the revolt of Mytilene, Athens had found herself in financial straits. She needed money for her fleet before the year's tribute arrived, and met the need by adopting the unwonted device of a direct tax upon her citizens. A sum of 200 talents was raised upon the capital value of the citizens' property, probably at the rate of one per cent. In the same year the four-yearly reassessment of the allies' contributions fell due. Under the wise guidance of the men who had rescued the tax-payers of Mytilene she made a few minor alterations, but left the total practically unchanged. It stood as high as was compatible with safe and inexpensive collection; and a time of crisis was not the moment to run the risk of further revolts.[2]

Two years had passed since then, and Athens had still been spending. Now came the offer of peace, not only with honour but with acknowledged victory. We have heard the speech of the Spartan envoys. What reply did the People give?

' The Athenians,' says Thucydides, ' having the men enclosed on the island, thought that the treaty would be ready for them whenever they chose to make it, and were in a mood for grasping at something further. Foremost to encourage them was Cleon,

rate, given in Thuc. iii. 17. 4, to have been usual : it was the ordinary wage for a day's work at this time. Moreover, the heavy-armed at Potidaea received two drachmas, one for themselves and one for an attendant. On the other hand, three months is perhaps too long a reckoning for the summer expeditions in 431.

[1] Thuc. ii. 24 ; cf. viii. 15 ; Ar. *Lys.* 174.

[2] Thuc. iii. 19 ; Cavaignac, p. 125. The supposed loan from the local authorities, mentioned in the first edition of this work, with a reference to Hicks and Hill, No. 58, was based upon one letter in an inscription which Wilhelm reads differently ἀ[ποδεκτôν] for δ[ημαρχôν]. See *Göttingische Gelehrte Anzeigen*, 1903, p. 775.

son of Cleaenetus, a popular speaker of the day and very powerful with the multitude.' Under Cleon's persuasion they demanded impossible conditions. The envoys did not refuse them, but showed the seriousness of their intentions by replying with reason and good temper. ' They asked that commissioners might be chosen with whom they could confer on each point, so as to talk the matter over quietly and attempt to reach some agreement.' They appealed from Philip drunk to Philip sober, from the Sovereign People in General Assembly to the Sovereign People in Committee. This gave the Parliamentarian his cue. ' He knew from the first, he said, that they had no right intentions; it was clear enough to all now. They were ashamed to speak before the People, preferring to confer in secret with two or three. No ! if they meant anything honest let them say it out before all.' Of course he had his way. ' The Lacedaemonians, seeing that whatever concessions they might be prepared to make in their humiliation it was impossible for them to speak before the multitude and lose credit with their allies for a negotiation in which they might after all miscarry, and, on the other hand, that the Athenians would never grant what they asked for upon moderate terms, returned home from Athens with their mission unfulfilled.' Thus, when victory came to her, Athens coldly averted her eyes. The winged and flighty goddess never came near her again.[1]

Cleon was now her acknowledged leader, and his foolish violence her evil genius. If the citizens desired to live in idleness, varied by the excitements of naval campaigning, it would be easy to find the money. No need to raise it at home when there was treasure overseas to be had for the asking, ' from the Black Sea to Sardinia.' Henceforward Athenians paid no more war-taxes. Cleon showed them a better way. Let their lazy subjects eastwards and westwards pay for the privilege of Athenian rule. In the autumn of this year Athens broke the Charter of her Empire—the contract drawn up two generations before by Aristeides the Just between Athens and her Allies—and doubled the rates of tribute.[2]

[1] Thuc. iv. 21, 22.
[2] Cavaignac, p. 128 ; cf. 124 and 132 (disappearance of the war-tax) and *Wasps* 700 ; cf. Francotte, *Finances*, pp. 99 and 115.

Portions of this revised tribute-list still remain to us. We have the title and the grand total, and a good many of the detailed entries. Let us set out the first dozen in the Province of the Islands, putting together the old rates with the new, in order to show how Cleon went to work.[1]

Paros	.	.	.	30 talents instead of 16 talents, 1,200 dr.
Naxos	.	.	.	15 „ „ „ 6 „ 4,000 dr.
Andros	.	.	.	15 „ „ „ 6 „
Melos	.	.	.	15 „
Siphnos	.	.	.	9 „ „ „ 3 „
Eretria	.	.	.	15 „ „ „ 9 „
Thera	.	.	.	5 „ „ „ 3 „
Ceos	.	.	.	10 „ „ „ 4 „
Carystos	.	.	.	5 „ „ „ 5 „
Chalcis	.	.	.	10 „ „ „ 6 „
Cythnos	.	.	.	6 „ „ „ 3 „
Tenos	.	.	.	10 „ „ „ 3 „

One entry here will have arrested the reader's attention. Why is there no earlier rate of payment for Melos? Because that island had hitherto been successful, alone in the Archipelago, in preserving its neutrality. It needed no protection from Athens, and had never provoked her hostility; so she had always allowed it to remain outside the meshes of her Aegean sea-power. It was a small rocky island with home-keeping Dorian traditions, which traced back its quiet history over seven hundred years of unbroken life. No one had thought it worth while to fit out an expedition against it, till Cleon, the great financier, entered it upon his revised list.[2]

For nine years the islanders remained upon the list; but they never paid. At last, in 416, during a temporary lull of the unending war, Athens bethought her of the arrears and deter-

---

[1] *I. G.* i. 37, printed in Hicks and Hill, No. 64, and partly in Cavaignac, p. 128. The heading is simply Τάξις φόρου, the total 960, against Aristeides' 460 (raised to 600 by the Samian Indemnity &c., see note on p. 415 above). Thucydides does not mention the assessment, but cf. iv. 51 for the consequent anxiety of Chios.

[2] Thuc. v. 112. 2. There is no suggestion in Thucydides or any other fifth-century writer, that the Melians abused their neutrality by indulging in piracy or privateering. In spite of the bareness of their country and their fine land-locked harbour, they remained agricultural, like their fellow Dorians in Crete. The market-place of their city has been identified by the British excavators. It lies at the highest point of the city (which lay on a steep hill slope), conveniently for transport with the interior, not with the harbour (*J. H. S.*, vol. xvii, p. 131; *B. S. A.*, vol. ii, pp. 77 ff., with photograph): this is probably the Agora mentioned by Thucydides in v. 115.

mined to compel them. Troops were dispatched to the island, and their generals sent envoys into the little rock-bound city to demand the money. An interchange of views followed between the island leaders and their visitors. Thucydides has selected the occasion for his most intense and ironical description of the war spirit at work. ' We shall not trouble you with specious pretences,' say the Athenians, with that chilling candour which their public speakers were now so proud to display, ' either of how we have a right to our Empire because we overthrew the Persians, or are now attacking you because of wrong that you have done us. You know as well as we do that right, as the world goes, is only in question between equals in power, while the strong do what they can and the weak suffer what they must.'

' As we think, at any rate,' pleaded the Melians, ' it is expedient that you should not destroy what is our common protection, the privilege of being allowed in danger to invoke what is fair and right. Surely you are as much concerned in this as any, since your fall would be a signal for the heaviest vengeance, and an example to all the world.'

' We feel no uneasiness about the end of our Empire, even if end it should,' came back the proud answer, as if to challenge the high gods ; ' a fellow Empire, like Lacedaemon—though it is not she who is our real enemy—is not so terrible to the vanquished as subjects who by themselves attack and overpower their rulers. This, however, is a risk that we are content to take.'

' And how, pray,' ask the Melians, ' could it turn out as good for us to be subjects as for you to rule us ? '

' Because you would have the advantage of submitting before suffering the worst, and we should profit by not having wiped you out.'

' Do your subjects accept this as a reasonable policy—to put strangers and neutrals in the same category with States that are most of them your own colonists and some of them even conquered rebels ? '

' So far as right goes,' replied the sea-power, ' our subjects consider that one has as much of it as the other : that if any maintain their independence it is because they are powerful, and that if we do not molest them it is because we are afraid. So that, besides extending our Empire, we should gain in security by your subjection; and the fact that you are islanders, and weaker than others, renders it all the more necessary that you should not succeed in baffling the masters of the sea.'

'But we know that the fortune of war is sometimes more impartial than the disproportion of numbers might lead one to suppose. To submit is to accept despair, while resistance still preserves for us a hope that we may stand upright.'

'Hope is ever danger's comforter,' was the prophetic answer. 'Let those take her to their breast who have abundance of resources. Wound them she may; she will have no power to kill. But her nature is to be a spendthrift; and, when men stake all upon her ventures, it is only in the hour of ruin that they behold her face unveiled.'

'You may be sure that we are as well aware as you of the difficulty of contending against your power and fortune, unless the terms are equal. But we trust that the gods may grant us fortune as good as yours, since we are just men fighting against unjust.'

The appeal to religion and morality, the last resort of the simple islanders, stirred the intellectual interest of their visitors from the great world. They had learnt their philosophy in a sterner school, not at the humble shrines of a backward island, but in the field of affairs and experience. They were practical men, and politicians; and they were proud to have faced the facts. So, with the mocking simplicity of the intellectual preaching sense to his country cousin, they end by expounding the creed which enlightened Athens now professed. It was more than a creed; it was a rule of life. So it is well for us, as it was for Melos, that she frankly stated it. 'When you speak of the favour of the gods we may as fairly hope for that as you, neither our pretensions nor our conduct being in any way contrary to what men believe of the gods, or practise among themselves. Of the gods we believe; and of men we know, that by a necessary law of their nature they rule wherever they can. It is not as if we were the first to make this law, or to act upon it when made. We found it in the world before us, and shall leave it in the world after us; all we do is to make use of it, knowing that you and everybody else, having the same power as we have, would do the same as we do. Thus, so far as the gods are concerned, we have no fear at all.'[1]

The Athenians withdrew from the conference, leaving the Melians to debate. Their decision was soon announced. ' Our resolution, men of Athens, is the same as it was at first. We will not in one moment deprive of liberty a city that can look back over seven hundred years of free life. We put our trust in the fortune by which the gods have preserved it until now, and in the help of men, that is, of the Lacedaemonians. So we will try and save ourselves.'

Neither gods nor men came to their aid. They held out through the autumn and made two successful sallies. At last, in the winter, the besiegers sent for reinforcements. ' The siege was now pressed vigorously ; and, some treachery taking place inside, the Melians surrendered at discretion.' Athens had grown too worldly-wise by now to repeat her clemency at Mytilene. ' The Athenians put to death all the grown men and sold the women and children for slaves. Later, they sent out five hundred settlers and inhabited the place themselves.'[2]

So Melos never paid Athens tribute. But there was once more corn in her little valleys and men sat in her city market-place drinking the sweet wine from her hillsides.

> Where bled her children hangs the loaded sheaf.
> Forgetful is green earth ; the Gods alone
> Remember everlastingly : they strike
> Remorselessly, and ever like for like.
> By their great memories the Gods are known.

Still hungry, the imperial city lifted up her eyes towards a better prey, from a small island in the East towards a larger in the West. Six months after the sack of Melos the Great Armada left port for Sicily.

---

[1] Thuc. v. 85–105. I have considerably abridged the conversation, but have not worried the reader by marking the omissions. The translation is substantially Crawley's.

[2] Thuc. v. *fin.* Remember, in reading this part of Thucydides, that the division into books is not his own. See *I. G.* xii. 1187 for an inscription dedicated by one of the Melians who betrayed his city, and was granted Athenian citizenship for his services. [See Appendix.]

APPENDIX

PAGE 25, note. 'Commander Binger, the French explorer, states that the lack of salt was one of the causes which promoted the slave trade in the region of the Upper Niger. For the salt came from the North, and in the absence of portable produce the vendors took slaves in payment.' Lugard, *The Dual Mandate in Tropical Africa*, p. 266. See now also Pauly, *s.v.* Salz (1920).

PAGE 27. The view that Carthaginian mystifications were responsible for the legendary character which the Atlantic assumed for the Greeks of the classical period is confirmed by recent investigation. See A. Schulten, *Fontes Hispaniae Antiquae*, Part i, *Avienus* (Barcelona, 1922), and *Tartessos, ein Beitrag zur ältesten Geschichte des Westens* (Hamburg, 1922). Schulten holds that the *Ora Maritima* of Avienus (fourth century A.D.) embodies valuable material from the early Greek geographers, and in particular from the περίπλους of a Marseilles writer of the sixth century B.C., and that Atlantis is a legendary memory of the Phocaean settlement at Tartessus (Cadiz), which was later wiped out, and its whereabouts obscured, by the Carthaginians. I am indebted for this reference to an article by Fritz Netolitzky, in the first (January, 1924) issue of *Cultura*, a periodical issued at Cluj, in Transylvania, in the Roumanian, Hungarian, German, and French languages. Netolitzky goes so far as to identify Atlantis with the island of Santipetri, twelve miles south of Cadiz. Compare the difficulties experienced by British seaman in penetrating eastwards from the Atlantic. The first recorded venture of an Englishman to the Levant in an English ship was that of Robert Sturmy of Bristol in 1458; he was captured and robbed by the Genoese on his way home because he was said to be bringing green pepper and other spices to plant in England, and so render the country independent of the Italian trade. See Williamson, *A Short History of British Expansion*, 1922, p. 28. For the first appearance of up-to-date British seamanship (in no very respectable guise), and, later, of British sea-power in the Mediterranean, see the fascinating account in Corbett, *England in the Mediterranean*, vol. i, ch. 2, and following.

PAGE 34. According to Rostovtzeff, *Iranians and Greeks in Southern Russia* (Oxford, 1922), the Greek colonies in the Crimea, e. g. Phanagoria, Nymphaeum, and Panticapaeum, were established in order to exploit the fisheries of the Sea of Azov and the Strait of Kertsch (the Cimmerian Bosporus). 'The same causes led to the creation of a fishing colony at the mouth of the Dnieper and the Bug; this colony was Olbia, and it had a branch on the island of Berezan' at the mouth of the Gulf (p. 44).

'In the course of the eighth and seventh centuries, the mouths of the great fishing rivers on this route, the Danube, the Dniester, the Bug, the Dnieper, were occupied, one after the other, by Milesian fishing colonies' (p. 63).

PAGE 36.   Rostovtzeff, *op. cit*, gives a full account of the Greek colonies in the climatic enclave mentioned in the text, and of their relations with the Scythians of the hinterland and the peoples subject to them.

PAGE 60.   It is interesting to note that privacy is more foreign to American than to traditional British arrangements.   American towns with their unwalled and unhedged garden plots are Greek rather than English in their democratic openness.

PAGE 74.   On the Indian influence in Plato see now Urwick, *The Message of Plato*, 1920, who bases his interpretation of the *Republic* upon Indian religious thought.   Unfortunately, considerations of space have compelled him to omit 'a long inquiry into the channels by which Indian thought penetrated Greece in the sixth and fifth centuries B. c.', so that his argument as it stands is based simply on internal evidence.

PAGE 82.   Mention must be made of the as yet (1924) unpublished work of Calhoun on the evolution of criminal law in Greece, several chapters of which are summarized by him in *Proceedings of the Classical Association*, xviii (1922), pp. 86 ff.

PAGE 87.   See now also in general substantiation of the account in the text Calhoun, *loc. cit.*, p. 93.

PAGE 89.   For the lotless man see now also Glotz, *Le Travail dans la Grèce ancienne*, Paris, 1920, pp. 37 ff., an admirable book, marred only by the omission of references.

PAGE 110.   On the early history of Sparta see now Toynbee in *J. H. S.* 1913, pp. 246 ff., and the brief but useful summary of the results of recent archaeological and historical research by Woodward in *History*, October 1923.   For the constitutional organization of Sparta in the historic period see Kahrstedt, *Griechisches Staatsrecht*, vol. i (Göttingen, 1922), which is almost wholly devoted to Sparta.   The long overdue incursion of jurists, such as Vinogradoff, Calhoun, and Kahrstedt, into the field of the Greek city-state is one of the most striking features of Greek study during the last decade.   This development might well have been consecrated by the inclusion of a chapter on Greek Law in the Oxford volume on *The Legacy of Greece* (1922), an omission which will perhaps be repaired later.   The defenders of Roman originality have been hard pressed by the discovery of Rome's debt to Greece in the last field that remained to them.   Compare the circumscribed and qualified claim made by de Zulueta in *The Legacy of Rome* (Oxford, 1923), pp. 186–8, with the confident attitude of Holland, who unreservedly credits the Roman jurisconsults with the 'beginnings' of the science of law.   See Holland's *Jurisprudence*, eleventh edition, pp. 2 ff., and Calhoun, 'Greek Law and Modern Jurisprudence', *California Law Review*, July 1923.

PAGE 111.   On κορυνηφόροι and κυνόφαλοι (not κυνόφιλοι) see now Pauly, *s.v.*: the Sicyonian club-carriers were, it appears, a bodyguard, not a class of dependents.

PAGE 113. As Glotz, *Travail*, pp. 114–18, points out in his excellent but too brief account of Sparta, the Perioeci were also largely engaged in industry, trade, fishing, and navigation. All these occupations were forbidden to Spartiates after the Lycurgan organization had put an end to the artistic development of which recent excavations have revealed us the traces. On Perioeci and Helots see now also Toynbee, *loc. cit.*, with map, showing the distribution of the various lands in Laconia and Messenia: also Kahrstedt, pp. 1–8 (the geographical distribution of the Spartan state) and pp. 57–81 ff. (status of Helots and Perioeci), where he points to the fact that the Helots were Doric-speaking as showing that they were not a primitive people conquered by the incoming Dorians, in which case, as he truly says, they would, according to historical analogy, have preserved their own language, like the Esthonians, Latvians, and Lithuanians of the Baltic coast under German feudal overlordship. See also Pareti, *Storia di Sparta arcaica*, Part i (Florence, 1920), pp. 154 ff.

PAGE 133. The Gortyn inscriptions have now been re-edited with a valuable commentary in systematic legal form by Kohler and Ziebarth, Göttingen, 1912.

PAGE 135. See now also Calhoun in *Proceedings of Classical Association*, xviii (1922), p. 88.

PAGE 143. For the silver coinage introduced by Pisistratus see now P. Gardner, *History of Ancient Coinage*, 1918, pp. 157–8. Its influence was felt as far afield as Sicily, where the tyrants of Syracuse issued money on the Athenian standard.

PAGE 164. See now Ledl, *Studien zur älteren athenischen Verfassungs geschichte*, Heidelberg, 1914, who argues (pp. 364 ff.), but not very convincingly, that the system of αἵρεσις ἐκ προκρίτων did not date from Solon or Cleisthenes but was first introduced in 411.

PAGE 176. On the Scythian bowmen see now also the well-illustrated article of Plassart in *Revue des Études grecques*, 1913, 151 ff.

PAGE 187. This has since been confirmed by Woodward, *B. S. A.* xv, pp. 243 ff.

PAGE 189. See now also Vinogradoff, *Jurisprudence of the Greek City-State* (1922), pp. 157 and 161.

PAGE 193. P. Gardner, *op. cit.*, p. 226, following Babelon, takes the view that Athens claimed a complete monopoly of the issue of coins where she was strong enough to enforce it, as opposed to the more liberal policy attributed to her in the text. He admits, however, that his conclusion is mainly based upon negative evidence, and the absence of local issues of the higher denominations in most of the Aegean islands and Asiatic cities (but not in other parts of the Athenian Empire), during the Periclean period may equally well be due to considerations of convenience. For the facts, besides Cavaignac, cited on p. 193 above, see Gardner, pp. 222 ff. and esp. pp. 285 ff., Weil in *Zeitschrift für Numis-*

matik, xxviii, pp. 357 ff., and Babelon, *Revue Numismatique*, 1913, pp. 457 ff. The electrum coins of Phocaea (Thuc. iv. 52) and Mytilene deserve special mention beside those of Lampsacus and Cyzicus : see Babelon, *loc. cit.*, p. 475, and Pauly, *s.v.* Cyzicenoi. Gardner however adduces a further argument, which he considers conclusive—the Siphnian decree in *I. G.* xii. 5 480. But the most probable date for that inscription, from its form and lettering, is between 420 and 415 (Weil, *loc. cit.*, xxv, p. 56), and there is no sufficient reason for putting the previous decree of Clearchus, mentioned in it, as much earlier. The well-known passage in the *Birds* (line 1040), the importance of which in this connexion was detected by Wilamowitz before the Siphnian inscription came to light, bears out this conclusion, which is that of Cavaignac, *Histoire*, ii, pp. 138-9.

PAGE 216, note. A small point worth noting is that Greek garments, as described in the text, had no pockets. As Halliday, *Growth of the City-State* (Liverpool University Press), points out, larger articles, such as paper, vegetables, or lap-dogs, could be carried in the folds of the ἱμάτιον. Small change, of necessity, was carried in the mouth. This is probably' one of the reasons, adds Halliday, why Attic small coins were of silver, and not of copper.

PAGE 233. See now Glotz, *Travail*, pp. 300 ff., who estimates that Attica produced at the most one quarter of Athenian needs (i. e. in oil and wine as well as corn).

PAGE 235. See now on this whole subject Heitland, *Agricola*, Cambridge, 1921, and Orth in Pauly, *s.v.* Landwirtschaft (1924), with bibliography, which, however, omits Heitland.

PAGE 243. Andreades (*Revue des Études grecques*, xxviii, pp. 377 ff.) has made an interesting study of what he describes, perhaps with excessive precision, as 'les finances de l'état homérique'. See esp. p. 393 (on 'Did the Homeric kings provide rations for their troops ?') and pp. 406 ff. entitled 'Extraordinary Receipts', which are discussed under two heads, (i) 'parasitic finance', i. e. the proceeds of warfare, piracy, &c., and (ii) 'royal revenues in time of war', i.e. the king's share of the booty.

PAGE 251. I leave the paragraph on pp. 245-6 unaltered, although, strictly speaking, it should be rewritten in the past tense. For there has now come into existence, embodied in the Covenant of the League of Nations, itself inserted in the four peace-treaties, a binding engagement against resorting to the arbitrament of war. It is true that, after a nine-months delay for processes of conciliation, war may still be legitimate under the Covenant, although even in that event territorial annexation is ruled out. But war between Great Powers within these constitutional limits, if theoretically admissible, has become practically inconceivable; and, as to war between lesser states, or between a Great Power and a lesser state, the experience of 1914 seems to show that such hostilities have become increasingly difficult to localize, both in Europe and outside it. We have entered in fact, since the paragraph was written, on a period of transition which will culminate, unless all our safeguards break down, in the general acceptance of force in international affairs no longer as the arbitrary and clumsy expedient of pre-war days, but as a collective sanction to be employed by the Society of States against a law-breaker. That the transition of thought and practise thus involved is difficult and full of danger will not escape any reader of this volume or any attentive student of democracy; that it is not only desirable but necessary and urgent is as clear to me now as it was when I penned the preface to the second edition.

PAGE 256. For those who wish to compare Greek and British methods of colonization there is now an excellent general account of the latter from the earliest days onward, with a good bibliography, in *A Short History of British Expansion* by James A. Williamson, London, 1922.

PAGE 258. For a recent example of the tendency referred to at the close of the note see Ure, *The Age of Tyrants* (1922).

PAGE 277. Labour conscription has recently been temporarily adopted in Bulgaria and, for week-end periods, in Soviet Russia. It was recommended on quite different grounds by William James in his essay on 'The Moral Equivalent of War' published in *Memories and Studies* (1911). His object is to 'breed the martial type of character without war'.

PAGE 302. The tendency referred to at the end of the note has been well—too well—illustrated in the discussions on the Reparations Question.

PAGE 303. See Babelon, *les Origines de la Monnaie*, pp. 93–134, who maintains that the earliest coins, in Greece as elsewhere, were struck by merchants and capitalists rather than by public authorities. He adduces many examples of this, both in the Old World and the New, to which it may be added that a merchant coinage of this kind is still in existence in the Northern Territory of Australia.

PAGE 304. P. Gardner, p. 68, believes that it was the Greek cities of Asia Minor and not the Lydian kings who were responsible for the earliest electrum coinage. But, as he admits, the balance of numismatic opinion is against him. In any case, it is certain that Croesus (560–546) superseded this electrum coinage of his predecessors by a gold and silver currency which, as Gardner believes (pp. 82–3), was the first of its kind. See also Babelon, *les Monnaies grecques* (Paris, Payot Manuals, 1921), pp. 10–11 and 24.

PAGE 332. See also van Hook in *Transactions of the American Philological Association*, 1920, pp. 134 ff.

PAGE 344. On the age of marriage see Plato, *Rep.* 460, *Laws* 785, Ar. *Pol.* 1335 (who lays down the best age for girls as from 16 to 20 and for men from 30 to 35), Eur. frag. 24 (Nauck), Aristoph. *Lys.* 597, and the whole tone of the description in Xenophon's *Oeconomicus*.

PAGE 372. Cary (*Classical Quarterly*, vii, pp. 198 ff.) argues that the 200 ships mentioned in Thuc. i. 104 refer to a force sent to Cyprus and subsequently divided, part going to Phoenicia, part to Egypt, and part, perhaps, remaining behind at Cyprus. This explanation, which is not precluded by Thucydides' words, would explain why the disaster to the expedition was not more fully exploited by the enemies of Athens. For Crete see Thuc. ii. 85. 5 (a πρόξενος at Gortyn, i. e. on the direct Egyptian route).

PAGE 389. See Heitland, *Agricola*, pp. 446 ff., on why there was never an 'Abolitionist' movement in antiquity.

PAGE 395 See also Glotz, *Travail*, pp. 254–7, and Brillant, *Les Sécretaires Athéniens*, Paris, 1911 ; also Lysias xxx. 2 ff. for the story of Nicomachus, who, having become in his servile profession as Clerk of the Court the most learned lawyer in Athens, was chosen as one, and evidently the most important, member of the body of ἀναγραφεῖς constituted to form a new code of laws after the Revolution of 411. For the Scythian slave police see p. 176 above.

PAGE 410. Dinsmoor, *American Journal of Archaeology*, 1913, pp. 64–5, has reconstituted the building accounts of the Acropolis buildings, and shown that the contribution from the funds of the Confederacy to the building of the Propylaea from 437–436 to 433–432 'is specified as $\frac{1}{60}$ of the annual tribute ', i. e. the sum rightfully due to Athena. The accounts for the Parthenon itself (447–446 to 438–437) are too much mutilated to show this item, but, in Dinsmoor's opinion, ' it is practically certain ' that the Confederacy contributed no more than the rightful sixtieth to the Parthenon itself. But it is difficult to reconcile this view with the very definite statement as to the controversy between Pericles and Thucydides the son of Melesias in Plut. *Per.* 12 ff. Dinsmoor's explanation is that Thucydides' charge against Pericles of misappropriating the Confederacy funds was a falsehood ; but on so important an issue this is hardly credible, nor is it consistent with Plutarch's account. It is simpler to hold, with Cavaignac, p. 93, that the main fund of the Confederacy was handed over to the treasurers of the goddess and that the treasurers of the Confederacy 'continued to occupy their posts, to receive the tribute and to defray current military expenses, but retained only small sums in their own hands '.

PAGE 411. Woodward, *B. S. A.* xvi, pp. 187 ff., and Dinsmoor, *loc. cit.*, have shown that the Parthenon sculptures, which it was generally thought were contemporaneous with the building itself, were being constructed from 439–438 to 433–432, when they were completed. As Pheidias was in disgrace after 438 it seems probable therefore that he did not supervise their execution.

PAGE 419. See now the full account of the Athenian financial system by Andreades in vol. i, pp. 229 ff., of ἱστορία τῆς Ἑλληνικῆς δημοσίας οἰκονομίας ἀπὸ τῶν ἡρωικῶν χρόνων μεχρὶ τῆς συστασέως τοῦ Ἑλληνικοῦ βασιλείου, who has gone most systematically over the whole ground.

PAGE 420. For the relations between Corinth and her colonies see now Kahrstedt, pp. 357 ff.

PAGE 443. For the compatibility of Thucydides' account with the epigraphical evidence see Woodward in *J. H. S.* xxxiv, p. 289, refuting Gardner. For Melos as a base for piratical operations in the fourth century, under its new population, see [Dem.] lviii. 56, attributed to Deinarchus. The Melians succeeded in cheating their Athenian victors to the extent of burying a small hoard of about a hundred coins from their local mint, which were not unearthed until 1907. See Jameson in *Revue Numismatique*, 1909, pp. 188 ff., Weil in *Zeitschrift fur Numismatik*, xxviii, p. 359, and Babelon in *Revue Numism.*, 1913, p. 471. See also p. 193 above and note in Appendix. The obverse of the coinage bears an apple ($\mu\tilde{\eta}\lambda o\nu$), the reverse varies, showing dolphins, the murex, a cartwheel, and religious symbols.

CHRONOLOGICAL TABLE

(Many of the earlier Dates must be regarded as merely approximate.)

B. C.

1300–900 First settlement of Greeks, in various tribal bodies, in Greece, the islands, and the coastlands of Asia Minor ; first Achaeans, later Dorians. Village life, beginning slowly to concentrate round fortified centres.

900–800 Spread of City-life, with Law interpreted by Magistrates, ' hereditary, with definite prerogatives.' Traditional Greek date of ' Hesiod ' and ' Homer ' (Hdt. ii. 53).

1000–700 Aegean trade mainly in hands of Phoenicians.

800–650 Growth of exploration, commerce, and colonization. The coining of money, adopted from Lydia, spreads throughout Greece, working an economic revolution. Influence of the Delphic Oracle as ' adviser to European Greece ', and of Hebrew Prophets (Amos 750, Hosea 743, Isaiah 720).

800–700 Spartan conquest of Messenia (First Messenian War).

776 Traditional Greek date of first Olympic festival.

750 Pheidon, ' King ' of Argos, introduces definite standard of weights and measures.

735 Traditional date of first Sicilian colony, Naxos, promoted by Apollo.

734 Traditional date of foundation of Syracuse.

721 Traditional date of foundation of Sybaris.

715 Traditional date of foundation of Zancle (Messina).

683–2 List of annual Governors (Archons) at Athens begins.

668 Traditional date of Spartan defeat by Argos at Hysiae.

664 Traditional date of great sea-battle between Corinth and Corcyra.

650–600 Age of Law-givers in Greece (623, finding of Book of Instruction in the Jewish Temple, and consequent reforms).

648 (April 6) Eclipse of the Sun mentioned by Archilochus.

640–30 Foundation of Greek settlement at Naucratis on the Nile.

630 Foundation of Cyrene (Tripoli, in North Africa).

630–600 Final reduction of Messenia by Sparta (' Second Messenian War ').

600 War between Athens and Mytilene on coast of Dardanelles. Sappho, Alcaeus, and Pittacus at Mytilene.

594–3 Solon ' Governor ' at Athens. Abolition of debt-slavery and ' Shaking-off-of-burdens '.

593–1 Continuation of Solon's legislation.

585 (May 28) Eclipse of the Sun. Thales (Wise Man) flourishes.

B. C.

605–562	Reign of Nebuchadnezzar of Babylon.
560	Croesus succeeds to throne of Lydia.
561–0	Pisistratus becomes ' tyrant ' of Athens.
559–6	Miltiades becomes ' tyrant ' of Thracian Chersonese (north coast of Dardanelles).
550	Spartan conquest of Thyreatis.
548–7	Temple of Apollo at Delphi burnt down.
546	Cyrus, King of Persia, conquers Lydia and dethrones Croesus.
546–5	Persian conquest of Asiatic Greeks.
538	Cyrus takes Babylon.
528–7	Death of Pisistratus.
526	Polycrates, ' tyrant ' of Samos, abandons alliance with Egypt and joins Persia.
525	Persian conquest of Egypt.
521	Accession of Darius of Persia.
514	Conspiracy of Harmodius and Aristogeiton.
512	First European expedition of Darius ; conquest of Thrace.
510	Fall of Pisistratid tyranny. Spartans in Attica. Athens joins Peloponnesian League. War of Sybaris and Croton.
508–7	Isagoras ' Governor ' at Athens. Spartans in Attica ; besieged on the Acropolis and capitulate. Supremacy of Cleisthenes.
503–2	First civil year on system of Cleisthenes.
499	Outbreak of Ionian Revolt against Persia.
498	Athens at war with Aegina.
497	Ionians with an Athenian contingent burn Sardis.
494	Defeat of Ionians at Lade ; Persians capture Miletus.
493–2	' Governorship ' of Themistocles.
492	Persians subdue Thrace and Macedonia.
490	Persian naval expedition to Greece. Destruction of Eretria. Battle of Marathon.
489	Expedition of Miltiades to Paros.
487	Athens at war with Aegina.
487–6	Governors begin to be appointed by lot out of elected candidates. Elected generals supersede ' Polemarch ' as chiefs in command.
485	Death of Darius. Accession of Xerxes.
483–2	Discovery of new vein in silver mines at Laureion. Large surplus.
482	Increase of Athenian fleet.
480	(Spring) Athens recalls ostracized citizens.
480	(August) Xerxes enters Greece. Battles of Artemisium and Thermopylae.
	(September) Battle of Salamis.
	(October 2) Eclipse of the Sun. Carthaginians invade Sicily and are defeated at Himera.
479	(Spring) Persians in Attica.
	(August) Battle of Plataea ; battle of Mycale ; Ionians revolt from Persia.

B. C.

479–8   (Winter) Fortification of Athens. Athenians capture Sestos on Dardanelles.

478–7   Organization of Confederacy of Delos by Aristeides.

476–5   Cimon captures Eion in Thrace.

474   Battle of Cyme ; defeat of Etruscans by Syracusans.

473–2   Cimon conquers pirates at Scyros.

472   The *Persae* of Aeschylus.

472–1   Athenians reduce Carystos in Euboea. Ostracism of Themistocles. ' Synoecisms ' of Elis and Mantinea.

471   Flight of Themistocles from Greece.

470–69   Revolt and reduction of Naxos.

468   First victory of Sophocles.

467 or 466   Battle of Eurymedon ; defeat of Persian land and sea forces.

465   Revolt of Thasos.

464   Earthquake at Sparta ; revolt of Helots. Siege of Ithome.

463   Surrender of Thasos ; increase of Athenian domain lands and mines. (April 30) Eclipse of the Sun.

463–2   Cimon in Messenia helping Sparta against Helots.

462–0   Pay introduced for judges at Athens. First appearance of Pericles.

461–0   Ostracism of Cimon. Alliance of Athens with Argos and Thessaly.

460–59   Athens wins over Megara. Long Walls of Megara built ; hostility between Athens and Corinth. Athenian expedition to Egypt.

459–8   Battles with Corinthians, Epidaurians, and Aeginetans in Saronic Gulf. Activity of Athens in Cyprus, Egypt, Phoenicia, Aegina, and Megara.

458   The Orestean Trilogy of Aeschylus. Building of Long Walls of Athens.

457   Battles of Tanagra and Oenophyta ; Athenian party supreme in Boeotia.

457–6   (Winter) Athenian conquest of Aegina.

456   Death of Aeschylus. Completion of Temple of Zeus at Olympia. Athens invites the Greeks to restore the temples burnt by Persians.

456–5   First appearance of Athenian fleet in Corinthian Gulf.

454   Catastrophe of Egyptian Expedition.

454–3   Treasury of Confederacy transferred from Delos to Athens.

453   Capture of Ithome. Expedition of Pericles to Corinthian Gulf. Messenians settled at Naupactus. Athenian treaty with Segesta.

452–1   Thirty years' Peace between Argos and Sparta. Five years' truce between Athenians and Peloponnesians.

451–0   Law at Athens confining citizenship to persons of Athenian birth on both sides. Settlers sent to Andros.

450–49   Cimon's expedition to Cyprus. Death of Cimon. Treaty with Miletus.

448   Peace between Athens and Persia ; delimitation of territorial waters.

447   Defection of Boeotia (battle of Coronea). Settlers sent to Thracian Chersonese (Dardanelles), Euboea, and Naxos. Work begun on the Parthenon.

B. C.

447–6 Revolt and reduction of Euboea. Defection of Megara. Abortive Peloponnesian invasion of Attica.

446–5 Thirty years' peace between Athenians and Peloponnesians.

443 Foundation of Thurii. Ostracism of Thucydides son of Melesias.

443–2 Division of Athenian Confederacy into five districts. Sophocles ' Steward of the Greeks '.

440 Revolt of Samos and Byzantium.

439 Their reduction. Pericles in the Black Sea.

438 Inauguration of the Parthenon. The *Alcestis* of Euripides.

436–5 Trouble at Epidamnus.

435 Sea victory of Corcyra over Corinth.

433 Defensive alliance of Athens with Corcyra. Athenians take part in battle against Corinthians.

433–2 Revolt of Potidaea.

432 (Autumn) The Megarian boycott enforced.

432–1 Assemblies at Sparta decide on war.

431 First year of the Peloponnesian War. First Peloponnesian invasion of Attica (May). The *Medea* of Euripides.

430 Second year of the War. Outbreak of plague at Athens. Second invasion of Attica. Pericles deposed from generalship, tried, fined, and reappointed for next year. Phormio operates in the west: surrender of Potidaea. Herodotus's *History* completed.

429 Third year of the War. Peloponnesians besiege Plataea. Death of Pericles (Autumn).

428 Fourth year of the War. Third invasion of Attica. Revolt of Mytilene. The *Hippolytus* of Euripides.

427 Fifth year of the War. Fourth invasion of Attica. Surrender of Mytilene. Surrender of Plataea. Civil war breaks out in Corcyra.

426 Sixth year of the War. Aetolian expedition of Demosthenes in hope of reaching Boeotia.

425 Seventh year of the War. Fifth invasion of Attica. Athenians send an expedition to Sicily. Occupation of Pylos. Rejection of Spartan Peace-terms by Athens. Capture of Spartans in Sphacteria. Athens raises the tribute of her allies. The *Acharnians* of Aristophanes. Probable date of ' Old Oligarch's ' pamphlet.

424 Eighth year of the War. Athens wins Oeniadae in Corinthian Gulf; captures Nisaea, with the Long Walls of Megara, and Cythera. Athenian invasion of Boeotia ; battle of Delium. Brasidas in Thrace. Revolt of Acanthus, Amphipolis, and other cities. Banishment of Thucydides, the historian. The *Knights* of Aristophanes.

423 Ninth year of the War. Negotiations for peace. One year's truce (March). Revolt of Scione. The *Clouds* of Aristophanes.

422 Tenth year of the War. Battle of Amphipolis. Deaths of Cleon and Brasidas. Peace negotiations. The *Wasps* of Aristophanes.

421 Eleventh year of the War. Peace of Nicias (March). The *Peace* of Aristophanes. Capture of Scione ; inhabitants killed or enslaved.

B. C.

421–20 Defensive alliance between Athens and Sparta.

420 Twelfth year of the War. Alliance of Athens with Argos.

419 Thirteenth year of the War.

418 Fourteenth year of the War. Defeat of Argos by Sparta at Mantinea Argos forms alliance with Sparta.

417 Fifteenth year of the War. Nicias in Thrace.

416 Sixteenth year of the War. Conquest of Melos. Embassy of Segesta to Athens.

415 Seventeenth year of the War. Athenian expedition to Sicily. The *Trojan Women* of Euripides.

414 Eighteenth year of the War. The *Birds* of Aristophanes. Siege of Syracuse. The Spartan Gylippus arrives in Sicily.

413 Nineteenth year of the War. Spartans occupy Decelea in Attica. Second Athenian expedition to Sicily. The *Iphigenia in Tauris* and *Electra* of Euripides. Great battle in the Syracusan Harbour (September 9). Total defeat of the Athenians.

412 Twentieth year of the War. Revolt of Athenian allies. Treaty of Miletus (between Sparta and Persia). The *Helen* of Euripides.

411 Twenty-first year of the War. Revolt of Rhodes. Revolt of Abydos and Lampsacus. Assembly at Colonus and provision made for a new Constitution (May). Council of Four Hundred comes into office (early in June), and governs till September. Revolt of Euboea (September). Four Hundred overthrown and Polity established (September). Battle of Cynossema in Dardanelles. *Lysistrata* and *Thesmophoriazusae* of Aristophanes.

410 Twenty-second year of the War. Battle of Cyzicus in sea of Marmora. Restoration of Democracy at Athens. Athens recovers Thasos.

409 Twenty-third year of the War. Athens recovers Colophon : loses Pylos and Nisaea.

408 Twenty-fourth year of the War. Athens recovers Chalcedon and Byzantium. The *Orestes* of Euripides.

407 Twenty-fifth year of the War. Prince Cyrus of Persia comes down to the coast.

406 Twenty-sixth year of the War. Battle of Arginusae. Trial and execution of the Generals in command. Deaths of Euripides and Sophocles.

405 Twenty-seventh year of the War. The *Frogs* of Aristophanes (January). Lysander becomes Spartan Admiral. Cyrus called to Susa. The *Bacchae* of Euripides produced. Battle of Aegospotami in Dardanelles (end of Summer).

405–4 Twenty-eighth year of the War. Blockade of Athens.

404 Surrender of Athens. Long Walls pulled down (April). Spartan garrison on the Acropolis.

401 *Oedipus at Colonus* of Sophocles (produced by his grandson).

399 Death of Socrates.

About **398** Thucydides' *History* published.

INDEXES

NOTE

A fuller description of each modern work will be found on the first page where it is cited. With regard to the ancient authorities cited, note :

Hellenica Oxyrhynchia refers to the fragment of a fourth-century Greek historian (perhaps Theopompus) discovered in Egypt in 1906, and since published in the Oxford Text Series, together with other fragments of its possible authors.

Old Oligarch refers to the anonymous treatise entitled Ἀθηναίων Πολιτεία, commonly printed among the lesser works of Xenophon, as in the Teubner Text. See Murray's *Greek Literature*, pp. 167-9. Its probable date (which can only be determined by internal evidence) is 425. It has been edited with a translation and full commentary by E. Kalinka (Leipzig, 1913). There is also an English translation by Francis Brooks (London, 1913).

Ways and Means refers to the anonymous treatise entitled Πόροι, commonly printed among the lesser works of Xenophon, whom some scholars still believe to have been its author. It dates almost certainly from the year 355.

I. G. refers to the Berlin series of *Inscriptiones Graecae.*

I. G. A. stands for *Inscriptiones Graecae Antiquissimae.*

INDEX OF MODERN WRITERS

This index includes every modern writer and periodical cited in the book. For the sake of readers in need of guidance I have put an asterisk against writers whom they are likely to find especially helpful.

Abrahams 216
Achad Haam 181–2
Addams, Jane 62, 68
American Journal of Archaeology 216, 238, App. 450
Angell, Norman 247, 414
Annual of British School at Athens 35, 195, 267, 306, 342, 384, 440, App. 447, 450
Ardaillon 400
Atchley 41, 45, 47
Athenische Mitteilungen 311

Beazley 267
Beloch 174
Bérard 28, 34, 35, 52, 86, 241, 318 (' law of the isthmus ' criticized)
Blümner 261
Böckh 297
Booth, Charles 275
Brants 322
British School, see *Annual*
Brocks 450
Brown, Horatio 217, 293
Browning 18, 94, 337
Bruns 337
Büchsenschütz 316
Bulletin de correspondance hellénique 167, 284
*Burke 59, 81, 180, 196
Burkitt 215
Burns, Rt. Hon. John 297
Bury : *History of Greece to the Death of Alexander the Great* 111 ; *Romances of Chivalry on Greek Soil* 70
Busolt 137, 277, 412, 427
Butler, Samuel 92

Cairnes 332, 386, 401
Calderini 394
Cambridge Modern History, 217, 293
Capps 331
Carcopino 169
Carpenter, Edward 344
*Cavaignac, Études sur l'histoire financière d'Athènes au Vme siècle,

Histoire de l'antiquité vol. ii, 86, 146, 174, 186–7, 193, 195, 277, 293, 308, 397–9, 405–14, 417, 437–40
Chadwick 76
Charleston Mercury, The 386
Ciccotti 394
Classen 191, 198, 201, 402
Classical Association, Proceedings of the 22, 41, 256
Classical Philology 154
Classical Review 169
Clausewitz 429
Clerc 177, 372, 383
Cobbett 279
Comptes rendus de l'Académie des Inscriptions et Belles-Lettres 270
Cornford 183
Crawley 248, 443
Cromer, Lord 323
Cunningham, H. J. 169
Cunningham, W. 117, 414
Curtius 124

Dakyns 176, 385
*Daremberg and Saglio, *Dictionnaire des antiquités* 52, 54, 136, 146, 165, 189, 266, 290, 293, 296, 313, 331, 400
Dareste 316
Darwin 181, 326
d'Avenel 224
Davis 310, 312
d'Azambuja 241
Delbrück 174, 429
Demolins 34, 70, 317
de Sanctis 117
Dickins 412
*Dittenberger, *Sylloge Inscriptionum Graecarum* (2nd ed.) 89, 176, 235, 254, 262, 271, 277, 283, 296, 297, 311, 361, 365, 384, 394
Donaldson 337, 340
Dörpfeld 86, 298

Eliot 167
Evans, Sir Arthur 303

Fawcus 174, 417
Ferguson 154
Ferrero 120, 310, 312, 358, 362
Fleckeisen's *Jahrbücher* 179, 339
France, Anatole 273
Francke 394
*Francotte :
  La Polis grecque 79, 80, 84, 90, 148, 149, 150, 154
  L'Industrie dans la Grèce antique 177, 230, 262–4, 322, 372
  Les Finances des cités grecques 219, 317, 407, 408, 412, 439
  Le Pain à bon marché 362
  De la condition des étrangers 362
Freeman, E. A. 76
Freeman, K. J. 297, 384
Furtwängler and Reichhold 52, 323, 343
Fustel de Coulanges 82, 89, 99

Galton, Sir F. 368
Gernet 174, 362
Gilliard 131
*Glotz :
  La Cité Grecque 162–4
  La Solidarité de la famille 82, 105, 106, 134, 136, 138
  Études sociales et juridiques 101, 102, 146, 331
  In *Bulletin de correspondance hellénique* 167
  Travail 225, 261, App. 446, 447, 448, 450
  In *Comptes rendus de l'Académie des Inscriptions et Belles-Lettres* 266
Goethe 18
Göttingische Gelehrte Anzeigen 438
Grenfell and Hunt, see *Oxyrhynchus Papyri*
Grote 134, 140, 117 (note in abridged ed.)
Grundy 49 (*Map), 85, 347
Guiraud 233, 266, 270, 324
Gwynn 256

Haekl 322
Haggard, Rider 103
Hahn 344
Hakluyt 41 (John Eldred), 254, 380
Haverfield 296
Head 303, 307
Headlam, J. W. 164, 166
Headlam, W. 177, 397
Hehn 55
Helbig 375
Helfferich 168
Hermes 303, 360, 365, 395 ; see also under Wilamowitz

*Hicks and Hill 179, 190, 191, 216, 254, 309, 315, 324, 359, 363, 372, 374, 389, 438, 440
Hill 187, 194, 195, 374
Holmes, Edmond 368

Inscriptions juridiques grecques 114, 235
Inscriptions, selected, see Dittenberger and Hicks and Hill
Iwan Müller 232, 233

Jacoby 375
Jahreshefte des österreichischen archäologischen Instituts 216, 269, 285, 323, 360
Jebb, *Theophrastus* 51, 64, 168, 217, 313, 323
  Sophocles 161, 271, 347
Journal of Hellenic Studies 174, 177, 267, 303, 396, 398, 417, 440, App. 446, 451

Keil, 176, 305, 410
Kiepert (*Festschrift für*) 296
Kinglake 27, 63
Kipling 26, 103, 356, 359
Klio 86, 277
Körnemann 86, 296

Leaf : *Troy* 28
  Homer and History 28, 32, 104, 317, 318, 421
Lécrivain 293
Lehmann-Haupt 303
Liddell and Scott 311, 317
Lincoln, Abraham 161, 200
Livingstone 368
Louvre Album 52

Maciver 368
Mackail 369
Mahaffy 237, 342
Malthus 326
Mansbridge 368
Marshall 213
Marx 400
Mediterranean Pilot 27, 28, 29, 32, 40, 42
Mélanges d'archéologie et d'histoire (Journal of French School at Athens) 31
Mélanges d'histoire ancienne 169, 174, 362
Mélanges Nicole 362
Meredith (*Odes in Contribution to the Song of French History*) 443
Merkel 297, 317

*Meyer, Eduard :
Forschungen zur alten Geschichte 76, 79, 174, 178, 233, 338, 375, 407, 412, 417, 427
Geschichte des Altertums 77, 80, 87, 89, 90, 111, 114, 133, 147, 148, 190, 194, 203, 254, 339, 351, 352, 372, 374, 375, 377, 427, 429
Kleine Schriften 117, 258, 396
Michel 321
Miller 19, 69
Milligan 331
Monro 76, 87
Montesquieu 213, 366, 379
Morris, William 287
Müller, O. 179, 339
Münchener Archäologische Studien 322
*Murray, Gilbert :
Ancient Greek Literature 198
Rise of the Greek Epic 28, 34, 50, 74, 75, 77, 121, 122
Euripides (Introduction to translations) 129, 136, 196, 343, 352
Euripides (notes to Greek text) 146
Translations :
Bacchae 389
Iphigenia in Tauris 255
Medea 90, 240, 337
Troades 21
*Myres :
Greek Lands and the Greek People 17, 47, 60, 233, 329
Herodotus and Anthropology 22, 48, 181, 337
The Geographical Aspect of Greek Colonization 22, 41, 256

Nation, The (London) 106
Neue Jahrbücher für das klassische Altertum 296
Nevinson 387, 391, 402
*Nietzsche :
Philologika (Works, vol. xvii) 15, 171, 343
Was ich den Alten verdanke (Works, vol. viii) 74, 200
Also sprach Zarathustra 198

Oxyrhynchus Papyri 331

Pater 113
Paterson, Alexander 68
Paterson, W. R. 396, 400
Pauly-Wissowa (Realencyclopädie) 105, 158, 163, 170, 266, 283, 290, 303, 304, 313, 316, 375, 446, 448

Pears, Sir Edwin 28
*Philippson 17, 36
Phillipson 179
Pohl 271
Pöhlmann 296, 352
Poland 270
Pottier 265, 322, 375
Punch 140
Putnam, Emily James 82, 274, 341

Quarterly Review, The 293

Renan 150
Revue archéologique 322, 375
Revue des études grecques 316, App. 447, 448
Belgique 322
Revue des études grecques 316
Ridgeway 84, 303, 304
*Riezler 218, 249, 304, 312, 316
Rodd, Sir Rennell 69, 242
Roscher (Lexikon) 76
Ruskin 257, 350
Rutherford 337

Sadler 21
Salvioli 272, 362
Schmitt 70
Schreiber 296
Seeley 108
Sociological Review 394, 401
Steup 201
Sudhoff 52
Sundwall 158, 163, 175
Sykes, Sir Mark 63

Tarde 225
Times, The 297
Tod 267, 342, 384
Todd, Canon 84
Tolstoy 94
Toynbee 196, App. 447
Trevelyan, G. M. 93
Trevelyan, Sir G. O. 346
Tucker 332
Turner, J. K. 402

Unamuno 242
Ure 396, 398
Uyehara 81

Wachsmuth 282
Walker 117
Wallas :
Human Nature in Politics 199, 268
The Great Society 224, 261
Wallon 111

Waszynski 395
Wellhausen 84
Wells, H. G. 224
Westermarck 227
Whitelaw 139
Wiegand 360
*Wilamowitz-Moellendorff :
  Aristoteles und Athen 53, 105, 117,
    131, 143 ff., 146, 148, 155–7, 163–5,
    170, 173–6, 183, 234, 338, 365, 394,
    417
  Aus Kydathen 86, 87, 130, 137, 150,
    173, 176, 191, 193, 268
  Ein Gesetz von Samos 312, 360
  Hippolytus 335
  Nord-Ionische Steine 133
  Oedipus 102
  Orestie 45, 77, 102, 124, 344
  Platon 198

Reden und Vorträge 357, 370 (where
    see note), 372, 375
Staat und Gesellschaft der Griechen
    133, 166, 167, 176, 293, 332, 339,
    344
Griechisches Lesebuch (text) 200, 203
Articles in *Hermes* 191, 337, 341,
    342, 383
*Wilhelm 146, 187, 269, 278, 285, 321,
    365
Withers, Hartley 301
Wordsworth 107, 198, 217

Yiddish-English Conversation Manual
    125
Young 216

Zangwill 280
Ziebarth 270, App. 447
Zimmern 368, 394, 401

ADDITIONS TO INDEX OF AUTHORS

American Journal of Archaeology
  App. 450
Andreades App. 448, 450

Babelon App. 448, 449, 451
Brillant App. 450

Calhoun App. 446, 447
Cary App. 449
Classical Quarterly App. 449
Corbett App. 445
Cultura App. 445

Dinsmoor App. 450

Gardner App. 447, 448, 449

Halliday App. 448
Hakluyt Society 242
Heitland 6, App. 448, 450
Holland App. 446
van Hook App. 449

James App. 449
Jameson App. 451

Kahrstedt App. 446, 447, 450
Kohler App. 447

Ledl App. 447
Lugard App. 445

Netolitzky App. 445

Orth App. 448

Pareti App. 447
Plassart App. 447

Revue Numismatique App. 448, 451
Rostovtzeff App. 445, 446

Schulten App. 445

*Transactions of American Philological
  Association* App. 449

Ure App. 449
Urwick App. 446

Vinogradoff App. 446, 447

Weil App. 447, 448, 451
Williamson App. 445, 449
Woodward 195, App. 446, 447, 450,
    451

Zeitschrift für Numismatik App. 451
de Zulueta App. 446

INDEX OF GREEK WORDS AND PHRASES

ἀασάμην 101
Ἀβροσῦνα 394
ἄγειν καὶ φέρειν 189
Ἀγορά, ἀγοράζειν 65
ἀγών 269
Ἀειναῦται 146
Αἰδώς 121, 122
αἰσχύνη 122
ἄλσος 45
ἀλώνητον 25
Ἄνακες 321
ἀνδράποδον 397
ἀνήκεστος 436
ἀξίωσις 65
ἄπαις 75
Ἀπάτορια 149
ἀποδεκτής 438
ἀπόρρητα 359
ἀποφορά 264
ἀπραγμοσύνη 204, 357
ἄριστον 50
ἀρχή 395
ἀρχὴ ἄνδρα δείξει 160
ἄρχοντες 141, 191
ἀστοι 109
ἀσυλία 316
ἀτίμητος μετανάστης 89
Ἀτλαντίς 26
αὐτόφορτος 317
αὐτόχθων 90
ἀφρήτωρ ἀθέμιστος ἀνέστιος 89
ἀχρεῖος 214

βαναυσία 273
βασανίζειν 304
βασιλεύς 89
βουλή 165

γεννῆται 148
γέροντες 89
γεωργοί 384
γνῶθι σεαυτόν 122
γνωρίσματα 332
γραμματεῖς 39ͼ
γραφαί 135
γυναικοκρατουμενοι 113

δαίμονες 321
δάνειον 313
δαμιόργιον 94
δεῖπνον 50
δένδρον 46
δεύτερος πλοῦς 317
δημιοῦργος 105, 174, 272
δῆμοι 156, 158

δημοκρατία 139
δῆμος τε πόλις τε 109
δημόσιον 405
δήμου ἡγεμόνες 109
δίκαι 135
δίκη 96
δοῦλοι 113
δραχμή 306
δρόμος 347
δυσέρωτες 195
δυσκολὸν θρέμμα 391

ἔγγραφοι 384
ἐγγύα παρὰ δ' ἄτα 116
ἔθνος 71
εἴριον ἀπὸ ξύλου 55
εἰς μεσον 63
ἑκατόμβοι' ἐννεαβοίων 302
ἑκτημόροι 117
ἐλευθερία, 180
Ἐλευθέριος 183
Ἑλληνοταμίαι 188
ἐμπορία 255
ἐμπόριον 256
ἔμπορος 317
ἐπίσκοποι 191
ἐπιστάτης 165, 262
ἐπώνυμοι 154
ἔργα ἀξιόλογα 85
ἔρανος 289, 312
ἐρασταί 195
Ἐρεχθεῖδαι 90
Ἑστία 72
ἑταίρα 340
τὸ εὖ ζῆν 83
εὐδαιμονία 198
εὔφρων 177
ἔφεσις 189
ἐχθρος 249

ζεῦγος 192
Ζεὺς πατρῷος 90
ζῆλος 269

ἡλιαία 137

θέμις 96
θεοὶ σωτῆρες 321
θεωρία 255
θίασος 269

ἴδιος 203
ἰδιώτης 214
ἱερομνήμονες 105
ἱμάτιον 215, 448
ἰσηγορία 382

ἰσονομία 125
ἰσόνομος 93, 130

κακοῦργοι 34
κακώσεως γραφαί 136
Καλλιρρόη 121
καρποῦσθαι τὴν ἀρχήν 175
καπηλεύειν 280
κατὰ κώμας 78
κατωνακοφόροι 111
κήρυκες 263
κίβδηλος 304
κλῆροι 88
κληροῦχοι 111
κληρωταί 111
τὸ κοινόν 59
κονίποδες 111
κορυνηφόροι 111, 447
κόσμος 108
κρισί 51
κυνόσουρα 26
κυνόφαλοι 111, 447
κωλακρέται 87, 405
Κωλίας 152
κῶμαι 78

λειτουργία 174
λειτουργεῖν 175, 289
Λύσανδρος 134

μελάνυδρος 121
μεταβάλλειν 181
μεταμανθάνειν 181
μέτοικοι 179
μετρίως 124
μνήμονες 96
Μυρίανδρος 328
Μύρμηξ 33

ναύκληρυς 322
Ναύκραροι 146
Νέμεσις 122
νοσεῖν 124
νόμος ἐπ' ἀνδρί 169

ξένος 249, 384
ξόανα 95
ξυμβόλαια 190
ξυμβολή 189
ξύμβολον 189

ὀβελοί 306
οἰκεῖς 114
οἰκέτης 88, 397
ὀλιγαρχία 130
ὁμογάλακτες 148
ὀργεῶνες 148
ὄργια 149
ὄψον 50

παῖς 397
παλλακή 340
παμβοιώτια 76
παραμονή 394
παράστασις 322
παρρησία 64
τὸ πάτριον 69, 72
πενιχροί 109
περίοικοι 109
περιορᾶν 207
περίπλοι 26, 33
περίπολοι 384
πόλεις 80
πολίτης 80
πουλυμαθίη 119
προφήτης 124
πρυτανεῖον 87, 147
πρυτάνεις 165
πρυτανεύειν 176

σῖτος 49
σκοπέειν τινὰ τὰ ἑωυτοῦ 131
στέλεχος 414
στιχυμυθία 61
συνέδριον 188
σύνταξις 408
συντελεῖς 194
σῶμα 397
σωφροσύνη 107, 122

τάξις φόρου 440
τόκος 116
τριεραρχία 290

ὕλη 46
ὑλοτόμος 278
ὑπηρέται 395

φίλος 177
φιλότης 101
φόρος 187, 408
φορτηγός 322
φράτριος 149
φρύγανα 47
φυλή 71

χειροτέχναι 271, 272, 402
χειρώνακτες 272
χιτών 215
χορηγία 290
χρέος 311, 313
χρημίτων κρείσσων 214
χωρὶς οἰκοῦντες 264

Ὠφελίων 394
ὢχ ὢχ 235

GENERAL INDEX

This index is drawn up for those who have already read the book and wish to refer back to topics mentioned in it. Special attention has therefore been paid to the footnotes, and subjects fully discussed, and easily discoverable from the Contents, have been passed over.

Abdul Hamid 34, 62
Academy, Plato's 53, 60 ; cf. 393 note
Acciajuoli 310
Acharnae 46, 164, 278
Acropolis building design 292, 296, 297, 367, 411
Adriatic 36 ; cf. 253, 256
Adramyttium, Bay of 377
Advertisements 138, 283
Aegina 303, 308, 322, 372, 376, 414
Aegospotami 50, 356
Aeneas Tacticus 68, 349
Aeschylus, epitaph 70 ; *Orestean Trilogy* 97 f. ; *Persae* 129 ; as an inventor 225 note ; quoted 83, 397
Aetolia 237, 437
Albania 344, 420
Albert Memorial 368
Alcibiades 185, 208, 372 ; cf. 357 note
Alexander 63, 330
Alluvial plains 42, 49, 66 ; cf. 347, 349
Amasis, King 63 ; vase-painter 266
Amateurs, in cricket and government 160, 163 ; cf. 294, 307
America 90, 180, 291 ; cf. 120, 296, 328
Amos 115, 117, 123
Anarchists 72, 130
Apaturia 149, 153 ; cf. 200, 407, 430
Archive, the first 96
Argo, who owned her ? 239
Argos 76, 80, 263, 277, 318, 355
Aristeides 169, 185, 187, 340, 407, 415, 439
Aristocracy, Greek different from English 91 ; see Oligarchy
Aristotle, aristocratic 119 ; on aliens 384 ; on education 295 ; on Law 128 ; on Parliament and Market 282 ; on population questions 327, 332 ; on respectability 119 ; on self-sufficiency 287, 351 ; on slaves 270, 295, 385, 389, 392–3 ; on

Solon's land-laws 134 ; on the City-State as a normal institution 67 ; on the early City 80 ; on the Model City 254, 327, 351 ; on Tragedy 84 ; on Virtue 123, 206, 343 ; on walls 86 ; on women 61 ; secular 106 ; socialistic 293 ; used a garden 60
Armour 346–7
Arms, manufacture of 265–6 ; wearing of 80, 237, 347–8
Art forms, Greek and modern 225
Aspasia 338, 340
Asphodel 47
Asylum, right of 316
Athenians, not 'Atticans' 79
Athletics 345
Atlantic, the 25
Atlantis 27
Aulis 32
Bacchae 343
Bathing 29, 52, 216 (end of note)
Battles at the Ships 30
Bedroom furniture 216–17
Beggars 105, 316
Bengal 297
Bimetallism 305
Black Sea, see Pontus
Blood-guiltiness 102, 436
Boeotia, Athenian trade with 316, 376 ; constitution of 130, 164, 167 ; name of 76, 79 ; relations with 356, 372, 422
Border-wars 47, 244 ff., 346, 356, 422
Bosporus 28–9, 355, 361 ff.
Boswell, a Greek 268
Boxes or 'levels' 48
Boycotting 323–4, 427
Brasidas 239
Brea Decree 324
Brotherhoods 71, 95, 149 ff. ; cf. 268–9
Budgeting 217–19, 404 ff., 418–19
Byzantium 28, 410

Calendar at Athens 166 ; at Ceos 234
Camp-fire talk 54, 184, 345
Capitalism 258, 260 ; cf. 400, 402
'Captains of industry' 319
Carthage and Carthaginians 26, 182 (in Sicily), 372, 376
Catalan Grand Company 242
Cataline 308
Cato 119 ; on worn-out slaves 401
Cavalry 92, 175–6, 416
Caves on Greek hillsides 238
Celibacy 74, 208, 334
Chalcedon 28–9
Chalcis 32, 146, 191, 440
Charcoal burning 46, 278
Childlessness, dread of 74, 329
Chilon 116
Chinese Law-courts 99, 106
Chios 133, 186, 190, 440
Christianity 73, 150, 206 ; cf. 432
Cicero 119, 360
Cimon 333–4 and 339 (wife and family of), 372, 381, 404, 409
Civil Servants 163, 177, 395 ; cf. 406
Classical education 17, 21
Cleanliness 52, 216 (end of note)
Cleisthenes 82, 90, 143 ff., 178–9, 327, 339
Cleon 101, 171, 234, 435, 436, 437, 438–40
Clerks 163, 271, 272
Clerks of the Market 282 ff., 365
Clocks, Greek 65, 67
Clothes 37, 52, 63, 183 (foreign fashions), 215, 216 (borrowed), 266 (working clothes)
Cnidos 94, 277
Coinage, Athenian 192–3, 306, 308, 401 ; see cover
Colonnades 60
Colour-prejudice 323
Comforts, absence of 215, 319
Commission-system 175 (secret), 322
Committees 166–7, 439
Communism 288
'Companions' at Athens 341 ; in Macedonia 146
Competition 224, 262, 268, 320 ; cf. 33, 94–5
Confirmation 152
Congo 103, 387
Conservatism, Greek 72, 223, 231, 335, 365
Constantinople 22, 69, 292 ; see also Byzantium
Continents, as boundaries 21–2
Contractors 261–3, 296 ; cf. 360, 413

Corcyra and Corcyraeans 33, 38, 357, 373, 374, 420 ff.
Corinth, currants = Corinths 51 ; fleet of 218 ; frontier of 47 ; good coinage of 307 ; loan to Athenians 311 ; in Funeral Speech 202 ; relations with Athens 289, 373, 375, 377, 378, 420 ff. ; serfs at 111 ; temple-slaves at 342 ; tyrants at 126
Corn Exchange 365
Corn and corn supply 49–50, 228 ff., 326–8, 355 ff., 425
'Corner' in olive-presses 52 ; in grain 364
Council at Athens 163 ff., 439
Craft-gilds (θίασοι) 269
Credit-built finance 247, 309
Crete 111, 133 ; cf. Minos
Croesus 181, 226–7
Currents 31 ; cf. 255
Customs and customs-houses 317, 324
Cyclops 83, 254
Cyprus 186, 193, 357, 361, 371, 372
'Cyrenaic' pottery 225

Dalmatia 23, 253, 389
Dardanelles 27–8, 142, 356, 361 ff., 425
Darius 175, 194, 304, 408
Darwinism misapplied 246 ; cf. 442
Death-rate 328
Debased currencies 304–5
Decelean War 44, 216, 401–2, 429
Delian League 187 ff., 408 ; treasuries 218 ; market 284, 358
Delphi, Croesus's gifts to 181 ; influence of 72, 122 ff., 130–1, 252 ; international centre for traders 316 ; loss of influence 182–3 ; plagiarism 29 ; rebuilding of temple 405–6 ; Sicyonian Treasury at 347 ; sides with Peloponnesians 357 ; treasury at 218, 311
Demes 155 ff., 162, 339, 347, 438
Democedes 65, 259, 267, 271
Democracy, modern 159 ; cf. 62, 139
Demosthenes as creditor 311
Demotionidae 149
Dionysus, on vases 342–3
Division, numbers of, in Athenian Parliament 169
Doctors 259, 271 ; cf. 60 and 65, 267
Dorians 89, 109 ff., 438
Dowries 330

Drachma, origin of 306
Drinking 51, 119–20 ; cf. 342–3

Earthquakes 23
Ebenezer (Winchester notion) 346
Ecclesia, see Parliament
Economics as an exact science 302
Education at Athens 295–6, 344–5 ;
    cf. 67, 223, 271, 368
Egotism 214
Egypt and Egyptians 179, 182–3,
    194, 323, 355, 361, 371, 372, 413 ;
    cf. 152
Electra 73, 334
Electrum 304, 193 note
Elis 78, 105, 374, 421
Elpenice 334
Emigration 62, 138 (modern), 252 ff.,
    318
Empiricism in politics 268
Emporia 256
Engineering, Greek 41, 276, 296,
    316–17
England, discoverers of 26
Epidamnus 420
Equality in Greek lands 62, 107
Erechtheum workmen 264, 414
Eretria 32, 369
Erythrae 190–1
Etesian winds 38
Etruria 194, 322
Eugenics 323, 332, 368
Eumaeus 88, 241 (his nurse's death),
    391
Euphrates, navigation on 40
Euripides, Bacchae of 343 ; choruses
    of, quoted 20, 255, 336–7, 388 ;
    countryman in Electra 234 ; Ion of
    395 ; later plays 352 ; on women
    336–7 ; scene of Orestes 60 ; cf. 171
Euripus 32
Evaporation 24
Examination tests 269
Exposure of infants 47, 330–2, 394

Fashion versus Custom 225
Fertile, Greece not 43, 50, 219, 326
Feudalism 91, 291
Fez, the Ottoman 132, 324
Fish and fishermen 34, 282, 358
Fleas (charm against) 235
Föhn, in Switzerland 38
Fool, the Shakespearian 342
Forests in Greece 44–6, 278
Forge as club-house 37, 95
Franks in Greece 19, 69, 241
Frederick the Great 429

Freedmen 178, 392–4
Freedwomen 341
French plays 284
Friendship 100–1, 177 note, 343–4 ;
    cf. 297 note
Fruits 55, 233, 235

Gallio 273
Gardens 60
Gaza 193–4, 372
Geishas 342
General Purposes Committee 147, 162
Gibraltar 25, 27, 29
Giotto's Campanile 259
Gipsies 317
Goats and goat pasture 45–8, 232
Gorillas 26
Gortyn, Laws of 133
Gramophones 224

Hanno 26, 33
Harbours 30, 38
Harpies 39
Hecataeus 34, 90
Hedges 48
Heliaea 137, 158, 172
Hellenistic cities 296, 320
Hellespont, see Dardanelles
Helots 55, 77, 85, 111–14, 353, 384
Herodotus at Thurii 374–5 ; journeys
    of 371 ; not self-conscious 342 ; on
    development 181 ; on free trade
    366 ; on oracles 182 ; on the Trojan
    War 101 ; on tyrants 127, 366 ; an
    Outlander 179 ; story of Adrastus
    103 ; stories of Arion, Nitocris and
    Gyges 131 ; story of Deioces 97 ff. ;
    story of Solon and Croesus 131, 181,
    226–7 ; story of the Andrians 219 ;
    story of the Cnidians 249 ; story of
    the expedition to Paros 249 ; story
    of the war in Thyreatis 250
Hesiod 39, 61, 72–3, 89, 93 ff., 96, 120
Hiero of Syracuse 374
Hippias 143, 306–7
Homer, aristocracy in 91 ; blindness
    of 259 ; debt collecting in 311 ;
    evidence of 71 ff. ; fighting in 347 ;
    Iliad 76, 86 ff., 100 ; Odyssey,
    geography of 34 ; poor widow in
    Iliad 341 note ; predecessors of
    18 ; shield of Achilles 43, 48, 86 ;
    slavery in 388–9 ; town-life in 83
Homeric hymn to Hermes 347
Home-sickness 19, 62 ; cf. 317
Horace 41, 193, 317
Horsemanship 175–6

Hotels 51, 298, 328
Housing conditions 215–16, 295–6, 298

Illiterate voters at Athens 169
Immigrants at Athens, see Outlanders
Imperialism 296 (territorial), 379, 433 ff.
Indemnities 414
Interdict 103, 104
International finance 310–11
International law 98, 189
Investments 312–13
Ionia 133, 186, 252 ; cf. 370
Iron Age 77, 108
Iron money 306
Isocrates 126, 159, 201, 269, 427

Japan 81, 183, 216, 342
Jews, the 85, 100, 181–2, 242 (Spanish), 308, 311 ; cf. 323
Joiners, as artists 79, 95
Jonah cited 349
Journalism 260
Judges 97, 137, 162 ff., 179 note, 187 note
Kings in Greece 89 ff.
King's Peace, the 365

Land-tax (Athenian) 142, (English) 151, (in Athenian Empire) 407
Landed tradition 89, 229 ff., 258
Landladies, Athenian 172
Law of the Isthmus criticized 318
Law Courts at Athens 162 ; cf. Heliaea
Letter, the earliest Greek 284
Light-armed troops 233, 416–17
'Liturgies' 173, 175, 290, 359, 405
Living-in 394
London, City of 80 ; County Council steamboats 154 ; Old London 267 ; situation of 370
Lot, election by 162, 164
Luncheon interval 50
Lyceum, slaves at 393 ; cf. 60
Lycia 194 ; cf. 404
Lycurgus 35, 91, 128, 131–3 ; cf. 306
Lysias and the corn-dealers 364
Lysicrates, monument of 290

Macedonia 146, 237, 359, 425 ; cf. 91
Machpelah, Cave of 116
Maenads 343
Magazines 219 (store-houses), 225 (light reading)

Malaria 329 ; cf. 44–5
Manchester 31, 302, 313
Mantinea 78, 84
Map-making 33
Marathon, battle of 85, 180, 184, 200, 356, 375, 434 ; mile ' run ' at 347
Maria Theresa dollars 193
Market-place 65, 87, 268 (shelter from), 281 ff. ; 365, 440, 443
Marriage laws 74, 339
Mayors 154 ; cf. 158
Meals, Greek 50, 95 ; cf. 168, also 100
Megarian Decree 323, 426–7
Melos 440–3
Merchant Service, Athenian 203, 321, 417–18
Messina, Straits of 31 ; cf. 373–4
Metics, see Outlanders
Mexico, labour conditions in 402
Miletus 31, 118, 126, 146, 318, 369, 370
Military commands at Athens 172–6
Mill work 55, 224, 260 (mill-catch)
Mining 259, 397 ff.
Minos and Minoan 33, 53, 219, 256
Mohammedanism 22, 73
Money 114, 192, 280, 301 ff., 412 (purchasing power), 416, 437–8, 440
Money-changers 193, 308
Monkeys 323 ; cf. 26, 181, 321
Montenegro 113
Mugwumps 204 ; cf. 214
Muses 93–4, 96
Museums 309, 415 ; cf. 265
Mycenaean period 75, 77, 301
Mytilenaean debate 101, 435

Naples 374
Naucraries 146
Naucratis 318
Nausicaa 30, 52
Naval officers, modern 81
Naxos, foundation of 256
Negroes 322, 323, 368
Night-dresses 266
Night voyages 39, 240, 345
Nomenclature 91–2, 134, 154, 157, 394
Non-intervention 357 ; cf. 355, 422–3
Norway 34
Nymphs 42 ; cf. 120–1

Oeantheia 315
Oligarchy 90, 130, 140, 167, 338, 340 ; cf. 175 note
Olive-oil 51, 419

Olive picking 37, 54
Olive-tree, the 53, 54, 55, 59, 134, 168, 231, 233, 235, 259, 428, 429
Olympia, inscription at 105 ; scene at 316 ; temple at 406, 409
Oracle, see Delphi
Orneates 111
Oropus 32 ; cf. 79 note
Orpheus 46
Ostracism 169
' Outlanders ' 138, 157, 177, 179, 191, 263, 278, 339 (Outlander women), 353 ff., 380 ff., 406, 416
Oxford 295, cf. 333 ; vase at 267

' Paganism ' 342 ; cf. 70
Palestine compared with Greece 39, 44, 66, 84, 106, 115 ; intercourse with Greece 372
Panathenaic procession 177, 407 note ; cf. 176
Panhellenism 184–5, 375 ; cf. 200 note
Parable of the Sower 44 ; of the labourers in the Vineyard 206 ; of the lost piece of silver 217 ; of the Talents 308
Parians, the 118, 249, 440
Parliament at Athens 159, 162, 208, 250, 281, 282, 429 ; debates in 171, 410, 422, 428, 432–3, 435 ; description of 165 ff.
Pasion 392
Patria potestas 99
Patriarchal system 71 ff., 83, 87
Pay for private work 169, 262, 271, 392–4, 419
Pay for public service 87, 95, 165, 169, 174–5, 406, 414, 418, 419
Pegae 373, 427
Pelasgian Wall 68
Pentelic marble 382 ; cf. 276
Pericles, death of 433–4 ; family of 92, 333 ; Funeral Speech of 199 ff. ; policy of 361 ff.
Persia 118, 180, 182, 185, 193–4, 368, 371–2, 403–4, 408
Personal remarks 64, 171
Phaeacia 30, 83, 230
Phaselis 190
Pheidon 133, 303
Philip of Macedon 37, 63
Phoenicians 35, 184, 255, 321, 371–2
Phormio 39, 85, 437
Phrygians in Attica 278, 392, 429
Pigs 47

Pindar 26, 90, 92, 124, 344
Piracy 33, 237 ff., 315
Pisistratus 27, 54, 141 ff., 351, 363, 398
Plague 38, 298, 431
Plantation-work 55, 390, 400, 402
Plataea 76, 200, 216, 333, 422, 434–5
Plato, aristocratic 119, 158 ; contemporary influence of 158–9 ; Critias of 287 ; model cities of 112, 254, 300, 351–2 ; myth of Protagoras 86 ; used a garden 60 ; on aliens 384 ; on Apollo 124, 131 ; on bargaining 282 ; on communism of husbands and wives 222 ; on currencies 305 ; on education 295 ; on food 50 ; on friendship 344 ; on general labourers 276 ; on immortality 74 ; on parliament and market 282 ; on population questions 253, 327, 332 ; on retail traders 279 ; on respectability 119 ; on slave-doctors 271 ; on slaves 390–1 ; on Sparta 113, 288, 305 ; on teaching for money 273 ; on the best life 108 ; on the philosopher king 130 ; on travelling 255 ; on wills 138 ; on wine 51 ; on women's questions 336–7
Plautus 34, 284
Polemarch, duties of 179
Police 135, 176, 295 ; cf. 321, 377
Polites 80   [(sea-police)
Polybius 38, 332, 390
Polycrates of Samos 239, 246
Pontus 36, 195, 362 ff., 372, 376–8, 439
Population of Athens 174, 177, 381, 399, 415
Portage 31, 118
Portuguese Africa 387, 402
Postage stamps 193, 307
Postal system 224, 295
Potidaea 418, 426, 437–8
Prefect-system, the 160
Prices, not fixed 284 ; rises in (at Athens) 414
Priesthood, not powerful in Greece 106, 182–3
Primogeniture, not Greek 89, 234
Professions and character 280
' Progress ' 181
Prometheus 224
Propylaea 86, 411–12, 420
Protection 323–4, 362
Prytaneis 147, 165 ; cf. 87
Psychology 166, 183, 280 ; cf. 268
Purple dye 34–5

Radicalism, Greek 72, 90, 148, 154 ; cf. 164 note, 220, 225 note
Railway cuttings 44
Rain in Greece 36, 39, 60
Rate of interest 313
Rates 292, 293
Referendum 160 ; cf. 140
Relief works 413–14
Rhamnus 155, 411
Rivers and river-beds 40
Roads 295, 316–17
Roman Empire 150, 312 ; Greekness of 22
Romance 18 ; cf. 223–4
Rome, wrongly associated with Greece 82, 202 (embassy to Athens), 296 (drains), 379 (not traders) ; policy of 190
Rotation of crops 233
Ruth cited 87

Salamis 21, 168, 182, 369, 375, 403
Salt 24
Samian War 199, 373, 410, 412, 415
Sanitation 295–6
Sappho 342
Schoolmasters 271, 272, 273
Scottish Lowlands 78 ; thrift 217
Scrub 47, 232, 237
Sea-power 33–4, 350 ff., 369 ff., 409, 417, 421 ff.
Secretaries 396
Segesta 194, 374
Self-sufficiency, 50, 225, 287, 305, 354, 375 (cf. 202), 427
Servant-keeping class 275
Sestos 363, 403
Shame (αἰδώς) 121 ; cf. 441–3
Sheep-dogs 48, 238, 316
Shepherds 47, 232, 316–17
Shipbuilding 46, 186, 358, 407
Shore, party of 34, 141
Sicily 182, 256, 370, 373, 443
Siege operations 346, 348, 355, 417
Siena 158
Siesta 37, 356
Sigeum 27, 143, 363
Siphnos, mines at 398
Siris 31, 318
Slavery and slaves, at Athens 178, 362, 380 ff., 397 ff. ; debt-slaves 117–18 ; Homeric 88 ; household 275 ; in crafts 263–4 ; in guilds 270 ; in National Balance-sheet 417 ; in workshops 266 ; join in public banquet 360 new definition of 109 ; ransom of 134, 349 ;

riches calculated in 301 ; Roman slaves 150, 401 ; runaway slaves 316 ; silver-bought slaves 121, 396 ; slave-infants 332 ; slave-market 282 ; slave nurse-girl 331 ; slave shop-keepers 281 ; slave-work 272
Smyrna 42, 377
Socialism 33, 220–2, 258, 293 ; cf. 404–5
Socrates, a stone-cutter 261 ; claim to public maintenance 175 ; could think standing 168 ; death of 82, 199, 339 ; double marriage of 340 ; family of 333 ; habits of 268 ; holds office as 'Chief' 166 ; personal appearance of 283 ; trial of 364
Solon 54, 106, 130 ff., 181, 189, 259 (on Athenian earners), 323, 351, 353 ff., 357, 405
Songs, labourers' 260
Soothsayers 105, 259–60
Sophocles, atmosphere of his plays 73–4, 124 ; chorus on the olive 54 ; *Oedipus Tyrannus* of 102, 316, 384 ; on Athens 136, 182, 195–6 ; on unmarried women 334 ; 'Steward of the Greeks' 188
Sparta and Spartans, armistice made by 378, 430 ; avoid Marathon 184 ; battle-speeches to 347 ; conquests of 128 ; discipline at contrasted with Athens 202 ; Helots at 112–13 ; in Attica 143 ; incredible to us 223 ; laws of 128 ; money at 193, 305, 306 ; place in narrative 132 ; potters of 225 ; reject Athenian proposal 406 ; situation of 49 ; unwalled 78, 85 ; war with Athens 422 ff.
Sport, war as a 251, 345 ff.
St. Francis 123
St. Paul's journey 38
State Insurance 358
Stirrups 176
Stock Exchange 311–12, 319
Stone-masons 261
Stores, Wholesale 215
Street-corner gatherings 168, 429
Subalterns 173
Subtropical cultivation 55
Suicide 227
Sunium 19, 45, 283, 364, 411
Surnames at Athens 92, 156–7
Switzerland 48, 134, 183 ; see Föhn
Sybaris 31, 270, 374
Synoecism 78–9

Syracusan Expedition 40, 357, 372, 432, 443
Syracuse 256, 373, 375, 376

Taormina 361
Tartessus (Tarshish) 25
Taxation, in money 142, 159, 289, 295–6, 306, 406 ; in time 167 note, 174–7, 289
Temperance 51 ; cf. 120–1, 342–3
Temple-slaves 342, 394–5
Tenancy 234
Tenos 316 ; cf. 298
Thasos 398 ; cf. 407
Theatre audience, 60, 170–1
Themistocles, and Athenian fleet 218 ; and Athenian wall 85 ; character of 294 ; encouraged aliens 178–9, 380 ; hoarded his money 309 ; journey of 374 ; mother of 339 ; policy of 371–2, 397
Theognis 108, 119–21
Theophrastus, *Characters* of 216–17 ; see Index I under Jebb
Thermopylae 85 ; cf. 182
'Theseus' 79, 84, 98, 129, 145, 147, 162, 163, 192
Thessaly, 76, 111–12, 233
Thucydides 198 (life) ; on 'mediaeval' Greece 76, 78 ; introduction to 432
Thurii 41, 374, 375, 424
Tides, absence of 29, 35
Timber-trade 46, 359, 419
Tin Islands 26–7
Tiryns 80
Town-life in Greece 83 ; cf. 67–8
Town-planning 296
Towpath by the sea 27
Trade and traders, commercial treaties 189–90, 315–18, 373–4 ; growth of trade 118, 242–3, 255 ; retail trade 279 ff. ; foreign trade 314 ff. ; trade and sea-power 350 ff. ; Athenian trade 202, 203, 365 ff., 382

Trade Unions 269
Tragedy, the Greek 73, 84
Treaty-rights 188–9, 315 ff., 423
Trident, uses of 34
Trojan War 76, 78, 87, 241
Troy 28
Truck, payment in 387
Turks 46, 225, 323, 344 ; cf. 292
Tyrants 63, 125 ff., 366, 396
Tyrtaeus 347

Unemployment 59, 263, 269, 413–14
Uniforms 35, 131, 176 ; cf. 216
Universities 119, 166–7, 333 ; cf. 295
Usury 115, 308
Utopias, ancient and modern 220 ff., 351

Valuation at Athens 292–3
Vari, cave near 238
Vase-painters 265 ff.
Vendetta 100
Venereal disease 342
Venice 42, 140, 217, 293, 318, 382
Village life 78

Wagoners 192, 276
Warfare 71, 198 ff., 244 ff., 344 ff., 403, 420 ff.
Water-supply 40, 78, 120–1, 296–7, 299
Winds 39, 345
Wine 51, 119–20 ; cf. 342–3
Winter, the Greek 37
Women 52 (washing arrangements for), 61, 150 (women officials), 150 (in secret societies), 209, 267, 274, 302, 333 ff., 349 (cannot throw)
Wooden horse, the 93, 259

Yamen 100
Yorkers 345

Zeus-born kings 89, 96
Zollverein 193 ; cf. 189